Juvenile Delinquency

BRIDGING THEORY TO PRACTICE

Robert Hartmann McNamara

The Citadel

JUVENILE DELINQUENCY: BRIDGING THEORY TO PRACTICE

Published by McGraw-Hill, a business unit of The McGraw-Hill Companies, Inc., 1221 Avenue of the Americas, New York, NY, 10020. Copyright © 2014 by Robert McNamara. All rights reserved. Printed in the United States of America. No part of this publication may be reproduced or distributed in any form or by any means, or stored in a database or retrieval system, without the prior written consent of The McGraw-Hill Companies, Inc., including, but not limited to, in any network or other electronic storage or transmission, or broadcast for distance learning.

Some ancillaries, including electronic and print components, may not be available to customers outside the United States.

This book is printed on acid-free paper.

1 2 3 4 5 6 7 8 9 0 DOW/DOW 1 0 9 8 7 6 5 4 3

ISBN   978-0-07-811151-8
MHID   0-07-811151-X

Senior Vice President, Products & Markets: *Kurt L. Strand*
Vice President, General Manager: *Mike Ryan*
Vice President, Content Production & Technology Services: *Kimberly Meriwether David*
Managing Director: *Gina Boedeker*
Brand Manager: *Bill Minick*
Director of Development: *Lisa Pinto*
Content Development Editor: *Betty Chen*
Marketing Manager: *Caroline McGillen*
Director, Content Production: *Terri Schiesl*
Project Manager: *Holly Irish, Jane Mohr*
Production Service: *Melanie Field, Strawberry Field Publishing*
Buyer: *Nicole Baumgartner*
Designer and Cover Designer: *Margarite Reynolds*
Cover Image: *© Richard Ross, www.juvenile-in-justice.com Santa Barbara County Juvenile Hall*
Interior Designer: *Ellen Pettengell*
Content Licensing Specialist: *Brenda Rolwes*
Photo Researcher: *Jerry Marshall*
Media Project Manager: *Jennifer Barrick*
Typeface: *10/12 Times*
Compositor: *Laserwords Private Limited*
Printer: *R.R. Donnelley Willard*

All credits appearing on page or at the end of the book are considered to be an extension of the copyright page.

Library of Congress Cataloging-in-Publication Data
McNamara, Robert Hartmann.
    Juvenile delinquency : bridging theory to practice / Robert Hartmann McNamara.—1st ed.
        p. cm.
    Includes bibliographical references and index.
    ISBN 978-0-07-811151-8 (alk. paper)—ISBN 0-07-811151-X (alk. paper) 1.
    Juvenile delinquency—United States. I. Title.
    HV9104.M357 2014
    364.36—dc23   2012037151

www.mhhe.com

To Carey and Connor: My love letters from God.

Brief Contents

Contents

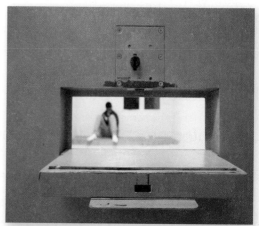

Theories in **Action**

By taking what they learn from *Juvenile Delinquency: Bridging Theory to Practice,* talking to real people, seeing real situations, and analyzing real programs, students are better equipped to offer explanations and to connect the data they collected with the theories they encounter.

PROVIDING THE BIG PICTURE

Content and context in *Juvenile Delinquency* serve to help students understand how information, statistics, and research studies apply to the bigger picture.

Learning Objectives open up each chapter to build knowledge beyond memorization by having students define, outline, interpret, assess, and come up with their own solutions based on the theories and data provided.

The Big Picture series of questions follow each chapter's public policy section, which concludes and synthesizes the chapter's discussion. They serve to guide students to better understand how the theories, issues, and practices are connected.

THE BIG PICTURE
Conclusions on Status Offenses

- Have judges misunderstood the motives behind many status offenders? Do youths reoffend because they are disobedient? Or are judges limited in the tools at their disposal to help, so they use punishment to get youths to refrain from engaging in these behaviors?
- Should juvenile justice officials be allowed to incarcerate and/or detain status offenders? Should status offenders continue to be under the authority of the juvenile justice system or should their cases be decided by some other treatment-oriented agency? Explain.
- What should parents do when their children continually disobey them by breaking curfews, binge drinking, or smoking?

BRINGING THEORY INTO PRACTICE AND ACTION

Activities in *Juvenile Delinquency* bridge academic learning and practical exposure to an issue.

Think about It questions ask students to review what they read and to draw conclusions to fulfill chapter learning objectives, to analyze visual data, and to assess case studies and real-life programs.

Theory and Practice Working Together features focus on existing programs for a realistic look at how theories are brought into practice to address juvenile delinquency issues. They also ask students to assess the effectiveness of the programs described.

THINK ABOUT IT

Treating Status Offenders

Can we separate the true status offenders from those who commit major crimes like shoplifting and trespassing? Should we try to consider the crimes that are likely linked to status offending (e.g., shoplifting) when viewing an offender's behavior?

FRANKIE'S CASE

Drawing Conclusions

Recall the issues Frankie is facing:

- brought a gun to school
- pulled the gun on gang members in a school bathroom
- was reported to school officials
- was expelled from school

Consider what you have learned about the structure of schools and the various responses of school officials to student offenses. More and more, schools are responding to potential problems by trying to assert control over students, as they do with harsh measures like zero-tolerance policies.

Now reconsider Frankie's case. Frankie did not bring the gun to school to show off or to intimidate or bully others. Instead, his decision was informed by fear of victimization, along with the belief that school officials could not or would not protect him.

Apply Theory to Reality assignments provide students with a chance to apply theory to social life. Early chapters will provide a suggested theory and scenario, but later chapters will ask students to select their own theories that offer the best "fit" in terms of explaining a particular event or circumstance in real life today.

Apply Theory to Reality ▶ Social and Cultural Influences

As we have discussed in this chapter, there are a number of programs in place to attempt to divert youths from gang allegiances and criminal activity. Given what you know about the influence of social culture on people's behavior, can you offer insight into the likelihood of gang-affiliated youths' reforming their behavior?[81]

STEPPING INTO VARIOUS SHOES

Through case studies, videos, and activities, students address preconceptions they bring to the course and question the myths about youth offenders based on media portrayals.

RYAN'S CASE

Is Birth Order a Factor?

Recall Ryan's situation:

- is a twelve-year-old boy
- lives in California with his mother and stepfather
- is a middle child of four children
- has a bad reputation in his neighborhood and school

Ryan's neighbors think that his delinquent behavior is the result of his position in the family, which allows him to behave as he likes. They believe his lack of supervision predisposes him to further delinquency.

The bigger the family, the harder it can be for parents to keep an eye on their children, leaving some youths free to get into trouble. In some families, particularly large ones, parents are also more likely to relax strict behavioral standards and boundaries. In fact, inadequate supervision is considered the most important variable in understanding the relationship between family position and delinquency.

Given the research on birth order, do you think that Ryan's position as a middle child is a factor in his delinquent behavior? If Ryan were the youngest, or even the first-born, might he have received more attention from his mother and stepfather?

THINK ABOUT IT

Case Studies of youths are given in each chapter to challenge commonly held assumptions about delinquency. Students put themselves into a youth's position and return to the particular youth's case throughout the chapter to consider what is known empirically, to ask and respond to whether a situation works with or against a theory, and to have a fuller picture of a scenario.

Make the Call activities provide scenarios that officials in the juvenile justice system face when dealing with delinquents. They challenge the students to appreciate the complexity and difficulty of those decisions, to consider the theories they learned, and to try their hands at "working" within the system.

Make the Call ▶ Status Offenses

Review the scenario below, and decide how you would approach this case.

YOUR ROLE: Juvenile court judge

DETAILS OF THE CASE

- A young man, fifteen years old, has been arrested for underage drinking.
- He is also charged with vandalism.
- This youth is a repeat offender: several instances of running away, two instances of truancy, and incorrigibility.
- You had previously ordered him to attend school every day, admonished him about being disobedient to his parents, and mandated that if he were to run away again, you would place him in a group home.
- You had also ordered a psychiatric evaluation and required him to attend therapy sessions offered by the Department of Social Services.

WHAT IS YOUR RULING?

Since he is a status offender, you are prohibited from detaining him as he has not been adjudicated a delinquent. The philosophy of the court is to offer treatment to status offenders. Clearly, he is defiant and is not interested in treatment, so how do you rule?

Consider:

- Has the youth violated a valid court order?
- Has the youth committed a crime for which he could be adjudicated as a delinquent?
- Is detention really in the best interests of the youth?
- What could be the reasons for the defiance and escape behavior? What are some of the ways you can determine the causes of the problem?
- Are you on solid legal ground if you detain the youth? What if there are no secure facilities to accomplish this goal? What if the only option is an adult jail? Are you still on solid legal ground?

Your Community ▶ Neediest Individuals

In addition to the information you glean from your readings, class lectures, and discussions, it is important to roll up your sleeves and immerse yourself in a topic as a researcher who gains an understanding of problem or issue by observing or experiencing it firsthand. Through such methods, you gain a much greater appreciation of the magnitude and scope of the problem than if you were only engaged in "armchair theorizing."

- Create a list of the organizations that might exacerbate the already difficult circumstances of your community's poorest individuals. Consider, for instance, the industry that rents furniture and appliances to people on a weekly or sometimes monthly basis, or the businesses

that cash checks for individuals without checking accounts, for a fee. You might also want to include pawnshops or "title loan" establishments.

- Visit one of these establishments, and explore the means by which they profit from those in the lowest income brackets.
- Determine whether the poor are being exploited. Are they required to pay more for goods and services than those who can afford to buy furniture, for instance, or those who have access to checking accounts?

After collecting your data and drawing from the relevant literature, prepare a report that discusses some of the social structural factors that contribute to your findings.

Your Community assignments ask students to roll up their sleeves to explore solutions in their communities and to develop their research skills. They become more aware of the scope of the problems when they read beyond what is given in readings and lectures, ask questions, and draw conclusions from data they collect on their own.

In Their Own Words are short videos, available online at **www.mhhe.com/mcnamarajd1e,** that offer students insights into the nature of delinquency and the juvenile justice process with firsthand accounts from ten youths at Pendleton Juvenile Correctional Facility and three practitioners.

This anecdotal evidence can be used as a valuable teaching tool. Call-outs to the videos can be found for particular topics, and excerpts are integrated into the chapters to offer a framework and context for understanding the information presented in the videos. Full-length, uncut interviews are available to instructors upon request.

YOUTHS INTERVIEWED

Anthony B.

Given a two-year determinate sentence as part of a plea bargain from being waived for grand theft auto and battery of staff at juvenile detention.

Anthony J.

Received a two-year determinate sentence for aggravated assault.

Austin

Reclassed from Camp Summit, where he was sent for reckless endangerment with a firearm.

Jose

Given an indeterminate sentence for burglary, and is part of the Future Soldiers Program.

Larry

Sentenced to one-and-a-half years for his latest charge, a repeat offender and part of the Future Soldiers Program.

Phillip

Sentenced in 2007 when his father brought him in to the police for sex offenses.

Richard

Taken away from his parents by the court for neglect, and ended up here after multiple placements for his own offenses.

Shun

Recommitted, this time for auto theft and possession of a firearm.

Walter

Placed here for running away repeatedly and resisting law enforcement, and headed to a residential placement facility after release.

Zachary

Received an indeterminate sentence for battery of staff at another placement.

PRACTITIONERS INTERVIEWED

Michael Corriero

Former Judge of New York County Supreme Court

Executive Director of New York Center for Juvenile Justice

Patrick Igneri

Retired Lieutenant, New York Police Department

Vidhya R. Kelly

Deputy Executive Director, Big Brothers Big Sisters of New York City

Juvenile Delinquency: Bridging Theory to Practice prepares students for future professions, whether they are looking to become sociologists, criminologists, psychologists, counselors, social workers, police officers, or public policy specialists. It also assists students in understanding overall issues affecting them in their society. These goals are accomplished through the information contained in the chapters, the larger framework of understanding or context to grasp the nature of delinquency, the exercises throughout the chapters, and the civic engagement opportunities.

The Online Learning Center at **www.mhhe.com/mcnamarajd1e** includes *In Their Own Words* videos, a test bank, an instructor's manual, and lecture PowerPoint slides.

CourseSmart offers thousands of the most commonly adopted textbooks across hundreds of courses from a wide variety of higher education publishers. It is the only place for faculty to review and compare the full text of a textbook online, providing immediate access without the environmental impact of requesting a printed exam copy. At CourseSmart, students can save up to 50 percent off the cost of a printed book, reduce their impact on the environment, and gain access to powerful Web tools for learning, including full text search, notes and highlighting, and email tools for sharing notes among classmates. Learn more at www.coursesmart.com.

McGraw-Hill Create allows you to create a customized print book or eBook tailored to your course and syllabus. You can search through thousands of McGraw-Hill texts, rearrange chapters, combine material from other content sources, and include your own content or teaching notes. Create even allows you to personalize your book's appearance by selecting the cover and adding your name, school, and course information. To register and to get more information, go to http://create.mcgraw-hill.com.

From the Author

At the risk of sounding immodest, I must confess to a good deal of excitement about *Juvenile Delinquency: Bridging Theory to Practice.* While my professional and personal interest in delinquency spans over forty years, and while I have been teaching courses on delinquency for nearly twenty-five, I have had a somewhat different perception of the role of a text in a delinquency course. A text should serve not only as a reference point or guidepost for students to know what is expected from them in a given course, but also as a source of insight and curiosity for them as they think through complex issues. It should also be a resource students return to long after the course has ended.

Rarely does a problem as complicated as delinquency or crime lend itself to simplistic solutions or explanations. Crime and delinquency are linked to other social problems like poverty, inadequate education, family discord, and the economy, to name a few. A comprehensive understanding of delinquency can occur only if those factors are considered, given that they impact people's perceptions of the world and their place in it, as well as their behavior. Too often, this context is overlooked, leaving many students thinking that delinquency is the result of a series of poor choices by an offender. While youths should be held accountable for their actions, what led to their decisions? *Juvenile Delinquency: Bridging Theory to Practice* offers a context of understanding and helps sociology and criminal justice students alike to gain a better insight into the nature of delinquency and the choices youths make.

Juvenile Delinquency: Bridging Theory to Practice presents information differently by making it "come alive" with integrated video content and a series of application exercises to help connect information to the real world. It also helps students to see the relevance of theory as a valuable tool for dealing with real problems, but not at the expense of exposure to the research and the information about a topic. There is a proverbial "sweet spot" where a balance between the two is optimal, and I hope *Juvenile Delinquency: Bridging Theory to Practice* gets closer to that ideal point for students and faculty.

Finally, one of the most important aspects of this program is the *In Their Own Words* videos. These clips (as well as the entire interviews) provide insight from the point of view of the offenders as well as practitioners and are deeply integrated with text material to highlight relevant concepts and theories. In addition, the videos can be used as a mechanism to generate class discussions or support other assignments. In sum, this text really lives up to its subtitle, bridging theory to practice, and provides enough information and research to be useful without overwhelming the student. It also provides sufficient opportunities for students to learn how to apply information and theory in a relevant way.

I hope you are as excited about reading *Juvenile Delinquency: Bridging Theory to Practice* and viewing the videos as I was writing it, because I think it will be one of those texts students will want to keep once the course has ended. To me, there could be no greater compliment.

Acknowledgments

At a certain point in the process of completing any project, but particularly a textbook, I suspect most authors question whether the decision to undertake the task was a smart one—that is, until the manuscript is complete and the finished product arrives in the mail. Scholarship in general, and writing in particular, is often an isolated and even lonely exercise, and while the author gets credit for the final product, anyone who knows the publishing industry recognizes that there are countless people who work behind the scenes and who rarely get credit for their efforts. While I cannot fix the larger problem of the lack of recognition in publishing, I can do something about it in my own projects. In fact, I take great pleasure in recognizing several of these individuals for their contributions to the project since it is as much their product as it is mine.

On the larger conceptual horizon is Katie Stevens, a brilliant publisher at McGraw-Hill Higher Education. Katie was my first editor, and I was immediately impressed with her talent, skill, creativity, and industry acumen. As many experts in sports have noted, there are many talented athletes, but only a select few who enhance the abilities and performance of those around them—Katie is one of those people in publishing. I am grateful for her insight, ideas, and vision for this text, and am honored to call her my colleague and friend.

My association and friendship with Katie came as a result of my relationship with Frank Mortimer. It was Frank who initially gave me the opportunity to work with McGraw-Hill, and from our first encounter, I asked Frank (and McGraw-Hill) to show me his character and integrity, and to demonstrate that he was interested in building a lasting and meaningful working relationship, and he did not let me down. Thank you Frank, for everything.

To continue recognizing members of the McGraw-Hill family, and to whom I owe a great debt of thanks on the practical side of the project, Bill Minick and Betty Chen deserve a lion's share of the credit for what appears in the coming pages. Betty, along with Elizabeth Murphy, took an inexperienced textbook author and made him appear thoughtful, creative, insightful, and a gifted writer. In reality, the two of them, particularly Betty, made this a far better manuscript than anything I could have accomplished on my own. Thank you, Betty and Elizabeth, for giving me valuable experience into understanding how students think, read, and digest information. I hope we get to work together again soon.

Similarly, one would be hard-pressed to find a more supportive and encouraging editor than Bill Minick. From the outset, Bill was open to ideas and thoughts about the project and found ways to implement them. His tireless efforts and diligence are the main reasons the video component of this text became a reality. This was in addition to all the other responsibilities he carried into the project. In short, I could not have had a better team to work with and believe that whatever success this book has in the future comes as a result of their efforts and commitment to it.

I also have several colleagues for whom I owe a lifetime of thanks. First and foremost is John Fuller at the University of West Georgia, a friend for nearly twenty years, and to whom I owe so much for introducing me to the academic publishing industry. Thank you, John, for your guidance, advice, friendship, jokes, and sympathetic ear over the years. You are a great friend, and there are few others I would want in my corner when the chips were down.

Similarly, old friends and colleagues Chip Burns and Chuck Crawford merit recognition as they tolerated my tardy responses and lackluster participation in other projects as this one took so much of my time. Thank you guys: I will do the heavy lifting in the future (and pay the bar tabs)—you are good friends and cherished colleagues—we still have much to learn and I am grateful we can do that together.

I would be remiss if I did not extend my thanks to the many students over the years who took my courses and taught me far more than I shared with them. As this text is the culmination of nearly twenty-five years of teaching, there are too many to name here, and many of them may not even realize the impact they had on my understanding of delinquency and crime. Thanks to all of you.

Finally, I owe my wife Carey and son Connor an important debt of thanks for those times when I needed to meet deadlines or escape into my office at home to write—their sacrifice can easily be overlooked, but it was no less essential in completing this project.

We are grateful to the many reviewers who generously offered comments and suggestions at various stages in the development of *Juvenile Delinquency: Bridging Theory to Practice.* Our thanks go to the following instructors:

Steven W. Atchley, *Delaware Technical and Community College*

Maldine Beth Bailey, *University of North Florida*

Nikki Banks, *Grand Rapids Community College*

Tiffany Barfield-Cottledge, *University of North Texas, Dallas*

Kristin Bates, *California State University, San Marcos*

William Blake, *Raritan Valley Community College*

Kelli Callahan, *Park University*

Jennifer Capps, *Metropolitan State College of Denver*

Mary Ann Czarnezki, *University of Wisconsin, Milwaukee*

Kristen E. DeVall, *University of North Carolina, Wilmington*

Eugene J. Evans, Jr., *Camden County College*

Robert Friedenbach, *Colorado Technical University*

Stephanie Frogge, *University of Texas at Austin*

Kelly Gould, *Sacramento City College*

Tiffiny E. Guidry, *University of Alabama*

Jay Paul Horner, *University of Maryland*

Hua-Lun Huang, *University of Louisiana*

Jessica Huffman, *Old Dominion University*

Jason Jolicoeur, *Cincinnati State Technical and Community College*

Soraya K. Kawucha, *University of North Texas*

Jeri Kirby, *West Virginia University*

Jonathan M. Kremser, *Kutztown University of Pennsylvania*

Todd M. Krohn, *The University of Georgia*

Adam Langsam, *Northeastern State University*

Diane Leamy, *Missouri State University*

JoAnne M. Lecci, *Nassau Community College*

Ruth X. Liu, *San Diego State University*

Jeff London, *Metropolitan State College of Denver*

Miriam Lorenzo, *Miami Dade College*

Frances Manino, *Herkimer County Community College*

Cid Martinez, *California State University, Sacramento*

Dorothy S. McClellan, *Texas A&M*

Dagmar Moravec, *Lansing Community College*

Timothy O'Boyle, *Kutztown University*

Neil Quisenberry, *McKendree University*

Cynthia Robbins, *University of Delaware*

Christine Rodriguez, *East Los Angeles College*

Stephen Schlereth, *San Diego State University*

Ellen Smith Chupik, *Moraine Valley Community College*

Michael Such, *Hudson Valley Community College*

Austin T. Turk, *University of California, Riverside*

William B. Waegel, *Villanova University*

Morag Walls, *Delta College*

Elvira M White, *Texas A&M Commerce*

Katina Whorton, *Delgado Community College*

Ivy Yarckow-Brown, *Missouri State University*

Thomas G. Ziesemer, *Central Florida Community College*

Finally we want to extend our thanks to the many people involved in the production of the video series for this textbook. They include:

Pendleton Juvenile Correctional Facility

Calamari Productions

mama siu productions

Cameron Kittrell

Hon. Michael Corriero, *New York Center for Juvenile Justice*

Patrick Igneri, *retired New York Police Department officer*

Vidhya R. Kelly, *Big Brothers Big Sisters of New York City*

—Bob Hartmann McNamara

1

After reading this chapter, you should be able to:

- Define juvenile delinquency and *parens patriae*.
- Trace society's historical treatment of children and how the juvenile justice system developed.

- Interpret the reasons for the different perceptions of delinquency from the public and policymakers.
- Examine and compare the general nature of adolescent behaviors over the past few generations.

- Assess the nature of delinquency and how public policy for juveniles differs from that for adults.

1

The Nature of Delinquency

CASE STUDY ON MARIO

Well-publicized episodes of extreme violence have helped to make the general public fearful of violent delinquents. However, violent delinquents represent only a small percentage of the population. Consider the following case about Mario:

- fourteen years old and lives with his father, younger sister, and grandparents in Alabama
- mother abandoned the family when Mario was young
- acts out when his father or grandparents set behavioral boundaries, talks back to teachers, and refuses to abide by school policies
- has started experimenting with drugs and alcohol

Mario has increasingly become withdrawn from his family and has only a few friends. Most of the time, he stays in his room alone playing video games and sleeping. He refuses to eat meals with the family or attend social functions or holiday gatherings. Mario's family believes he is suffering from depression, but they do not know how to help him.

Recently, Mario has come into conflict with his neighbors, some of whom have accused him of vandalizing their cars and antagonizing their pets, although no one has actually observed him committing these acts. One night, after seeing Mario sitting on the curb in front of his house, alone, after midnight, a neighbor called the police. This particular resident wanted to press charges against Mario because she believed him to be in violation of the local juvenile curfew, which prohibits youths from being outdoors without an adult after 11 pm.

In order to get a better grasp on Mario's behavior, we will need to explore the larger context of delinquency, its definitions, and its causes and effects. This chapter will explore the nature of adolescence, as well as cultural influences that shape ideas about and definitions of delinquency. In addition, it will examine the social and political context in which the juvenile justice system was developed, including the differences between the juvenile and adult systems.

Recent explanations of delinquency seem to focus on punishment and detention of youths who engage in delinquency, but should all offenders be treated the same way?

A police officer or social worker approaching Mario's case might ask the following questions:

- Has Mario committed an offense for which he could be arrested?
- Why does the neighbor want to press charges?
- If Mario is arrested, what is likely to happen to him?
- Should Mario's father seek professional help for Mario, or is his behavior pattern typical of most teenagers?

Definitions of Juvenile Delinquency

juvenile delinquency
Behavior that violates the criminal code and is committed by youths who have not reached majority age.

Juvenile delinquency is a complex issue that requires a thorough understanding of the physical, social, economic, legal, and political context in which it occurs. Delinquency also encompasses a wide range of activities, making it difficult to define. How one defines delinquency has a lot to do with how it is measured, understood, and addressed. Sometimes we apply the legal definition. Although this definition works to standardize the behaviors associated with delinquency to some degree, it is not always inclusive of what the general public believes delinquency to be.

In most states, the legal definition of delinquency consists of behavior that violates the criminal code and is committed by youths who have not reached majority age of eighteen. Because each state has its own definition of delinquency, there is a wide variation in the age at which youths remain under the jurisdiction of the juvenile court. Table 1-1 lists the youngest ages at which offenders can be prosecuted by state, while Table 1-2 lists the states that target the upper age limits for youths in juvenile court.

Historically, many states have failed to distinguish between youths who commit criminal acts and youths who are victims of abuse, neglect, or other mistreatment.[1] With the passage of federal legislation separating minor offenders from serious ones—most notably, the Juvenile Justice and Delinquency Prevention Act—many states began to distinguish between delinquents and **status offenders,** those who engage in activities that could be committed only by youths, such as truancy, running away, or underage drinking.[2]

status offenders
Those who engage in activities that could be committed only by youths, such as truancy, running away, or underage drinking.

Legally, delinquent acts are those for which youths can be arrested and sentenced—a process referred to in juvenile court as adjudication. While legal definitions provide narrower designations for delinquent acts, others define *delinquency* much more broadly. Parents and siblings, for example, may use the term *delinquent* to define a wide array of behaviors, such as refusing to complete household chores, hanging out with people they

TABLE 1-1 Lowest Age for Juvenile Court Jurisdiction in Delinquency Matters by State[3]

Age 6	Age 7	Age 8	Age 10
North Carolina	Maryland Massachusetts New York	Arizona	Arkansas Colorado Kansas Louisiana Minnesota Mississippi Pennsylvania South Dakota Texas Vermont Wisconsin

Youths as young as six years old can be held accountable for their behavior in the juvenile justice system in some states.

Note: All other states have no specified lower age limit.

TABLE 1-2 Oldest Age for Juvenile Court Jurisdiction in Delinquency Matters by State[4]

Age 15	Age 16	Age 17		
Connecticut	Georgia	Alabama	Iowa	North Dakota
New York	Illinois	Alaska	Kansas	Ohio
North Carolina	Louisiana	Arizona	Kentucky	Oklahoma
	Massachusetts	Arkansas	Maine	Oregon
	Michigan	California	Maryland	Pennsylvania
	Missouri	Colorado	Minnesota	Rhode Island
	New Hampshire	Delaware	Mississippi	South Dakota
	South Carolina	DC	Montana	Tennessee
	Texas	Florida	Nebraska	Vermont
	Wisconsin	Hawaii	Nevada	Virginia
		Idaho	New Jersey	Washington
		Indiana	New Mexico	West Virginia
				Wyoming

How often do you think young offenders are waived to adult court?

think are troublemakers, or listening to rap music. The way that youths dress and talk, and the people with whom they associate do not necessarily mean they are breaking any laws. While parents may complain to social workers, counselors, or even probation officers, these types of behaviors are not likely to be considered delinquent acts by the juvenile justice system.

There is a great deal of interpretation and subjectivity associated with delinquency. As we will discuss at length in Chapter 5, delinquency can be a form of negative labeling. How behavior and offenders are perceived, positively or negatively, is an important consideration in the study of delinquency.

Defining Delinquency

Consider the ways in which our perceptions shape our interpretations of others' behavior. Are there times when behavior is misinterpreted because the person engaging in it is seen in a negative light?

THINK ABOUT IT

History of Juvenile Delinquency in the United States

The law has historically differentiated juveniles from adult offenders, but the degree of that distinction has varied during different eras and for many reasons. In early U.S. history, the law was heavily influenced by the common law of England, which governed the American colonies.

One of the most important English lawyers of the time was William Blackstone, whose *Commentaries on the Laws of England,* first published in the late 1760s, was read widely by our nation's founders.[5] Blackstone identified two criteria by which to hold someone accountable for a crime. First, the person had to have a "vicious will," the intent to commit a crime. Second, the person had to commit an unlawful act. If either the will or the act was lacking, no crime had occurred.

There are groups of people who are incapable of committing a crime based on these two criteria. One group is made up of infants, or children who are too young to fully understand their actions. Those under the age of seven were classified as infants and could not be guilty of a felony or serious crime such as burglary, kidnapping, or murder. Children over the age of fourteen were said to be able to understand the significance of their actions and so were treated like adults if found guilty of a crime.[6]

For Blackstone and his contemporaries, the ages between seven and fourteen were more difficult to categorize, because children in this age range were generally presumed incapable of committing crimes. If, however, children appeared to understand the difference between right and wrong, then they could be convicted and suffer the full consequence, such as a prison sentence, or even the death penalty in a capital crime.[7]

NINETEENTH-CENTURY UNITED STATES

In the early nineteenth century, the United States experienced significant social and economic changes as a result of the Industrial Revolution. Economic growth, coupled with immigration, urbanization, and industrialization, had an adverse effect on many families. Many poor families had to migrate from farms to cities and take jobs in factories in order to survive. Many children were forced to work long hours in those same factories to help their families. Child labor laws were developed to prevent the exploitation of children, but because parents were working long hours, many children did not receive adequate supervision, which led to a rise in neglect and abuse of children, as well as increases in crime and delinquency.

During this time, several reform movements emerged in an effort to protect children. One of the earliest came in New York City, which had many orphans, runaways, and throwaway children. To remedy the problem, Reverend Charles Loring Brace, who established the **Children's Aid Society** to help homeless children, came up with an innovative idea. Believing that one of the main reasons for juvenile crime stemmed from the negative influence of the urban environment, Brace created **Orphan Trains,** which transported city youths to rural farms, where families assumed custody of and responsibility for them as apprentices.

At regularly scheduled dates, farming families would go to their local train stations and select orphaned children to live with them. The children and their families had one year to decide whether they would stay together. At the end of the year, if either party decided to part ways, the child would be returned to the Children's Aid Society and board the next train, to be selected by a family in another location.[8]

The Orphan Trains strategy was a popular one since many families were moving west and could use help operating their farms. It also provided orphans with a family environment and got them away from dangers found in cities. Unfortunately, some host families considered orphans to be little more than cheap labor, and so treated them harshly. While the practice of shipping children to unknown families was questionable, with some evidence that this was yet another form of exploitation by adults, some experts cite success stories associated with the experience.[9]

Another attempt to address juvenile crime and child exploitation was the **Child Savers Movement,** which consisted primarily of philanthropists and social reformers who felt that the exploitation of children ultimately resulted in juvenile crime and a host of other problems. Child Savers attempted to enact laws that would allow children to be placed in reformatories or other institutions. As with the Orphan Trains, the thought was that if children were placed in country settings where they could be taught the value of hard work, away from the negative influences of the city, their lives could be improved.

Unfortunately, the noble goal of creating a better life for children often resulted in youths being warehoused in institutions where they were treated poorly and their needs were not met. Some experts note that the Child Savers were unrealistic in their efforts to reform troubled youths. The false expectation that urban, immigrant children would easily and willingly adopt rural Protestant values often resulted in misbehavior.[10]

For those youths who did not participate in Orphan Trains or reside in institutions in rural areas, **Houses of Refuge** were created. The first House of Refuge opened in New York in 1825 as a facility exclusively for children. By the 1840s, an additional fifty-three houses had been built around the country. Houses of Refuge did not limit their services to children who had committed crimes. They were also homes for poor children, orphans, and any children thought to be incorrigible or wayward. The average number of children in a House was 200, but some, like the New York House of Refuge, housed over 1,000 youths at any given time.[11]

Children's Aid Society
Established by Reverend Charles Loring in 1853; assisted homeless children, orphans, runaways, and throwaway children. Today, it helps all children in need and their parents through counseling, housing, health care, and preparatory programs.

Orphan Trains
The vehicles used to transport city youths to rural farms, where families assumed custody of and responsibility for them as apprentices.

Child Savers Movement
Individuals consisting primarily of philanthropists and social reformers who felt that the exploitation of children ultimately resulted in juvenile crime and a host of other problems, and sought to enact laws that would allow children to be placed in reformatories or other institutions.

Houses of Refuge
Started in 1825; facilities exclusively for children, whether poor, orphaned, incorrigible, or wayward.

THEORY AND PRACTICE WORKING TOGETHER

Orphanages

Problems stemming from abuse and neglect, as well as from the increasing number of **broken homes** in the United States, have led to a resurgence of support for orphanages. While some of these facilities have a history of charges of abuse and neglect, others have been quite successful in helping youths overcome the obstacles they face and in providing them with a chance to be successful.

- In 2001, Place of Hope, located in Palm Beach Gardens, Florida, was established by a Christian pastor and his wife. Place of Hope currently provides long-term care for up to thirty-six children, who live in six cottages. Most children served by Place of Hope are between the ages of six and ten, although some are older. House parents live with youths five days a week, providing care in a Christian environment that includes daily devotionals and nightly prayers. While some children eventually are reunited with their parents, many end up staying at Place of Hope until they reach the age of eighteen. The Fellowship of Christ Church raised a portion of the money to build Place of Hope, and operational funding for its $1.5-million annual budget comes from the state, grants, private donations, and corporate gifts.
- Hope Village for Children in Meridian, Mississippi, is another recent successful effort to establish an orphanage. Opened in 2002 by actress Sela Ward, this privately funded nonprofit organization provides long-term residential care for children in two cottages: one housing ten girls and another housing ten boys. While reunification

and adoption of residents is possible through Hope Village, its residential group homes are designed to provide a permanent home for children who do not thrive in foster care and who cannot be returned to their families. Children can stay until they reach adulthood and are given the opportunity to go to college.

- San Pasqual Academy, located in San Diego, California, is a long-term-care placement alternative that houses 250 youths. As in other successful orphanages, residents live in family groups of six to eight children, in residence halls where adult staff serve as role models and advisors. San Pasqual Academy is funded by a combination of private and public money. The county committed $7 million toward the project; the Child Abuse Prevention Foundation contributed $5 million; Metabolife Foundation pledged another $5 million over ten years; and Qualcomm made a $1.5-million gift in the form of computers.

While there is some controversy about the use of orphanages to help children, these three programs have shown considerable success in providing care and opportunities for their participants. Many advocates, social service agencies, and experts have cited these programs as being models for others to emulate.[12]

THINK ABOUT IT   What is a missing but important component that many children raised in orphanages do not receive?

As the needs of children surpassed the ability of the Houses of Refuge to safely care for them, with problems such as overcrowding, deplorable living conditions, and reports of abuse by staff, training schools were developed in the mid-nineteenth century. **Training schools** were larger facilities that placed a greater emphasis on education and vocational training. Consistent with contemporary thinking at the time, the city was the source of temptation, and a rural setting would offer youths a simpler and more virtuous way of life. Such thinking led to many of the new facilities being built outside of cities.[13]

While the twentieth century brought the development of individualized diagnosis and treatment, new kinds of rehabilitative therapy, and improved educational programming, the training school model of concentrating large numbers of juvenile offenders in one institution has persisted.[14] The twentieth century also brought about a resurgence of orphanages, discussed in the Theory and Practice box.

DELINQUENCY IN THE EARLY TWENTIETH CENTURY

In the late nineteenth century, in response to continuing problems associated with juvenile crime, child neglect, and the exploitation of children, the Child Savers and other reformists attempted to establish a separate court for juveniles. In 1899, after years of development and months of compromise, the Illinois legislature passed a law permitting counties in the state to designate one or more of their circuit court judges to hear all cases involving

broken homes
A family situation in which family members are separated, due to either divorce, separation, or criminal charges against one or more parents. Children from broken homes often end up in foster care or living with relatives.

training schools
Larger facilities that placed a greater emphasis on education and vocational training.

dependent, neglected, and delinquent children younger than age sixteen. The law stipulated that these cases were to be heard in a special courtroom that would be designated as the juvenile courtroom, generally referred to as the juvenile court. Thus, the first juvenile court in Cook County, Illinois, was not a new court, but a division of the existing circuit court with original jurisdiction over juvenile cases.

By 1910, thirty-two states had established juvenile courts and/or probation services. By 1925, all but two states had followed Illinois's lead in creating a separate court for juveniles. Borrowing from British thinking, the doctrine *parens patriae* (the state as parent) served as the foundation for the state to intervene and to provide protection for children whose parents did not provide adequate care or supervision.[15]

parens patriae
The foundation for the state to intervene and provide protection for children whose parents did not provide adequate care or supervision.

In line with their "parental" role, juvenile courts tried to focus on the best interests of children. They emphasized an informal, nonadversarial, and flexible approach to cases—there were few procedural rules that the courts were required to follow. Cases were treated as civil (noncriminal) actions, and the ultimate goal was to guide juvenile offenders through adolescence to become responsible, law-abiding adults. The juvenile court could, however, order that young offenders be removed from their homes and placed in juvenile reform institutions as part of their rehabilitation program.[16]

In subsequent years, most juvenile courts had exclusive jurisdiction over all youths under age eighteen who were charged with violating criminal laws. Only if the juvenile court decided to waive its jurisdiction in a case could children be transferred to criminal court and tried as adults. **Transfer** decisions were made on a case-by-case basis, using a "best interests of the child and public" standard.[17]

transfer
The turning over of youths charged with violating criminal laws to criminal courts to be tried as adults.

By this stage in the development of the juvenile court, there were significant differences in the juvenile and adult criminal court systems. The focus of the juvenile court was on the offender, not on the offense, and the juvenile court could be much more flexible and informal than the adult criminal court. Additionally, the focus was on rehabilitation rather than punishment. There was a wide range of options available to judges at the sentencing phase: judges were not limited to punitive sanctions stemming from the particular offense.[18]

DELINQUENCY IN THE 1960S–1970S

In the 1950s and 1960s, treatment strategies available to juvenile justice professionals were called into question. Although the goal of rehabilitation through **individualized justice**—the basic philosophy of the juvenile justice system—was not in question, professionals were concerned about the growing number of juveniles who were being institutionalized indefinitely in the name of treatment. In a series of decisions beginning in the 1960s, the U.S. Supreme Court required that juvenile courts become more formal, like the criminal courts.[19]

individualized justice
A guiding principle of the juvenile justice system, that each case should be decided on its own merits and the punishment or treatment be tailor-made to a particular offender.

Formal hearings were required in waiver situations, and delinquents facing possible confinement were given protection against self-incrimination and rights to receive notice of the charges against them, to present and question witnesses, and to have an attorney present during the proceedings. The burden-of-proof standard for adjudication changed from merely a preponderance of evidence to the much more rigorous proof beyond a reasonable doubt. The Supreme Court, however, still held that there were enough "differences of substance between the criminal and juvenile courts . . . to hold that a jury is not required in the latter."[20]

Take, for example, the case of Morris Kent, whose circumstances set precedent in the landmark Supreme Court decision known as *Kent v. the United States*. Kent first entered the juvenile court system at the age of fourteen, following several housebreakings and attempted thefts. Two years later, his fingerprints were found in the apartment of a woman who had been robbed and raped. Detained and interrogated by police, he admitted to the crimes. Kent's mother hired a lawyer, who arranged for a psychiatric examination of the boy. The examination concluded that Kent suffered from "severe psychopathology" and recommended that he be placed in a psychiatric hospital for observation.[21]

The juvenile court judge had authority to **waive jurisdiction** in Kent's case to a criminal court, where Kent would be tried as an adult. Kent's lawyer opposed the waiver and offered to prove that if Kent were given proper hospital treatment, he would be a candidate for rehabilitation. The juvenile court did not respond to the motions made by Kent's lawyer and, without a hearing, waived jurisdiction to adult court.[22]

In a majority opinion authored by Justice Abe Fortas, the U.S. Supreme Court ruled that Kent was entitled to a hearing and to a statement of the reasons for the juvenile court's decision to waive jurisdiction. The majority of the justices also expressed concerns that the juvenile courts were not living up to their potential and speculated "that there may be grounds for concern that the child receives the worst of both worlds [in juvenile courts]: that he gets neither the protections accorded to adults nor the solicitous care and regenerative treatment postulated for children."[23]

A year after the Kent decision, the case of *in re Gault* was heard by the U.S. Supreme Court[24] and fundamentally changed the way juvenile courts processed cases. Gault, a fifteen-year-old Arizona boy, was accused of making an indecent phone call to a neighbor. The victim, who recognized Gault's voice, called the police. Officers arrived at Gault's home and took him into custody, without leaving notice to Gault's parents that their son had been arrested. Before Gault's adjudication hearing, neither Gault nor his parents received notification of the specific charges against him. At the hearings, there were no sworn witnesses, and no record was made of the proceedings. Not even the neighbor who had made the complaint about the phone call was present.[25]

At the end of the hearings, the judge committed Gault to Arizona's State Industrial School until he turned twenty-one, a six-year sentence. An adult convicted of using vulgar or obscene language would have received a maximum penalty of a $50 fine and imprisonment for no more than two months. Gault's parents argued that he had been denied due process of the law and that his constitutional rights to a fair trial had been violated. The case eventually made its way to the Supreme Court, which ruled in Gault's favor.[26]

While the U.S. Supreme Court was protecting the constitutional rights of juveniles accused of committing crimes, Congress was attempting to determine the types of crimes and offenders that warranted special attention. In 1968, Congress passed the **Juvenile Delinquency Prevention and Control Act,** recommending that children charged with noncriminal (status) offenses be handled outside the court system. A few years later, Congress passed the **Juvenile Justice and Delinquency Prevention Act of 1974,** which prohibited states from incarcerating status offenders and required them to detain juvenile offenders in separate facilities from adult offenders.[27]

DELINQUENCY IN THE 1980S–2000S

During the 1980s and 1990s, many politicians and policymakers asserted that not only were instances of serious juvenile crime increasing, but the juvenile justice system was too lenient with offenders. In response, many states attempted to limit the authority of the juvenile courts over some types of delinquents. Changes included mandatory waivers and/or sentences for certain offenses, and a reduction in protections normally afforded to juveniles, such as changes to confidentiality laws, fingerprinting and photographing suspects during booking procedures, using a juvenile's prior record at the sentencing stage of the process, and allowing juvenile hearings to be open to the public.

Over the past thirty years, the media have painted a picture of juveniles as violent and chronic offenders, and many policymakers and politicians claim that delinquency is out of control. But the vast majority of juvenile offenders are not violent, nor are they chronic in their misbehavior, and the juvenile justice system appears to be able to adequately deal with the challenges they present to their respective communities.[28] Ample research also suggests that incarceration does not rehabilitate juvenile offenders.[29] Instead, it may contribute to the delinquency problem, as youths are more likely to commit additional crimes after being incarcerated.[30]

waive jurisdiction
The move of a youth from juvenile to criminal court, where he or she would be tried as an adult.

Juvenile Delinquency Prevention and Control Act
A 1968 act that prohibited states from incarcerating status offenders and required them to detain juvenile offenders in separate facilities from adult offenders.

Juvenile Justice and Delinquency Prevention Act of 1974
A pioneering act that distinguished between youths who committed criminal acts and status offenders so that the latter did not suffer from the stigmatizing label "juvenile delinquent," and that turned care of status offenders over to community agencies.

Public Perceptions of Adolescents and Delinquents

According to the U.S. Census Bureau, in 2008, there were 16.9 million high-school-age children (ages fourteen to seventeen), or 5.6 percent of the total population (see Table 1-3). Collectively, the under-eighteen age group consists of nearly 74 million people, or approximately 24 percent of all U.S. residents.[31] Additionally, current projections indicate that this segment of the population will increase by 14 percent between 2000 and 2025, and the population will have grown by 33 percent between 2000 and 2050.[32] This latest generation of teenagers is different in many ways from their historical counterparts. According to many experts, teenagers today have been raised with high expectations of social, economic, and political success; possess a strong sense of economic and social entitlement; and have a high level of confidence in their abilities.[33] As a result, some teen behaviors, including status offenses, and even serious delinquency, may be a reflection of a changing value system and family structure rather than of individual decisions.

PUBLIC PERCEPTIONS OF CRIME AND DELINQUENCY

The public perceives youths in general, and delinquents in particular, with a combination of fear and compassion.[34] Public opinion polls show that most Americans are still committed to treating juvenile offenders rather than simply punishing them.[35] According to a 2007 poll sponsored by the National Council on Crime and Delinquency, most Americans favor rehabilitative services for young people, are largely opposed to prosecuting youths in adult courts, and oppose incarcerating youths in adult facilities:

- 90 percent agree that youth crime is a major problem in our communities.
- 66 percent believe that decisions to transfer youths to adult court should be made on a case-by-case basis and should not be simply a matter of statute or public policy.
- 91 percent believe that rehabilitative services and treatment for incarcerated youths could help prevent future crimes.
- More than 80 percent think that spending on rehabilitative services and treatment for youths will save tax dollars in the long run.
- Approximately 70 percent feel that putting youths under the age of eighteen in adult correctional facilities makes them more likely to commit future crimes.
- Nearly 68 percent *disagree* that incarcerating youths in adult facilities teaches them a lesson and deters them from committing future crimes.[36]

A number of other polls, such as a report by the National Juvenile Justice Network, indicate that politicians and policymakers may have misread the public's concerns about delinquency and offenders. Polls from the Center for Children's Law and Policy, the MacArthur Foundation Research Network on Adolescent Behavior and Juvenile Justice,

TABLE 1-3 Population Distribution in the United States by Age, 2008[37]

Age Group	Size	Percent of Total U.S. Population
Under age 5	21 million	6.9%
Age 5–13	36 million	11.8%
Age 14–17	16.9 million	5.6%

The growing size of the adolescent population presents a number of challenges to society, including what to do when teens misbehave.

and the National Council on Crime and Delinquency have found that the public generally believes in rehabilitation and a separate system for youths:

- The public believes that rehabilitation and treatment can reduce crime and is willing to pay additional taxes to provide those services.
- The public prefers rehabilitation, even for young people who commit violent crimes, over punishment.
- The public opposes mandatory waiver laws for juveniles who commit felonies at a certain age.
- The public believes strongly in a separate juvenile justice system.[38]

In general, these polls, as well as others conducted during the 1990s when the punitive sentiments toward delinquents were at their peak,[39] suggest that the public is supportive of the treatment philosophy and practices of the juvenile justice system even when it considers youth violence to be a major problem.[40] Citizens do not think the "get-tough" approach is the solution to delinquency.

POLICYMAKERS' PERCEPTIONS OF CRIME AND DELINQUENCY

Many policymakers and politicians believe the juvenile justice system has gone "soft" on holding youths accountable for their actions. They believe that teens are not deterred by the potential consequences of the system and that **recidivism,** the rate at which offenders are re-arrested, is out of control. They see a need for tougher sanctions on juveniles. Advocates of a "get-tough" approach often point to gang-related violence and a "super predator" class of violent youths as the reason behind the increase in juvenile crime delinquents.

recidivism
The re-arrest for a crime by an offender.

The leading proponents of the so-called super predator phenomenon were professors John DiIulio of Princeton University and James Fox of Northeastern University. According to this theory, juvenile super predators are sociopaths with no moral conscience, who are not deterred by the sanctions of the juvenile justice system. Some experts even argue that this new breed of offenders has a different DNA makeup from their predecessors: these former "crack babies"—the result of substance abuse by their mothers while pregnant—are genetically predisposed toward violent crime.[41] Because this cohort of disturbed youths is so violent and irrational, any attempt to change their thinking or behavior is futile. The only reasonable solution is to increase punitive sanctions and to treat these offenders as the violent future adults they will eventually become.[42]

In response to this growing "threat" of juvenile offenders, and the subsequent fear it generated, in the early 1990s, nearly every state changed how their justice system responded to violent juveniles. These changes were designed to increase the flow of juveniles into the adult criminal justice system, where the punishments were more severe. For instance, many states adopted the following legislation:

- juveniles will be charged with certain violent crimes and tried as adults
- expansion of the list of crimes excluded from juvenile court jurisdiction
- increase in the discretion given to prosecutors to file certain juvenile cases in either juvenile or adult court
- broadened the range of offenses for which juveniles could be tried as adults
- lowering of the age at which juvenile court judges could transfer youths to adult criminal court[43]

How do youths' outward appearances affect the public's perception of them?

While the prediction of a super predator cohort of youths failed to materialize, concern about violent juvenile offenders remains high, and many of the policies and laws enacted during the 1990s remain in effect.

As we will discuss in subsequent chapters, what is perceived to be the cause of the problem shapes public policy. In the case of violent offenders, the "get-tough" philosophy witnessed in the juvenile justice system comes largely from the perception that these individuals make up the bulk of the juvenile offender population[44] and from fears about delinquents engaging in senseless violence, dissatisfaction with the level of accountability offered by the juvenile justice system, and the belief that these youths cannot be rehabilitated. The United States may be moving farther and farther away from treatment and rehabilitation and focusing more and more on punishment.[45]

Have we really seen an increase in violence by teens, or has society taken typical adolescent behavior and recast it in a more negative light? Given that our perceptions are often a function of what we have seen and heard, what role has the media played in shaping our understanding of the nature of crime in general and delinquency in particular?

MEDIA PORTRAYAL OF DELINQUENTS

While the media's impact in the study of adult crime has been studied rather extensively, in terms of both the news media's and Hollywood's portrayals of criminals, much less attention has been given to depictions of delinquents. Consequently, very little research has explored the media's influences on the public's perception of juveniles. However, one study found that while adult crimes make up a significant portion of television news stories, only about one-third of crime stories involve juveniles; of those, the vast majority focus on homicide and violent crime.[46] Another study pointed out that the extent and type of juvenile crime, as well as the nature of offenders, are distorted in the news media.[47] Still another study reported that only one in twelve local news reports and only one in twenty-five national news stories involved youths, but nearly half (46 percent) of these stories involved crime victimization, accidents, or violent juvenile crimes. The study also found that the public's perceptions of youths as often troubled and violent were less likely to change even if factual information was presented that ran counter to these stereotypes.[48]

What these and other studies suggest is that for most citizens who have little direct experience with the juvenile justice system, the most available and accessible information on the incidence and nature of juvenile crime comes from the news media.[49] If the few stories offered about juveniles involve homicide or other violent crimes, it makes sense that the result is a high level of fear, both of the nature of the problem and of potential victimization by juveniles.[50] In turn, this fear has been misinterpreted by policymakers and politicians as a call for more punitive measures.

What is the media's role in affecting the public's perceptions of juveniles? In particular, how are delinquent youths portrayed on television and in movies?

THINK ABOUT IT

Perceptions of Delinquency

Consider the media's focus on violent criminal activities and portrayal of juvenile delinquents. Why do you think the public maintains its emphasis on rehabilitation, despite these often frightening images of criminal behavior? How might you go about informing policymakers of the benefits of rehabilitation of youths?

The Nature of Adolescence

If the media's images of delinquent youths are exaggerated, particularly for violent crimes, what is normal adolescent behavior? The teenage years can be a trying time for both parents and youths. Sociologists and psychologists tell us that part of the normal development of teenagers involves taking on new roles and identities in an attempt to discover who they are and what is important to them.

Adolescence involves a great deal of experimentation, including friends, clothes, hairstyles, music, and even piercings and tattoos.[51] For some youths, this stage of life may also mean experimenting with drugs, alcohol, and sexual behavior. During this period, a teenager's brain is still developing, and the parts that allow the youth to engage in logical thinking and memory are not completely formed, which can lead to poor judgment and risky behavior.[52]

According to the American Academy of Pediatrics, five types of behavior are considered typical for teens:

- changes to appearance where efforts to "fit in" with various groups may lead to wardrobe changes and other alterations involving hairstyles, piercings, and makeup
- withdrawal from family life and group activities
- clashes with parents over independence, rules, and boundaries
- emotional and hormonal changes, which can lead to dramatic mood swings and behaviors typically uncharacteristic for that youth
- experimentation with drugs and alcohol[53]

Not every teen will engage in all five types of behavior, and some youths will have varying levels of intensity in adopting any one of them, but these are generally considered to be typical behavioral issues for teenagers.[54]

Keeping up with trends and fashions is an important part of being a teenager, so it is common for this age group to experiment with different "looks," or to have a preoccupation with physical appearance. This is particularly true for girls, who learn at this age to equate their value with their appearance. At its most extreme, this behavior can be a warning sign for more serious problems, such as eating disorders.[55]

It is also reasonable to expect that teenagers are less likely to want to spend time with the larger family unit. Adolescence places a great deal of emphasis on friendship and independence from the family, which may include not wanting to be seen in public with parents or siblings. While it is reasonable to allow teenagers some latitude during this stage, experts and counselors often caution parents to set boundaries for youths so that they maintain some level of contact with and commitment to the family.[56]

When you were a teenager, did you or your friends alter your appearances in dramatic ways? If so, can you recall your reasons for doing so? What did you hope to communicate using your outward appearance and body language?

Because adolescents desire independence and are generally unwilling to conform to rules, confrontations with parents are more common. These arguments often include attempts to manipulate parents to give them more freedom. Additionally, teenagers often justify behavior by telling their parents that other parents grant such permission to their children, thereby making the behavior or activity seem acceptable and reasonable.[57]

A good deal of emotional turmoil accompanies adolescence, and its unpredictable nature can be a source of concern for parents. Particular issues or interactions, the sources of problems, their intensity, and a teen's social networks can all vary on any given day. At times, it may even appear that the youth is suffering from depression and anxiety when, in fact, the behavior is likely to change and improve soon after it is displayed. This wide range of emotions can be particularly troublesome for the teens themselves, since they often recognize they are experiencing different moods and emotions and are surprised by their own behavior.

While not all youths do so, it is likely that most will experiment with drugs or alcohol at some point. But most either do not like the experience or, if they do, manage to control usage at low or moderate levels. Obviously, extreme behavioral changes could be an indication that the youth has developed a dependency problem, which could be reflected in persistent levels of moodiness or argumentativeness, or even extreme forms of dress and physical appearance. Despite the fears and concerns of parents during this phase, while most youths will experiment with alcohol or drugs, most do not become addicted or dependent.[58]

GENERATIONAL DIFFERENCES

In addition to normal adolescent development, cultural and generational values, attitudes, and beliefs can shape behavior as well. Notions of deviant and acceptable behavior are redefined over time and generations, and can vary according to worldview. While it seems that each generation finds something wrong with the ones preceding or succeeding it, knowledge about other generations can provide insight into certain behaviors. Baby Boomers, Generation X, and Generation Y receive the most focus. Whatever the particular label or designation, the bulk of teenagers today belong to Generation Y; their parents generally fall into one of the other two generational groups.

Baby Boomers

After World War II, the United States experienced an explosion of births, nearly 76 million from 1946 to 1964. While it is difficult to provide exact dates for when any generation begins or ends, many sociologists define those born during those years as **Baby Boomers.** This group currently represents about 28 percent of the U.S. population and is responsible for some of the most dramatic changes in American history. From the Civil Rights Movement to the Vietnam War protests to the rise of feminism, Baby Boomers have been at the center of debate, discussion, and social change. This group, many of whom turned sixty-five years old in 2011, comprises some of the country's leading politicians, entertainers, and social activists.[59]

Baby Boomers have also been referred to as the "Me" generation for their narcissism and focus on individual pleasure. They have changed the way most Americans conceive of the aging process as they remain healthy and active in their retirement years.[60] Their focus on careers and leisure activities led many to delay having children or to remain childless, and as a result, an anticipated second Baby Boom generation did not occur.[61]

Generation X

Following the Baby Boomers is a smaller generation consisting of about 41 million people, born roughly between 1968 and 1979. This group is often referred to as Generation X (Gen Xers), which many experts argue has been too often ignored and misunderstood.[62] Gen Xers are generally marked by their lack of optimism for the future and an absence of trust in traditional values. In the early 1990s, the media portrayed Gen Xers as a group of overeducated, underachieving "slackers," who were preoccupied with tattoos and body piercings and who spawned the grunge music movement.[63]

Gen Xers grew up during the era of the Cold War and the Reagan presidency, and witnessed the economic depression of the 1990s. Many watched their parents cope with the loss of careers and jobs due to outsourcing, deindustrialization, and corporate mergers. This experience had a profound impact on many Gen Xers, who realized that company loyalty and personal sacrifices did not always pay off.

Having witnessed what their parents faced during the economic hard times, many Gen Xers did not take advantage of their education or talents and ended up with jobs in the lowest-paying sectors of the market, often working for minimum wages. These social and economic experiences left many of this generation with a strong sense of cynicism about their lives, their future, and the country as a whole. This group is also generally critical of the Baby Boomer generation, which they see as self-centered, selfish, and unrealistic in its expectations and lifestyles.[64]

Generation Y

Generation Y (Gen Yers), those born approximately between 1977 and 1994, makes up over 20 percent of the U.S. population, or about 70 million people.[65] This group is likely to have a significant impact on the nation's social and economic landscape in the future, perhaps as much as Baby Boomers. Generation Y is characterized by three main elements.

First, members are comfortable with and tolerant of racial, ethnic, and cultural diversity.[66] Second—and perhaps most importantly—the parents of Generation Y children are very

Baby Boomers
The generation born post–World War II, representing about 76 million Americans responsible for some of the most dramatic social changes in American history, such as the Vietnam War protests, the Civil Rights Movement, and the rise of feminism.

involved in their daily lives and decision making. Parents often help Gen Yers plan their lives, take part in their daily activities, and strongly encourage them to succeed. One consequence of this support and involvement by parents is a sense of self-confidence: Gen Yers generally believe they can accomplish anything. Their relationship with their parents also makes it more likely for Gen Yers to believe they can return home for support and assistance.[67]

Third, Gen Yers tend to be more sophisticated in their computer skills than previous groups because of exposure to technology at an early age. In the United States, three out of four teenagers are online, and 93 percent of youths between fifteen and seventeen are computer users. Their time spent online consists of gaming, emailing, and instant messaging, according to the National Center for Health Statistics.[68] In short, this group is educated and technologically adept, and has been encouraged to achieve the goals they set for themselves. Not surprisingly, then, this group has a strong sense of entitlement to want the best in life and to think they deserve it.

It also means that this group is accustomed to instant gratification. Paying one's dues in a profession, or working one's way up the corporate ladder, is minimized in importance or even considered unacceptable to most Gen Yers. If they have the skill and talent, they believe, they should not have to wait to be promoted. Besides being smart, talented, and technologically savvy, and having a strong support mechanism, this ambitious, goal-driven group often is willing to cheat, if necessary, to achieve objectives.[69]

Because of the differing value systems, as well as having parents who are intimately involved in their lives both personally and professionally, members of Generation Y have grown up expecting success to come quickly and easily. The term used to describe the parents of Gen Yers is "helicopter parent": one who hovers just above the child and ensures that every need is met. While involvement and concern by a parent is normal and expected, when taken to such extremes, one result is that children are not allowed to experience the normal obstacles and difficulties associated with growing up.[70]

The social world of today's teenager is very different from that of previous generations. Technology largely drives social interactions and relationships: TiVo, Netflix, and YouTube allow teens to remain physically distant from each other while they watch movies on laptops, on iPhones, or at home. Text messaging and social networks like Facebook and Twitter are a primary, but also a physically distant, vehicle for social interaction and relationships. Coupled with demographic shifts in a postmodernist world, these changes have created a number of unique challenges for today's teens.

MARIO'S CASE

Defining Delinquency

Recall Mario's situation:

- struggling with the loss of his mother
- withdrawn from interacting with his family and community
- experiencing a strained relationship with his neighbors, who believe he has vandalized their properties

Thinking that Mario has violated the local curfew ordinance, a fed-up neighbor calls the police and insists that the youth be arrested. Although Mario did not break any laws by sitting on the curb in front of his house, the officer has limited options in responding to this type of situation.

Recall the difference between legal definitions of delinquency and those held by the general public. How might you define delinquency according to Mario's neighbor? If you were the officer in this scenario, would you categorize Mario's behavior as delinquent? Consider our discussion of the developmental issues that contribute to teenagers' behaviors. Do you think Mario is displaying typical teenage behavior?

THINK ABOUT IT

SOCIAL PROBLEMS AND YOUTHS

In addition to the developmental issues and cultural challenges, a number of structural problems, beyond the control of youths and their parents, can place youths at risk for engaging in delinquency. There are societal-level problems that impact the quality of life of youths and that influence the life chances or opportunities they have access to. In Chapter 4, when we examine social structural explanations of delinquency, we will discuss the four main challenges faced by youths today: poverty, unemployment, housing, and education.

Poverty

According to the U.S. Census Bureau, about 36 million people are defined as poor[71] because they do not earn enough money to meet their living expenses. If a family is at or below certain income thresholds, it is entitled to assistance or welfare from the government in the form of food stamps, subsidized housing, and/or Medicaid.

There is a belief that those who are poor lack a strong work ethic.[72] While this may be true in some cases, many impoverished individuals work one, and sometimes two, full-time jobs. Statistics show that approximately 76 percent of the poor are full-time employees[73] and that 25 percent of U.S. workers earn less than $16,000 per year (or about $7.69 per hour).[74] Most of the working poor are employed in minimum-wage jobs, with no health or retirement benefits. With such jobs, it is virtually impossible for people to earn an adequate living.[75] Poverty has a strong relationship to delinquency in that youths who live in poor areas or who cannot get jobs themselves may turn to crime as a solution. The nature of inner-city neighborhoods also places youths at risk to join gangs or to be victimized by others.

Unemployment

A central concern in the life of the poor is employment. At one time, individuals who graduated from high school could find well-paying jobs that afforded them a respectable standard of living. American-made products were far superior to those produced in other countries, and U.S. industrial workers were well paid. However, technological advances helped countries like Japan emerge as international powers in the consumer market (think of the rise of the automaker Toyota and the electronics giant Sony).

As a result, U.S. companies have gotten out of certain markets entirely or have outsourced the manufacturing of those products to lower-wage countries.[76] This has meant fewer jobs for American workers, greater competition for the jobs that remain, and the emergence of new industries, primarily high-tech, that require specialized training.

Consequently, many nonskilled and semi-skilled workers with a high school education or less find themselves without jobs or opportunities that would have been accessible to them a generation earlier. And many of the jobs available for these types of workers are in the lowest-paying sectors of the market.[77] Also, as well-paying jobs become more difficult to find, many people are taking jobs for which they are overqualified. This has a ripple effect throughout the labor market, with those at the bottom either stuck in low-wage jobs or squeezed out of the market entirely.[78] For teenagers, and particularly minorities, who have the highest unemployment rate of any group, finding a job in such an economy is especially difficult, and they may turn to delinquency as a result.

Housing

While most financial experts estimate that an individual or family should spend only about 30 percent of their income on housing, most low-income workers end up spending a lot more. According to one estimate, approximately 60 percent of people living in low-income areas spend 50 percent or more of their income on housing.[79] Although the recent economic downturn has resulted in a depression of the housing market, along with an increased number of foreclosures, the costs of housing remain high for many people.

As an option for housing, renting has traditionally been considered less expensive than home ownership. However, the housing crunch has raised the expenses of renting. According to the National Housing Trust Fund, the costs of renting have been steadily increasing since 2003, and increases in rents actually exceeded the rate of inflation in 2007. Rents are rising faster than people's incomes.[80]

Data from the Michigan Consumer Report show that the median monthly rent for an apartment (meaning half the rents were above and half were below) in 2008 in the United States was $815.[81] The practical realities involved in obtaining housing, such as security deposits and moving expenses, prevent many people from moving or improving their situations. When trying to manage these costs, some families must face the difficult decision of asking older children to leave home. This reality contributes to the number of homeless youths, as well as rates of criminal activity, which homeless youths engage in for survival.

Education

Many people think that educational or **academic achievement** opens the door to better job opportunities and a better quality of life, but educational opportunities are not equally distributed. Some experts argue that education can serve to reinforce one's social class position: if the quality of education is much lower in inner-city communities, then not all students are given the tools, knowledge, and skills they need to attend college or obtain well-paying jobs. Certainly, children living in poor areas tend to receive an inferior education compared to children from well-to-do families.[82]

Many inner-city public schools lack advanced preparation (AP) classes, up-to-date equipment, new technology, a sufficient number of current textbooks, well-trained teachers, and funding for innovative programs. Gang presence, crime, and drugs on school grounds limit the amount and quality of learning that can take place. Teachers in inner-city public schools spend more time maintaining order than actually providing instruction.[83] All of these influences affect academic achievement and future life chances.

To be fair, education does provide a path out of poverty for some individuals: a small number of people manage to succeed despite the obstacles described above. However, for too many youths, negative experiences in school result in their dropping out all together or finding other ways to earn a living. The relationship between education and delinquency will be further discussed in another chapter; but for now, note that education tends to reinforce an inner-city child's socioeconomic position. A Better Chance program, described in the box on page 18, offers some promise for remedying the inadequate education of minority youths.

RISK AND PROTECTIVE FACTORS

In addition to responding to the structural problems of poverty, unemployment, housing, and education, many teens also engage in a variety of behaviors that place them at risk to either be injured, killed, or involved with the juvenile justice system. These are called **risk factors,** or behaviors that place youths at higher risk of engaging in delinquency. These include drug and alcohol use, underage drinking and smoking, drug dealing, the use of violence to solve problems, running away, truancy, dropping out of school, weapons possession, vandalism, and theft. While some of these activities are considered typical teenage behaviors and are understood as part of a teenager's search for identity and independence, they do place youths at greater risk for getting into trouble.[84]

A related concept in understanding adolescent risky behaviors is what some psychologists call the **illusion of invulnerability.** This is the tendency of teenagers to believe that they are immune to the negative consequences of high-risk activities. This is not

academic achievement
Success in school that opens the door to better job opportunities and a better quality of life, although educational opportunities are not equally distributed.

risk factors
Behaviors that place youths at higher risk to engage in delinquency; anything that increases the probability that a person will suffer harm.

illusion of invulnerability
The tendency of teenagers to believe that they are immune to the negative consequences of high-risk activities.

THEORY AND PRACTICE WORKING TOGETHER

A Better Chance Program

In urban areas across the country, minority students have had to rely predominantly on public schools, which tend to have fewer resources and provide fewer opportunities for success, both of which result in considerable gaps in academic achievement. For instance, a study conducted in 2007 by the National Center for Education Statistics found that, among eighth graders, African Americans and Latinos scored lower than whites in standardized math, reading, and writing tests.

Academic struggles like these affect job opportunities and income. The American Medical Association notes that in 2006 almost 56 percent of physicians were white, while 4 percent were African American and 5 percent were Latino. Only about 15 percent of college graduates were African American and Latino (compared to almost 30 percent for whites), and African Americans accounted for only about 8 percent of MBA students at the top twenty-five business schools and only 3 percent of senior management positions in the United States.[85]

In 1963, at the height of the Civil Rights Movement, twenty-three headmasters of selective independent schools made a mutual commitment to change the profiles and compositions of their student bodies. By creating A Better Chance (ABC) program, they would broaden their enrollment to include students of color who were economically disadvantaged but academically talented.

Chosen for their motivation and demonstrated achievement, fifty-five students from low-income families were given the opportunity to complete their secondary education at these founding independent schools. Since it began, ABC has enjoyed considerable success. The program has grown from 55 students enrolled in nine schools to nearly 1,900 students enrolled in numerous schools during the 2008–2009 school year. To date, more than 96 percent of ABC-graduating seniors have gone on to college, and new ABC scholars have received over $6.5 million in financial aid. The latter statistic is significant since approximately one-third of ABC scholars live at or below the federal poverty line, and virtually all come from working-class families, with more than 65 percent coming from single-parent households.

 THINK ABOUT IT Do you think that intelligence and/or academic talent is based on innate factors, or does the environment play an important role in educational achievement?

to say that youths do not recognize the risks associated with extreme behaviors; rather, they often mistakenly believe that the potential or real consequences of those activities will not affect them—or that bad things only happen to other people. With the illusion of invulnerability, teens believe they possess some quality, trait, or characteristic that prevents them from being harmed or caught, or from experiencing any negative consequences.[86]

Most youths avoid getting into trouble, and if they do, their inappropriate behavior is often sufficiently addressed and does not require further intervention on the part of the juvenile justice system. As we will see in Chapter 7 on families and delinquency, some youths who experience obstacles and pressures that put them at risk of engaging in delinquency somehow manage to overcome them and become productive and healthy adults. Much of the work on resiliency focuses on what are called **protective factors**, or those that shield or minimize the risk factors to which youths are exposed.[87]

The research on resiliency indicates that these protective factors can be identified and nurtured through the use of what researchers refer to as developmental assets. Experts believe that there are forty developmental assets that allow youths to be resilient in the face of adversity.[88] Most youths possess about twelve, but the more assets a youth possesses, the greater the likelihood he or she will be resilient. These assets consist of positive experiences, relationships, opportunities, and personal qualities that young people need to grow up healthy, caring, and responsible.[89]

For example, research suggests that youths involved in constructive outlets during their free time are less likely to become involved in delinquency.[90] Spending time at home with family has a host of benefits, such as improving communication and the development of positive relationships with parents. Thus, attachments to family, good friends, a safe school, and a concerned and committed larger community can help youths withstand peer pressure and avoid risky behaviors.[91]

protective factors
Influences or variables that reduce youths' chances of offending and minimize the risks to which they are exposed.

MARIO'S CASE

Conclusions

Recall Mario's situation:

- struggling with the loss of his mother
- withdrawn and expressing symptoms of depression
- accused of breaking curfew

The neighbor's reaction to Mario's behavior is likely a result of the community's negative perception of him. Mario is obviously upset about something, and his behaviors indicate this. However, his community's reactions to him—and more significantly, their perception of him as a delinquent—may actually result in a greater likelihood of misbehavior, as we will explore further in our discussion of the labeling effect.

Does Mario's behavior, which is stressful for his father, his grandparents, and his community, qualify as criminal or delinquent? Do you think Mario's depressive behaviors are misunderstood by his community as signs of delinquency? What do think the officer might do to address Mario's problems? Moreover, how might the officer address the concerns of his neighbors?

Generational Differences

Describe the studied differences between the various generations we have discussed: Baby Boomers, Gen Xers, Gen Yers. How do the beliefs and behaviors of adolescents in particular contribute to our understanding of these generations?

Differences in Public Policy for Juveniles and Adults

During the 1990s, many laws were changed to reflect a more punitive approach to delinquency, and a number of the safeguards afforded to juveniles during the justice process were relaxed or eliminated. Today, the juvenile justice system maintains certain features that distinguish it from the adult system. As we have discussed, there are philosophical differences between the two systems; for example, in contrast to the adult justice process, the juvenile system emphasizes treatment, rehabilitation, and preservation. This framework influences many of the procedures that officials follow when a juvenile is taken into custody and processed in the system.

Many of these philosophical differences are applied symbolically to the terminology used at each stage of the process. The objective, of course, is to prevent youths from being damaged, harmed, or stigmatized by a negative label commonly associated with adult criminals. Table 1-4 offers insight into the main differences between the two systems of justice.

In the adult system, police officers arrest suspects, whereas in juvenile cases, the suspects are "taken into custody." While this term has come to mean practically the same thing, the original meaning of *taken into custody* was that officers brought youths to the police station in order to find alternative ways of handling them. Under the adult system, when an officer makes an arrest, a booking procedure follows, where the suspect is

TABLE 1-4 Terminology Differences between Adult and Juvenile Court Proceedings

Adult	Juvenile
Arrest	Taken into custody
Complaint or indictment	Petition
Defendant	Respondent
Bail hearing	Detention hearing
Trial	Fact-finding hearing
Verdict	Adjudication
Guilty	Delinquent
Sentence	Disposition

The differences in the various steps of the process reflect the treatment and rehabilitative philosophy of the juvenile justice system.

complaint
A formal charge against a suspect.

photographed, fingerprinted, and sometimes required to participate in a lineup. In most cases of juveniles who have committed acts of delinquency, these procedures are not allowed.[92]

In adult court, a formal charge against a suspect is sometimes referred to as a **complaint,** an information, or an indictment. The prosecutor, or a grand jury, determines the facts of the case and makes a decision about a formal charge. In juvenile cases, however, while it serves to formally ask the juvenile court to intervene in a particular case, a petition can be filed by a prosecutor, a parent, a teacher, or some other adult.

Trials in adult court are public events, where the defendant has an attorney and the prosecution puts forth evidence to a judge (and sometimes a jury). The steps involved are formal and structured, and include pretrial motions to exclude evidence or testimony, procedural questions during the trial, and the judge's rulings. In the juvenile court, however, the proceedings are much less formal, with cases often resembling business meetings. The court is given a great deal of flexibility in how to handle particular cases. In most cases, juveniles do not have an attorney, juries, and public attendance. However, juveniles still have constitutional protections. For example, transcripts and court records for juvenile cases are sealed and not available to the public.

Should an adult suspect be found guilty of his or her crimes, the verdict is read in open court, and sentencing occurs at a later date. In juvenile court, guilt or innocence is not the standard; the judge is interested in determining the facts of the case and rendering a decision that is in the best interests of the youth. Thus, the term *trial* is avoided; instead, a fact-finding hearing takes place. In a criminal trial, the defendant is found either guilty or innocent. In juvenile court, if the facts show that a crime was committed, the youth is adjudicated a delinquent rather than found guilty of a crime.

At such time, a determination or disposition is made as to how to rehabilitate the delinquent youth. A disposition is similar in nature to a sentence for an adult, but juvenile court judges have more options in deciding on an appropriate outcome. While adults can appeal their sentences and verdicts in criminal court cases, juveniles do not have a constitutional right to an appeal. Most states, however, have some sort of appeal process to provide constitutional rights to juveniles in criminal cases.

Many states are attempting to change the juvenile justice process to make it more like the adult system, with an emphasis on waiving youths to adult court for serious crimes. But there remain a number of substantial differences because most juveniles do not commit serious or violent crimes, and the rehabilitative focus of the juvenile justice system requires greater flexibility in solving cases informally. Most of the cases that come to the juvenile justice system are handled informally before getting to the juvenile court stage. And even then, judges often order some type of diversionary strategy, such as probation, in order to avoid the stigma associated with youths who are adjudicated a delinquent or detained in a facility.

THE BIG PICTURE

Conclusions on the Nature of Delinquency

- Why would state legislators pass more punitive laws regarding the treatment of juveniles when the public continues to believe in rehabilitation for most delinquents?
- Why did society's perceptions of children change in the late 1800s to become more humanitarian?
- Should the public use a legal or a social definition of delinquency? Explain.
- What social conditions in the 1960s led to changes in the way delinquent youths were processed and detained?
- Does youth incarceration have a positive impact on future behavior? Explain.

Key Terms

recidivism

illusion of invulnerability

status offenders

risk factors

protective factors

Orphan Trains

Children's Aid Society

Child Savers Movement

House of Refuge

training schools

parens patriae

individualized justice

waive jurisdiction

Juvenile Delinquency Prevention and Control Act

Juvenile Justice and Delinquency Prevention Act of 1974

Make the Call ▶ Nature of Delinquency

Review the scenario below, and decide how you would approach this case.

YOUR ROLE: Probation officer

DETAILS OF THE CASE

- A couple comes into your office to complain about their son, Austin.
- They want to file charges of ungovernability against the youth, because they claim he has threatened them with violence and refuses to obey the rules of the household.
- Austin also refuses to go to school and has been charged with truancy, resulting in a fine the parents had to pay.
- The parents further claim that Austin has stolen money from them in the past and even taken the family car, despite the fact that he does not even have a driver's license.
- You interview Austin, who claims that his parents are too strict, demand too much from him, and have unfair parenting practices, which is why he does not comply with their wishes.
- Austin also says that he is perfectly willing to comply, but his parents are being unreasonable in their demands and have unrealistic expectations of him.

WHAT DO YOU DO?

After hearing accounts from the mother and father, interviewing the youth and his teachers, and reviewing his file, you consider your options. If you process Austin as per the parents' instructions, you will have officially entered him into the juvenile justice system. Considering the difficulties Austin has had with regard to school, you believe the problem is not limited to his relationship with his parents. However, having Austin adjudicated will not necessarily change his behavior.

Consider:

- Do you recommend intensive therapy for Austin?
- Do you advise the parents about workshops and seminars for disobedient children?
- Do you revoke Austin's probation and allow him to be detained overnight in a secure facility, with a recommendation to the judge that he be ordered to participate in a psychological evaluation?
- Do you contact Child Protective Services and have them begin an investigation of the parents?
- Do you explain to the parents that this is a family matter that does not require the intervention of the juvenile justice system? Do you tell them that some of this behavior is normal for teenagers, but it is okay to set some reasonable boundaries?

Apply Theory to Reality ▶ Drift Theory

Skip ahead to Chapter 5 and read about Matza and Sykes's techniques of neutralization, better known as *drift theory*. Use this theory as a framework for understanding the behaviors associated with youths in this chapter.

Your Community ▶ Experiences of Adolescence

In addition to the information you glean from your readings, class lectures, and discussions, it is important to roll up your sleeves and immerse yourself in a topic as a researcher who gains an understanding of a problem or issue by observing or experiencing it firsthand. Through such methods, you gain a much greater appreciation of the magnitude and scope of the problem than if you were only engaged in "armchair theorizing."

■ Interview two close friends about their experience of their teenage years.

■ Then interview their parents to hear what they have to say about that period of their children's lives.

■ Compare the two responses. How do the events differ among the accounts? How are they similar?

■ Determine whether the events described by your friends or their parents constitute a legal definition of delinquency.

■ After collecting your data and drawing from the relevant literature, prepare a report or presentation of your findings that relates to our discussion of delinquency in Chapter 1. In particular, discuss the correlation between the behaviors attributed to youths and the legal and social definitions of delinquency.

Notes

[1] Juvenile Justice and Delinquency Prevention Act of 1974. P.L. 93-415, 88 Stat. 1109.

[2] See McNamara, R. H. 2008. *The Lost Population: Status Offenders in America.* Durham, NC: Carolina Academic Press.

[3] King, M., and Szymanski, L. 2006. "National Overview." *State Juvenile Justice Profiles.* Pittsburgh, PA: National Center on Juvenile Justice. Available at http://www.ncjj.org/state/profiles/.

[4] Ibid.

[5] See Simpson, A. W. 2010. *Blackstone's Commentaries on the Laws of England.* New York: Nabu Press.

[6] Ibid.

[7] Ibid.

[8] See, for instance, O'Connor, S. 2001. *Orphan Trains.* Boston: Houghton Mifflin.

[9] Ibid.

[10] Ibid.

[11] Tanenhaus, D. S. 2005. *Juvenile Justice in the Making.* New York: Oxford University Press.

[12] Freundlich, M. 2004. *A Return to Orphanages.* New York: Children's Rights. Available at http://www.childrensrights.org/wp-content/uploads/2008/06/return_to_orphanages_sept_2004.pdf.

[13] Tanenhaus, 2005.

[14] Marrus, E. 2007. *Children and Juvenile Justice.* Durham, NC: Carolina Academic Press.

[15] See, for instance, the Center on Juvenile and Criminal Justice at http://www.cjcj.org/juvenile/justice/juvenile/justice/overview.

[16] Tanenhaus, 2005.

[17] Ibid.

[18] Marrus, 2007.

[19] U.S. Department of Justice, Office of Justice Programs, Office of Juvenile Justice and Delinquency Prevention. 2006. *Juvenile Offenders and Victims 2006: A National Report.* http://www.ojjdp.ncjrs.gov/ojstatbb/nr2006/downloads/chapter4.pdf.

[20] Ibid.

[21] *Kent v. United States,* 383 U.S. 541 (1966).

[22] Ibid.

[23] Ibid.

[24] *In re Gault,* 387 U.S. 1 (1967).

[25] Ibid.

[26] Ibid.

[27] Ibid.

[28] Marrus, 2007.

[29] See Mendel, R. A. 2002. *Less Hype, More Help: Reducing Juvenile Crime: What Works and What Doesn't.* Washington, DC: America Youth Forum; Krisberg, B. 2005. *Juvenile Justice: Redeeming Our Children.* Los Angeles: Sage; Mackenzie, D. L. 2006. *What Works in Corrections.* Boston: Cambridge University Press, pp. 271–303.

[30] Ibid.

[31] http://www.census.gov/Press-Release/www/releases/archives/population/013733.htm.

[32] Ibid.

[33] See Bauerlein, M. 2008. *The Dumbest Generation.* New York: Penguin.

[34] Krisberg, B., and Marchionna, S. 2007. *Attitudes of U.S. Voters toward Youth Crime and the Justice System.* Washington, DC: National Council on Crime and Delinquency. Available at http://www.nccd-crc.org/nccd/pubs/zogby_feb07.pdf.

[35] Ibid.

[36] Ibid.

[37] http://www.census.gov/Press-Release/www/releases/archives/population/013733.htm.

[38] National Juvenile Justice Network. 2009. *Polling on Public Attitudes about Treatment of Young Offenders.* Washington, DC. Available at http://www.njjn.org/media/resources/public/resource_633.pdf. See also *Rehabilitation Versus Incarceration of Juvenile Offenders: Public Preferences in Four Models for Change States,* http://modelsforchange.net/pdfs/WillingnesstoPayFINAL.pdf; Nagin, D. S., and Piquero, A. R. 2006. "Public Preferences for Rehabilitation Versus Incarceration of Juvenile Offenders: Evidence from a Contingent Valuation Survey." *Criminology & Public Policy,* 5(4), November; National Council on Crime and Delinquency, 2007; Mears, D. P., Carter, J., Gertz, M., and Mancini, C. 2007. "Public Opinion and the Foundation of the Juvenile Court." *Criminology,* 45(1): 57–79.

[39] See, for instance, *Report of the Virginia Commission on Youth on the Study of Juvenile Justice System Reform,* House Document No. 37(1996); Soler, M. 1999. *Public Opinion on Youth, Crime and Race: A Guide for Advocates.* Washington, DC: Building Blocks for Youth. http://www.buildingblocksforyouth.org/advocacyguide.pdf.

[40] National Juvenile Justice Network, 2009.

[41] Juvenile Violent Offenders—The Concept of the Juvenile Super Predator. http://law.jrank.org/pages/1546/Juvenile-Violent-Offenders-concept-juvenile-super-predator.html#ixzz0auiTs8YR.

[42] Ibid.

[43] Marrus, 2007.

[44] Ibid.

[45] Ibid.

[46] Yanich, D. 2005. "Kids, Crime, and Local Television News." *Crime and Delinquency,* 51(1):103–132; see also Goidel, R. K., Freeman, C. M., and Procopio, S. T. 2006. "The Impact of Television Viewing on Perceptions of Juvenile Crime." *Journal of Broadcast and Electronic Media,* March, pp. 1–19; Gilliam, F., and Iyengar, S. 2001. "Prime Suspects: The Influence of Local Television News on the Viewing Public." *American Journal of Political Science,* 44: 560–573; Gilliam, F., and Iyengar, S. 2000. "Super-predators or Victims of Societal Neglect? Framing Effects in Juvenile Crime Coverage." In Callaghan, K., and Schnell, F. (eds.), *The Framing of American Politics* (pp. 148–166). Pittsburgh: University of Pittsburgh Press.

[47] Ibid. See also Cottle, J., and Perrault, R. 2009. "The Juvenile Delinquent Stereotype." Paper presented at the meeting of the American Psychology–Law Society, San Antonio, TX.

[48] Gilliam, F., and Bales, S. 2003. "Strategic Frame Analysis: Reframing America's Youth." *Social Policy Report,* 15: 3–21.

[49] Busselle, R. W. 2001. "Television Exposure, Perceived Realism, and Exemplar Accessibility in Social Judgment Process." *Media Psychology,* 3: 43–68; Busselle, R. W., and Shrum, L. J. 2003. "Media Exposure and Exemplar Accessibility." *Media Psychology,* 5: 255–282.

[50] Tamborini, R., Zillmann, D., and Bryant, J. 1984. "Fear and Victimization: Exposure to Television and Perceptions of Crime and Fear." In Bostrom, R. N. (ed.), *Communication Yearbook* (pp. 492–513). Beverly Hills, CA: Sage; Taylor, D. G., Scheppele, K. L., and Stinchcombe, A. L. 1979. "Salience of Crime and Support for Harsher Criminal Sanctions." *Social Problems,* 26: 413–424; Weaver, J., and Wakshlag, J. 1986. "Perceived Vulnerability to Crime, Criminal Victimization Experience and Television Viewing." *Journal of Broadcasting and Electronic Media,* 30: 141–155; Wilson, B. J., Colvin, C. M., and Smith, S. 2002. "Engaging in Violence on American Television: A Comparison of Child, Teen and Adult Perpetrators." *Journal of Communication,* 52: 36–60.

[51] See University of California, Irvine Medical Center. 2010. *Troubled Teen 101.* Available at http://www.troubledteen101.com/articles12.html.

[52] Ibid. See also Ponton, L. E. 1997. *The Romance of Risk: Why Teenagers Do the Things They Do.* New York: Basic Books.

[53] See the American Academy of Pediatrics at http://www.aap.org/.

[54] Ibid.

[55] University of California, Irvine Medical Center, 2010.

[56] Ibid.

[57] Ponton, 1997. See also Sachs, B. E. 2005. *The Good Enough Teen: How to Raise Adolescents with Love and Acceptance.* New York: Harper.

[58] Ibid.

[59] See Tulgan, B. 2000. *Managing Generation X: How to Bring out the Best in Young Talent.* New York: Norton.

[60] U.S. Census Bureau, 2006.

[61] Tulgan, 2000.

[62] IT Management. 2006. "Generation X for Dummies." www.eweek.com/article.

[63] Ibid.

[64] Tulgan, 2000.

[65] Ibid.

[66] Tulgan, B., and Martin, C. A. 2001. *Managing Generation Y.* Amherst, MA: HRD Press.

[67] Ibid.

[68] See Zemke, R., Raines, C., and Filipczak, B. 2000. *Generations at Work: Managing the Clash of Veterans, Boomers and Xers and Nexters in Your Workplace.* New York: American Management Association.

[69] Ibid.

[70] See Wiseman, R. 2006. *Queen Bee Moms and Kingpin Dads.* New York: Crown.

[71] U.S. Census Bureau, 2007. Poverty Thresholds. http://www.census.gov/poverty/incomethresholds.html. Accessed June 2, 2008.

[72] See, for instance, Henry, J. F. 2007. "Bad Decisions, Poverty, and Economic Theory—The Individualist and Social Perspective in Light of the American Myth." *Forum for Social Economics,* 36(1): 17–27.

[73] Kantowiz, M. 2007. *The Financial Value of a Higher Education.* Washington, DC: Institute for Higher Education Policy.

[74] The Economic Policy Institute. Minimum Wage: Frequently Asked Questions, 2005. Available at www.epinet.org.

[75] See, for instance, Allegratto, S. A. 2005. "Basic Family Budgets: Working Families' Incomes Often Fail to Meet Living Expenses around the U.S." Economic Policy Institute Briefing Paper #165. http://www.epi.org/publications/entry/bp165/.

[76] Congressional Research Reports for the People. 2004. "Deindustrialization of the U.S. Economy: The Roles of Trade, Productivity and Recession." April 15. Accessed June 1, 2008, at http://opencrs.dct.org.

[77] According to the U.S. Bureau of Labor Statistics, it is estimated that during his eight years in office, President Clinton created 23.1 million new jobs. In contrast, President Bush created a total of 6.0 million jobs as of 2008. See, for example, "Bush on Jobs: The Worst Record on Record." *Wall Street Journal,* January 9, 2009. Available at http://blogs.wsj.com/economics.2009/01/09/bush-on-jobs-the-worst-track-record-on-record/.

[78] Banglore, A. 2006. Noteworthy Aspects about the Participation Rate (2000–2005). Northern Trust Economic Research: Daily Global Commentary, January 10, 2006. http://www.northerntrust.com/library/econ_research/daily/us/dd011006.pdf.

[79] Bernstein, J., and Schmitt, J. 2000. "The Impact of the Minimum Wage: Policy Lifts Wages, Maintains Floor for Low-Wage Labor Market." Briefing Paper No. 96. Washington, DC: Economic Policy Institute.

[80] See, for instance, the National Housing Trust Fund fact sheet at http://www.nlihc.org/doc/factsheets/NHTFFactSheet-RentsvsInflation.pdf.

[81] See http://www.thomsonreuters.com/products_services/financial/financial_products/investment_management/research_analysis/umichigan_surveys_of_consumers.

[82] See, for instance, Margolis, E. (ed.). 2005. *The Hidden Curriculum in Higher Education.* New York and London: Routledge. See also Kozol, J. 1999. *Savage Inequalities.* New York: Crown.

[83] For a discussion of the social class differences in public education, see Kozol, J. 2006. *The Shame of the Nation.* New York: Crown.

[84] Shader, M. 2007. *Risk Factors for Delinquency: An Overview.* Washington, DC: U.S. Department of Justice, Office of Justice Programs, Office of Juvenile Justice and Delinquency Prevention. Available at http://www.ncjrs.gov/pdffiles1/ojjdp/frd030127.pdf.

[85] See http://www.abetterchance.org/abetterchance.aspx?pgID=967.

[86] Sagarin, B. J., Cialdini, R. B., Rice, W. E., and Serna, S. B. 2002. "Dispelling the Illusion of Invulnerability: The Motivations and Mechanisms of Resistance to Persuasion." *Journal of Personality and Social Psychology,* 83(3): 526–541.

[87] Goldstein, S., and Brooks, R. (eds.). 2005. *Handbook of Resilience in Children.* New York: Kluwer Academic Press.

[88] Ibid.

[89] See, for instance, Luthar, S. S. 2006. *Resilience in Development: A Synthesis of Research across Five Decades.* New York: Wiley. See also Elias, M. 2008. "Laws of Life: A Literacy-Based Intervention for Social-Emotional and Character Development and Resilience." *Perspectives in Education,* 26: 75–79. See also Heller, S. S., Larrieu, J. A., D'Imperio, R., and Boris, N. W. 1999. "Research on Resiliency to Child Maltreatment: Empirical Considerations. *Child Abuse and Neglect,* 23(4): 321–338. See the discussion of developmental assets and how to nurture their development at http://www.search-institute.org/.

[90] Ibid.

[91] Search Institute brochure. http://www.search-institute.org/. Accessed July 15, 2008.

[92] Marrus, 2007.

After reading this chapter, you should be able to:

- Understand the various methods of how delinquency is measured, including the FBI's Uniform Crime Report (UCR), the National Crime Victimization Survey (NCVS), and self-report studies.

- Construct the current offense patterns or trends in delinquency based on statistics and reports.

- Recognize the correlates of delinquency and determine how gender, race, social class, and age relate to delinquency.

- Examine why juveniles are at risk for victimization and its implications.

- Understand how delinquency is measured and how that measurement affects public policy.

Measuring Delinquency

Given that our society has wide access to technology, it would seem that information about the frequency and type of delinquency some youths commit would be readily available. While data exist on a wide range of topics, information related to delinquency is limited by a number of factors, including the nature of the measuring tools and the data itself. Consider the following situation about Audrey.

Audrey's profile:
- is eleven years old
- is a white female in a Northeast suburban middle school
- is a popular student, friendly and helpful to others at her school

Incidents at school:
- Two weeks ago, Audrey's locker was broken into and her iPod stolen.
- Audrey was so upset that she did not report the theft or the vandalism to the school principal.

Current status:
The next day, two girls confronted Audrey in the school's restroom and threatened to assault her if she did not surrender her lunch money. One girl even produced a knife to underscore the threat. Audrey did not share these events with teachers or friends, and the next day told her parents that she was not feeling well enough to go to school. When she returned several days later, no further incidents occurred, and Audrey's life returned to normal. No teachers or administrators were made aware of the incidents, nor were the police notified.

When trying to understand Audrey's situation, we might ask ourselves the following questions:
- Why did Audrey refrain from telling the principal about the stolen iPod?
- Why did Audrey fail to tell the principal about the vandalism?
- Was Audrey afraid of retaliation by the two girls?
- Is this type of event common in suburban middle schools?
- How might Audrey's unwillingness to report the incidents affect the outcome of future incidents like these?

There are a number of challenges to measuring the amount of crime and delinquency, such as how often victims report crimes to the police. What are some ways we can address the challenges?

Based on the scenario presented, how might you explain Audrey's response to the theft and the threats?

This chapter will explore the different ways in which delinquency is measured, as well as the limitations of these methods and the general trends that inform them. For example, we will examine the types of sources the media draw from in order to report the changes in rates of juvenile delinquency. In doing so, we will also focus on factors that give us insight into the nature of delinquency–gender, race, social class, and age–known as the *correlates of crime.*[1]

Measuring Crime and Delinquency

Chapter 1 discussed legal and social definitions of delinquency. Using these definitions, we are better able to measure the rates at which certain behaviors occur.

For the sake of measurement, the various tools used to assess delinquency tend to adhere to the legal definition of delinquency: behaviors carried out by youths, not of majority age, that violate the criminal code. There is also a category of offender that fits the social definition of delinquency more closely: status offenders, or youths who engage in behavior that would not be considered a violation if committed by an adult. Status offenses include truancy, running away, underage drinking, underage smoking, and incorrigibility. Although information is collected on status offenses, the indicators of delinquency mostly focus on traditional criminal behavior.

In our attempt to understand the different ways of measuring delinquency, we should note that most experts contend that there are three elements to every crime, sometimes referred to as the *crime triangle:* victim, offender, and location. This model suggests that unless all three elements exist, crime cannot occur.[2] The crime triangle also helps to conceptualize the different ways in which delinquency is measured. Instead of containing a victim, an offender, and a location, we can think of the crime triangle as including the police, the victim, and the offender (see Figure 2-1).

Each of the three main instruments used to measure crime focuses on a different dimension of crime and delinquency. The police generally use the Uniform Crime Reports (UCR) to collect information on crimes that are reported to them, as well as arrest information. Victimization surveys, such as the National Crime Victimization Survey (NCVS), focus on victims' experiences with crime, and self-report studies ask offenders about their experiences with criminal activity, particularly those in which they were not caught or arrested.

FIGURE 2-1   Crime Measurement Triangle
The crime triangle represents the three elements of a crime: victim, offender, and location. Each element is necessary for a crime to occur.

UNIFORM CRIME REPORTS (UCR)

In 1927, the International Association of Chiefs of Police (IACP) attempted to develop a system in which national crime statistics could be collected and analyzed. The goal was to use this information to determine how best to allocate law enforcement resources and to identify effective strategies to reduce crime. The IACP recognized that there were both an absence of data collected by many departments and problems in how certain crimes were defined. In trying to standardize the process, the IACP focused on the crimes that were the most serious and the most frequent; the result was the **Uniform Crime Reports** program, created in 1929.[3]

From the beginning, there was a concern about collecting crime data from police departments, since each state had different criminal codes and varying punishments for the same offense. Consequently, the UCR had to create its own standardized definition of these crimes for the purpose of reporting and measuring crime across the country. Part I and Part II crimes are classified as follows:

- **Part I crimes** consist of seven main classifications of violent crime, which are known as the **Crime Index.** These include murder and non-negligent manslaughter, forcible rape, robbery, aggravated assault, property crimes such as burglary and larceny, and motor vehicle theft. Congress added arson to the Crime Index in 1979.

- **Part II crimes** are offenses that provide a broad picture of less serious and danger-ous crimes. Twenty-one crimes fall under this classification, including simple assault, fraud, forgery, counterfeiting and embezzlement, vandalism, gambling, disorderly conduct, liquor law violations, offenses against family members, weapons possession, vagrancy, curfew violations, and status offenses.[4]

Using this classification structure, the UCR is able to offer a yearly glimpse of the nature of crime across the United States.[5]

In 1930, the attorney general of the United States designated the Federal Bureau of Investigation (FBI) to be the agency responsible for collecting and disseminating UCR data. Information on crimes known to the police is currently collected on a monthly basis. Police agencies around the country tabulate the number of offenses known to them based on reports from victims, officers who discover crimes on their own, and other sources. The data are sent to the FBI regardless of whether anyone was arrested or prosecuted, or whether any property was recovered. This information, along with other data, is presented in a yearly report titled *Crime in the United States.* The FBI lists the number of Index or Part I crimes, expressed as a rate per 100,000 people, which makes comparisons between different locations much easier.[6] The formula to calculate the crime rate is:

$$\frac{\text{Number of crimes known to police}}{\text{Size of total population}} \times 100{,}000$$

For instance, consider the differences in crime rates between New York City and Washington, DC. Simply examining the total number of crimes known to the police does not give a clear picture of the crime situation in each locale, because the two cities are different in size. New York City has many more crimes than Washington, DC, because it has a much larger population. However, by expressing it as a rate, the nature of the crime problem in both cities becomes clearer. In 2008, New York City had a crime rate of 2.37 per 100,000 people (198,419 crimes known to the police divided by 8,345,075, the size of the population, and multiplied by 100,000), whereas Washington, DC, had a crime rate of 6.23 per 100,000 people (36,894 offenses divided by a population of 591,833 and multiplied by 100,000).[7] Thus, the crime rate is actually higher in Washington, DC, than in New York City. In addition to calculating the overall crime rate for a given location, the rate for a particular crime (e.g., a murder rate, rape rate, or motor vehicle theft rate) can be calculated simply by taking the total number of crimes for those particular offenses (instead of all crimes known to the police) and applying the same formula.

Besides the number of crimes known to the police, arrest data are also collected along with the **clearance rate,** or the percentage of crimes "solved" by arrest. The clearance rate does not imply guilt or innocence, but rather represents a general assessment of law

---

Uniform Crime Reports
A system created by the International Association of Chiefs of Police (IACP) in 1927 to document the number of crimes, its data used to determine how to allocate law enforcement resources and to identify effective strategies to reduce crime.

Part I crimes
Seven main classifications of violent crime, which are known as the Crime Index, that include murder and non-negligent manslaughter, forcible rape, robbery, aggravated assault, property crimes such as burglary and larceny, and motor vehicle theft.

Crime Index
Seven main classifications of violent crime, including murder and non-negligent manslaughter, forcible rape, robbery, aggravated assault, property crimes such as burglary and larceny, and motor vehicle theft.

Part II crimes
Offenses that provide a broad picture of less serious and danger-ous crimes, such as simple assault, fraud, forgery, counterfeiting and embezzlement, vandalism, gam-bling, disorderly conduct, liquor law violations, offenses against family members, weapons possession, vagrancy, and curfew violations.

clearance rate
The percentage of crimes solved by arrest.

enforcement's ability to address crime.[8] Think of the clearance rate as a form of "batting average" of how many crimes occur and how many offenders the police apprehend. The clearance rate is calculated by dividing the number of arrests made by the number of crimes known, and then multiplying by 100 to express the rate as a percentage:[9]

$$\frac{\text{Number of arrests}}{\text{Number of crimes known to police}} \times 100$$

There are two primary ways in which a crime can be cleared for the purposes of the UCR. The first is by arrest. A person is arrested for a particular crime either because he or she confesses to committing that crime or because sufficient evidence exists to make the arrest. The second way is through *exceptional means,* which occurs when the police know the identity of the suspect but cannot make the physical arrest for some reason. For example, if a suspect commits suicide before being arrested or if a crime victim suddenly decides not to cooperate with law enforcement after the offender has been identified, the police cannot make an arrest.[10]

Another instance of exceptional means occurs when suspects commit an offense in another jurisdiction, are arrested, and are prosecuted for that crime. One interesting feature of the clearance rate is that the UCR counts the number of offenses that are cleared, not the number of people arrested. The arrest of one person may clear several crimes while the arrest of a group of offenders may clear only a single offense.[11]

Limitations of the UCR

One of the most glaring limitations of the UCR is that it collects information only on crimes that are known to the police. A great deal of unknown crime may not be present in the findings. This limitation, often called the **dark figure of crime,** prevents the UCR from providing the full crime picture. Some experts argue that nearly twice as much crime occurs as what is reported in the UCR.[12] This is because people often fail to report crimes to the police for various reasons:

dark figure of crime
Unknown crime that may not be present in UCR findings, resulting in an inability to have the entire crime picture.

- **Fear of retaliation:** victims may be unwilling to report crimes to the police for fear that the offender will return and victimize them again.
- **Lack of confidence in police:** victims do not always have faith in the police department to solve the case.
- **The belief that nothing can be done:** victims may not believe the offender will ever be caught or may feel that nothing can be done to repair the harm. For example, if you came out of your house one morning and discovered that the wheels on your car had been stolen, you might be tempted to call the police, especially since insurance companies routinely require a police report to accompany a claim. However, in this instance, you might also realize that you have a large deductible on your auto insurance policy (the amount you must pay out of pocket before the insurance company covers the rest), higher than the cost of the wheels. Thus, filing a police report will not help—you will have to replace the wheels completely at your expense. As a result, you may not report the crime to authorities.
- **Embarrassment/humiliation:** victims may be embarrassed, think they should have known better, or feel partially responsible for their **victimization.** Some may have been so traumatized by their experience that they do not want to relive it by telling the story again and again. This is particularly true for victims of sexual assault, who have to tell their story to several people including police officers, medical personnel, and the court.
- **Misunderstanding of the circumstances:** victims may not think an actual crime occurred. For example, if a victim thinks she lost her purse, she would not report it as stolen.[13]

victimization
The situation in which individuals become the receivers of crime and are sometimes made to feel embarrassed, think they should have known better, or feel partially responsible for their trauma by the retelling of their story to several parties.

UCR data also limit how crimes are defined by the program. While a common definition is necessary for police departments to submit standardized data, problems sometimes emerge as a result. For instance, the UCR defines forcible rape as "the carnal knowledge of a female forcibly and against her will. Rapes by force and attempts or assaults to rape, regardless of the age of the victim, are included. Statutory offenses (no force used—victim under age of consent) are excluded."[14] This definition restricts data collection on rape to only females and adults. Such a narrow definition limits our understanding of the extent of rape crime and cases if the UCR is the only source used.

Another limitation of the UCR relates to how crimes are recorded. When officers respond to a call, an actual crime must have taken place for the incident to be on record with the UCR. A resident may contact the police department because he or she thinks someone is breaking into a neighbor's home. But if upon examining the home and surrounding area, the officers find no evidence that a crime has occurred, the incident is declared *unfounded* and is not included in the UCR monthly totals. **Unfounded crimes,** therefore, become important in our discussion of manipulating the crime count.[15]

Only the most serious charge in an incident gets recorded. Let's revisit the situation discussed earlier. If the responding officers discover a suspect during a breaking-and-entering incident, and in the process, the suspect attempts to flee by holding a neighbor hostage, stealing a car, and shooting at the officers, only the most serious offense—which is the attempted murder of a police officer—gets recorded for UCR purposes. Other crimes that took place during this scenario will not appear in the UCR monthly totals. This rank-ordering of offenses for the UCR count is sometimes referred to as a **hierarchical line** and contributes to an artificial evaluation of the amount and frequency of actual crime that exists.[16]

Finally, the UCR suffers from the *politics of policing,* when data are manipulated to give the appearance that crime is either increasing or decreasing, depending on the given police department's needs. Issues of funding for additional officers and equipment might be given greater consideration during appropriations time in a given community if there is an apparent increase in the crime rate. Similarly, sometimes a "promise" of a decrease in crime by a local politician or police chief is made and then proven correct by the data. While we are not suggesting that police chiefs are openly dishonest about the data, there may be instances in which political pressure influences recording practices. One way to manipulate the crime rate relates to unfounded crimes: if a department declares many crimes as unfounded, overall, fewer crimes will be reported in the monthly UCR total. Conversely, if every incident, no matter how trivial, is declared to be a crime, the result will be a dramatic increase in the overall crime rate.

unfounded crimes
Incidents in which a crime has been reported but no evidence has been found to indicate a crime has occurred.

hierarchical line
Rank-ordering of offenses for the UCR count.

National Incident-Based Reporting System (NIBRS)

Given the limitations of the UCR program, in the 1980s, law enforcement agencies called for the modernization of the program. In 1988, the FBI developed the UCR program's National Incident-Based Reporting System (NIBRS) to collect data on each reported crime incident, instead of information only on the types of crime and arrests.[17] The NIBRS requires local police agencies to provide a brief account of each incident and arrest, including information on the victim and offender. Police departments provide information on each criminal incident related to the seven Part I crimes and to an expanded list covering fifty-six specific offenses, including blackmail, embezzlement, drug offenses, and bribery. The gathering of such information led to the development of a national database on the nature of crime, victims, and criminals.[18]

The FBI began accepting NIBRS data from a handful of agencies in January 1989. Based on 2008 data submissions, thirty-one states submitted NIBRS data in some way to the FBI, while thirteen states submitted all their data via the NIBRS. The remaining states either are in various stages of testing the NIBRS or are planning to implement it in the near future.[19]

In June 2004, the FBI discontinued use of the Crime Index in the UCR program. Recall that the Crime Index, first published in *Crime in the United States* in 1960, was the name used for a summary of the seven main offenses (Part I offenses). The Modified Crime Index, used after 1979, tabulated the seven Index offenses plus arson. Neither were good indicators of criminality, however, because they were inflated by so many larceny-theft crimes.[20] Because larceny-theft is the most frequently reported crime, those jurisdictions that had exceptionally high numbers of the offense often had a higher overall crime rate than other locations with more serious crimes. The UCR provided a measure of only volume of crime, not seriousness. For this reason, the UCR abandoned its Crime Index and now uses a violent crime and property crime index for comparison purposes.[21]

VICTIMIZATION STUDIES

Many of the problems stemming from the UCR—in particular, the issue of the dark figure of crime—led to the development of other measures to capture the extent of crime in the United States. One method involves asking victims about their experiences with crime, instead of the police.

In 1972, in response to the substantial volume of crime not reported to the police, the U.S. Census Bureau began conducting studies to determine the extent of crime. The *National Crime Survey,* later renamed the **National Crime Victimization Survey (NCVS)** in 1990, was created to give policymakers a better idea of the extent and scope of crime. The NCVS is a telephone survey of victims. The 2008 sample consisted of approximately 135,000 people representing 76,000 households across the United States. Only people ages thirteen and older were interviewed; information about younger residents of a household was obtained from adults. Approximately once a year, research staff from the NCVS contact respondents involved in the survey and pose a series of baseline questions to determine whether they were victims of one or more of the crimes of interest. Those who answer "yes" are provided with additional questions that explore the nature and circumstances of the crime.[22]

The NCVS is a comprehensive survey of victims since it collects data on both personal and household crimes. Personal crimes include crimes of violence such as rape, robbery, and assault, and crimes of theft, which consist primarily of larceny. Homicide is not included in the NCVS list of offenses because homicide victims cannot be interviewed or asked to complete a questionnaire.[23]

Burglary, household larceny, and motor vehicle theft are among the eight household crimes known as *crimes of interest,* selected based on the likelihood that victims will report them to the police. In 1993, the Bureau of Justice Statistics took over responsibility for administering the NCVS from the Census Bureau and redesigned it because the survey did not collect data on certain crimes, such as sexual assault and domestic violence. Victims began reporting more types of criminal incidents, and victims are now more likely to report aggravated and simple assault, and unwanted or coerced sexual contact.[24]

The NCVS helps to uncover the dark figure of crime, as well as some of the reasons victims do not report crime to the police. It has also revealed a great deal of information about the characteristics surrounding certain types of crime, including the relationships between victims and offenders. According to the 2008 NCVS, only about half of all violent crimes and 40 percent of all property crimes were reported to the police. Common reasons for not reporting the crime to the police include the following:

- The respondent thought the situation was a private or personal matter (20 percent).
- The incident was not considered important enough to report (17 percent).
- The situation was reported to someone else (14 percent).[25]

Of the property crimes listed in the NCVS, motor vehicle theft (80 percent) had the highest reporting levels.

Limitations of the NCVS

Like all measuring tools, the NCVS is not without its limitations. The first involves the relatively small number of crimes for which data are collected. Second, the NCVS is a measure of victimization that asks respondents to recall the number and circumstances of crimes in the recent past. It is often difficult for people to remember such information. Researchers have identified five main problems related to NCVS data:

- Respondents often fail to recall all the events within the last six months or year.
- Respondents "telescope" their experiences—that is, they remember only the most recent event—affecting the overall estimation of victimization.
- People simply do not tell the truth about their experiences—they fabricate crimes.
- Respondents fail to discuss crimes out of embarrassment. This is particularly true for adolescents who have been victimized by peers or family members.
- Sampling errors occur. This is a chronic problem with all types of survey research: respondents in the sample might not be representative of the overall population, which

---

National Crime Victimization Survey (NCVS)
A telephone survey of victims that gives policymakers a better idea of the extent and scope of crime.

raises questions about the ability of researchers to generalize the findings from the sample to the entire population from which they were selected.[26]

The NCVS collects data using a scientific sampling procedure, with households as the main source of respondents. But this means that those who do not have residences, such as homeless youths, are excluded from the sample.[27] This segment of the juvenile population is frequently victimized, but the extent and characteristics of those crimes are not included in the NCVS.

Victimization Surveys and the UCR

Given the relationship between the UCR and the NCVS, how can each be used to obtain an accurate picture of the extent of crime? Both are independent measures of crime, meaning they use different methodologies and subjects. Therefore, if we find consistency in the frequency of a particular crime, we can be confident that the estimated number is accurate. For example, if we take the number of motor vehicle thefts reported in the UCR (956,846) and compare it to the number offered by the NCVS (979,640), we can generally conclude that this is a good approximation of how many cars were stolen in the United States in 2008.[28]

MEASURING CRIME: SELF-REPORT STUDIES

While the UCR and the NCVS help us to understand general crime and delinquency trends, there remain a number of crimes that are not reported to the police or revealed in the NCVS. What these measures do not tell us is how many youths committed crimes but were not arrested. Neither the UCR nor the NCVS tells us much about the individual offenders in terms of their attitudes, values, and beliefs. **Self-report studies,** which are primarily surveys or interviews, ask youths about their experiences with criminal activity.

There are many self-report studies conducted on a number of topics relating to teen behavior, including serious crime. Other studies focus primarily on risk-taking behavior or minor forms of delinquency such as sexual behavior, drug and alcohol use, and underage smoking. One of the most widely used self-report measures to assess youths' drug use and health behaviors is the National Drug Use and Health Study (NDUHS), an annual nationwide survey involving interviews with approximately 70,000 randomly selected individuals ages twelve and older. Adults in the household convey the information about victimization of anyone under the age of twelve in that household. The NDUHS is a study conducted by the Substance Abuse and Mental Health Services Administration, which is a division of the U.S. Department of Health and Human Services.[29]

Another important national self-report study is called Monitoring the Future (MTF), an annual survey involving about 46,000 eighth-, tenth-, and twelfth-grade students in nearly 400 secondary schools across the country. The MTF study is conducted by researchers at the University of Michigan's Institute for Social Research. The purpose is to gauge the behaviors, attitudes, and values of American secondary school students, college students, and young adults.[30] Included in previous versions of the MTF study were questions relating to teenagers' involvement in criminal behavior, such as larceny, vandalism, and assault.[31]

The National Youth Risk Behavior Survey (YRBS), conducted by the federal Centers for Disease Control, monitors behaviors that contribute to the leading causes of death, disability, and social problems among youths and adults in the United States. The YRBS is conducted every two years and provides data representative of ninth- through twelfth-grade students in public and private schools throughout the United States.[32]

The information gathered from self-report studies has been invaluable in understanding the nature and extent of crime and delinquency in the United States. Researchers have found that more than 90 percent of juveniles have committed acts that could have resulted in incarceration had they been caught and prosecuted. Self-report studies have also shown more insight into the nature of the dark figure of crime—approximately four to ten times more crime occurs than what is reported in the UCR.[33] Perhaps most importantly, self-report studies have helped juvenile justice officials and researchers to better understand the racial and ethnic biases in the juvenile justice system.[34]

Some people question whether self-report data are reliable. After all, self-report studies generally make use of smaller samples, and subjects' responses may be problematic. When asked to recount their experiences with delinquency, some youths may forget about events

self-report studies
Primarily surveys or interviews that ask individuals about their experiences with criminal activity.

that occurred, may exaggerate the circumstances or even lie about certain events to make themselves appear more deviant, or may withhold information out of embarrassment.[35]

How do researchers determine the accuracy of what is being reported? Recent developments in the methodology of self-report studies have given researchers greater confidence in analyzing the responses of subjects—for example, the use of polygraph tests, comparisons of youths' responses to official police records, reinterviews with youths to see if their answers remain consistent, or conversations with youths' friends to corroborate the accounts.[36] Much of the concern about *reliability* (the consistency of the response over time) and *validity* (the accuracy of the response) is less of an issue with researchers.[37] Studies have found that self-report surveys are a reliable and accurate indicator of delinquent activities despite the potential drawbacks.[38]

The main limitation of self-report studies is that serious and chronic offenders are often missed—they rarely participate in surveys. This can lead observers to underestimate the overall extent of the delinquency problem and to overlook the most active offenders, who are qualitatively different from the average delinquent.[39]

AUDREY'S CASE

Measuring Delinquency

Recall Audrey's situation:

- is an eleven-year-old white female in a suburban middle school
- was the victim of theft and, later, physical threats
- failed to report the theft, vandalism, or bullying to the school principal

Audrey refused to tell her teachers, the principal, or her parents about either incident. She even lied to her parents about the loss of her iPod, telling them that she had misplaced it. It seems to go without saying that Audrey should have informed someone of these incidents. However, she later admitted to feeling embarrassed and even humiliated by what happened.

How might Audrey's failure to report these crimes affect the measurement of official crime at her school? What might teachers or administrators at her school do to encourage students to step forward when they have been victimized?

Measuring Crime

Recall the various methods for measuring delinquency, including the UCR, the NCVS, and self-report studies. What are some of the limitations of each method? Which do you think is the most accurate approach to measuring crime, and why?

General Trends in Delinquency

As was mentioned, one of the ways to overcome the deficiencies of any one measure of juvenile crime is to use multiple sources to determine whether there is consistency in the trends for certain types of crime. For instance, if the number of motor vehicle thefts is similar across independent measures, that consistency provides researchers with confidence that the number is an accurate one. To identify recent trends in delinquency, we draw on a number of sources including UCR and NCVS data, reports from the Office of Juvenile Justice and Delinquency Prevention (OJJDP), as well as statistics generated from the National Center on Juvenile Justice.

One of the most comprehensive reports on the nature of delinquency is derived from the OJJDP. Titled *Juvenile Offenders and Victims,* this report relies on data developed by a number of sources, including:

- NCVS
- Bureau of Labor Statistics 1997 National Longitudinal Survey of Youth
- Centers for Disease Control's (CDC) Youth Risk Behavior Surveillance Survey
- UCR's Supplementary Homicide Reports
- NIBRS and the Monitoring the Future study

Information on gangs is drawn from the National Youth Gang Survey, supported by the OJJDP, and data on the association between offenses and contacts with the juvenile justice system come from the OJJDP's Causes and Correlates Studies. The 2006 report, which collected data from all of these sources, provided a comprehensive picture of delinquency in the United States while avoiding the limitations found in any single measurement tool.[40]

OFFICIAL STATISTICS

What proportion of crimes can be attributed to delinquents? According to official reports, juveniles are responsible for about 15 percent of all crimes committed in the United States. Despite media attention on violent crimes and drive-by shootings, juveniles are arrested for only about 10 percent of all homicides. As Figure 2-2 shows, contrary to popular

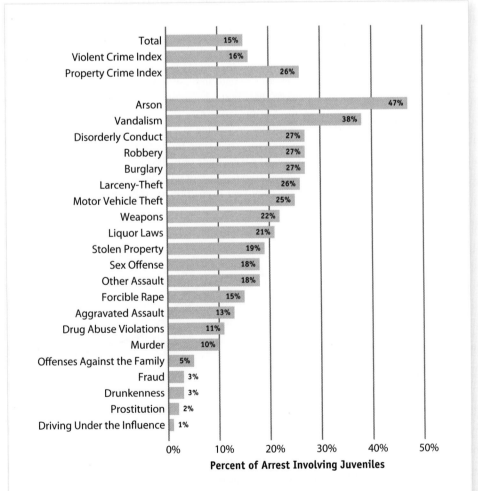

FIGURE 2-2 Percentage of Juvenile Arrests by Offense

Juveniles commit a small proportion of violent crimes despite media attention.

Source: *Crime in the United States 2008.* Washington, DC: Federal Bureau of Investigation, 2009, Table 38.

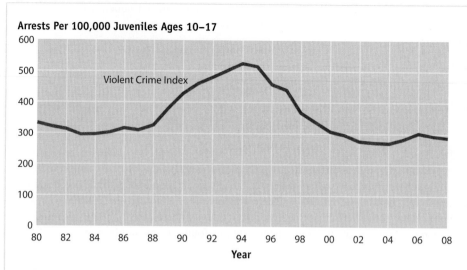

FIGURE 2-3 Trends in Juvenile Violent Crime Index

Violent crimes committed by juveniles have continued to decline.

Source: Analysis of arrest data from the FBI and population data from the U.S. Census Bureau and the National Center for Health Statistics.

belief, juveniles are responsible for a relatively small percentage of motor vehicle thefts (about 25 percent) and vandalism (38 percent), traditionally thought of as crimes committed primarily by juveniles.[41]

According to the UCR, in 2008, there were an estimated 2.11 million arrests of persons younger than age eighteen in the United States, a decrease of about 3 percent from 2007. While the UCR's Violent Crime Index rates had increased in both 2005 and 2006, arrests for violent crimes fell about 2 percent. As Figure 2-3 demonstrates, recent data show that while there are some exceptions, most crime categories showed a decrease.[42]

With regard to property crime, a similar decreasing arrest trend has been noted, with one exception. If we examine the Juvenile Property Crime Index between 1994 and 2006, the number of arrests fell by half. However, if we examine only the last two years, the number of juvenile arrests for property crimes increased because of a higher number of juvenile arrests for larceny-theft, which rose 8 percent each year from 2006 to 2008 (see Figure 2-4).[43]

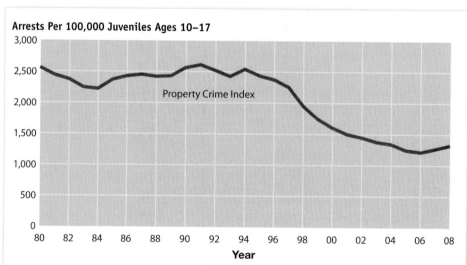

FIGURE 2-4 Trends in Juvenile Property Crime Index

Why did the number of juveniles arrested for property crimes show a steady decline until 2007? Was it because of tougher laws or other factors?

Source: Analysis of arrest data from the FBI and population data from the U.S. Census Bureau and the National Center for Health Statistics.

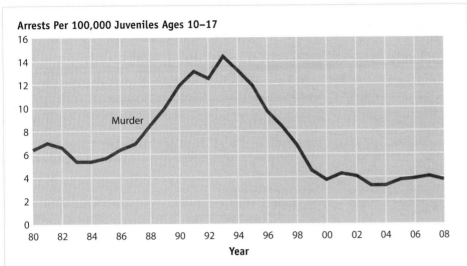

Arrests Per 100,000 Juveniles Ages 10–17

Murder

FIGURE 2-5 Arrests for Juvenile Homicide, 1980–2008

Why is so much media attention given to juvenile homicides when the rates are so low?

Source: Puzzanchera, C. 2009. *Juvenile Arrests 2008*. Washington, DC: U.S. Department of Justice, Office of Justice Programs, Office of Juvenile Justice and Delinquency Prevention.

Arrest rates of juveniles for murder have also decreased in recent years. As indicated in Figure 2-5, during a ten-year period from the mid-1980s to 1993, the juvenile arrest rate for murder more than doubled. This growth is often attributed to the increase in drug trade, specifically crack cocaine, and fights over gang territory. A great deal of effort was made to reduce gang violence after 1993, which led to a decrease in the juvenile arrest rate for homicide through 2004. The rate began to increase again in 2004 but decreased in 2008.[44]

These data raise the question of what can be done to reduce juvenile homicides. Operation Night Light (see the box on page 36) offers a program with promise.

DELINQUENT TRENDS: SELF-REPORT STUDIES

Self-report studies indicate that delinquency includes a wide range of activities. While the UCR data tend to focus more on street crimes and to provide information on serious crimes, self-report studies cover a much broader swath of delinquent activities, particularly minor violations such as drug use, underage drinking, and smoking.[45] Consistent with official statistics like those provided by the UCR and NCVS, self-report studies show that boys report involvement in a greater number of offenses than girls. They also show that boys commit a wider variety of crimes. Older adolescents tend to report more offenses than younger ones. This may be attributed to the fact that older youths are more willing to take greater risks than their younger counterparts.

According to the YRBS, in 2009, about 18 percent of students carried a weapon at least one day in the last thirty, about 6 percent carried a gun, and nearly a third had been in a physical fight in the last twelve months. Nearly 10 percent of teens had hit, slapped, or physically hurt their boyfriend or girlfriend the previous year.[46]

According to the NDUHS, in 2008, an estimated 70.9 million Americans ages twelve and older were current users (using within the past thirty days) of a tobacco product, representing about 28 percent of the population. About 84 percent (59.8 million persons) of tobacco users in 2008 were cigarette smokers.[47] The NDUHS also reported that about 10 million persons age twelve to twenty reported alcohol consumption. Approximately 6.6 million (about 17 percent) were binge drinkers, those having five or more drinks on the same occasion or within a few hours on at least one day in the past thirty; and 2.1 million (about 6 percent) were heavy drinkers, those having at least five or more drinks on the same occasion on each of five or more days in the past thirty.[48]

Findings from the 2009 MTF survey indicate that drug use among teenagers has declined somewhat. But perhaps the most important finding in that year's results was

THEORY AND PRACTICE WORKING TOGETHER

Reducing Juvenile Homicides: Operation Night Light

Probation is a common disposition in juvenile cases, and the number of youths placed on probation has increased substantially in the last three decades. However, during this time, resources and the staffing of probation offices have remained the same or have been reduced. Probation officers sometimes have caseloads of 150 probationers or more, making adequate supervision difficult, if not impossible. Often officers must resort to telephone contact with probationers and spend much more time working from their offices. As a result, many youths, particularly probationary high-risk offenders, go unsupervised.

One of the more common parameters of probation agreements is a curfew, which requires the probationer to be at home by a certain time. Probation officers typically work from 8:30 am to 4:30 pm. With fewer probation officers able to venture out into the community, restrictions set by curfews are unenforceable. This enforcement responsibility could not fall to the police during these hours since officers working night shifts have no way of knowing whether a particular youth is on probation. Moreover, whereas probation officers have wide latitude to stop, search, and detain youths on probation, police officers are limited in their ability to stop and search youths in general. All of these issues have resulted in higher rates of recidivism for youths on probation, particularly high-risk offenders.

In 1992, Operation Night Light began as an informal collaboration between probation officers in the Dorchester, Massachusetts, District Court and police officers in Boston's Anti-Gang Violence Unit. Initially, the program paired one probation officer with two police officers as backup to make surprise visits to the homes, schools, and work sites of high-risk juvenile probationers from 7 pm to midnight. These visits were important in conveying to probationers the seriousness of their offenses and in making them aware of the higher probability of getting caught if they violated their probation agreements. The presence of police officers also ensured probation officers' safety while visiting these areas. Since its inception, the program has expanded to include dozens of police and probation officers, who spend at least 20 percent of their time in the community during evening hours.

The success of Operation Night Light is notable. Initially coupled with a larger violence-reduction strategy, juvenile homicides in the Boston area were reduced from 152 to 31 between 1990 and 1999. Compliance with probation agreements more than doubled to 70 percent during the same time period. Some evaluations demonstrated a higher level of cooperation and information sharing between the police and probation departments, as well as higher levels of morale within each agency.[49] The success of Operation Night Light has led many other jurisdictions to adopt it as a strategy to address juvenile crime. In fact, Operation Night Light has been so successful that it has been identified as an "exemplary" program by the OJJDP.[50]

THINK ABOUT IT

Did increasing the patrol hours of probation officers have an impact on juvenile homicide, or are there other explanations for this trend?

---

that marijuana use had begun to increase after a decade of gradual decline. In general, use of other drugs, such as LSD, cocaine, crystal methamphetamine, and sedatives, showed a decrease in 2009, whereas the use of drugs such as ecstasy, heroin, and other opiates such as OxyContin, Vicodin, and Rohypnol, as well as tranquilizers, remained steady.[51]

THINK ABOUT IT

Patterns of Delinquency

Consider the trends of various types of delinquency discussed in this chapter. What does the research suggest about the likelihood that some youths will progress to become violent adult criminals? Do you think that these projections are accurate? If so, how might future criminal behavior be deterred?

Correlates to Delinquency

Delinquency does not occur randomly, but follows patterns and trends. A number of factors can help us to better understand how, when, where, and why delinquency occurs. These factors are sometimes called *correlates* to delinquency and consist primarily of gender, race, social class, and age.

GENDER

In 2008, there were 629,800 arrests of females younger than age eighteen. Over the past decade, the number of juvenile females arrested has decreased at a lower rate than that of their male counterparts in most offense categories.[52] According to Table 2-1, police officers are more likely to arrest females than in the past. In fact, the rate of female arrests has increased noticeably over the last ten years.

For example, girls are more likely than boys to be arrested as runaways. There are two possible explanations for this. It might be that girls are more likely than boys to run away from home; or it could be the case that the police view the female runaway as the more serious problem and are therefore more likely to process females through official juvenile justice channels.

Girls are also more likely than boys to be arrested for simple assault, DUI, disorderly conduct, and larceny. Once again, the implications of these data are ambiguous: they might suggest that more females are engaging in these crimes or that police officers are more willing to arrest females than they once were.

In the past, the tendency not to arrest females was explained as the result of paternalistic practices by officers who believed that girls were more likely to get in trouble if they were on the street. This is sometimes referred to as the *chivalry hypothesis,* which we will discuss in more detail in Chapter 11.

RACE

According to official statistics, the racial composition of the U.S. juvenile population age ten to seventeen in 2008 was 78 percent white Americans, 16 percent black Americans, 5 percent Asian/Pacific Islanders, and 1 percent American Indians.[53] Of all juvenile arrests for violent crimes in 2008, 47 percent involved white youths, 52 percent involved black youths, 1 percent involved Asian youths, and 1 percent involved American Indian youths.[54] As Table 2-2 shows, the proportion of arrests for black youths is much higher for all crimes except liquor law violations.

In general, black youths are arrested for a disproportionate number of murders, rapes, robberies, assaults, and other crimes, whereas white youths are arrested for a disproportionate number of arson offenses and alcohol-related violations. The Violent Crime Index arrest rate in 2008 for black juveniles was about five times the rate for white juveniles, six times the rate for American Indian juveniles, and thirteen times the rate for Asian juveniles.[55]

TABLE 2-1 Changes in Percentage of Juvenile Arrests, 1999–2008[56]

Most Serious Offense	Percent Change in Juvenile Arrests, 1999–2008	
	Female	Male
Violent Crime Index	−10%	−8%
Robbery	38	24
Aggravated assault	−17	−22
Simple assault	12	−6
Property Crime Index	1	−28
Burglary	−3	−16
Larceny-theft	4	−29
Motor vehicle theft	−52	−50
Vandalism	3	−9
Weapons	−1	−3
Drug abuse violations	−2	−8
Liquor law violations	−6	−29
DUI	7	−34
Disorderly conduct	18	−5

Are the differences between males and females really the result of different offending patterns or are other factors at work?

TABLE 2-2 Proportion of Arrests for Black Youths[57]

Most Serious Offense	Black Youths' Proportion of Juvenile Arrests in 2008
Murder	58%
Forcible rape	37
Robbery	67
Aggravated assault	42
Simple assault	39
Burglary	35
Larceny-theft	31
Motor vehicle theft	45
Weapons	38
Drug abuse violations	27
Vandalism	19
Liquor law violations	6

Are black youths getting arrested more often because they commit more crimes, or are the police using selective enforcement?

As seen in Figure 2-6, for property crimes, the rate for black juveniles was more than double the rate for whites and nearly six times the rate for Asian juveniles.[58] Experts often refer to the higher arrest rate as a reflection of a type of systematic discrimination against African Americans in the juvenile justice system. African American youths are more likely to be stopped, searched, and arrested by the police compared to white youths.[59] Some argue that the reason blacks are overrepresented in the arrest statistics is that they commit more crimes. One way to examine this issue is to compare the racial differences in self-report data with those found in official delinquency records. If there is little difference between the number of crimes reported by whites and African Americans, then some support may be given to the discrimination argument.

The evidence, such as the MTF study, shows that whites and African Americans have similar offending patterns,[60] suggesting that racial differences in the official crime data may reflect the fact that African American youths have a much greater chance of being

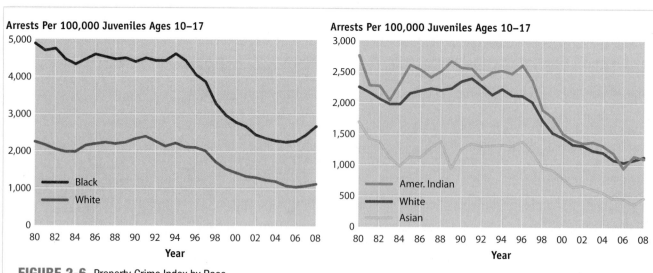

FIGURE 2-6 Property Crime Index by Race

What explains the low rate of arrests for Asian youths?

Source: Puzzanchera, C. 2009. *Juvenile Arrests 2008.* Washington, DC: U.S. Department of Justice, Office of Justice Programs, Office of Juvenile Justice and Delinquency Prevention.

arrested and officially processed than white youths. However, some experts warn that African American youths may underreport more serious crimes, which limits self-report data as a good indicator of racial differences in delinquency and treatment by the juvenile justice system.[61] Other data indicate that police officers routinely search, question, and detain African American males. Additionally, other studies show that African American youths are more likely to be formally processed in the juvenile justice system, more likely to be adjudicated a delinquent, and more likely to be detained rather than having their cases diverted than white youths.[62]

Why is this the case? Perhaps juvenile court judges see offenses committed by African American youths as more serious than those committed by white offenders. Judges also seem more willing to give white defendants lenient sentences if they can demonstrate strong family ties or if they live in two-parent households. This initial contact with the juvenile justice system is critical, since having a formal juvenile record increases the likelihood that police officers will arrest youths rather than release them with a warning. It also means that youths are eligible for more severe punishment should they return to juvenile court and be adjudicated a delinquent.[63]

Some experts argue that the reason African American youths are arrested at a disproportionate rate has nothing to do with bias or discrimination. Rather, the differences are attributed to higher rates of offending—in other words, they are arrested more often because they commit more crimes.[64] Others argue that the main explanation for higher rates of offending has to do with access to social and economic success. Low employment rates, for example, particularly among African American males, put a strain on marriages, weaken the family structure, leading to a lack of adequate supervision of children in the household, and limit a family's ability to control youths' behavior.[65]

This lack of social and economic access can be attributed to the more general exclusion of blacks from educational and economic opportunities, a circumstance that leads some youths to attempt to succeed through illegitimate means. In Chapter 4, we will examine social structural factors as they relate to delinquency in more depth. For now, we should note that this lack of opportunity, coupled with an exposure to violence and crime, contributes to greater rates of delinquency.

SOCIAL CLASS

The relationship between economic status and delinquency appears, at first glance, to be pretty straightforward: youths who are poor or lack resources and opportunities to succeed are the most likely to use criminal activities to achieve their goals, the basis of Merton's strain theory (see Chapter 4). Merton and other structural theorists argue that youths who live in communities where there is little chance to achieve economic or social success are more likely to commit crimes than teenagers growing up in affluent families with greater access to good schools and other social networks.[66]

However, this relationship is more complicated than it appears, and the research on the subject—much of which was conducted primarily between the 1970s and 1990s—has yielded mixed results. For example, research based on official data, such as the UCR, has found that lower-class youths are arrested and detained more often than middle- or upper-class youths.[67] But a number of factors contribute to this trend. The police are more likely to formally intervene and arrest juveniles for behaviors in lower-class neighborhoods that they might ignore in affluent ones. More criminal activities, like illegal drug purchases, tend to occur in lower-class neighborhoods. These types of neighborhood influences translate into higher official recorded delinquency for some types of youths than for others. Some criminologists refer to this as the *ecological fallacy*, when conditions found in poorer neighborhoods render higher delinquency patterns.[68]

Because of variables that influenced the relationship between social class and delinquency in official statistics, criminologists began using self-report data. The early studies found no solid proof that lower-class youths were the only ones committing crimes. Many studies found that when asked about their activities, middle- and upper-class youths reported committing as many delinquent acts as their lower-class counterparts.[69]

These dramatic and controversial findings led to additional research. Some experts noted that the relationship between delinquency and social class depends on the particular methodology of a given study. Official data collected during the 1940s showed a strong relationship between delinquency and social class; that relationship all but disappeared by the 1970s. Later studies have found a weak relationship.[70]

Despite criticisms of various studies, the weight of the evidence suggests that there is a significant class difference, particularly as it relates to serious crimes.[71] This is especially true when we consider the fact that some studies include minor crimes and infractions, such as using a false ID or underage drinking by middle-class youths.[72] We are left to question why such a distinction exists. Considerable controversy about the relationship between social class and delinquency continues as experts on both sides of the argument present contradictory claims. Some criminologists have suggested that our understanding of the relationship between social class and delinquency has progressed no further since the argument began.[73]

AGE

aging out process or **maturational effect**
The process by which juvenile offenders engage in less delinquent and criminal activity as they get older.

Age is inversely related to crime. As juvenile offenders get older, they tend to engage in delinquent and criminal acts less frequently,[74] also known as the **aging out process** or **maturational effect.** Explanations as to why the aging out process occurs include:

- **Growing up:** as sociologists point out, sometimes the belief that one has no viable future results in living for the moment, or *present orientation.* Most people, however, tend to start thinking about the future as they age and realize that the potential allure and benefits of crime simply do not fit into their larger plans.

- **Resolving conflicts:** during adolescence, when youths' reasoning abilities are not fully developed, rash decisions and quick fixes are common. With maturity, however, youths develop the cognitive ability to create multiple solutions to problems.

- **Assuming greater responsibility:** as youths grow older, they take on more responsibility, and the risks associated with petty crimes are simply not worth the potential consequences.

- **Changing personality:** personalities can change with age. As youths mature, they usually develop a greater ability to engage in impulse control as well as recognizing societal influences and rewards for conforming behavior.

- **Breaking away from peer influences:** as youths get older, the ability of their peers to influence their behavior also changes. Adults are less likely to want to engage in risky activities simply because their friends are encouraging them to do so. This is not the case with many adolescents, however.[75]

ONSET

age of onset
The time period when juveniles begin committing offenses and crimes.

While people tend to stop committing crimes as they get older, when they begin, the **age of onset,**[76] is a component to understanding delinquency. Some research shows that people who demonstrate problem behaviors at a very early age are more likely to commit crimes frequently and for a longer period of time.[77] According to this view, there are two classes of offenders. The first begin committing crimes in late adolescence, typically with their peers, but eventually desist altogether as they enter young adulthood. These youths begin to avoid illegal activities as they mature and realize that crime is too dangerous, physically taxing, and unrewarding to continue. The second group of delinquents begin offending careers early and continue engaging in a high rate of offending throughout their lives. Early onset of crime is a significant marker for chronic offending patterns.

CHRONIC OFFENDING

Although most adolescents age out of crime, a relatively small number begin to violate the law early and continue at a high rate well into adulthood. These offenders are resistant to change and seem immune to the effects of punishment. Arrest, prosecution, and conviction do little to slow down their offending careers. These so-called **chronic offenders** are responsible for a significant amount of delinquent and criminal activity, and many grow up to become career adult criminals.[78]

The concept of the chronic or career offender is most associated with the work of criminologist Marvin Wolfgang.[79] Wolfgang used official records to follow the criminal careers of a cohort of 9,945 boys born in Philadelphia in 1945, from the time of birth until 1963, when they reached eighteen years of age. Using police records, Wolfgang determined that one-third of the sample (3,475 boys) had experienced some contact with the police. Each delinquent's offense was given a seriousness score, which allowed Wolfgang and his colleagues to differentiate among certain types of crime, such as between a simple assault and an armed robbery. Wolfgang also collected information from the youths' school records, including IQ scores, grades, and attendance.[80]

The most well-known discovery was that of the 3,475 boys who had some contact with the police, 54 percent (1,862) were repeat offenders while the remaining 46 percent (1,613) were one-time offenders. The repeat offenders could be further broken down into what Wolfgang referred to as *chronic recidivists* and *nonchronic recidivists.* The latter consisted of 1,235 boys who had been arrested more than once but less than five times. Chronic recidivists were those youths who had been arrested five or more times. As Figure 2-7 indicates, this group made up about 6 percent of the total sample.[81]

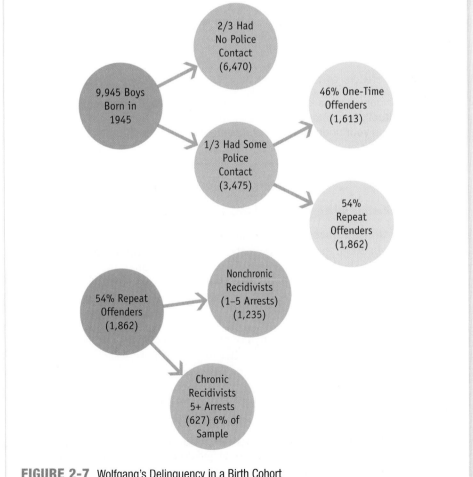

FIGURE 2-7 Wolfgang's Delinquency in a Birth Cohort
Wolfgang offered evidence that a small number of youths commit most of the crimes.

chronic 6 percent
Chronic recidivists or serious repeat offenders responsible for more than half of all offenses.

Chronic recidivists are also known as the **chronic 6 percent,** a term now used to describe all serious repeat offenders. These offenders were responsible for 52 percent of all offenses: 71 percent of homicides, 73 percent of rapes, 82 percent of robberies, and 70 percent of all aggravated assaults. More importantly, Wolfgang discovered that being arrested by the police and being processed by the juvenile court did not deter an offender's behavior. Such experience was inversely related to chronic offending: the stricter the disposition or punishment, the more likely the youth was to engage in repeated criminal behavior.[82]

The findings were so dramatic that Wolfgang decided to conduct another study to see how juvenile behavior patterns changed over time. The second sample consisted of Philadelphia youths born in 1958, observed until they reached majority age. The second cohort was larger, consisting of 28,000 youths. It also included females: there were approximately 13,500 males and 14,500 females in the sample. Similar to the first study, a small number of offenders had five arrests or more. This time this group of offenders represented 7.5 percent of the sample. Chronic males accounted for 61 percent of total offenses: 76 percent of rapes, 73 percent of robberies, and 65 percent of aggravated assaults. The 1958 group was actually more involved in violent crime than the original sample. The violent crime rate for the second cohort was 149 per 100,000 people compared to 47 per 100,000 in the original study. Thus, the second cohort was three times more violent than the first one.[83]

As was the case in the original study, involvement in the formal justice process had little impact on changing youths' behavior: the more often juveniles in the cohort were arrested, the more likely they were to be arrested again. These findings have a number of implications regarding chronic offenders. First, the research tells us that a small group of individuals is responsible for a great deal of delinquency and crime. Second, this group of offenders begins their criminal careers very early and remains active in their offending habits. Finally, conventional methods to rehabilitate or punish this type of offender actually result in higher rates of criminal behavior.

THINK ABOUT IT

Correlates of Delinquency

Consider what we know about the maturation effect—that most youths eventually lose interest in criminal activity as they get older. How might you use your understanding of this studied effect to deter delinquent behavior?

Victimization and Delinquency

When it comes to crime, juveniles are not always the offenders; in many instances, they are the victims. In 2008, the NCVS indicated that about 21 million criminal incidents occur each year. While that may seem like a very large number, the trend for the past several years shows that victimization rates are stable or have been declining for most crime categories.[84] For example, consider the following statistics on the dynamics of victimization:

- **Extent of victimization:** according to a Bureau of Justice Statistics report that summarizes NCVS data, juveniles age twelve to seventeen were about 2.5 times more likely than adults (ages eighteen and older) to be the victims of violent crimes. Compared with adults, youths age twelve to seventeen were twice as likely to be robbery or aggravated assault victims, 2.5 times as likely to be victims of a rape or sexual assault, and almost three times as likely to be victims of a simple assault.[85]

- **Victim/offender relationship:** between 1993 and 2003, most offenders whose victims were youths age twelve to seventeen were acquaintances or others well known to the victim (61 percent and 47 percent, respectively). For these two age groups, a small proportion of offenders were family members or intimates (5 percent and 10 percent, respectively).[86]

- **Time and place of victimization:** the number of violent crimes with adult victims peaked between 9 pm and midnight. In contrast, on school days, the number of violent crimes with juvenile victims peaked between 3 pm and 4 pm, fell to a lower level in the early evening hours, and declined substantially after 9 pm. On nonschool days, however, the juvenile victimization pattern mirrored the general adult pattern, with a peak in the late evening hours.[87] School was the most common setting for violent victimizations: 53 percent of victimizations of youths age twelve to fourteen and 32 percent of victimizations of youths age fifteen to seventeen occurred at or in school.[88]

VICTIMIZATION RISK

As with delinquency, victimization does not occur randomly. Personal behavior, social status, and lifestyle all affect the risk of victimization. The factors increasing the likelihood that an adolescent will become a victim of violent crime are:

- **Family status:** youths being raised in single-parent households are victimized more often than youths from two-parent families (60 out of every 1,000 children vs. 40 out of every 1,000). The overall risk for violence is about 50 percent higher among youths living in single-parent families than among those in two-parent families.

- **Community composition:** youths living in economically disadvantaged communities will have the greatest chance of becoming crime victims. Neighborhood residents lack a sense of connection to or integration with one another. The sociological term for this is a lack of *social cohesion*. As the number of single-parent households increases, neighborhoods lose the resources to protect their children because fewer adults are available to monitor youths' activities.

- **High-risk lifestyle:** youths who use alcohol and illegal drugs, and who also commit delinquent acts, have a much greater chance of being victimized. Runaways are at a high risk of victimization, particularly so the longer they are exposed to street life. Teenagers who use fake IDs to get into bars or those who get high with their friends put themselves at greater risk for victimization than youths who avoid risky lifestyles and behaviors.[89]

THE YOUNGEST VICTIMS

Children under age six are often the target of criminal and sexual assaults. In 2006, there were approximately 6 million allegations of child maltreatment made to child protective service agencies in the United States. An estimated 3.6 million children received an investigation or assessment, and 905,000 children were determined to be victims of abuse or neglect. However, there are problems with reporting rates of child abuse, so it is likely this figure is underestimated.[90]

Infants are most likely to be the victims of physical abuse. As Figure 2-8 indicates, the percentages decrease as the child gets older, likely due to the ability of the child to flee the parent or victimizer by running away or leaving home.[91] Parents are the most frequent offenders when it comes to physically abusing their children. According to Figure 2-9, nearly 80 percent of the time, it is a parent who is responsible for abusing or neglecting their children.[92]

Sexual abuse can occur in both rural and urban areas, at all socioeconomic and educational levels, and across all racial and cultural groups. Statistics indicate that girls are more frequently the victims of sexual abuse, but estimates suggest that boys account for 25–35 percent of child sexual abuse victims. Boys tend not to report sexual abuse as often as girls, perhaps because they fear appearing weak and vulnerable.[93]

The majority of sexual abuse of children is committed by someone the child knows. Sexual abuse can occur within the family (by a parent, stepparent, guardian, older sibling,

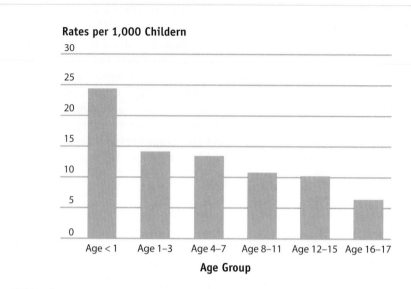

FIGURE 2-8 Physical Abuse Victimization Rates by Age Group, 2006
Older youths, more so than younger children, are able to protect themselves from some types of victimization. Why are they able to better protect themselves?

Source: Adapted from Snyder, H. N., and Sickmund, M. 2008. *Juvenile Offenders and Victims 2006 National Report.* Washington, DC: U.S. Department of Justice, Office of Juvenile Justice and Delinquency Prevention.

or relative) or outside the family (often by a person the child and family know well). Relatives have the highest rate of sexual abuse, representing about 30 percent of offenders, followed by day care staff, who make up about a quarter of offenders. Unlike with physical abuse, parents represent only about 3 percent of sexual abuse offenders.[94]

In 90 percent of child sexual abuse cases, the offender is male. Other common offender characteristics include a history of abuse (either physical or sexual), alcohol or drug abuse, little satisfaction with sexual relationships with adults, a lack of control over emotions, and, occasionally, evidence of severe mental illness.[95]

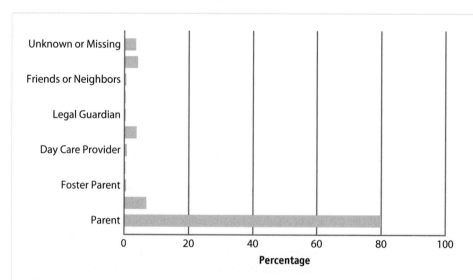

FIGURE 2-9 Physical Abuse Perpetrators by Relationship to Victims, 2006
Parents, and not strangers, are often the ones abusing their children.

Source: Adapted from Snyder, H. N., and Sickmund, M. 2008. *Juvenile Offenders and Victims 2006 National Report.* Washington, DC: U.S. Department of Justice, Office of Juvenile Justice and Delinquency Prevention.

Females can also be perpetrators of sexual abuse against children. However, unlike male offenders, who tend to use threats or actual force, females tend to use persuasion. Boys are more likely than girls to be abused by a female. Sexual abuse is a serious issue and has links to delinquency in a variety of ways, especially for victims.[96]

AUDREY'S CASE

Preventing Victimization

Recall Audrey's situation:

- is a popular student at a suburban middle school
- was a victim of theft and armed robbery on school campus
- did not report the incidents to anyone

People fail to report crimes for a number of reasons. These might include a lack of confidence in authorities' ability to solve the crime, a fear of retaliation by the offender, or humiliation at the thought of telling others about their victimization. Audrey was the victim of what could easily be categorized as felonies; nevertheless, she preferred to let the problem go unreported, hoping it would go away without affecting her social standing at school.

Recall our discussion of adolescence in Chapter 1. What role might Audrey's age have played in her decision not to report these crimes?

Understanding Victimization

What kinds of delinquent behaviors are likely to be linked to the fear of victimization? What reasons might youths have for bringing weapons to school, for instance?

Measuring Delinquency and Public Policy

As we have seen in this chapter, the measures used to record the extent of juvenile crime are limited in a number of ways. Because funding for programs, legislation designed to address delinquency, and the attitudes of the general public are largely based on what is known about the problem of delinquency, it is important that we understand these limitations and do what we can to correct them.

For example, if the information used to study a specific type of delinquency is flawed, or if the data are misinterpreted, the strategies developed to address it will likewise be limited in scope and effectiveness. While most citizens do not pay close attention to how delinquency is measured or analyzed, it remains the case that both considerations are the basis for public policy regarding delinquency and the treatment of offenders.

The degree of accuracy with which this information is collected and interpreted has a considerable impact on how crime is addressed in our communities. This fact underscores the need for scientifically sound methods of collecting data and drawing objective conclusions. One example of a program addressing juvenile violence and victimization based on accurate data is the Safe Start Initiative, discussed in the Theory and Practice box.

THEORY AND PRACTICE WORKING TOGETHER

The Safe Start Initiative

Throughout the United States, millions of children are exposed to violence, either as witnesses or as actual victims. The impact of this exposure to violence is seen in higher rates of depression, anxiety, anger, substance abuse, and decreased academic achievement, all of which have links to delinquency. Children who are exposed to violence have an increased risk of becoming violent themselves. In fact, abused children commit crimes at younger ages, commit them nearly twice as often, and are arrested more frequently than nonabused children.

In 1999, in response to this alarming trend, the OJJDP worked with the Department of Justice and the Department of Health and Human Services to develop the Safe Start Initiative. The purpose of this initiative is to prevent and reduce the impact of family and community violence on young children (primarily from birth to age six) and their families. Exposure to violence includes witnessing domestic or other forms of violent crime in the community, in addition to being an actual victim.

The goal of the Safe Start program is to expand existing partnerships among service providers in key areas such as early childhood education and development, health, mental health, child welfare, family support, substance abuse prevention and intervention, domestic violence and crisis intervention, law enforcement, courts, and legal services. Safe Start seeks to create a comprehensive service delivery system that will meet the needs of children and their families. The OJJDP has undertaken several research-based evaluations to assess the overall impact of Safe Start and has given the program an "exemplary" status in terms of its ability to prevent and reduce violence among youths.

 THINK ABOUT IT

Consider the correlation between exposure to violence and the commission of violent acts. What types of mental health and welfare services do you think a program like Safe Start might offer for reducing juveniles' exposure to violence?

THE BIG PICTURE

Conclusions on Measuring Delinquency

- Despite its limitations, why do scholars and policymakers continue to use the UCR as the primary source to explain trends in delinquency in the United States?

- What is the value of self-report studies? What is the likelihood that juveniles will distort the extent to which they have been involved in crime?

- Why is there a disproportionate percentage of black Americans involved in the juvenile justice system? Do black youths commit more crimes than white youths, or do existing racial biases within the system cause them to be targeted?

- Is there a correlation between a growing concern about chronic offenders and "get-tough" approaches to crime? Will treating chronic juvenile offenders like adults prevent them from committing crimes in the future? Why or why not?

- Consider how many gang-related homicides actually take place in the United States each year. Why is there such a dramatic difference between media coverage of these events and the actual frequency of their occurrence?

Key Terms

crime triangle
Uniform Crime Reports
Part I crimes
Crime Index
Part II crimes

clearance rate
dark figure of crime
unfounded crimes
hierarchical line
National Crime Victimization Survey

self-report studies
aging out process or maturational
  effect
age of onset
chronic offenders

Make the Call ▶ Researching Delinquency

Review the scenario below, and decide how you would approach this case.

YOUR ROLE: Police chief in a small town

DETAILS OF THE CASE

- During a community meeting, several residents complain to you about an increase in auto thefts by juveniles.

- These incidents are underscored by recent dramatic episodes, such as when the mayor's son was arrested for stealing a car and joyriding around town.

- Angry residents demand some type of action from you to address what they perceive as a growing problem.

HOW DO YOU RESPOND?

Before responding to the community's concerns, consider the research on the nature of auto thefts and the perpetrators of those crimes. Recall that it is no longer common for teens to steal cars for joyriding. On the other hand, keep in mind that members of the community are feeling generally distrustful of youths these days, on account of particular recent incidents. How might you respond to residents in this situation? Consider:

- Do you promise to assign officers to an auto theft task force, even though you do not have sufficient resources to do so?

- Do you downplay the significance of the recent episodes and attribute them to a few "bad apples"?

- Do you avoid dealing with the issue entirely, particularly because of the potential political fallout from arresting the mayor's son?

- Do you promise to study the issue thoroughly and get back to residents with a plan of action?

Apply Theory to Reality ▶ Cognitive Psychology

A great deal of attention has been given to the relationship between violent video games like *Grand Theft Auto* and actual acts of violence. Skip ahead to Chapter 6 to read more about cognitive psychology. Based on your reading, do you think cognitive psychology offers any insight into the nature of violent behavior and its possible correlation to violent games and media?

Your Community ▶ Studying Crime Rates

In addition to the information you glean from your readings, class lectures, and discussions, it is important to roll up your sleeves and immerse yourself in a topic as a researcher who gains an understanding of a problem or issue by observing or experiencing it firsthand. Through such methods, you gain a much greater appreciation of the magnitude and scope of the problem than if you were only engaged in "armchair theorizing."

- Contact your university's public safety office and obtain a copy of its crime report on campus. Then access the UCR for your state. Read over both reports and then compare the crime rate on your campus to the crime rate in your state.

- Identify the particular crimes that occur more frequently on campus. Why do you think these are more common? Which crimes appear to be more unique to the larger community? Why are these more common?

- Note that some of these similarities and differences may have to do with the location of the campus in relation to the community (e.g., an urban campus versus a suburban or rural campus).

After collecting your data and drawing from the relevant literature, prepare a report that addresses the types of strategies you would use to address campus crime in particular. Discuss how these strategies might be different from those the local police chief would implement.

Notes

[1] See, for instance, Antonaccio, O., Tittle, C., Botchkovar, E., and Kranidioti, M. 2010. "The Correlates of Crime and Deviance: Additional Evidence." *Journal of Research in Crime and Delinquency,* 47(2). Available at http://jrc.sagepub.com/content/early/2010/04/22/0022427810365678.abstract.

[2] See, for example, Felson, M., and Boba, R. 2009. *Crime and Everyday Life,* 4th. ed. Los Angeles: Sage.

[3] See Department of Justice, Federal Bureau of Investigation. 2009. *Crime in the United States, 2008.* http://www.fbi.gov/ucr/cius2008/about/about_ucr.html.

[4] Ibid. http://www.fbi.gov/ucr/cius2008/about/offense_definitions.html.

[5] Ibid. http://www.fbi.gov/ucr/cius2008/about/about_ucr.html.

[6] Ibid.

[7] U.S. Department of Justice, Federal Bureau of Investigation. 2009. *Crime in the United States, 2008.* Table 8. Washington, DC. Available at http://www.fbi.gov/ucr/cius2008/data/table_08_ny.html.

[8] U.S. Department of Justice, Federal Bureau of Investigation. 2009. *Crime in the United States, 2008.* http://www.fbi.gov/ucr/cius2008/offenses/clearances/index.html.

[9] Ibid.

[10] Ibid.

[11] Ibid.

[12] See, for example, Fazari, G. M. 2004. "Research Strategy for Bringing to Light the Dark Figure of Campus Crime." *Campus Law Enforcement Journal,* 34(6): 32–36. http://www.iaclea.org/pubs/.

[13] See, for instance, Lewis, L. 2003. "Many Victims Don't Report Crimes." *National Public Radio,* March 10. Available at http://www.npr.org/templates/story/story.php?storyId=1188140.

[14] See http://www.fbi.gov/ucr/cius2008/about/offense_definitions.html.

[15] Ibid.

[16] Ibid.

[17] See http://www.fbi.gov/ucr/cius2008/about/about_ucr.html.

[18] Ibid.

[19] Ibid.

[20] Ibid.

[21] Ibid.

[22] Ibid.

[23] See U.S. Department of Justice, Office of Justice Programs, Bureau of Justice Statistics. 2010. *Victims.* Available at http://bjs.ojp.usdoj.gov/index.cfm?ty=tp&tid=9.

[24] Ibid. http://bjs.ojp.usdoj.gov/index.cfm?ty=tp&tid=91.

[25] Ibid.

[26] Ibid.

[27] Ibid.

[28] See Rand, M. R. 2009. *Criminal Victimization 2008.* Available at http://bjs.ojp.usdoj.gov/content/pub/pdf/cv08.pdf. See also U.S. Department of Justice, Federal Bureau of Investigation. 2009. *Crime in the United States, 2008.* Washington, DC. http://www.fbi.gov/ucr/cius2008/offenses/property_crime/motor_vehicle_theft.html.

[29] U.S. Department of Health and Human Services, Office of Applied Studies. 2008. *National Survey on Drug Abuse and Health.* Washington, DC. Available at http://www.oas.samhsa.gov/nhsda.htm.

[30] For a general description of the study, see the Monitoring the Future website at http://monitoringthefuture.org/index.html.

[31] Ibid.

[32] Centers for Disease Control. 2009. *National Youth Risk Behavior Survey.* Available at http://www.cdc.gov/HealthyYouth/yrbs/pdf/us_violence_trend_yrbs.pdf.

[33] Thornberry, T. P., and Krohn, M. P. 2000. *The Self-Report Method for Measuring Delinquency and Crime.* Washington, DC: U.S. Department of Justice. Available at http://www.ncjrs.gov/criminal_justice2000/vol_4/04b.pdf.

[34] Ibid.

[35] Ibid.

[36] Ibid.

[37] Babbie, E., and Maxfield, D. 2010. *Research Methods in Criminal Justice,* 6th. ed. Upper Saddle River, NJ: Prentice-Hall.

[38] See, for instance, Thornberry and Krohn, 2000.

[39] Ibid.

[40] Snyder, H., and Sickmund, M. 2006. *Juvenile Offenders and Victims: 2006 National Report.* Washington, DC: U.S. Department of Justice, Office of Justice Programs, Office of Juvenile Justice and Delinquency Prevention. http://www.ojjdp.ncjrs.org/ojstatbb/nr2006/downloads/NR2006.pdf.

[41] U.S. Department of Justice, Federal Bureau of Investigation. 2009. *Crime in the United States, 2008.* Washington, DC. http://www.fbi.gov/ucr/cius2008/offenses/index.html.

[42] Puzzanchera, C. 2009. *Juvenile Arrests 2008.* Washington, DC: U.S. Department of Justice,

Office of Justice Programs, Office of Juvenile Justice and Delinquency Prevention.

[43] Ibid.

[44] Ibid.

[45] Thornberry and Krohn, 2000.

[46] Centers for Disease Control, 2009.

[47] U.S. Department of Health and Human Services, Office of Applied Studies, 2008.

[48] Ibid.

[49] Reichert, K. 2002. *Police-Probation Partnerships: Boston's Operation Night Light.* Washington, DC: University of Pennsylvania Jerry Lee Center of Criminology Forum on Crime and Justice.

[50] U.S. Department of Justice, Office of Justice Programs, Office of Juvenile Justice and Delinquency Prevention. 2009. *Exemplary Programs.* Available at http://www.ojjdp.ncjrs.gov/pubs/jaibgbulletin/exemp.html.

[51] Johnston, O'Malley, Bachman, and Schulenberg. 2009. *Monitoring the Future: National Results on Adolescent Drug Use.* Available at http://monitoringthefuture.org/pubs/monographs/overview2009.pdf.

[52] U.S. Department of Justice, Federal Bureau of Investigation. 2009. *Crime in the United States, 2008.* Table 33.Washington, DC: Available at http://www.fbi.gov/ucr/cius2008/data/table_33_ny.html.

[53] Puzzanchera, 2009.

[54] U.S. Department of Justice, Federal Bureau of Investigation. 2009. *Crime in the United States, 2008.* Table 43.Washington, DC: Available at http://www.fbi.gov/ucr/cius2008/data/table_43_ny.html.

[55] U.S. Department of Justice, Federal Bureau of Investigation, 2009, Table 43.

[56] U.S. Department of Justice, Federal Bureau of Investigation, 2009, Table 33.

[57] Ibid.

[58] Ibid.

[59] Ibid.

[60] Johnston et al., 2009.

[61] See, for instance, Farrington, D., Loeber, R., Stouthammer-Loeber, M., Van Kammen, W. B., and Schmidt, L. 1996. "Self-Reported Delinquency and a Combined Delinquency Seriousness Scale Based on Boys, Mothers, and Teachers: Concurrent and Predictive Validity for African-Americans and Caucasians." *Criminology,* 34: 493–514. See also Thornberry and Krohn, 2000.

[62] See, for instance, Puzzanchera, C., and Kang, W. 2008. *Juvenile Court Statistics Databook.* Available at http://ojjdp.ncjrs.gov/

ojstatbb/jcsdb/. See also Sickmund, M. 2009. *Delinquency Cases in Juvenile Court 2005.* Washington, DC: Office of Juvenile Justice and Delinquency Prevention. http://www.ncjrs.gov/pdffiles1/ojjdp/224538.pdf

[63] See Sickmund, 2009.

[64] Elliott, D. S., and Huizinga, D. 1983. "Social Class and Delinquent Behavior in a National Youth Panel 1976–1980." *Criminology,* 21(2): 149–177. See also Tittle, C., Villemez, W., and Smith, D. 1978. "The Myth of Social Class and Criminality." *American Sociological Review,* 43: 643–656; Tittle, C., and Meier, R. 1990. "Specifying the SES/Delinquency Relationship." *Criminology,* 28: 271–299.

[65] See, for instance, Wilson, W. J. 2004. *When Work Fails.* Chicago: University of Chicago Press. See also Wilson, W. J. 1997. *The Truly Disadvantaged.* Chicago: University of Chicago Press; McWhorter, J. 2001. *Losing the Race: Self-Sabotage in Black America.* New York: HarperCollins.

[66] Merton, R. 1957. *Social Theory and Social Structure,* 2nd. ed. New York: Free Press.

[67] See Tittle, C. R., and Meier, R. F. 1991. "Specifying the SES/Delinquency Relationship by Social Characteristics of Contexts." *Journal of Research in Crime and Delinquency,* 28(4): 430–455.

[68] Hennessy, M., Richards, P. J., and Berk, R. A. 2006. "Broken Homes and Middle Class Delinquency: A Reassessment." *Criminology,* 15(4): 505–528.

[69] See also Triplett, R. 2000. "Juvenile Delinquency and Social Class." In Rafter, N. (ed.), *Encyclopedia of Women and Crime.* Phoenix, AZ: Oryx Press. See also Tittle and Meier, 1990.

[70] Ageton, S. S., and Elliott, D. S. 1978. *The Incidence of Delinquent Behavior in a National Probability Sample of Adolescents.* Boulder, CO: Behavioral Research Institute.

[71] Farnworth, M., Thornberry, T. P., Krohn, M. D., and Lizotte, A. J. 1994. "Measurement in the Study of Class and Delinquency: Integrating Theory and Research." *Journal of Research in Crime and Delinquency,* 31(1): 32–61. See also Braithwaite, J. 1989. *Crime, Shame, and Reintegration.* New York: Cambridge University Press; Hindelang, M., Hirschi, T., and Weis, J. 1979. "Correlates of Delinquency." *American Sociological Review,* 44: 495–1014.

[72] Farnworth et al., 1994; Ageton and Elliott, 1978. See also Dunaway, G., Cullen, F., Burton, V., and Evans, T. D. 2000. "The Myth of Social Class and Crime Revisited." *Criminology,* 38: 589–632.

[73] Tittle and Meier, 1990. See also Dunaway et al., 2000.

[74] See, for example, McCord, J., and Conway, K. P. 2002. *Patterns of Juvenile Delinquency and Co-Offending.* Washington, DC: U.S. Department of Justice. Available at http://www.ncjrs.gov/pdffiles1/nij/grants/192288.pdf.

[75] Cusick, G. R., Courtney, M. E., Havlicek, J., and Hess, N. 2010. *Crime during the Transition to Adulthood.* Washington, DC: U.S. Department of Justice. Available at http://www.ncjrs.gov/pdffiles1/nij/grants/229667.pdf.

[76] See Loeber, R., and Farrington, D. P. 2001. *Child Delinquency: Development, Intervention and Service Needs.* Belmont, CA: Sage.

[77] Ibid.

[78] See, for instance, Street Crime Working Group, BC Justice Review Task Force. 2009. *Beyond the Revolving Door: A New Response to Chronic Offenders.* http://www.bcjusticereview.org/working_groups/street_crime/scwg_report_09_29_05.pdf.

[79] Wolfgang, M. E., and Figlio, R. M. 1972. *Delinquency in a Birth Cohort.* Chicago: University of Chicago Press.

[80] Ibid.

[81] Ibid.

[82] Wolfgang, M., Thornberry, T., and Figlio, R. 1987. *From Boy to Man, from Delinquency to Crime.* Chicago: University of Chicago Press.

[83] Ibid.

[84] Rand, 2009.

[85] Snyder and Sickmund, 2006.

[86] Ibid.

[87] Ibid.

[88] Ibid.

[89] Ibid.

[90] U.S. Department of Health and Human Services, Administration of Children and Families. 2005. National Child Abuse and Neglect Data System. 2005. *Child Abuse and Neglect of Children under Age 18.* Washington, DC: U.S. Government Printing Office.

[91] Ibid.

[92] Ibid.

[93] Ibid.

[94] See Snyder and Sickmund, 2006.

[95] Prevent Child Abuse America. 2008. *Fact Sheet on Sexual Abuse.* http://member.preventchildabuse.org/site/DocServer/sexual_abuse.pdf?docID=126.

[96] Ibid.

After reading this chapter, you should be able to:

- Distinguish status offending from juvenile delinquency.

- Explain the complexity of runaway youths by putting together a profile of one.

- Consider the factors contributing to truancy, and determine whether children should be held accountable.

- Debate the issue of incorrigibility, and form an analysis of whether incorrigible individuals can be changed.

- Examine the arguments for and against curfews, and discuss whether curfews are effective.

- Evaluate the causes of underage drinking, and consider policies that would prevent this status offense.

- Demonstrate how education and the media discourage and/or encourage underage smoking.

Status Offending

The public generally thinks that many of the behaviors labeled as status offenses are typical teen behaviors; however, consider the following case about Virginia.

Virginia's profile:
- is a fifteen-year-old from Seattle, Washington
- is a good student
- has near-perfect attendance

Her family:
- lives in a low-income neighborhood
- mother works as a housekeeper
- stepfather, recently laid off from his job at a local factory, makes Virginia feel uncomfortable
- has stormy relationship with parents

Her behavior over the past year:
- began skipping classes and then missing school altogether for days at a time
- last year, ran away from home and lived on the streets but continued to attend school, in part because of free lunches and friends
- after a period of time, stopped going to school altogether

Current status:
One night, around 1 am, Virginia was arrested for shoplifting in a twenty-four-hour convenience store. She was also charged with violating Seattle's curfew law, which prohibits youths under the age of eighteen from being in a public place unaccompanied by a parent or legal guardian after 11 pm. When the officer checked Virginia's criminal record, he found that she had been arrested two weeks earlier for trespassing and vandalism. When the officer asked Virginia about these charges, she said she broke the window of an abandoned building in order to sleep there that night. The arresting officer also discovered a bottle of liquor in Virginia's backpack. Upon reviewing her rap sheet, which showed the

Status offenses like underage drinking may not seem to be serious crimes, but their negative impact on individual offenders and society is considerable. What are some consequences of status offenses?

51

trespassing and vandalism charges, the officer decided to proceed with the shoplift-ing, curfew, and underage drinking charges.

When trying to explaining why juveniles such as Virginia commit status offenses, the following perceptions may come up:

- Virginia's actions show that she is clearly on the road to a career as a chronic offender and should be adjudicated as a delinquent.
- Virginia is emotionally unstable and is in need of an evaluation by a licensed psychologist.
- Virginia's behavior is not uncommon; some youths "act out" by engaging in minor forms of vandalism or underage drinking. Her behavior should not be a cause for concern, and she will likely grow out of it.

THINK ABOUT IT   Based on the scenario provided, what is your current perspective of Virginia's behavior, and why?

status offenses
Acts, such as truancy, incorrigibil-ity, and curfew violations, that are considered against the law, but are not viewed as criminal, based on the age of the offender.

Making sense of Virginia's behavior might be easier if we explore the larger picture. Her actions are often considered **status offenses:** acts that are defined as criminal based on the age of the offender. For example, it is legal for an adult to purchase cigarettes, but it is a status offense for a teenager to do so. Status offenses cover a host of behaviors but the ones most commonly seen include running away, truancy, ungovernability (sometimes called incorrigibility), curfew violations, underage drink-ing, and underage smoking.[1] These are not serious offenses, and they do not typi-cally present a significant threat to the general public; however, they can carry risks for the youths who engage in them. For instance, smoking has serious health conse-quences, and runaway teenagers may face dangers on the streets. Status offenses are differentiated from juvenile delinquency in that neither the acts nor the youths who commit them are considered criminal.

This chapter explores the nature and types of status offenses, the controversial connection between status offenses and delinquency, and the much-debated issue of handling status offenses as a matter of public policy, community action, and judicial action.

A Brief History of Status Offending

As far back as the 1700s in the United States, disobedient or runaway youths often were placed in orphanages or houses of refuge, discussed in Chapter 1. Young people who com-mitted criminal acts, on the other hand, were generally treated like adults.[2]

Until the 1970s, no significant legal distinction existed among a juvenile who com-mitted a criminal act, a juvenile who was considered a wayward youth, and a child who came from a home with poor or deceased parents. Under the doctrine of *parens patriae,* or "parent to the nation," the state acts as a parent when a child is in need of protection. Within the broad parameters of *parens patriae,* courts could intervene in any behavior or circumstance involving a child, whether the behavior was delinquent or not. As a result, many jurisdictions handled a wide range of situations involving youths, many of which did not involve any criminal acts.[3]

Given that there were few options available to the court in addressing youths' needs, institutionalization, even for nondelinquent youths, was a common practice. This attempt by the court to handle an array of juvenile issues led to a number of unintended conse-quences. Sometimes, for example, a teenager was placed in an institution of some kind simply because his parents failed to adequately provide for him. Many youths in this situation remained under state care until they came of age. They might have been institutionalized longer than teens who had actually committed crimes.

In addition, many youths who had not committed a serious crime were incarcerated with serious offenders. They often were victimized by more hardened offenders and learned more about the "criminal lifestyle."[4]

THE JUVENILE JUSTICE DELINQUENCY PREVENTION ACT (JJDPA)

As observers began to recognize the unfortunate consequences of incarcerating noncriminal teens, they began to effect changes in public policy.[5] More than two decades ago, the National Council on Crime and Delinquency, an influential, privately funded think tank, recommended removing status offenders from the jurisdiction of the juvenile courts. These calls for reform prompted a number of states to experiment with replacing juvenile court jurisdiction over most status offenders with community-based treatment programs.

Meanwhile, at the federal level, perhaps the most significant piece of legislation as it relates to status offenders occurred in 1974 with the passage of the **Juvenile Justice Delinquency Prevention Act** (JJDPA). The act was a pioneering effort in two ways: how status offenders are labeled and how they are handled. First, the JJDPA made a legal distinction between youths who committed criminal acts and status offenders so that status offenders did not suffer from the stigmatizing label "juvenile delinquent." Second, care of status offenders was now turned over to community agencies. In effect, status offenses were "deinstitutionalized"—it was illegal to institutionalize or incarcerate juveniles when they had not committed a crime.

The passage of the JJDPA changed the treatment of status offenders (see Table 3-1). For example, when status offenders are detained, they must be completely separated from adult offenders and prevented from having any type of contact with them.[6] There are exceptions to this, of course, but in general, the emphasis is on providing treatment rather than punishment to status offenders.

Juvenile Justice Delinquency Prevention Act
A pioneering act that made a legal distinction between youths who committed criminal acts and status offenders so that status offenders did not suffer from the stigmatizing label "juvenile delinquent," and that turned care of status offenders over to community agencies.

AMENDMENTS TO THE JJDPA

The judiciary reacted negatively to the JJDPA because it limited the authority of juvenile court judges. In 1980, judges successfully lobbied Congress to amend the JJDPA to allow them to remand status offenders who violated a valid court order to secure detention. This amendment, known as the **valid court order amendment,**[7] made several exceptions to the requirement that juveniles would not be detained in adult jail and lockups. Juveniles being tried as adults for felonies and juveniles with felony convictions can be sent to an adult jail or lockup. They can also be held in an adult jail or lockup for six hours in urban areas and up to twenty-four hours in rural ones, if secure detention is required and no alternative arrangements can be made.[8]

Not all judges opposed deinstitutionalization. In a 1990 report, the National Council of Juvenile and Family Court Judges argued that status offenders were most often victims, not offenders, and should not be treated as delinquents. The report called for court intervention only as a last resort, when all other community resources had failed.

valid court order amendment
Legislation that allows juveniles being tried as adults for felonies or juveniles with felony convictions to be sent to an adult jail or lockup and to be held for six hours in urban areas and up to twenty-four hours in rural ones, if secure detention is required and no alternative arrangements can be made.

TABLE 3-1 Status Offenders

Categories of Status Offenders
CHINS (Children in Need of Supervision)   MINS (Minors in Need of Supervision)   PINS (Persons in Need of Supervision)
The JJDPA created three categories of status offenders; the differences are based on the age of the offender, but all groups consist of youths who require guidance and assistance by the court.

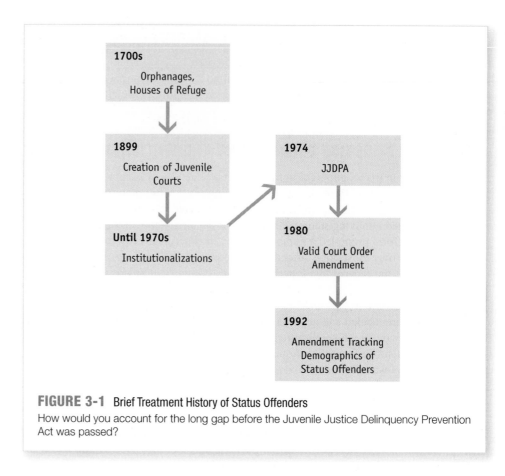

FIGURE 3-1 Brief Treatment History of Status Offenders
How would you account for the long gap before the Juvenile Justice Delinquency Prevention Act was passed?

A 1992 amendment to the JJDPA represented an effort to address the disproportionately high percentage of status offenders who are members of minority groups, particularly African Americans (see Figure 3-1). That amendment requires juvenile justice agencies to track the race and ethnicity of status offenders. If the percentage of minority offenders is disproportionately high relative to the group's population in the state, the agency must determine why that is the case and take steps to reduce it.[9]

STATUS OFFENDERS VERSUS DELINQUENTS

Some experts on delinquency contend that juvenile courts routinely circumvent federal law by incarcerating status offenders rather than sending them to community agencies for treatment, such as anger management, family therapy to resolve issues with parents and siblings, or counseling for exposure to violence and abuse. The courts bypass the law in two ways: bootstrapping and reclassifying status offenders as mentally ill.

Bootstrapping is a process whereby a juvenile court classifies (or bootstraps) a status offender as a delinquent after repeated violations of the same offense. For example, suppose a child skips school and is identified as truant. He is brought before the court, and the judge issues a formal court order to the child to attend school. What if the child defies the court's request and continues to be truant? If he is again caught and brought before the court, a judge can elevate the status offense to a delinquent offense on the charge of contempt of court. Once the child is classified as a juvenile delinquent, the judge has more options in dealing with the youth, such as holding him in a detention center.[10]

Another type of bootstrapping that can result in incarceration occurs when a juvenile court judge sends a status offender to a group home for running away and the youth runs away from this facility as well. Although the youth's behavior did not change, the act of running away is now a violation of a court order, and the juvenile's status changes from runaway to delinquent.[11]

bootstrapping
A process whereby a juvenile court classifies a status offender as delinquent after repeated violations of the same offense.

Another way to detain status offenders is through the use of treatment facilities, such as mental hospitals and substance abuse treatment centers, which does not violate the mandates of the JJDPA.[12] Youths sent to these places are sometimes labeled **hidden delinquents** because they rarely show up in official statistics on delinquency or even status offending.

Hidden delinquents are usually afforded less due process even though they have not committed a crime. In the landmark case of *Parham v. J. R.,* the U.S. Supreme Court held that parents may commit their child to a mental hospital as long as an impartial party conducts a hearing and finds evidence of a mental disorder. In those instances, the child may be held until either the parents request their child's release or there is evidence that the child no longer suffers from a mental illness.[13]

Placing minors in mental institutions and other treatment facilities is controversial because it is seen as an alternate way of incarcerating status offenders. A minor may not be suffering from a mental illness, but the offense he or she committed is used as evidence of the need for treatment. The "hidden system" is not limited to substance abuse facilities or mental hospitals, however; as long as a status offender is not placed in a secure detention facility or a training school, juvenile court judges can use a variety of **residential programs** or out-of-home placements such as group homes. These institutions provide an alternative to detention centers and state schools, and are not subject to JJDPA deinstitutionalization guidelines. While youths are not placed with adult criminals, they may still face victimization and other consequences in such environments.

hidden delinquents
Detained status offenders who rarely show up in official statistics because they are detained in treatment facilities, such as mental hospitals and substance abuse treatment centers, which does not violate the mandates of the JJDPA.

residential programs
Out-of-home placements that provide an alternative to detention centers and state schools and are not subject to JJDPA deinstitutionalization guidelines.

VIRGINIA'S CASE

Status Offending or Delinquency?

Recall Virginia's situation:

- skipped, then dropped out of school
- ran away from home
- arrested for trespassing and vandalism
- shoplifted
- violated curfew law

Consider the definition of status offenses, as well as local and federal laws. Then reflect on Virginia's behavior. Experts tend to lump status offenders and delinquents together, as the boundaries between the two populations are blurred when status offenders sometimes engage in more serious crimes.

Retracing the history of and legislation on status offenses, and bearing in mind the definition, should Virginia be taken into custody, and should the juvenile justice system intervene?

THINK ABOUT IT

THE CHANGING NATURE OF STATUS OFFENDING

More than twenty years ago, the National Council on Crime and Delinquency recommended removing status offenders from the juvenile court. But even today, juvenile court judges strongly resist removal of these offenders from their jurisdiction because it interferes with their ability to help youths before they get into serious trouble. Their concerns are fueled by research, which shows that many status offenders, especially runaways living on the street, have serious emotional problems and engage in a variety of self-destructive behaviors.[14] The juvenile court is the only way to force repeat offenders into compliance, especially in states that do not have community-based programs or funding to help these youths.

Is discipline needed? Many youths regularly engage in status offenses, such as underage smoking and drinking, and truancy; therefore, it makes little sense to have the juvenile court intervene in the lives of teenagers who are engaging in what has become routine behavior.[15]

The debate over whether courts should retain jurisdiction over status offenses also minimizes the importance of the different types of status offenders. Some act out in ways similar to delinquents while others, who are not serious offenders, have different motives and intentions. A juvenile court experience can be harmful to true status offenders who are not committing serious, violent acts, and can escalate the frequency and seriousness of criminal behaviors.

Even chronic status offenders are different from traditional delinquents. The reasons children run away from home do not change simply because the child has been arrested and the court ordered him or her to stop committing this offense. The difficulties in distinguishing between the different types of offenders often result in an oversimplification of the problems and issues surrounding status offending.

THINK ABOUT IT

Treating Status Offenders

Can we separate the true status offenders from those who commit major crimes like shoplifting and trespassing? Should we try to consider the crimes that are likely linked to status offending (e.g., shoplifting) when viewing an offender's behavior?

Runaways

Each year as many as 2 million children leave home without a destination in mind, and tens of thousands of other children are pushed out of the home or abandoned by parents or guardians.[16] Runaways can become involved in a cycle of poverty, drugs, prostitution, and various forms of victimization. At times, caregivers may be aware of where the youths are located but do not want to find them or bring them back home. While most runaways leave home because of family problems, some youths find they prefer to be on their own. In such cases, rarely do youths find a better life on the streets.

DEFINITION

Defining a runaway seems simple: a youth who runs away from home. However, the definition is more complicated because criteria used to describe these youths frequently overlap and are not mutually exhaustive or exclusive.

The term *homeless youth* is often used as an umbrella term for a large variety of young people including runaways, throwaways, and street youths. The Runaway and Homeless Youth Act defines a **homeless youth** as one who is "not more than 21 years of age for whom it is not possible to live in a safe environment with a relative and who has no other safe alternative living arrangement"[17]; however, there are debates over what constitutes a young person. While most people tend to use under the age of eighteen as the main criterion for status offenses, when it comes to homeless youths, it can also include young people up to age twenty-one.[18]

The varying criteria official agencies use to qualify certain behaviors present another issue in understanding runaway behavior.[19] According to the U.S. Department of Health and Human Services, a runaway is a youth who is away from home without permission of his or her parents or legal guardian at least overnight. A **throwaway youth** is generally defined as a young person who either is asked to leave home by a parent or other adult in the household or is away from home overnight and prevented from returning.[20] The term **street youths** has been used to refer to those who reside in high-risk, nontraditional locations, such as under bridges, in abandoned buildings, or in vehicles. The National Center for Unaccompanied and Homeless Youth defines street youths as "those who run away or who are indefinitely or intermittently homeless and spend a significant amount of time on the street or in other areas that increase their risk for sexual abuse, sexual exploitation, prostitution, or drug abuse."[21]

homeless youths
Young people up to the age of twenty-one who do not have a safe living space outside of or within a relative's home.

throwaway youths
Young individuals who either are asked to leave home by parents or other adults in the household or are away from home overnight and prevented from returning.

street youths
Young individuals who reside in high-risk, nontraditional locations, such as under bridges, in abandoned buildings, or in vehicles.

TABLE 3-2 Types of Runaways

Broad Scope Runaways	Juveniles who leave or stay away from home without permission	—Teenagers, age fifteen or older, who have permission to be out but break curfews, are an exception —Two nights are necessary for such teenagers to be considered Broad Scope Runaways
Policy Focal Runaways	Minors who, along with fitting into the Broad Scope definition, are also endangered due to not having a familiar and safe place to stay	—Youths who leave home and spend time on the streets, in cars, or in shelters —Garners the most attention from policymakers and law enforcement officials
Runaway Gestures	Youths who leave home only for a matter of hours but do not stay overnight	—Runaways who leave notes and older teenagers who stay out overnight without permission also fall under this category —Typically omitted from national figures on runaway incidents

NISMART-1, which is based on three components—the National Household Survey of Adult Caretakers, the National Household Survey of Youth, and the Juvenile Facilities Study—identifies these three types of runaways.[22] NISMART also distinguishes between youths who run away from home and those who are referred to as *Non-Household Runaways,* which include those children who run away from institutions, group homes, or other facilities.

Because the definitions are complicated and they overlap, our definition of **runaways** includes homeless youths, throwaways, and street youths. To get a sense of the different types of runaways (see Table 3-2), estimates suggest that many children are conceptualized as "voluntarily missing," which helps to distinguish them from abducted and lost children. However, as the National Incidence Studies of Missing, Abducted, Runaway, and Throwaway Children (NISMART-1) discovered, children who leave home often do so as a result of family conflict. In these instances, the term "voluntary" does not apply and is a bit misleading.

runaways
Youths who leave home without permission for more than twenty-four hours.

PROFILES

While there is no single cause for why teens run away, most of the reasons given can be grouped into three broad, interrelated categories: family problems (which include the behaviors of both parents and youths), economic problems, and residential instability.[23]

Youths are usually financially, emotionally, and legally dependent on their parents, but the majority of those who leave home do so because they need to escape dysfunctional or abusive (physical, sexual, or psychological) family situations, or their parents or other adults in the household coerce them into leaving.[24] Consider Walter's relationship with his family, which led to his decision to run away. He says:

Well, uh, I got up. And I knew it was just going to be another trouble day, 'cause every day's trouble. And uh, at this time, I, I was like about seven, maybe, eight, maybe. And uh, I peed in my pants when I was sleeping, and it got all over my bed. So my mom got mad and took everything out of the room. So I was just like, okay, I'm mad, and I'm going to act up. So I started cussing, screaming, pounding on the door, punching holes in the walls, and she was like, either you sit there, or I'm going to call the cops. So I sat there, and I, I sat there for about three, four hours. And I was like, I can't sit here anymore. So I got up, dug a hole through the wall. And my dad's office is right next to my door. So, I mean—well, it's right next to my room. So, when I dug through there, it led right into his office. And I got in there, and I was under his desk. So, I mean, I crawled out from under his desk, and I used his pocketknife that was laying on his desk to cut out the screen. And I hopped out the, the screen and ran through my backyard to my school. And I jumped up on the monkey bars and sat there for about forty-five minutes. And then, I was like, I'm going to run away from here, and I'm leaving the country, something. Uh, I just—I didn't want to be here. So, I jumped off there and I started running, as fast as I could, as hard as I could. And, and it didn't matter what direction I went. I just wanted to leave.

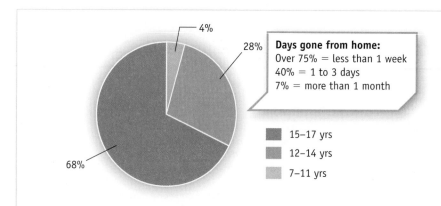

Days gone from home:
Over 75% = less than 1 week
40% = 1 to 3 days
7% = more than 1 month

- 15–17 yrs
- 12–14 yrs
- 7–11 yrs

FIGURE 3-2 Percentage of Runaways by Age

According to NISMART-2, the follow-up study to NISMART-1, an estimated 1,682,900 youths had a runaway episode. Many youths who run away from home do so for only a short while, a majority for less than one week. Less than 10 percent are away from home for more than a month. How do you think the youths who run away for more than a month get by?

Source: Hammer, H., Finkelhor, D., and Sedlak, A. 2002. Runaway/Throwaway Children: National Estimates and Characteristics. *National Incidence Studies of Missing, Abducted, Runaway and Throwaway Children.* NISMART-1.

For more on running away, watch *Running Away: Zachary, Running Away and Status Offenses: Jose,* and *Running Away: Walter* at www.mhhe.com/mcnamarajd1e

Runaways with poor family relations have difficulty forming relationships with service providers because they have trust issues with adults. This stems largely from their experiences with being exploited, neglected, or traumatized by their parents, relatives, and others. As a result, they have limited ability to access all the existing services that could support them in transitioning to a more stable lifestyle.[25] See Figure 3-2 for a breakdown of runaways by age and length of incidence.

A clear relationship exists between physical, sexual, and psychological abuse of youths and their decisions to run away.[26] In addition to violence and abuse, other family-related factors that influence young people to leave home include neglect, parental substance abuse, and parental control issues.[27]

For some youths, economic problems and residential instability may lead to their decisions to run away[28] or, more specifically, become part of the throwaway youth population. One study of over 1,200 runaway youths reported that about 40 percent were from families that received public assistance or lived in public housing.[29] Low wages lead some families to ask their children to leave home because they can no longer care for them.

Sociologist James Wright says throwaways typically experience episodes of residential instability, where family members are living in doubled-up housing[30] or living with other friends or relatives in households not designed to accommodate such a large number of people. An unstable physical home, along with a lack of financial resources, sometimes forces youths to seek other housing alternatives.[31]

PROGRAMS FOR RUNAWAY YOUTHS

Since 1974, Congress has funded three types of programs under the Runaway and Homeless Youth Act. In 2005, with $84 million in funding, these three types of programs—street outreach, basic or walk-in centers (shelters), and transitional living—operated in hundreds of communities around the country. Street outreach workers try to pass on counseling, medical, and mental health treatment information to young people living on the streets to keep them safe and to show them ways to improve their circumstances. In extreme cases, workers try to bring the youths into shelters for more intensive help. Walk-in centers offer short-term shelter, food, clothing, medical assistance, and counseling to reunify families

VIRGINIA'S CASE

Motives for Running Away

Recall Virginia's family and background:

- lives in a low-income neighborhood
- mother works as a housekeeper
- stepfather, recently laid off from his job at a local factory, makes Virginia feel uncomfortable
- has a stormy relationship with her parents

Consider the factors leading youths to running away. Virginia may want to have freedom, but she may also have an economic or emotional motive. Like some youths who run away, Virginia has not returned home. This suggests that whatever the problems are, they are not likely to be resolved if she is reunited with her parents.

If the approach by the juvenile justice system is to return runaways to their families, what happens if Virginia's motive has to do with abuse or rejection? Are officials then increasing the chances that she will run away again?

THINK ABOUT IT

when possible and appropriate. Agency staff can also try to place young people, age sixteen to twenty-one, who are unable to return home, in transitional living programs that provide housing and comprehensive social services aimed at achieving self-sufficiency.

One promising avenue in seeking to decrease the problems associated with runaway youths involves the school system, because most runaways want to go to school and think their education is very important.[32] For these youths, school attendance offers them a chance to maintain relationships with friends who can provide emotional support, as well as to develop networks and skills that will help them cope with their situations and become independent. In short, attending school has a host of social and economic benefits, particularly for youths who do not feel safe at home or on the streets. Education is a strong predictor of the likelihood that the youth will overcome poverty and become independent; without an education, a runaway youth may never have the opportunity to acquire critical life skills.[33] Unfortunately, up to three-quarters of older runaway youths drop out of school because they are displaced and lack emotional, financial, and residential support.[34]

In an extraordinary turn of events relating to throwaway youths, in 2008, Nebraska passed a new "safe-haven" law, which allows parents to abandon unwanted children at hospitals without any level of accountability. What is different about Nebraska, compared to other states that have similar laws, is that the new statute permits parents to drop off a child of any age, up to nineteen years old. The law does not absolve people of possible criminal charges, such as if a child has been beaten, but it does not require officials to inquire why parents are absolving their responsibility to the youth. The law also allows anyone, not just a parent, to legally surrender custody; most states narrowly define the role of the person surrendering the child.[35]

Runaway youths present a number of challenges to agencies in terms of both individual needs and the circumstances surrounding the decision to run away. The Theory and Practice Working Together box offers some promising opportunities.

Runaways may leave home due to abuse or neglect. In some instances, they are forced out. As a way to cope with street life, many become involved in drugs and petty crimes. Why is it important that we make this status offense an issue that should not be ignored?

THEORY AND PRACTICE WORKING TOGETHER

CASAA's Homeless and Runaway Youth Program and Life Link

The University of New Mexico's Center on Alcoholism, Substance Abuse and Addictions (CASAA) Runaway and Homeless Youth Program has recently partnered with The Life Link, a nonprofit organization offering housing and behavioral health services for teens. Together, they offer best-practice treatment models and extensive homeless outreach and prevention services.

CASAA's Homeless and Runaway Youth Program began with a research grant to determine whether providing different forms of assistance to homeless and near-homeless youths, including pretreatment and follow-up assessments, would be successful. For years, CASAA has provided assistance for troubled youths through its evidence-based therapeutic technique known as the Community Reinforcement Approach (CRA), which has been successful in helping youths to cope with adversity, learn life-skills, and remain optimistic about their futures.

While the CASAA program is a research-based program rather than an ongoing operational one, The Life Link in Santa Fe has been operating the Homeless Adult and Family Program for years, using the same treatment modality that CASAA has been using with its clients. Recently, The Life Link was awarded the "Best in America" seal of approval from the Independent Charities of America Association. This partnership is a good example of how research and policy interrelate. While the CASAA program was originally designed to explore effective treatment for homeless youths, once the grant money ran out, it turned the operation over to an advocacy group that has a great deal of experience in addressing the needs of the homeless. Visit The Life Link's website to learn more about its mission and programs.

 THINK ABOUT IT Why is it so difficult to address the needs of homeless and runaway youths?

 THINK ABOUT IT

Profiling and Assisting Runaway Youths

Why would runaway youths want to remain in school? What does this mean in terms of the school's obligation to help youths living on the streets?

Truancy

truancy
The act of skipping school.

People tend not to think of students skipping school, or **truancy,** as a national problem with a host of social, economic, and political implications. Every day hundreds of thousands of students are absent from school, many without an excuse. Although national data on truancy rates are unavailable, partly because no uniform definition of truancy exists, many cities wrestle with this problem.[36] A national study in public schools found that principals identified student absenteeism, class cutting, and tardiness as the top discipline problems.[37] In addition, according to the Office of Juvenile Justice and Delinquency Prevention (OJJDP), adults who were truant at an early age are much more likely to have poorer physical and mental health, lower-paying jobs, higher likelihood of living in poverty, more reliance on welfare support, and children who exhibit problem behaviors.[38] Figure 3-3 depicts the links between truancy and juvenile delinquency.

With regard to demographic variables, a few trends are noteworthy. For instance, the relationship between race and truancy is not well established. Some data suggest that whites are underrepresented in petitioned cases, partially because many African Americans tend to have lower academic achievement levels than white students. The frustration of not doing well in school, as well as the perceived lack of relevance of getting an education, may lead some African American students to regularly avoid school. Repeated truancy is then likely to be seen by school officials and the juvenile court as a form of defiance. Consequently, these youths may be more likely to experience formal processing than white students.[39] The frustration felt by some students who do not perform well in school, as well as the feeling that education is not important, is underscored by other studies showing that African Americans and Latinos from lower-income homes consistently have the highest truancy and **dropout** rates of all categories of students.[40] While the relationship between income and truancy is not well known, experts generally believe that students from low-income families have higher rates of truancy.[41]

dropout
A student enrolled in school who voluntarily chooses not to return and complete the requirements for graduation.

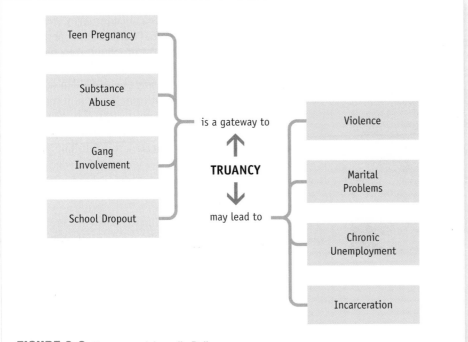

FIGURE 3-3 Truancy and Juvenile Delinquency
Besides the educational implications, according to the U.S. Department of Education, truancy is the most powerful indicator of juvenile delinquent behavior. It is a gateway to additional behavioral problems and serious forms of delinquency, and may lead to negative adult behaviors. Is truancy as serious a problem as experts portray it to be? Do you think it will lead to negative behaviors and adult crimes in the long term?

Finally, there is some evidence that boys and girls are about evenly divided in the truancy statistics.[42] While girls tend to demonstrate a slightly higher rate of absenteeism in high school than boys, the latter are more likely to become chronically truant, especially in later grades when their lack of proficiency in the classroom becomes more apparent. It is also likely to be a result of the fact that boys in later grades believe that obtaining an education is unlikely, given their grades. As a result, they find other ways to spend their time, including using drugs and committing crimes for financial gain.[43]

CAUSES

According to the National School Safety Center, about 5 percent of students in grades nine through twelve skip school because they feel unsafe on their way to or from school, or while they are on school grounds. Others miss school because of family health issues, financial demands, substance abuse, or mental health problems. Factors contributing to truancy stem mainly from four areas: school configuration, academic performance, family involvement, and community characteristics.[44]

School Configuration
According to the National Center for Education Statistics, large school systems in low-income, inner-city urban school districts have higher rates of absenteeism and truancy compared to suburban and rural school systems. The incidence of truancy is greater when attendance is not made a priority and when constructive interaction does not take place between teachers and parents.

Research consistently reports high absenteeism rates for urban schools, with approximately 8 to 10 percent of these students labeled chronically truant.[45] Educators' behaviors and performances shape their students' behaviors. Uncertified teachers,[46] low teacher expectations, high teacher absenteeism, and inconsistent discipline are contributing factors to truancy.[47]

Serious delinquency may come out of truancy. The vast majority of serious offenders started out as truants and then dropped out of school. How much should parents participate in children's education? Could too much parental attention lead to truancy or other status offenses?

> You know, it gets old, the same thing every day. And you know, I just—I didn't feel like going through school.
>
> AUSTIN

Academic Performance

Typically, the problems of absenteeism and truancy stem from a child's experience in the classroom. Poor academic performance often causes students to lose interest in school. As a result, they fall behind and begin to avoid class, then stop going to school altogether. The school's response is usually punitive, often suspension, which further alienates the student from the institution.[48] Given limited budgets, teachers and administrators sometimes "write off" these students, focusing instead on those that are present and interested. These circumstances create a self-fulfilling prophecy: once a student begins to fail and gives up, the system does not have effective mechanisms in place to get him or her back on track.

Family Involvement

A long-standing relationship exists between parental involvement, social class, and children's academic achievement. When parents participate in their children's education, whether it is monitoring homework, helping to improve reading ability, or attending PTA meetings, the probability of truancy decreases.[49] Parents with high socioeconomic status (SES) tend to be more involved with teachers and schools, as well as being more involved with their children's educational and learning development.[50]

Affluent parents tend to have more resources and time to devote to their children, and they place a high value on education. At the other end of the spectrum are youths from low-income, single-parent homes, who tend to have higher rates of absenteeism and truancy.[51] For many of these youths, the single parent has to work, sometimes at more than one job, and may not have the time and resources to tutor and be more active in the child's education and attendance. The links to truancy may not only be about money; some studies show that regardless of social class, weak or nonexistent parenting styles may contribute to truancy because children are given too much autonomy in decision making and are not held accountable for their misbehavior.[52] Part of the challenge with truancy is that many youths do not like school and refuse to attend. Consider Zach's remarks regarding skipping school:

> I never wanted to go to school. I'd always refuse. Like my mom and stuff would tell me, get up and go to school. I'd just say "no, I'm not goin' to school." I got myself in a little bit of trouble. . . . I'd just wake up in the morning and say, "I'm not goin'.". . . School didn't interest me. I don't know. It's just not my thing. A lot of kids don't [like school.]

Neighborhood and Community Factors

Children living in low-income and/or inner-city neighborhoods are more likely than suburban youths to experience violence, maltreatment, neglect and abuse, and below-average education. This living environment, in turn, affects student motivation about education in general and school attendance in particular.

Related to social class are the physical conditions of neighborhoods in which children live, which suggest a link with truancy.[53] Exposure to mental and physical health stressors (e.g., abuse, neglect, domestic violence, family strife) and to other signs of disorder (e.g., abandoned buildings and cars, condemned housing, illegal drug markets) is related to truancy.[54] The links between neighborhood conditions and delinquency will be discussed further in the next chapter, but for now, consider what can be done about truancy. One type of program that has shown some effectiveness in reducing truancy is Accountability Courts. The Theory and Practice Working Together box offers an explanation of one such program in Charleston, South Carolina.

00:20 / 01:02

For more on truancy, watch *Truancy: Austin* **and** *Truancy: Zachary* **at www.mhhe.com/mcnamarajd1e**

THEORY AND PRACTICE WORKING TOGETHER

South Carolina's Anti-Truancy Program

In many states, the courts have become the main vehicle for addressing truancy. South Carolina has three categories of truancy:

- truant: a child who has three consecutive unlawful absences or a total of five unlawful absences during the school year
- "habitual" truant: a child who does not comply with the intervention plan developed by the school, the child, and the parents or guardians, and who accumulates two or more additional unlawful absences
- "chronic" truant: a child who has been through the school intervention process, has reached the level of "habitual" truant, and has been referred to Family Court and placed under an order to attend school, but continues to accumulate unlawful absences

The Barrett Lawrimore Juvenile Drug Court and Accountability Court was created in 2006 in response to a serious truancy problem in Charleston. The program is a collaborative effort between twelve different agencies ranging from the Department of Juvenile Justice, the Charleston County School District, the Department of Mental Health, the Public Defender's Office, Family Services, Inc., and the Charleston County Family Court.

Once a child is brought before the court, he or she is placed on probation, and the parents are placed under a court order to ensure that their child attends school. If the parents and child successfully complete the program, the case is reopened, and the charges are dismissed and removed from the child's juvenile record. The program consists of three phases, summarized in the following table:

	Child's Responsibility	Parent's Responsibility	Both
Phase One (12 weeks)	▪ life-skills counseling program ▪ school attendance ▪ good behavior ▪ tutoring participation ▪ satisfactory grades ▪ 7 pm curfew	▪ parenting course ▪ enforcement of children's school attendance ▪ one-hour homework session each night ▪ school attendance with children (if deemed necessary)	▪ weekly court appearance ▪ subject to drug and alcohol testing
	Penalties: If the child skips school or a class, he or she spends each weekend in detention at the Department of Juvenile Justice until his or her school attendance record is acceptable to the court. If the child misbehaves in school, he or she is subject to detention, community service, or counseling.	**Penalties:** If a parent violates the rules, he or she is subject to a contempt of court charge, which carries a sentence of up to one year in jail, a $1,500 fine, and/or 300 hours of community service. If the parents do not make sure the child gets to school, they can be fined $50 each day the child misses school.	**Penalties:** Should the parents or child not complete Phase One successfully, they will be assessed by the Department of Mental Health to determine what should be added to the program to successfully complete it the second time around.
Phase Two (12 weeks)	▪ life-skills counseling program ▪ school attendance ▪ good behavior ▪ tutoring participation ▪ satisfactory grades ▪ *8 pm curfew	▪ enforcement of children's school attendance ▪ one-hour homework session each night ▪ school attendance with children (if deemed necessary	▪ monthly court appearance
			Penalties: If the participants begin violating the rules, they return to Phase One and are assessed for additional services.

*Phase Three: If the participants complete Phase Two successfully, the youth's curfew is increased to 9 pm, and they do not have to appear in court as long as they continue to comply with the stipulations and rules of the program.

The Accountability Court tries to address the short- and long-term issues relating to truancy in Charleston by including an internal evaluation of the program.

THINK ABOUT IT

Does it make sense to fine parents for the behavior of their children? Does having both parents and children participate in programs with distinct phases help to alleviate truancy issues?

VIRGINIA'S CASE

Impact of Her Truancy

Recall Virginia's truant actions:

- began skipping classes
- while living on the streets, continued to attend school, in part because of free lunches and friends
- started missing school for days at a time
- after a period of time, stopped going to school altogether

Virginia was a good student with near-perfect attendance. Her character did not seem to fit with those who engage in truancy; however, some factor, perhaps family issues, led her to start skipping classes. She stayed in school for a while for food and socialization, but even those incentives could not keep her from dropping out of school.

In addition to the loss of her educational opportunities, what other problems might Virginia encounter if she remains truant? What impact will this have on her future?

Holding Children Accountable

Do parents know that truancy is connected to delinquency? Would they hold their children more accountable for attending school if they did? Why or why not?

Incorrigibility

Parents commonly lament that their children do not listen to or obey them or the rules of the household. Those with teenagers are especially sensitive to disobedience: the teen years are usually the most difficult ones for a family to overcome.[55] But some parents have acutely difficult and uncontrollable children who are considered incorrigible or ungovernable.

By definition, **incorrigibility** refers to juveniles who habitually do not obey their parents. This type of behavior received a lot of attention during the 1970s. With *parens patriae* still operating at this time, many juveniles were incarcerated for incorrigibility. This incarceration exposed juveniles to much more severe criminality and sometimes even sexual and physical abuse. In short, juveniles came out of the system worse than when they entered it.

incorrigibility
The habitual disobedience of juveniles toward their parents or guardians.

HISTORICAL ROOTS

During the seventeenth and eighteenth centuries, interest in improving child-rearing practices grew. Church and school officials promoted the idea that children were special and fragile, but also corruptible. The church, the family, the community, and the school were to join in fostering children's development and controlling misbehaviors. Principles emerged that stressed discipline, modesty, chastity, hard work, and obedience to authority. Such Puritan values were very influential, if not universal, in the North American colonies.

As it was the case with adults, most social policies ignored those who were considered unworthy of assistance, and this same attitude applied to children. The Massachusetts "stubborn child" offense, used as late as the 1970s, was passed in 1654 when the House of

Deputies of the Massachusetts Bay Colony in New England determined that children often misbehaved and treated authority figures with little or no respect. The colony provided corporal punishment such as whippings for young offenders.[56] Over time, amendments were made, but as late as 1971, the state's Supreme Court upheld the stubborn child statute against a complaint that the statute was so vague and indefinite as to violate constitutional due process requirements.[57]

Numerous social and societal changes, particularly the influence of humanitarianism found in the philosophy of the Enlightenment, contributed to the desire to help the less fortunate. But the focus was on adults, not children. Wayward youths commonly were held, not helped, in impoverished almshouses and regularly sentenced to jail where they lived side by side with adult inmates.[58]

As discussed in Chapter 1, beginning about 1825, specialized institutions, such as orphan asylums for abandoned children and houses of refuge for runaway, disobedient, or vagrant youths, were founded. Later, training schools and reformatories for young offenders were established, but jailing remained common. Accurate data of the official handling of incorrigibility are still difficult to come by; however, an examination of archival data of the offenses recorded for juveniles committed to the Wisconsin State Reform School between 1880 and 1899 found that 50 percent of inmates had been committed for "incorrigibility."[59]

INCORRIGIBILITY AND THE JUVENILE JUSTICE SYSTEM

The general trend has been to detain status offenders in secure facilities despite the fact that the JJDPA prohibits such practices. A 2004 report by the Office of Juvenile Justice and Delinquency Prevention found that in those cases where the offense could not be handled informally or through probation, an increasing percentage of detained juveniles were being held in locked facilities. As Table 3-3 shows, almost 20 percent of incorrigibility offenders were confined under locked security arrangements. Incorrigibility offenders were the least likely of all status offenders to be detained in locked security locations because there is minimal threat of escape, and the youths' safety is a concern. On the other hand, underage drinkers, runaways, and even curfew violators may pose a risk to themselves, thus requiring a more restrictive environment.[60]

Of all the status offenses, incorrigibility is perhaps the least understood empirically and has the fewest programs or alternatives available to curtail it. Because of the lack of programs, police officers will often charge youths with some other offense rather than incorrigibility. Parents are the ones who typically petition the court to intervene because they are unable to control their children. This is often a last resort, since parents will usually try many other options before involving the juvenile court, which explains the lower number of petitioned cases for incorrigibility in juvenile court statistics.

TABLE 3-3 Profile of Adjudicated Status Offenders by Type of Detention Facility

	Locked	Staff-Secure
All status offenses	**29%**	**71%**
Underage drinking	51	49
Runaway	40	60
Curfew violation	40	60
Incorrigibility	18	82
Other status offenses	33	67

Underage drinkers, runaways, and even curfew violators may pose a risk to themselves, thus requiring a more restrictive environment. Do you agree that incorrigible offenders, in comparison to other status offenders, pose minimal risks to themselves and are less likely to try to escape?

Dealing with Incorrigible Children

Should there be some sort of criteria for parents to know when they should bring their disobedient children to court?

Curfew Violations

curfew violations
Status offenses involving ordinances that prohibit youths of certain ages from being in a public place during late evening or nighttime hours unless they are accompanied by an adult or are traveling to or from some acceptable activity.

Curfew violations are status offenses because curfew laws impose restrictions based solely on age. A typical curfew law generally prohibits youths under the age of sixteen or seventeen from being in a public place during late evening or nighttime hours. These ordinances vary greatly from location to location, and most contain exceptions for children who are accompanied by an adult or who are traveling to or from some acceptable activity.[61]

Curfews have a long history of use in this country, dating back hundreds of years. Curfews had fallen out of favor for a time, but more recently, the public's fear of violent crime, which some youths engage in, has resulted in a renewed interest. In the mid-1990s, a survey of America's largest 200 cities showed that 73 percent had curfew ordinances. Of those surveyed cities, 21 percent had the curfews in place for one year or less. More recently, in 2008, the FBI reported 104,168 arrests for curfew violations for offenders under the age of eighteen, an increase of about 5 percent since 2004.[62]

Like arrests for incorrigibility, arrests for curfew violations have witnessed a steady decrease since the 1990s for similar reasons. For example, there were 149,800 arrests for curfew violations in 1995[63] compared to 104,168 in 2008.[64] Police officers are less likely to make an arrest for such a charge if there are a few options available to them to address the problem.

Curfews are controversial, with proponents believing that they reduce crime and opponents arguing that they stigmatize underclass minority youths. Without sufficient empirical evidence, there remain a number of questions about the effectiveness of curfew laws.[65] Evaluations of curfews are typically conducted by agency personnel, and the instruments used are methodologically flawed since they usually measure crime only during a specific period of time, such as before and after the implementation of the curfew. A variety of factors may contribute to a reduction in crime and delinquency other than the curfew. Additional problems include the lack of control groups in evaluations of the effectiveness of curfews. This is not to suggest that curfews, by themselves, are ineffective in reducing delinquency; rather, it means there is an absence of definitive data regarding whether they work.[66] Figure 3-4 highlights some links between curfews and delinquency.

PROPONENTS AND OPPONENTS OF CURFEWS

Community residents, activists, and politicians justify curfews not only as a way to control youth gangs and as a deterrent to delinquency in general, but also as a way to protect youths from victimization. Advocates argue that curfews can also be a part of a larger outreach program to help at-risk youths, and can give the police more resources with which to fight crime in their communities.[67]

There are two main arguments against the use of curfews: they are discriminatory and they are ineffective. Perhaps the loudest criticism relates to the uneven enforcement of curfew laws against minority youths in less affluent neighborhoods. For example, in San Jose, California, nearly 60 percent of juveniles detained under the city's curfew law are Latino, which was disproportionate to the size of that segment of the population.[68] Confinement to home is less problematic

Many cities have attempted to address concerns about serious juvenile crimes by establishing curfews. Data suggest that curfews may have little actual impact on juvenile crimes, as most of these activities occur at times outside of curfew. What is your opinion on the effectiveness of curfews?

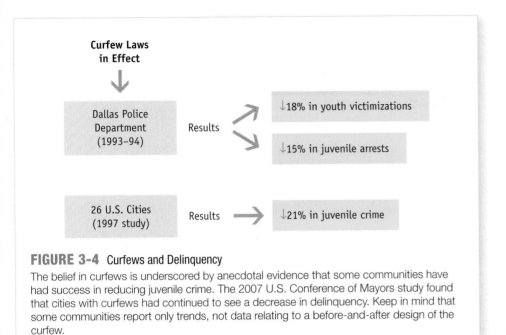

FIGURE 3-4 Curfews and Delinquency

The belief in curfews is underscored by anecdotal evidence that some communities have had success in reducing juvenile crime. The 2007 U.S. Conference of Mayors study found that cities with curfews had continued to see a decrease in delinquency. Keep in mind that some communities report only trends, not data relating to a before-and-after design of the curfew.

when there is ample room in the house and many things to do. Thus, because of economic inequalities, minority youths are unfairly punished by curfews and are more likely to violate these laws.[69]

The overall impact of curfews on reducing crime is questionable. Methodologically, virtually all of the studies on curfews fail to construct a control group to make empirical comparisons. Often, success is measured only in terms of a decrease in the crime rate in a given community. However, a host of factors contributes to a drop in crime, and parceling out the role of the curfew is virtually impossible without some sort of control mechanism. Care must be taken when interpreting overall decreases in crime. While an overall drop in the crime rate may occur shortly after a curfew law is enacted, one must consider not only the overall crime rate in a given area but also the rates of crime for the target population. It makes no sense, for example, to cite a decrease in crime as a result of a curfew law only to discover that juvenile crimes actually increased while adult crimes dropped.[70]

Consider what happened in San Diego, California. After enacting a curfew law, the city witnessed an overall drop in arrests for juvenile crime during the program's first year. Thus, the data "proved" that the curfew program was a success. However, the data actually demonstrated that the crime rate during curfew hours remained essentially unchanged (233 arrests in one year vs. 222 a year later) while the crime rate during noncurfew hours dropped dramatically. San Diego credited its juvenile curfew program with a decline in crime, but the vast majority of the change in crime occurred during the period when the curfew was *not* in effect. Additional analysis showed that less than 15 percent of all arrests for violent juvenile crimes in San Diego occurred during curfew hours.[71] This was and continues to be consistent with national data indicating that juvenile crime peaks at 3 pm and then again at 6 pm, well before curfews take effect.[72] Even if curfews were effective, they would account for only a small percentage of the reduction in juvenile crimes committed in a community.[73]

THE LEGALITY OF CURFEWS

Some legal experts also question the validity of curfew laws. The American Civil Liberties Union has taken a strong stance against juvenile curfews, essentially arguing that they constitute house arrests of youths with no due process. While no case has come before the U.S. Supreme Court regarding the constitutionality of juvenile curfews, appellate courts have maintained their viability as long as states that enact them carefully describe their parameters and criteria (see Table 3-4).

TABLE 3-4 Curfews and the Courts

Case	Court Ruling
Bykofsky v. Borough of Middletown	The stipulations of the curfew did not violate juveniles' First Amendment rights or parents' rights to raise their children as they saw fit[74] because "[t]he parents' constitutionally protected interest . . . which the ordinance infringes only minimally, is outweighed by the Borough's interest in protecting immature minors."[75]
Johnson v. Opelousas	Curfew struck down because it provided no exceptions for minors attending religious or school meetings, going to or from their jobs, or engaging in interstate travel.
Waters v. Barry	"The right to walk the streets or to meet publicly with one's friends for a noble purpose or for no purpose at all, and to do so whenever one pleases is an integral component of life in a free and ordered society."[76]
Qutb v. Strauss	Dallas's curfew law upheld because of its precise nature, which makes it a standard model for other communities: 1. unaccompanied minors (younger than seventeen or eighteen) prohibited from using public spaces at night (usually between 11 pm and 6 am during the week and midnight and 6 am on weekends) 2. exceptions for minors who are on the street due to emergency, work reasons, interstate travel, attendance of a sponsored event, participation in First Amendment activities, or an errand for a parent[77]

The courts have consistently upheld the validity of curfew laws despite the fact that they may lead to constitutional challenges with regard to issues of freedom and due process. Should the matter of curfews be settled by the courts or by parents?

There are three legal arguments against curfew laws. One of the main challenges comes in the form of contesting the infringement on the freedom of minors. Curfew laws tend to violate youths' right to freedom of speech and assembly. They also encroach upon parents' rights to raise their children as embodied in the Ninth Amendment and in the due process clause of the Fourteenth Amendment.

A second legal challenge focuses on the content of curfew laws. If curfews are considered legal on constitutional grounds, what types of parameters are in place to prevent their abuse? The Fifth Circuit Court of Appeals has ruled that a statute is invalid if it is too general and its "standards result in erratic and arbitrary application based on individual impressions and personal predilections."[78] Statutes that broadly restrict juveniles when less rigid measures are available may be voided by the courts. Therefore, when cities and states create curfews, they must not only meet a minimum test relating to the constitutional issues mentioned but also ensure that the legislation is precise in language and specific in terms of its restrictions.

A third legal issue involving juvenile curfews relates to the JJDP Act of 1974, which addresses the deinstitutionalization of status offenders. Recall that this legislation prohibits agencies from detaining status offenders in a secure facility. The only exception is if the youth is detained only for a brief period, not to exceed twenty-four hours exclusive of weekends and holidays. The statute also makes exceptions that allow detention if the offender violates a valid court order or commits a felony. With these restrictions in mind, cities creating curfew laws must establish comprehensive, community-based programs that allow officers to bring curfew violators in for temporary detention pending their release to parents or some other disposition. Otherwise, curfew arrests become little more than "catch and release" in form and function.

THINK ABOUT IT

Effectiveness of Curfews

If most juvenile crime takes place between 3 pm and 6 pm, can curfews really be effective in reducing the problem?

Underage Drinking

In 2007, the Surgeon General called underage drinking an "epidemic" and urged parents to recognize the problem it presents to all Americans. Underage drinking impairs judgments and may lead to consequences harmful to both the underage drinker and others. Citing the psychological and physical threats underage drinking presents to society, Kenneth Moritsugu, the acting Surgeon General from 2006 to 2007, issued a National Call to Action to stop underage drinking and to keep others from starting: "alcohol remains the most heavily abused substance by America's youth. This Call to Action is attempting to change the culture and attitudes toward drinking in America. We can no longer ignore what alcohol is doing to our children."[79]

Each year, over 3 million teens between the ages of twelve and seventeen take a drink of alcohol for the first time. Despite many programs related to the war on drugs, most high school students are touched by alcohol far more extensively than any other type of drug (see Figure 3-5). By their senior year in high school, nearly 81 percent of teens have tried alcohol. This figure exceeds the percentage of seniors who have smoked cigarettes or have used marijuana. About 29 percent of high school seniors have used an illegal drug other than marijuana.[80] Thus, despite the fear associated with **inhalants** and drugs like **crack, cocaine, heroin, marijuana,** and other illicit drugs, and despite the many efforts to educate youths on the dangers of using them, such as the Drug Abuse Reduction through Education (D.A.R.E.) program, alcohol

A police officer conducts a DUI stop. Are there other methods that can be employed to prevent underage drinking?

inhalants
Any toxic substances, such as glue or paint thinner, whose fumes are inhaled for their euphoric effect.

crack
A cheaper, yet more potent and pure, form of cocaine that solidifies in the purification process to assume a rocklike form; is often smoked and is considered highly addictive.

cocaine
An alkaloid extracted from coca leaves that is commonly used as an illicit drug.

heroin
A highly addictive narcotic that is more potent than morphine and is used illegally for its euphoric effects.

marijuana
A drug, usually smoked, that is derived from the dried leaves and female flowers of the hemp plant.

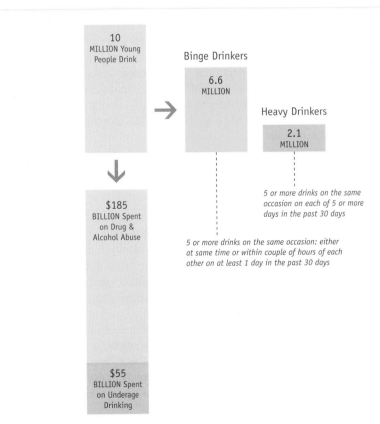

10 MILLION Young People Drink

Binge Drinkers
6.6 MILLION

Heavy Drinkers
2.1 MILLION

5 or more drinks on the same occasion on each of 5 or more days in the past 30 days

$185 BILLION Spent on Drug & Alcohol Abuse

5 or more drinks on the same occasion: either at same time or within couple of hours of each other on at least 1 day in the past 30 days

$55 BILLION Spent on Underage Drinking

FIGURE 3-5 2008 NDUHS Study of Young Drinkers and 2002 CASA Study of Alcohol and Drug Abuse Costs
According to the latest figures, specifically the 2008 National Drug Use and Health Survey (NDUHS), about 10 million persons age twelve to twenty reported alcohol consumption.

For more on drug use, watch *Drugs and School Life: Austin* at www.mhhe.com/mcnamarajd1e

Students who abuse alcohol or are at high risk for alcohol abuse are more prone to repeating a grade, being absent, or being suspended from school. What is the appeal of drinking for high school students?

presents the biggest threat to American teens. Underage drinkers are also more likely than persons ages twenty-one and older to use illicit drugs within two hours of alcohol use. The most commonly reported drug used by underage drinkers in combination with alcohol was marijuana (1.6 million persons).[81]

Underage drinking is not simply a high school phenomenon. While more teens drink as they get older, many have their first alcoholic drink before age thirteen.[82] Early alcohol use can have long-lasting consequences. People who begin drinking before age fifteen are four times more likely to develop alcohol dependence at some time in their lives compared with those who have their first drink at age twenty or older.[83]

The real problem with alcohol consumption at an early age, even if it is to simply experiment, is that most who try it do not stop; further, they abuse it. Students who engage in regular alcohol use as teens have the greatest risk for becoming binge drinkers in college. Research has shown that students who enter college as nondrinkers will likely remain that way throughout their first two years on campus. High school students who have a history of drinking, on the other hand, are likely to drink in their freshman year of college.[84] The upshot of these figures is that preventing student alcohol use and abuse during the early teen years is perhaps the most effective way of reducing the high rates of alcohol use and binge drinking in college.

Underage drinking is associated with various physical and emotional issues. According to the National Center for Health Statistics, alcohol is related to the three leading causes of death among teens age twelve to eighteen: accidents (including motor vehicle traffic fatalities and drowning), homicides, and suicides.[85] Underage drinking is also associated with teenage pregnancy and has been linked to poor educational achievement, delinquency, and drug abuse.[86] High school students who use alcohol or other substances are five times more likely to drop out of school than nonusers.[87]

Young drinkers also run the risk of developing numerous health problems early on in life due to alcohol use, such as coronary heart disease, stroke, liver cirrhosis, and various forms of cancer. In addition, alcohol abuse is related to bulimia and anorexia nervosa, as well as to depression and anxiety disorders, particularly among girls.[88]

Alcohol use is also closely related to teen sexual activity. Teenagers who drink are more likely than teens who do not drink to have sex and to have more partners. About 5.6 million fifteen- to twenty-four-year-olds report having unprotected sex because they were drinking or using drugs at the time. Perhaps more importantly, while the majority of high-school-age drinkers and drug users report using condoms, a large percentage of teens are still at risk for HIV, other sexually transmitted diseases, and pregnancy.[89]

Suicide is a leading cause of death for young people fifteen to twenty-four years old, and alcohol use is a significant risk factor for suicide attempts: it is estimated to be involved in about 10 percent of teen suicides. In one study of suicide among adolescents, 70 percent of young people who attempted suicide reported frequent use of alcohol and/or other drugs.[90] Additionally, adolescent heavy drinkers and binge drinkers are more than twice as likely as nondrinkers to say they contemplate suicide.[91]

Finally, alcohol-related motor vehicle fatality rates are nearly twice as great for those between the ages of eighteen and twenty compared to those over age twenty-one.[92] In an effort to reduce traffic fatalities associated with alcohol consumption, the National Minimum Drinking Age Act of 1984 required all states to increase the age at which individuals can legally purchase and publicly possess alcohol to twenty-one. Failure to comply with the act resulted in states losing federal highway funds under the Federal Highway Aid Act. By 1987, all states had complied with the twenty-one minimum drinking age law.[93] However, restricting access to alcohol does not necessarily translate into a decrease in alcohol use.

"Shock" Programs

Do you think "shock" programs, which show the potential effects of excessive drinking, make a difference in changing youths' behavior? Why or why not?

THINK ABOUT IT

Underage Smoking

Although it is considered a status offense, and even though it is not noted in the Uniform Crime Reports or the Juvenile Court Statistics, teen smoking is considered a serious social problem in the United States, affecting millions of teenagers each year (see Figure 3-6). The use of tobacco products, which includes cigarettes, cigars, and smokeless tobacco products such as "chew" and "snuff," causes a host of problems for parents, teens, and the general public because it has links to alcohol abuse and other forms of illicit drug abuse.[94]

EXTENT

Perhaps the two most comprehensive measures of teen smoking come from the 2008 National Drug Use and Health Survey (NDUHS) and the 2008 Monitoring the Future Study (MTF). According to the MTF, nearly half of American youths have tried cigarettes by the twelfth grade, and nearly a quarter of twelfth graders are current smokers. An equal number of eighth graders have tried cigarettes, and about 10 percent of that population are considered current smokers. Recently, some experts expressed a high level of optimism concerning the decline in teen cigarette use in the 1990s, which continued through 2008, at which time the rates showed an even greater decline.[95]

The decline in cigarette smoking in the early 1990s is attributed to the reduction in cigarette advertising and to antismoking campaigns funded by tobacco companies as part of their overall legal settlement with the government concerning the effects of smoking. Further, the cost of cigarettes, which rose substantially during this period, was seen as a deterrent among teens (these costs were designed in part to offset the expenses associated

FIGURE 3-6 Adolescents and Cigarette Smoking

Approximately 90 percent of smokers begin smoking before the age of twenty-one. Adolescents who smoke regularly can have just as hard a time quitting as long-time smokers. Of adolescents who have smoked at least 100 cigarettes in their lifetime, most of them report that they would like to quit but are not able to do so.

with the tobacco settlement, as well as providing a source of revenue for states in the form of increased excise taxes).[96]

Another source of concern is smokeless tobacco, which comes in two forms. "Snuff" is finely ground tobacco usually sold in tins, either loose or in packets. It is held in the mouth between the lip or cheek and the gums. "Chew" is a leafy form of tobacco, usually sold in pouches. It is held in the mouth and can be chewed. Smokeless tobacco is also sometimes called "spit" tobacco because users spit out the tobacco juices and saliva stimulated by the tobacco that accumulates in the mouth. While this represents a much smaller segment of the tobacco-using teen population, the changes in use patterns and availability are similar to those for cigarettes.[97]

According to the NDUHS, in 2008 an estimated 70.9 million Americans ages twelve and older were current users of a tobacco product (defined as using within the past thirty days). This represents about 28 percent of the population in that age category. About 84 percent (59.8 million persons) of tobacco users in 2008 were cigarette smokers, with another 5 percent consisting of cigar smokers, and about 4 percent smokeless tobacco users. Among underage smokers, those between the ages of twelve and seventeen, there were 3.3 million users of tobacco products in 2008, of whom 2.7 million used cigarettes. As with their adult counterparts, cigarettes are the preferred tobacco product among underage youths. Smokeless tobacco rates were only about 2 percent for the twelve-to-seventeen age group compared to about 5 percent for the eighteen- to twenty-five age group.[98]

Among adults, cigarette use also tends to be related to education levels. Since 2002, those with more education have tended to smoke less. Among adults ages eighteen and older, current cigarette use in 2008 was reported by about 34 percent of those who had not completed high school, about 31 percent of high school graduates, 26.6 percent of persons with some college, and about 14 percent of college graduates (see Figure 3-7).

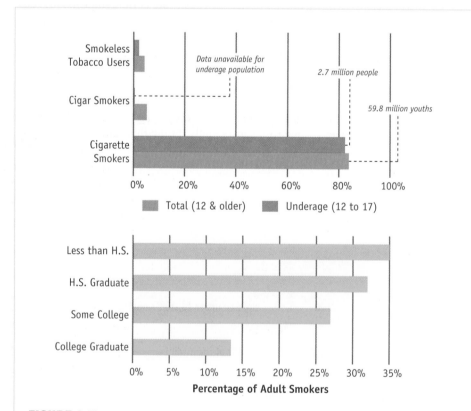

FIGURE 3-7 Tobacco Use and Education Level

According to the NDUHS, in 2008, an estimated 70.9 million Americans ages twelve and older were using tobacco products (defined as using within the past thirty days). As with adults, cigarettes are the preferred tobacco product among underage youths. Among adults, cigarette use also tends to be related to education levels, with those with more education tending to smoke less. Why would those with more education tend to smoke less? How does what you do as a youth affect your behavior as an adult?

EFFECTS OF SMOKING

Cigarette smoking during childhood and adolescence produces significant health problems, including an increase in the number and severity of respiratory illnesses, decreased physical fitness, and a potential reduction of lung function. An estimated 440,000 Americans die each year from diseases caused by smoking.[99]

Nicotine causes arterial blood vessels to become clogged, so that blood cannot flow through them properly. Nicotine also constricts blood vessels causing the heart rate, blood pressure, and blood flow to increase. This requires the heart to work harder. Carbon monoxide from cigarettes takes the place of oxygen in the blood, which means the tissues are not getting the oxygen they need. Carbon monoxide also makes it easier for bad cholesterol to get into the blood vessels.

Some experts argue that heavy cigarette smoking is problematic but that those who smoke only occasionally are not nearly as at risk as heavy smokers. However, in a study published in 2006 in the *Journal of Epidemiology and Public Health,* Danish researchers reported that smoking as few as three to five cigarettes per day substantially increases the risk of heart attack and death. This finding was true for both men and women, but especially for women, for whom "light" smoking (those who smoke only a few cigarettes a day) resulted in a 50 percent higher incidence of both heart attack and death as compared to men.[100] This study was accomplished by analyzing data from the Copenhagen City Heart Study, in which 14,223 individuals without evidence of heart disease were followed from 1976 to 1998. A relatively large proportion of these people turned out to be smokers. The researchers found that the more cigarettes one smokes per day, the higher the risk. But the risk remains substantial all the way down to three cigarettes per day. What this means is that cigarette smokers who convince themselves that "cutting back" is good enough are still vulnerable.[101]

REASONS TEENAGERS SMOKE

Given the health risks associated with smoking, why would teens do it? Perhaps it has something to do with modeling the behavior of parents—one study revealed that adolescents whose parents smoked were four times more likely to be a smoker than their peers whose parents had never smoked. This same study found that if parents quit smoking while their children were still young, the chances of them becoming smokers as teenagers were dramatically reduced.[102] Other researchers point to the influence of friends and older siblings as a main factor in decisions to start smoking. Additionally, ad campaigns that portray smoking as glamorous, sexy, or sophisticated, or that foster other positive attitudes, increased the likelihood of a teen smoking.[103]

Young people may find social "rewards" associated with smoking. For instance, smokers provide other smokers with social interaction, companionship, and a common bond. People who smoke go to designated areas, usually outside, and congregate around the person who has a cigarette lighter. In addition to providing opportunities for social interaction, cigarette smoking offers other social "benefits." Research has shown that nicotine has the ability to suppress appetite for food and is a good way to obtain relief from troubles and feelings of insecurity.[104]

MEDIA CAMPAIGNS AND TEENAGE SMOKING

The usage rates of tobacco products are decreasing in part due to antismoking campaigns, cost increases, and the tobacco industry's refusal to target teens in ad campaigns. With regard to the latter, some controversy exists. While tobacco-makers emphatically deny that they target young people, many of their promotions appeal to underage smokers. These efforts seem to be pitched at three levels. First, like the alcohol industry, tobacco manufacturers have begun

Besides potential health problems associated with smoking and tobacco use, what behavioral effects does smoking and tobacco use cause?

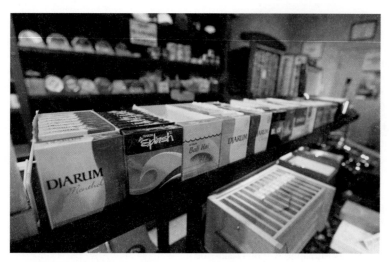

Might the packaging of these flavored cigarettes tempt teenagers to try smoking? Are tobacco companies trying to target a younger audience?

marketing flavored products—cigarettes with names such as Kauai Kolada, Twista Lime, and Mandarin Mint—giving curious teens new reasons to try smoking. R. J. Reynolds, which markets the Camel "exotic blends," says they are not aimed at teens. Yet, according to surveys released in May 2004 by the Roswell Park Cancer Institute in Buffalo, New York, about 20 percent of smokers age seventeen through nineteen tried a flavored cigarette, compared with less than 9 percent of smokers older than nineteen. Only about 2 percent of people ages fifty-five and older expressed any interest in flavored tobacco products.

Second, similar to alcohol companies, the tobacco industry seems to have increased its spending on promotions despite agreeing to curtail or stop certain types of marketing. According to a Federal Trade Commission report in 2003, since signing a deal in 1998 with state officials across the country to curtail certain types of marketing, the industry has more than doubled its expenditures on advertising and promotions. In 2003, major tobacco companies spent $15.1 billion—$22 for every dollar the states spent on tobacco prevention.

Finally, tobacco companies have also tried to renege on the settlement agreement they signed in the late 1990s. As part of the 1998 settlement, tobacco companies agreed to help fund a national antismoking advertising campaign aimed at teens. But in 2002, the Lorillard Tobacco Company threatened to sue the group running the campaign, claiming it violated the deal by vilifying the tobacco industry. In 2003, a Delaware judge ruled that the advertising campaign did not violate the terms of the tobacco compromise. While the rates of smoking are changing and questions remain about the value of deterrent advertising and price hikes, it is interesting that the industry claims not to target teens but objects when teens are given antismoking information.

VIRGINIA'S CASE

Conclusions

Recall the issues Virginia is facing:

- dropped out of school
- ran away from home
- broke curfew law
- shoplifted and trespassed

Consider factors that may contribute to her behavior. She may be fleeing some type of conflict or abuse at home. The causes of her actions need to be taken into account.

Extended time on the streets for teenagers leads to a host of survival behaviors that can result in criminal charges. Because she had run away from home, Virginia shoplifted for food, trespassed to find shelter, and broke curfew. While these are criminal behaviors for which she should be held accountable, the course of action is complicated because of the roots of her problems.

THINK ABOUT IT Consider what you know about Virginia. What are some possible reasons for her behaviors? What kinds of programs could have prevented her from running away in the first place? Currently, most programs provide safe places for youths, similar to shelters for homeless adults. Should that be the extent of society's assistance?

Status Offenders and Public Policy

The shift in philosophy in the juvenile justice system, which currently focuses more on accountability and fosters a "get-tough" attitude, has affected status offenses. Given that many status offenders also commit delinquent acts, it may seem reasonable to treat these types of offenders like delinquents, but the circumstances are more complicated, and many offenders are average teenagers who commit minor crimes. The actions of juvenile court judges add more layers to the issues by engaging in bootstrapping and hidden delinquency, perhaps due to the failure of many youths to comply with court orders. However, recidivism may not be a result of defiance; many youths run away because of abusive home situations. Thus, reoffending might be an appropriate response even though these youths should be complying with official judicial orders. The frustration felt by judges, who are attempting to prevent youths from getting into serious trouble but are constrained by federal law, is understandable. The end result of such policy decisions means that the original intent of the JJDPA is being ignored, with runaways, truants, and curfew violators being cast together with their more hardened juvenile counterparts.

Other behaviors, such as curfew violations, incorrigibility, and underage drinking and smoking, while problematic from a public health perspective, have been routinely ignored by the police, largely because little can be done to punish offenders. Despite the potential risks involved in engaging in underage drinking, police officers avoid making arrests for such violations since the offenders likely will not be punished in any significant way.

THE BIG PICTURE

Conclusions on Status Offenses

- Have judges misunderstood the motives behind many status offenders? Do youths reoffend because they are disobedient? Or are judges limited in the tools at their disposal to help, so they use punishment to get youths to refrain from engaging in these behaviors?

- Should juvenile justice officials be allowed to incarcerate and/or detain status offenders? Should status offenders continue to be under the authority of the juvenile justice system or should their cases be decided by some other treatment-oriented agency? Explain.

- What should parents do when their children continually disobey them by breaking curfews, binge drinking, or smoking?

Key Terms

status offender	deinstitutionalization	homeless youths
Juvenile Justice Delinquency Prevention Act	valid court order amendment	street youths
	bootstrapping	truancy
CHINS	hidden delinquency	incorrigibility
MINS	runaways	curfew violations
PINS	throwaway youths	

Make the Call ▶ Status Offenses

Review the scenario below, and decide how you would approach this case.

YOUR ROLE: Juvenile court judge

DETAILS OF THE CASE

- A young man, fifteen years old, has been arrested for underage drinking.

- He is also charged with vandalism.

- This youth is a repeat offender: several instances of running away, two instances of truancy, and incorrigibility.

- You had previously ordered him to attend school every day, admonished him about being disobedient to his parents, and mandated that if he were to run away again, you would place him in a group home.

- You had also ordered a psychiatric evaluation and required him to attend therapy sessions offered by the Department of Social Services.

WHAT IS YOUR RULING?

Since he is a status offender, you are prohibited from detaining him as he has not been adjudicated a delinquent. The philosophy of the court is to offer treatment to status offenders. Clearly, he is defiant and is not interested in treatment, so how do you rule?

Consider:

- Has the youth violated a valid court order?

- Has the youth committed a crime for which he could be adjudicated as a delinquent?

- Is detention really in the best interests of the youth?

- What could be the reasons for the defiance and escape behavior? What are some of the ways you can determine the causes of the problem?

- Are you on solid legal ground if you detain the youth? What if there are no secure facilities to accomplish this goal? What if the only option is an adult jail? Are you still on solid legal ground?

Apply Theory to Reality ▶ Differential Association Theory

Underage drinking and smoking are two of the most significant forms of drug abuse for youths today. Use Differential Association theory, discussed in Chapter 5, as a framework to understand why so many youths engage in drinking and smoking despite knowledge of the risks.

Your Community ▶ Programs for Runaways

In addition to the information you glean from your readings, class lectures, and discussions, it is important to roll up your sleeves and immerse yourself in a topic as a researcher who goes out and gains an understanding of the problem by observing or experiencing it firsthand. Through such methods, you gain a much greater appreciation of the magnitude and scope of the problem than if you were only engaged in "armchair theorizing."

- Go to the Web or visit your local Department of Juvenile Justice or Department of Social Services agency to determine what programs exist for runaways in your community.

- Read up on the details of these programs. See if you can interview the director and agency staff members to learn about runaways in your community. What are some of the reasons for running away? What are some of the effects of running away?

- After collecting your data, and drawing from the relevant literature, prepare a report or presentation of your findings regarding the programs offered in your community.

Notes

[1] Puzzanchera, C. 2009. *Juvenile Arrests 2007.* Washington, DC: Office of Juvenile Justice and Delinquency Prevention.

[2] Tyler, J., Segady, T., and Austin, S. 2000. "Parental Liability Laws: Rational, Theory, and Effectiveness." *Social Science Journal,* 37: 79–97.

[3] Steinhart, D. J. 1996. "Status Offenses." *The Juvenile Court,* 6(3), Winter.

[4] Tyler, Segady, and Austin, 2000.

[5] Maxon, C., and Klein, M. 1997. *Responding to Troubled Youth.* New York: Oxford University Press.

[6] Hutzler, J. 1982. *Juvenile Court Jurisdiction over Children's Conduct: 1982 Comparative Analysis of Juvenile and Family Codes and National Standards.* Pittsburgh, PA: National Center for Juvenile Justice.

[7] Steinhart, 1996.

[8] Del Carmen, R. V., and Trulson, C. R. 2006. *Juvenile Justice: The System, Process and Law.* Belmont, CA: Wadsworth.

[9] Ibid.

[10] Steinhart, 1996.

[11] Ibid.

[12] Del Carmen and Trulson, 2006.

[13] 442 U.S. 584 (1979).

[14] Flowers, R. B. 2001. *Runaway Kids and Teenage Prostitution.* Westport, CT: Praeger.

[15] Van Wormer. 2003. "Homeless Youth Seeking Assistance: A Research-Based Study from Duluth, Minnesota." *Child & Youth Forum,* 32(2): 89–103.

[16] Puzzanchera, 2009.

[17] 42 U.S.C. 5732a.

[18] Hammer, H., Finkelhor, D., and Sedlak, A. 2002. Runaway/throwaway Children: National Estimates and Characteristics. *National Incidence Studies of Missing, Abducted, Runaway and Throwaway Children.*

[19] Van Wormer, 2003.

[20] Hammer, Finkelhor, and Sedlak, 2002.

[21] See Moon, M., Binson, D., Page-Shafter, K., and Diaz, R. 2001. "Correlates of HIV Risk in a Random Sample of Street Youths in San Francisco." *Journal of the Association of Nurses in AIDS Care,* 12(6): 18–27; Auerswald, C. L., and Eyre, S. L. 2002. "Youth Homelessness in San Francisco: A Life Cycle Approach." *Social Science & Medicine,* 54: 1497–1512.

[22] See Moon et al., 2001; Auerswald and Eyre, 2002.

[23] National Coalition for the Homeless. 1999. *Breaking the Foster Care–Homelessness Connection,* September/October; van Wormer, 2003; Wilder Research Center. 2005. *Homeless Youth in Minnesota: 2003 Statewide Survey of People without Shelter.* St. Paul, MN.

[24] National Coalition for the Homeless, 1999; Powers, J., Eckenrode, J., and Jaklitsch, B. 1990. "Maltreatment among Runaway and Homeless Youth." *Child Abuse and Neglect,* 14(1): 87–98; Whitbeck, L. B., and Hoyt, D. R. 1999. *Nowhere to Grow: Homeless and Runaway Adolescents and Their Families.* New York: Aldine de Gruyter; Wilder Research Center, 2005.

[25] Kipke, M., Montgomery, S., Simon, T., Unger, J., and Johnson, T. 1997. "Homeless Youth: Drug Use Patterns and HIV Risk Profiles according to Peer Affiliation." *AIDS and Behavior,* 1(4): 247–259.

[26] Bao, W., Whitbeck, L., and Hoyt, D. 2000. "Abuse, Support, and Depression among Homeless and Runaway Adolescents." *Journal of Health and Social Behavior,* 41: 408–420.

[27] Hagan, J., and McCarthy, B. 1997. *Mean Streets: Youth Crime and Homelessness.* Cambridge, MA: Cambridge University Press, Institute for Children and Poverty; Rotheram-Borus, M., Mahler, K., Koopman, C., and Langabeer, K. 1996. "Sexual Abuse History and Associated Multiple Risk Behavior in Adolescent Runaways." *American Journal of Orthopsychiatry,* 66: 390–400.

[28] Hagan and McCarthy, 1997.

[29] Van Wormer, 2003.

[30] Wright, B., Caspi, A., Moffitt, T., and Silva, P. 1998. "Factors Associated with Doubled-up Housing—A Common Precursor to Homelessness." *Social Service Review,* 72(1): 92–111.

[31] Ibid.

[32] Slavin, P. (2001). Life on the run, life on the streets. Children's Voice Magazine. Retrieved February 11, 2005, from http://library.adoption.com/print.php?articleid=3950

[33] Nunez, R. 1995. *An American Family Myth: Every Child at Risk.* New York: Homes for the Homeless.

[34] Cauce, A., Paradise, M., Ginzler, J., Embry, L., Morgan, C., and Lohr, Y. 2000. "The Characteristics of Mental Health of Homeless Adolescents: Age and Gender Differences." *Journal of Emotional and Behavioral Disorders,* 8(4): 230–239.

[35] Ortiz, J. 2008. "Neb. 'safe-haven' law allows abandonment of teens." Associated Press.

[36] See, for instance, Henry, K. L. 2007. "Who's Skipping School? Characteristics of Truants in 8th and 10th Grade." *Journal of School Health,* 77(1): 29–35; Baker, M. L., Sigmon, J. N., and Nugent, M. E. 2001. *Truancy Reduction: Keeping Students in School.* Washington, DC: U.S. Department of Justice, Office of Juvenile Justice Programs, Office of Juvenile Justice and Delinquency Prevention.

[37] Heaviside, S., Rowan, C., Williams, C., and Farris, E. 1998. *Violence and Discipline Problems in U.S. Public Schools: 1996–1997.* Washington, DC: U.S. Department of Education, Office of Educational Research and Improvement, National Center for Education Statistics.

[38] Baker, Sigmon, and Nugent, 2001. See also Zhang, D., Katsiyannis, A., Barrett, D., and Wilson, V. 2007. "Truancy Offenders in the Juvenile Justice System." *Remedial and Special Education,* 28(4): 244–256; Puzzanchera, C., Stahl, A. L., Finnegan, T. A., Tierney, N., and Snyder,

H. N. 2003. *Juvenile Court Statistics 2008.* Washington, DC: U.S. Department of Justice, Office of Juvenile Justice and Delinquency Prevention; Dryfoos, J. G. 1990. *Adolescents at Risk: Prevalence and Prevention.* New York: Oxford University Press; Catalano, F. R., Arthur, M. W., Hawkins, J. D., Berglund, L., and Olson, J. J. 1998. "Comprehensive Community and School-Based Interventions to Prevent Antisocial Behavior." In Loeber, R., and Farrington, D. (eds.), *Serious and Violent Juvenile Offenders: Risk Factors and Successful Interventions.* Thousand Oaks, CA: Sage; Snyder, H. N., and Sickmund, M. 1995. *Juvenile Offenders and Victims: A National Report.* Washington, DC: U.S. Department of Justice, Office of Juvenile Justice and Delinquency Prevention.

[39] See Henry, 2007. See also Bell, A. J., Rosen, L. A., and Dynlacht, D. 1994. "Truancy Intervention." *The Journal of Research and Development in Education,* 27: 203–211; Puzzanchera et al., 2003.

[40] Kaufman, P., Alt, M. N., and Chapman, C. D. 2001. *Dropout Rates in the United States, 2000.* Washington, DC: U.S. Department of Education, National Center for Education Statistics. See also Zhang et al., 2007.

[41] Henry, 2007; Bell et al, 1994.

[42] Puzzanchera et al., 2003.

[43] Allen-Meares, P., Washington, R. O., and Welsh, B. L. 2000. *Social Work Services in Schools.* Boston: Allyn and Bacon. See also Zhang et al., 2007.

[44] Ibid.

[45] Epstein, J. L., and Sheldon, S. B. 2002. "Present and Accounted For: Improving Student Attendance through Family and Community Involvement." *Journal of Educational Research,* 95: 308–318. See also Henry, 2007.

[46] Dougherty, J. W. 1999. "Attending to Attendance," *Phi Delta Kappa Fastbacks,* 450: 7–49; Epstein and Sheldon, 2002; Henry, 2007.

[47] Baker, Simon, and Nugent, 2001; Strickland, V. P. 1998. *Attendance and Grade Point Average: A Study.* East Lansing, MI: National Center for Research on Teacher Learning. See also Zhang et al., 2007.

[48] Allen-Meares, Washington, and Welsh, 2000.

[49] Epstein and Sheldon, 2002.

[50] Ibid.

[51] Oman, R. F., McLeroy, K. R., Versely, S., Aspy, C. B., Smith, D. W., and Penn, D. A. 2002."An Adolescent Age Group Approach to Examining Youth Risk Behaviors." *American Journal of Health Promotion,* 16: 167–176.

[52] Oman et al., 2002; Rohrman, 1993.

[53] Epstein and Sheldon, 2002; Teevan, J. J., and Dryburgh, H. B. 2000. "First Person Accounts and Sociological Explanations of Delinquency." *Canadian Review of Sociology and Anthropology,* 37(1): 77–93.

[54] Wandersman, A., and Nation, M. 1998. "Urban Neighborhoods and Mental Health: Psychological Contributions to Understanding Toxicity, Resilience, and Interventions," *American Psychologist,* 53: 647–656.

[55] See, for instance, Lamanna, M. A., and Riedmann, A. 2008. *Marriage and Families: Making Choices in a Diverse Society.* Boston: Pearson; Shaffer, D. R. 2008. *Social and Personality Development.* Boston: Pearson.

[56] Steinhart, 1996.

[57] *Commonwealth v. Brother,* Supreme Court of Massachusetts, 270 N.E. 2d 389 (Mass.), 1971.

[58] Steinhart, 1996.

[59] Ibid.

[60] Office of Juvenile Justice Delinquency Prevention, 2004.

[61] Juvenile Justice Digest. 2003. "Indiana Uses Curfews to Cut Summer Crime," 31(15): 3; Steinhart, D. J. 1996. "Status Offenses," *The Juvenile Court,* 6(3), Winter.

[62] U.S. Department of Justice, Federal Bureau of Investigation. 2006. *Crime in the United States.* Table 36. Washington, DC: U.S. Government Printing Office. http://www.fbi.gov/ucr/cius2006/data/table_36.html. Accessed August 28, 2008.

[63] U.S. Department of Justice, Federal Bureau of Investigation. 1995. *Crime in the United States.* Washington, DC: U.S. Government Printing Office. http://www.fbi.gov/ucr/Cius_97/95CRIME/95crime4.pdf.

[64] U.S. Department of Justice, Federal Bureau of Investigation. 2008. *Crime in the United States.* Washington, DC: U.S. Government Printing Office. http://www.fbi.gov/ucr/cius2008/data/table_38.

[65] Bannister, Carter, and Schaefer, 2001; Juvenile Justice Digest, 2003; Lersch, K. M., and Sellers, C. S. 2000. "A Comparison of Curfew and Noncurfew Violators Using a Self-Report Delinquency Survey." *American Journal of Criminal Justice,* 24(2): 259–270.

[66] Bannister, Carter, and Schafer, 2001. See also, for instance, http://www.citymayors.com/society/usa-youth-curfews.html.

[67] Aitken, M. 2003. *Community Curfews for Youth: Punitive or Positive?* Ann Arbor, MI: The Search Institute.

[68] See, for instance, Boyle, P. 2006. "Curfews and Crime." *Youth Today,.* http://www.youthtoday.org/publication/article.cfm?article_id=306. See also Privor, B. 1999. "Dusk Till Dawn: Children's Rights and the Effectiveness of Juvenile Curfew Ordinances," *Boston University Law Review,* 79: 415–489.

[69] See Boyle, 2006; Males, M. A., and Macallair, D. 1998. *The Impact of Juvenile Curfew Laws in California.* San Francisco: Justice Policy Institute.

[70] See Adams, K. 2007. "Abolish Juvenile Curfews." *Criminology and Public Policy,* 6(4): 663–670; Budd, J. 1999. *Juvenile Curfews: The Rights of Minors vs. the Rhetoric of Public Safety.* Washington, DC: American Bar Association.

[71] Ibid.

[72] See, for instance, Butts, J., and Snyder, H. 2008. *Arresting Children: Examining Recent Trends in Preteen Crime.* Chicago: Chapel Hill Center for Children at the University of Chicago.

[73] Adams, 2007; Budd, 1999.

[74] *Bykofsky v. Borough of Middletown.* 401 F. Supp. 1242 (M.D. Pa. 1975).

[75] Ibid.

[76] *Waters v. Barry.* 711 F. Supp.1125 (1989).

[77] *Qutb v. Strauss.* 11 F.3d 488, 492 (5th Circuit Court of Appeals 1993).

[78] Ibid.

[79] National Center for Health Statistics. 2008. *Ten Leading Causes of Death, United States: 2008.* http://www.cdc.gov/nchs/.

[80] The National Center on Addiction and Substance Abuse (CASA). 2002. *CASA Analysis of Substance Abuse and Mental Health Services Administration.* New York: Columbia University.

[81] U.S. Department of Health and Human Services. 2008. *Results from the 2008 National Survey on Drug Use and Health. National Findings.* Available at http://oas.samhsa.gov/NSDUH/2k8NSDUH/2k8results.cfm#3.1.

[82] Ibid.

[83] Grant, B. F., and Dawson, D.A. 1997. "Age of Onset of Alcohol Use and Its Association with DSM–IV Alcohol Abuse and Dependence: Results from the National Longitudinal Alcohol Epidemiologic Survey." *Journal of Substance Abuse,* 9:103–110.

[84] Kluger, J. 2001. "How to Manage Teen Drinking (the smart way)." *Time,* 157, pp. 42–44. See also http://www.surgeongeneral.gov/library/publichealthreports/sgp124-1.pdf.

[85] See, for instance, Centers for Disease Control and Prevention. 2006. *Youth Risk Behavior Surveillance: United States, 2005.* http://apps.nccd.cdc.gov/yrbss/CategoryQuestions.asp?cat=1&desc=Unintentional Injuries and Violence.

[86] Greenblatt, J. C. 2000. *Patterns of Alcohol Use among Adolescents and Associations with Emotional and Behavioral Problems.* Rockville, MD: Substance Abuse and Mental Health Services Administration.

[87] Ibid.

[88] Centers for Disease Control and Prevention, 2006.

[89] National Institute on Alcohol Abuse and Alcoholism. 2000. *10th Special Report to Congress on Alcohol and Health: Highlights from Current Research.* Rockville, MD: U.S. Department of Health and Human Services, National Institute on Alcohol Abuse and Alcoholism; National Institute on Alcohol Abuse and Alcoholism. 2000. *Make a Difference: Talk to Your Child about Alcohol.* Rockville, MD: U.S. Department

of Health and Human Services, National Institute on Alcohol Abuse and Alcoholism.

[90] Ibid.

[91] See, for instance, Center for Science in the Public Interest at http://www.cspinet.org/booze/enforcing.htm. See also Levy, D. T., Miller, T. R., and Cox, K. 1999. *Costs of Underage Drinking.* Calverton, MD: Pacific Institute for Research and Evaluation.

[92] Centers for Disease Control and Prevention, 2006.

[93] National Highway Traffic Safety Administration. 2000. *Traffic Safety Facts 2000: Alcohol.* Washington, DC: U.S. Department of Transportation. See also http://www.surgeongeneral.gov/library/publichealthreports/sgp124-1.pdf.

[94] Mei-Chen H., Davies, M., and Kandel, D.B. 2006. "Epidemiology and Correlates of Daily Smoking and Nicotine Dependence among Young Adults in the United States." *American Journal of Public Health,* 96(2): 299–308.

[95] National Institute on Drug Abuse. *Monitoring the Future 2005.* Ann Arbor: University of Michigan.

[96] Sussman S., Sun P., and Dent C. W. 2006. "A Meta-analysis of Teen Cigarette Smoking Cessation." *Health Psychology,* 25(5).

[97] National Institute on Drug Abuse, 2008.

[98] Department of Health and Human Services, Office of Applied Studies. 2008. *National Drug Abuse and Health Survey.* Washington, DC: U.S. Government Printing Office.

[99] American Heart Association, 2006.

[100] Mei-Chen, Davies, and Kandel, 2006.

[101] Ibid.

[102] Sussman, Sun, and Dent, 2006.

[103] Ibid.

[104] See, for instance, Palmatier, M., Liux, M., Donny, E., Caggula, A. R., and Sved, A. F. 2008. "Metabotropic Glutamine 5 Receptor Antagonists Decrease Nicotine Seeking But Don't Affect Reinforcement Enhancing Effects of Nicotine." *Neuropsychopharmacology,* 33(9): 2139–2147. See also Miyasato, K. 2001. "Recent Advances in Research on Nicotine Dependence." *Folic Pharmacological Japonica,* 117(1): 27–34; Goode, E. 2008. *Drugs and Society,* 8th ed. New York: McGraw-Hill.

OBJECTIVES

After reading this chapter, you should be able to:

- Relate how factors such as poverty contribute to social disorganization and delinquency.

- Recall the origins of social structural theories of delinquency and how they evolved.

- Define social disorganization theory and illustrate how it relates to delinquency.

- Describe strain and anomie theories, and demonstrate how they explain delinquency.

- Analyze how subcultural theories apply to the study of delinquency.

- Support social structural theories of delinquency with public policy applications.

4

Social Structural Theories of Delinquency

A popular belief is that parental neglect causes delinquency. When parents do not provide proper supervision, children become delinquents. Consider the following case about James:

James's profile:
- is a fourteen-year-old boy
- lives in a low-income housing project in a large metropolitan area with his mother and three younger siblings
- mother works full-time at a local Wal-Mart for minimum wage and often takes extra shifts to supplement her low income

James's school:
- frequently skips school to care for his younger brothers and sister
- avoids school because gang members have been harassing him to join the gang
- has been caught shoplifting food
- has been suspended from school for truancy

Current status:
The juvenile court gave James probation for his shoplifting and truancy, but additional offenses might land him in a detention facility. James is a smart young man, earning good grades when he attends school. He is also caring and sensitive to other people, and is loyal to his family, as he demonstrates by taking care of his younger siblings. When asked, he states that shoplifting and skipping school were necessary to feed and protect his family.

When trying to make sense of James's behavior, we might explain his situation in one of the following ways:

- James's mother is irresponsible in caring for her children.
- James lacks opportunities to address the problems in his life.
- James is making poor choices and getting into trouble as a result.

Structural factors, such as neighborhood conditions and shifts in the labor market, contribute to the likelihood of delinquency. How have structural factors changed through time?

81

THINK ABOUT IT Based on what you know about James's situation, how would you explain his behavior? Would you describe his shoplifting and truancy as delinquent acts? Why or why not?

In this chapter, we will explore some of the external influences that relate to delinquency, such as poverty, a changing economy, housing costs, and limited educational opportunities. These factors are all part of social structure, or the way that society is organized.

social structural theories
Explanations of how some children, especially those who are members of minority groups or are poor, do not receive the same opportunities for success as white middle-class children and, as a result, turn to crime.

Social structural theories of delinquency are the subject of this chapter. These theories explain delinquency by stating that because of the way society is organized, some children, especially those who are members of minority groups or who are poor, do not receive the same opportunities for success as white middle-class children. As a result, despite their individual talent, discipline, drive, or willingness to sacrifice, some young people turn to crime. Can these theories help us explain James's delinquency? Can understanding the social causes of delinquency improve the potential outcome for him and many other young people like him? What do these theories imply about the kinds of social policies that might help James and other young people like him?

Students in criminal justice classes often ask why they have to study theory. Theory is a tool that helps us understand the world around us and put things and events in perspective. Applying theory to a behavior or a social phenomenon will get us a bit closer to finding an explanation or solution for it. A good analogy is when engineers try to build a strong bridge to replace one that failed. They need to know why the original bridge did not hold up—in other words, they need to know the theory of mechanics—to figure out how to build a better bridge. Similarly, in order to explain certain events and behaviors of juvenile delinquency, we need to know the relevant theories and how to apply them.

It is sometimes helpful to think of theory as a stepping-stone toward new ideas and practical applications. Rarely will you find a new program targeted at delinquents that does not have a theoretical basis. Theory helps criminologists understand how different elements—social factors, individuals, families, schools, communities—can be expected to work together. Without theory, discovery becomes little more than trial and error, a very slow way to learn.

Social Structural Influences

Social structural theories link delinquency and crime to elements in the fabric of society such as poverty, chronic unemployment, racism, lack of affordable housing, low wages, and inadequate education. These large-scale problems can have devastating effects on individuals and families. In response to these obstacles, which prevent youths from achieving success in conventional ways, some youths turn to crime and delinquency. To understand social structural theories, it helps to understand the various social issues and how they affect the poor. The effects of such social conditions can be strong even on individuals with a fine work ethic or a determination to succeed. For example, a young man may work hard, but if the only school available to him does not teach him the skills he needs to get a good job, he probably will remain poor. As a result, the young man may see little hope for success, and criminal opportunities may become attractive to him. In this section, we will focus on four important social problems that influence delinquency: poverty, deindustrialization, the housing crunch, and public education.

POVERTY

According to the U.S. Census Bureau, about 36 million Americans are defined as poor.[1] This means they do not earn enough money to meet their living expenses. If a family is at or below what are called "income thresholds," it is entitled to assistance from the government in the form of food stamps, subsidized housing, Medicaid, and other benefits. Another 50 million Americans are defined as **near poor,** meaning their incomes are too high to qualify them for government assistance but not high enough to cover basic expenses for food, clothing, and shelter. In many ways, the near poor are the hardest hit by most structural problems, since they do not have the safety net of government assistance but do not make enough to live comfortably.[2] While the poor and near poor are different in terms of the help they receive, both are confronted with the effects of social structural problems. To keep things simple, when we refer to the poor and the problems they experience, we will include the near poor group as well.

near poor
Those who have incomes too high to qualify for government assistance but not high enough to cover basic expenses for food, clothing, and shelter.

Many people, including some scholars, think that people are poor because they are lazy or lack a strong work ethic.[3] However, while this may be true for some individuals, many impoverished families and individuals work one and sometimes two full-time jobs. For instance, statistics show that approximately 76 percent of the poor are full-time employees[4] and that 25 percent of U.S. workers earn less than $16,000 per year (or about $7.69 per hour).[5] Most of the working poor are employed in minimum-wage jobs, with no health or retirement benefits. Such jobs make it virtually impossible for people to earn an adequate living.[6]

Consider this example (see Table 4-1): suppose you and your spouse are both working full-time in minimum-wage jobs. At the current level, $7.25 per hour, that is $580 per forty-hour workweek, or $30,160 per year. Assume that you have two children who require day care while you and your spouse work. Estimates vary, but let's assume you find day care for $150 per week per child, which is about average in many parts of the country. That is $15,600 per year. Then there is housing to consider. According to national statistics, housing should cost no more than 30 percent of a family's income, which would be $9,048. Food costs are estimated to be approximately 20 percent of a family's income: that amounts to $6,032. These expenses total $30,680. Compared with your income, that leaves a deficit of $520 and does not include the cost of utilities, transportation, clothing, and other expenses, such as birthday or holiday presents or a vacation. Most important, it assumes that both spouses work all year without any illnesses or injuries that require medical attention or result in loss of wages. If these individuals are working full-time jobs, can a family of four really make it on minimum wage?[7]

What factors might contribute to the poverty issues so many individuals face?

Chances for obtaining better jobs are also slim for people who live in poverty since they tend to lack **social capital,** the networks that provide opportunities for well-paying

social capital
The development of networks that provide opportunities for well-paying jobs and a chance to succeed.

TABLE 4-1 Minimum Wages and Expenses

	Yearly Income	Yearly Expenses (Basic)
You:	$15,080	$15,600 day care for two children
Your spouse:	$15,080	$9,048 rent
		$6,032 food
Total income:	$30,160	Primary expenses: $30,680
	Deficit: **$520***	
Given the high cost of living, can anyone really be expected to make it on the minimum wage?		

*Does not include utilities, clothing, transportation, medical care, vacation, gifts, or loss of work due to illnesses.

jobs and a chance to succeed, networks that can get you a job because you have a friend or relative who plays golf with someone whose company has an opening.[8] People who grow up with solid social networks, such as those in the middle class or the wealthy, have many more opportunities or **life chances.** It is simply more difficult for the poor to achieve success in the form of well-paying jobs because they typically do not know anyone who can provide them with an opportunity to get one.

life chances
Extensive opportunities for individuals who grow up with solid social networks, usually those in the middle class or the wealthy.

DEINDUSTRIALIZATION AND THE ECONOMY

A central concern in the life of the poor is employment. At one time, individuals who graduated high school could find well-paying jobs that afforded them a respectable standard of living. U.S.-made products were far superior to those produced in other countries, and U.S. industrial workers were well paid. However, that is not the case today, as technological advances have helped countries like Japan to emerge as international powers in the consumer market (think of companies like Toyota and Sony). As a result, the U.S. economy has suffered from **deindustrialization,** meaning that U.S. companies have either gotten out of a certain market entirely or outsourced the manufacturing of those products to lower-wage countries.[9] That means fewer jobs, more competition for the ones that remain, and the emergence of new industries, primarily in technology, that require specialized training. Consequently, many nonskilled and semi-skilled workers with a high school education or less have found themselves without jobs or opportunities that would have been available to them a generation earlier. Recall the case study that opened this chapter: James's mother holds a low-wage job at Wal-Mart, not a high-wage manufacturing job, and prospects for James may not be much better.

deindustrialization
The process through which companies either get out of a certain market entirely or outsource their operations to lower-wage countries resulting in fewer jobs, more competition for the remaining ones, and the emergence of new industries, primarily in technology, which require specialized training.

Currently, the jobs in the lowest-paying sectors of the market, such as James's mother's job, come with low wages, no benefits, and little in the way of job security.[10] Also, as well-paying jobs have become harder to find, people are taking jobs for which they are overqualified. This has a ripple effect throughout the labor market, and those at the bottom either remain stuck in low-wage jobs or are squeezed out entirely.[11]

THE HOUSING CRUNCH

Along with the problems in the economy related to wages and unemployment comes an increased cost of housing. Approximately 60 percent of people living in low-income areas spend 50 percent or more of their income on housing.[12] (Most banks and financial experts estimate that a person or family should spend only about 30 percent of income on housing.) Not only is the cost of housing skyrocketing, but the practical realities of obtaining affordable housing, such as having enough money for security deposits, prevent many people from moving or improving their situations.

Home ownership has become increasingly difficult for the poor, forcing many to become long-term renters instead of buyers. Upfront costs, such as down payments, closing costs, and repairs, have made it unrealistic for many low-wage workers to afford home ownership. Renting has traditionally been considered the less expensive option; however, the housing crunch has also made renting more expensive. In fact, according to the National Housing Trust Fund, the costs of renting have been steadily increasing since 2003, and in 2007, the increases in rents exceeded the rate of inflation.[13] According to data from the Michigan Consumer Report, the median (meaning half the rents were above and half were below) monthly rent for an apartment in 2008 in the United States was $815.[14]

gentrification
An influx to inner-city neighborhoods of affluent people who want to enjoy the advantages of living near a downtown metropolitan area, where they are likely to work, creating an environment with a strong sense of responsibility and purpose that comes with home ownership, but also causing property values and real estate tax rates to increase.

Added to this already complex problem is the phenomenon of **gentrification,** a long-standing trend involving the restoration of inner-city neighborhoods by affluent people who improve home and property values and who enjoy the advantages of living near a downtown metropolitan area, where they are likely to work.[15] Gentrification creates an environment with the strong sense of responsibility and purpose that comes from home ownership. However, it also causes property values and real estate taxes to increase. Landlords pass those tax increases in the form of higher rents on to tenants, who may find that they can no longer afford to live in their neighborhood. As a result, poorer residents move out, and remaining low-income urban areas become overcrowded. Gentrification therefore accelerates the decline of low-income neighborhoods, resulting in increased crime and gang activity. Thus, while gentrification and revitalization benefit some groups and communities, they have a corresponding negative impact on others.[16]

PUBLIC EDUCATION

Many people in our society think of education as the path out of poverty and assume that educational achievement results in credentials and skills that will open the door to better job opportunities. However, educational opportunities are not equally distributed. In fact, some argue that instead of being the path out of poverty, education may serve to reinforce one's social class; because of unequal educational opportunity, poor people's children tend to stay poor while rich people's children tend to stay rich.[17]

In what ways might a factor like gentrification contribute to the issues faced by inner-city public schools?

These conclusions may seem contradictory at first glance, and to be fair, education does provide a path out of poverty for some individuals. In general, however, the opportunities provided in many inner-city schools do not give students the tools, knowledge, and skills they need to succeed to attend good colleges or to obtain well-paying jobs. For example, many inner-city public schools lack advanced preparation (AP) classes, up-to-date equipment, new technology, a sufficient number of textbooks, well-trained teachers, and funding for innovative programs. In addition, the nature of the inner-city school environment limits the learning that can take place there. Factors such as higher rates of gang activity, crime, and drug dealing than are found in affluent schools are at work here. Teachers in inner-city public schools may spend more time maintaining order than actually providing instruction.[18] The relationship between education and delinquency will be further discussed in another chapter, but for now, note that education tends to reinforce an inner-city child's socioeconomic position.

JAMES'S CASE

Structural Influences

Recall James's case:

- is a fourteen-year-old boy who lives in a low-income housing project with his mother and siblings
- has a mother who works full-time for a low wage and often takes extra shifts to supplement her low income
- is a good student when he attends, but frequently skips school to care for his younger brothers and sister
- has been caught shoplifting food for his family

James's mother works as many hours as she can at Wal-Mart. Some might argue that a mother with young children should work fewer hours so as to be able to care for them, or that she should put her younger children in day care so James can attend school regularly. Others might argue that she should move her family to another school district so James does not skip school to care for his siblings or to avoid gang members. Still others might contend that James's shoplifting is a form of "acting out" in response to his family situation.

Given what you have learned so far, how would you respond to these explanations and arguments? How might structural factors be affecting James and his family?

THINK
ABOUT
IT

Far too often, experts on delinquency try to explain why someone commits a delinquent act without really considering the larger factors that might contribute to the behavior. All the structural problems we have discussed create a context for delinquency and will help explain why people in certain circumstances turn to crime and delinquent behaviors.

Industrial Revolution
A transition, beginning in the late eighteenth century in Great Britain and afterwards spreading throughout the world, from a simple, pre-industrial society to a complex, modern, multicultural one.

Consider what you already know about occupational conditions in postindustrial America. How might these factors have contributed to the study of criminal justice?

The Origins of Social Structural Theories of Delinquency

Modern social structural theory developed in the late nineteenth century in response to the social problems that arose out of the Industrial Revolution. Beginning in the late eighteenth century in Great Britain, and afterwards spreading throughout the world, the **Industrial Revolution** represented a dramatic transition from a simple, preindustrial society to a complex, modern, multicultural one. The structure of society changed as people migrated from small towns and villages—where most individuals had similar backgrounds and performed similar kinds of agricultural labor—to large urban environments, where there was great diversity.[19]

This dramatic transformation occurred slowly in some places and almost overnight in others. It resulted in a host of pathologies that observers struggled to understand: poverty, crime, and disease, to name just a few. Most of what we now call *classical social theory,* such as the work of Karl Marx, Max Weber, and Emile Durkheim, began as an attempt to solve these problems.[20] In many ways, early theorists were a lot like criminal justice researchers today: they focused on the particular problems of society and attempted to develop solutions to them. One can discover the solutions only after arriving at a firm understanding of the problems.[21]

EMILE DURKHEIM

For someone like Emile Durkheim (1858–1917), one of the greatest thinkers of modern times, crime, suicide, and other forms of deviant behavior were a result of a breakdown of the moral fabric of society. More specifically, these problems could be linked to the level of connectedness people felt to the larger society.

Durkheim characterized the transition from agrarian to industrialized society as a shift in the type of social solidarity people felt for one another. **Social solidarity** is the connectedness people have to the larger group. Prior to the Industrial Revolution, societies were characterized by **mechanical solidarity,** based on the fact that most people performed the same tasks (farming), lived in sparsely populated rural areas, and tended to know their neighbors. People had a strong sense of **homogeneity,** or shared similar views of the world and their place in it.[22] In this type of community, people had the same ideas about how they wanted to live their lives, so they had a strong sense of morality and connectedness.

In contrast, in modern urban societies, people are dependent on each other not because of similar backgrounds or personal relationships, but because of the division of labor in society. In the modern world, people tend to perform specialized tasks. This specialization creates a dependency based on need rather than emotion or morality. In the modern city, I cannot grow my own food, so I have to rely on a grocery store for food; I do not own my home, so I have to rely on a landlord to provide housing. Societies like this are

social solidarity
The connectedness people feel for the larger group.

mechanical solidarity
A situation in which most people performed the same tasks such as farming, lived in sparsely populated areas, and tended to know their neighbors.

homogeneity
Shared or similar views of the world, as well as what is acceptable and unacceptable behavior.

characterized by **organic solidarity,** a type of cohesion based on interdependence and need.

Because people come from many different parts of the world to live close to where they work, modern cities contain great **heterogeneity,** or diversity. With diversity come different attitudes, values, and beliefs about how things should be accomplished, as well as what is acceptable and unacceptable behavior.[23]

In describing the morality of society, Durkheim used the term **collective conscience** to refer to the way the group or society responds to moral or ethical situations. When the collective conscience is strong, the group's sense of morality is clear, and everyone agrees about what is acceptable and what is not. This is more likely to be the case in societies with mechanical solidarity than in large, diverse, industrial or postindustrial societies. The collective conscience is weak in heterogeneous societies because everyone has different ideas about how things should be done, as well as different lifestyles.[24] Think about the diversity of lifestyles you see on your campus, in your neighborhood, or even on your block if you live in a large city. Today we live in a diverse society with a weak collective conscience.

CONTEMPORARY APPLICATIONS

Today, Durkheim's theory remains an important way of understanding social life, and it has links to the study of crime and delinquency. Think, for example, of the differences between living in a big city and in a small town. One of the things people often say they enjoy about living in a small town is that they know many of the residents, have personal relationships with them, and understand their place in the community. They may also say they like the fact that people share values. Like the theme song from the old sitcom *Cheers* says, people like to go "where everybody knows your name." Many experts argue that we all need to feel connected in some way to something larger than ourselves.[25]

In contrast, in a big city, there are many people from different backgrounds and cultures, and with different perspectives and worldviews. Living in a big city can be exciting and can broaden one's horizons, but these urban areas also have many problems such as crime, pollution, and poverty, to name just a few. A large number of people occupying a concentrated area also can increase demand and competition for existing resources, making such problems more likely to occur.

Durkheim's theory helps us understand the well-known rural versus urban distinctions relating to crime rates;[26] but it also helps us to understand things like neighborhood instability, citizens' fears of victimization, the popularity of community crime prevention programs, and even community policing. The most important component of Durkheim's model is the notion of trust. Without trust, people are fearful of others, and there is little **informal social control,** the process by which community residents solve their own problems without the use of the formal agents of control, such as the police. If you grew up in a neighborhood where the families all knew each other, and someone was likely to tell your parents if they saw you do something wrong, you have experienced strong informal social control. The more formal the social control, the less likely the neighborhood is to feel like a place where residents want to remain.[27]

There is an inverse relationship between informal and formal social control: the more informal social control in a community, the less likely formal means are needed. Conversely, when little informal social control is generated, there is a greater need for law enforcement and other formal mechanisms to solve problems.[28] This is one of the reasons the police maintain high levels of visibility in disorganized neighborhoods—the community cannot solve its own problems. In such neighborhoods, residents never develop a sense of community, which in turn means that informal social control does not develop. If they can, people tend to leave these areas since they do not feel safe.[29]

Durkheim's model helps us to understand how low levels of integration in a given community can result in high crime rates and high rates of delinquency. It also helps us understand that certain **delinquency prevention** programs, those that rely heavily on sources of strength within a community, tend to be successful. The program described in the box on page 88 is one example.

organic solidarity
A type of cohesion based on interdependence and need.

heterogeneity
Diversity of attitudes, values, and beliefs about how things should be accomplished, as well as what is acceptable and unacceptable behavior.

collective conscience
The way a group or society responds to moral or ethical situations; when the group's sense of morality is clear, everyone agrees on what is and is not acceptable.

informal social control
The process by which community residents solve their own problems without the use of formal agents of control, such as the police.

delinquency prevention
Various programs to either discourage youths from engaging in delinquency or keep delinquency from occurring in the future.

THEORY AND PRACTICE WORKING TOGETHER

Weed and Seed Programs

Many of Durkheim's ideas about the value of social cohesion and solidarity are reflected in programs like Weed and Seed, which is managed by a division of the U.S. Department of Justice. The Weed and Seed strategy includes six basic components: law enforcement, community policing, crime prevention, offender intervention, drug treatment, and neighborhood restoration.

The Weed and Seed program is a two-pronged approach that begins with law enforcement weeding out the criminal element through aggressive patrol tactics, repeat offender projects that target chronic offenders, and police crackdowns. Once the offenders are removed from the area and the crime problem begins to lessen, the seeding portion of the program begins. This includes drug rehabilitation and treatment, crime prevention, neighborhood restoration in the form of physical improvements to the community, and economic redevelopment through the enticement of businesses to invest in the neighborhood.

Much of the theory behind Weed and Seed is rooted in the idea that if residents begin to see that an area is salvageable and that others are interested in improving local conditions, they too will become involved. Once that happens, the stakeholders in communities (usually home owners) will begin to organize and rally around common community concerns and issues. Weed and Seed fosters a sense of trust and understanding between residents and police, as well as a spirit of cooperation that contributes to

an atmosphere of optimism. When that happens, residents feel as though their efforts matter, and they remain committed to the program. This ultimately leads to greater success in solving crime and other neighborhood problems.

Evaluations of Weed and Seed demonstrate that programs are most successful when they target smaller criminal populations and work closely with community groups to solve local problems. For example, in Clearwater, Florida, the North Greenwood community was experiencing a host of problems ranging from prostitution and drug dealing to vandalism and homelessness. With the police department and community groups working together, guided by the Weed and Seed initiative, Clearwater experienced dramatic decreases in crime as a result of aggressive police efforts. In addition, community groups established drug treatment and GED and job training programs, and even created a homeless transitional shelter for runaway youths. While not a panacea or cure-all, Weed and Seed programs across the country demonstrate the impact a community can have when residents develop reasonable goals and work together to solve problems.[30]

 THINK ABOUT IT People tend to get involved in solving community problems when they think there is a chance that a particular effort will be successful—and when they start to see results. How can community programs generate this type of enthusiasm and support?

---

broken windows theory
A theory that explores how small problems and signs of disorder or social control, such as graffiti, trash, and broken windows, can become bigger ones if left unaddressed.

Durkheim's ideas are also reflected in the **broken windows theory** of crime. While we will discuss this theory in more detail in another chapter, for now recognize that the broken windows theory is based on the idea that signs of disorder in the community generally create a climate of fear for citizens, who then avoid using those public spaces. When that happens, crime actually increases since there is an absence of informal social control. The key to reducing crime and fear, then, involves reducing the signs of disorder: graffiti, trash, broken windows in abandoned buildings, and so on. By taking care of the small problems, a community can avoid bigger ones later on. Put another way, if people feel an area is worth saving and take steps to solve smaller problems or issues that affect their quality of life, and do so before those problems grow, citizen fear levels are reduced and crime decreases as well.[31]

 THINK ABOUT IT

Social Structural Theories

Consider the origins of social structural theories like Emile Durkheim's model of social control. What are some of the contemporary applications of Durkheim's theories? How would you compare Durkheim's model to the broken windows theory, for instance?

Social Disorganization Theory

Durkheim developed his social control theory in France in the late 1800s. A short time later, in the early twentieth century in the United States, sociologists were trying to piece together an explanation for the problems they were seeing in their cities. From their studies emerged the **social disorganization** perspective, which concentrates on the community's lack of structure and ability to control its residents' behaviors. Social disorganization theorists believe that if a community fails to realize its common values, social disorganization is likely to result.

At the turn of the twentieth century, the city of Chicago was struggling with overcrowding, a shortage of affordable housing, and high rates of poverty, suicide, crime and delinquency, and mental illness. Researchers, policymakers, and other experts searched for solutions to these problems, as well as an explanation for their development.[32] Sociologists and activists at the University of Chicago, who created a school of thought that came to be known as the Chicago School, developed a theory of social disorganization to explain these problems. According to this theory, a host of structural problems, such as migration, housing discrimination, economic change, and segregation, combined with other problems, such as family disruption, residential turnover, and concentrated pockets of poverty, caused certain areas within the city to become "disorganized."[33]

Researchers such as Ernest Burgess, Robert Park, Thomas Znaniecki, and W. I. Thomas, among others, were fascinated to notice that disorganization did not occur uniformly throughout the city. When they mapped out areas where the problems seemed to be the worst, they found that crime, poverty, mental illness, suicide, and other social maladies were all highly concentrated in particular areas (see Figure 4-1).[34]

CONCENTRIC ZONES

As Figure 4-1 shows, the researchers discovered that the city could be mapped as a series of concentric zones. Moving outward from the center of the city, these ranged from the central business district at the core to wealthy suburbs in outlying areas. Each zone had its own unique population and organizational style. In other words, people living in each zone had attitudes, values, and beliefs that were similar to those of other residents of that zone, but different from those of residents of other zones. Even though still connected to the larger city, each zone was a kind of integrated community, which Durkheim referred to in his discussion of mechanical solidarity.[35] Each zone was also dependent on the others in an interrelated whole, what Durkheim referred to as organic solidarity: the kind of cohesion that comes as a result of an interdependency of need.[36]

When the map was completed, the researchers found that most urban problems were concentrated in an area they called the **Transitional Zone,** an area of rapid social change and heterogeneity. This area was close to the central business district, which contained

social disorganization
A community's lack of structure and ability to control its residents' behaviors.

Transitional Zone
A concentrated urban area, usually near the central business district, with affordable housing and job opportunities, but undergoing rapid social change and achieving heterogeneity.

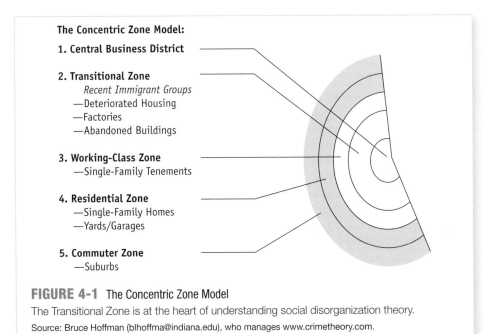

The Concentric Zone Model:
1. **Central Business District**

2. **Transitional Zone**
   Recent Immigrant Groups
   —Deteriorated Housing
   —Factories
   —Abandoned Buildings

3. **Working-Class Zone**
   —Single-Family Tenements

4. **Residential Zone**
   —Single-Family Homes
   —Yards/Garages

5. **Commuter Zone**
   —Suburbs

FIGURE 4-1 The Concentric Zone Model
The Transitional Zone is at the heart of understanding social disorganization theory.
Source: Bruce Hoffman (blhoffma@indiana.edu), who manages www.crimetheory.com.

Recall the characteristics that describe a Transitional Zone. Can you identify the Transitional Zone of the city nearest you? Which zone best describes where you live?

many of the jobs in the city. As a result, this was also where much of the affordable housing was located. People looking for work tended to live in this area. In particular, new immigrants, who typically came to the city to find work, lived here. Because of the rapid social changes, poor housing conditions, and high rates of diversity, the Transitional Zone had the highest rate of social disorganization. Related to this were high rates of delinquency, truancy, adult crime, mental illness, prostitution, gambling, suicide, poverty, and infant mortality.[37]

Initially, at least, researchers thought that there was a cultural explanation for social disorganization. They believed that as various immigrant groups came to live in the Transitional Zone, they brought with them sets of attitudes, values, and beliefs that supported involvement in crime and deviant behavior. However, over time, as members of one group after another—Irish, Germans, Jews, Italians, southern blacks—improved their standard of living and moved to the Working-Class Zone, they left behind the attitudes and behaviors of the Transitional Zone. Moreover, regardless of which group moved into the Transitional Zone, the problems remained.[38]

Thus, the explanation for the problems in the Transitional Zone could not be found in the cultural attitudes and values of a particular group. Rather, it must have had something to do with the structural characteristics of that zone. Clifford Shaw and Henry McKay provided perhaps the most famous explanation of the relationship between social disorganization and delinquency: the breakdown of traditional control mechanisms, such as the family.

DISORGANIZATION AND DELINQUENCY

In 1929, Clifford Shaw and Henry McKay noted that there were significant variations in rates of truancy, delinquency, and adult crime in the different zones of Chicago. The rates of all these social problems were highest in the Transitional Zone and lowest in the Commuter Zone, with each zone having progressively lower rates as it radiated out from the Transitional Zone. These rates remained high over time and did not change depending on the characteristics of the population.[39]

Breakdown in Control

To explain their findings, Shaw and McKay suggested that, as a result of living in disorganized zones, many youths turned to delinquency and adopted the attitudes, values, and beliefs of a delinquent lifestyle instead of embracing traditional ones. These attitudes, like all components of culture, were passed on from one generation to the next.

In 1942, Shaw and McKay published *Juvenile Delinquency and Urban Areas,* a classic work on the theory of social disorganization and delinquency. This report was based on an analysis of 55,998 juvenile court case records compiled in Chicago over approximately thirty years. In subsequent years, Shaw and McKay extended their analysis of the ecological distribution of delinquency to cities in other parts of the nation. Their findings support the central tenets of disorganization theory.[40]

Reasons for Delinquency

Shaw and McKay argued that youths living in the Transitional Zone might become delinquent for a variety of reasons. First, they were at an age when issues of identity and conformity came into question, but they were also in a place that was so socially disorganized that inappropriate behavior was considered acceptable: it is very hard to stay out of trouble when everyone you know belongs to a gang. Thus, children living in disorganized communities were exposed to contradictory standards that required them to choose a pattern of behavior that could lead them to chronic offending.

In later works, Shaw and McKay concluded that the social life of the local community was less significant in explaining delinquency than the economic and occupational structure of the larger society. Members of lower-class groups remained in

THEORY AND PRACTICE WORKING TOGETHER

The Chicago Area Project

The Chicago Area Project (CAP) was created in the 1930s by Clifford Shaw to address the problems of delinquency in poor areas of Chicago. The mission of CAP is to reduce and ultimately eliminate delinquency by improving the quality of neighborhoods and solving economic and social problems that young people and their families face. This is accomplished by offering programs that foster community empowerment alongside collaborative efforts by community agencies.

CAP uses a three-pronged attack on delinquency: direct service, advocacy, and community involvement. It empowers neighborhood residents to work together to improve neighborhood conditions and to ensure the overall well-being of their children. CAP also focuses on using existing neighborhood institutions, such as churches and clubs, rather than creating new agencies or institutions. This approach fosters a sense of ownership of the problems within the community since established resources are used. In addition, whereas most social service agencies provide assistance on a case-by-case basis, CAP takes a more holistic approach and focuses on the neighborhood as a whole. By making the entire neighborhood conscious of the problems of delinquency and the welfare of its children, and by enhancing the physical environment, everyone becomes a stakeholder in seeing the area improve. Finally, unlike most programs, which are operated by professionals, CAP empowers residents of the neighborhood to plan and operate the programs.

One example of the many CAP programs is the Juvenile Justice Diversion Project. CAP has worked with the Cook County Juvenile Court to divert youths who have committed delinquent acts into programs that will prevent them from becoming hard-core offenders. The program targets delinquents who are first-time offenders, repeat petty offenders, and marginal gang members. Youths become involved in community service projects that develop and strengthen their ties to the larger community and connect them with positive adult mentors, who can show them appropriate behaviors and a different way of life. Evaluations of the program indicate that many youths have been diverted from more serious offenses.

 THINK ABOUT IT Why should the juvenile justice system be concerned with generating a sense of community among residents? What value do such efforts have?

---

levels of independence and will say things like "I make my own decisions" or "No one is going to tell me what to do." Miller says this attitude is in contrast to actual behavior, whereby many youths seek out jobs that are highly structured and restrictive. The explanation for this relates to how the circumstances are perceived. For many youths, structure and inflexibility are taken to mean the youth is cared about.

- **Excitement** focuses on the search for thrills, dangers, and risks. Miller argues that lower-class life is boring and uneventful, and that many youths seek excitement through excessive drinking, fighting, gambling, and sexual activity. Having something exciting to share with friends is status enhancing and builds one's reputation.

- **Fate** consists of the belief that life is unpredictable and that certain events are beyond the control of individuals. Being considered lucky or unlucky serves as an explanation for what happens to these youths. It also helps to alleviate any sense of responsibility for their actions.

- **Smartness** refers to being "street smart" or having the ability to take advantage of others. It also refers to the ability to avoid being victimized.

- **Toughness** relates to the ability to demonstrate one's manhood. It can consist of physical prowess in the form of strength and endurance, but it can also involve mental and emotional toughness. Examples might include the willingness to withstand a beating or to not inform on a friend or fellow gang member.

- **Trouble** is one of the most important focal concerns since it relates to all the others. Getting into and out of trouble is an important mechanism by which youths gain status. Some experts even argue that this is a preoccupation among people in the lower class.[52]

Miller asserts that the more lower-class youths identify with these values, the more likely they are to commit crime. The reason, of course, is that they are living up to the expectations of their community.[53]

The primary strength of the disorganization perspective is that it rejects many of the individualistic theories of crime and delinquency. In other words, it asks us to imagine that criminals and delinquents are people just like us. What separates us from criminals or delinquents is that the latter are exposed to the disruptive forces of rapid social change.[54] If we were suddenly confronted with the same obstacles, disorganization theorists argue, we would likely find ourselves committing similar types of acts. Disorganization theory, then, focuses on environmental factors such as the physical and social structure of a neighborhood, as well as the attitudes, values, beliefs, and norms of the people living in those areas. However, the theory is not without its critics.

For instance, some opponents argue that the meaning of "disorganization" is not clear. Part of the reason for this confusion stems from the lifestyles and experiences of disorganization theorists, who tend to be disproportionately male, middle class, and white. Often, because they are insulated to some degree by their own social class experiences, disorganization theorists can fail to appreciate the ways that people from other social class, cultural, or ethnic backgrounds organize their worlds. In other words, what may look like disorganization to these theorists may simply be a different type of social organization.[55]

THINK ABOUT IT

Social Disorganization Theory

Do you think there is a relationship between fear levels and delinquency within a community? Why or why not?

Strain and Anomie Theories

The term **anomie** literally means normlessness, and Emile Durkheim used it in the nineteenth century to describe a situation in which a norm that regulates behavior no longer applies or does not exist.[56] The consequences of anomie can include fear, frustration, and anxiety. Typically, anomie occurs when there is a breakdown in the social mechanisms that normally control or regulate people's behavior. You might be thinking that this sounds similar to disorganization theory. In fact, anomie and disorganization are both seen as consequences of social change, and both are also characterized by a lack of significance of the rules of society.[57]

There are several important differences between social disorganization and anomie, however. Social disorganization is often presented as a problem affecting particular parts or zones of a society that are exposed to rapid social changes. But once these changes subside, the part or zone returns to a somewhat organized state. Anomie, on the other hand, is a problem that affects an entire society during a particular era, such as transition from the traditional to the modern world. Durkheim suggested that anomie caused problems on such a broad scale that the only way to solve them was a massive, society-wide reorganization.[58]

ROBERT MERTON'S STRAIN THEORY

While Durkheim's theory grew out of the crisis of early-twentieth-century European society, Robert Merton extended the anomie perspective into a formal theory of deviance in the mid-twentieth century in the United States. For Merton, a social crisis arose out of the disparity between the promise of the American Dream and the reality of actual possibilities for people. According to Merton, not everyone has an equal chance of achieving the American Dream because the legitimate means of doing so are unequally distributed in society. This produces a **strain,** or sense of anxiety, in people who want to achieve the goals but do not have access to the institutional means to do so. Anomie results because people do not know how to cope with such a dilemma.

Merton's theory examines the relationship between two aspects of social life: cultural goals and socially available means of attaining them. Merton argues that every society establishes markers of success, or cultural goals. In the United States, traditionally, those goals include a house in the suburbs, two late-model cars, and lots of fancy appliances. In addition, society creates acceptable means of achieving those goals, such as hard work and a good education. In the United States, the cultural message is that America is the land of opportunity, and through hard work and sacrifice, anyone can succeed. These cultural values are promoted through every agent of society: schools, family, peers, and the media. Because U.S. culture typically relates people's social identities to material possessions, the more one can acquire, the more status one is accorded.[59] The problem is that not everybody has an equal or fair chance to succeed. For Merton, then, the American Dream is possible for only a small segment of society. Those who lack resources and networks will inevitably be excluded from achieving success. And for some individuals, criminal behavior becomes the path to success. To Merton, crime is a normal by-product of such a system: "A cardinal American virtue, 'ambition,' promotes a cardinal American vice, 'deviant behavior.'"[60] Merton's theory of anomie is illustrated by Shun's comments on his motives for engaging in crime. For him, the American Dream can be achieved only through unconventional means. He says:

> Uh, it's, it's basically, if, if—any—in any city, if you get a group of kids that doing somethin' that—what they do, then it's going to be trouble. We just do that shit. Anything I do, I don't know about anybody else, but anything I do got to be a profit to it. So, that's, that's basically why I do mine, there's a profit to it.

In his description of innovation, Merton recognized that crime and delinquency are but one response or adaptation to the strain such a situation creates. Table 4-2 shows five different ways in which individuals may respond to societal strain, as well as the types of goals and the means of achieving them held by people who use each adaptation. For example, a person who chooses conformity accepts society's goals as legitimate, indicated by a plus sign (+), and uses socially acceptable ways of achieving them, also indicated by a plus sign. In contrast, when a person accepts the goals set out by society, but does not accept or agree with the means of achieving those goals, as indicated by a minus sign (−), the person still believes in the markers of success as defined by society, but uses different means, such as delinquency or crime, to achieve those goals.

- **Conformity:** most people who encounter obstacles to success conform or continue working within the system. The conformist accepts both culturally prescribed goals and the socially legitimate means for reaching those goals (as indicated by two plus signs). He or she accepts the goals and plays by the rules. According to Merton, conformity is the most common adaptation to socially structured goals and means. If this were not so, the stability and continuity of society could not be maintained.

- **Innovation:** while most people conform to social goals and use socially approved means of achieving them, inequality can lead to other responses. Innovators are individuals who accept society's goals (+) but do not accept society's means of

TABLE 4-2 Cultural Goals and Means Adaptations

Adaptation	Goals	Means
Conformity	+	+
Innovation	+	−
Ritualism	−	+
Retreatism	−	−
Rebellionism	+/−	+/−

There are a number of ways to respond to blocked opportunities. Most people continue to follow the rules of society and conform; however, some choose delinquency as their only way to adapt to the strain of not achieving societal success.

achieving them (−). For most innovators, the normal means of achieving success are simply unavailable. In such cases, criminal activities present a way for people to achieve the culturally acceptable goals. Think of drug dealers—some achieve considerable wealth. How do they spend their money? They buy the same kinds of things other wealthy people purchase, the things society recognizes as symbols of success. According to Merton, innovators are the most likely of the five groups to become criminals.

- **Ritualism:** ritualists adapt to strain by giving up a belief in the goals (−) and focusing instead on the rules (+). Examples might include a low-level employee who focuses on the minutiae of the job or a person who focuses on religious rituals or the rules and customs of a fraternity. In these situations, people do their jobs but lose sight of the larger reason for performing those tasks. A ritualist will know exactly what is expected and will adequately perform those duties and responsibilities, but will also be very legalistic. If something falls outside the parameters of the job, the ritualist will not take the initiative and complete the task. Ritualists are often burned-out employees who are interested in just getting by.

- **Retreatism:** as the name implies, some people respond to anomie or strain by accepting neither the goals of society nor the means of obtaining them. Merton includes the mentally ill, artists, homeless people, and drug addicts in this category, and offers drug addicts as perhaps the best example of those who withdraw from society in significant ways. Merton describes them as "included as members of the society, but only in a fictional sense . . . people in the society but not of it."[61]

- **Rebellionism:** people who choose rebellion attempt to replace conventional society's goals and normative activities with new ones. Think of terrorists or revolutionaries.

What types of material possessions or status symbols do you associate with success?

Typically, these rebels do not define their goals in the terms of the present culture. Rather, they want to change what society defines as success and how one acquires it.[62] This is true despite the fact that they may accept or reject goals and means of society selectively—hence the "+/−" in the table for means and goals. Their underlying objective, though, is to replace the system entirely.

According to Merton, each of these adaptations is a normal product of a stratified society. In terms of specific limitations of Merton's theory, it does not tell us why some people choose one mode of adaptation over another. It also does not tell us why some people choose a particular strategy within one type of adaptation. Why, for example, does one innovator choose auto theft while another chooses drug dealing? While no theory is perfect and each has its own limitations, these questions remain unanswered by Merton.

A variation on Merton's ideas is found in the book *Crime and the American Dream,* by Steven Messner and Richard Rosenfeld. The authors argue that the problem of crime is essentially a function of a conflicting set of values within U.S. culture. For example, a defining feature of U.S. culture is individualism. However, while there are many advantages to allowing people the right to pursue life, liberty, and happiness, individualism can present a challenge to the need for conformity and obedience to the larger society—an unwillingness to follow laws and rules because they are not in one's best interests—and so can result in crime.

Another defining feature of American society is its emphasis on materialism and the acquisition of "things," such as large homes, fancy cars, designer clothing, and the latest electronic gadgets, all of which are considered measures of success. The emphasis on the "stuff" of our culture, rather than on how to obtain it, can easily lead to crime.

In addition, Messner and Rosenfeld argue the preoccupation with money and material goods tends to make it more difficult to place a value on behaviors that do not have a clear economic value, such as parenting or teaching as an occupation. While both of these jobs are essential to society, Messner and Rosenfeld argue that their importance is devalued in many ways.[63]

ROBERT AGNEW'S GENERAL STRAIN THEORY

Merton's theory helps us to understand crime across society, but it does not explain why an individual might feel pressure to commit criminal acts. Robert Agnew revised strain theory to suggest that crime and delinquency are adaptations to stress. In his **general strain theory,** Agnew proposes three different sources of strain:

- **Strain caused by the disjunction between just or fair outcomes and actual ones.** When a hard-working individual observes that others receive more than they seem to merit, whether it is based on social networks, family relationships, or some other source, that person begins to experience feelings of stress and strain over the inequality.

- **Strain caused by the removal of positively valued stimuli from the individual.** This kind of strain results from personal losses: loss of a job, suspension from school when the youth really wants to go, the death of a loved one, or divorce. Some individuals attempt to compensate for the loss and to cope with the stress through crime or delinquency.

- **Strain caused by the presentation of negative stimuli.** Negative stimuli can include nearly anything an individual finds offensive: physical abuse, personal victimization, corporal punishment, or poor relationships with parents, peers, teachers, or coworkers. They may also include environmental conditions such as pollution, noise, overcrowding, or inadequate housing. Stressors are created when the individual is subjected to the adverse effects of these stimuli. For instance, the rates of crime and delinquency increase during summer months, in part because youths are out of school, but also because of the weather—high heat and humidity create stress, and people often react violently.[64]

Agnew argues that each type of stress increases the chances that negative emotions, such as depression, fear, and anger, will arise. Because emotions often drive behavior, negative emotions like anger increase the possibility that a person will engage in unacceptable actions.

However, crime is not the only option for people who experience stress and strain. Coping strategies enable individuals to deal with these emotions through legitimate means. These include:

- **Minimizing the importance of the event:** a young man who is suspended from school decides that education is not important.

- **Ignoring the negative event:** a young woman pretends that her mother's boyfriend has not molested her.

- **Focusing on the positive aspects of the situation:** a youth whose parents are in jail decides that it is better to learn how to take care of himself at as young an age as possible.

- **Accepting responsibility for the negative outcome:** a teen decides that it is appropriate for him to get a job to pay for the windows he broke at school.[65]

The evidence suggests that the greater the stress and the lower the person's ability to cope with it, the more likely the youth will turn to delinquency. For example, adolescents who have negative emotions, such as feeling stressed or angry, are more likely to engage in criminal behavior.[66] Agnew's theory incorporates and expands on Merton's ideas, and has become the subject of a great deal of empirical testing.

general strain theory
A theory of how crime and delinquency are adaptations to stress coming from different sources of strain, such as the disjunction between just or fair outcomes and actual ones, the removal of positively valued stimuli from the individual, and the presentation of negative stimuli.

JAMES'S CASE

Choice Theory

Recall James's case:

- is a fourteen-year-old boy from a low-income neighborhood
- skips school; has been suspended for truancy
- has been caught shoplifting

Some people might argue that the reason James is getting into trouble is simply that he is making poor choices. The basis of choice theory is that people make rational decisions based on what is good for them. But James's behavior is not benefiting him as much as it is his family: for example, he skips school even though he likes going to class and is a bright student; however, he needs to take care of his younger siblings. Is it possible that James is making poor choices in terms of his behavior but that his choices are influenced by structural factors?

THINK ABOUT IT — What elements of Agnew's version of strain theory might help you to understand the motives behind James's delinquent behavior?

DIFFERENTIAL OPPORTUNITY

differential opportunity
The concept that because legitimate means of success are blocked and illegitimate ones may be as well, the path juveniles choose to follow is dependent on the nature of the community and the opportunities it offers.

Richard Cloward and Lloyd Ohlin attempted to synthesize key elements of Merton's anomie theory with Edwin Sutherland's theory that delinquency is learned behavior in terms of what is called **differential opportunity**.[67] Cloward and Ohlin use as a starting point Merton's idea that crime and delinquency result from blocked opportunities for or access to legitimate avenues of success. Cloward and Ohlin take this idea a step further by arguing that not only are legitimate means of success blocked, but illegitimate ones may be blocked as well. In other words, criminals do not have equal access to illegal means to achieve societal goals. Just as not everyone who wants to be a doctor can go to medical school, not every criminal who wants to head a drug ring will get that chance.[68] Cloward and Ohlin suggest that there are three different types of gangs: the criminal gang, the conflict gang, and the retreatist gang. Which one a juvenile selects depends on the nature of the community and the opportunities it offers.

The criminal gang is organized around criminal activities. It typically develops in stable, lower-class neighborhoods where adult role models can train youths in certain types of lucrative criminal activities. These adult role models also control delinquents' activities, which prevents unnecessary violence that might draw the attention of the police. In such neighborhoods, a working relationship is established between offenders and others who can assist them should they get caught. This support group includes attorneys, bail bondsmen, and others who can minimize the impact of the criminal justice system. Examples of this type of gang would include some Chinese American gangs that have greater levels of organization within the gang, as well as integration with adult criminals.[69]

Conflict gangs are found in disorganized slums, where many people move in and out and where there are few lucrative criminal opportunities or adult role models to serve as mentors. Adult criminals who are present are unsuccessful, and there is no organizational structure to recruit new gang members. There is also no cooperation with lawyers or politicians, since the adult criminals in the area have little to offer them in exchange for their assistance. Thus, in the absence of financial gain and interpersonal connections, criminals vent their frustrations and win reputations for toughness by turning to violence. An example of a conflict gang might be neo-Nazi skinheads, who, while organized to some degree, essentially use violence as a marker of identity.[70]

Finally, there are retreatist gangs. Whereas some criminals are eager to succeed in criminal ventures and others stake their reputations on the use of violence, this group withdraws from society. Because so-called retreatists cannot make it in conventional society and have few opportunities in the illegitimate markets, Cloward and Ohlin refer to them as "double failures."[71] Examples of retreatists might include drug addicts and even the homeless, who are content to remain on the fringes of society.

As an illustration of Cloward and Ohlin's concept of criminal gangs, consider the comment by Shun about role models in the community. In some cases, these are mentors from whom aspiring criminals learn the attitudes, values, and beliefs associated with being a criminal, while in other cases, there are constructive role models who embody conforming behavior:

Based on your reading so far, why might it be important for gangs to be organized in some way?

> Everybody, everybody who is older than you, you want to be like him, so the drug dealers, they get money. So you want to get money. And all that, that's just like people that are younger than me now look up to me, because I was doing the same thing. I was looking up to people.

In some neighborhoods, there are positive role models, who attempt to steer youths in positive directions. These are community elders or young adults who have some level of credibility with the criminal population. While clearly a smaller segment of the population, these role models can sometimes peacefully coexist with their criminal counterparts. Larry says:

For more on role models, watch *Neighborhood Role Models: Larry* at www.mhhe.com/mcnamarajd1e

> Uh, a friend of mine that was cool with my sister, named Tony, he's from my neighborhood. He was positive. He'd never done anything retarded to get locked up. And he was just—I ain't, I ain't goin' to say perfect, 100 percent, but he was doin' what he was supposed to do. When he sees something that's not right, he hit a 180 instead of a 360, 'cause if you hit that 360, you goin' to get in trouble. If you throw a half degree, which is a 180, and go the other way, you positive. You straight. You won't get in trouble.

Like Merton, Cloward and Ohlin believe that delinquency stems from pressures to succeed and the obstacles that members of lower-class neighborhoods face in their attempts to do so. If there were equally legitimate opportunities for these youths, it is likely that delinquency rates would decrease. However, because legal opportunities are limited and even illegal ones are unevenly distributed, the delinquent's chance of success, even as a criminal, is low.

Strain and Anomie Theories

Compare and contrast the explanations for delinquency provided by strain and anomie theories. What types of social services or remedies would a proponent of each type of strain theory advocate?

THINK ABOUT IT

Subcultural Theories of Delinquency

What social structural factors might lead youths to embrace a retreatist lifestyle?

Strain theorists paint a picture of U.S. society in which everyone is bound together in a common commitment to pursuit of the great American Dream. But is our culture really as homogeneous as Merton suggests? While many mainstream values and goals do characterize U.S. culture, our perceptions of the American Dream are influenced by factors such as our ethnic group, our place of residence, our age, and our social class. For example, in a study of homeless women, many of whom were teenagers and young adults, participants were asked to describe their ideal job. At the time of the study, the vast majority of the women were either unemployed or working in minimum-wage jobs.

Most said that their ideal job paid about $8 an hour. When asked to define success—which, to many middle-class people, means a nice home, a good job, and disposable income—most homeless women said one of two things: having a dry and warm place to stay that night, or not living in fear of their husband's abusive behavior.[72] Not everyone has the same idea of what success is or even what the American Dream entails.[73]

Subcultural theories explain delinquency based on people's group memberships, and the attitudes, values, and beliefs of those groups. Membership can be based on geography, gender, race and ethnicity, or some other criteria. Subcultural theories of delinquency are usually age-based and consider the values and attitudes that make delinquency acceptable. **Cultural deviance theory** focuses specifically on groups of criminals and delinquents who assert certain values and pass them down from generation to generation. Albert Cohen's theory and the subculture of violence hypothesis are two important examples of subcultural theories of delinquency.

subcultural theories
Explanations for delinquency that are based on age and that consider the values and attitudes that make delinquency acceptable.

cultural deviance theory
A theory that the values of a group, in this case delinquents or criminals, transmit from one generation to the next.

ALBERT COHEN'S THEORY

Albert Cohen's theory has a fairly straightforward and simple message. In *Delinquency Boys,* Cohen begins by describing what he believes to be the main characteristics of delinquency. The first is *maliciousness,* or behaviors committed out of spite. Youths derive pleasure from harassing other people, whether they are children, adults, teachers, coaches, or anyone else.

Another characteristic of delinquency is *negativism,* the tendency for delinquent boys to think their behavior is right precisely because it is wrong according to the norms or rules of the larger culture. A third characteristic is *non-utilitarianism,* or the lack of useful value. According to Cohen, delinquents' activities do not produce any real social or economic benefits. For instance, Cohen argues that many delinquents steal things they do not plan to use; they steal merely for the thrill of getting away with it. This view that delinquents are simply out for kicks is directly in opposition to Merton, who emphasizes the economic or social gains connected to delinquency.

Yet another central feature of delinquency is the fact that many offenders engage in *short-run hedonism.* In other words, the pleasure they derive from a given act is not sustained. The inability to stay focused on a given criminal act demonstrates delinquents' impatience. Finally, delinquency is characterized by an emphasis on *group autonomy,* meaning that delinquents are close to the other members of the gang but hostile toward outsiders such as parents, teachers, and even other youths.

If Cohen is correct and this is a fair characterization of delinquents, how do they acquire these traits? Middle-class parents, teachers, and social workers apply a set of values or standards that Cohen calls *middle-class measuring rods.* All children, not just middle-class ones, are expected to live up to these expectations. However, not all children find it easy to do so. Lower-class children, for example, either are not taught these standards or receive insufficient exposure to them. Consequently, many lower-class children have great difficulty following or living up to these expectations. The costs of failure to adopt these standards, however, are steep: children who do not measure up in school lose status or prestige. Teachers and fellow students look down on these children. In response, those children may hang out together and collectively decide to reject the standards, a phenomenon Cohen calls *reaction formation.*

However, these youths become trapped, since once they gain status from their delinquent peers, they lose status in the wider society. Perhaps most significantly, once they are identified as delinquent, youths can never turn back. In other words, delinquency may be understood as a process of *status frustration,* or the inability to live up to middle-class standards. These feelings are then expressed in terms of hostility toward middle-class norms and values.[74]

For example, suppose your teachers repeatedly tell you that you are not a good student because you have no work ethic—you do not study or try to improve your grades. Your gym teacher scolds you because you cannot meet minimum fitness requirements, and your neighbors and parents are constantly saying that you are lazy and need to learn responsibility. In response, you decide that you do not want to get a job, do not want to try to improve, and do not accept the idea that working hard is important. You also decide to hang out with others like you. You may start getting into trouble, but at least you feel as though you are accepted and understood.

Let's also suppose that at some point you decide you want to change your ways and look for new outlets and friends. Perhaps you want to rethink your approach to others and to life in general: you want to work, want to get an education, and want to pursue a different lifestyle. Cohen says that this is unlikely to happen because you rejected mainstream society, which does not think you will ever change and continues to view you as a delinquent—hence the term *status frustration*—you are frustrated in your current status. Because of what you perceive to be an unfair judgment, you grow even more hostile toward society.

Cohen's work represents a significant contribution to the delinquency literature and has links to that of many other theorists, including Cloward and Ohlin. The greatest value in Cohen's work lies in its view of delinquency as a consequence of the interaction between youths and others. That is, delinquency gradually becomes a product of the interaction. For example, one of the concerns we have about detaining juvenile delinquents in adult prisons is based on the fear that as youths are exposed to adult offenders, they are likely to learn more about crime and criminality.

As with all theories, questions remain about the assumptions on which subcultural theory is based. For instance, some critics argue that most delinquents go on to become law-abiding citizens, despite the fact that their social class position does not change. Others question whether delinquents really reject mainstream societal values in general. Rather, it could be that they reject societal values only under certain circumstances. Critics also argue that Cohen's characterization of delinquents as non-utilitarian may apply only to certain individuals at certain times. Clearly, there are instances in which delinquents commit crime for profit or some other purpose, such as creating or sustaining one's reputation. Finally, Cohen offers no empirical evidence to support his theory. Still, the questions and criticisms of his theory have resulted in numerous advances in delinquency theory.[75]

SUBCULTURE OF VIOLENCE

Suppose you are walking down the street in a low-income neighborhood in your hometown. You see a teenager on the other side of the street walking in the opposite direction. You hold the youth's gaze a little longer than you might in another setting. Suddenly, that person curses at you, makes a menacing gesture, and begins to cross the street toward you uttering threats of violence. What do you do? You were simply looking at the guy, and all of a sudden he is threatening to injure or even kill you. Does this make any sense? How did the situation deteriorate so quickly?

An explanation for this situation might be found in the idea of a **subculture of violence** offered by Marvin Wolfgang and Franco Ferracuti to explain the unequal distribution of violent behaviors among certain groups. Unlike other subcultural theorists, Wolfgang and Ferracuti begin with the assumption that the use of violence does not result from the rejection of mainstream societal values. In fact, they see it as a reflection of the violence in the larger society. The difference, of course, is in the degree of violence, the speed with which it is used, and its social acceptability by the members of the community.[76]

subculture of violence
The assumption that the use of violence does not result from the rejection of mainstream societal values, but is a reflection of the violence in the larger society.

In this subculture, violence is not a substitute for other values but rather a versatile problem-solving tool. It is also a way of enhancing one's status, since its use is socially acceptable—the more intense the violence inflicted on another, the greater the status accorded the offender. Because the person is not violating any cultural parameters, there is no reason to feel guilt. Violence is simply a prevalent theme that runs throughout all aspects of social life, including the socialization of children, interpersonal relationships, conflict resolution, and business deals.[77]

> Why respect is so important, basically, I mean, you can't have nobody just dogging you ever. It's, it's like I'm on release. Like I—today I go for my release. And so, there will be a chance to go home, but if somebody just disrespected me to the fullest, and I—then nobody can't—can nobody be seen as, uh, they soft, you feel me? They don't like to be seen as soft. So respect is a big thing, just to be respected.
>
> **SHUN**

The subculture of violence hypothesis suggests that the use of violence is a learned response that allows individuals to survive in environments where mainstream mechanisms are not effective. What is interesting about this phenomenon is that even in communities where violence is considered an acceptable problem-solving tool, there are limits on its use. The threat of violence often controls group members' behavior, since everyone knows that the threat is real. It is also the case that in those situations, community sympathy is unlikely. The idea of a subculture of violence is most useful for explaining certain groups and environments in which violence and its use is highly valued. The best examples are prisons, juvenile detention centers, military schools, and gangs.[78]

While the subculture of violence hypothesis was developed in the late 1960s, Elijah Anderson reexamined it in his 1999 book *Code of the Street: Decency, Violence, and the Moral Life of the Inner City.* Anderson describes the unwritten set of rules that regulate social life in the inner-city. That code involves the use of violence in many instances. Giving and receiving respect is an important part of the code. People who are not treated properly by others on the street are required to "stand up for themselves" and to use violence to remedy the situation. In sociological terms, this use of violence is a form of informal social control, a means by which inner-city communities maintain order.[79]

For more on subculture of violence, watch *Subculture of Violence: Anthony J.* at www.mhhe.com/mcnamarajd1e.

Anderson found that families in his study area are required to abide by the code, even if they do not believe in the use of violence. This is a means of self-preservation, since residents of inner-city communities typically do not believe the police will protect them. Consequently, they exert the kind of social control over one another that the police cannot. Thus, even law-abiding families must teach their children how to act appropriately and how to respond should the situation require it. Failure to do so can not only result in a loss of status but also lead to victimization because the person failed to uphold community values.[80]

Anderson's work, as well as that of Wolfgang and Ferracuti, suggests that because disadvantaged youths may have only their personal relationships or street reputation to mark their identity, any threat to it is a serious one. Whereas middle-class youths might define themselves through their families, their resources, or their accomplishments, lower-class youths have only their reputations. This not only explains why relatively minor threats can trigger violent responses but also shows why youths are more concerned with preserving their status than anything else.

Subcultural Theories of Delinquency

How does the subculture of violence theory help us to understand the lack of remorse or guilt that some delinquents exhibit?

THINK ABOUT IT

Social Structural Theories and Public Policy

Social structural theories and social disorganization theories contend that, because of factors such as neighborhood disorganization, a failure to live up to middle-class standards, limited opportunities to achieve success, or membership in a particular subculture, young people may be exposed to a variety of criminal influences and turn to delinquency and crime as a way of reaching their goals.

In general, delinquency is symptomatic of a set of larger problems. That is, as long as poverty, inadequate education, substandard housing, and other problems are present, they will continue to have an adverse effect on children. Some of these youths, in response to these conditions, will turn to crime. In one sense, the challenge for society is not to solve its delinquency problem as much as it is to solve the problems that cause delinquency in the first place.

Social structural theories have greatly enhanced our understanding of problems like delinquency and crime, largely by demonstrating that certain behaviors do not happen by accident or are not simply the result of poor decision making. Granted, the decision to commit a delinquent act is a choice, but social structural explanations offer us insight into why that particular choice was made. To that end, strategies and policies designed to eliminate or reduce delinquency must also take into account the surrounding influences. If, for example, delinquency is, in part, a result of poverty, then policies that attempt to reduce poverty will likely have an effect on delinquency as well.

Similarly, if delinquency is a function of neighborhood conditions, whereby some areas contain many abandoned buildings, are littered with trash and graffiti, and boast few home owners, policies addressing those issues will likely improve the social and physical landscape as well. Weed and Seed is perhaps the best example of such a focus in policy. Another example of how residents are putting theory into practice to improve their neighborhoods is the Safe Streets program, outlined in the box on page 104.

One of the challenges relating to public policy is the creation of programs that are effective in achieving their goals. Too often, programs are created with a noble intent, but fail to deliver on their stated objectives. Added to this problem are the poorly designed evaluations of such programs. It was not that long ago that evaluations of programs consisted mainly of internal assessments. In this form of evaluation, the person who was responsible for operating the program—and who had a vested interest in seeing the program succeed—often conducted the evaluation. It is very difficult for people to be objective in such circumstances since they are so heavily invested in the outcome. Programs that are created based on policy need to contain an objective and impartial evaluation. In fact, some organizations have been created specifically to address this problem and to guide politicians in effective decision making with regard to policy.

That said, many programs have been shown to have a lasting effect in reducing the problem behavior. One program, which relates specifically to James's family situation, is the Minnesota Family Investment Program (MFIP). This welfare reform program helps low-income families with children achieve self-sufficiency by getting a job. This program

THEORY AND PRACTICE WORKING TOGETHER

Safe Streets Program

The Safe Streets program was created in 1989 in Tacoma, Washington, in response to rising crime rates and concerns about community safety. Nearly 2,500 residents attended a meeting with local police because they wanted to make their neighborhood safe again. Originally a cooperative agreement between the city and county government, the school district, and the local United Way, the Safe Streets campaign has become a nonprofit organization that attempts to empower individuals, families, youths, neighborhoods, and organizations to promote safety within the community. This is accomplished through numerous programs designed to give youths choices in terms of their behavior, such as the Our Youth Leading Change program, which provides individual role models and mentors to teach youths leadership skills. The program also provides "block" mentors, who involve youths in community projects. All of these efforts are designed to foster leadership and to create future stakeholders in the community, while reducing the chances that youths will become involved in drugs, crime, and gangs.

Other programs focus on specific problems and tap into the resources of local residents, businesses, and community organizations. One example is a methamphetamine education program called "Meth Watch," which educates residents on the connection of drugs to gang violence, truancy, and other types of crime. Safe Streets believes that only through education and awareness can community residents have a positive impact on their neighborhoods.

Residents also take issue with the signs of disorder that threaten the community. More than 5,000 Block Watch groups, representing nearly a half million people, have been formed, with 1,700 groups operating in Tacoma/Pierce County alone. Members paint over graffiti, and citizen patrols conduct surveillance of known drug areas and report gang activity to the police. The impact of Safe Streets has been considerable: between 1990 and 2003, gang membership in the Tacoma area dropped from 2,500 to 500. Moreover, the program has received awards from President Clinton and DEA Director Asa Hutchinson. By making the area cleaner, physically and socially, the streets become safer, and residents' fear levels subside.

 THINK ABOUT IT What is the relationship between Durkheim's concept of the collective conscience and a strategy like community policing?

provides both cash and food assistance. When most families first apply for cash assistance, they participate in the Diversionary Work Program (DWP), a four-month program that helps parents go immediately to work rather than receive welfare. Some families may be referred to MFIP when they first apply for assistance or after they finish four months of DWP. Parents are expected to work and are supported in working. Most families can get cash assistance for only sixty months.

A longitudinal study, which began over ten years ago, tracked 2,000 recipients to see what impact the MFIP program had on their long-term needs. Two groups were selected at the start of the study: *recipients,* who had been receiving economic assistance, and *applicants,* who were then new to assistance. The study showed that new applicants left MFIP more quickly—half in the first year and two-thirds by the end of two years. In comparison, recipients took much longer—two to four years—to reach those milestones. Thus, the comprehensive efforts involved in addressing the many needs of newer applicants had a significant effect in terms of their ability to live independently.

Public policies like welfare can have an impact on delinquency by trying to alter some of the chronic conditions that exist for some families. While not a cure-all, some programs show promise in their ability to solve problems. With additional funding or with day care assistance, James's mother would not have to work as many hours. She might then be able to spend more time with her family and provide the necessary supervision of James at this critical stage in his life. It might also allow James to attend school more regularly. Food stamps might also deter shoplifting and keep James out of the juvenile justice system. Some critics might oppose these types of programs and policies by arguing that they enable families or are excessively expensive. But consider the costs taxpayers are going to have to incur, either in the form of programs that could empower families to improve or in the form of costs related to crime, delinquency, and the administration of justice.

JAMES'S CASE

Conclusions

Recall James's case:

- comes from a low-income family in an inner-city neighborhood
- skips school to care for his siblings
- shoplifts to feed his family

The problems that James and his family are encountering are difficult to resolve because they are embedded in the structure of society. James's mother works full time but does not make enough money to support her family. The high costs of housing eat up much of what she earns, leaving little money for other expenses. Moreover, James's family cannot afford to move.

James's behavior, in response to his family's struggles, could lead to bigger problems down the line. Although most teens and families do not resort to crime to solve these kinds of problems, some do. Circumstances like James's require that we take a thoughtful and balanced view of the problems families and youths encounter, and seek to understand the context in which those problems occur.

Consider some of the public policies discussed earlier, such as welfare and food stamps programs. What types of programs might be of the most immediate assistance to James and his family? While these programs might not solve all of this family's problems, which issues do you think might be effectively addressed?

THINK ABOUT IT

THE BIG PICTURE

Conclusions on Social Structural Theories

- Should living in a low-income neighborhood minimize youths' accountability for delinquent behavior? Why or why not?
- Can structural theories explain delinquency committed by middle-class youths? Why or why not?
- How would you use the subculture of violence hypothesis to explain violent acts committed by youths who typically do not get into trouble?
- Why is trust such a critical component of Durkheim's theory?
- Give several examples of the value of social capital. Why do you think that the lack of social capital is so important to disadvantaged youths?

Key Terms

social capital
social solidarity
mechanical solidarity
homogeneity
heterogeneity
organic solidarity

collective conscience
informal social control
broken windows theory
Transitional Zone
social ecology model
anomie

strain
focal concerns
general strain theory
differential opportunity
subcultural theories
subculture of violence

Make the Call ▶ Structural Theories

Review the scenario below, and decide how you would approach this case.

YOUR ROLE: Juvenile court judge in a major metropolitan area

DETAILS OF THE CASE

- You receive a case about a young man who committed assault against another youth from the same neighborhood. The victim suffered a broken nose as well as numerous cuts and bruises around his head and neck.
- The offending youth contends that the victim "had it coming," meaning the assault was justified because he failed to show the offender proper respect.
- You read the facts of the case and learn that the situation consisted of the victim looking at the offender's girlfriend in school, whereby the offender proceeded to assault the victim with a textbook in the presence of the entire class and the teacher.

- The offender does not think he has done anything wrong and feels no remorse for the injuries he caused. His mother is outraged at her son's behavior.

WHAT IS YOUR RULING?

The public defender has asked you to consider social disorganization theory to explain the offender's behavior, citing the fact that he is from a single-parent family, whose mother works two jobs to make ends meet and cannot adequately supervise the youth. The attorney believes that the boy simply started hanging out with the wrong crowd and emulated their behavior, and so asks you to consider granting his client probation instead of detention. You are familiar with the theory of social disorganization. How do you rule?
Consider:

- What sentence would you give this youth?
- Does this explanation limit the youth's responsibility in this case?
- Does the lack of remorse factor into judges' decisions in most cases?

Apply Theory to Reality ▶ Social and Cultural Influences

As we have discussed in this chapter, there are a number of programs in place to attempt to divert youths from gang allegiances and criminal activity. Given what you know about the influence of social culture on people's behavior, can you offer insight into the likelihood of gang-affiliated youths' reforming their behavior?[81]

Your Community ▶ Neediest Individuals

In addition to the information you glean from your readings, class lectures, and discussions, it is important to roll up your sleeves and immerse yourself in a topic as a researcher who gains an understanding of problem or issue by observing or experiencing it firsthand. Through such methods, you gain a much greater appreciation of the magnitude and scope of the problem than if you were only engaged in "armchair theorizing."

■ Create a list of the organizations that might exacerbate the already difficult circumstances of your community's poorest individuals. Consider, for instance, the industry that rents furniture and appliances to people on a weekly or sometimes monthly basis, or the businesses that cash checks for individuals without checking accounts, for a fee. You might also want to include pawnshops or "title loan" establishments.

■ Visit one of these establishments, and explore the means by which they profit from those in the lowest income brackets.

■ Determine whether the poor are being exploited. Are they required to pay more for goods and services than those who can afford to buy furniture, for instance, or those who have access to checking accounts?

After collecting your data and drawing from the relevant literature, prepare a report that discusses some of the social structural factors that contribute to your findings.

Notes

[1] U.S. Census Bureau, 2007. Poverty Thresholds. http://www.census.gov/poverty/incomethresholds.html. Accessed June 2, 2008.

[2] See, for instance, Press, E. 2007. "The Missing Class." *The Nation,* July 26. http://www.thenation.com/doc/20070813/press/single. Accessed June 2, 2008.

[3] See, for instance, Henry, J. F. 2007. "Bad Decisions, Poverty, and Economic Theory—The Individualist and Social Perspective in Light of the American Myth." *Forum for Social Economics,* 36(1): 17–27.

[4] Kantowiz, M. 2007. *The Financial Value of a Higher Education.* Washington, DC: Institute for Higher Education Policy.

[5] The Economic Policy Institute. Minimum Wage: Frequently Asked Questions, 2005. Available from www.epinet.org.

[6] See, for instance, Allegretto, S. A. 2005. "Basic Family Budgets: Working Families' Incomes Often Fail to Meet Living Expenses around the U.S." Economic Policy Institute Briefing Paper #165. http://www.epi.org/publications/entry/bp165/.

[7] Source: for wages: U.S. Department of Labor, Employment Standards Administration; for poverty figures: U.S. Census Bureau, Poverty Thresholds 2009.

[8] See, for instance, Swartz, D. L. 2003. "How the Concept of Cultural Capital Was Imported into American Sociology of Education." Paper presented at the meeting of the American Sociological Association, Atlanta, GA.

[9] Congressional Research Reports for the People. 2004. "Deindustrialization of the U.S. Economy: The Roles of Trade, Productivity and Recession." April 15. Accessed June 1, 2008, at http://opencrs.dct.org.

[10] According to the U.S. Bureau of Labor Statistics, it is estimated that during his eight years in office, President Clinton created 23.1 million new jobs. In contrast, President George W. Bush created a total of 6 million jobs as of 2008. See, for example, "Bush on Jobs: The Worst Record on Record." *Wall Street Journal,* January 9, 2009. Available at http://blogs.wsj.com/economics/2009/01/09/bush-on-jobs-the-worst-track-record-on-record/.

[11] Banglore, A. 2006. Noteworthy Aspects about the Participation Rate (2000–2005). Northern Trust Economic Research: Daily Global Commentary, January 10, 2006. http://www.northerntrust.com/library/econ_research/daily/us/dd011006.pdf.

[12] Bernstein, J., and Schmitt, J. 2000. The Impact of the Minimum Wage: Policy Lifts Wages, Maintains Floor for Low-Wage Labor Market. Briefing Paper #96. Economic Policy Institute.

[13] See, for instance, the National Housing Trust Fund fact sheet at http://www.nlihc.org/doc/factsheets/NHTFFactSheet-RentsvsInflation.pdf.

[14] See http://www.thomsonreuters.com/products_services/financial/financial_products/investment_management/research_analysis/umichigan_surveys_of_consumers.

[15] Ley, D. 1994. "Gentrification and the Politics of the New Middle Class." *Environment and Planning: Society and Space,* 12: 53–74.

[16] See Freeman, L. 2005. *Does Gentrification Equal Displacement? Explaining Neighborhood Change in Gentrifying Neighborhoods.* New York: Institute for Social and Economic Research and Policy, Columbia University.

[17] See, for instance, Margolis, E. (ed.). 2005. *The Hidden Curriculum in Higher Education.* New York and London: Routledge. See also Kozol, J. 1999. *Savage Inequalities.* New York: Crown.

[18] For a discussion of the social class differences in public education, see Kozol, J. 2006. *The Shame of the Nation.* New York: Crown.

[19] Ashton, T. S. 1969. *The Industrial Revolution.* London: Oxford University Press.

[20] Coser. L., 2006. *Masters of Sociological Thought,* 5th ed. Long Grove, IL: Waveland Press.

[21] Ibid.

[22] Durkheim, E. 1997. *The Division of Labor in Society.* New York: Free Press.

[23] Coser, 2006.

[24] Ibid.

[25] See, for example, Durkheim, E. 1997. *Suicide.* New York: Free Press.

[26] See U.S. Department of Justice, Federal Bureau of Investigation. 2007. *Crime in the United States.* Washington, DC: U.S. Government Printing Office.

[27] Durkheim, 1997, *Division of Labor in Society.*

[28] See Black, D. J., and Reiss, A. J., Jr. 1970. "Police Control of Juveniles." *American Sociological Review,* 35(1): 63–77.

[29] See Kelling, G., and Wilson, J. Q. 1982. "Broken Windows." *The Atlantic Monthly.* Available at http://www.theatlantic.com/doc/198203/broken-windows.

[30] Dunworth, T., and Mills, G. 2005. *National Evaluation of Weed and Seed.* Washington, DC: U.S. Department of Justice.

[31] Kelling and Wilson, 1982. See also Haller, M. H. 1972. "Organized Crime in Urban Society: Chicago in the Twentieth Century." *Journal of Social History,* 5(2): 210–234.

[32] Coser, 2006.

[33] Park, R., and Burgess, E. (eds.). 1925. *The City.* Chicago: University of Chicago Press.

[34] Ibid.

[35] Ibid.

[36] Durkheim, 1997, *Suicide.*

[37] Park and Burgess, 1925.

[38] Ibid.

[39] Shaw, C. R. 1929. *Delinquency Areas.* Chicago: University of Chicago Press.

[40] Shaw, C., and McKay, H. 1942. *Juvenile Delinquency and Urban Areas.* Chicago: University of Chicago Press.

[41] Ibid.

[42] Ibid.

[43] Park, R., and Burgess, E. 1929. *Human Communities.* Chicago: University of Chicago Press.

[44] Ibid.

[45] Ibid.

[46] Bursik, R. J. 1988. "Social Disorganization and Theories of Crime and Delinquency: Problems and Prospects." *Criminology,* 26: 519–552.

[47] See Spelman, W. 1993. "Abandoned Buildings: Magnets for Crime?" *Journal of Criminal Justice,* 21: 481–493.

[48] See Wilson, W. J. 2004. *When Work Fails.* Chicago: University of Chicago Press.

[49] See, for instance, DeCoster, S., Heimer, K., and Wittrock, S. 2006. "Neighborhood Disadvantage, Social Capital, Street Context, and Youth Violence." *Sociological Quarterly,* 47: 723–753.

[50] See, for instance, Wilcox, P., Quisenberry, N., and Jones, S. 2003. "The Built Environment and Community Crime Risk Interpretation." *Journal of Research in Crime and Delinquency.* 40: 322–345.

[51] See, for instance, Bursik, R., Jr. 1986. "Ecological Stability and the Dynamics of Delinquency." In Reiss Jr., A., and Tonry, M. (eds.), *Communities and Crime,* vol. 8. Chicago: University of Chicago Press, p. 36.

[52] Miller, W. 1958. "Lower-Class Culture as a Generating Milieu of Gang Delinquency." *Journal of Social Issues,* 14: 5–19.

[53] Ibid.

[54] Little, C. B. 2000. *Deviance and Control: Theory, Research, and Social Policy,* 5th ed. Itasca, IL: Peacock.

[55] Pfhol, S. 1994. *Images of Deviance and Social Control,* 2nd ed. New York: McGraw-Hill.

[56] Durkheim, 1997, *Suicide.*

[57] Durkheim, 1997, *Division of Labor in Society.*

[58] Pfhol, 1994.

[59] Merton, R. 1957. *Social Theory and Social Structure,* 2nd ed. New York: Free Press.

[60] Ibid.

[61] Ibid, p. 157.

[62] Ibid.

[63] See Messner, S. F., and Rosenfeld, R. 1996. *Crime and the American Dream,* 2nd ed. Belmont, CA: Wadsworth.

[64] Agnew, R. 1992. "Foundations for a General Strain Theory of Crime and Delinquency," *Criminology,* 30: 47.

[65] Agnew, 1992.

[66] Mazerolle, P., Burton, V., Cullen, F., Evans, D. T., and Payne, G. 2000. "Strain, Anger, and Delinquent Adaptations Specifying General Strain Theory," *Journal of Criminal Justice,* 28: 89–101.

[67] Cloward, R., and Ohlin, L. E. 1955. *Delinquency and Opportunity: A Theory of Delinquent Boys: The Culture of a Gang.* Glencoe, IL: Free Press.

[68] Ibid.

[69] Ibid.

[70] Ibid.

[71] Ibid.

[72] See McNamara, R. H., Flagler, C., and Hauser, A. 2004. *Boundary Dwellers: The Lives of Homeless Women in Transitional Housing.* New York: Cummings and Hathaway.

[73] Ibid.

[74] Cohen, A. K. 1955. *Delinquent Boys.* New York: Free Press.

[75] Rabow, J. 1966. "Delinquent Boys Revisited: A Critique of Albert K. Cohen's *Delinquent Boys.*" *Criminology,* 4(1): 22–28.

[76] Wolfgang, M., and Ferracuti, F. 1967. *The Subculture of Violence: Towards an Integrated Theory in Criminology.* London: Tavistock.

[77] Ibid.

[78] Ibid.

[79] Anderson, E. 1999. *Code of the Street: Decency, Violence and the Moral Life of the Inner City.* New York: Norton.

[80] Ibid.

[81] Dohrmann, G., and Evans, F. 2007. "The Road to Bad Newz." *Sports Illustrated,* November 20. http://sportsillustrated.cnn.com/2007/football/nfl/11/20/vick1126/1/html. Accessed June 2, 2008.

After reading this chapter, you should be able to:

- Recognize the connection between delinquency and social interaction.

- Identify various social learning theories, and explain why some delinquents are able to drift between criminal activity and appropriate behavior.

- Demonstrate how the theories of social control emphasize a connection between attachment to society and inappropriate behavior.

- Examine how labeling can be used to explain delinquency.

- Analyze how social conflict theories offer reasons for why some youths are more prone to status offenses and delinquency.

- Link the social process theories to the development of public policy for juveniles.

5 Social Process Theories of Delinquency

CASE STUDY ON BOB

It is a popular assumption that we can judge youths' propensity for violence and crime by their social background and upbringing. However, consider the following case about Bob:

Bob's profile:

- was raised in the inner-city
- has three older brothers, one in prison
- is involved in gangs and drugs

His school and foster family:

- has been arrested several times for assault, vandalism, truancy, and larceny
- was placed in foster care after his mother abandoned him
- is currently a fifteen-year-old sophomore at a high school in the suburbs, where most of the students are from middle- and upper-class families

Current status:

Bob is having trouble fitting in at school. His classmates tease him about his less privileged background, and teachers tend to be impatient with him as he struggles to catch up academically. Moreover, when teachers and students learn where Bob grew up, many become fearful and keep him at a distance.

Recently, a teacher accused Bob of threatening assault and sent him to the principal's office. The police were contacted, and Bob was asked for his account of the events. He explained that he simply did not agree with the teacher's grade on an assignment. When he asked for a more detailed explanation, the teacher panicked and overreacted. No voices were raised, and no one was threatened or assaulted during the conversation. Another student even witnessed the interaction, but she initially refused to get involved. She later revealed that Bob's version of the events was accurate and that the teacher did not handle the situation appropriately.

What is the connection between delinquency and social interaction? How does understanding social process theories help with development of public policy?

Disbelieving Bob's story, the principal suspended Bob for a week for "insubordination." When Bob's social worker interviewed teachers and students to learn what happened, many of them said that they "knew" he would eventually act out in this way.

When trying to understand the situation Bob has found himself in, we should consider the following questions:

- Did Bob actually threaten the teacher, or did the faculty member overreact because of Bob's reputation?
- Is Bob coming up with excuses to justify his poor grades?
- Is Bob unable to cope with different environments? Can he adapt to his new surroundings?
- Has the school community already made up its mind about Bob, regardless of his actual behavior?

THINK ABOUT IT   **Based on what you know about Bob's background, what do you think of the principal's charge of "insubordination"?**

In the last chapter, we focused on structural factors involved in delinquency, such as how a neighborhood's framework can allow delinquency to take hold by limiting opportunities and creating a culture that makes crime acceptable. In this chapter, we will look at social process theories, which suggest that delinquency is learned behavior.

Learning Theories and Delinquency

socialization
The process by which people in a given culture learn the accepted attitudes, values, beliefs, and behaviors of that group.

Socialization is the process by which people in a given culture learn the attitudes, values, beliefs, and behaviors of that group. Many researchers contend that socialization is a factor in delinquency as well. Just as children are taught to follow traffic laws, practice common courtesy, and obey their parents, delinquency is the product of learning a different set of behaviors and attitudes—in this case, delinquent behavior and thinking.[1]

The good news, according to social process theorists, is that exposure to delinquents does not necessarily lead to delinquency. Social process theorists argue that most youths can overcome the societal barriers that put them at risk for delinquency if they feel good about themselves and are surrounded by people who model acceptable behavior.[2] Research shows that self-confident youths are likely to continue to make good decisions and have greater opportunities to succeed in life, even when exposed to delinquent behavior.[3]

Consider, for example, a youth who comes from an abusive family where he experiences and witnesses physical, emotional, and psychological abuse by siblings and his biological mother. His stepfather also physically abuses him.

- This youth lives in a crime-ridden neighborhood where many of his friends and colleagues are involved in gangs and commit a wide assortment of crimes.
- This youth enjoys going to school each day and has a teacher who spends a lot of time with him, encouraging him to use education as a stepping-stone to college and a better life.

Consider what you have learned about social structural theories of delinquency. How would you compare these theories to those offered by social process theorists?

- This teacher points to other examples of youths just like him and how they made it out of a bad situation.

- The teacher also provides emotional support to the youth by listening to his troubles and offering sound advice on how to solve some of the problems he faces.

In contrast, think of another youth who lives in the same neighborhood and has similar family experiences:

- This youth's parents are abusive or absent.

- This youth's siblings are involved in crime.

- Unlike the first youth, this one does not enjoy school, and his teachers view him as a troublemaker.

- This youth does not have mentors who provide counsel and emotional support.

In this latter situation, the youth is more likely to spend time with siblings and other friends who are involved in criminal activities, and is more likely to become involved in delinquency.

What separates these two youths and puts them on different life paths are the people around them, from whom they learn about life. Social process theories generally offer insight into the way people learn and how this translates into behavior, with each having a slightly different focus. There are four types of social process theories:

- **Social learning theory:** suggests that there is nothing unique about individuals who engage in delinquency. Rather, they have been exposed to people who find criminal behavior acceptable and have been taught how to be delinquent.

- **Social control theory:** argues that people are inherently driven to pursue their own self-interests and need to be compelled to follow society's rules. To prevent delinquency, society has to create meaningful connections among individuals, and these connections must trump the otherwise selfish interests of individuals. Otherwise, delinquency and crime can flourish.

- **Labeling theory:** argues that people are stigmatized by labels, which become part of their identity. Once that happens, labeled individuals may seek out others who have been similarly labeled. Often, they will engage in inappropriate behavior as a result of their associations.

- **Social conflict theory:** looks at how the very structure and institutions of our society relate to how we label and treat offenders.

Social process theories may sound very theoretical, but they do have practical application in terms of how social policy is shaped. For instance, much of the deinstitutionalization movement, discussed in Chapter 3 on status offenders, was an attempt to minimize or limit the impact of the label "delinquent" on certain types of offenders. Similarly, the conflict approach to delinquency translates into public policy as we consider issues of minority youths, who are overrepresented in detention facilities and are more likely to be formally processed in the juvenile justice system.

Social process theories also have a connection to the restorative justice movement. Restorative justice takes as a starting point the need for offenders to recognize the harm they have caused society in general and victims in particular, and also attempts to find nonlabeling ways to repair the injuries offenders inflict. Restitution, juvenile arbitration, and mediation programs, along with community service and letters of apology, are designed to develop in delinquents the attachments necessary to their understanding the consequences of their actions and realizing the effect of their behaviors on the community.

THINK ABOUT IT

Delinquency and Social Interaction

Do you think it is possible for people to change the course of their behavior by surrounding themselves with positive role models and influences?

Social Learning Theory

According to social learning theory, children become delinquents when they learn delinquent behavior from their environments. In other words, their behaviors are not inherent, but are learned. Two theories that fall under the social learning school of thought are differential association theory and drift theory.

EDWIN SUTHERLAND'S DIFFERENTIAL ASSOCIATION THEORY

The best-known learning theory of delinquency is sociologist Edwin Sutherland's Differential Association theory. This theory argues that crime is a behavior that is learned from others, such as family members and delinquent peers, who believe that criminal behavior is acceptable. Sutherland created nine propositions to outline his theory. They apply generally to how criminal behavior is learned, but they are used by researchers and policymakers to explain juvenile delinquency as well:

1. **Criminal behavior is learned.** People learn to commit crime in the same way they learn to tie their shoes, drive a car, or dress fashionably. In the same way that people learn to internalize societal norms and values, they can learn to reject them as well.

2. **Criminal bevavior is learned through the process of communication.** People learn societal norms and values by observing others. Criminal behavior is more prevalent in individuals who associate and interact with individuals who engage in criminal activities, and who have norms and values that support it.

3. **Criminal behavior is learned from family, friends, and close companions.** People's behaviors are primarily influenced by their families, who teach children fundamentals about their culture, such as morality—what is right and wrong. Behavior is also influenced by peer groups—one's friends and classmates—and by people with whom they have intimate relationships.

4. **Learning criminal behavior involves learning techniques, motivations, drives, rationales, and attitudes.** Learning to become a criminal extends beyond the "tricks of the trade" in terms of the techniques of how to commit a particular crime. In addition, one needs to learn a set of rationalizations to justify delinquent behavior. In *The Professional Thief,* Sutherland discusses this process in more detail:

   A person can become a professional thief only if he is trained by those who are already professionals. It is ridiculous to imagine an amateur deciding to become a pickpocket, con man, penny-weighter (jewelry thief), or shake man (extortioner) without professional guidance. He knows nothing of the racket, its techniques or operations, and he can't learn these things out of books.[4]

5. **The specific direction of motives and attitudes is based on interpretations of the legal code as favorable or unfavorable.** The justification for one's actions might be based in part on the cultural distinctions of what constitutes a crime. In a highly heterogeneous society like the United States, where there are many interpretations of acceptable and unacceptable behavior, how one group interprets behaviors and activities has a lot to do with whether they are perceived as crimes. In those instances, cultural norms can conflict with societal ones, making somewhat obvious criminal behavior acceptable.

6. **A person becomes a criminal when there is an excess of interpretations favorable to violations of the law as opposed to unfavorable interpretations.** Delinquents are more likely to learn how to commit crimes from people who think

criminal behavior is more appropriate than noncriminal behavior. This is a crucial step in understanding the essence of differential (different) association (or affiliation).

7. **Differential associations vary in frequency, duration, priority, and intensity.** When people learn more from criminals than conventional people, they are more likely to engage in criminal behavior.[5] While children may have delinquent friends and family members, not all of them commit crimes. Exposure to delinquent individuals does not result in people's automatic involvement in crime. The nature and types of relationships with significant others matter. Sutherland identifies four dimensions of relationships that influence individuals' decisions to engage in crime:

> **Priority:** potential offenders place an emphasis on the relationship with criminals.
>
> **Frequency:** potential offenders spend a lot of time with criminals.
>
> **Duration:** potential offenders have known criminals for a long time.
>
> **Intensity:** potential offenders respect criminals and feel close to them.

   The greater the priority, frequency, duration, and intensity of these relationships, the more likely these interactions will lead potential offenders to learn and engage in delinquent acts.[6]

8. **The process of learning criminal behavior involves all the mechanisms involved in any other learning.** Criminal behavior, like any other learned behavior, is adopted through a variety of mechanisms, and is not simply the result of being exposed to others or observing their crimes. For example, as we will see in Chapter 7, about 30 percent of children abused by their parents end up abusing their own children when they become adults. In these cases, a negative experience with violence, either directly or indirectly, teaches children how to commit domestic violence.[7]

9. **Although criminal behavior is an expression of general needs and attitudes, criminal bevavior and motives are not explained or excused by the same needs and attitudes.** Attempting to explain crime by drives, such as the need for money, does not explain criminal behavior in particular, since it can also explain other types of behavior as well. For example, thieves who steal to earn money share their essential motives with legally employed people, who work for the same reason.[8]

For Sutherland, the learning process involves three stages:

- learning to define certain situations as opportunities for delinquency
- mastering the techniques associated with a particular criminal activity
- acquiring the motives, drives, attitudes, and rationalizations that justify breaking the law[9]

Sutherland's theory is captured in the story of Jack Henry Abbott, who, while in prison in 1980, wrote *In the Belly of the Beast,* which depicts how prison violence teaches people how to survive while incarcerated but not how to exist in mainstream society. The book was so well received that it got Abbott an early parole, largely through the help of writer Norman Mailer, who felt Abbott was a rehabilitated criminal.

Shortly after his release in 1981, Abbott was involved in an argument with a waiter in a New York City restaurant. When Abbott told the waiter he needed to use the restroom, the waiter informed him that one was not available and instead escorted Abbott outside so he could urinate in an alley. Abbott felt that he was going to be attacked. In response to a perceived threat, Abbott stabbed and killed the waiter. Charged with murder, Abbott claimed that because he had spent most of his life in prisons and institutions, he had learned that violence was the proper way to deal with such situations and people. He was convicted of manslaughter and sent back to prison.[10]

If exposure to strong influences suggesting that delinquency and crime are acceptable actually leads to such behavior, then presumably almost anyone could engage in such acts. However, there are many people who resist such influences. As we will see in Chapter 7, some youths manage to thrive in these situations, despite a heavy exposure to delinquents and criminals.

SYKES AND MATZA'S NEUTRALIZATION THEORY

drift theory
The theory that offenders learn rationalizations in an effort to protect themselves against the condemnation of society by downplaying the negative impact of their crimes.

Criminologists Gresham Sykes and David Matza were interested in the rationalizations offenders learn in an effort to protect themselves against the condemnation of society.[11] These techniques of neutralization are also referred to as the **drift theory** because they allow criminals or delinquents to "drift" back and forth between conventional behavior and delinquency and not have their identities damaged. As the label suggests, these techniques "neutralize" the negative impact of the violation in the minds of the offenders. These techniques include the following:

- **Denial of responsibility ("I didn't do it").** Matza and Sykes see two ways in which delinquents employ this technique. First, an offender can claim that the crime was an accident, and therefore no one is responsible. Second, an offender might say that her actions were the result of some outside force beyond her control. For example, a youth who steals a car but gets into a traffic accident because the car had faulty brakes will likely argue that the damage is not his fault but the car's. In either case, the offender claims to have no culpability in a particular act.[12]

- **Denial of injury ("I didn't hurt anyone").** A delinquent might contend that since no one was hurt by his actions, he should not be punished.[13] For example, he might rationalize graffiti by arguing that the cost of repainting the area is covered by insurance, or he might argue that the wall was unattractive and his artistic enhancement actually improved the neighborhood's aesthetic value.

- **Denial of victim ("They deserved it").** Some delinquents claim that their actions really had no victim or, if one existed, the victim did something to warrant the outcome. For example, a prostitute might argue that her involvement in the sex trade really has no victim since no one is injured by the exchange of sex for money. Or a youth who beats a man he sees flirting with his girlfriend might argue that the victim made a choice to flirt and has to accept the consequences of his actions.[14] The restorative justice movement, which will be discussed in a later chapter, makes the impact of an offender's behavior a strong consideration in minimizing the effectiveness of neutralization techniques. In many programs that operate under the philosophy of restorative justice, youths meet face to face with their victims, who then show the juveniles the consequences of their actions, thus negating justifications or rationalizations.

- **Condemnation of the condemners ("I learned it from watching you").** Delinquents use this technique to deflect the responsibility for what they did by focusing attention on larger issues.[15] For example, a youth who is arrested for smoking marijuana may point out that many adults abuse alcohol but are not punished. Or students who cheat on exams may criticize teachers and administrators, claiming that school officials manipulate students' test scores in order to receive bonuses or additional funding for their school.

- **Appeal to higher loyalties ("I didn't do it for me").** In some situations, youths are faced with the dilemma of adhering to the values of society or those of their individual group. Most universities have conduct codes that regulate student behavior with regard to academic dishonesty. Many students, even those who attend colleges with honor codes, are often conflicted about turning in others who cheat because the student culture is stronger than the moral guidance offered by a university's behavior code. By acting on their loyalties to their fellow students, students who do not turn in their peers will argue that they did not profit from their actions. Similarly, delinquents may claim they did not commit a crime for themselves but for the gang, their relatives, their teammates, or some other group with whom they are allied.[16]

DRIFT THEORY

The techniques of neutralization offered by Matza and Sykes are part of the larger drift theory, which helps to account for the fact that the majority of youths commit occasional delinquent acts but then go on to become law-abiding citizens as adults. However, the theory is not infallible. A youth who rationalizes his delinquent behavior may still feel remorse about it. Still, other youths are so isolated from mainstream society that they feel no real need to rationalize their behavior.[17] While many of the youths interviewed for this text demonstrated examples of the techniques of neutralization, Anthony's explanation to his mother about how he got into trouble is a good but subtle example of the appeal to higher loyalties. Notice how the decision to stay and get into trouble actually sounds like a noble effort:

> I'll come to mama telling the truth, but it'd start off like mama, it ain't nothin' but a little party, if something get to going on, I'm gonna leave. But it don't always be like that, because if—if I'm in the party and everything get to goin' on when I get ready to leave. And my brother, he—he into it with somebody, I'm not gonna leave, as much as I done promised my mama and told her I would, I end up stayin' anyway.

RONALD AKERS'S SOCIAL LEARNING THEORY

Criminologist Ron Akers has spent much of his career developing a theory of social learning that builds upon the work of Sutherland and others. The elements of his theory include imitation, differential reinforcement, definitions, and differential association.[18]

For more on family and friends, watch *Friendships & Relationships: Richard* and *Sibling Influence: Anthony B.* at www.mhhe.com/mcnamarajd1e

Imitation suggests that individuals learn how to make the decision to engage in crime by modeling other criminals' behavior. Perhaps a youth observes a friend or a respected older family member engaging in crime and being rewarded for that behavior. The youth may attempt to emulate that act. A simple example might be a youth who sees a friend shoplifting an mp3 player and getting away with it. The friend gets the benefit of either using the mp3 player or selling it without spending much time or expending much effort. Of greater importance than who did it, however, is the reward attached to the behavior. Akers believes that rewarded behavior is likely to be repeated and that once the reward is removed (or the person is punished), the behavior will stop.[19]

imitation
The decision to engage in crime by modeling other criminals' behavior.

Individuals have different ideas of what constitutes a "reward," however. While most of us would agree that money or material items would constitute a reward, so might prestige or feelings of importance in the eyes of others. A youth might be given status for being able to demonstrate courage and ability during a physical fight with others. Or a person may be given recognition for gambling skills or creativity in burglarizing local businesses. In all of these instances, the behavior was positively rewarded by others, making the individual more likely to repeat his or her delinquent behavior.

BOB'S CASE

Learning Delinquency

Recall Bob's situation:

- was raised in the inner-city
- has been arrested several times for assault, vandalism, truancy, and larceny
- was placed in foster care after his mother abandoned him
- is currently a fifteen-year-old sophomore at a high school in the suburbs

Recall that Bob spent his childhood surrounded by friends and family members who were involved in crime. He, too, got involved in an assortment of delinquent acts. When he was placed in an upscale school district with classmates from different backgrounds, Bob encountered problems. Most significantly, his background made him the subject of criticism and ridicule, as well as some degree of condemnation by his teachers.

What can learning theories tell us about Bob's behavior at this point? Should Bob's exposure to middle- and upper-class standards of behavior cause him to adopt those attitudes, values, and beliefs?

THINK ABOUT IT

negative reinforcement
Refraining from certain behaviors because of an absence of reward or the application of punishment.

mandatory sentence
A sentence that requires a particular type of punishment; often used for serious offenders who are waived to adult court, mandatory sentences are determined by the law and do not allow judges to alter or modify the sentence.

differential reinforcement
A concept that relates to social learning theory, which states that certain types of rewards and punishments have a different effect on certain types of people.

definitions
Justifications from youths to rationalize certain inappropriate behaviors, which allow them to square their self-images with the obvious harm of their actions.

differential association
A theory arguing that crime is a behavior learned from others, such as family members and delinquent peers, who feel that criminal behavior is acceptable.

People also might refrain from certain behaviors because of an absence of reward or the application of punishment. This is sometimes referred to as **negative reinforcement.** An example of the absence of reward for behavior might be graffiti artists who "tag" buildings to make some sort of statement with their art only to discover that the building has been coated with a graffiti-resistant substance. In this case, there is no payoff for the graffiti artist to engage in tagging behavior since the reward (showing off their work) cannot occur.

The second type of negative reinforcement is much easier to understand: the punishment for committing the delinquent act is greater than any perceived benefit. This is the basis of deterrence theory: making the costs outweigh the rewards. Examples might include **mandatory sentences** for youths who commit felonies or statutory waivers to adult court for some criminal offenses. Thus, for Akers, the idea that there are different types and levels of reinforcement means that all of these must be taken into account in understanding whether delinquent behavior is learned, which leads to the second component to the theory: **differential reinforcement,** for which Akers borrows heavily from psychology and behaviorism.[20]

A third key concept in Akers's social learning theory, **definitions,** describes how youths are often able to find ways to rationalize certain inappropriate behaviors, which allow them to square their self-images with the obvious harm of their actions. In the same way that a terrorist justifies killing and injuring people for altruistic or religious reasons, delinquents can claim that their actions were not harmful or that the impact on the victims was minimal.[21] Definitions theory shares common ground with the techniques of neutralization discussed in Matza and Sykes's drift theory. But the definitions element to this theory is more elaborate in that it suggests many other ways to justify behavior than simply the techniques used in the drift theory.

The heart of Akers's social learning theory focuses on Sutherland's notion of **differential association.** Akers extends Sutherland's analysis by examining the type of exposure to others. His studies show that certain groups, such as parents, teachers, coaches, pastors, adult mentors, and peers, are more likely to have an impact on others.

An area often overlooked in discussing social learning is the role of the media in shaping youths' ideas and values about the appropriateness of certain behaviors. Thus, while direct association or contact is important, indirect association via the media, particularly the Internet, can also influence youths in terms of what is learned, how well it is learned, and whether it is put into practice.[22] The Theory and Practice box outlines an exemplary program called Aggression Replacement Training (ART) that offers insight into how social learning works and how it can change people's behavior.

Social learning theories have been given a significant amount of attention by criminologists and researchers who study delinquency. Youths who commit crimes are no different from other youths except that the offenders have been rewarded in some way for engaging in inappropriate behavior. While the early learning theories lacked substantial empirical support, more recent versions have shown that delinquency is learned just like any other behavior.[23] Walter's and Anthony's comments speak to key issues in social learning theory, particularly as they apply to Akers's theory. Walter discusses the need to earn social acceptability and to fit in with his new colleagues as the motivation behind imitating their behavior:

> Well, it, it wasn't so much of somebody being negative and in a—like monkey-see, monkey-do. It wasn't so much of that. It was just, I seen every—I seen everybody else try to be cool. So, I was like, I'm going to try to be cool, too 'cause I was new in the neighborhood. I didn't, I didn't fit in anywhere, so I started doing bad, started acting up, doing dumb stuff, started getting along with a lot of people. But, my parents didn't like it very much. So, it started problems at home. That's when I started getting locked up.

On the other hand, Anthony seems to be one of those individuals others imitate:

> No. I sometimes had to talk them into it [stealing cars], because they ain't want to do it. But other times, I don't know. I was goin' to get in it, regardless, if they was gettin' in it with me or not. I don't even like to walk . . . I'd just say they scared and stuff, make them feel like they was not—so they was scared of doing the thing. Eventually, they'd do it, because, uh, one time they didn't want to do it with me, and I left them. And I guess they didn't want me to leave them again.

Here is an example of what Sutherland's Differential Association theory attempts to explain about criminal behavior: not only does it consist of the techniques of how to steal

THEORY AND PRACTICE WORKING TOGETHER

Controlling Anger Management in Teens through Aggression Replacement Training (ART)

Teenagers commonly have difficulty learning to control their emotions. While some parents might think that their children should be able to self-regulate their feelings, often these problems stem from a lack of adequate training in understanding and channeling emotions. One program that has shown extraordinary success is Aggression Replacement Training (ART).

ART is a ten-week, thirty-hour intervention administered to eight- to twelve-year-old juvenile offenders. Youths attend three one-hour sessions per week, one in each of the three specific intervention areas:

- **skill streaming,** which uses modeling, role-playing, and performance feedback to teach acceptable behavior to youths
- **anger control training,** which teaches youths how to better respond to situations in which someone or something is aggravating them
- **training in moral reasoning,** which teaches youths how to better understand the notions of fairness and justice with regard to the needs of others

Youths are also taught more about empathy and how to put themselves in other people's situations when facing moral dilemmas. ART uses repetitive learning techniques to teach youths how to control their impulses and anger, and to replace impulsive reaction with more appropriate behaviors.

This program has been highly rated by the Office of Juvenile Justice and Delinquency Prevention (OJJDP) for reducing aggressive behavior in teens. It has also been extensively evaluated by researchers and found to be both effective and inexpensive. Compared with control groups, program participants commit fewer felonies, demonstrate reduced levels of impulsiveness, and show an increased ability to identify and cope with stressful situations.

 THINK ABOUT IT Since anger issues are common ones among adolescents, should anger management be a part of the school curriculum?

---

a car, it also includes an assessment of the justifications and rationalizations needed to engage in the behavior. While Anthony learned how to steal cars, the justifications others used did not make sense to him, in part because of his concern about getting caught by his victims and their willingness to use violence against him. This dimension of Sutherland's theory is important since both techniques and rationalizations/justifications are necessary for the individual to engage in criminal behavior. When asked about how he even knows how to break into a house or a car, Anthony responded with:

> Like, you know, friends you hang around. You be with them and they do it, and you just take heed and then say like, they, they get something out of it. And you'd be like, 'dang, I need to do that, too, because they just got a whole lot of money, so I got to get me some. . . . It was just like night, probably 2:00 in the morning, something like that. We just walk in. Some car doors be open, like, my friends, they just open, mess with the door and I just jump in with them. I just watch them just break the steering column off and do all the other crazy stuff. I'm like it's crazy, man. How they used to start somebody's car up and leave. You just, I be I should think like I wonder how them people feeling about their car, that's why I didn't do it.

Given the powerful influence of peers in shaping youths' behavior, consider how difficult it is for them to pull away from their colleagues who engage in crime. The data suggest that youths who are in situations like Anthony's are less likely to be able to refrain from committing any further criminal activity, in part because crime-prone friends encourage it.

"My top priority I'm gonna go look for me a job, you feel me? I'm a apply for college, and I'm gonna be trying to make somethin' of myself. So if you all ain't trying to help me, bro, or you all ain't supporting me, bro, I'm not messin' with you all. I'm gonna just tell them like it is."

ANTHONY J.

00:20 / 01:02

For more on learning theory, watch *Learning Theory: Anthony J.* at www.mhhe.com/mcnamarajd1e

Drift Theory

How would you assess the juvenile justice system's ability to change youths' behavior using the reward and punishment system? What methods would you propose for dealing with youths who drift between criminal activity and socially appropriate behavior?

Social Control Theory

social control theory
Studies that look into why most people internalize the norms of their group and engage in conforming behavior most of the time, and how criminal behavior can be changed through resocialization.

There are four versions of **social control theory,** each offering a slight variation on the main idea that youths who commit delinquency have not been adequately taught or socialized to follow society's rules and norms.

Social learning theorists often begin with the question of why delinquents and criminals commit crimes. Social control theorists, on the other hand, tend to ask why most people internalize the norms of their group and engage in conforming behavior most of the time. Social control theorists often contend that criminal behavior can be changed through resocialization: a stronger influence of family, school, church, and law-abiding schoolmates can change individuals' delinquent behaviors. These theorists also concentrate on the process by which social bonds are created and strengthened or weakened.[24]

ALBERT J. REISS'S PERSONALITY AND CONTROL THEORY

Sociologist Albert J. Reiss, Jr., offered one of the first theories of social control. Drawing in part on Freud's model of psychoanalysis, Reiss was one of the first scholars to recognize the importance of the interaction between social control and an individual's personality, which ultimately could lead that person to engage in delinquency. Reiss does not focus as much on individual choices to explain delinquency as he does on the mechanisms in place that constrain an individual's selfish impulses. Under normal circumstances, elements of informal social control (friends, family, and peer influence) and formal social control (the juvenile and criminal justice systems) regulate youths regardless of their individual interests. However, if society or parents fail to properly teach youths how to control behavior and thoughts, or if some event causes these regulatory mechanisms to break down, the individual is much more likely to engage in crime and delinquency.[25] Reiss's theory contains three elements: a lack of development of internal controls, a breakdown of internal controls, and disruptions in the social world.

A lack of development of internal controls is at the heart of the socialization argument for delinquency. According to Reiss, if parents do not adequately teach their children self-control, such as controlling their temper and refraining from impulsive physical behavior such as hitting other children or not respecting their toys, then the children will be more likely to engage in delinquent behaviors.[26]

If children are properly socialized, Reiss asserts, they may still be tempted to engage in illegal activity if their normal inhibitions are reduced—for example, under the influence of drugs or alcohol. If teenagers have been drinking beer or smoking marijuana, they may be more inclined to break into a commercial business after hours with their friends.[27] Stressful events such as parents' divorce or a move to a new school can weaken youths' internal social control mechanisms and make them vulnerable to delinquent behavior.[28]

WALTER RECKLESS'S CONTAINMENT THEORY

Walter Reckless's containment theory is sometimes referred to as a "push/pull" theory in that it looks at internal influences on youths' behaviors that either "push" or "pull" them to delinquency.[29]

Reckless proposed that youths are "pushed" into delinquency because of inadequate *inner containment*. These individuals have drives, motives, frustrations, hostility, and feelings of inferiority that encourage them to become involved in crime. People with greater self-control over their emotions are more likely to resist delinquent influences.

Youths are "pulled" into crime because of pressures from *outer containment* influences such as poverty, blocked opportunities, family discord, and other environmental factors that present crime as an attractive alternative. Reckless felt that people with strong outer containment influences, such as positive role models, proper and effective discipline by parents, and healthy outlets for constructive behavior, would be less likely to engage in delinquent acts.[30] He proposed that inner containment is a more significant factor in delinquency because how people feel about themselves has significant effects on their behavior. While one might be able to alter outer containment factors by providing positive role models, for example, inner containment is much more difficult to change since it contains within it an element of personality.[31]

TRAVIS HIRSCHI'S BONDING THEORY

Travis Hirschi is widely associated with social control theory. While some theories argue that youths' position in the social structure determines whether they will engage in crime, in his classic book *Causes of Delinquency,* Hirschi argues that the level of connection youths feel toward society and significant others will determine whether or not they engage in delinquency.[32] If a youth has a very weak connection to the larger society, then that individual is free to pursue self-interests without concern for society's condemnation. In contrast, if an individual has tight bonds to social groups such as family, school, or peers, he or she is less likely to commit delinquent acts.[33] Hirschi's theory looks at four factors that describe the bonds that individuals form to society: attachment, commitment, involvement, and belief.

- **Attachment** refers to an individual's connection to or level of integration with others. Hirschi asserts that attachment involves the ability to adopt or internalize societal norms and the development of a conscience. It also refers to the intimate connections to and relationships with significant others, such as teachers, parents, and friends; however, Hirschi argues that the attachment to parents is a key component to preventing delinquency.[34]

- **Commitment** refers to a willingness to dedicate time, resources, and energy to conventional goals such as education and development of a good reputation. Commitment is important because the risk of losing the respect of significant others or damaging one's reputation by engaging in delinquency is one of the most significant factors in youths' conforming behavior.[35]

- **Involvement** relates primarily to time management. Commitment to conventional goals such as education or community service requires a heavy involvement in activities such as studying or helping others. This means there are fewer opportunities to engage in delinquent acts because so much of the person's time is spent doing other things.[36]

- **Belief,** Hirschi believes, is at the root of delinquency. He argues that delinquency results from a belief system that suggests criminal behavior is acceptable. Respect for the law and the legal system, which is modeled by parental behavior, means the youth believes in the value of the system and does not wish to damage it by engaging in unacceptable behavior.[37]

Consider Hirschi's four factors to describe the bonds individuals form to society: attachment, commitment, involvement, and belief. Can you think of an example of each that would apply to youths today?

While Hirschi's theory does not explain all delinquency, it has gained acceptance because it has been validated by scientific research. What control theory leaves unanswered are the factors that create and weaken social bonds.

Consider a recent trend in delinquency. Some middle- and upper-class "good" kids who have intact families, adequate education, and no gang affiliation have participated in murders

How can we explain violent and harmful behaviors when they are committed by youths who apparently have strong connections and commitments to society?

and aggravated assaults, often referred to as *sport killings,* typically of homeless people. In 2008, a homeless man died after two youths set him on fire as he slept in his cardboard box in New York City.[38] Other incidents have made headlines as well:

- In January 2007, in Fort Lauderdale, Florida, a surveillance camera captured two teens beating a homeless man with baseball bats. Prosecutors say a seventeen-year-old skateboarder, an eighteen-year-old hockey team captain, and a third teen assaulted two more homeless men that night.

- In August 2005, two youths, both nineteen years old, beat a fifty-six-year-old homeless man with baseball bats. The victim emerged from a coma three weeks later with dents in his skull, permanent scars, and no vision in one eye.[39]

Some offenders stated that they got the idea from watching a video series called *Bumfights,* in which homeless people were given a few dollars to square off in a mock boxing match. This series was sold on the Internet, and distributors have claimed sales of hundreds of thousands of copies.[40] A quick Google search of the issue brings up numerous blogs arguing that sport killing offenders lack any type of morality and should be treated like violent adult offenders. Others have argued that the explanation for such behavior is to be found in the absence of remorse or guilt many offenders feel over their actions.[41] Here the youths involved clearly have all of the elements Hirschi discusses in his bonding theory, but engage in violent acts anyway. Could it be the case that these youths have been influenced or socialized into the acceptability of bum fights by watching it over the Internet? Or have these youths failed to develop an attachment to society as outlined by Hirschi?

GOTTFREDSON AND HIRSCHI'S GENERAL THEORY OF CRIME

A recent trend in delinquency and criminology involves integrated theories, which provide much more comprehensive explanations than any one theory can. An example is Michael Gottfredson and Travis Hirschi's "general theory of crime." More popularly called *self-control theory,*[42] it argues that most crimes share these common characteristics:

- The individuals who commit crimes or delinquent acts experience immediate gratification.

- The individuals who commit crimes or delinquent acts find them exciting, risky, or thrilling.

What types of crimes do you think share the common characteristics proposed by Gottfredson and Hirschi's self-control theory?

- Little skill or planning is needed for most crimes.

- Victims' pain and discomfort result in physical and psychological control over them.[43]

These characteristics convinced Gottfredson and Hirschi that crime is basically a problem of low self-control. The general theory of crime declares that some individuals have certain traits, such as impulsivity, insensitivity, self-centeredness, and lower-than-average intelligence. These traits, which are established early in life through inadequate socialization by parents, inhibit an individual's ability to accurately calculate the consequences of his or her behavior.

Unlike Hirschi's early version of social control theory, the general theory of crime is focused on the individual rather than external sources of control. The theory presumes that criminals have no special motivations—all individuals have access to the same motivations. The real problem is that some individuals have low levels of self-control, which results in a wide variety

BOB'S CASE

Social Control Theory

Recall Bob's situation:

- is fifteen years old
- was raised in the inner-city
- was abandoned and placed in foster care
- has been placed in a high school in the suburbs

Because Bob was not previously exposed to affluent culture and the rules governing expected behavior, he is unable to effectively interact with teens at his new school. As a result, Bob withdraws from interacting with most of his peers and is reluctant to ask teachers for help. Similarly, his classmates and teachers are unprepared and ill-equipped to deal with Bob's upbringing and experiences. They cannot relate to him and so keep him at a distance.

As a result, Bob struggles to attach himself to his new community. For example, Bob attempted to emulate his peers by asking his teacher about the grading criteria in a courteous way. However, when he did not simply accept the teacher's explanation and wanted further clarification, his teacher concluded that Bob was on the verge of a physical confrontation.

Recall the basis of social control theories, such as a lack of adequate socialization. What does control theory offer in the way of an explanation for Bob's situation?

THINK ABOUT IT

of behaviors, only one of which is crime. Any action taken to raise self-control will not only affect crime but also decrease other undesirable social behaviors such as truancy or alcohol abuse.[44]

Many researchers have built on Gottfredson and Hirschi's theory. In particular, the theory has given way to new research on the impact of a lack of self-control and its relationship to delinquency and crime.[45]

Social Control Theory

Consider the tenets of social control theory. Do you think that people are, by nature, selfish? Do they need to be coerced or convinced to conform to society's rules?

THINK ABOUT IT

Labeling Theory

Labeling theory, sometimes referred to as the *societal reaction perspective* or the *interactionist perspective,* asserts that society creates criminals, delinquents, and deviants based not on the harm caused by their acts but on the way in which society labels such behavior. A consequence of being labeled is that it can cause an individual to commit even more delinquent acts or crimes.

In a philosophical sense, labeling theorists argue that criminal or delinquent behaviors are not deviant in and of themselves. Deviance is in the eye of the beholder: if society finds these behaviors criminal or unacceptable, then these behaviors become so. Howard Becker, one of the pioneers in the development of this theory, states that "deviance is not a quality of the act a person commits but rather a consequence of the application by others of rules and sanctions to an offender. The deviant is one to whom the label has successfully been applied; deviant behavior is behavior that people so label."[46]

labeling theory
The societal reaction or interactionist perspective, which asserts that society creates criminals, delinquents, and deviants based not on the harm caused by their acts but on the way in which society labels such behavior.

The juvenile justice system was created in part because of a concern about the stigma of being a "criminal" would have on youthful offenders. However, even the juvenile justice process engages in a form of labeling, since "juvenile delinquent" carries with it a host of practical and symbolic consequences for youths. In keeping with the labeling perspective, some theorists argue that being labeled a delinquent leads to further acts of delinquency, which led to the deinstitutionalization of status offenders in the late 1960s and early 1970s.[47]

In general, researchers have studied three issues related to labeling theory: the application of labels to certain types of people, the labeling process, and the symbolic and practical consequences of being labeled.

APPLICATION OF LABELS

The origins of the labeling perspective can be found in a 1918 essay by sociologist George Herbert Mead, who pointed out that the labeling of criminals enhances the social cohesion of a community by uniting conforming members of society against a common enemy or threat.[48] In 1938, sociologist Frank Tannenbaum used the term **tagging** to describe the assignment of a label to delinquents; however, he saw the real danger as lying in what he referred to as the **dramatization of evil**—the process by which society's reaction to the negative label results in the offender engaging in further criminal or delinquent behavior.[49]

Edwin Lemert built on the ideas of Mead and Tannenbaum in his 1951 book *Social Pathology*. His concepts of primary and secondary deviance offer insight into the consequences of labeling. **Primary deviance** is the type of behavior that goes unnoticed, or, if the individual is caught, the impact of the behavior is minimized or explained.[50] For example, suppose a high school teacher catches a "good" student plagiarizing material for a written assignment. The behavior might be explained as an error on the part of the student, who did not know he or she was engaging in academic dishonesty. Thus, it is unlikely that formal charges will be brought against the student. Even if charges are brought, teachers and administrators might protect the student's reputation and not stigmatize him or her with the formal label of "cheater." However, what if the student is an underperformer whose integrity is in doubt? In that case, it is likely that teachers and administrators will believe that the student deliberately cheated and label the student accordingly. This type of perception and labeling can translate into **secondary deviance,** or the kind of systematic deviance that comes as a result of the label. Thus, Lemert argued that while people may initially engage in inappropriate behavior for any number of reasons, once they are caught and labeled, the reaction to deviance may itself cause further deviance.[51]

In his classic book *The Outsiders,* Howard Becker further elaborates on the selective (and unfair) way labels are applied. Becker argues that the labeling process is employed only with certain types of people, meaning only some laws are enforced and, even then, only for particular types of people.[52] For instance, a number of cities have recently passed ordinances about the use of public space. These laws often limit the amount of time people can sit on park benches or use public space before having to move to a different location. The laws target homeless people, who are more likely to occupy park benches and other forms of public space for lengthy periods of time.[53]

Imagine that you are sitting on a park bench in one of these cities and are so engrossed in this delinquency textbook that you lose track of time. Assuming you do not look like a homeless person, do you think it is likely that a police officer will issue you a ticket or ask you to move to a different location? What if you are a shabbily dressed person doing the same thing? Despite the fact that the laws should apply to everyone, in reality only certain people are likely to get the attention of authorities, and those people are more likely to be formally labeled.

But why has something like the use of public space acquired the label of deviance in the first place? How do deviant labels come about? Becker suggests that labels arise as the result of the efforts of powerful "moral entrepreneurs," who attempt to get laws passed or change public policy to deal with important issues. Moral entrepreneurs are individuals who have economic, social, and/or political power and who identify certain

---

tagging
The assignment of a label to delinquents.

dramatization of evil
The process by which society's reaction to a negative label results in further criminal or delinquent behavior on the part of offenders.

primary deviance
The type of behavior that goes unnoticed or, if the individual is caught, the impact of which is minimized or explained.

secondary deviance
The kind of systematic deviance that comes as a result of labeling.

issues and activities as a threat to the entire society. At times, these individuals go on "crusades" to stamp out whatever threat a certain group or behavior supposedly poses to society. In the process, moral entrepreneurs spend a considerable amount of time trying to get the rest of society to align with their cause or crusade.[54]

Mothers whose children were victims of drunk drivers started one such crusade. Mothers Against Drunk Driving (MADD) is instrumental not only in changing the laws as they relate to driving while intoxicated but also in increasing sanctions for repeat offenders. Most importantly, MADD is instrumental in shaping the public's opinion about the seriousness of drunk driving and how it affects everyone in the United States.[55]

While it is easier to understand why people get labeled for their behavior, sometimes they are given a negative label simply for how they look. In his book *Stigma: Notes on the Management of a Spoiled Identity*,[56] Erving Goffman argues that stigmatized persons, or those in danger of becoming stigmatized, will attempt to restrict the amount of information the community has about them to avoid acquiring a negative label. Most people, but especially those who are given labels based on how they look, attempt to engage in **impression management,** creating a favorable impression of themselves for others. In the case of the physically disabled, where people have already been given an obvious label, they may engage in **covering** to minimize the effects of the disability and the stigma connected to it, and to "prove" they are as capable as "normal" people.

Sometimes an individual attempts to hide attributes that might stigmatize him or her. For example, a gay teen may not want his friends and peers to know about his sexual identity. Goffman uses the term **passing** to describe the process by which people will attempt to hide potentially stigmatizing attributes.[57] In this instance, the teen may try to pass himself off as a heterosexual rather than risk the dangers of "coming out." Other examples include teens and college students who suffer from eating disorders but give the appearance that they are healthy and active.[58]

What are the consequences of labeling someone a criminal or delinquent?

impression management
Creating a favorable impression of oneself for others.

covering
The attempt to minimize the effects of a disability and the stigma connected to a label.

passing
The process by which people will attempt to hide potentially stigmatizing attributes.

THE LABELING PROCESS

We have talked about some of the more important concepts associated with labeling theory, but before we discuss the consequences of having a label, we should outline the process by which one is acquired:

1. **The deviant act.** This is the first step in acquiring a criminal or delinquent label. Obviously, an important component at this stage is getting caught. It is here that Lemert's concept of primary deviance plays a role. If the matter is handled informally, no further action is taken. Most youths who get into trouble with the law have their situations resolved by the police officer without an arrest being made.

2. **Status degradation ceremony.** This is the next step in the process of acquiring a label. If the crime is serious enough, the matter must be turned over to the juvenile court for resolution. Because the impact can be so severe, juvenile court proceedings are not usually open to the public. It is also why there is such an emphasis in the juvenile justice system on handling matters informally rather than going forward in the judicial process. When offenders are publicly proclaimed and formally labeled as criminals, deviants, or delinquents, they are made to take responsibility for their actions.[59]

3. **Master status.** At this stage, the individual's master status, or dominant position in society (e.g., teenager, mother, college student), is altered, and the label is applied in its place. Depending on the seriousness of the act, individuals' entire identities are shaped by this new label. For example, a student who joins a gang, commits an initiation crime, and is arrested and convicted will be seen not as a teenager, but as a gang member or perhaps even a felon.

How might the process of labeling juvenile delinquents as such lead to a self-fulfilling prophecy?

self-fulfilling prophecy
The occurrence that takes place when individuals live out their labels.

4. **Retrospective interpretation.** Once individuals are stigmatized by a label, their community is likely to reevaluate their past behavior in light of this new label. That is, family, friends, and others will look back *retrospectively* and *interpret* offenders' behavior in light of this new label.[60]

5. **Internalization of the label.** The old saying that "if enough people tell you something long enough you begin to believe it is true" applies to this stage of the labeling process. With the community's condemnation and the reassessment of offenders' identities, offenders may begin to internalize their new labels and then attempt to live up to them. This can lead to Lemert's secondary deviance—more systematic or patterned deviant behavior. In other words, people may begin to believe that they are "bad," as society claims, and act accordingly.

6. **Deviant career.** Because society excludes certain labeled groups, and because humans need others for social interaction, offenders may turn to deviant subcultures made up of other similarly labeled individuals. For instance, juveniles who commit sexual assault will likely be shunned by teachers, parents, and other youths. As a result of this ostracism, they may turn to other sex offenders for relationships. By association and interaction, coupled with the previous step of internalization, individuals may embark upon delinquent or deviant careers, not because they choose to, but rather because it has been chosen for them. This is the **self-fulfilling prophecy** at work: individuals living out their labels.[61]

Suppose you are in high school and one of your teachers is convinced you are a poor student. The self-fulfilling prophecy suggests that the teacher will treat you as if you cannot learn. Then, if you do not grasp concepts easily or fail exams, the teacher will conclude that his or her initial assessment of you was correct: you are a poor student. However, the self-fulfilling prophecy states that the way the teacher treated you has more to do with your failing the exams or struggling to learn concepts than any predictive powers of that teacher. Anthony J. offers a thoughtful example of the labeling process when he discusses how the prosecuting attorney described him to the judge:

> The prosecutor's gonna make you feel like you really just all out you just, just cutthroat killer, like you really out to get everybody. He, he, god, he's just violent, he got numerous cases in the past, he's just hurtin' people, he got batteries, he got this, he be carryin' guns, this and that. He just repeated his violent history, and he just don't care. Ma tries to help him, he, he bends the rules at home, he goes out, do what he want. They just make you seem like, like you just the worstest person in the neighborhood, and you just feel like it's all on you. Everythin' that go on in the neighborhood they tryin' to, like if they tryin' to pin it on you. You just, you just look at her [the prosecutor] like—what can you what can you do? And the judge, you look at the judge, you be lookin' at him, he just takin' it all in and then it just stink at the end.

CONSEQUENCES OF LABELING

Labeling theory has had a major impact on our understanding of crime, delinquency, and deviant behavior. It has also helped us to understand and clarify how easily and quickly negative labels can be applied. Perhaps even more importantly, scholars have begun to explore the consequences of those labels on individuals. If individuals who commit crimes pay the price for doing so, should their debt to society be erased? Even if so, what types of lingering effects do negative labels have for offenders?

Research on labeling shows that it is difficult for a label to disappear, particularly when a person has committed serious offenses. Relocating often does not work, since someone in a new location may discover the offender's past.[62] Ex-convicts, drug addicts, and others who have been convicted for serious offenses sometimes try to use their label for constructive purposes, by giving lectures and testimonials in the hope that the audience will learn the lesson that they should not follow in the offender's footsteps. Sociologists call this "legitimating the ex-status."[63] However well-intentioned these types of programs are, they do not remove the label: the person remains an "ex" convict or "ex" drug addict.

Another way to destigmatize a label might be to recast the behavior in light of offenders' lack of responsibility for their actions. This is often referred to as the *medicalization of deviance*—redefining the behavior in such a way as to make it more acceptable and to hold those engaging in it less responsible for their actions. For instance, in the past, alcoholism was considered unacceptable behavior, and alcoholics were looked upon by society as deviants. However, when alcoholism was redefined as a "disease," it relieved offenders of some of the responsibility for engaging in this activity. Just as a person is not necessarily responsible for contracting cancer or some other disease, alcoholism is now understood and explained in terms of a medical model.[64] But medicalization does not remove the label; it transforms the label into something less deviant. While we might offer a person more sympathy and less responsibility for engaging in certain behaviors, the label, and the stigma, remains.

Finally, at least theoretically, a deviant label presumably can be erased if society's morality changes. During Prohibition, the manufacture, distribution, and sale of alcohol were illegal, and bootleggers who engaged in the trafficking of alcohol were considered criminals. What happened to bootleggers once Prohibition was repealed? They were still thought of as criminals. Even when a society's norms or laws shift, members of society still tend to view certain people or groups as deviant based on past norms or laws.[65]

Thus, while society is quick to affix labels on individuals, negative ones are difficult to remove, particularly if the crime is serious enough. Most labeling theorists contend that offenders, at best, can only minimize their label's impact. Sociologist Albert Reiss, Jr., for example, argued that three variables are important in determining the impact of the label: the seriousness of the act, the amount of time elapsed from the commission of the crime, and the remorse and contrition shown by the offender.[66]

Many youths who have been incarcerated have difficulty making the transition back into mainstream society, what experts refer to as **reentry.** They are stigmatized by their labels, and they encounter problems finding jobs, enrolling in school, and reuniting with their families and friends. Perhaps more importantly, they are thrust back into the neighborhoods that got them into trouble in the first place. The Theory and Practice box describes a program that helps juvenile offenders reintegrate themselves into the community while staying away from the influences that initially got them into trouble.

reentry
The transition back into mainstream society.

While most labeling theorists argue that affixing labels to youths is likely to result in continued delinquency, some contend that perhaps the labeling effect can be positive. Sometimes youths who have been labeled as juvenile delinquents can be motivated to change their behavior, just as the stigma of being obese can serve as a motivating factor for some people to lose weight and maintain a healthy lifestyle.[67] There may also be a deterrent effect in labeling. That is, youths who see the challenges faced by those labeled as delinquents may avoid going down that path themselves.[68]

Criminologist John Braithwaite discusses the phenomenon of **shaming,** the public embarrassment of offenders for engaging in inappropriate behavior, and distinguishes between two types of shaming: *disintegrative* and *reintegrative*. Disintegrative shaming is consistent with the traditional understanding of labeling theory. The juvenile justice system affixes a negative label, which has a host of negative consequences for the individual. For instance, labeling can have an isolating effect on individuals, who have limited access to employment and educational opportunities, and who are denied the right to vote if convicted of a felony. As a result, the juvenile delinquent will likely turn to other similarly labeled offenders and become part of a delinquent subculture. In these instances, shaming has no potential positive effect; in fact, it increases the likelihood of further delinquency.

shaming
The public embarrassment of offenders for engaging in inappropriate behavior, sometimes used to refrain youths from committing crimes in the future.

In reintegrative shaming, however, the impact of the label is tempered with community forgiveness. In these cases, family, friends, and neighbors condemn the act, not the actor. While they may express disappointment in youths for making poor choices, and while the offenders may still receive some type of punishment, reintegrative shaming is more

THEORY AND PRACTICE WORKING TOGETHER

Operation New Hope

Operation New Hope, a program operated out of Corona, California, is designed to help high-risk chronic offenders between the ages of twelve and fifteen, who have been recently released from a detention facility, cope with the problems of everyday life. Operation New Hope is based on six principles that help offenders reintegrate into society:

- Improve basic socialization skills, which are necessary for a successful transition.
- Significantly reduce the amount and seriousness of future criminal activity.
- Eliminate alcohol and substance abuse dependency.
- Enhance quality of life by providing participants with job training, education, and social capital.
- Reduce dependency on gangs for emotional, social, and financial support.
- Reduce the chance of a parole revocation.

The program consists of thirteen consecutive weekly meetings, each lasting three hours, that concentrate on a variety of coping skills to achieve these six objectives, such as dealing with emotions or living with an addiction.

The primary evaluation of this program showed that ninety days after release from a secure facility, control group youths (nonparticipants) were twice as likely as members of the experimental group (participants) to have been re-arrested, to be unemployed, and to lack the resources to find and hold a job. Control group youths were also three times more likely to associate with former gang members and to have serious family relationship problems. A year later, control group youths were still twice as likely to be arrested, to be unemployed, and to lack job prospects. They were also twice as likely to have violated terms of their parole and three times more likely to have abused drugs or alcohol.

The OJJDP has identified this program as an effective tool in preparing youths for reentry into society, suggesting that this type of intervention has a demonstrable effect in reintegrating youths into society and minimizing the effects of negative labels.

 THINK ABOUT IT Can a changed self-image result in different behaviors for youths and different perceptions about their place in the world?

For more on motives for engaging in crime, watch *Recidivism: Shun* and *Respecting & Teaching: Shun* at www.mhhe.com/mcnamarajd1e

proactive and can reintegrate youths into the larger society as full participants and law-abiding citizens.[69] Thus, Braithwaite argues that reintegrative shaming can actually result in fewer episodes of delinquency and can be used as a tool to prevent delinquency. Drug courts, which effectively use formal programs of reintegrative shaming, typically process offenders differently than traditional juvenile courts, with an emphasis on making restitution to victims and, where possible, mitigating the harm done by offenders, such as by repairing vandalized property or writing letters of apology. While there is some evidence to indicate that such an approach can be a positive experience for youths, the research findings are mixed. In some cases, efforts to redirect youths through shaming have led to an increase in delinquency rates because offenders are not sufficiently punished for their actions, making shaming less important than the benefits they receive from committing crimes.[70]

Reintegrative shaming has become an important part of the restorative justice movement in the juvenile justice system. It gives young people an opportunity to recognize their mistakes, take responsibility for them, and repair the harms that they have inflicted. In the process, hope is created for youths since they are not "written off" or cast aside as unsalvageable.[71]

Clearly, the labeling perspective has a different focus than the other theories discussed thus far. One of the main criticisms levied against the labeling perspective is that it does not explain the causes of delinquency, but that was never really the intent of the theory. Other theories attempt to identify the root causes of delinquency, but labeling theorists are more interested in how rules are created, how a person gets labeled, and what happens to that individual once a label has been applied.

BOB'S CASE

Was Bob Labeled?

Recall Bob's situation:

- was raised in the inner-city
- was abandoned and placed in foster care
- has been enrolled in a high school in the suburbs
- is unfairly accused of threatening assault on a teacher

It seems likely that Bob's limited experience with middle-class culture did not adequately prepare him to make the transition to his new school and the people there. It is also likely that the school community formed a quick impression of Bob early in its relationship with him and affixed a negative label on him as a result. For example, students ridicule Bob for his poor academic performance and his lack of social skills, and teachers fear him because of his violent family background.

What does labeling theory offer us in terms of understanding Bob's situation? Do you think a self-fulfilling prophecy was at work in his case? Why or why not?

THINK
ABOUT
IT

Labeling Theory and Delinquency

How does an understanding of labeling theory help us to explain delinquency? Do you think the same understanding can help us prevent delinquency from occurring in the first place? If so, how?

THINK
ABOUT
IT

Social Conflict Theories

Social process and social structural theories take as a given that we have reached a consensus on how society is structured, and they explain delinquency in terms of attitudes, values, beliefs, and behaviors that deviate from that established system. Criminal behavior is unacceptable because it threatens the existing order.

However, conflict theorists contend that no such consensus exists in the first place; instead, they question the legitimacy of existing social institutions. They argue that much of social life centers on conflict among and competing interests of various groups, and that the legal system is a mechanism by which those in power further their interests. Unlike consensus theories, which frame delinquency and crime as a by-product of an established system, conflict theories assert that delinquents and criminals are those who do not have enough social, economic, or political power to have their interests furthered. As a result, they are more likely to be labeled as criminals. This perspective leads conflict theorists to argue that there are two forms of justice in the United States: one for the wealthy and one for the poor.

There are many different versions of conflict theory, each offering a slightly different focus. Some conflict theorists—for example, Karl Marx and Friedrich Engels—have emphasized the importance of social class in explaining the economy, and social life in general, including whether one is likely to be perceived by the wealthy as a potential threat to their way of life. Inevitably, those individuals perceived as a threat will violate some law, culminating in their arrest and punishment.

The related theories of radical or critical criminology focus not on a single group, as Marx and Engel do, but on various interest groups. Other conflict theories, such as those offered by Max Weber, John Hagan or Richard Quinney, focus on power and authority. These theorists argue that public perceptions of what constitutes a threat to society, as well as its severity, is determined by those in power, who exploit the public's fear of being victimized to further their own economic, political, and social interests.[72]

Still other conflict theories emphasize cultural conflict. Thorsten Sellin and George Vold, for example, argue that cultural conflicts, such as differing norms and value systems found in some neighborhoods, result in an individual choosing to follow a different set of norms from conventional society.[73] Sellin, in his book *Culture and Conflict in Crime*, was one of the first to argue that delinquency is a by-product of conflicting norms. Sellin makes a distinction between two different types of norms: *conduct* and *crime*.[74]

Crime norms are those that spell out the specific rules and laws of, and the behaviors prohibited by, society, as well as their corresponding punishments. These norms, says Sellin, are created because they are essential to the survival of the social order and of society in general. Examples of crime norms include homicide, larceny, and robbery. Conduct norms, in contrast, reflect the values, attitudes, and beliefs of informal social groups. These are the working norms, found in every group and organization, for how people develop relationships with one another. These are not the norms found in the criminal law, and they may even conflict with other groups' norms, but they have a profound influence on how people behave.

As societies become more heterogeneous, meaning many different types of people come together in groups, all with different ideas about what is appropriate and inappropriate behavior, conduct norms and crime norms are likely to merge, resulting in higher delinquency rates. As a result, the ability of heterogeneous society to resolve its differences informally is limited, creating the need for formal mechanisms, such as the legal system, to handle problems and conflicts. In other words, instead of people working out the problems they have with one another, people and groups will turn to the courts and the police to work out their issues.[75]

Suppose a community resident discovers that his neighbor's teenage son is using his swimming pool without permission. The teenager invites his friends, and they leave the pool area a mess. Normally, the resident would resolve this problem informally by having a talk with the teenager's father and allowing the parents to handle it. But Sellin argues that the resident will likely contact the police instead and threaten to have the teenager charged with trespassing.

At the core of the various aspects of conflict theory are Marx's ideas about how certain groups are exploited, feel powerless to affect the existing system, and ultimately work to change the system. For Marx, change meant a revolutionary upheaval of the entire economic system.

MARX AND ENGEL'S CONFLICT THEORY

Karl Marx and Friedrich Engel's theory is based on the idea that certain groups in a capitalistic society have greater advantages over others since they control the **means of production,** the resources needed to produce wealth, such as factories, equipment, land, and raw materials. Writing in the nineteenth century during the Industrial Revolution, Marx noted that the **bourgeois,** or capitalists, owned the means of production and that their goal, as in all of capitalism, was the pursuit of profit. Others in the capitalist society had only their labor to sell. These people were referred to as the **proletariat,** or working class, which consisted of former sharecroppers and others who worked the land before the Industrial Revolution.[76]

According to Marx, having no other resources, the proletariat had to sell their labor to the bourgeois to earn a living. While the bourgeois and the proletariat needed each other to produce wealth and contribute equally to creating a commodity, only the bourgeois profited from the exchange. This setup, what Marx referred to as **false consciousness,** initially seemed acceptable to the workers. Since the bourgeois were taking all the risks of the business, they should be able to hire workers at whatever salary they thought was fair. For their part, the workers felt as though they had a choice: they could decide whether or not to work in the factory. So, the relationship appeared to be a reasonable one.

Over time, however, the bourgeois became highly exploitative in an effort to squeeze as much productivity (which ultimately translated into profit) out of each worker. Conditions in the factories during the era when Marx wrote were generally deplorable; workers

means of production
The resources, such as factories, equipment, land, and raw materials, needed to produce wealth.

bourgeois
Capitalists or owners of the means of production whose goal is the pursuit of profit.

proletariat
Those who have only their labor to sell; the working class.

false consciousness
In the state of false consciousness, the worker accepts the lower wages and exploitation of the bourgeois as an acceptable condition of employment.

were required to work upwards of twenty hours per day for sometimes less than a dollar in wages. Even given the value of the dollar during that era, it was barely enough to survive.[77] The intent by the bourgeois was to pay workers just enough so they could feed their families and eke out a living. This would make the proletariat more dependent on the bourgeois and thus more accepting of exploitation.[78]

At some point, Marx proposed, the workers would come to recognize that this type of treatment could not continue. They would also begin to realize that they should benefit from their efforts beyond a simple salary because both the means of production and labor were needed to produce a commodity. Given that the bourgeois and the proletariat contributed equally, workers argued, fairness would dictate that they share equally in the profits as well.

The awakening, or **class consciousness,** of the workers in recognition of their contributions to the economy led to demands for better working conditions and higher wages, but the bourgeois resisted because any increase in wages would have been subtracted from their profits. Marx's famous phrase "Workers of the world unite" served as a rallying cry in one of his most famous works, *The Communist Manifesto,*[79] urging workers to overthrow the bourgeois and take over the means of production. Only after the workers wrestled control away from the bourgeois would a fair and equitable system emerge. A revolution would not guarantee a better system, but without any dramatic changes, life for workers would go from bad to worse. While the exploitation was not personal, it was driven largely by the pursuit of profit by the bourgeois.[80]

To Marx and his contemporaries, the state and the legal system were tools used by the bourgeois to further their economic, political, and social interests, and to prevent the proletariat from controlling the economic system, thus ensuring poverty, alienation, and extreme dissatisfaction among the workers. The legal system prevented attempts to change the system by prosecuting those who called attention to its unfairness. This strained relationship between worker and capitalist highlighted the flaws of capitalism and, Marx argued, would ultimately result in capitalism's downfall.

class consciousness
The awakening of workers in recognition of their contributions to the economy, which led to demands for better working conditions and higher wages; however, the bourgeois resisted because any increase in wages would be subtracted from their profits.

MODERN CONFLICT THEORY

In *The Social Reality of Crime,* Richard Quinney builds upon Marx's ideas about the elite using the legal system to control those without power. Quinney notes how the criminal justice system is a tool used by the elite to ensure that those groups with social, economic, and political power maintain their interests by defining certain acts as criminal and using the criminal justice system to keep people from gaining access to their resources.[81] Because they control the system, as well as the media, the elite can control not only who becomes a criminal, and what their punishment and long-term future consist of, but also the public's perceptions of crime.

Can you think of a present-day example of a group that demonstrates class consciousness?

Many experts argue that the extent and seriousness of crime is severely distorted by the media, which only heightens the public's fear of certain classes of people.[82] All of this is designed by the elite to maintain their interests. Quinney points out that white-collar crime is far more harmful to society than street crime, but when asked about their primary fears and concerns, most people identify various types of street crimes and criminals.[83]

Modern conflict theories, such as those offered by Quinney, suggest that the reason for the higher rates of delinquency among minority youths relates to their position in society. The use of the system as a tool can be linked to the labeling perspective, since the poor are much more likely to be labeled criminals.[84] The Marxist approach and the modern conflict theories suggest that delinquency is rooted in class and economic conflict in the capitalist system. Delinquency occurs largely because the wealthy and powerful define certain behaviors as criminal since they are contrary to their economic, social, or political interests.

One way to use Marx's theory, or even the modern conflict approach, to understand delinquency is to examine the disproportionate number of African Americans who are detained by the juvenile justice system. According to a recent report by the OJJDP, the racial disparity in the juvenile justice system is highlighted in the proportion of cases in the court system, as well as their outcomes. Blacks are more than three times as likely as whites to be charged with a violent crime, more than twice as likely to be charged with a property crime or public order crime, and about one and a half times as likely to be charged with a drug offense.[85]

In addition to being more likely to be sent to a detention facility, blacks are disproportionately represented in the juvenile justice system, particularly in terms of arrests. In fact, one of the amendments to the Juvenile Justice Delinquency Prevention Act of 1974 included a provision mandating that states investigate whether there is a racial bias in their juvenile justice system, collect data to document such a trend, and develop effective solutions to reducing the problem.[86]

The research suggests that the reason for the difference stems from early stages of case processing. Black youths are less likely to be diverted from the court system and more likely to receive sentences involving detention. About 60 percent of all juveniles in custody are minorities, and almost three-quarters of youths held in custody for violent crimes are minorities.[87] One explanation as to why blacks are identified, arrested, convicted, and detained at higher rates than whites or other groups is because they represent a threat to the status quo and generate fear among those in power.

One criticism of conflict theory is that the law does not always operate for the exclusive benefit of the elite and powerful, who do not have as much control of the system as many conflict theorists suggest. If they did, white-collar crimes, such as those committed by Martha Stewart, Bernie Madoff, and the tobacco industry, would not be prosecuted because they would not be considered as crimes.[88] This approach is largely theoretical since conflict theory has not been supported by a wide body of empirical evidence.

THINK ABOUT IT

Social Conflict Theories

What reasons do social conflict theories offer for why some youths are more prone to delinquency than others? Do these theories offer valid explanations for the effects of social and class differences on crime rates?

Social Process Theories and Public Policy

There are a variety of ways in which social process theories apply to public policy. For instance, much of the deinstitutionalization movement, discussed in Chapter 3 on status offenders, represented an attempt to minimize or limit the impact of the label "delinquent" on certain types of offenders. Similarly, the conflict approach to delinquency calls for changes in public policy to ensure that minority youths are not overrepresented in detention facilities and are more likely to be formally processed in the juvenile justice system.

The restorative justice movement offers another example of social process theory's impact on public policy. Restorative justice takes as a starting point the need for offenders to recognize the harm they have caused society in general, and victims in particular; it also attempts to find nonlabeling ways to repair the injuries inflicted by offenders. Programs involving restitution, juvenile arbitration, mediation, and community service, as well as letters of apology, try to instill in delinquents a sense of attachment to their communities. In doing so, youths learn to understand the consequences of their actions and to realize the entire community is affected by their behavior.

THE BIG PICTURE

Conclusions on Social Process Theories

- Can differential association explain most delinquent acts?
- Can you think of examples of people who regularly come into contact with criminals, but who do not engage in crime?
- How does bonding or social control theory explain the lack of remorse some youths feel over their involvement in some crimes?
- What is the impact of the labeling of delinquents? Can a label ever be removed? Why or why not? What factors determine whether or not a label is minimized?

Key Terms

socialization

differential association

techniques of neutralization

belief

tagging

dramatization of evil

moral entrepreneurs

status degradation ceremony

retrospective interpretation

master status

means of production

false consciousness

class consciousness

Make the Call ▶ Social Control Theory

Review the scenario below, and decide how you would approach this case.

YOUR ROLE: A parent who decides to take in a foster child

DETAILS OF THE CASE:

- You and your spouse decide to take in a foster child named Peter, who is a fifteen-year-old boy from a dysfunctional home. You learn that he was left alone for much of his childhood and that he has had to panhandle for money as his parents are substance abusers and were rarely at home.

- After a short time, you learn that Peter steals from you, is verbally abusive toward his teachers, and is withdrawn or surly with almost everyone around him.

- After six months, you learn that Peter has been in and out of foster care since he was five years old and that he has been placed with over a dozen foster families and group homes.

WHAT DO YOU DO?

Peter does not seem to mind the punishments you create for his unacceptable behavior, nor does he seem interested in changing his method of dealing with you or anyone else. As a potential solution, you seek professional guidance only to discover that after one visit, Peter refuses to attend any sessions.
  Consider:

- Can you force Peter to attend counseling, either alone or with you, as a condition of his staying with you and your family? Will it do any good if he fails to cooperate with the counselor?

- Do you contact the local Department of Social Services in the hopes that perhaps one of the caseworkers can offer insight?

- Do you tell Peter he can no longer stay with you because he does not seem interested in being a part of the family nor in abiding by the rules of the household?

Apply Theory to Reality ▶ Co-Offending

A recent study sponsored by the National Institute of Justice examined the issue of co-offending, or the tendency of youthful offenders to commit acts with others rather than alone. The report found that offenders ages thirteen and under are more likely to commit crimes in pairs and groups than sixteen- and seventeen-year-old offenders. Overall, about 40 percent of juvenile offenders commit crimes with partners. Choose a theory discussed in this chapter that offers insight into the nature of co-offending, particularly among younger offenders.

Your Community ▶ Departments of Juvenile Justice

In addition to the information you glean from your readings, class lectures, and discussions, it is important to roll up your sleeves and immerse yourself in a topic as a researcher who gains an understanding of a problem or issue by observing or experiencing it firsthand. Through such methods, you gain a much greater appreciation of the magnitude and scope of the problem than if you were only engaged in "armchair theorizing."

- Contact your local Department of Juvenile Justice, and try to interview a judge or probation officer.

- Ask them about the impact of labeling and its consequences for youths. Also ask them about what they think causes delinquency: is it genetic, learned behavior, or are some other factors involved?

- After collecting your data, and drawing from the relevant literature, prepare a report that discusses your findings according to the social process theories discussed in this chapter.

Notes

[1] See Kornblum, W. 2006. *Sociology*, 9th ed. New York: McGraw-Hill.

[2] See Fuller, J. R. 2010. *Criminology: Mainstream and Crosscurrents.* New York: McGraw-Hill.

[3] See, for instance, Luthar, S. S. 2006. *Resilience in Development: A Synthesis of Research across Five Decades.* New York: Wiley. See also Elias, M. 2008. "Laws of Life: A Literacy-Based Intervention for Social-Emotional and Character Development and Resilience." *Perspectives in Education*, 26: 75–79. Heller, S. S., Larrieu, J. A., D'Imperio, R., and Boris, N. W. 1999. "Research on Resiliency to Child Maltreatment: Empirical Considerations. *Child Abuse and Neglect*, 23(4): 321–338. See the research by the Search Institute at http://www.searchinstitute.org.

[4] Sutherland, E. 1937. *The Professional Thief.* Chicago: University of Chicago Press, p. 21.

[5] Ibid.

[6] Ibid.

[7] About 30 percent of children of abuse go on to abuse their children as parents. See National Child Abuse Center Statistics at http://www.childhelp.org/resources/learning-center/statistics.

[8] Sutherland, E. 1947. *Principles of Criminology.* Philadelphia: J. B. Lippincott.

[9] Ibid.

[10] Abbott wrote a second book about his experiences titled *My Return*, and, along with film rights, earned an estimated $100,000. In 1990, he was sued by the waiter's family for an estimated $10 million. A court ruled that the family was entitled to damages and, under the Son of Sam law, Abbott was not allowed access to any of the money earned from the proceeds of his books or films. See Sullivan, R. 1990. "Author Facing Damages for Murder." *New York Times*, June 6. http://query.nytimes.com/gst/fullpage.html?res=9C0CE4D6103BF935A35755 C0A966958260. Accessed June 8, 2008.

[11] Sykes, G. M., and Matza, D. 1957. "Techniques of Neutralization: A Theory of Delinquency." *American Sociological Review*, 22: 664–666; see also Matza, D. 1967. *Delinquency and Drift.* New York: Wiley.

[12] Ibid.

[13] Ibid.

[14] Ibid.

[15] Ibid.

[16] Ibid.

[17] Ibid.

[18] Ibid.

[19] Ibid.

[20] Ibid.

[21] Ibid.

[22] Ibid.

[23] See, for instance, Akers, R., and Jensen, G. 2002. "Social Learning Theory and the Explanation of Crime: A Guide for the New Century." *Advances in Criminological Theory*, 11. Somerset, NJ: Transaction.

[24] Hirschi and other social control theorists have historical links to Emile Durkheim for his insight into the value and purpose of social integration. See Shoemaker, D. 2005. *Theories of Delinquency: An Examination of Explanation of Delinquent Behavior.* New York: Oxford University Press.

[25] Ibid.

[26] Reiss, A. J., Jr. 1951. "Delinquency and the Failure of Personal and Social Controls." *American Sociological Review*, 16: 196–207.

[27] Ibid.

[28] Ibid.

[29] Reckless, W. 1955. *The Crime Problem.* New York: Appleton-Century-Crofts.

[30] Ibid.

[31] Ibid.

[32] Hirschi, T. 1969. *Causes of Delinquency.* Berkeley: University of California Press.

[33] Ibid.

[34] Ibid.

[35] Ibid.

[36] Ibid.

[37] Ibid.

[38] See "Burned New York Man Dies." http://news.yahoo.com/s/ap/20071014/ap_on_re_us/homeless_attack;_ylt=AlaBJrjKUHzcUBQB-VnisnExvzwcF.

[39] See Fantz, A. 2007. "Teen Sport Killings on the Rise." February 20, 2008.

[40] See http://www.bumfightsdump.com.

[41] See http://technorati.com/videos/tag/bumfights.

[42] Gottfredson, M. R., and Hirschi, T. 1990. *Towards a General Theory of Crime.* Palo Alto, CA: Stanford University Press.

[43] Ibid.

[44] Ibid.

[45] See, for instance, Evans, D. T., Cullen, F. T., Burton, V. S., Dunaway, R. G., and Benson, M. L. 2006. "The Social Consequences of Self-Control: Testing the General Theory of Crime." *Criminology*, 35(3): 475–504.

[46] Becker, H. 1969. *The Outsiders.* Chicago: University of Chicago Press, pp. 8–9.

[47] See, for instance, Triplett, R. A., and Jarjoura, G. R. 1994. "Theoretical and Empirical Specification of a Model of Informal Labeling," *Journal of Quantitative Criminology*, 10: 243.

[48] Mead, G. H. 1918. "The Psychology of Punitive Justice," *American Journal of Sociology*, 23: 577–602.

[49] Tannenbaum, F. 1938. *Crime and the Community.* New York: Columbia University Press.

[50] Lemert, E. 1951. *Social Pathology.* New York: McGraw-Hill.

[51] Ibid.

[52] Becker, 1969.

[53] National Coalition for the Homeless. 2007. *A Dream Denied: The Criminalization of Homelessness in U.S. Cities.* "Narratives of Meanest Cities, #9—Santa Monica, California." Washington, DC.

[54] Becker, H. (ed.). 1961. *The Other Side.* Chicago: University of Chicago Press.

[55] For a discussion of crusades by moral entrepreneurs, see Gusfield, J. 1986. *Symbolic Crusade: Status, Politics and the American Temperance Movement.* Urbana: University of Illinois Press. MADD has had a significant impact on shaping legislation and policy, including influencing congressional changes of laws regulating blood alcohol levels from .10 to .08, creating drunk driving checkpoints, and increasing sanctions for drunk driving offenses. Perhaps most significant is the impact of these efforts in the reduction of alcohol-related fatalities. See National Highway Transportation Safety Administration report: Traffic Safety Facts, Alcohol Impaired Driving at http://www.nrd.nhtsa.dot.gov/pubs/811155.pdf.

[56] Goffman, E. 1963. *Stigma: Notes on the Management of a Spoiled Identity.* New York: Simon and Schuster.

[57] Ibid.

[58] Ibid.

[59] See, for instance, Doubt, K. 1989. "Garfinkel before Ethnomethodology," *The American Sociologist,* 20(3): 252–262.

[60] Schur, E. 1971. *Labeling Deviant Behavior.* New York: Harper and Row.

[61] Becker, 1969.

[62] Albert J. Reiss Jr. personal communication 1990.

[63] Ibid.

[64] See Conrad, P. 1980. "Implications of Changing Social Policy for the Medicalization of Deviance." *Contemporary Crises,* 4: 195–205. See also Szaz, T. 1984. *From Badness to Sickness.* St. Louis: C.V. Mosby.

[65] For a discussion of the creation and changes to morality as it relates to deviant behavior, see, for instance, Gusfield, 1986. See also Cohen, S. 1972. *Folk Devils and Moral Panics: The Creation of the Mods and the Rockers.* UK: MacGibbon and Kee.

[66] Ibid.

[67] See, for instance, Martin, D. 2002. "From Appearance Tales to Oppression Tales." *Journal of Contemporary Ethnography,* 31(2): 158–206. See also Laslett, B., and Warren, C. 1975. "Losing Weight: The Organizational Promotion of Behavior Change." *Social Problems,* 23(1): 69–80.

[68] See, for instance, Akers, R., and Sellers, C. 2004. *Criminological Theories,* 4th ed. Los Angeles: Roxbury.

[69] Braithwaite, J. 1989. *Crime, Shame, and Reintegration.* Cambridge, UK: Cambridge University Press.

[70] See, for instance, Makkai, T., and Braithwaite, J. 1994. "Reintegrative Shaming and Compliance with Regulatory Standards." *Criminology, 32*: 361–386. See also Zhang, L., and Zhang, S. 2004. "Reintegrative Shaming and Predatory Delinquency." *Journal of Research in Crime and Delinquency,* 41: 433–453; Miethe, T., Lu, H., and Reese, E. 2000. "Reintegrative Shaming and Recidivism Risks in Drug Court: Explanations for Some Unexpected Findings." *Crime and Delinquency,* 46: 522–541; Sherman, L. 2003. "Reason for Emotion: Reinventing Justice with Theories, Innovations, and Research." The American Society of Criminology 2002 Presidential Address.

[71] See, for instance, Rodriguez, N. 2005. "Restorative Justice, Communities, and Delinquency: Whom Do We Reintegrate?" *Criminology and Public Policy,* 4: 103–130.

[72] See, for instance, Quinney, R. 2001. *The Social Reality of Crime.* Piscataway, NJ: Transaction.

[73] Shoemaker, 2005.

[74] Sellin, T. 1938. *Culture and Crime in Conflict.* New York: Social Science Research Council.

[75] Ibid.

[76] See Coser, L. 1978 *Masters of Sociological Thought.* Chicago: University of Chicago Press.

[77] Ibid.

[78] Ibid.

[79] Marx, K., and Engels, F. 2007. *The Communist Manifesto.* London: Filiquarian.

[80] Ibid.

[81] Quinney, 2001.

[82] See Felson, M. 2002. *Crime and Everyday Life,* 3rd ed. Thousand Oaks, CA: Sage.

[83] Quinney, 2001.

[84] See Schwendinger, H., and Schwendinger, J. S. 1985. *Adolescent Subcultures and Delinquency.* New York: Praeger.

[85] Snyder, H., and Sickmund, M. 2006. Juvenile Offenders and Victimss: 2006 National Report. Washington, DC: U.S. Department of Justice, Office of Justice Programs, Office of Juvenile Justice and Delinquency Prevention. http://www.ojjdp.ncjrs.org/ojstatbb/nr2006/downloads/NR2006.pdf.

[86] For a description of the racial disproportionality clause of the JJDPA, see http://www.njjn.org/federal_activity_156.html.

[87] Office of Juvenile Justice and Delinquency Prevention, 2006.

[88] See, for instance, "Martha Stewart's Conviction Upheld." 2006. *Money,* January 6. http://money.cnn.com/2006/01/06/news/newsmakers/martha/index.htm. See also Frank, R., and Efram, A. 2009. "Evil Madoff Gets 150 Years in Epic Fraud." *Wall Street Journal,* June 30. http://online.wsj.com/article/SB124604151653862301.html; Freund, C. P. 2002. "Government Smokes: The Tobacco Settlement." http://reason.com/archives/2002/06/01/government-smokes.

After reading this chapter, you should be able to:

- Describe the Classical School of Criminology and its connection to delinquency.

- Discuss how biological factors such as exposure to violence and twin studies offer explanations for delinquency.

- Assess the psychological explanation for delinquency, including psychoanalysis, behaviorism, and cognitive theories.

- Compare and contrast a number of psychological disorders, and discuss how they contribute to delinquency.

- Formulate public policy based on individual views of delinquency.

6

Individual Views of Delinquency

Many people believe that violent youths suffer from some form of mental illness, which would explain their criminal and delinquent behavior. Consider the following case about Kevin.

Kevin's background:

- is thirteen years old
- lives in an inner-city neighborhood in an industrial city in the Midwest
- has a long history of violent behavior: as a toddler, Kevin took toys away from other children and punched them if they objected

As he got older, Kevin routinely reacted to relatively minor circumstances with an overly aggressive response, including throwing tantrums and threatening violence. Kevin's mother once commented that Kevin used violence to solve all of his problems. He has two siblings who are not prone to violence, while his father and uncles have violent tempers.

Perspectives on Kevin's outbursts:

- Kevin continues to make poor choices in terms of his behavior, and this gets him into trouble.
- Kevin's behavior is a learned response.
- Kevin has a deeply rooted psychological problem that manifests itself when he is frustrated.
- Kevin has never been held accountable for his actions and does not understand boundaries and limits to his behavior.
- Kevin is biologically predisposed toward violence.

One of the most important components to successful therapy involves offenders taking responsibility for themselves and their actions.

THINK ABOUT IT Based on what you know about Kevin's background, what explanation might you offer for his behavior?

In the previous two chapters, we discussed sociological explanations for delinquency. Social structural theories attribute delinquency to factors related to the operation of society or the physical conditions of neighborhoods. Social process theories link delinquency to learned behavior or the impact of being stigmatized and exploited by society.

One question that typically arises in the discussion of delinquency involves the actual decision to act. Regardless of the source or influence, the youth has to make the decision to engage in illegal behavior. Is delinquency a matter of some type of choice? An argument could be made that delinquents are rational actors who weigh the potential costs and benefits of their actions, and when the benefits are perceived to be greater, they engage in delinquency. The solution, then, is to increase the costs to the offender so that he or she chooses conformity over illegal behavior. This is a popular view of delinquency, as many people like to think that choices are made based on a simple and rational line of thinking. Such an approach to crime is also popular since it is consistent with an overall "get tough" philosophy.

While delinquency may be explained as a function of choice, some would argue that biological or genetic factors lead people to commit certain types of crime. Many politicians and activists scoff at these explanations, largely because the early research on the subject was flawed. However, there is evidence to suggest a link between biology and delinquency.[1]

There is also a long-standing discussion of the relationship between personality and criminal behavior. People with particular personality traits may be more susceptible to criminal influences than others. While psychological theories are discounted by many sociologists and criminal justice experts, there is value in considering both individual and environmental factors in predicting behavior. The reason for this is that neither sociology nor psychology alone has discovered a way to explain behavior consistently. A combined approach could provide a more comprehensive explanation of why youths commit delinquent acts.[2]

In this chapter, we will explore biological and psychological factors to explain delinquency. Included in this discussion will be the research on the connection between biology and crime, as well as psychological explanations for some of the more common disorders related to delinquency.

Rational Choice and Delinquency

Many factors contribute to the decision to commit delinquent acts. For some offenders, it is the benefit they receive from committing that act, or the lack of punishment. As we saw in the previous chapter on social learning theory, rewarded behavior, or behavior that goes unpunished, is likely to be repeated.

But not all delinquency is explained by rational choice. Sometimes the acts are impulsive, or offenders ignore the potential consequences. An individual's intelligence or biology also can contribute to delinquency.[3] Nevertheless, "choice theory," as it is sometimes called, remains a popular explanation for delinquency. Choice involves some type of discernment or calculation, which makes the discussion of rational actors and punishments an important one.

CLASSICAL CRIMINOLOGY

Classical School of Criminology
The particular conception of crime and criminal behavior that emerged in the eighteenth century with a focus on lawmaking and legal processing.

The particular conception of crime and criminal justice that emerged in the eighteenth century is known as the **Classical School of Criminology,** a term commonly used because its members gave rise to some of the early ideas about how to operate the criminal justice system. The Classical School was not interested in studying criminals per se, but it gained its association with criminology through its focus on lawmaking and legal processing.[4]

The eighteenth century was a period of major social change. The existing sociopolitical system, ruled by the aristocracy, was corrupt, and the type of justice one received depended on one's social position. Additionally, anyone who questioned the existing political or legal system usually faced severe punishment. Sometimes called *reformists* because of their desire to reform the existing legal system to make it more equitable, writers of the classical period called for changes in the justice process.[5]

The major explanation for human behavior during this era was hedonism—people acted on the basis of trying to maximize pleasure and minimize pain—and this concept was incorporated into the legal system. The best way to address problems like crime, then, was to make the consequences of engaging in it so difficult or painful that most people chose to avoid it altogether. The Classical School was focused on preventing crime in the first place and was responsible for the development of the concept of the **proportionality of crime,** whereby the punishment given is related to the seriousness of the offense.[6]

Under the rational choice model of crime, delinquent behavior occurs when an offender decides to break the law after considering his or her personal motivations or goals (such as the desire for money or status), his or her values and morality (such as the

How would you assess the rational choice explanations for delinquency?

proportionality of crime
A concept whereby the punishment given is related to the seriousness of the offense.

attachment to conventional society and other people), and situational factors (such as if the target appears to be an easy one and the chances of getting caught are low).[7] While it is easy to understand certain motivations, such as economic ones for property crimes, there is also something to be said for thrill-seeking as a motivating factor in the decision to commit delinquent acts. In *Seductions of Crime,* criminologist Jack Katz points out that excitement is an important factor in explaining why youths engage in shoplifting and vandalism.

According to Katz, youths choose to commit crime because of its seductive qualities: the excitement, the thrill, and the enhancement of one's self-esteem and status with peers.[8] Similarly, Albert Cohen's argument on subcultural influences notes that most delinquents engage in short-run hedonism and in delinquent acts for no other reason than to relieve the boredom many youths experience. When asked about the reason for stealing cars, Anthony B. explains:

> It was—I just—it was fun. I don't know. I just—the adrenaline rush, probably, knowin' that I just took somebody's car, and then—I don't know. Just, it was fun. If it's a nice car, I don't know, we—it just depends on what kind of car it is. Like the nicer cars, we try to act like it's ours, so everybody see us in a nice car and think it's ours. So, I don't know. We just drive around and use them as transportation.

DETERRENCE

As part of its preventive philosophy, the Classical School devoted a great deal of attention to deterring people from committing crimes. There are two types of deterrence. *General deterrence* seeks to change the behavior of an entire group of people, largely through the threat of punishment sufficient to discourage members from engaging in inappropriate acts. *Specific deterrence* uses the punishment of an individual as an example to others and involves punishing someone with an eye toward preventing that person from committing future criminal acts.[9]

How the sanction is applied can play a role in deterring criminal behavior. In order for a punishment to deter behavior, it must be swift, severe, and certain. The punishment has to occur shortly after the crime is committed, has to outweigh the benefits an offender might achieve from the crime, and has to make the offender believe that he or she will be caught and punished. If all three characteristics are operating, then the punishment can act as a deterrent to delinquent behavior.[10]

The juvenile justice process is often invoked only as a last resort, making swiftness of punishment less likely. It could be said that youths are generally not deterred by the severity of punishment because the juvenile justice system is based on *parens patriae,* which limits the power of the law since children are to be treated, not punished. Because most juvenile matters are handled informally, by either the police or juvenile court officials, the certainty of punishment is lacking as well. In general, then, the punishment offered by the juvenile justice system does not deter youths from committing delinquent acts.

"I pressured them into gettin' in the car, but, still, it was their decision. I ain't hold a gun to them. I ain't done none of that thing. They got in, their own free will."

ANTHONY B.

For more on choice theory, watch *Choice Theory: Anthony B. and Larry* and *Therapy, Guilt, Shame: Richard* at www.mhhe.com/mcnamarajd1e

In recent years, the increase in teen violence, gang activity, and drug abuse has prompted a reevaluation of deterrence strategies. Juvenile court judges have been willing to waive youths to adult court, and prior records may outweigh an offender's need for treatment and rehabilitation. Legislators also seem more willing to pass laws with mandatory sentences for very severe cases such as homicides committed by juveniles. These strategies are part of a larger movement toward treating juveniles like adult offenders. The emphasis, however, has been to increase the severity of punishment rather than to enhance all three components of the deterrence triangle. All three are needed in order for punishment to change behavior.[11]

Deterrence is based on the notion of a rational offender who makes a choice about what is in his or her best interests. If the costs are not likely to be incurred or are not sufficiently painful, the act is more likely to occur. Because they are immature, most delinquents fully comprehend neither the seriousness of their acts nor the consequences they face. This lack of understanding inhibits their ability to make good choices about their behavior.[12]

While it is easy to grasp the logic behind the rational choice perspective, several questions remain unanswered. For instance, why do most youths continue to follow the rules and laws of society even though they are poor, have little chance of gaining economic success, and may even realize that the juvenile court is limited in how severely it can punish offenders? Some youths have every reason to try to maximize their pleasure, particularly since the costs of engaging in delinquency are low; yet they do not. Conversely, why do some affluent youths break the law when they have everything to lose and little to gain? In addition, violent crimes are not adequately explained by rational choice. While some crimes might be the result of a thoughtful decision-making process, such as revenge killings, violent crimes tend to be impulsive and emotional. Offenders often do not consider the consequences before acting. Although choice theories can contribute to understanding criminal events and victim patterns, they leave a number of major questions unanswered.

KEVIN'S CASE

Did Kevin Choose Delinquency?

Recall Kevin's background:

- is thirteen years old
- lives in an inner-city neighborhood in an industrial city in the Midwest
- has a long history of violent behavior
- has male family members with anger issues

Given what you have read about rational choice theory, what do you make of Kevin's actions? Is it the case that Kevin is simply making poor choices? It seems that his behavior is getting rewarded in some way, either in actual rewards (e.g., status among peers) or in the absence of punishment (e.g., no real sanctions for his outbursts). Some experts would argue that his behavior is likely to continue until the punishment outweighs the crime.

THINK ABOUT IT In our culture, we tend to focus on severity of punishment, but what about certainty and swiftness? An emphasis on which element do you think would result in changes in behavior?

Positivist Theories

Some experts believe it is wrong to conclude that all youths choose to commit crime simply because the benefits outweigh the risks. Instead, mental and physical characteristics influence decisions. Youths who choose to engage in repeated criminal behavior may have abnormal or missing traits that influence their choices, such as a lack of impulse control.[13] These explanations are sometimes referred to as **determinism,** the belief that delinquency is not a result of **free will,** but is *determined* by other factors beyond the control of the individual, such as body configuration. A scientific approach to understanding and identifying the biological connections to criminal behavior is often called **positivism.** Physical characteristics can distinguish delinquents from nondelinquents, and those features can be observed and measured in order to predict who will become criminals.[14]

The first attempt to discover why criminal tendencies develop focused on the physical makeup of offenders, what is sometimes called *trait theory*. In *The Criminal Man,* published in 1876, Cesare Lombroso asserted that criminals were different from noncriminals and that this distinction could be seen in terms of their physical features.[15] Criminals were "biological throwbacks" to an earlier stage of human evolution.[16] After working as a physician in the Italian army, where he spent time in mental hospitals, Lombroso became convinced that there was something biologically related to criminal behavior. In his analysis of soldiers and inmates, he concluded that criminals possessed certain **atavisms,** or physical features such as large ears, protruding jaws, large canine-looking teeth, an abundance of tattoos and scars, and broad cheekbones.[17]

One of the criticisms of Lombroso's theory is that his conclusions were based only on his subjects; he never used a control group, nor did he use subjects from the general population. In other words, his research sample was skewed or biased, and his conclusions were not *generalizable,* or not applicable to the general population. The importance of his work, however, is its suggestion that there might be biological factors beyond the control of the individual that lead him or her to commit crimes.[18]

Another early explanation for delinquency and crime focused on the shape of criminals' bodies. According to this theory, criminals possessed a certain body type that lent itself to criminality. The most famous theorist in this category was William Sheldon, who wrote *Varieties of Delinquent Youth* (1949), in which he outlined his *somatyping* theory.[19] Sheldon identified three body types—endomorphs, ectomorphs, and mesomorphs—and argued that a person's attitudes, values, beliefs, and behaviors were connected to these body structures (see Figure 6-1). **Endomorphs** are round and overweight individuals. They typically have outgoing personalities but can be lazy and do not usually have the psychological drive to commit crime. In contrast, **ectomorphs** are thin and frail-looking individuals who tend to be more introverted and shy. Unlike endomorphs, these individuals exhibit a great deal of self-control over their desires and behaviors and have higher levels of motivation. However, ectomorphs also have an assortment of minor physical ailments, such as asthma, that prevent them from getting involved in the physical aspects of crime. Finally, **mesomorphs** are muscular, strong, and athletic. These individuals are active, confident, and assertive, and possess the physical and psychological makeup such that criminal acts are attractive and possible.

While Sheldon did not believe anyone fit the typology perfectly, and while a particular body type did not guarantee the person would commit crimes, the classification system uncovered how body type may be related to crime. Through a study of delinquent youths in Boston involving nearly 4,000 college students, Sheldon discovered that mesomorphs were the most likely to engage in criminal activities because they possessed the physical and psychological makeup to engage in crime.[20]

determinism
The belief that delinquency is not a result of free will, but is determined by other factors beyond the control of the individual.

free will
The ability of an individual to choose a particular course of action.

positivism
A scientific approach to understanding and identifying the biological connections to criminal behavior.

atavisms
Assumed physical features, such as large ears, protruding jaws, large canine-looking teeth, tattoos, scars, and broad cheekbones, of those prone to crime.

endomorphs
Round and overweight individuals who tend to be outgoing but lazy.

ectomorphs
Thin and frail-looking individuals who tend to be more introverted and shy.

mesomorphs
Muscular and athletic individuals who are active, confident, and assertive.

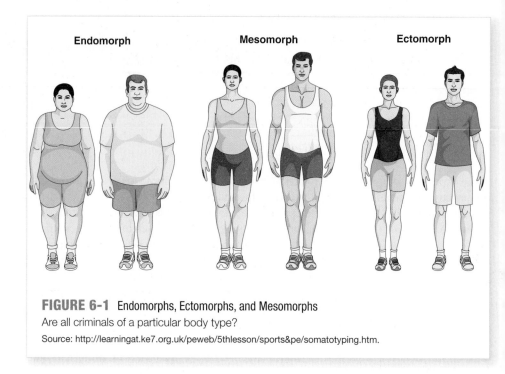

FIGURE 6-1 Endomorphs, Ectomorphs, and Mesomorphs

Are all criminals of a particular body type?

Source: http://learningat.ke7.org.uk/peweb/5thlesson/sports&pe/somatotyping.htm.

biosocial theorists
Those who believe in the interaction between biology and the environment as an explanation for delinquency.

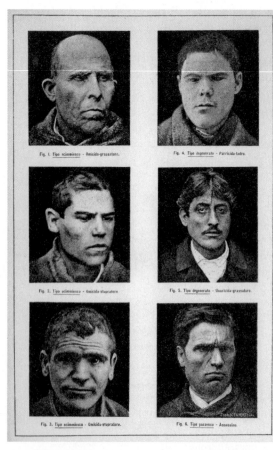

What are some of the dangers of focusing on biological links to deviance? What positive outcomes have resulted from such studies?

These early views portrayed deviant, delinquent, or criminal behavior as a function of a single factor or trait, such as body build or defective intelligence.[21] While many of the early biological explanations for delinquency were discounted due to extravagant claims or methodological flaws, today those who believe there is some type of biological basis for delinquency argue that no two people respond the same way to environmental stimuli, in part because of their biological makeup. These scholars, often referred to as **biosocial theorists,** believe there is an interaction between biology and the environment that explains delinquency.[22]

BIOCHEMICAL FACTORS

Biosocial theory focuses on three main areas:

- biochemical factors, such as the connection between ingesting lead and subsequent violent behavior
- neurological impediments, such as malfunctions in the brain that inhibit the ability to understand and grasp information
- genetic influences, such as the connection between heredity and delinquency[23]

While much has been learned about the impact of lead poisoning on behavior, there is also evidence that diet, food allergies, and certain vitamin deficiencies play a role in explaining hyperactivity, depression, and aggressive behavior.[24]

In 2005, researchers at the University of Pittsburgh School of Medicine found that exposure to lead was one of the most significant causes of violent behavior in teenagers. Humans can be exposed to lead in paint, dust, air, drinking water, food, and contaminated soil. According to Herbert Needleman, a professor of psychiatry and pediatrics, and one of the authors of the study, "exposure to lead, at doses below those which bring children to medical attention, is associated with increased aggression, disturbed attention, and delinquency. A meaningful strategy to reduce crime is to eliminate lead from the environment of children."[25]

The study showed that even very low levels of lead can affect brain development, and about 30 percent of all delinquency cases in Pennsylvania's Allegheny County could be attributed to lead.[26]

While it seems logical that chemical poisoning can create a wide variety of problems for youths, including delinquent acts, what about diet? Poor nutrition alone does not cause delinquent behavior. But might a healthy diet improve brain functioning, impulse control, school performance, and decision making? There are a number of studies, in the United States and in other countries, that consistently demonstrate a relationship between good nutrition and conforming behavior. Conversely, poor diets, especially those lacking in vitamin B, have been linked to antisocial behavior.[27] Programs that offer children vitamin supplements have witnessed physical, social, and behavioral impacts on participants.[28]

Consider the proposed correlations between environment and behavior. How might you go about preventing children's exposure to lead, for instance, or improving diet?

NEUROLOGICAL ISSUES

Neurological explanations tend to focus on imbalances in or damage to youths' brains as an explanation for their aggressive behavior, what is sometimes referred to as **minimal brain dsyfunctions (MBD).** A variety of factors such as low birth weight, injury to the brain, or inherited diseases or abnormalities can affect brain function and development.[29]

minimal brain dysfunctions (MBD)
Neurological focus on imbalances in or damage to youths' brains as a explanation for aggressive behavior.

One specific type of MBD is learning disabilities. The relationship between learning disabilities and delinquency is a controversial one. Some studies show that children who are arrested and incarcerated have higher rates of learning disabilities than children in general.[30] However, it is difficult to connect learning disabilities as a causal factor to delinquency because the data may reflect an environmental influence in how learning-disabled children are treated rather than problems related to the disability itself.[31]

Suppose you suffer from a learning disability that results in poor academic performance in school. It is a fixable problem, but you do not receive treatment for the disability. Consequently, the frustration of not performing well in class leads you to act out, which causes you to end up in the principal's office or detention, or even suspended from school. Even though teachers know or suspect you have a learning disability, they begin to treat you as if you cannot learn or, worse, to think of you as a troublemaker. And to top things off, the punishment you receive at school, coupled with your poor grades, gets you punished at home. In retaliation for being grounded by your parents, you and a friend throw rocks through the windows of a convenience store. You get caught, and when you are petitioned to juvenile court, officials examine your school record and learn that you have a history of acting out, getting into trouble, and receiving poor grades. This record is then used as part of the justification for your treatment.

Juvenile justice officials, teachers, and parents should consider other factors in addition to the learning disability that may have contributed to your behavior (recall the labeling perspective, discussed in Chapter 5). The way children are treated may better explain the relationship between learning disabilities and delinquency than the disorder itself. Some research has found that a child with a learning disability may not be any more susceptible to delinquent behavior than the child without one, but the link is related to the way the juvenile justice system treats children with learning disabilities.[32] Many questions remain unresolved about the relationship between these two factors, and further research is needed to separate the environmental influences from the biological ones.[33]

GENETIC INFLUENCES

Biosocial theorists also study the genetic makeup of delinquent offenders. These theorists believe that some youths inherit genes that predispose them toward violence and aggression. In the same way that people inherit genes for eye color or other physical features, antisocial behavior characteristics and mental disorders may be passed down from one generation to the next.[34] If antisocial tendencies are inherited, children of criminal parents should be more likely to become criminals than children whose parents have noncriminal backgrounds. Some studies demonstrate such a link, although the research should be viewed with caution since the number of cases in each study, as well as the overall number of studies, is small.[35]

Do studies of twins demonstrate a biological connection to delinquency?

twin studies
Research, using identical twins separated at birth, that would identify a genetic link to delinquency.

Some of the most famous studies identifying the genetic link to delinquency are called **twin studies.** For example, imagine two identical twins who are separated at birth. One twin goes to a conventional, loving, intact family, and the other goes to a dysfunctional, deprived, crime-prone one. Over time, both twins end up engaging in criminal behavior despite having been raised in very different environments. Is there a genetic link? There may be, but very few cases have such dramatic circumstances. The chance of having twins, even with the increased use of fertility treatments, is relatively rare.[36] Identical twins are even rarer, and the chances of twins being separated at birth and going to dramatically different households are unlikely too. The point is that while a genetic link to delinquency and crime may be real, the number of studies that demonstrate this link is quite small, which makes generalizing the conclusions of such studies to the entire population more difficult.[37] That said, twins tend to be similar in their behavior.[38] This is especially true of identical or monozygotic twins, who have delinquent behavior patterns more similar than those of fraternal or dizygotic twins.[39] All of this suggests that heredity plays some type of role in behavior.

Though the research appears to support the genetics argument, similar behavior might also be explained by the fact that identical twins get treated alike, suggesting an environmental link. Thus, while a genetic link to delinquency may exist, it is very difficult to isolate the biological factors from environmental influences in explaining behavior.

Adoption studies also demonstrate a genetic link. The basis of these studies involves children with criminal parents who have been adopted by noncriminal families, but who still become involved in delinquency. Many youths share stories about their parents' involvement with crime that are similar to what Walter describes:

> So, he [my father]—I mean, he's like—he's worse than me, really. Like, he's shot at cops before and done a whole bunch of—drank, smoked crack and marijuana and coke and all kinds of stuff. My mom was the same way.

Generally, adopted children appear to share many of the behavioral and intellectual characteristics of their biological parents even when those parents are not present in the children's lives or when the children's environment in their adoptive homes is not conducive to criminal activity.[40] While there is some type of link between parents' and their children's behavior, the research on adopted children is inconclusive.[41]

KEVIN'S CASE

Is Biology a Factor?

Recall Kevin's background:

- is thirteen years old
- lives in an inner-city neighborhood in an industrial city in the Midwest
- has a long history of violent behavior
- has a father and uncles with aggressive tendencies

It is unclear whether Kevin's behavior is caused by biological or environmental factors. Some members of Kevin's family, particularly on his father's side, have a history of violence, which might lead some to explain his tantrums in biological terms. Kevin also lives in an industrial city in a poor neighborhood. It is possible, too, that the physical dimensions of his neighborhood and contaminants in the air are causing his angry outbursts.

THINK ABOUT IT

Do you think it is reasonable to believe research that links genetics to a predisposition toward violence? Why or why not?

Another example of biological and environmental links to delinquency involves females. Traditionally, researchers who study female delinquency have concluded that girls' involvement in criminal activity could be explained in environmental terms—namely, their social affiliation with boys who engaged in delinquency.[42] Recent research suggests that perhaps biology plays a role as well: in another study, which attempted to explain female delinquency, early puberty was an important factor when it was coupled with peer group relations. Girls who go through puberty earlier than their peers are more likely to be involved in delinquency.[43] Obviously, an important question in examining this relationship is whether this tendency is due to hormonal changes or to social factors, such as peer groups.[44]

For example, in one study, girls who were physically developed compared to their peers had a 27 percent higher rate of involvement in minor delinquency (e.g., shoplifting) compared to those with average prepubescent physical development. The study also found that early-developing adolescents involved in romantic relationships had a 35 percent higher rate of involvement in smoking cigarettes and marijuana, drinking alcohol, lying to parents, and school truancy. In addition, early development often results in girls expanding their social networks. The girls in this particular study were twice as likely to have friends who participated in delinquency than girls of typical development.[45] Other studies have shown a connection between early puberty and delinquency as well.[46]

For more on parents and genetics, watch *Adoptive & Biological Parents: Zachary* at www.mhhe.com/mcnamarajd1e

INTELLIGENCE AND DELINQUENCY

Do youths get involved in crime because they are not smart enough to see the impact it can have on their lives? One of the most controversial genetic links to crime relates to intelligence. Low intelligence as an explanation for delinquency was popular in the 1960s and 1970s, and there remain a number of theorists today who argue that some youths are more likely to engage in criminal activities because of it. The primary explanation for this relationship is the fact that low intelligence inhibits one's ability to learn impulse control, as well as the value and importance of appropriate behavior.[47] Even more controversial are the beliefs held by experts who link low intelligence, as measured by IQ test scores, to race, which is then used to explain the higher crime rates among African Americans.[48]

The relationship between race and intelligence is a complicated one, largely because there may be other factors at work that cloud that relationship. While African Americans consistently score about fifteen points lower on IQ tests than the mean score for whites, this finding may have little to do with actual intelligence. Perhaps, as some critics contend, the lower score is the result of biases in the tests, which actually measure knowledge of mainstream middle-class culture more than intelligence.[49] Similarly, other critics point out that IQ tests are really designed to measure how well someone will do in an academic setting, and those students who have low levels of academic achievement tend to score lower on the test—it is not a test of intelligence as much as it is of academic achievement.

There may be factors that interfere with this relationship as well, such as the quality of the academic program, which tends to be less rigorous in inner-city schools than in affluent ones. Students from inner-city schools also tend to be poor and to not have been exposed to the same information as their affluent counterparts. Thus, these students end up scoring lower on these tests not because of intelligence but because of a lack of exposure to and familiarity with the information.[50]

In their now famous book titled *The Bell Curve,* James Q. Wilson and Richard Herrnstein contended that there is an inverse relationship between intelligence and certain types of adult crime, meaning the less intelligence a person possesses, the more likely he or she is to be involved in crime.[51] But the relationship between intelligence and delinquency is unclear. There may be genetic factors at work; some people might suffer from brain dysfunction as a result of complications at birth or from some other genetic predisposition that results in low intelligence. The level of intelligence could also be a result of some indirect relationship such as environmental influences.[52]

While much of the biological explanation for delinquency is dismissed as outdated or irrelevant, these theories do offer some insight into delinquent behavior. We know that, by themselves, they do not offer compelling explanations of delinquency since there are environmental and psychological factors that interact with genetic ones. However, there can be little doubt that there is some type of linkage; what remains unanswered is the *extent* to which genetics and biological factors play a role in delinquency.

THINK ABOUT IT

Positivist Theories

Imagine a scenario in which the study of twins would be of particular significance. Describe the study you would propose. What would you hope to learn about biological and biosocial explanations for delinquency?

Psychological Theories

As we have seen, purely biological or sociological theories cannot adequately explain delinquent behavior since there is usually an interaction between individuals and their environments. Psychological theories can be categorized in many subfields, but we will focus on four broad areas:

- **Psychodynamic theories** are rooted in the work of Sigmund Freud and his analysis of repressed emotions or obstacles created in childhood.

- **Behaviorism** argues that all behavior is learned and based on past experiences, a system of rewards and punishments, or the presence of certain stimuli that cause individuals to model the behavior of others they respect.

- **Cognitive psychology** focuses on how people understand, interpret, and process information in the decision on how to act. Included in this category is the development of moral codes that people use to guide their behavior.

- **Developmental psychology** tends to focus on the stages of development a person goes through in shaping his or her identity and behavior.

PSYCHODYNAMIC THEORY

The work of Sigmund Freud played an important part in the development of psychodynamic theory. The basis of psychodynamic theory is the assumption that human behavior is controlled by unconscious mental processes developed early in childhood.[53] For Freud, criminal behavior was the result of some type of abnormality in the individual's personality, which affected his or her decision making. These abnormalities formed early in life but had a lifelong impact on the person's thoughts and behaviors.

Freud argued that the human personality contains three components: the *id,* the *ego,* and the *superego.* The id is the internal portion of the personality, sometimes referred to as the *pleasure principle,* that continually seeks pleasure and attempts to avoid pain. The superego is created through the individual's socialization into society. This part of the personality is often equated with a person's conscience, or what society expects the person to do. It is in contrast to the id, which reflects what the individual *wants* to do. The ego, also developed in the context of being a member of society, acts like a referee in the tension between the id and the superego, providing a balance in the individual's personality that allows him or her to achieve some of what he or she wants and also what society expects of this person, as illustrated in Figure 6-2.[54]

In mentally healthy children, the three parts of the personality work together, resulting in good decision making and moral and ethical behavior. For example, suppose you are eleven years old, and one of your friends gets a brand-new bicycle for his birthday. It is a

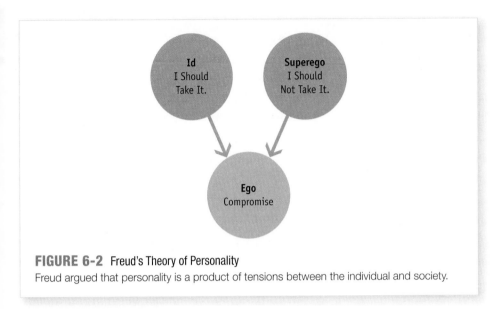

FIGURE 6-2 Freud's Theory of Personality
Freud argued that personality is a product of tensions between the individual and society.

very cool bike, and you really want to ride it. Your id urges you to take the bike from your friend and go for a ride. However, your superego tells you that stealing is wrong and you should not do it. Your ego might step in and cause you to conclude that perhaps your friend will let you ride it with his permission on occasion.

When the three elements of the personality are in conflict, however, children may be more susceptible to engaging in delinquency. For Freud, the motivations for behavior were essentially a reflection of two unmet needs—sex and aggression—and behavior was often symptomatic of those hidden or unmet needs.[55]

Psychodynamic theory suggests that events early in a child's life can result in long-term psychological difficulties. For example, if parents are more concerned with achieving their own individual pleasure than with developing their child's sense of duty, responsibility, and morality (the superego), the child's id will come to play a dominant role in his or her personality. The result could be a manifestation of self-gratification, a lack of compassion, or narcissism in relationships with others. Id-driven youths are only interested in satisfying their own immediate desires.[56]

As it relates specifically to delinquency, the psychodynamic perspective generally suggests that delinquent behavior is motivated by an unconscious urge to be punished. Children who feel unloved at home assume the reason must be their own inadequacy; hence, they deserve punishment.[57] Given the problems of interpretation and subjectivity, where the motives of individuals are not easily identified or understood, care must be taken in attributing delinquent behavior to some unobservable unmet need. In fact, there are a host of other reasonable explanations for delinquent behavior that go beyond some undefined need to be loved or to be aggressive. This is one of the limitations of Freudian theory: the absence of empirical verification, as well as the heavily subjective interpretive framework used to assess individuals' motivations.[58]

BEHAVIORAL THEORY

The discussion in the previous chapter on social learning theory draws heavily from behavioral psychology, which argues that an individual's personality, as well as his or her behavior, is learned throughout life during interactions with others. Behaviorist psychologists argue that individuals learn by observing how people react to behavior and whether that action is rewarded. If the behavior is rewarded, it is likely to be repeated. If the behavior is punished, however, it is likely to desist. This is sometimes referred to as the *Skinnerian model,* named after the "father" of operant conditioning, B. F. Skinner.[59] One promising program that uses behavioral therapy for juveniles at risk for delinquent behavior is discussed in the Theory and Practice box on page 148.

THEORY AND PRACTICE WORKING TOGETHER

The Behavioral Monitoring and Reinforcement Program

The Behavioral Monitoring and Reinforcement Program (BMRP) is a school-based intervention that helps to prevent juvenile delinquency, substance use, and school failure for high-risk adolescents. The BMRP connects behaviors to outcomes and consequences, both positive and negative. The program is often used with students who demonstrate low academic motivation, experience family problems, or have frequent or serious school discipline issues.

This two-year program begins in seventh grade and heavily monitors participants' behavior, rewarding it when appropriate and providing a high level of communication among teachers, students, and parents. For instance, program staff check school records for participants' daily attendance, tardiness, and official disciplinary actions, and they contact parents by letter, phone, and occasional home visit to inform them of their children's progress. Teachers are also involved by submitting weekly reports assessing students' punctuality, preparedness, and behavior in the classroom. The emphasis is on positive reinforcement, helping the students connect good behavior choices to some type of reward.

But the program is not just about monitoring student activity. An essential part of the process is teaching students how to make good choices in the first place and why they should do so. Each week, students meet with a staff member to review their recent behaviors, discuss the relationship between actions and their consequences, and role-play healthy and productive alternatives to problem behaviors. They are also rewarded for refraining from disruptive behavior.

Evaluations of the BMRP have demonstrated short- and long-term positive effects. At the end of the program, when compared to control students, participants had higher grades and better attendance. Moreover, results from a one-year follow-up study showed that these students, compared to a control group of students who did not participate in the program, had fewer incidents of self-reported delinquency, drug abuse, and school-based problems, including suspensions, tardiness, and low academic achievement. Additionally, a five-year follow-up study found that participants also had fewer incidents with the juvenile justice system than a control group of students.

THINK ABOUT IT

Which aspect of the BMRP do you think is most responsible for its success? Besides behavioral theory, what other theories of delinquency apply to the program?

COGNITIVE THEORY

Cognitive psychologists focus on the way people perceive the world around them and how they use information to solve problems. They argue that people use a particular process when making decisions. The first step involves acquiring the information needed to make a decision and redefining the information until it is understood. The psychological term used to describe this process is **encoding.** Once the information is digested, individuals choose from an array of responses, picking the one that is most appropriate for their needs.[60]

encoding
The process of acquiring the information needed to make a decision and redefining the information until it is understood.

One of the early psychologists, Albert Bandura, developed the concept of *self-efficacy,* which refers to the belief in one's ability to function and achieve goals in life. People who have weak self-efficacy are less confident in their own abilities to interact with others and to develop relationships with them. Self-efficacy is also related to how people interpret and respond to information and stimuli, which ultimately results in certain behaviors.

One term used to describe this process is *social cognition.* An example of social cognition that is of particular interest to researchers of delinquency is how youths process exposure to violence in the media and how that information shapes their subsequent behavior.

Violence and the Media

It is difficult to determine a causal relationship between seeing violence and carrying out violent behavior. Some research suggests that youths learn to be aggressive and engage in violence largely because they have been influenced by the media's widespread depiction of it.[61] Recent research reports extensive violence in the media, and many children and youths spend an inordinate amount of time consuming it. Some researchers conclude that reducing exposure to media violence will reduce aggression and violence in children.[62]

For instance, one study concluded that there is a strong connection between media violence and aggressive behavior in children. The researchers conducted what is called a *meta-analysis,* whereby they examined a number of different studies on violence and behavior, and found that the media teach children that violence is an effective problem-solving tool. Heavy exposure to violence in the media also results in youths becoming emotionally desensitized to the violence that exists in the real world—it does not really faze them when they hear about it on the news. Finally, media violence gives youths the impression that the world is a violent and dangerous place; therefore, they fear being victimized in a violent manner.[63]

On the other hand, some criminologists and delinquency experts argue that while the media contribute to aggressive behavior in youths to some degree, other factors play a more instrumental role in explaining juvenile violence, such as the breakdown of the family, the availability of handguns, and a cultural understanding of violence as an acceptable course of action. They assert that violence is not caused by any one factor, but that it occurs as a result of a set of circumstances and influences.[64]

A related controversy was generated in the late 1990s with the introduction of ultra-violent video games that targeted youths,

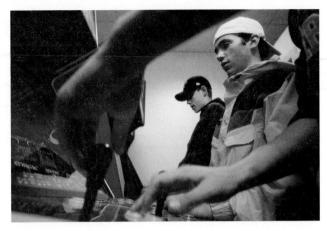

Did you play video games as a child? Do you still? Would you agree with the research that links certain aggressive behaviors to violence in the media, and video games in particular?

such as *Grand Theft Auto*. These games, experts say, desensitize youths to the impact of violence on others and glorify it so that it becomes more likely to be imitated.[65] According to one study led by Rowell Huesmann, a professor of communications and psychology at the University of Michigan, playing or watching these types of games significantly increases the risk that a viewer or player will behave aggressively both in the short term and over an extended time. Huesmann also points out that American children spend an average of three to four hours a day watching television, with more than 60 percent of television programs containing violence and about 40 percent of that percentage containing extreme violence.[66]

While there are a few studies that show some link between playing video games and acting violently, the research on this topic parallels that on the relationship between media exposure to violence and aggressive behavior.[67] In part due to the consistency of the research findings, the American Psychological Association recently concluded that viewing violence on television and other mass media contributes to aggressive behavior, especially in children.[68]

The ways in which teenagers process information can teach us about other problem behaviors as well. While the behaviors associated with aggression are certainly a problem worth addressing among today's youths, so are the behaviors that can result from psychological conditions like depression, as discussed in the Theory and Practice box on page 150.

Cognitive Skills of Youths

Cognitive psychology identifies some of the factors that go into the interpretation and use of information in youths' decision making. Some adolescents can interpret and use information properly, resulting in better, faster, and more logical decisions, even in situations that involve an array of emotions.[69] Thus, in stressful situations, youths who can objectively evaluate information and use reason and logic to come up with the right decision are much less likely to engage in delinquency.[70] This is the basis of resiliency, which we will discuss in more depth in the next chapter.

Those youths who have not had much practice or who are not adept at this process often make poor choices and engage in delinquency. One of the explanations offered by cognitive psychologists as to why delinquents seem to have poor cognitive skills, particularly under stress, is that they have not been exposed to other forms of thinking and reasoning.[71] A potential solution, then, would be to teach youths different models or lifestyles so they have an array of choices in making decisions. Many programs, such as Big Brothers/Big Sisters, incorporate this strategy through the use of mentors and positive role models.[72]

Similar to social learning theory, **cognitive theory** suggests that children who engage in delinquency may be modeling the behavior of others in similar situations. Delinquents often use a template for problem solving that tells them how to interpret and process information, as well as which conclusions to draw and the appropriate behavioral response.[73] Some children may have had early exposure to violence, which increases their sensitivity to teasing and maltreatment. Thus, if they see another person using aggression to stop teasing,

cognitive theory
The theory that delinquents use a template for problem solving that tells them how to interpret and process information, as well as which conclusions to draw and the appropriate behavioral response.

THEORY AND PRACTICE WORKING TOGETHER

Coping with Stress Course for Teenagers

The Coping with Stress (CWS) course targets adolescents who are at risk for depression. The program involves cognitive-restructuring techniques in which participants learn to identify and challenge negative or irrational thoughts that may contribute to the development of mood disorders, such as depression.

The theory behind the CWS model is that teaching adolescents new coping strategies and strengthening their current coping skills provides them with an ability to alter their moods. These skills, in turn, lower their risk of experiencing an episode of depression or some other psychological disorder.

The program uses a group-based intervention model and targets youth at risk for depression. Groups consist of six to ten adolescents who meet for forty-five- to sixty-minute intervals over a period of fifteen weeks. Separate parent meetings at the beginning, middle, and end of each adolescent course are also offered. During these sessions, parents are informed about the general topics discussed in the course, the skills taught in the adolescent groups, and the

rationale for the use of the selected techniques. The sessions are led by school psychologists and counselors who have expertise in clinical, counseling, or educational psychology, and who have experience working with teenagers.

Several studies demonstrate CWS's positive impact on youths. Further, the Promising Practices Network has shown that incidences of depression among youths who participated in the program were much lower than among those who did not. The program's impact has been shown to last for more than a year following participation.

 THINK ABOUT IT

Do you think that youths can learn how to encode new information so that the "triggers" that cause problem behavior are minimized? What types of techniques do you think a program like the CWS uses to teach youths how to cope with stress and depression?

then they may misperceive that person's behavior and conclude that violence is the solution to the problem. Given the apparent effectiveness of violence as a problem-solving tool, it is easily mistaken for an acceptable response.[74]

While violence may solve some problems immediately, over time, aggressive youths become overly sensitive and tend to overreact to any type of provocation because it is the only way they have learned how to process information. As these children mature, they use fewer cues than most people to process information. When they attack others, they may believe they are defending themselves, even though they may be misreading the situation.[75]

Piaget's Stages of Cognitive Development

Swiss biologist Jean Piaget developed a four-stage model of how the human mind processes new information. He argued that children progress through four stages of cognitive development and that they all do so in the same order:

- **Sensorimotor stage** (birth to two years old): infants build an understanding of themselves and of the objects surrounding them through interactions with the environment. Furthermore, they become able to differentiate between themselves and other objects. Learning takes place via what Piaget calls *assimilation,* or the organization and assimilation of information into what a child already knows. Learning also occurs through *accommodation,* which happens when assimilation does not work and information or objects have to be modified to fit into the existing framework of understanding.

- **Preoperational stage** (age two to four): in this stage, children are not yet able to think abstractly and need concrete physical explanations. Objects are classified in simple ways, especially by their important features.

- **Concrete operations** (age seven to eleven): Piaget argued that as children increase their experiences with the physical world, they develop a number of examples with which to compare new information. This leads to greater use of accommodation. Children begin to think abstractly and to create varying frameworks that explain their experiences and the objects with which they come into contact.

- **Formal operations** (age eleven to fifteen): in this final stage, youths have fully developed cognitively. They no longer require concrete objects to make rational judgments. Instead, they are capable of deductive and hypothetical reasoning. Their ability to think abstractly is much like an adult's.[76]

One of the important dimensions of Piaget's theory, particularly as it relates to delinquency, is that processing information occurs in a series of steps that must be completed in the proper sequence—children cannot skip a step in developing their ability to identify, understand, and use information. Another important aspect involves making decisions on how to act. While it is one thing to be able to discern and identify information that will influence children's behavior, it is quite another for them to develop the ability to make moral and ethical decisions about their actions—for instance, determining whether a certain behavior aligns with society's definition of appropriateness.

While Piaget offered an explanation about the early moral development of children, a more elaborate theory is provided by Lawrence Kohlberg.

Kohlberg's Theory of Moral Development

Explanations for delinquency tend to focus on children's and teenagers' moral development. This is particularly true of delinquent acts for which youths show little remorse. Some experts argue that youths lack morality because society has failed to teach moral codes or because youths are either unable or unwilling to learn them.[77] Whatever the case, it is worth discussing how moral behavior develops and occurs.

Psychologist Lawrence Kohlberg argued that as people mature, they progress through stages of moral development in which they cultivate a sense of integrity, fairness, and ethics. Kohlberg asserted that until they become teenagers, children are not cognitively mature enough to make many moral decisions. According to Kohlberg, moral development occurs in three stages: *pre-conventional, conventional,* and *post-conventional* (see Table 6-1).

Kohlberg believed that teenagers who were morally immature were more likely than mature youths to engage in delinquent behavior and were also less likely to recognize such actions as inappropriate. Since the theory was first presented, additional research has documented a trend suggesting that delinquent youths are morally immature and have an almost childlike self-centeredness. They are often driven by their own self-interest.[78]

DEVELOPMENTAL PSYCHOLOGY

The subfield of developmental psychology focuses on changes that occur in human beings as they age. While the subfield was originally designed to focus on infants and children, more recently, it has explored issues surrounding adolescence and the entire life span. Its relevance to juvenile delinquency involves how and in what ways individuals develop through the accumulation of information that can result in paradigm shifts or different perspectives.[79]

Developmental psychology also focuses on whether children are gifted with knowledge from birth or learn to solve problems through experiential learning.[80] As it relates to delinquency, psychologist Terrie Moffitt made one of the most significant discoveries in understanding youth behavior using a life-course perspective of crime by identifying two types of delinquents. Moffitt tries to make sense out of the fact that most youths stop

TABLE 6-1 Three Stages of Moral Development

Pre-Conventional Stage	Conventional Stage	Post-Conventional Stage
■ Children's lives are controlled by adults. ■ Children obey rules to avoid punishment.	■ Children abide by the rules. ■ Children put rules above their own self-interests. ■ Children have the cognitive capacity to understand the need for social order. ■ Children are too young to understand the implications of their actions.	■ People create their own rules in terms of attitudes, values, and beliefs they have chosen to follow.[81]
Kohlberg realized that the post-conventional stage does not guarantee people will be moral actors—there is a difference between knowing what the right thing to do is and actually doing it.		

engaging in delinquent behaviors at some point and go on to lead productive lives as adults. Others, however, start committing delinquent acts early and continue committing crimes throughout their adult lives. She refers to these two types as life-course persistent offenders and adolescence-limited offenders.[82]

Life-course persistent offenders begin their criminal careers early and remain involved in criminal activity over their life-course. In trying to explain this type of rare but dangerous offender, Moffitt argues that perhaps these offenders have limited cognitive abilities, or exhibit hyperactivity, limited self-control, and impulsivity. These types of offenders tend to see a limited array of behavioral choices in response to difficult situations.[83] Moffitt argues that physical problems are compounded by a social environment in which parents are also more likely to engage in criminal behavior, increasing the likelihood that children will model this behavior. The combination of cognitive deficiencies, poor parenting, and poverty is more likely to produce this type of offender.

In contrast, *adolescence-limited offenders*—a category that includes most juveniles—display short-term delinquency or deviant behavior, and only in certain situations. These types of offenders can choose from a host of behaviors when a situation calls for it. The deviant behavior is not ingrained in their personality, and it is easier to avoid delinquency in adulthood, because it is not understood as holding the value it did when they were youths. These offenders can distinguish when they can engage in delinquent acts and how far they can go in these activities while still engaging in conventional and socially appropriate behaviors.[84]

KEVIN'S CASE

Explaining Delinquency

Recall Kevin's background:

- is thirteen years old
- lives in an inner-city neighborhood in an industrial city in the Midwest
- has a long history of violent behavior, as does one side of his family

At this point, it is hard to know what is causing Kevin's outbursts. According to our discussion in this chapter so far, the following explanations could apply to Kevin:

- He may be modeling the behavior of his father and uncles.
- He may be getting rewarded for his actions, making them more likely to continue.
- He may have a genetic cause for his behavior.

The explanation may also be cognitive in nature. For most youths, a script, or behavior pattern, is based on the circumstances, the people involved, and the youth's feelings about the situation. Delinquents tend to have learned only one script and thus have to apply it to all situations they encounter.

 THINK ABOUT IT

Consider your reading thus far. Which explanation for Kevin's behavior seems most reasonable to you? What type of intervention would you recommend?

 THINK ABOUT IT

Psychological Theories of Delinquency

Is delinquency always a choice? Why do you think most people attribute delinquency to the bad choices made by youths? What other factors contribute to delinquent behaviors?

Psychological Disorders

Delinquent acts can often be traced back to some form of psychological or emotional disorder. In our attempt to gain a comprehensive understanding of delinquency, it helps to highlight a few common behavioral disorders. These include Oppositional Defiant Disorder (ODD), Conduct Disorder (CD), Attention-Deficit/Hyperactivity Disorder (ADHD), Bipolar Disorder, and psychopathy. Children who exhibit any of these behaviors and do not receive proper attention or treatment have higher chances of turning to delinquency.

OPPOSITIONAL DEFIANT DISORDER (ODD)

While most children are disobedient from time to time, more serious are those cases in which this behavior is more intense and lasts longer than in most children. ODD is a condition in which a child is consistently hostile toward and uncooperative with people in authority. This is particularly problematic when it disrupts normal daily activities at school, in day care, and elsewhere.[85] Many children and teenagers with ODD have other behavioral problems, such as ADHD, and various learning disabilities. They can also suffer from depression and anxiety disorders. Some children with ODD also eventually develop a more serious behavior disorder called Conduct Disorder. Symptoms of ODD include the following:

- throwing repeated temper tantrums
- excessively arguing with adults
- actively refusing to comply with requests and rules
- deliberately trying to annoy or upset others, or being easily annoyed by others
- blaming others for mistakes
- having frequent outbursts of anger and resentment
- being spiteful and seeking revenge
- swearing or using obscene language
- saying mean and hateful things when upset[86]

The exact cause of ODD is not known, but it is believed that a combination of biological, genetic, and environmental factors may contribute to it. For instance, some studies suggest that defects in or injuries to certain areas of the brain can lead to serious behavioral problems in children.[87] In addition, ODD has been linked to abnormal neurotransmitter levels. Neurotransmitters help nerve cells in the brain communicate with each other. If these chemicals are out of balance or are not present at sufficient levels, messages may not make it through the brain, leading to symptoms of ODD, and even other mental illnesses.[88]

In addition, environmental factors such as a family disruption, a family history of mental illnesses and/or substance abuse, and inconsistent discipline by parents may contribute to the development of ODD. Estimates suggest that 2–16 percent of children and teenagers have ODD. In younger children, ODD is more common in boys. In older children, it occurs about equally in boys and in girls, but it typically begins by age eight.[89]

Treatment is based on many factors, including age, the severity of symptoms, and children's ability to participate in specific therapies. Treatment may consist of some form of *psychotherapy,* a type of counseling that helps children to develop more effective ways to express and control their anger. *Cognitive-behavioral therapy* is also fairly common in the treatment of ODD. This type of therapy attempts to improve behavior by changing the way youths process information. *Family therapy* is another commonly used treatment since it serves to improve interactions and communication with family members. It also involves training parents on how to alter their children's behavior in positive ways.[90]

While there is no effective medication to treat ODD, various medicines may be used to control some of the symptoms, as well as any other mental illnesses that may be present, such as ADHD or depression. Early diagnosis and treatment is critical with this disorder; children with ODD may experience rejection by classmates and other peers because of their poor social skills, and may respond with aggressive and annoying behavior. When it is started early, treatment is usually effective in eliminating the problem.[91]

CONDUCT DISORDER (CD)

Untreated cases of ODD can result in CD, persistent patterns of behavior in which the child or adolescent simply ignores or breaks the rules of society and violates the rights of others. The child or adolescent usually exhibits these behavior patterns at home, in school, or anywhere others are present, which has a significantly negative impact on their social relationships with others.[92] Behaviors characteristic of CD include the following:

- aggression, such as bullying or intimidating others, getting into fights with friends or classmates, and being physically cruel to animals
- the destruction or vandalism of property, including setting fires
- consistent lies to parents or friends about a wide range of behaviors and activities
- property crimes, such as larceny and burglary
- status offenses, such as staying out at night when prohibited, running away from home, or regularly skipping school[93]

What types of behavior would you look for before diagnosing a child with ODD? Do you know any children who exhibit these behaviors on occasion, but who would not qualify for this diagnosis?

Many youths with CD have trouble feeling and expressing empathy for others or remorse for their own actions. They also have difficulty understanding the intent of others' behavior and other social cues. Typically, youths with CD misinterpret the actions of others as being hostile or aggressive and respond by escalating the situation into conflict.

CD is more common among boys than girls, with studies indicating that the rate among boys in the general population ranges from 6 to 16 percent, while the rate among girls ranges from 2 to 9 percent. CD can occur as early as age ten, creating social relationship problems.[94] However, recent research on CD has been very promising. For example, most children and adolescents with this disorder do not have behavioral problems or difficulties with the law as adults, and most become socially and occupationally productive adults.[95]

CD has both genetic and environmental components. Although the disorder is more common among the children of adults who themselves exhibited CD when they were young, many other factors are believed to contribute to the development of the disorder. For example, youths with CD have difficulty processing social information and social cues, which may be the result of some type of social rejection by peers at an earlier age.

Several recent reviews of the literature have identified promising approaches to treating children and adolescents with CD. The most successful approaches intervene as early as possible, are structured and intensive, and address the multiple contexts in which children exhibit problem behavior, including family, school, and the community.[96] Examples of effective treatment approaches include functional family therapy, multisystemic therapy, and cognitive-behavioral approaches that focus on building skills such as anger management. Like ODD, CD tends to occur simultaneously with other emotional and behavioral disorders of childhood, particularly ADHD and depression.[97]

ATTENTION-DEFICIT/HYPERACTIVITY DISORDER (ADHD)

ADHD is a chronic condition and is the most commonly diagnosed behavioral disorder among children and adolescents. ADHD is found in as many as one in every twenty children, and boys are four times more likely than girls to have it.[98]

Children and adolescents with ADHD are at risk for many other mental disorders. In fact, sometimes children or adolescents will have two or more of these disorders in addition to ADHD. For example, about half of those with ADHD also have ODD or CD,

TABLE 6-2 Signs of ADHD

Signs of Inattentive ADHD	Signs of Hyperactive-Impulsive ADHD
■ Short attention span ■ Easily distracted ■ Inattention to details ■ Prone to making mistakes ■ Failure to finish tasks ■ Trouble with memory ■ Inability to listen ■ Disorganization[99]	■ Fidgety ■ Inability to stay seated or play quietly ■ Too much running, climbing, and talking when not allowed ■ Blurting out responses before questions are completed[100] ■ Disregard for taking turns ■ Interruptions of others[101]
What are the similarities and differences between inattentive and hyperactive-impulsive ADHD?	

and about one-fourth have anxiety disorders. As many as one-third suffer from depression, and about one-fifth have learning disabilities. Children with ADHD are also at risk for developing personality and substance abuse disorders when they are adolescents or adults.[102]

Children and adolescents with ADHD have difficulty controlling their behavior in school and in social settings. They also tend to be accident-prone. Although some of these young people may not earn high grades in school, most have normal or above-normal intelligence.[103] There are three different types of ADHD, each with different symptoms. The types are Inattentive, Hyperactive-impulsive, and Combined Attention-Deficit/Hyperactivity disorder.

The most common version of ADHD is the Combined Attention-Deficit/Hyperactivity Disorder, which, as the name implies, is a combination of the inattentive and the hyperactive-impulsive types. A diagnosis of one of these disorders is usually made when children display several of the symptoms listed in Table 6-2 that begin before age seven and last at least six months. Generally, symptoms have to be observed in at least two different settings, such as home and school, before a diagnosis is made.[104]

Many potential causes of ADHD have been studied, but no one cause seems to apply to all young people with the disorder. Viruses, harmful chemicals in the environment, genetics, problems during the mother's pregnancy or delivery, or anything that impairs brain development can play a role in causing the disorder.[105]

Numerous medications have been used to treat ADHD. The most widely used drugs are stimulants. Stimulants increase activity in parts of the brain that appear to be underactive in children and adolescents, and experts believe this increased activity will improve attention and reduce impulsive, hyperactive, or aggressive behavior. For some children and adolescents, certain antidepressants may also help alleviate symptoms of the disorder.[106]

Like most medications, those used to treat ADHD have side effects. These medications may cause some children to lose weight, have reduced appetites, and temporarily grow more slowly. Other children may develop sleeping issues. Many doctors believe the benefits of these medications outweigh the possible side effects. Often, health care providers can alleviate side effects by adjusting the dosage.[107]

Another treatment approach, behavior therapy, involves using techniques and strategies to modify the behavior of children with the disorder. Behavior therapy may include the following:

■ instruction for parents and teachers on how to manage and modify children's or adolescents' behavior, such as by using rewards

■ daily report cards to link efforts between home and school, whereby parents reward children or adolescents for good school performance and behavior

■ special classrooms that use intensive behavior modification[108]

BIPOLAR DISORDER

Bipolar disorder (manic-depression) affects close to 1 million children and adolescents in the United States.[109] Abrupt swings of mood and bursts of energy that occur multiple times within a day, intense outbursts of temper, an inability to tolerate frustrating situations, and oppositional defiant behaviors are commonplace in juveniles experiencing the onset of bipolar disorder. These children can be silly, goofy, giddy, and elated, and then just as easily descend into periods of intense boredom, depression, and social withdrawal—some even have suicidal thoughts. Recent studies have found that from the time of initial manifestation of symptoms, it takes an average of ten years before a diagnosis is made.[110]

Bipolar disorder was once thought to be rare in children. Now researchers are discovering that not only can bipolar disorder begin very early in life, but it is much more common than ever imagined. Yet the illness is often misdiagnosed or overlooked because the symptoms of bipolar disorder may be initially mistaken for normal emotions and behaviors of children and adolescents. But unlike with normal mood changes, bipolar disorder significantly impairs functioning in school, with peers, and at home with family.

Another reason bipolar disorder is often misdiagnosed is that the disorder manifests itself differently in children and there is an overlap of symptoms with other disorders such as ODD, CD, or ADHD. Consequently, children may be treated with stimulants or antidepressants, but these medications can actually worsen the bipolar condition.[111] Manic symptoms include these:

- **severe changes in mood:** either extremely irritable or overly silly and elated
- **overly inflated self-esteem**
- **decreased need for sleep:** ability to go with very little or no sleep for days without tiring
- **increased talking:** talking too much, too fast; changing topics too quickly; unable to be interrupted
- **distractibility:** attention moving constantly from one thing to the next
- **hypersexuality:** increased sexual thoughts, feelings, or behaviors; use of explicit sexual language
- **disregard of risk:** excessive involvement in risky behaviors or activities[112]

Depressive symptoms include these:

- persistent sadness or irritable mood
- loss of interest in activities once enjoyed
- significant change in appetite or body weight
- difficulty sleeping or oversleeping
- physical agitation
- loss of energy
- feelings of worthlessness or inappropriate guilt[113]

Symptoms of mania and depression in children and adolescents may manifest in a variety of different behaviors. When manic, children and adolescents, unlike adults, are more likely to be irritable and prone to destructive outbursts than to be elated or euphoric. When depressed, children may offer physical complaints such as headaches, muscle aches, stomach aches, or tiredness. They may also start to experience frequent absences from school, poor academic performance, irritability, unexplained crying, social isolation, and extreme sensitivity to rejection or failure.[114]

Existing evidence indicates that bipolar disorder beginning in childhood or early adolescence may be a different and possibly more severe form of the illness than older-adolescent and adult bipolar disorder. When the illness begins before or soon after puberty, it is often characterized by a continuous cycle of irritability and mixed symptoms that may occur with disruptive behavior disorders, particularly ADHD or CD. Youths experiencing early bipolar disorder might also initially demonstrate symptoms of ODD or CD. In contrast, later-adolescent- or adult-onset bipolar disorder tends to begin suddenly, often with a classic manic episode, and has a more episodic pattern, with relatively stable periods between episodes.[115] Because of the nature of the behavior, some youths are diagnosed with multiple disorders, requiring medication for each one. For example, consider Austin's comments about his experiences:

> I've been diagnosed with almost everything. I have, uh, ADHD, bipolar, ADD, OCD, uh, conduct disorder, cannabis, cannabis abuse disorder. Well, it's cannabis dependence, CD, and then, um, that's pretty much all of it. But, you know, I've even been diagnosed with Tourette's, and I, I know I don't have Tourette's. . . . And you know, uh, it's probably going to follow me, because when you're diagnosed with bipolar, it prevents a lot of things. They look at that, because it's on your record. I won't be able to join the military 'cause I'm bipolar, none of that. Right now, I'm on Remeron and Wellbutrin, Remeron's to help me—you know, with mood stabilization, and then just helps me, helps me sleep at night. And then, the Wellbutrin—and they try to say I have depression, but I really don't. I'm one of the happiest kids in here. And uh, I take that for mood disorder. I, I don't like meds. They, they make me—well, these ones right here, they're okay. But most of them make me feel like I'm a zombie. You know, I'm always, you know, slow and with—my head's all light-headed and stuff. I don't like that. So, I'm, I'm happier off meds, than I am on meds. But, some of them do help and some of them don't. I plan on staying on my sleeping medication because I don't, I don't sleep at all at night. I have insomnia.

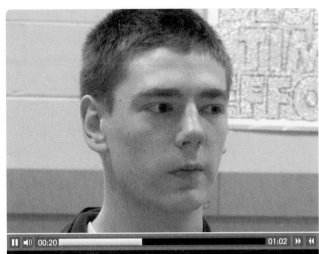

For more on psychological disorders, watch *Diagnosis of Disorders & Choice Theory: Austin* and *Testing & Counseling: Phillip* at www.mhhe.com/mcnamarajd1e

PSYCHOPATHY

Think of the most vicious and violent offender imaginable, perhaps an adult serial killer. The research on this segment of the criminal population is considerable, and many books have been written on various characteristics of individuals who engage in such crimes.[116] The FBI's Behavioral Sciences Unit dedicates itself to identifying and tracking serial killers. They have even developed a method to profile serial killers and have used it to catch some of society's most dangerous killers.[117] One of the more fascinating things we have learned about adult serial killers is that they begin their criminal behavior when they are younger and do not stop. In fact, their skills and techniques in killings are so well developed that law enforcement has a difficult time apprehending them.[118]

As it relates to juveniles, some of their crimes are so violent that experts conclude that such behavior is characteristic of a psychopathic personality, very much like their adult counterpart, the serial killer.[119] In fact, juveniles who display these tendencies may be early versions of adult offenders. Psychopathy is a serious personality disorder that is closely linked to severe antisocial behavior. The disorder is more likely to occur in boys and cuts across all racial, ethnic, and social class lines. Psychopathic individuals tend to be aggressive, narcissistic, and impulsive. They often get into trouble early in life and do not mature out of crime as many delinquents do. Psychopathic delinquents lack feelings of guilt and have little or no anxiety. They are manipulative and are unable to form intimate and lasting relationships with other people. They do not appear to be intimidated by society's sanctions and are essentially without a conscience.[120]

One of the most noted scholars of psychopathy has been Robert Hard, who developed an assessment tool called the Psychopathy Checklist Revised (PCL-R).[121] Table 6-3 outlines Hard's list of characteristics of psychopathic individuals. One of the more fascinating dimensions of psychopathy is that the problems are seen early in the person's life, even as young as three years old.[122]

Some experts distinguish between what are called *primary psychopaths,* who are youths suffering from an inability to express and process emotion, such as empathy or compassion, but whose behavior does not manifest itself in criminal activities,[123] and *secondary psychopaths,* who have the same characteristics of primary psychopaths, but whose problems

TABLE 6-3 Psychopathy Checklist Revised—Characteristics of Psychopathic Individuals

Interpersonal Relationships		Affective Dimensions to Personality	
Communicating with articulation and glibness		Lacking in guilt over actions	
Pathological lying to others		Lacking empathy toward others	
Manipulating others		Failing to accept responsibility	
Possessing high levels of self-worth		Having no ability to feel intimacy	
Antisocial Behavior		**Lifestyle**	
Having low levels of self-control		Impulsive	
Demonstrating criminal and delinquent behavior		Irresponsible	
Beginning to engage in delinquent acts at an early age		Thrill-seeking	
		Unrealistic goals[124]	

Given these characteristics, what role does guilt or remorse play in the person's thought process?

and the behaviors are developed as a way of coping with parental abuse, rejection, or some other serious trauma. Because of its environmental influences, some criminologists use the term *sociopath* to describe these types of individuals. In either case, whether it is due to environmental or biological factors, the problems such individuals present to parents, teachers, peers, and society in general make it difficult for them to fit into the larger community. Psychopathic individuals are also known for sadistic and extreme levels of violence.[125]

What is perhaps most perplexing about youths who are suffering from psychopathy is that the causes of the behavior are not completely known. Most experts contend that there are both biological and sociological factors at work. However, most of the research on psychopathic individuals focuses on adult offenders. Little is actually known about whether the standard treatment practices would be successful if used on juveniles.[126]

Some research suggests that treatment can actually make psychopaths more dangerous.[127] How? By learning to behave in socially acceptable ways and by learning how others respond emotionally, psychopaths might be able to improve their ability to manipulate and exploit others. This is not to suggest that society should not attempt to treat psychopathic youths. Rather, care must be taken in the course of the treatment that the information and skills developed are used in appropriate ways.

THINK ABOUT IT

Psychological Disorders

Compare and contrast some of the psychological disorders thought to contribute to delinquency. When diagnosed early, which of these disorders seem most treatable, and by what means?

Individual Theories and Public Policy

While there are limitations to most of the individual theories of delinquency, there remain a number of questions about the role they play in understanding youthful offenders. While the public—including some policymakers—scoff at a proposed biological or genetic connection, the fact remains that there are likely some links. As long as we perceive delinquency as simply a matter of choice, we will likely continue to view delinquents as miniature adults. It is also likely that such a narrow view will limit our understanding of delinquency, the contexts in which it occurs, and the most effective treatments and punishments to apply. As we learn more about the linkages between biology and behavior, perhaps our understanding of delinquents will demonstrate that the decision to commit a criminal act is still a choice, but there may be biological or genetic factors that influence that decision. However, until science catches up with people's perceptions, it is likely that delinquents and criminals will continue to be viewed as rational actors who make a conscious decision to commit crimes.

THE BIG PICTURE

Conclusions on Individual Views of Delinquency

- How does rational choice theory explain impulsive crimes or violent acts?
- Which of the three factors, with regard to punishment that aims to deter people's behavior, is given most attention in the United States? How would you explain such attention?
- Do you accept the notion that twin studies and adoption research help us to understand a link between biology and delinquency? Why or why not?
- Do learning disabilities, and other disorders like them, have an effect on delinquency, or do environmental influences, such as other people's responses to these disorders, have a greater impact?

Key Terms

choice theory
trait theory
Classical School of Criminology
proportionality of crime
determinism

positivism
atavisms
endomorphs
ectomorphs
mesomorphs

biosocial theorists
minimal brain dsyfunctions
encoding
twin studies
psychopaths

Make the Call ▶ Familial and Social Factors

Review the scenario below, and decide how you would approach this case.

YOUR ROLE: Counselor in a youth treatment facility

DETAILS OF THE CASE

- Most of your clients are minor offenders who have committed previous offenses, which resulted in them being sent to your facility.
- One of your clients, Steven, has made significant progress in his treatment plan and has earned the right to have visitors.
- One Saturday his father, a convicted felon with a long record of violent behavior, visits him. After the visit, Steven gets into a fight with another client, and as you intervene to break it up, Steven attacks you, breaking your wrist.
- As you and your colleagues are giving statements about the incident, one of them says that Steven should be sent to a more secure facility.

- You disagree and cite his previous record of exemplary behavior.

WHAT IS YOUR RULING?

Your supervisor asks you if you want to press charges against Steven. He points to your injury and says, "Steven made a bad choice. Now he needs to be held accountable for his actions."

WHAT DO YOU DO?

Consider:

- Did Steven's father's visit cause him to lash out?
- Are you afraid to work with your client, now that he has attacked you?
- Has Steven's previously stellar behavior convinced you that he can be rehabilitated?
- Do you think a harsh punishment—like moving Steven to another facility—would deter future outbursts?

Apply Theory to Reality ▶ Biosocial and Psychological Theories

Consider a family in which four boys, now middle-aged, were raised by parents who come from families with a history of alcoholism, drug abuse, mental illness, and antisocial behavior. Three of the sons have graduated from college, and two have gone on to receive postgraduate degrees. The third-born son, however, has a history of criminal behavior, substance abuse, chronic unemployment, and homelessness. Select one of the biosocial theories or psychological explanations discussed in this chapter to describe his behavior in relation to his brothers'.

Your Community ▶ Psychological Disorders and Academic Achievement

In addition to the information you glean from your readings, class lectures, and discussions, it is important to roll up your sleeves and immerse yourself in a topic as a researcher who gains an understanding of a problem or issue by observing or experiencing it firsthand. Through such methods, you gain a much greater appreciation of the magnitude and scope of the problem than if you were only engaged in "armchair theorizing."

■ Contact a local high school, and interview school psychologists, administrators, and teachers on campus.

■ Ask questions that will help you understand the nature of psychological disorders as they relate to academic achievement. Also ask interviewees about the relationship between these disorders and delinquent activity on campus.

■ After collecting your data, and drawing from the relevant literature, prepare a report that explains the relationship between the disorders discussed in this chapter and student learning in general.

Notes

[1] See, for instance, Hagan, J., and Foster, H. 2003. "S/He's a Rebel: Toward a Sequential Stress Theory of Delinquency and Gendered Pathways to Disadvantage in Emerging Adulthood." *Social Forces*, 82: 53–86.

[2] Ibid.

[3] Reynolds, M. 1985. *Crime by Choice: An Economic Analysis*. Dallas: Fisher Institute.

[4] See Martin, R., Mutchnick, R., and Austin, T. W. 1990. *Criminological Thought: Pioneers Past and Present*. New York: Macmillan.

[5] Vold, G., Bernard, T., and Snipes, J. 1998. *Theoretical Criminology*. New York: Oxford University Press.

[6] Ibid.

[7] Ibid.

[8] Katz, J. 1988. *Seductions of Crime*. New York: Basic Books.

[9] For the latest discussion of deterrence and crime, see Kennedy, D. 2008. *Deterrence and Crime Prevention: Reconsidering the Prospect of Sanction*. New York: Routledge.

[10] Ibid.

[11] Ibid.

[12] See, for instance, Nagin, D., and Pogarsky, G. 2003. "An Experimental Investigation of Deterrence: Cheating, Self-Serving Bias and Impulsivity." *Criminology*, 41: 167–195.

[13] See, for instance, Einstadter, W., and Henry, S. 1995. *Criminological Theory: An Analysis of Its Underlying Assumptions*. New York: Harcourt Brace.

[14] Ibid.

[15] Ibid.

[16] Ibid.

[17] For a discussion of all revised editions of Lombroso's work, see Lombroso, C., Gibson, M., and Rafter, N. H. 2006. *The Criminal Man*. Durham, NC: Duke University Press.

[18] Ibid.

[19] Sheldon, W. 1949. *Varieties of Delinquent Youth*. New York: Harper.

[20] Ibid.

[21] Einstadter and Henry, 1995.

[22] See, for instance, Shah, S. A., and Roth, L. H. 1974. "Biological and Psycho-physiological Factors in Criminality." In Glaser, D. (ed.), *Handbook of Criminology*. Chicago: Rand McNally.

[23] Ibid.

[24] See, for instance, Werbach, M. R. 1995. "Nutritional Influences on Aggressive Behavior." *Journal of Orthomolecular Medicine*. Available at http://www.orthomolecular.org/library/articles/werbach.shtml.

[25] Lanphear, B. P., Hornung, R., Khoury, J., Yolton, K., Baghurst, P., Bellinger, B. C., Canfield, R. L., Dietrich, K. N., Bornschein, R., Greene, T., Rothenberg, S. J., Needleman, H. L., Schnaas, L., Wasserman, G., Graziano, J., and Roberts, R. 2005. "Low-Level Environmental Lead Exposure and Children's Intellectual Function: An International Pooled Analysis." *Environmental Health Perspectives*, 113(7):

894–899. http://www.ncbi.nlm.nih.gov/pmc/articles/PMC1257652/.

[26] Ibid.

[27] See, for instance, Schoenthaler, S., and Bier, I. 2000. "The Effect of Vitamin-Mineral Supplementation on Juvenile Delinquency among American Schoolchildren." *Journal of Alternative and Complementary Medicine*, 6:7–17.

[28] Ewin, J., and Horrobin, D. 2001. *Fine Wines and Fish Oil*. London: Oxford University Press.

[29] See, for instance, Fayed, N., Modrego, P., Castillo, J., and Davila, J. 2007. "Evidence of Brain Dysfunction in Attention Deficit-Hyperactivity Disorder: A Controlled Study with Proton Magnetic Resonance Spectroscopy." *Academic Radiology*, 14 (9): 1029–1035.

[30] See Coalition for Juvenile Justice. 2001. *Abandoned in the Back Row: New Lessons in Education and Delinquency Prevention*. Available at http://www.juvjustice.org. See also National Center on Education, Disability and Juvenile Justice. 2005. *Special Education in Correctional Facilities*. http://www.edjj.org/Publications/pub05_01_00.html.

[31] See, for instance, the National Research Center on Learning Disabilities. http://www.nrcld.org/symposium2003/kavale/kavale9.html.

[32] Ibid.

[33] Ibid.

[34] Boutwell, B. B., and Beaver, K. M. 2007. "A Biosocial Explanation to Delinquency Abstention." Paper presented at the annual meeting of the American Society of Criminology, Atlanta.

http://www.allacademic.com/meta/p189528_index.html.

35 See, for instance, Cassells, E., and Bernstein, D. A. 2007. *Criminal Behavior.* New York: Routledge.

36 See American Society for Reproductive Medicine at http://www.asrm.org/.

37 Button, T. M., Stallings, M.C., Rhee, S. H., Corley, R. P., Boardman, J. D., and Hewitt, J. K. 2007. "Perceived Peer Delinquency and the Genetic Predisposition for Substance Dependence Vulnerability." *Drug and Alcohol Dependence,* 100(1-2): 1–8.

38 See Rutter, M. 2007. *Genes and Behavior: Nature and Nurture Explained.* Malden, MA: Blackwell.

39 See, for instance, Jones, C. M. 2007. "Genetic and Environmental Influences on Criminal Behavior." http://www.personalityresearch.org/papers/jones.html.

40 DiLalla, L. F., and Gottesman, I. I. 1989. "Heterogeneity of Causes for Delinquency and Criminality: Lifespan Perspectives." *Development and Psychopathology,* 1(4): 339–349.

41 See, for instance, Kendler, K. S., Jacobson, K., Myers, J. M., and Eaves, L. J. 2008. "Genetically Informative Development Study of the Relationship between Conduct Disorder and Peer Deviance in Males." *Psychological Medicine,* 37(7): 1001–1011.

42 Cauffman, E., Farruggia, S. P., and Goldweber, A. 2008. "Bad Boys or Poor Parents: Relations to Female Juvenile Delinquency." *Journal of Research on Adolescence,* 18(4): 699–712.

43 Ibid.

44 Haynie, D. L. 2003. "Contexts of Risk? Explaining the Link between Girls' Pubertal Development and Their Delinquency Involvement." *Social Forces,* 82(1): 355–397.

45 Ibid.

46 Ibid.

47 See, for instance, West, D. J., and Farrington, D. P. 1973. *Who Becomes Delinquent?* London: Heinemann.

48 See, for instance, Kirkegaard-Sorensen, L., and Sarnoff, A. 1977. "A Prospective Study of Predictors of Criminality: Intelligence." In Mednick, A., and Christiansen, K.O. (eds.), *Biosocial Basis of Criminal Behavior.* New York: Gardner.

49 See, for instance, Jencks, C., and Phillips, M. (eds.). 1998. *The Black-White Test Score Gap.* Washington, DC: The Brookings Institute.

50 Ibid.

51 Wilson, James Q., and Herrnstein, R. J. 1985. *Crime and Human Nature.* New York: Simon and Schuster.

52 See Ward, D. A., and Tittle, C. 1994. "IQ and Delinquency: A Test of Two Competing Explanations." *Journal of Quantitative Criminology,* 10: 189–200. See also Hirschi, T. 2002. *The Craft of Criminology: Selected Papers.* New Brunswick, NJ: Transaction; Nash, C. L.,

Stutzman, M., Ullman, D., Hansen, D., and Flood, M. F. 1998. "The Relationship of Individual and Family Factors with Clinical Profiles of Delinquent Youth: Implications for Assessment and Intervention." *American Sociological Review,* 42: 512–587.

53 See, for instance, Berzoff, J., Flanagan, L. M., and Hertz, P. 2002. *Inside Out and Outside In: Psychodynamic Clinical Theory and Practice in a Multicultural Context.* Lanham, MD: Rowan and Littlefield.

54 See Feldman, R. S. 2004. *Child Development.* Upper Saddle River, NJ: Prentice-Hall.

55 Freud, S. 2004. *The Origin and Development of Psychoanalysis.* New York: Kessinger.

56 Ibid.

57 Ibid.

58 Ibid.

59 Ferster, C. B., and Skinner, B. F. 1957. *Schedules of Reinforcement.* Washington, DC: American Psychological Association.

60 See, for instance, Eysenck, M. W., and Keane, M. T. 2005. *Cognitive Psychology.* New York: Psychology Press.

61 See, for instance, Loeber, R., and Hay, D. 1997. "Key Issues in the Development of Aggression and Violence from Childhood to Early Adulthood." *Annual Review of Psychology,* 48: 371–410.

62 See, for instance, Anderson, C., Berkowitz, L., Donnerstein, E., Huesmann, R., Johnson, J., and Linz, D. 2004. "The Influence of Media Violence on Youth." *Psychological Science in the Public Interest,* 4(3): 81–110.

63 See, for instance, Olson, C. 2004. "Media Violence Research and Youth Violence Data: Why Do They Conflict?" *Academic Psychiatry,* 28: 144–150.

64 See, for instance, Boxer, P. 2009. "The Role of Violent Media Preference in Cumulative Developmental Risk for Violence and General Aggression." *Journal of Youth and Adolescence,* February.

65 For a discussion of the facts and myths regarding the influence of video games and youth violence, see Anderson, C. 2003. "Violent Video Games: Myths, Facts, and Unanswered Questions." *Psychological Science Agenda,* 16(5). Available at http://www.apa.org/science/psa/sb-anderson.html.

66 University of Michigan. 2007. "Violent TV, Games Pack A Powerful Public Health Threat." *ScienceDaily.* Retrieved October 17, 2009, from http://www.sciencedaily.com/releases/2007/11/071127142134.htm.

67 See, for instance, Ferguson, C. 2007. "Evidence for Publication Bias in Video Games Violence Effects Literature: A Meta-analytic Review." *Aggression and Violent Behavior,* 12: 470–482.

68 See, for instance, Rowell Huesmann, L. R., Moise-Titus, J., Podolski, C., and Eron, L. D. 2003. "Longitudinal Relations between Children's Exposure to TV Violence and Their Aggressive

and Violent Behavior in Young Adulthood: 1977–1992." *Developmental Psychology,* 39(2): 201–221.

69 See, for instance, Tugade, M. M., and Fredrickson, B. L. 2001. "Positive Emotions and Emotional Intelligence." In Feldman, B. L., and Salovey, P. (eds.), *The Wisdom of Feelings: Processes Underlying Emotional Intelligence.* New York: Guilford.

70 Ibid.

71 See, for instance, Mitchell, J. P., Macrae, C. N., and Banaji, M. R. 2004. "Encoding-Specific Effects of Social Cognition on the Neural Correlates of Subsequent Memory." *Journal of Neuroscience,* 24(1): 4912–4917.

72 This is the basis of programs that use mentors or positive role models such as Big Brothers/Big Sisters. For more information, see http://www.bbbsa.org.

73 See, for instance, Coralijn, N., de Catro, B. O., and Koops, W. 2005. "Social Information Processing in Delinquent Adolescents." *Psychology, Crime and Law,* 11: 363–375. For a discussion of "scripts" used by delinquents, see Huesmann, R. L., and Eron, H. 1989. "Individual Differences and the Trait of Aggression." *European Journal of Personality,* 3: 95–106.

74 See, for instance, Williams, L. M., and Herrera, V. M. 2007. "Child Maltreatment and Adolescent Violence: Understanding Complex Connections." *Child Maltreatment,* 12: 203–207.

75 Ibid.

76 See, for instance, Keene, T. 2009. *An Introduction to Child Development,* 2nd ed. Los Angeles: Sage.

77 See, for instance, Turiel, E. 2002. *The Culture of Morality: Social Development, Context, and Conflict.* Oxford, UK: Cambridge University Press.

78 Kohlberg, L. 1981. *Essays on Moral Development, Vol. I: The Philosophy of Moral Development.* San Francisco: Harper and Row.

79 Shaffer, D. R., and Kipp, K. 2009. *Developmental Psychology: Childhood and Adolescence,* 9th ed. New York: Cengage Learning.

80 Ibid. See also Bransford, J., Brown, A., and Cocking, R. (eds.). 1999. *How People Learn: Brain, Mind, Experience and School.* Washington, DC: National Academic Press.

81 Kohlberg, 1981.

82 Moffitt, T. E. 1993. "Adolescent-Limited and Life-Course-Persistent Antisocial Behavior: A Developmental Taxonomy." *Psychological Review,* 100: 674–701.

83 Ibid.

84 Ibid.

85 Essau, C. (ed.). 2003. *Conduct and Oppositional Defiance Disorders: Epidemiology, Risk Factors, and Treatment.* Mahwah, NJ: Lawrence Erlbaum.

86 Ibid.

87 Breen, M. J., and Alterpeter, T. S. 1990. *Disruptive Behavioral Disorders in Children.* New York: Guilford.

[88] Ibid.

[89] For a discussion of the symptoms and incidence of ODD, see American Academy of Child and Adolescent Psychiatry. "Oppositional Defiance Disorder." Available at http://www .aacap.org.

[90] Essau, 2003.

[91] Ibid.

[92] See American Academy of Child and Adolescent Psychiatry. 1997. "Practice Parameters for the Assessment and Treatment of Children and Adolescents with Conduct Disorder." *Journal of the American Academy of Child and Adolescent Psychiatry,* 36 (supplement); 122S–139S.

[93] U.S. Department of Health and Human Services, Substance Abuse and Mental Health Administration. *Children's Mental Health Facts: Children and Adolescents with Conduct Disorder.* http://mentalhealth.samhsa.gov/child.

[94] Ibid.

[95] See, for instance, Robins, L. N. 1996. "Deviant Children Grown Up." *European Child and Adolescent Psychiatry,* 5(1): 44–46. See also Pruitt, D. 2000. *Your Child: Emotional, Behavioral and Cognitive Development.* Washington, DC: American Academy of Child Psychiatry.

[96] See, for instance, Hill, J., and Maughan, B. 2001. *Conduct Disorders in Children and Adolescents.* Oxford, UK: Cambridge University Press.

[97] Ibid.

[98] See National Institute of Mental Health. *Attention-deficit/ Hyperactivity Disorder Fact Sheet.* Available at http://www.nimh.nih.gov/. . ./attention-deficit-hyperactivity-disorder/complete-index.shtml.

[99] See U.S. Department of Health and Human Services, Department of Mental Health Administration. *Mental Health Facts: Children and Adolescents with Attention-deficit/Hyperactivity Disorder.* Available at http://family.samhsa.gov/redirect.asp?ID=286.

[100] Ibid.

[101] Ibid.

[102] National Institute of Mental Health, *Attention-deficit Hyperactivity Disorder Fact Sheet.*

[103] Ibid.

[104] U.S. Department of Health and Human Services, Department of Mental Health Administration, *Mental Health Facts: Children and Adolescents with Attention-deficit Hyperactivity Disorder.*

[105] National Institute of Mental Health. *Attention-deficit/ Hyperactivity Disorder Fact Sheet.*

[106] Ibid.

[107] Ibid.

[108] U.S. Department of Health and Human Services, Department of Mental Health Administration. *Mental Health Facts: Children and Adolescents with Attention-deficit/Hyperactivity Disorder.*

[109] Castle, L. R., and Whybrow, P. C. 2003. *Bipolar Demystified: Mastering the Tightrope of Manic Depression.* New York: De Capo Press.

[110] Ibid.

[111] See, for instance, Miklowitz, D. J., and George, E. L. 2007. *The Bipolar Teen.* New York: Guilford.

[112] National Institute of Mental Health. 2009. *Bipolar Disorder.* Available at http://www.nimh.nih.gov/health/publications/bipolar-disorder/complete-index.shtml.

[113] Ibid.

[114] See American Academy of Child and Adolescent Psychiatry. 2008. *Bipolar Disorder in Children and Teens.* Available at http://aacap.org/page.ww?name=Bipolar+Disorder+In+Children+And+Teens&section=Facts+for+Families

[115] Ibid. See also Miklowitz and George, 2007.

[116] See, for instance, Keppel, R., and Birnes, W. J. 2007. *The Psychology of Serial Killer Investigations.* New York: Academic Press. See also Douglas, J. 2000. *The Anatomy of Motive.* New York: Pocket.

[117] See http://www.fbi.gov/hq/td/academy/bsu/bsu.htm.

[118] See, for instance, Fox, J. A. 2005. *Extreme Killing: Understanding Serial and Mass Murder.* Belmont, CA: Sage.

[119] Ibid.

[120] Breen, M. J., and Alterpeter, T. S. 1990. *Disruptive Behavioral Disorders in Children.* New York: Guilford; Patrick, C. 2006. *Handbook of Psychopathy.* New York: Guilford. See also Herve, H., and Yuille, J. 2006. *The Psychopath: Theory, Research, and Practice.* Mahwah, NJ: LEA Press.

[121] Hare, R. D. 1991. *The Hare Psychopathy Checklist Revised.* Toronto: Multi-Health Systems.

[122] Glenn, A., Raine, A., Venables, P., and Mednick, S. 2007. "Early Temperamental and Psychophysiological Precursors of Adult Psychopathic Personality." *Journal of Abnormal Psychology,* 116: 508–518.

[123] See, for instance, Vaughn, M., Litschge, C., DeLisi, M., Beaver, K., and McMillen, C. 2008. "Psychopathic Personality Features and Risks for Criminal Justice System Involvement among Emancipating Foster Youth." *Children and Youth Services Review,* 30: 1101–1110.

[124] Adapted from Hare, R., and Neumann, C. 2008. "Psychopathy as a Clinical and Empirical Construct." *Annual Review of Clinical Psychology,* 4: 217–246.

[125] Porter, S., Woodworth, M., Earle, J., Drugge, J., and Boeer, D. 2003. "Characteristics of Sexual Homicides Committed by Psychopathic and Non-psychopathic Offenders." *Law and Human Behavior,* 27: 457–470.

[126] See Harris, G., and Rice, M. 2006. "Treatment of Psychopathy: A Review of Empirical Findings." In Patrick, C. (ed.), *Handbook of Psychopathy.* New York: Guilford.

[127] See, for instance, Rice, M., Harris, G., and Cormier, C. 1992. "A Follow-up of Rapists Assessed in a Maximum Security Psychiatric Facility." *Journal of Interpersonal Violence,* 5: 435–448.

After reading this chapter, you should be able to:

- List the characteristics of good parenting and its implications.

- Discuss resiliency in children and how it reduces delinquent behavior.

- Employ the different types of families in highlighting current trends in family structure.

- Describe the societal changes that have resulted in restructuring American families.

- Identify and analyze the relationship between aspects of family structure, such as family size and birth order, and delinquency.

- Trace how problems such as abuse, neglect, divorce, and foster care lead to delinquency issues.

- Interpret how family structure relates to delinquency and public policy.

7

Family and Delinquency

Many people believe that delinquency is caused by birth order or family size. That is, younger children, particularly those in large families, are more likely to get away with inappropriate behavior than their older siblings and are also more likely to become delinquent. However, consider the following case about Ryan.

Ryan's family situation:

- is a twelve-year-old boy
- lives in California with his mother and stepfather
- is one of four children; has an older brother, Timmy, age thirteen, and two younger sisters, Susie, age ten, and Grace, age eight

Ryan's reputation:

- has thrown rocks at neighbors' windows, broken into their vehicles and stolen personal items, and vandalized school property
- has threatened his teachers, bullied his classmates, gotten into fights with other students, and broken into their lockers after school

Teachers, school administrators, and neighbors have all talked to Ryan's parents about his behavior and have even called the police on several occasions. His parents are surprised and exasperated since Ryan's siblings are "model" children, and they believe they have done a good job raising their children. However, despite stern lectures and revocation of privileges, Ryan's behavior has not changed. Some of the neighbors think it is because his parents do not set adequate boundaries for Ryan, who has gotten "lost" in a large family with many children, too many activities, and frazzled parents who fail to maintain some level of order.

When trying to find an explanation for Ryan's behavior, community members seem to be asking the following questions:

- Does Ryan's birth order and family size play a role in his delinquency?
- Might the high level of social activity at home allow Ryan to go unsupervised?
- Is Ryan's behavior simply a matter of poor judgment and choices?

How do family structure, parenting, abuse, and neglect contribute to delinquency?

THINK ABOUT IT Given what you know about rational choice theory and social and psychological explanations for delinquency, how might you approach Ryan's case?

As we saw in Chapter 4 on social structural theories, before we can understand the impact of social institutions on delinquency, we must have a context or framework for understanding their connection. The structure of families, for example, has changed greatly in recent decades and is continuing to change. The general assumption is that this has had an impact on delinquency. For instance, cohabitation, divorce, and the entry of women into the workforce have all had an effect on the development of children and their likelihood of adopting delinquent behaviors.

In this chapter, we will also explore the ways in which parents can reduce their children's risk of becoming delinquent. For instance, dynamics *within* the family and the social interaction between parents and children, or between siblings, may also offer a key to understanding the nature of delinquency.

According to the U.S. Census Bureau, a **family** consists of "two or more people, one of whom is the householder, related by birth, marriage, or adoption and residing in the same housing unit." A family differs from a household, which "consists of all people who occupy a housing unit regardless of relationship. A household may consist of a person living alone or multiple unrelated individuals or families living together."[1]

The function of a family is to meet its members' needs for food, shelter, and intimacy, as well as to provide socialization and the transmission of culture from one generation to the next.[2] Most discussions of family and delinquency center around the **nuclear family,** which is a family unit composed of parents and their children.[3] This smaller unit contrasts with the extended family, which often includes grandparents, uncles, aunts, and others living in the household with the nuclear family. The nuclear family was the standard structure in the United States for many years.

In recent years, however, this structure has changed dramatically. The result is the creation of a variety of family units, such as the following:

- **Single-parent families:** while many people think of single-parent families as those that live in poverty or are the product of divorce, these are not the only explanations for this circumstance. The death of a spouse can create one, as can the situation in which one of the parents is unknown, is absent from the family, or has abandoned the spouse and children. Social class plays an important role in the success of a single-parent family. Parents who have sufficient wealth or extended family members who can offer assistance in raising the children tend to be better able to adapt to such a circumstance.[4]

- **Blended families:** these types of families consist of two adults who remarry after a divorce and bring their children with them into the new marriage. They can also consist of couples who already have children from a previous marriage and decide to add to the family once they have remarried. It is likely that in such situations, the children will experience some period of adjustment, during which they may act out or rebel in response to the new relationship.[5]

- **Cohabitating parents:** the institution of marriage has lost some of its appeal in many people's minds. As a result, many adults choose to live together without being formally married.[6] Some of these couples have children from previous relationships, while others decide to start a family without being married.[7]

- **Same-sex families:** gay and lesbian couples are also families. They might have children from a previous heterosexual relationship, or they might adopt a child or use a surrogate

family
A group of individuals related by blood, marriage, or adoption who meet its members' needs for food, shelter, and intimacy, as well as providing socialization and transmitting culture from one generation to the next.

nuclear family
A smaller unit composed of parents and their children, but not including grandparents, uncles, aunts, and others living in the household.

to conceive one. While there is disagreement as to whether gays or lesbians can provide a safe and healthy environment for children as parents, the reality is that they do raise children adequately despite the disapproval expressed by a portion of society.[8]

Good Parenting

What is the difference between a good parent and a bad one? The research tells us that there are documented behaviors that parents can display that protect or insulate youths from engaging in delinquent acts.[9] According to some experts, **good parenting** involves honesty, empathy, self-reliance, kindness, cooperation, self-control, and cheerfulness. Good parenting also promotes the development of intellectual curiosity in children, the pursuit of academic success, the motivation to learn, and a desire to succeed in life,[10] and guards against destructive behaviors by teaching youths how to cope with stress and avoid anxiety, depression, delinquency, and other problems.[11] In sum, good parenting helps children to become better adjusted psychologically and sociologically. The research consistently shows that being a good parent involves clarity, consistency, flexibility, and love.[12]

What terms would you use to describe your family unit?

CLARITY

Clarity refers to parents setting a clear example of appropriate behavior and being clear in their expectations for their children's behavior. Psychologists remind us that children model or imitate their parents' behavior, which means that parents must always be mindful of the impact their actions can have on their children.[13] Parents who model conforming behavior tend to have children who behave that way; conversely, children of criminals tend to imitate their parents' behavior.[14]

good parenting
Behaviors, such as honesty, empathy, self-reliance, kindness, cooperation, and self-control, that parents can display that protect or insulate youths from engaging in delinquent acts.

Clarity also refers to the detail with which parents explain their expectations to children. If you are a parent and tell your daughter that she is not to wear "revealing" clothing to school, you are leaving a lot of room for interpretation. While you have conveyed your expectations about appropriate behavior, you have not adequately articulated what "revealing" really means. On the other hand, if you are explicit in your definition and provide examples to illustrate your point, then your daughter will better understand your standards and expectations. While your daughter might not agree with the explanation or the reasons for it, you have modeled appropriate behavior and been very clear in defining what is acceptable and what is not.

CONSISTENCY

Related to clarity is consistency. Children need boundaries, and parents need to establish and enforce those boundaries.[15] An example of setting boundaries would be teaching your children to inform you where they are at all times, whom they are with, and what they doing. While it may seem excessive, or even an invasion of their privacy, research suggests that setting reasonable boundaries for children is a key component in preventing delinquency.[16]

If parents are going to the trouble of establishing rules, they also need to be consistent in their application of them. Psychologists remind us that children need structure *and* consistency so they can learn the boundaries of acceptable behavior.[17] If the rules vary too much or are unpredictable, children will have no sense of where their parents draw the line. Parents also need to let children know on which issues there is no negotiating (e.g., crossing the street alone as a toddler or taking the car without permission as an adolescent) and which ones can be discussed (e.g., curfew on weekends, if there is a special event such as a prom or important game).

FLEXIBILITY

Flexibility refers to the ability of parents to adapt their parenting style to each child and to know when discipline or corrective action is needed. While most children think that there should be a "one size fits all" model of parenting whereby all the children in the household are treated the same way, it is more important to tailor the parenting style to fit the learning abilities of each child.[18]

Suppose you have an older sister who was self-motivated and responsible, and did not need a lot of direction or counsel. As a result, your parents took a hands-off approach with her. But what if you were the type of child who needed a lot of structure and guidance? Just because the hands-off approach worked with your sister does not mean it was the best approach for your parents to take with you.

When boundaries are broken, how parents respond is critical to children's development. Research shows that physical punishment is the least effective way of disciplining children.[19] Children who are spanked, hit, or slapped are more prone to fighting with other children, more likely to become bullies, and more likely to use aggression to solve disputes with others.[20] We will have more to say on this later in the chapter, but for now, note that not only are physical forms of discipline ineffective, but they can cause a host of problems for children later in life.[21]

LOVE

Some parents think that buying gifts for their children is the way to show love. Or they may feel that ignoring certain misbehaviors demonstrates an understanding of what it is like to be a teenager. While this may work for some children, physical expressions of warmth and affection are more important to the proper development of children than gift giving or leniency.[22] Good parenting is about showing children genuine affection and love. The absence of love can easily lead children to act out and engage in delinquent behavior.

While it may be easier to imagine good parenting in affluent or highly educated families, good parenting knows no social class limits. Good parenting benefits youths who grow up in disadvantaged families and neighborhoods as well as wealthy ones. What makes good parenting especially important in poorer neighborhoods is that there are fewer opportunities for success and more influences that can lead youths astray.

As we saw in Chapter 4, in the discussion of social disorganization theory, one of the problems that can lead youths to crime and delinquency is a lack of consistency in the value systems of some neighborhoods. In Shaw and McKay's explanation, for example, delinquency occurs because youths have to choose between conventional (family) values and those of their delinquent peers. Similarly, Miller's classification of focal concerns suggests that delinquency occurs because of a different value system that exists in lower-class culture. Additionally, the subculture of violence hypothesis suggests that violence is socially acceptable in some areas largely because conventional means of solving problems do not work.

Despite these influences, some youths manage to thrive in such situations. This adaptability in the face of adversity, sometimes referred to as **resiliency,** has its origins in the lessons good parents teach their children. Some youths grow up in neighborhoods where they are at much greater risk of getting involved in crime, gangs, drugs, and delinquency, but do not. What makes these youths different? What allows them to withstand the pressures and to overcome the obstacles of disadvantaged communities or families? As you read through the section on resiliency, think about what happens to young people who do not possess these characteristics or parents who do not promote them in their families.

resiliency
Adaptability in the face of adversity.

Resiliency

While a host of family problems can contribute to the development of delinquent behavior, few children who come from troubled families actually go on to become delinquents. In fact, depending on their levels of resiliency, some youths are able to withstand and overcome significant social, physical, and economic obstacles and trauma in their lives, and become law-abiding citizens. Table 7-1 summarizes the key characteristics of resilient children and youths.

The research on resiliency indicates that characteristics of resilient children can be identified and nurtured through the use of what are referred to as *developmental assets*. Experts believe that there are forty developmental assets that allow youths to be resilient in the face of adversity;[23] these assets are listed in Table 7-2. Most youths possess about twelve, but the more assets, the greater the likelihood of resiliency. As Table 7-2 illustrates, these assets consist of positive experiences, relationships, opportunities, and personal qualities that young people need to grow up healthy, caring, and responsible.[24]

Surveys of almost 2.2 million students in grades six to twelve reveal that developmental assets have powerful influences on adolescent behavior. Regardless of gender, ethnic heritage, economic situation, or geographic location, these assets promote positive behaviors and attitudes, and help protect young people from many problem behaviors. For example, research suggests that delinquency is more likely when youths have few constructive outlets to occupy their time.[25] Thus, assets 17–19 focus on keeping young people involved in productive activities outside the classroom, while assets 23 and 25 focus on spending time completing homework or reading for pleasure. Asset 20 focuses on spending time at home with family, which has been shown to improve communication and help children develop positive relationships with parents.

In addition, research suggests that the development of these assets can result in higher levels of academic success, increase a young person's sense of responsibility to volunteer in their communities, and improve their confidence and self-esteem. These attachments to

TABLE 7-1 Characteristics of Resilient Children and Youths

Temperament	Have an easygoing disposition, are not easily upset, have a good sense of self-control
Problem-Solving Skills	Are able to engage in high levels of abstract thinking, are flexible, adapt to stressful situations
Social Competence	Demonstrate empathy and caring, good communication skills, and a sense of humor; get along with others
Autonomy	Have a sense of self-awareness, are able to act independently, demonstrate self-efficacy and an internal focus of control
Sense of Purpose and Future Orientation	Are able to plan for the future, to establish goals, to be achievement-oriented and persistent, and to hold religious beliefs that convey a sense of meaning in life
Sense of Optimism	Maintain a hopeful outlook, employ effective coping strategies
Academic and Social Success	Excel in reading comprehension and math skills[26]

Resilient children tend to be optimistic, handle adversity well, and tend to be introspective.

TABLE 7-2 Developmental Assets for Youths Age Twelve to Eighteen

External Assets

Support
1. *Family support.* Parents and relatives provide love and nurturing.
2. *Positive family communication.* Youths have good relationships with parents.
3. *Other adult relationships.* Three or more nonparental adults offer support.
4. *Caring neighborhood.* Neighbors care about youths.
5. *Caring school climate.* Schools encourage and care about youths.
6. *Parental involvement in school.* Parents are actively involved in education.

Empowerment
7. *Community values.* Youths believe that adults in the community value them.
8. *Youth as resources.* Youths are given a meaningful role within the community.
9. *Service to others.* Youths volunteer in the community one or more hours per week.
10. *Safety.* Youths feel physically safe at home, in school, and in the community.

Boundaries and Expectations
11. *Family boundaries.* Parents set clear rules and consequences, and monitor activities.
12. *School boundaries.* Schools provide clear expectations and rules.
13. *Neighborhood boundaries.* Residents are responsible for supervision of youth.
14. *Adult role models.* Parents and other adults model responsible behavior.
15. *Positive peer influences.* Close friends model responsible behavior.
16. *High expectations.* Parents and teachers want youths to succeed.

Constructive Use of Time
17. *Creative activities.* Youths spend three-plus hours per week in lessons in music, arts, or theater.
18. *Youth programs.* Youths spend three-plus hours per week in sports, clubs, or community groups.
19. *Religious programs.* Youths devote one or more hours per week to religious activity.
20. *Time at home.* Youths spend five nights at home per week.

Internal Assets

Commitment to Learning
21. *Achievement motivation.* Youths are motivated to succeed academically.
22. *School engagement.* Youths are actively involved in learning new things.
23. *Homework.* Youths spend one hour every school day on homework.
24. *Bonding to school.* Youths care about their school.
25. *Reading for pleasure.* Youths spend three-plus hours per week on reading for pleasure.

Positive Values
26. *Caring.* Youths place value on helping others.
27. *Equality and justice.* Youths place a high value on reducing hunger and poverty.
28. *Integrity.* Youths stand up for their beliefs.
29. *Honesty.* Youths tell the truth even when it is difficult to do so.
30. *Responsibility.* Youths accept personal responsibility for themselves.
31. *Restraint.* Youths avoid sex, drugs, and alcohol.

Social Competencies
32. *Planning and decision making.* Youths know how to plan and make good decisions.
33. *Interpersonal competence.* Youths have empathy and sensitivity, and can make friends.
34. *Cultural competence.* Youths are comfortable around different types of people.
35. *Resistance skills.* Youths can avoid dangerous situations and resist peer pressure.
36. *Peaceful conflict resolution.* Youths resolve conflict without violence.

Positive Identity
37. *Personal power.* Youths feel they have some control over events in their lives.
38. *Self-esteem.* Youths feel good about themselves.
39. *Sense of purpose.* Youths feel their lives have meaning.
40. *Positive view of future.* Youths feel their individual futures are bright.

Assets are a combination of community support and an internal sense of control. Individuals with a lot of community support will likely feel better about themselves and their future.

Source: Adapted from http://www.search-institute.org.

family, friends, school, and community also mean youths are better able to withstand peer pressure and avoid risky behaviors during their adolescent years.[27]

As Table 7-2 shows, there are actually two types of developmental assets: external and internal. External assets involve developing and nurturing youths by supporting and empowering them, setting boundaries and expectations, and keeping them actively involved in constructive activities such as three or more hours of sports or an hour or more per week in religious activities. Support consists of emotional support and encouragement by parents and adult role models, parental involvement in schools, and caring neighbors. Empowerment involves conveying to youths that the community values them, and they volunteer for more than one hour per week.

External assets also include families who set clear expectations, provide firm boundaries, and establish consequences with regard to youths' behavior. Similarly, schools and neighborhoods must provide a set of expectations and boundaries for youths when they are in the classroom, on campus, or in the community. Not only should these expectations be clear, but adult role models within all of these settings should carry out responsible behaviors. This sends a message to youths about what is expected of them.

Internal assets include a commitment to learning positive values, displaying sensitivity to others, and building a positive identity and sense of well-being. Internal assets are developed by promoting an active engagement in learning, meaning that the young person is motivated to do well in school, does at least one hour of homework every day, and reads for pleasure three or more hours per week.

Positive values include a desire to help other people, a sense of integrity, honesty, and personal responsibility for one's actions, which includes refraining from the use of alcohol or drugs. Youths who cultivate internal assets also develop an ability to plan ahead and make positive and constructive choices related to their behavior and future. They also develop healthy friendships, resist negative peer pressure, and resolve conflict without resorting to violence. They believe that their lives have a purpose and that they have control over their own destinies. This, in turn, makes them optimistic about their future.[28]

Resiliency

How can good parenting contribute to youths' resiliency? What is the community's role in fostering positive values among its youths?

Family Structure

Family structure can have a big impact on delinquency. However, problems related to family structure are complex and multifaceted. For example, research shows that a lack of adequate parental supervision has significant links to delinquent behavior.[29] We might conclude that requiring parents to spend time with their children would decrease delinquency rates. But what if the reason for the lack of supervision is not apathy or disinterest, but long work hours? Suppose a child lives in a single-parent household and her father or mother works two full-time jobs so that he or she can pay the exorbitantly high rents that keep the daughter in a good school district and a safe neighborhood. Or consider that same single parent, in addition to working long hours at a low-wage job, trying to finish college so he or she can get a better-paying one? Understanding structural problems—such as single-parent families, high rents, and low wages—has contributed to the design of programs that will help solve family problems and reduce delinquency.

Family Structure and Delinquency

Consider what you have read about the correlation between family dynamics and delinquent behaviors. Does studying family structure provide an adequate means of measuring risks of delinquency? Why or why not?

External Structural Changes to Families

In Chapter 4, we saw that poverty, deindustrialization, and high housing costs are social structural factors that contribute to delinquency. These factors all place a strain on families as they reduce the amount of time parents can spend supervising their children and likewise limit family resources.

Other social changes that affect the structure of families include an increase in cohabitation and unwed childbirth, changes in divorce laws that make it easier to dissolve a marriage, and the increased presence of women in the workforce. Note that many of our perceptions of the family are rooted in traditional thinking about family structure that is reflective of the 1950s. Many people still think of the "typical" family in this way, even though only 7 percent of U.S. households fit this definition.

Since the 1970s, the proportion of nuclear families has steadily decreased, and the average household size decreased from 3.4 people in 1960 to 2.5 people in 2008.[30] People are also waiting longer to get married. In 1970, median age at first marriage was 21 for women and 23 for men; in 2008, those numbers were 25.6 and 27.4 respectively. In addition, many couples are deciding not to have children. In 2008, over half, or 55 percent, of married couples had no children in the household.[31] Finally, some women are deciding to have children without husbands. In 2008, the birthrate for unmarried women age fifteen to forty-four was 47.5 births per 1,000, the highest rate in more than sixty years.[32]

COHABITATION AND CHILDBEARING

Since the 1960s, sex and childbearing outside of marriage have become more common. The development of effective contraception, as well as the availability of safe and legal abortions, reduced the risk of pregnancy and the likelihood of unwanted pregnancy. This trend, combined with the rising independence of women, encouraged the delay of marriage and childbearing, particularly for women who are highly educated and have well-paying jobs.

At the same time, cohabitation has become a popular alternative to marriage. According to the National Marriage Project, by 2006, the rate of cohabitation had increased 1,100 percent in forty years, and about half of married couples had lived together before marriage. These trends are continuing: the U.S. marriage rate decreased by almost 20 percent from 1995 to 2005.[33] People often think of cohabitation as something young people do before they begin a family. However, many are starting families without being married. According to one estimate, almost 40 percent of cohabiting households include children.[34]

There is considerable debate about the value of cohabitation. According to one school of thought, supported by the National Marriage Project, arguments against cohabitation are based on findings from earlier studies showing that children of cohabiting couples were more likely than children of married couples to experience emotional problems, alcoholism, and drug abuse.[35] On the other hand, some sociologists suggest that the problems children experience when couples live together may be due to related factors—the instability of the relationship or financial problems—rather than cohabitation itself.[36]

Additionally, cohabitation explains only a portion of the births by unmarried women. In 2005, 37 percent of all births in the United States occurred outside of marriage, and the majority of these births were to unwed mothers who did not have a cohabiting partner.[37] Note, therefore, that about 63 percent of births—less than two-thirds—were to married couples.[38]

multiple-partner fertility
Mothers attempting to have children by different fathers.

Another trend is the tendency for mothers to have children by different fathers. This phenomenon, called **multiple-partner fertility,** may make it more difficult for the mother to find a husband.[39] According to a recent study, about 17 percent of fathers age sixteen to forty-five have had children with more than one woman. Additionally, about 73 percent of multiple-partner-fertility men have three or more children.[40] Fathers who have children with more than one partner provide less financial support and spend less time with their nonresident children. Black, Hispanic, and young men and women are especially likely to experience multiple-partner fertility.[41]

TABLE 7-3 Divorce Rates for First and Subsequent Marriages

Number of Marriages	Rate of Divorce
First	43%
Second	66%
Third	74%

Higher rates of divorce in subsequent marriages suggest that perhaps the factors that led to the first divorce reproduce themselves in later marriages.

Source: U.S. Census Bureau. 2005. *Current Population Survey, March and Annual Social and Economic Supplements, 2005 and Earlier.* http://www.census.gov/population/socdemo/hh-fam/ms2.pdf.

DIVORCE

Even with couples who are married, the availability and convenience of divorce has changed the face of American families. According to the Census Bureau, about 43 percent of first marriages end in divorce. Remarriage also occurs fairly regularly, as shown in divorce rates for subsequent marriages. Divorce rates for second and third marriages are even higher than those for first marriages: according to Table 7-3, 66 percent of second marriages and 74 percent of third marriages end in divorce.[42] Twenty percent of first marriages end within five years.[43]

Factors that tend to diminish the chance of divorce include religion (Catholics are substantially less likely than Protestants to get divorced), older age, higher income, more education, absence of divorce in family history, and a child after marriage.[44] For many years, the prevailing view has been that divorce is very traumatic for children. Extensive studies of divorced couples have found that about 75 percent of children of divorce do not have serious psychological, social, or academic problems. However, the other 25 percent, which in absolute terms represents a large number of children, have significant problems.[45]

The first two years after a divorce are often physically, emotionally, and psychologically draining for everyone in the family. Erratic behavior, depression, and physical ailments are common. Divorce is especially traumatic for children whose parents have kept their problems hidden; these children experience a greater sense of loss.[46]

On the other hand, children whose parents' marriage created a chaotic environment often find things a bit more peaceful after divorce in a stable single-parent household. Interestingly, children from nondivorce, high-conflict homes have problems similar to those of children from divorced homes, which suggests that "staying together for the sake of the children" is not beneficial if the home is not a peaceful one.[47]

Preschool-age children can find coping with divorce especially difficult. Young children often regress in their behavior through action such as baby talk, clinging, or thumb sucking. Young boys, who typically have greater difficulty coping with and adjusting to divorce than young girls, frequently act out, even becoming aggressive with peers and others. Single parents often have great difficulty disciplining their sons in these situations. To make things worse, divorce often results in fathers leaving the household and spending less time with their sons, which causes numerous problems, including weakened father-son bonds. In addition, absent fathers tend to be lenient about chores, homework, and discipline. This can create problems when children return home and the mother tries to maintain normal discipline.[48]

Mothers who experience divorce face other types of problems. Particularly with daughters, mothers run the risk of blurring the lines between parent and child when the mother inappropriately confides in her daughter about her marriage, finances, or dates. Another potential problem occurs when mothers give children too much responsibility for household chores. This creates an unhealthy relationship between parent and child,[49] with the child expected to behave like an adult at a time when he or she is not cognitively prepared to do so. Worse are situations in which mothers regress and begin to act like children while the child becomes the responsible "parent."[50] All of this is understandable, since the mother, feeling isolated and overwhelmed, attempts to draw comfort from her immediate family. At its most extreme, however, this scenario can cause difficulties for everyone involved.

The good news is that for the vast majority of children, including teenagers, these problems do not cause long-term harm. Teens who do well in such situations tend to have a strong connection to at least one adult, although not necessarily a biological family member. The school may also provide important ways for teens to feel a sense of belonging and to experience success.[51]

WOMEN IN THE WORKFORCE

As more women enter the labor market and have professional careers, many have also started to rethink the value of marriage and childbearing as a form of identity and self-fulfillment. Of course, these trends are interrelated: women who expect to have fewer children, and who see less value in marriage as a form of identity, will dedicate more time to pursuing their education and careers and less to finding a husband.

As evidence of the changing social role of women, statistics that show women now attend college at higher rates than men, particularly those from disadvantaged families.[52] Moreover, women attend professional school in numbers equal to or greater than men; for instance, approximately 60 percent of law students and 50 percent of medical students are women.[53] Census Bureau data also show that most women are working. Additionally, 75 percent of married mothers and 78 percent of single mothers with children between the ages of six and seventeen are employed.[54]

The emphasis on education and professional training translates into higher earning potential. The median earnings of full-time year-round working women reached 76 percent of men's earnings in 2003. In 2009, President Obama signed into law a bill requiring employers to pay women and men equal wages for identical work. This law was designed to eliminate the wage gap for women doing the same jobs as men, and it shows that women are a significant presence in all dimensions of the labor force.[55] A recent study found that about 25 percent of married working women now earn more than their husbands.[56]

latchkey kids
Children age six to twelve who spend five or more hours per week unsupervised or in the care of an older sibling, and who are at much greater risk for engaging in delinquent behavior than children who have an adult provider in the home.

For married women with children, having a career, and all that comes with it, changes the structure of the family. For instance, the wife's career affects the family's parenting styles, financial situation, decision making, and choices about how to use their time. While college-educated women who are active in their professional lives have more stable marriages than those without college educations, they also tend to have fewer children, and the dynamics of decision making in their families tend to be more egalitarian. Because they contribute financially, women want more say in how finances are handled and more input in all decisions within the household. Traditionally, the husband handled the finances and made all the important economic decisions but this is changing.[57]

For those working women who decide to have a family, the reality is that they tend to spend less time with their children. Some mothers try to compensate for their absence by getting less sleep or participating in fewer leisure activities; however, this creates other challenges. For mothers with adolescents in particular, spending quality time is especially difficult, and the research on the amount of time working mothers spend with their adolescent children has shown a consistent decline in recent decades.[58]

In those cases where there are two parents present in the household and the marriage is a stable one, with both parents working, child care becomes an issue. The lack of parental supervision is a critical variable in explaining delinquency. According to one estimate, more than 3 million children age six to twelve spend five or more hours per week unsupervised or in the care of an older sibling, and more than 10 percent of these children spend ten or more hours alone while their parents are at work. These **latchkey kids,** as they are sometimes called, are at much greater risk for engaging in delinquent behavior than children who have an adult provider in the home.[59]

Did your mother work when you were growing up? If so, how did her career affect the structure of your family, if at all?

The solution, it seems, is to find adequate day care. But this is much more difficult than most people realize. Currently, about 60 percent of children under age six are cared for on a regular basis by people other than their parents, and nearly 80 percent of children under age five are in some sort of child care arrangement during a typical week.[60] Preschoolers spend an average of twenty-eight hours per week in child care. These numbers are especially significant considering that children who spend more time in day care than they do being cared for by their parents are more likely to develop behavioral problems.[61] Because of the problems associated with finding high-quality day care (including the costs, and often, the waiting lists), some married mothers with very young children have chosen to leave the workforce and stay home—what is informally referred to as *opting out*.[62]

It would be easy to conclude that the changes and problems in American families are related to women becoming more involved in the workforce. However, generally, the growing number of women in the workforce has not been shown to contribute to delinquency.[63] Some critics claim that if we simply went back to the family structure of the 1950s, many of our problems would disappear. This type of thinking blames women for social problems and calls for a return to **traditional family values,** which means that women should be in the home raising children. It is unreasonable, however, to blame women for the massive changes in society over the past fifty or sixty years. Social changes have many causes, not all of them are harmful, and most children emerge unscathed from even the most difficult home situations.

> "And my little brother, he—I'm a bad influence on him, too. But, I tried to guide him right away. He got waived to adult court."
>
> **ANTHONY**

traditional family values
The family structure of the 1950s, when women stayed home to raise the children.

THE CHANGING ROLE OF FATHERS

Traditionally, the husband and father was seen as the primary economic provider, but over the past decade, an increasing number of fathers have taken on primary caregiving responsibilities in the United States and in several other countries.[64] While more women are pursuing career opportunities, men have also been making different career decisions. For some, the decision to stay at home and raise their children is an attractive alternative to climbing the corporate ladder of success. In 2007, stay-at-home dads made up almost 3 percent of the nation's stay-at-home parents, which is three times what it was in 1997. According to a recent estimate, in 2009, the number of stay-at-home dads rose to 158,000, an increase of more than 10 percent from 2008, when 140,000 married men spent at least one year at home caring for children under fifteen while their wives worked.[65] Additionally, since 2005, the percentage of stay-at-home dads has steadily increased,[66] with 63 percent of stay-at-home dads being responsible for two or more children.[67]

The emergence of fathers as primary caregivers can be attributed in part to economic changes, as unemployment rates for males have been higher than for females. In some instances, the career path of the wife results in her earning more than her husband. As families calculate the costs of day care or nannies to care for the children if both spouses work, in many cases, it makes more sense for the father to remain at home. In other instances, fathers may intentionally decide to forego career advancement in favor of spending time with their children.

In addition, some men can remain employed while staying at home with their children.[68] **Telecommuting,** in which full-time employees can work from home, has become increasingly possible through technological advances, and allows parents to spend more time at home with their children. Such a situation provides fathers with the best of both options: earning a salary and still remaining actively involved in their children's lives.[69]

telecommuting
The ability for a full-time employee to work from home.

Besides the Census Bureau data that outline the steady increases in the number of fathers who assume caregiving responsibilities, the number of books and articles written about stay-at-home dads, along with forums, networks, and organizations that cater to this segment of the population, has grown as well. For instance, in his 2009 book *The Daddy Shift: How Stay at Home Dads, Breadwinning Moms and Shared Parenting Are Transforming the American Family,* Jeremy Adam Smith examines the changes to the American family as a result of fathers taking on the mother's traditional role. Such a change has a ripple effect throughout the family, including the relationship the father has with his children, spouse, and relatives, and society as a whole. Such a trend, Smith argues, forces society to reexamine the notion of parenting in general and fatherhood in particular.[70]

Self-help books provide practical tips on how to be a successful stay-at-home dad.[71] While clearly not a panacea to the challenges facing the twenty-first-century family, the fact that consideration is given to fathers who choose to stay home and raise their children, and to mothers who choose to embrace a career, suggests that much of what we understand about traditional roles and the structure of families will likely continue to change in this century.

Changing Family Structures

When you hear the word "family," do you think of a father who is the sole breadwinner, a stay-at-home mother who raises the children, and one or more children in the household? If not, describe the image of a family that does come to mind. What societal changes contribute to your definition of family?

Internal Family Dynamics

While large-scale structural changes have had a significant impact on families, internal family dynamics also contribute to delinquency. Factors include birth order, family size, family violence, and discipline methods.

BIRTH ORDER

In the 1970s and even into the 1980s, while many people thought that the youngest child was most likely to be delinquent, empirical evidence suggested that middle children were more likely to exhibit delinquent behavior than first-borns and youngest children.[72] The rationale was that the eldest and youngest children generally received more attention, and as a result, middle children were given more latitude in terms of their behavior. Even then the research was unclear about the relationship between birth order and delinquency. Many experts suggested that the relationship was attributable to a lack of parental supervision rather than to some genetic factor.[73]

After the mid-1980s, the amount of research done on birth order and delinquency decreased substantially. More recently, evidence suggests that birth order has a less important relationship to delinquency than previously thought. In 2005, one study in France examined this relationship and found, consistent with earlier research, that ordinal position (birth order) plays only a moderate role in delinquent behavior and that this effect is partly related to different levels of parental control.[74]

FAMILY SIZE

Does family size affect delinquency patterns? Most measures of family variables use a family of four as a general standard. Thus, a "large" family would include five or more people living in the same household.[75] Young people who engage in delinquent behavior tend to come from larger families.[76] However, as we have discovered, this is not a causal relationship; growing up in a family with many siblings does not *cause* someone to become delinquent.

Some research indicates that family size really does matter. For example, a 2006 study found that delinquency, as measured by both the total number of offenses and their seriousness, was approximately three times more frequent and four times more

For more on siblings and birth order, watch *Birth Order & Family Life: Larry* and *Family Environment: Jose* at www.mhhe.com/mcnamarajd1e

RYAN'S CASE

Is Birth Order a Factor?

Recall Ryan's situation:

- is a twelve-year-old boy
- lives in California with his mother and stepfather
- is a middle child of four children
- has a bad reputation in his neighborhood and school

Ryan's neighbors think that his delinquent behavior is the result of his position in the family, which allows him to behave as he likes. They believe his lack of supervision predisposes him to further delinquency.

The bigger the family, the harder it can be for parents to keep an eye on their children, leaving some youths free to get into trouble. In some families, particularly large ones, parents are also more likely to relax strict behavioral standards and boundaries. In fact, inadequate supervision is considered the most important variable in understanding the relationship between family position and delinquency.

Given the research on birth order, do you think that Ryan's position as a middle child is a factor in his delinquent behavior? If Ryan were the youngest, or even the first-born, might he have received more attention from his mother and stepfather?

THINK ABOUT IT

serious for children from large families. Furthermore, the relationship observed between large family size and delinquency remained even when the researchers controlled for household income, marital status, and parents' occupation. These findings suggest that perhaps family size is more important in predicting delinquency than previously thought.[77]

It is likely that certain aspects of a large family, such as difficulties in parental supervision, boundary enforcement, and discipline, contribute to delinquent behavior. Related to these aspects is another explanation suggesting that older siblings are often given child-rearing tasks in larger families, and they may not provide sufficient boundaries and limitations to those in their care. Still another explanation for the relationship between family size and delinquency might be that larger families tend to be poorer than smaller ones. Thus, the connection of family size to delinquency may be a result of other, larger factors.[78]

Regardless of family size, many parents of delinquent children often become frustrated because they do not know how to evoke a change in their son's or daughter's behavior. Most conclude that the decision to commit delinquent acts is a personal one, over which they have no control. However, new evidence suggests that parents of delinquent children can reduce rates of misbehavior by teaching them how to effectively cope with stress. In fact, the lessons learned about stress have a lasting effect; not only do they reduce delinquency in the short term, they can reduce the risk of mental illness and other physical ailments later in life.[79]

A recent study at the New York University School of Medicine included ninety-two families with a child who had been in trouble with the law. Some families were assigned to take part in a family intervention program that included twenty-two group sessions and ten home visits from mental health professionals over an eight-month period. During these sessions, the children learned how to effectively socialize with peers, to identify their feelings and emotions, and to follow and understand rules.

Other families were assigned to a control group that received no intervention. Cortisol (a stress hormone) levels were checked to assess stress in the children before and after a socially stressful situation, such as interaction with a group of unfamiliar children. The children in the intervention group showed a normal cortisol response while those in the control group showed a response pattern similar to that seen in older delinquent youths. "Our findings demonstrate the powerful influence of the care-giving environment on children's biology," said Michael Brotman, the lead author of the study. "We have known for some time that parents play an important role in how young children behave. We have shown that parents of delinquent youth can improve their parenting, and these changes result in lower rates of problems in their young children."[80]

FAMILY VIOLENCE

Family violence is an umbrella term that includes physical and sexual abuse of children, child neglect and maltreatment, intimate partner violence, and elder abuse. Children do not

> " I still sometimes have those moments where I just want to hit somebody or—when it's quiet and stuff, I'll just—it'll just pop up, and watch the images in my eyes. "
>
> Zachary

have to be direct victims of abuse to be harmed by it: witnessing violence in their homes makes them indirect victims. Children who witness abuse often have the same types of problems as those who experience it: low self-esteem, depression, stress disorders, poor impulse control, and feelings of powerlessness. They are also at high risk for alcohol and drug use, sexual acting out, running away, isolation, fear, and suicide.[81]

There are clear links between delinquency and exposure to violence, but what can the police or social workers do to help children in such situations? The Theory and Practice box on page 179 offers insight into one program that attempts to reduce the risks of delinquency associated with family violence.

Sadly, children exposed to violence at an early age are likely to become either perpetrators of abuse or victims of violence in adulthood.[82] In fact, boys who have witnessed abuse of their mothers are ten times more likely to batter their female partners as adults.[83]

Consider some other facts about the impact of family violence:

- Children of battered women are fifteen times more likely to be battered as adults than children whose mothers are not abused.

- Because abusers often use children's behavior as an excuse for battering the woman, children come to blame themselves for their mother's abuse.

- Divorced and separated women, who compose only 10 percent of all women, account for 75 percent of all battered women and report being battered fourteen times as often as women still living with their partners.[84]

For more on domestic violence, watch *Domestic Violence: Zachary* and *Father's History and Childhood Abuse: Austin* at www.mhhe.com/mcnamarajd1e

In trying to make sense of family violence, particularly as it relates to children and teens, many experts agree that it involves a *cycle of violence,* where parents and caregivers discipline children using violence because that is the way they were raised. The upshot, of course, is that victims of such abuse can become violent offenders themselves as they get older.[85] As we will see later in this chapter, a young person who is a victim of neglect or abuse is more likely to become a delinquent than one who is not mistreated. For instance, one study compared the arrest records of 908 abused or neglected children, age eleven or younger at the time of abuse or neglect, with arrest records of 667 children who were not abused or maltreated. The study found that being abused or neglected as a child substantially increased the likelihood of arrest as a juvenile or as an adult. It also increased the chances of being arrested for a violent crime.[86] Furthermore, children who do not become offenders or victims are likely to suffer from attention deficits, educational difficulties, substance abuse, mental health problems, symptoms of post-traumatic stress disorder, and lack of appropriate social skills.[87]

THEORY AND PRACTICE WORKING TOGETHER

Exposure to Violence and Community Policing

In 1996, the Charlotte-Mecklenburg Police Department created the CD-CP program, which was designed to help police officers and caseworkers identify children who have been exposed to violence and to provide some type of clinical intervention to help them cope with the trauma. The program began in New Haven, Connecticut, as a joint effort by the Yale University Child Study Center and the New Haven Police Department.

The rationale behind this program finds its origins in a wealth of psychological research suggesting that early exposure to violence can lead to subsequent violence. Part of the challenge for social workers and police officers is recognizing the signs and symptoms of a child who is suffering from that type of trauma. The CD-CP program helps officers and clinicians to understand this link and teaches them how to help victims cope with the experience.

The program consists of collaboration between police supervisors, mental health therapists, and child protective service (CPS) workers in the classroom, as well as in cross-training. Clinicians and CPS workers go on police ride-alongs, learning about routine police operations and the neighborhoods served. An important part of the training is

teaching officers more about abuse, neglect, and available services for victims.

Following the cross-training between the social workers and police officers, CD-CP teams, consisting of an officer and a clinician, provide in-service training to officers and social workers in each agency about the effects of violence on child development and when and how to make appropriate referrals. While only preliminary data are available, it appears that officers are intervening early and are directing families and children who have been exposed to violence to the help they need. For instance, in 2005:

- Over 6,100 cases were referred, with an average of two children per case. A total of 1,425 families were referred.
- Approximately 55 percent of the cases involved at least one child five years old or younger.
- Over half of all referrals were a result of domestic violence.

 THINK ABOUT IT Why would police officers and social workers need a reason to collaborate? What is the goal of cross-training?

Not only are children directly or indirectly affected by domestic violence, but the extent and seriousness of domestic violence has a clear and studied impact on women. Some experts contend that intimate partner violence, which includes domestic violence, is the most common violent crime in the United States.[88] Data indicate that one in every four women will experience domestic violence in her lifetime. Additionally, an estimated 4.8 million incidents of physical assault by an intimate partner occur each year, with 75 percent of those victims females. In 2008, 1,181 women were murdered by an intimate partner—an average of three women every day. Of all the women murdered in the United States, about one-third were killed by an intimate partner.[89]

DISCIPLINE

Discipline is an essential part of being a parent. Recall that one of the most important variables in parenting is setting and sticking to boundaries. Another basic principle is that the discipline must be reasonable. When punishment is needed, it should not include spanking, hitting, or otherwise physically hurting children. There is a long-standing debate about whether the use of corporal punishment, or spanking, is an effective disciplinary tool. While in an earlier time most people believed that "sparing the rod spoiled the child," today, even though most people in the United States approve of spanking,[90] the issue is much more controversial.

What is the difference between punishment and discipline? Although the two are related and often used together, as a general rule, *discipline* is a tool that parents and other adults use to effectively socialize and teach children about boundaries and limitations. *Punishment,* on the other hand, places less emphasis on teaching and more on accountability for misbehavior. So discipline is proactive, and it includes all

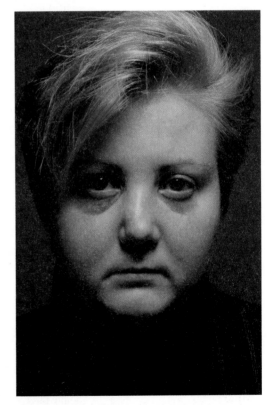

Are the data on domestic violence presented in this chapter surprising to you? How do the media cover domestic violence as an issue? According to your reading so far, are the media's portrayals and conclusions accurate?

Consider the differences between discipline and punishment. What are some examples of each? In what instances might a combination of these be used?

the means that parents use to guide their children's behavior: setting limits, stating consequences, providing positive role models, and giving reinforcement for good behavior. Punishment, on the other hand, happens after the fact and acknowledges only misbehavior.

Spanking

Spanking can include a range of corporal punishments, from simply hitting the child on the buttocks to slapping the child's hand or face. Murray Straus, a well-known researcher in the field of family violence, defines corporal punishment as the use of physical force with the intention of causing bodily pain, but not injury, for the purpose of correction or control.[91] Corporal punishment that causes injury is, by definition, child abuse.

Many psychologists and pediatricians say that parents should never strike a child. Frequent and impulsive spanking, hitting children with objects, or even simply yelling at them, are detrimental to development and can lead to delinquency and even adult crime.[92] According to the American Academy of Pediatrics, spanking can escalate into physical abuse and contribute to later emotional and behavioral problems. Many recent studies have shown that spanking is linked to higher rates of domestic violence and assault.[93]

Perhaps the most compelling argument against spanking is that it simply does not work. If the objective behind spanking is to change the behavior of children, other disciplinary tactics are more effective and less traumatic.[94] On the other hand, some psychologists argue that low levels of corporal punishment are acceptable, do not lead to long-term damage, and can be an effective disciplinary tool. While advocates of spanking argue it is always better to provide correction through explanation, light spanking may reinforce other forms of correction, such as a time-out.[95]

Verbal Assault

verbal assault
Yelling at or disparaging children.

Most experts also warn parents against **verbal assault,** yelling at or disparaging children. Frequent verbal reprimands become ineffective and even reinforce undesired behavior. In fact, verbal hostility may actually lead to more detrimental consequences than physical abuse. One study of more than 3,000 parents and their children younger than eighteen years of age linked both verbal and physical aggression by parents to aggressive behavior, delinquency, and interpersonal problems in their children—and the psychological abuse was the more harmful of the two. Those connections applied to both boys and girls, regardless of age.[96]

 THINK ABOUT IT

Family Structure and Delinquency

What has the cycle of violence taught us about the risks of delinquency and violent behaviors?

Neglect and Abuse

What is the difference between a bad parent and a neglectful one? This is not an easy question to answer, but it is one that caseworkers, police officers, and child welfare advocates face every day.

neglect
A situation created when parents or guardians do not provide the kind of care needed, even though they have the ability to do so.

For some families, failure means inadequate care or neglect, while for others, it means more obvious forms of abuse. Child neglect is the most prevalent form of child maltreatment in the United States. **Neglect** occurs when parents or guardians do not provide the kind of care needed, even though they have the ability to do so. The National Child

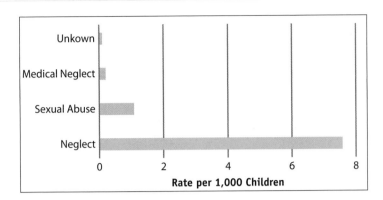

FIGURE 7-1 Child Abuse and Neglect among Children under Age 18 by Type of Maltreatment, 2005

Neglect is by far the most common form of child maltreatment.

Source: Adapted from Administration on Children, Youth and Families, National Child Abuse and Neglect Data System, 2005.

Abuse and Neglect Data System (NCANDS) defines neglect as "a type of maltreatment that refers to the failure by the caregiver to provide needed, age-appropriate care although financially able to do so or offered financial or other means to do so."[97]

Neglected children suffer from poor hygiene, weight loss, and frequent absence from school; extreme neglect is usually easily recognized. Physicians, nurses, day care personnel, relatives, and neighbors often suspect and report neglect in infants, toddlers, and younger children. Once children are in school, teachers and administrators usually notice the aforementioned characteristics of child neglect.[98]

According to the NCANDS, approximately 899,000 children in the United States were victims of abuse and neglect in 2005. As Figure 7-1 shows, according to NCANDS data, about 73 percent of child maltreatment cases involved neglect only.[99]

TYPES OF NEGLECT

While neglect can be a difficult concept to define, and while there are a wide range of activities that can be considered neglectful, experts and treatment professionals typically characterize neglect according to five types: physical, educational, emotional/ psychological, medical, and abandonment.

- **Physical neglect** occurs when the parent or caregiver does not provide the child with basic necessities (adequate food, clothing, and shelter). Examples include malnutrition; serious illness; physical harm in the form of cuts, bruises, burns, or other injuries due to the lack of supervision; and a lifetime of low self-esteem. This accounts for the majority of maltreatment cases.[100]

  Physical neglect also includes inadequate supervision and failure to provide for children's safety and physical and emotional needs. Physical neglect can severely impede children's development by causing *failure to thrive* (FTT).[101]

  FTT refers to a child whose growth is below normal levels. FTT is a controversial issue since it can result not only from neglect but also from real medical problems such as reflux disease, diarrhea, and other ailments that limit the body's ability to absorb nutrients. Environmental factors

Describe some of the physical characteristics you might expect a neglected child to display. If not neglect, what else may be causing these outward signs?

can play a role in FTT as well. These include maternal high blood pressure, cigarette smoking, and alcohol use, as well as maternal drug use or maternal infections or viruses.[102]

- **Educational neglect** involves the failure to enroll a child in school or to provide appropriate home schooling or needed special educational training. Recall from our discussion of status offending in Chapter 3 that parents may be punished for educational neglect when their children are chronically truant. Educational neglect has links to disruptive behavior, chronic delinquency, and adult unemployment and poverty. Thus, not only does this type of neglect negatively affect children and their emotional and psychological growth, it also has implications for their adulthood.

- **Emotional/psychological neglect** includes actions such as engaging in chronic or extreme spousal abuse in the presence of children, allowing children to use drugs or alcohol, refusing or failing to provide needed psychological care, constantly belittling children, and withholding affection. This form of neglect can be as simple as ignoring children by failing to respond to their needs for encouragement, failing to acknowledge their presence, refusing to show affection, or isolating them from normal relationships with other children. Emotional and psychological neglect can also include encouraging children to engage in antisocial or destructive behavior. This type of maltreatment is the most difficult to identify and prosecute because the trauma is not as evident as with other types of neglect.

- **Medical neglect** is the failure to provide appropriate health care for a child even though the parents are able to do so. According to the NCANDS, in 2005, 2 percent of children in the United States were victims of medical neglect. Medical neglect is most evident when a parent refuses emergency treatment for a child, but it also occurs when a parent ignores recommendations for treatment of a chronic illness or disease.

    Child protective services agencies can intervene in certain situations, such as when children:

    - are in need of medical treatment in an emergency
    - are suffering from a life-threatening disease and are not receiving medical treatment
    - have a chronic disease that can cause disability or disfigurement if left untreated

    In situations that are life-threatening or can cause disfigurement, a court order is required to provide medical treatment.[103]

    Another form of medical neglect is rooted in the behaviors of the mother during pregnancy. An example would be excessive drinking during pregnancy, which can cause fetal alcohol syndrome (FAS). FAS is one of the leading known preventable causes of mental disability and birth defects. Children with FAS are at risk for psychiatric problems, criminal behavior, unemployment, difficulty getting along with others, and incomplete education.[104]

- **Abandonment** is the desertion of a child without arranging for reasonable care and supervision. This category includes cases in which children were left by parents or substitutes, the children are not claimed within two days, and their caregivers have no information about the parent's whereabouts.[105]

REASONS FOR NEGLECT

Why do some parents fail to practice good parenting skills and end up neglecting their children? This is a difficult question to answer, but some experts argue that one reason some parents neglect their children is that they hold a **present orientation,** or an inability to think about or plan for the future. This living-for-the-moment mentality prevents these parents from thinking about buying clothes for their children, purchasing groceries, cleaning the house, or planning for emergencies. They simply do not grasp the importance of planning ahead for their children's needs.[106]

Another explanation for neglect, which relates to a lack of planning, involves a lack of knowledge. Many people, particularly teenage mothers, have children at an early age and

present orientation
An inability to think about or plan for the future; a living-for-the-moment mentality.

do not know how to manage a household or meet their children's needs. This knowledge was not passed along to them from their parents because it is likely *they* had children at an early age and failed to learn adequate life skills or to understand the psychological and emotional needs of children. The result is that new parents do not really know how to properly care for children and end up neglecting them at some point.

A third explanation for neglect focuses on poor judgment. Some parents assume their children can handle responsibility before they are ready. Examples might include not requiring a curfew for teens or overlooking experimental drug use because the parents believe their children appear to be responsible and "can handle it." While some parents may have good intentions and want to teach their children to be responsible adults, excessive or nonexistent boundaries can easily lead to neglect.

Finally, some parents simply give up on providing adequate care for their children. For some, this may be due to a feeling of being overwhelmed with the responsibilities of being a parent, while others may simply ignore their children.[107]

CHILD ABUSE

While neglect is perhaps the most common form of family disruption, there also appears to have been a steady increase in child abuse cases in recent years. **Child abuse** and neglect are defined by federal and state laws. The Child Abuse Prevention and Treatment Act (CAPTA) is the federal legislation that provides minimum standards that states must incorporate in their statutory definitions of child abuse and neglect. The CAPTA definition of "child abuse and neglect" refers to "any recent act or failure to act on the part of a parent or caretaker, which results in death, serious physical or emotional harm, sexual abuse or exploitation, or an act or failure to act which presents an imminent risk of serious harm."[108]

According to the NCANDS, in 2006, there were approximately 6 million allegations of child maltreatment made to child protective services (CPS) agencies in the United States. An estimated 3.6 million children were the subject of an investigation or assessment, and 905,000 children were determined to be victims of abuse or neglect. Obviously, there are problems with reporting rates of child abuse, so it is likely that this figure is underestimated.[109] Parents are the most frequent offenders when it comes to physically abusing their children. As illustrated in Figure 7-2, nearly 80 percent of the time, it is parents who are responsible for neglecting their children.

child abuse
Any act or failure to act on the part of a parent or caregiver that results in death, serious physical or emotional harm, sexual abuse, or exploitation of a minor.

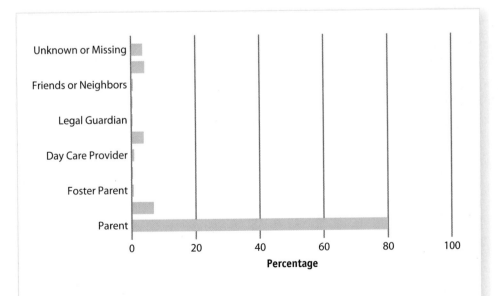

FIGURE 7-2 Perpetrators by Relationship to Victims, 2006
Parents are the most common offenders in child neglect cases.

Source: Adapted from Snyder, H. N., and Sickmund, M. 2008. *Juvenile Offenders and Victims 2006 National Report*. Washington, DC: U.S. Department of Justice, Office of Juvenile Justice and Delinquency Prevention.

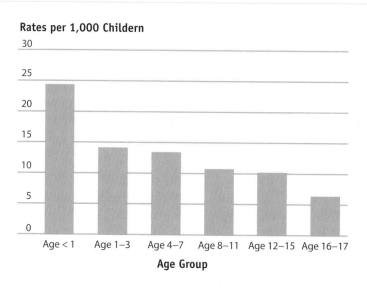

Rates per 1,000 Children

FIGURE 7-3 Victimization Rates by Age Group, 2006

Infants have the highest rates of physical abuse, largely due to the fact that they cannot protect themselves.

Source: Adapted from U.S. Department of Health and Human Services, Administration on Children, Youth and Families. 2008. *Child Maltreatment 2006.* Washington, DC: U.S. Government Printing Office.

Infants are the most likely of all age groups to be the victims of physical abuse (see Figure 7-3). The percentages decrease as children get older, likely due to the ability of these children to flee their parents or victimizers by running away or leaving home. Unlike neglect, which may be more difficult to detect, physical abuse results in signs and symptoms that are more obvious. However, we must be careful to distinguish between injuries sustained by youths as a result of normal childhood activity and those caused by abusive parents.

While physical abuse can occur in a variety of forms, medical experts contend that the three main signs of such abuse are bruises, burns, and fractures. The skin is the most commonly injured organ system and the easiest to examine. Certainly, bruises can be a result of normal childhood activity, depending on the child's age (bruises are rare in infants who do not walk or crawl). Children frequently fall, and scrapes or bruises on the shins, knees, hands, elbows, nose, and forehead are normal.[110]

In contrast, unexplained injuries to protected parts of the body such as the buttocks, thighs, torso, ears, and neck are suggestive of child abuse. The shape or pattern of the injury may also suggest abuse. Bruises in the shape of handprints or belt buckles are considered sufficient to make a claim of physical abuse. The dating of bruises by color can also be used as an indicator of abuse. Bruises at different ages and of various sizes may signify ongoing physical abuse.[111]

Children may also be abused by burning, which can result in disfigurement and even death. Cigarette burns leave centimeter-sized circular marks on the skin. Scald marks on the hands, feet, or buttocks that display certain patterns may have been caused by deliberate immersion of the child in a sink or bathtub of hot water.[112]

Fractures can also be related to abuse. While fractures do occur in the normal course of childhood activity, this type of injury must be placed in an age-related context. Some fractures suffered by members of certain age groups would not raise any suspicion, such as an eight-year-old boy who falls out of a tree and breaks his arm. Even certain types of skull fractures, while more serious, can occur during normal play activity. However, younger children sustaining such injuries, particularly those who

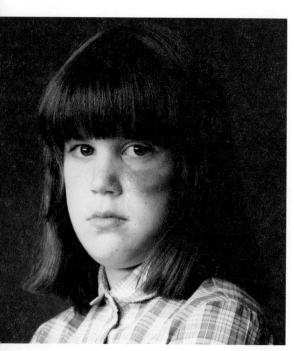

Emotional and verbal abuse can be more difficult to identify than certain types of physical abuse, which can leave visible marks. What might be some of the signs of emotional and verbal abuse of children?

have less mobility, are scrutinized more carefully. Certain types of fractures, such as spiral fractures, which occur when a child's arm has been grabbed and twisted, or complex skull fractures, and sternum and shoulder fractures, or even a history of fractures in general, will often arouse suspicion.[113] Other warning signs that may indicate abuse include a delay in seeking medical attention for injuries and inconsistent explanations by parents as to what happened. Sometimes children get hurt during normal activities, and parents do not always have every detail of what happened, but the more inconsistency between their explanation and the injury, the greater the likelihood that some type of abuse has occurred.[114]

SEXUAL ABUSE

The sexual abuse of children has generated a lot of media attention in recent years. There have been a number of highly publicized cases of sexual abuse, such as those involving members of the clergy, family members, or care providers who sexually abuse the children in their care. The Child Abuse Prevention and Treatment Act (CAPTA) definition of *sexual abuse* includes

the employment, use, persuasion, inducement, enticement, or coercion of any child to engage in, or assist any other person to engage in, any sexually explicit conduct or simulation of such conduct for the purpose of producing a visual depiction of such conduct; or the rape, and in cases of caretaker or interfamilial relationships, statutory rape, molestation, prostitution, or other form of sexual exploitation of children, or incest with children.[115]

Sexual abuse can occur in all populations. It happens to children in both rural and urban areas, at all socioeconomic and educational levels, and across all racial and cultural groups. Statistics indicate that girls are more frequently the victims of sexual abuse, but that the number of boys who are victimized is also significant. Estimates suggest that boys account for 25–35 percent of child sexual abuse victims. Boys tend not to report sexual abuse as often as girls, perhaps for fear of appearing weak and vulnerable.[116]

The majority of sexual abuse of children is perpetrated by someone the child knows. Sexual abuse can occur within the family (by a parent, stepparent, guardian, older sibling, or relative) or outside the family (often by a person the child and family know well). As demonstrated in Table 7-4, relatives have the highest rate of sexual abuse, representing about 30 percent of offenders, followed by day care staff, who make up about a quarter of offenders. Parents represent only about 3 percent of sexual abuse offenders.[117]

In 90 percent of child sexual abuse cases, the offenders are male. Other common offender characteristics include a history of abuse (either physical or sexual), alcohol or drug abuse, little satisfaction with sexual relationships with adults, a lack of control over emotions, and, occasionally, evidence of severe mental illness.[118]

TABLE 7-4 Maltreatment Perpetrator Relationship to Victim

	Total	Parent	Parent's Partner	Other Relative	Foster Parent	Day Care	Facility Staff
Type of Maltreatment							
Neglect	57%	62%	38%	38%	50%	48%	46%
Physical abuse	11	11	17	10	17	13	19
Sexual abuse	7	3	11	30	6	23	11
Psychological or other abuse	9	9	14	6	7	2	8
Multiple types	16	15	20	1 6	20	13	15

While parents are more likely to neglect their children, other relatives and day care workers are more likely to engage in sexual abuse.

Note: Columns may not total 100 percent because of rounding.

Source: Snyder, H., and Sickmund, M. 2008. *Juvenile Victims and Offenders 2006: A National Report.* Washington, DC: Department of Justice, Office of Justice Programs, Office of Juvenile Justice and Delinquency Prevention, p. 55.

Females can also be perpetrators of sexual abuse against children. Unlike male offenders, who tend to use threats or actual force, females tend to use persuasion. Boys are more likely than girls to be abused by a female. Because juveniles can be both victims and offenders when it comes to sexual abuse, juvenile sex offenders are discussed in Chapter 9 in more detail. It is important to recognize that sexual abuse is a serious issue and has a variety of links to delinquency, especially for the victims.[119]

How can a parent tell if his or her child has been sexually abused, especially if the child will not talk about it? One way is to pay attention to the child's behavior. Significant changes in the way he or she acts may be indicators of sexual abuse. Parents should be aware of the following symptoms and behaviors:

- loss of appetite
- regression to infantile behavior (bed-wetting, thumb sucking, excessive crying)
- fear of being left alone with a particular person or at a particular place
- frequent lying
- delinquent behavior or a sudden drop in grades at school[120]

Children who have been sexually abused may also express unusual interest in sexual matters, express affection in inappropriate ways, or act out sexual behaviors such as intercourse or masturbation. Victims may have difficulty getting along with other children and have a desire to engage in self-destructive behavior, such as pulling out their hair or inflicting some other type of injury upon themselves.[121]

CHILD PROTECTIVE SERVICES

Child Protective Services (CPS), which is usually a division within state and local social services agencies, is at the center of every community's child protection efforts. In most jurisdictions, CPS is the agency mandated by law to conduct an initial assessment or investigation of reports of child abuse and neglect. It also offers services to families and children where maltreatment has occurred or is likely to occur.

While not the only agency charged with handling child abuse cases, CPS is typically the lead agency in coordinating efforts to protect children. Often CPS workers collaborate with police officers, mental health professionals, family and juvenile courts, hospitals, and other agencies to investigate and treat child abuse and neglect cases. According to the National Association of Public Child Welfare Administrators (NAPCWA), the mission of the CPS agency is to:

- assess the safety of children
- intervene to protect them from harm
- strengthen the ability of families to protect their children
- provide either a reunification or an alternative safe family for the child

Generally, when a report of child abuse or neglect has been made, CPS workers follow a process that consists of seven stages: intake, initial assessment or investigation, family assessment, case planning, provision of services, ongoing assessment, and case closure.[122]

Intake
CPS is responsible for receiving and evaluating reports of suspected child abuse and neglect. Agency staff determine if the reported information meets the statutory and agency guidelines for child maltreatment, and also assesses the urgency with which the agency must respond.

Initial Assessment or Investigation
If the report is valid, CPS conducts an initial assessment or investigation to determine if child maltreatment occurred, if the child's immediate safety is a concern, and if so, what steps can be taken to protect the child while not removing him or her from the family. Examples include when a parent neglects a child and CPS places that child in the custody of a grandparent or other relative. CPS workers also consider if there is a risk of future maltreatment, the level of that risk, and whether agency services are needed to address any effects of child maltreatment and to reduce the risk of future issues.

The ultimate goal is usually the reunification of the family at some point in the future. While this is not always possible, the general belief is that being with the biological family is in the best interests of the child. Many of the efforts of CPS workers are designed to reunify the family by solving the problems that led to the neglect or abuse in the first place.[123]

Family Assessment

Once a determination of child abuse or neglect has been made and the child's immediate safety has been ensured, the next step is to conduct a family assessment. During this stage, the caseworker attempts to understand family members' strengths and needs. This includes identifying some type of foundation that can be used as a basis for changing family members' behavior, identifying and addressing those factors that place children at risk, and helping the children to cope with the effects of maltreatment.[124]

Case Planning

In order to achieve the goals of the agency, a permanent solution to the problem— sometimes referred to as *child permanency*—in the form of a treatment plan or intervention, must occur. There are essentially three types of plans, all of which are typically used in abuse and neglect cases:

- **A safety plan** is developed whenever it is determined that the child is at risk of imminent harm. This plan outlines how and in what ways the child's safety will be ensured both in the immediate and distant future.

- **A case plan** identifies the goals and outcomes the worker wants the family to achieve and describes how the family will accomplish those objectives. This plan may consist of anger management workshops, drug treatment, life skills classes, job training, or some other type of constructive activity to help the family address the underlying conditions that led to the abuse or neglect.

- **A concurrent permanency plan** identifies how reunification can be achieved, or, if that is not possible, how permanency with a new family can occur. This can include revoking parental rights or making the child eligible for adoption or long-term care by legal guardians.[125]

Provision of Services

This is the stage during which the case plan is implemented. CPS arranges and coordinates the delivery of services to children and families. CPS workers have a lot of discretion in terms of what services are provided, how often they are provided, and the responsibility of each family member receiving those services.

Ongoing Assessment

Assessment occurs throughout the process and includes what happens when services are provided. Essentially, this is a follow-up by CPS workers to ensure that the plan is being adhered to or to make whatever changes are necessary. When evaluating family progress, caseworkers focus on:

- ensuring the child's safety
- reducing the risk of maltreatment
- addressing any of the effects of maltreatment on the child and family
- achieving the goals and tasks in the case plan[126]

Case Closure

The process of ending the relationship between CPS and the family involves a review of the progress made throughout the relationship. Optimally, cases are closed when families have achieved their goals and the risk of maltreatment has been reduced or eliminated. Some closings occur when families do not meet the goals of the treatment plan and the parents' rights are terminated, making the child eligible for adoption. Other cases are closed when a relative agrees to become the permanent guardian for the child.[127]

For more on foster care, watch *Foster Care: Richard* and *Foster Care: Zachary* at www.mhhe.com/mcnamarajd1e

foster care
A system whereby the state provides care to neglected, abused, or abandoned children in place of their parents.

FOSTER CARE

When cases of abuse or neglect are substantiated, one alternative available to CPS workers is to remove children from their homes until family problems can be resolved. Children may remain with other relatives, or they may be temporarily placed with foster families, group homes, or institutions.

About 513,000 children and teenagers participated in the **foster care** system in 2006, the vast majority of whom were abused or neglected by parents. Once in foster care, they tend to stay: the average length of a placement for a foster child is thirty months with three different families. Teenagers, who make up one-third of the population, typically have longer and more frequent placements.[128]

Youths who are involved in the foster care system must cope with two sources of trauma: the experience that brought them into the system in the first place and their actual experiences while in the system.[129] Compared to nonfoster children, they are more likely to suffer from mental disorders, health-related illnesses, low academic achievement, substance abuse, and delinquency. Recall from Chapter 3 on status offenders that many foster children engage in truancy, running away, or conduct that results in placement in juvenile detention facilities. This is in addition to the issues within the family that resulted in their being placed in foster care. Consider Zach's experiences with foster care when he says, "Foster care has been good for me. . . . [Y]ou can't get attached to 'em [foster parents] because then it's too hard."

RYAN'S CASE

Conclusions about Ryan

Recall Ryan's situation:

- is a twelve-year-old boy
- lives with his mother and stepfather
- is a middle child of four children
- has a bad reputation in his neighborhood and at school

Perhaps the most important factor in Ryan's behavior is his parents' inability to provide him with the time and attention he needs to develop good behavior habits. Whether his behavior is the result of inadequate supervision, too much leniency, or a lack of accountability for his actions, it seems likely that it will continue until there is a change in his family situation.

THINK ABOUT IT
What steps do you think Ryan's parents can take to change Ryan's current behavior? Do you think Ryan's parents are fostering resiliency in him, or are they increasing the likelihood of further delinquency?

THINK ABOUT IT
Neglect, Abuse, and Delinquency
Recall the theories that link exposure to family violence to delinquency. Based on your reading so far, do you agree that such a link exists? Why or why not?

THEORY AND PRACTICE WORKING TOGETHER

The Strengthening Families Program

The Strengthening Families Program (SFP) was created by the U.S. Department of Health and Human Services to help parents improve their parenting skills and, ultimately, to reduce rates of delinquency among children.

SFP involves elementary school–aged children (six to twelve years old) and their families in family skills training sessions. SFP attempts to increase resiliency and reduce the risks of behavioral, emotional, academic, and social problems by improving family relationships and parenting skills, and youths' social and life skills. SFP's curriculum is a fourteen-session behavioral skills training program of two hours per session. Parents meet separately with two group leaders to learn how to increase desired behaviors in children by increasing attention to and rewards for positive behaviors.

Parents also learn about clear communication, effective discipline, substance abuse, problem solving, and limit setting. Children meet separately with two trainers who help them learn how to understand their feelings, control anger, resist peer pressure, comply with parental rules, solve problems, and communicate effectively. Children also develop their social skills and learn about the consequences of substance abuse. During the second hour of the session,

families practice therapeutic child play, learn communication skills, and reinforce positive behaviors in each other.

SFP has been extensively evaluated by a number of state and federal agencies, and has been recognized as a model parent skills training program by the U.S. Department of Health and Human Services, the National Institute on Drug Abuse, the National Institutes of Health, the U.S. Department of Justice, and the Department of Education. The findings of various studies have consistently demonstrated that appropriate behaviors in children were increased, fewer instances of aggression and depression symptoms occurred in children, and substance abuse by parents and children decreased. Perhaps most promising is a five-year follow-up study showing that 92 percent of families continued to use parenting skills learned in the program and over two-thirds still used family meetings as a tool in collective decision making.

THINK ABOUT IT Should a national training program be required for everyone who wishes to be a parent?

Source: U.S. Department of Health and Human Services, Substance Abuse and Mental Health Services Administration, Center for Substance Abuse Prevention. http://www.samhsa.gov.

Families, Delinquency, and Public Policy

Even as we better understand the connections between changes in family structures and rates of delinquency, we continue to struggle with the various and complex problems accompanying abuse and neglect. Often, we are left to wonder what the government can do to address some of these issues. Some groups have pushed for legislation that makes it more difficult for couples to divorce, so that families are more likely to stay together and work out their problems. Others have made efforts to create a child care system that is affordable, safe and nurturing, and accessible to all types of families. While these suggestions might seem reasonable, they would be incredibly difficult to implement.

Perhaps a more reachable goal would be to offer parents workshops and seminars that help them develop good parenting skills and reduce the risks associated with abuse, neglect, and other trauma. These types of programs can improve family dynamics and ultimately influence problems like delinquency. Since about a third of all parents who have been victims of abuse and neglect inflict the same trauma on their children, seminars on healthy parenting might prevent some incidents of abuse and neglect.[130]

It is understandable, then, that many parents need help in this area and would benefit from programs such as the one described in the Theory and Practice box above.

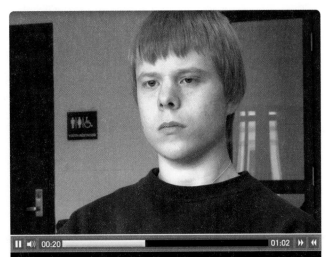

For more on family issues and delinquency, go to www.mhhe.com/mcnamarajd1e

THE BIG PICTURE

Conclusions on Families and Delinquency

- Do you think that making divorce more difficult for couples would have an impact on delinquency rates? Explain.
- Consider families who choose to withhold medical treatment for their children on religious grounds. Do you think this qualifies as abuse? Why or why not?
- Take a position in the debate on corporal punishment for children, and make an argument for or against its use. Should states be able to pass laws criminalizing this behavior?
- Visit the Search Institute's website at http://www.search-institute.org, and review the ways that communities can develop social assets in youths. Which ones seem to be the most easily implemented, and which ones seem unrealistic? On balance, do you think the assets framework is effective? Why or why not?

Key Terms

family
good parenting
resiliency
cohabitation
multiple-partner fertility

latchkey kids
birth order and delinquency
family size and delinquency
spanking
verbal assaults

child neglect
present orientation
child abuse

Make the Call ▶ A Case of Neglect?

Review the scenario below, and decide how you would approach this case.

YOUR ROLE: Recent graduate with a Master's Degree in Social Work (MSW), just hired as a CPS worker

DETAILS OF THE CASE

- On the first day of your new job, you are contacted by a community member who reports that two children are being neglected. You arrive at the home and find that the family is unkempt. There is some food, although not a lot, in the refrigerator.
- The oldest child, Brendon, is a twelve-year-old boy who appears relatively clean, although his clothes are dirty. His younger sister, Tiffany, is three years old and is running around the house crying while wearing only a dirty diaper. It appears that this child has not had a bath in a while and looks a little thin for her age and height.
- When you call Brendon's mother at work, she tells you she works two full-time jobs, but her sister watches the two children while she is away.
- Brendon tells you that his aunt just left to go to the store to buy milk and will be right back. However, there does

not appear to be any indication that someone else has been in the home.

WHAT DO YOU DO?

You suspect that the children are not being given proper care. You want to help this family, but you also know what will happen if you place the children in foster care. Based on what little information you have, can you assess whether these children are being neglected? What course of action do you take?

Consider:

- Do you take the children into protective custody?
- Do you bring the children to a local shelter or church until the mother returns home from work?
- Do you ask the mother to contact someone to supervise Brendon and Tiffany?
- Do you decide that Brendon is old enough to adequately supervise his sister, so you leave after giving him your phone number?
- Do you contact a more experienced colleague and ask for advice on what to do?
- Do you give the children a bath, feed them, and play with them until their aunt or mother comes home?

Apply Theory to Reality ▶ Cycles of Abuse

About 30 percent of victims of child abuse become abusers of their own children. While some experts identify chemical imbalances or emotional disorders as causal factors, others offer a more sociological point of view. Draw on your understanding of the various theories discussed in Chapters 4, 5, and 6. Consider learning theories, socialization theories, cultural theories, or perhaps even some of the psychological and biological explanations for this trend. Which theory do you think holds the most compelling explanation for child abuse, and why?

Your Community ▶ Spectator Behavior and Violence among Youths

In addition to the information you glean from your readings, class lectures, and discussions, it is important to roll up your sleeves and immerse yourself in a topic as a researcher who gains an understanding of a problem or issue by observing or experiencing it firsthand. Through such methods, you gain a much greater appreciation of the magnitude and scope of the problem than if you were only engaged in "armchair theorizing."

- Review the literature on spectator behavior at school sporting events, with an emphasis on inappropriate conduct by parents.

- Attend a sporting event and observe parents' behavior. In your study, aim to understand the connection between violence among youths and the problematic behaviors displayed by parents who promote a win-at-all-costs mentality.

- Interview all those involved in this issue: parents, leaders of organizations, officials, players, coaches, and so on.

- After collecting your data and drawing from the relevant literature, prepare a report that connects your observations and your research to issues of family dynamics and delinquency. Consider how the attitudes, values, beliefs, and behaviors of parents impact their children in the use and acceptability of violence.

Notes

[1] U.S. Census Bureau. 2005. Question and Answer Center. Retrieved July 7, 2005, from https://ask.census.gov/cgi-bin/askcensus.cfg/php/enduser/std_alp.php.

[2] See, for instance, Kornblum, W. 2008. *Sociology in a Changing World.* New York: McGraw-Hill.

[3] See, for instance, Parkin, R. 1997. *Kinship: An Introduction to Basic Concepts.* Oxford, UK: Blackwell.

[4] See, for instance, Wen Ming, S. 2005. "Single-Parent Family Structure, Child Development, and Child's Well-being." Paper presented at the annual meeting of the American Sociological Association, Philadelphia, August 12. http://www.allacademic.com/meta/p23369_index.html.

[5] See, for instance, Wallerstein, J. S., and Blakeslee, S. 2004. *What about the Kids?* New York: Hyperion. See also Dillon, F., Pantin, H., Robbins, M. S., and Szapocznik, J. 2008.

"Exploring the Role of Parental Monitoring of Peers on the Relationship between Family Functioning and Delinquency in the Lives of African American and Hispanic Adolescents." *Crime and Delinquency,* 54(1): 65–94; Pasley, K. 1997. "Does Living in a Step-Family Increase the Risk of Delinquency in Children?" *Stepfamilies,* 17(4). Available at http://www.stepfamilies.info/education/pdfnl/17-4.pdf.

[6] Jayson, S. 2008. "More View Cohabitating as Acceptable Choice." *USA Today,* June 8. http://www.usatoday.com/news/nation/2008-06-08-cohabitation-study_N.htm?POE=click-refer. Accessed January 30, 2009.

[7] Ibid.

[8] See, for example, *Gay and Lesbian Families,* a publication of the Jordan Institute for Families at the University of North Carolina at Chapel Hill's School of Social Work. See also Masci, D. 2008. *Two Perspectives on Gay Marriage.*

Pew Research Center. http://pewresearch.org/pubs/820/two-perspectives-on-gay-marriage.

[9] See, for instance, U.S. Department of Health and Human Services, Children's Bureau. 2009. *Strengthening Families and Communities: Resource Guide.* Available at http://www.childwelfare.gov-/pubs/res_guide_2009/. See also Moeller, T. G. 2001. *Youth Aggression and Violence: A Psychological Approach.* New York: Lawrence Erlbaum.

[10] See, for instance, Lamanna, M. A., and Riedmann, A. 2008. *Marriage and Families: Making Choices in a Diverse Society.* Boston: Pearson. See also Shaffer, D. R. 2008. *Social and Personality Development.* Boston: Pearson; Samalin, N., and Whitney, C. 2003. *Loving without Spoiling.* New York: McGraw-Hill; Townsend, J. 2006. *Boundaries with Teens.* New York: Zondervan.

[11] U.S. Department of Health and Human Services, Children's Bureau, 2009.

[12] See, for instance, Shaffer, 2008; Samalin and Whitney, 2003; Steinberg, L. 2006. *The Ten Basic Principles of Good Parenting.* New York: Simon and Schuster. http://www.chiff.com/a/good-parenting.htm.

[13] For a good discussion of imitative behavior in children, see Seigler, R. S., DeLoache, J. S., and Eisenberg, N. 2006. *How Children Develop.* New York: Macmillan.

[14] See, for instance, Bandura, A., and Walters, R. H. 1963. *Social Learning and Personality Development.* New York: Holt, Rinehart and Winston.

[15] See, for instance, Lamanna and Riedmann, 2008; Townsend, 2006.

[16] See, for instance, Thornberry, T., and Krohn, M. 2003. *Taking Stock of Delinquency.* New York: Springer; Hoghughi, M., and Long, N. 2004. *Handbook of Parenting: Theory and Research.* Los Angeles: Sage. See also Smentana, J. G. 2005. *Changing Boundaries of Parental Authority during Adolescence.* New York: Free Press.

[17] Hoghughi and Long, 2004; Shaffer 2008; Moeller, 2001.

[18] See, for instance, Smart, D. 2007. *Tailoring Parenting to Fit the Child.* AFRC Briefing Paper #4, Australian Institute of Family Studies. Available at http://www.aifs.gov.au/afrc/pubs/briefing-/briefing4.html. See also Mosier, J. 2001. *Parenting Styles: A Cross Cultural Perspective.* Pittsburgh: Pennsylvania Child Welfare Training Institute. Available at http://www.pacwcbt.pitt.edu/Curriculum-/307ParentingStylesACrossCulturalPerspective/Content/Content.pdf; Frost, S. L., Wortham, S. C., and Refel, S. 2008. *Play and Development of Children.* Boston: Pearson; Wills, M., and Hodson, V. K. 1999. *Discover Your Child's Learning Style.* New York: Crown.

[19] Steinberg, 2006.

[20] Straus, M. A. 1993. *Ten Myths about Spanking Children.* Durham: Family Research Laboratory, University of New Hampshire. See also Harder, B. 2007. "When Parents Lift Their Hands." http://articles.latimes.com/2007/feb/19/health/he-spanking19. Retrieved July 17, 2008.

[21] See Steinberg, 2006.

[22] Castiglia, P. 1999. "Growth and Development: Affectionate Behavior." *Journal of Pediatric Healthcare,* 13(1): 34–36. See also Oldham, J. M., Skodol, A. E., and Bender, D. S. 2005. *The American Psychiatric Association Textbook of Personality Disorders.* Washington, DC: American Psychiatric Association.

[23] Goldstein, S., and Brooks, R. (eds.). 2005. *Handbook of Resilience in Children.* New York: KluwerAcademic Press.

[24] See, for instance, Luthar, S. S. 2006. *Resilience in Development: A Synthesis of Research across Five Decades.* New York: Wiley. See also Elias, M. 2008. "Laws of Life: A Literacy-Based Intervention for Social-Emotional and Character Development and Resilience." *Perspectives in Education,* 26: 75–79; Heller, S. S., Larrieu,

J. A., D'Imperio, R., and Boris, N. W. 1999. "Research on Resiliency to Child Maltreatment: Empirical Considerations." *Child Abuse and Neglect,* 23(4): 321–338. See the discussion of developmental assets and how to nurture their development at http://www.search-institute.org/.

[25] Ibid.

[26] See the Search Institute brochure. http://www.search-institute.org/. Accessed July 15, 2008.

[27] Ibid.

[28] Ibid.

[29] See, for instance, Junger-Tas, J. 2009. *The Prevention of Delinquent Behavior.* New York: Springer. See also Brezina, T., Agnew, R., Cullen, F. T., and Wright, J. P. 2004. "The Code of the Street." *Youth Violence and Juvenile Justice,* 2(4): 303–328.

[30] See U.S. Census Bureau. 2008. *America's Family and Living Arrangement 2008.* Table AVG1 at http://www.census.gov/population/www/socdemo/hh-fam/cps2008.html.

[31] Ibid.

[32] See U.S. Census Bureau. 2008. *America's Family and Living Arrangement 2008.* http://www.census.gov/population/www/socdemo/hh-fam/cps2008.html.

[33] Jayson, 2008.

[34] Popenoe, D., and Whitehead, B. 2006. *The State of Our Unions, 2006.* The National Marriage Project. New Brunswick, NJ: Rutgers University.

[35] Jayson, 2008.

[36] Ibid.

[37] Ventura, S., Abma, J., Mosher, W. D., and Henshaw, S. 2008. "Estimated Pregnancy Rates by Outcome for the United States, 1990–2004. "*National Vital Statistic Reports,* 56(15): 1–26. Accessed from the CDC National Center for Health Statistics at http://www.cdc.gov/nchs/.

[38] Lundberg, S., and Pollak, R. A. 2007. "The American Family and Family Economics." *Journal of Economic Perspectives,* 21(2): 3–26.

[39] Mincy, R. 2002. "Who Should Marry Whom? Multiple Partner Fertility among New Parents." Center for Research on Child Well-Being, working paper 02-03-ff.

[40] Logan, C., Manlove, J., and Ikramullah, E. 2006. *Men Who Father Children with More Than One Woman: a Contemporary Portrait of Multiple-Partner Fertility.* Child Trends, Research in Brief, November. http://www.childtrends.org/Files//Child_Trends-2006_11_1_RB_MultiplePartners.pdf.

[41] Ibid.

[42] National Center on Health Statistics, 2007. *Divorce Data.* http://www.cdc.gov/nchs/products/elec_prods/subject/divorce.htm. Accessed July 21, 2008.

[43] Family Research Council, 2004. *The Family Portrait.*

[44] Popenoe and Whitehead, 2006.

[45] Hetherington, E. M., and Kelly, J. 2002. *For Better or Worse: Divorce Reconsidered.* New York: Norton.

[46] Ibid.

[47] Ibid.

[48] Ibid.

[49] Amato, P. R., and Keith, B. 1991. "Parental Divorce and the Well-Being of Children: A Meta-analysis." *Psychological Bulletin,* 110: 26–46.

[50] Dunn, J., Davies, L. C., O'Connor, T. G., and Sturgess, W. 2001. "Family Lives and Friendships: The Perspectives of Children in Step-, Single-Parent, and Nonstep Families." *Journal of Family Psychology,* 15: 272–287.

[51] Ibid.

[52] See Education Portal. 2007. "Leaving Men Behind: Women Going to College in Ever-Greater Numbers." http://education-portal.com/articles/Leaving_Men_Behind:_Women_Go_to_College_in_Ever-Greater_Numbers.html. See also Attewell, P., and Lavin, D. 2007. *Passing the Torch: Does Higher Education for the Disadvantaged Pay Off across the Generations?* New York: Russell Sage Foundation.

[53] See http://www.aamc.org/newsroom/reporter/feb05/deans.htm. Accessed July 19, 2008.

[54] U.S. Bureau of Census. *Statistical Abstract of the United States,* 12th ed. Washington, DC: U.S. Government Printing Office.

[55] Superville, D. 2009. "Obama Signs First Bill into Law on Equal Pay." Associated Press, January 29. http://news.yahoo.com/s/ap/20090129/ap_on_go_pr_wh/obama. Retrieved February 5, 2009.

[56] Winkler, A. E., McBride, T. D., and Andrews, C. 2005. "Wives Who Outearn Their Husbands: A Transitory or Persistent Phenomenon for Couples?" *Demography,* 42(3): 523–535. See also Murrell, S. 1974. "Relationship of Family Size and Ordinal Position to Psychosocial Measures of Delinquency." *Journal of Abnormal Psychology,* 2(1): 39–46; Rahav, G. 1981. "Family Size and Delinquency." *Sociology and Social Research,* 66(1): 42–51; Green, A. E., Gesten, E. L., Greenwald, M. A., and Salcedo, O. 2008. "Predicting Delinquency in Adolescence and Young Adulthood: A Longitudinal Analysis of Early Risk Factors." *Youth Violence and Juvenile Justice,* 6: 323.

[57] Ibid.

[58] See, for instance, Bianchi, S. M., Robinson, J. P., and Milkie, M. A. 2006. *Changing Rhythms of American Family Life.* New York: Russell Sage Foundation. See also Eberstadt, M. 2001. "Home Alone America: The Consequences of Children Raising Themselves." *Policy Review,* 107. Available at http://www.hoover.org/publications/policyreview/3476711.html. See also Plionis, E. M. 1990. "Parenting, Discipline and the Concept of Quality Time." *Child and Adolescent Social Work Journal,* 7(6): 513–540.

[59] See, for instance, Gottfredson, D., Weisman, S., Womer, S., and Soule, D. 2003. *Not All After School Programs Good for Latchkey Kids: Some*

May Offer Little or No Benefit in Delinquency and Drug Use. Washington, DC: Society for Prevention Research. See also Hanson, G. R., Venturelli, P. J., and Fleckenstein, A. 2005. *Drugs and Society,* 9th ed. New York: Jones and Bartlett; Robinson, B., Coleman, M., and Rowland, B. 1998. *Latchkey Kids: Unlocking Doors for Children and their Families.* Los Angeles: Sage.

[60] See, for instance, Belsky, J., Burchinal, M., McCartney, K., and Vandell, D.L. 2007. "Are There Long-Term Effects of Early Child Care?" *Child Development,* 78(2): 681–701; Hickman, L. N. 2006. "Who Should Care for Our Children?" *Journal of Family Issues,* 27(5): 652–684; Lowry, R. 2001. "Nasty, Brutish and Short: Children in Day Care and the Mothers Who Put Them There." *National Review,* May 28, pp. 36–42. See also Loeb, S., Bridges, M., and Rumberger, R. W. 2007. "How Much Is Too Much? The Influence of Preschool Centers on Children's Social and Cognitive Development." *Economics of Educational Review,* 26(1): 52–66.

[61] Ibid.

[62] Day, J., and Downs, B. 2009. "Opting Out: An Exploration of Labor Force Participation of New Mothers." Available at http://www.census.gov/hhes/ioindex/opting-out-paper.pdf. See also Stone, P. 2008. *Opting Out? Why Women Really Quit Careers and Head Home.* Berkeley: University of California Press.

[63] See, for instance, Belsky, J., and Eggebeen, D. 1991. "Early and Extensive Maternal Employment and Young Children's Socioemotional Development: Children of the National Longitudinal Survey of Youth." *Journal of Marriage and the Family,* 53: 1083–1110.

[64] See, for instance, a study in England regarding the trend toward stay-at-home fathers. http://www.telegraph.co.uk/finance/personalfinance/7561254/stay-at-home-fathers-have-increased-ten-fold-in-ten-years.html.

[65] Lyttle, L. 2010. "How Stay-at-Home Dads Bounce Back from Career Hiatus." ABC News. http://abcnews.go.com/Business/role-reversal-unemployment-creates-stay-at-home-fathers/story/id=11983642#.Tvi3BXN66-8.

[66] Shaver, K. 2007. "Stay-at-Home Dads Forge New Identities, Roles." *The Washington Post,* June 17. Available at http://www.washingtonpost.com/wp-dyn/content/article/2007/06/16/AR2007061601289.html.

[67] Ibid. These statistics only account for married stay-at-home dads; there are other children being cared for by single fathers or gay couples.

[68] Gill, L. 2001. *Stay-at-Home Dads: The Essential Guide to Creating the New Family.* New York: Penguin.

[69] Ibid.

[70] Smith, A. 2009. *The Daddy Shift.* Boston: Beacon Press.

[71] Baylies, P. 2004. *The Stay-at-Home Dad Handbook.* Chicago: Chicago Review Press.

[72] See, for instance, Tibbetts, R., and Gilbert, J. 2006. "The Effects of Family Size on the Development of Delinquency." Paper presented at the annual meeting of the American Society of Criminology (ASC), Los Angeles. See also Mullin, J. 1973. "Birth Order as a Variable of Probation Performance." *Journal of Research in Crime and Delinquency,* 10(1): 29–34; Begue, L., and Roche, S. 2005. "Birth Order and Youth Delinquent Behavior: Testing the Differential Parental Control Hypothesis in a French Representative Sample." *Psychology, Crime and Law,* 11(1): 73–85.

[73] Ibid.

[74] See, for instance, Begue and Roche, 2005.

[75] See, for instance, "Family Size in America: Are Large Families Back?" 2006. http://www.babycenter.com/0_family-size-in-america-are-large-families-back_1503367.bc?showAll=true.

[76] See Kristin, Y., Mack, K. Y., Leiber, M. J., Featherstone, R. A., and Monserud, M.A. 2007. "Reassessing the Family-Delinquency Association: Do Family Type, Family Processes, and Economic Factors Make a Difference?" *Journal of Criminal Justice,* 35(1): 51–67; Sathyanarayana Rao, T. S. 2007. "Criminal Behavior: A Dispassionate Look at Parental Disciplinary Practices." *Indian Journal of Psychiatry,* 49: 231. Available from http://www.indianjpsychiatry.org/text.asp?2007/49/4/231/37661; Loeber, R., and Stouthamer-Loeber, M. 1986. "Family Factors as Correlates and Predictors of Juvenile Conduct Problems and Delinquency." In Tonry, M., and Morris, N. (eds.). *Crime and Justice: An Annual Review of Research.* Chicago: University of Chicago Press, pp. 29–149.

[77] Tibbetts and Gilbert, 2006.

[78] Ibid.

[79] Preidt, R. 2009. "Intervening in Preschool Years Can Prevent Juvenile Delinquency, Sessions Alter At-Risk Kids' Stress Responses, Study Suggests." ABC News, March 23. http://abcnews.go.com/Health/Healthday/Story?id=4508955&page=1.

[80] Ibid.

[81] Ibid.

[82] Bureau of Justice Statistics. 2000. *Intimate Partner Violence,* Washington, DC: U.S. Department of Justice. http://www.ojp.usdoj.gov/bjs/pub/pdg/jpv.pdf. Retrieved February 3, 2009.

[83] Redden, G. 2008. *Violence in the Family.* National Association of Children of Alcoholics. http://www.nacoa.org/famviol.htm.

[84] Ibid.

[85] Department of Justice, Office of Juvenile Justice Delinquency Prevention. 2001. *The Nurturing Parenting Programs.* Washington, DC. http://www.ncjrs.gov/pdffiles1/ojjdp/172848.pdf. Retrieved February 3, 2009.

[86] National Institute of Justice. 2001. *An Update on the Cycle of Violence.* Washington, DC. Available at http://www.ncjrs.gov/pdffiles1/ojjdp/184894.pdf.

[87] U.S. Department of Justice, Office of Juvenile Justice and Delinquency Prevention. 2000. *Safe from the Start: Taking Action on Children Exposed to Violence,* Washington, DC.

[88] Redden, 2008.

[89] Bureau of Justice Statistics. 2007. *Homicide Trends in the U.S.* Washington, DC: U.S. Department of Justice. http://www.ojp.gov/bjs/homicide/intimates.htm.

[90] The most recent survey on this issue was conducted in 2002: an ABC News poll that shows 65 percent of Americans believe spanking is acceptable. http://www.pollingreport.com/life.htm. According to some experts, this is identical to what a Gallup Poll found a decade earlier. See http://www.icrsurvey.com/Study.aspx?f=ABC_Spanking_1102.html.

[91] Straus, 1993.

[92] Harder, 2007.

[93] Ibid.

[94] Ibid.

[95] Ibid.

[96] Ibid.

[97] Ibid.

[98] Redden, 2008.

[99] U.S. Department of Health and Human Services. *Study of National Incidence and Prevalence of Child Abuse and Neglect.* http://www.childwelfare.gov/pubs/usermanuals/neglect/neglectb.cfm.

[100] Ibid.

[101] Ibid.

[102] See http://kidshealth.org/parent/food/weight/failure_thrive.html.

[103] U.S. Department of Health and Human Services, Children's Bureau. 2007. *Child Maltreatment 2005.* Washington, DC: U.S. Government Printing Office. Retrieved July 12, 2008 from http://www.acf.hhs.gov/programs/cb/pubs/cm05/index.htm.

[104] U.S. Department of Health and Human Services, Centers for Disease Control and Prevention. http://www.cdc.gov/ncbddd/FAS/fasask.htm.

[105] U.S. Department of Health and Human Services. *Study of National Incidence and Prevalence of Child Abuse and Neglect.*

[106] See, for instance, McNamee, S. J., and Miller, R. K. 2004. "The Meritocracy Myth." *Sociation Today,* 2(1). Available at http://www.ncsociology.org/sociationtoday/v21/merit.htm. See also Zimbardo, P. G., and Boyd, J. 2008. *The Time Paradox.* New York: Simon and Schuster; Banfield, E. 1970. *The Unheavenly City Revisited.* Chicago: University of Chicago Press; Orford, J. 2008. *Community Psychology: Challenges, Controversies, and Emerging Consensus.* New York: Wiley.

[107] See, for instance, Wallace, H. 2005. *Family Violence: Legal, Medical and Social Perspectives,* 4th ed. Boston: Allyn and Bacon.

[108] See http://www.childwelfare.gov/systemwide/laws_policies/statutes/define.cfm.

109 U.S. Department of Health and Human Services, Administration of Children and Families. 2005. National Child Abuse and Neglect Data System. 2005. *Child Abuse and Neglect of Children under Age 18.* Washington, DC: U.S. Government Printing Office.

110 Pressel, D. M. 2009. "Evaluation of Physical Abuse in Children." http://www.aafp.org-/afp/20000515/3057.html.

111 Ibid.

112 Ibid.

113 Ibid.

114 See "Warning Signs of Abuse and Neglect." http://www.helpguide.org/mental-/child_abuse_physical_emotional_sexual_neglect.htm.

115 Pressel, 2009.

116 Ibid.

117 See, for instance, Snyder, H., and Sickmund, M. 2006. *Juvenile Offenders and Victims: 2006 National Report.* Washington, DC: U.S. Department of Justice, Office of Justice Programs, Office of Juvenile Justice and Delinquency Prevention. http://www.ojjdp.ncjrs.org/ojstatbb/nr2006/downloads/NR2006.pdf.

118 Prevent Child Abuse America. 2008. *Fact Sheet on Sexual Abuse.* http://member.prevent-childabuse.org/site/DocServer/sexual_abuse.pdf?docID=126.

119 Ibid.

120 See "Warning Signs of Abuse and Neglect."

121 Ibid.

122 DePanfilis, D., and Salus, M. K. 2003. *Child Protective Services: A Guide for Case Workers.* Washington, DC: U.S. Department of Health and Human Services, Administration for Children and Families, Administration on Children, Youth and Families, Children's Bureau, Office on Child Abuse and Neglect. http://www.childwelfare.gov/pubs/usermanuals/cps/cps.pdf.

123 Ibid.

124 Ibid.

125 Ibid.

126 See, for instance, Brittain, C., and Grant, D. E. 2004. *Helping in Child Protective Services: A Competency-Based Casework Handbook.* New York: Oxford University Press.

127 DePanfilis and Salus, 2003.

128 See Child Welfare League of America at http://www.cwla.org.

129 Ibid.

130 About 30 percent of children of abuse go on to abuse their children as parents. See National Child Abuse Center Statistics at http://www.childhelp.org/resources/learning-center/statistics.

After reading this chapter, you should be able to:

- Underline the difficulties in defining "gang" and terms such as "gang-related" crimes.

- Identify and describe the different types of gangs and their common characteristics.

- Discuss some of the latest trends in gang behavior and how those trends attract youths to join gangs.

- Construct an argument for why gangs are prone to drug-related and violent activities.

- Explain the criminal justice system's response to gangs, and support your findings.

8 Gangs and Delinquency

Many people believe that gangs are a serious problem in the United States, but they also have many misconceptions about the nature of gang life. When people think about gangs, they tend to imagine a violent group of individuals who engage in drive-by shootings of rival gang members, are heavily involved in the drug trade, and pose a threat to public safety. While such activities do form the nature of some gangs, consider the following scenario.

Andre's profile:
- is an eleven-year-old African American
- lives in a large southwestern city with his grandmother

His friends:
- Together with Andre, they form a gang called the Black Cobras.
- Kenny is an aspiring artist who draws a picture of a black cobra on the back of each of the boys' jackets.
- They proudly display their "colors" while riding their bicycles around the neighborhood.
- They enjoy the thrill of scaring residents in the neighborhood by projecting an image of themselves as dangerous by occasionally vandalizing property and shoplifting from local stores.

Current situation:
The boys formed the Black Cobras after they were approached to join a chapter of the Crips, a dangerous gang in the area. They thought that by forming their own group, they could have a way out of the dangers of Crips membership. When the Crips members learned of the Black Cobras, they decided that the Black Cobras should not be allowed to travel in Crips-controlled areas. The leader of the Crips tells Andre that they have to have a "sit down" or meeting, which is often a prelude to a gang war. Clearly, the Black Cobras cannot win this battle, but at the same time, they do not want to join the Crips.

The dilemma the boys face is serious, but consider whether the Black Cobras are really a gang and why the boys formed the group in the first place. In such a situation, can the police play a role in settling the dispute?

How does the justice system typically respond to young people in gangs?

THINK ABOUT IT What will happen when Andre meets with the Crips leader? What can he do or say to prevent a gang fight?

A gang member may be one of the most enduring images people have when they think of delinquency. Media portrayals of gangs tend to exacerbate our fears of victimization, but what is really meant by *gang,* and what threats do gangs actually pose to a community? If we were to simply follow the news or heed the claims made by politicians, we would have to conclude that drive-by shootings and gang wars are common, that all gang members are violent, and that gang members are more likely to commit murder than ever before. But crime data from the Uniform Crime Reports in 2009 indicate that youths in general are responsible for only 16 percent of all violent crimes.[1] Additionally, consider the following statistics:

- A study from the Bureau of Justice Statistics shows that only 10 percent of homicide convictions were for youths under the age of 18.[2]

- The Uniform Crime Reports indicates that less than 8 percent of all homicides in 2009 were gang-related.

- According to the National Youth Gang Survey, more than half of suburban areas and more than 75 percent of rural counties recorded no gang-related homicides in 2007.[3]

In this chapter, we will explore what gangs are, what types of gangs exist in the United States, and why youths join gangs, as well as common gang activities. But note that we may be seeing a significant shift in the way gangs operate. Traditionally, the bond that members had with each other was one of the most important reasons for joining a gang. Gang wars are typically based on rivalries between gangs over turf or allegiance to one group or another. Today, researchers are noticing a blurring of those lines, which suggests that different reasons for gang membership may be emerging.

Definition of Gangs

gang
A small group of adolescents who loiter on a street corner, but also applicable to graffiti artists, drug users, neo-Nazi Skinheads, or any other group of highly organized youths whose purpose is to generate money from drug dealing or other criminal activity.

The term **gang** evokes a number of images. For some, a gang is a small group of adolescents who loiter on a street corner. For others, the term applies to graffiti artists, drug users, neo-Nazi Skinheads, or any other group of highly organized youths whose purpose is to generate money from drug dealing or other criminal activity. The definition of *gang* is complicated because the term could apply to various groups of people with different characteristics. The diversity in perceptions of gangs, as well as the way the public defines them, presents particular challenges to communities as they attempt to deal with the problem. The success or failure of community-wide attempts to address gangs rests in part on how the problem is understood and diagnosed.[4]

There is also the issue of according responsibility for criminal behavior to gangs instead of to individual offenders. The term *gang-related* has become a marker to describe much of the crime that exists in many neighborhoods, but the extent to which gangs are responsible for crime is often overstated.

The media, the public, and community agencies use the term *gang* more loosely than the law enforcement community. While drug distribution is a featured activity of some gangs, the public's perception has become that all gangs are highly organized and heavily involved in the drug trade.[5] Additionally, the public has come to perceive drive-by shootings as a common characteristic of gang life.[6]

In contrast, politicians and law enforcement officials tend to rely on legal parameters to define a gang. These formal definitions often reflect only high-profile, violent gangs that present the most pressing problems for police departments. For example, the Miami

Police Department defines a gang as "a group of persons joined together to commit acts of violence or any other anti-social behavior."[7] The Los Angeles Police Department defines a gang as "a group of juveniles and/or adults in a geographic area whose activities include the unlawful use of force, violence, or threats of force and violence to further the group's purpose."[8] The LAPD's description is the most common definition used by police departments across the country, but it fails to recognize the fact that many gangs do not engage solely in criminal acts, or even highly visible ones.

Even experts on gangs have great difficulty in reaching a consensus on an acceptable definition of a gang. Part of the problem is that there is a qualitative difference between a youth gang and a delinquent group, which were viewed as identical in the 1950s and 1960s. One way to distinguish them is to compare *gang* behavior with *delinquent group* behavior. Gang youths engage in more criminal behavior and have higher rates of police contact, arrests, and drug-related offenses.[9] Moreover, gang membership tends to inhibit the maturational effect, discussed in Chapter 2. Generally, as youths mature, they become less likely to engage in further criminal behavior.[10]

While there is diversity, three criteria, according to gang experts David Curry and Scott Decker, do set a standard for defining a street gang:

- community recognition as a group or collectivity
- group recognition of itself as a distinct group of either adolescents or young adults
- consistent negative response from law enforcement and/or neighborhood residents due to illegal activities[11]

Even this approach presents problems, however, since it implies a negative relationship between the community and the gang. Some gangs have a positive relationship with their local communities and often solve neighborhood problems informally.[12] Even though delinquents may commit acts with others, sometimes referred to as **co-offending,** which is more common than solo acts of delinquency, these offenders do not necessarily constitute a gang.

co-offending
The act of committing offenses or crimes with others, but not necessarily as part of a gang.

One way to conceptualize gangs is to think of them as part of a larger continuum that represents how adolescents come together in groups. The teenage years are an important period in the lives of youths, and the groups they choose to connect with shape their social identities. But not all groups are bad for a youth's development (see Figure 8-1). Gang expert James Howell describes the continuum. On one end are simple play groups and

FIGURE 8-1 The Gang Continuum
What is it that distinguishes a group of adolescents who hang around together from a street gang?
Source: Adapted from Howell, J. C. 2003. *Preventing and Reducing Juvenile Delinquency: A Comprehensive Framework.* Thousand Oaks, CA: Sage.

gang-related
An often misused term to describe the criminal activities of an individual member rather than the coordinated activities of the gang itself.

member-based definition
Classification of an incident as gang-related simply because the individual involved is a gang member.

motive-based definition
Classification of an incident as gang-related if offending individuals act on behalf of the gang.

at the other are criminal groups. Most youths affiliate with one or more of these types of groups during adolescence.

While association with a group or groups is part of youths' development, they mostly act on their own. The term **gang-related** is often misused to describe the criminal activities of an individual member rather than the coordinated activities of the gang itself. The police often classify an incident as gang-related simply because the individual involved is a gang member. Cheryl Maxson and Malcolm Klein refer to this as a **member-based definition.** Other police departments may use a **motive-based definition** to classify an incident as gang-related if the individual acts on behalf of the gang.[13] It makes sense to separate the crimes a youth commits while acting as a gang member, such as assaulting rival gang members, from his or her own individual behavior, such as robbing a convenience store for personal gain; however, the police tend to include most crimes committed by individuals as related to their membership in an organization.

Many police departments have been confronted with another aspect of gang membership involving youths who are on the fringes of a gang, sometimes referred to as associates or *wanna-be* members. These youths hang around full-fledged gang members but may not be recognized either by the particular gang or by others as a full member. Determining if a youth is a member or merely a wanna-be is important since they often engage in very different types of activities. Some police departments require a youth to meet specific characteristics to be documented as a gang member. These include having gang tattoos, wearing gang colors, spraying gang graffiti, participating in gang-related drive-bys, or committing felonies with other gang members.[14]

REASONS FOR JOINING

Why do youths join gangs in the first place? What are the motivating factors that propel some individuals in a neighborhood to join a gang while others avoid the influence? While we cannot know for certain what motivates all youths in the decisions they make, several factors play a significant role in the process.

One extensive sixteen-year-long study of high-risk youths in New York reveals two essential factors: stimulation and survival. Youths who join gangs learn that drugs, girls, and excitement come from membership. They also realize that the only way to be protected from other gangs is to join one.

Other research on gang membership tends to indicate that a variety of factors place adolescents at increased risk of joining a gang. Those factors include the following:

- early involvement in delinquency, especially with violence and drug use
- troubled family relationships
- low attachment to school and poor grades
- association with youths involved with gangs, including older siblings
- residence in neighborhoods with gangs[15]

The more of these factors that exist in children's lives, the greater the likelihood that they will join a gang. Hanging out with delinquent peers, school failure at the elementary level, and sexual activity at an early age are among the stronger predictors of gang membership.[16] As Anthony points out, associating with other delinquents can create a situation in which an individual youth is in jeopardy:

> It's just if you know these dudes on the next block don't like you, well, don't like the people you hang with, and if you walk through there then it's more than likely that they know you hang with them, so they gonna try to get at you. Like, say, one of my friends shot his cousin. If he see me, he gonna try to kill me just out of retaliation because he can't get to the—it just— I'm not going to let it happen. So I see him, he, he pull him, draw him on it. We at it. Whoever get hit, they hit, and we gone.

We will return to the discussion of risk and protective factors in Chapter 12 when we discuss the nature of delinquency prevention, but for now, recognize that there are variables that play an important role in understanding why some youths choose to become involved in gangs while others do not.[17] See Table 8-1 for some reasons youths join gangs.

TABLE 8-1 Reasons Youths Join Gangs

Identity or Recognition	Being part of a gang allows members to achieve a level of status they feel is impossible outside the gang culture.
Protection	Because they live in a gang area, they are subject to violence by rival gangs; membership guarantees support in case of attack and retaliation.
Fellowship	A gang functions as an extension of the family and may provide companionship lacking in gang members' home environments. Older siblings and relatives may belong or have belonged to gangs, and often socialize younger brothers and sisters into gang life.
Intimidation	Some members are forced to join if their membership will contribute to the gang's criminal activity. Some youths join to intimidate residents and other youths in the community.
Criminal Activity	Some join gangs in order to financially benefit from involvement in the drug trade and other crimes.[18]

According to the Los Angeles Police Department, youths join gangs for these reasons. Are there other factors that you can think of for why youths get involved in gangs?

While gang members are more likely than other delinquents to become chronic adult offenders, most eventually leave their gangs.[19] This *aging out* process, whereby the youth matures and finds other activities that take priority over the gang, is common among most delinquents. Some simply get tired of the gang lifestyle and seek new challenges. As they get older, most gang members get married, find legitimate jobs, and settle down.[20]

The study of gangs in the United States demonstrates a wide variety of reasons members become involved in the first place, as well as the benefits of gang affiliation. If policymakers, community leaders, and police officials are to design and implement effective strategies to control gang activity, they must understand the diversity of gangs in terms of their characteristics and the numerous functions they serve.

For more on reasons for joining gangs, watch *Gang Involvement: Shun, Respecting & Teaching: Shun* and *Friends & Gang Life: Larry* at www .mhhe.com/mcnamarajd1e

MEDIA DISTORTION

Throughout various periods in American history, gangs have received quite a bit of attention from the media, especially during the 1970s and 1980s. Moreover, whether it was movies, television, radio, magazines, newspapers, or documentaries, the image created about gangs was a consistent one: they are heavily involved in the drug trade and are exceptionally prone to violence.[21]

There are two primary reasons for this characterization. First, there is a commonality of interests that are being served with exaggerated portrayals of gangs and gang life. The news media are in a profit-making business. The more exciting or dramatic the story, the more likely it will capture the general public's interest. Given the propensity to associate gangs with violence and mayhem, whenever a story carries a great deal of interest, members of the media seek to relate that drama to gangs.[22]

Second, the media have a limited amount of time and space in which to present the story, and very often the reporter reinterprets the information to fit a preconceived framework. In cases for which the details of a particular crime are unknown, reporters commonly recast this description and broadly categorize it as "gang-related."[23] With limited access to gangs, reporters gain their understanding through other media accounts and attempted interviews with gang members, which may or may not be successful.

Gangs also benefit from media distortion. Those living the so-called street life have a need to enhance their reputation. In the absence of more traditional status-conferring mechanisms, a person or a gang moves up the social hierarchy and gains the marker of being tough, savvy, or a "bad-ass" through the media. The more negative or violent the characterization, the more it serves the interests of the individual and the gang.[24]

Another distortion the media presents about gangs relates to their ethnic and racial composition. Gangs are not exclusively a minority phenomenon. Although poor non-white communities have produced the largest number of gangs, lower-class white communities have a long history of gang involvement. It is more accurate to say that ethnicity and race do not explain the allure of gang life as much as a marginalized social status does. The race-related portrayals of gangs perpetuate existing myths that contribute to the gang problem.

ANDRE'S CASE

The "Threat" of the Black Cobras

Recall Andre's dilemma:

- He and his friends formed the Black Cobras to avoid the pressure of joining the Crips.
- They engage in minor crimes, such as vandalism, to establish an identity in the neighborhood.

However we might define a gang, the Black Cobras do not pose a large threat to community residents and do not possess the criminal intentions that gangs such as the Crips do. Because the Black Cobras are a small group that does not have economic motivations, they could be considered posers seeking attention rather than a legitimate gang.

THINK ABOUT IT Is turf control still the basis of violence among gangs, or is some other factor the cause?

ORIGINS OF GANGS

Gang studies have focused on three fairly distinct eras in the twentieth and twenty-first centuries (see Figure 8-2). The earliest studies at the University of Chicago were part of the more general concern with social disorganization in rapidly growing urban areas.[25] The most influential study of gangs in the early twentieth century is Fredrick Thrasher's *The Gang,* published in 1927, which identified 1,313 different gangs in Chicago and provided the foundation for generations of gang phenomena researchers. Thrasher's study

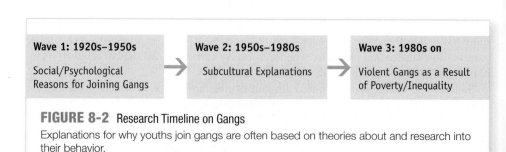

FIGURE 8-2 Research Timeline on Gangs
Explanations for why youths join gangs are often based on theories about and research into their behavior.

was the first truly sociological analysis that attempted to do more than simply describe the gang problem; he addressed some of the social psychological issues, such as the quest for adventure, that prompt individuals to join gangs.[26]

Thrasher also looked at how gangs are organized, how leaders emerge, and how authorities attempt to deal with them. Similarly, recall the discussion of social disorganization theory in Chapter 4, in which Clifford Shaw and Henry McKay argued that central areas of social disorganization, often the neighborhoods of the poorest and most recent immigrants, have high rates of street crime and delinquency due to a breakdown in their capacity to control residents. Thus, in this first wave of studies, the explanation for gangs centered on the squalor of urban areas.[27]

The second wave of studies focusing on community subcultures began in the mid-1950s and lasted for approximately thirty years.[28] Albert Cohen, in his version of strain theory (discussed in Chapter 4), argued that delinquent gangs are primarily a lower-class, male phenomenon because legitimate opportunities to succeed are often severely restricted. In response, these boys create a subculture, or gang.

In contrast, Walter Miller, whose theory was also discussed in Chapter 4, held that there is no need to create a delinquent subculture because lower-class culture itself embodies a set of focal concerns or characteristics (e.g., toughness, smartness, trouble, excitement) that account for higher rates of delinquency and gang life. Crime is a natural reaction to living up to the expectations found in a distinct and lower-class culture.[29] Both perspectives attributed the creation of gangs, and the problems associated with their existence, to social structural elements, either urban social ecology or social class opportunities.

Beginning in the 1980s, the third wave of research on gangs has resembled the research of the 1920s. There continues to be a tendency to associate gangs and violence with urban poverty; gang life becomes a source of social identity in the face of impoverished living conditions. The lack of opportunities and the living conditions for some groups have not improved or have become worse. As a result, gang life appears more severe. Individuals who become gang members join earlier and remain for longer periods of time. The gangs themselves have become increasingly entrenched in economically depressed communities.[30]

Definition of Gangs

Why is it difficult to define terms such as "gang" and "gang-related crimes"? How do their definitions influence social policy and programs?

THINK ABOUT IT

Extent and Types of Gangs

According to the National Youth Gang Survey (NYGS), an annual study of gangs and gang activity across the country, gang problems declined significantly in the mid-1990s. This trend lasted about a decade; since 2001, gang activity has been steadily rising. In 2007, there were an estimated 788,000 gang members and 27,000 active gangs in the United States. Rural counties experienced the most dramatic increase even though gang activity is predominantly an urban phenomenon—between 2002 and 2007, the number of gang problems in rural areas increased by nearly 25 percent.[31]

While the media portray gang membership as primarily a juvenile phenomenon, the data indicate that adults in larger cities comprise the greatest proportion of gang members. According to the National Gang Center, in 2007, two-thirds of all gang members were adults. Gangs that exist in rural areas or smaller cities tend to be made up of juveniles: the NYGS indicates that approximately three-quarters of gang members in these locations are juveniles, while gangs in larger cities tend to attract adult members.[32]

Larger cities have a much longer, more extensive history of gang problems—nearly half have experienced ongoing gang problems since before the 1990s. In contrast, very few

gang cycles
Consistently changing patterns of gang activity and violence.

rural counties have long-standing gang problems. In its 2007 report, the NYGS reported that an overwhelming majority of agencies noted a fluctuating trend of gang activity, characterized by alternating periods of increasing and decreasing seriousness of the local gang problem, rather than a general increase. These findings highlight **gang cycles,** or consistently changing patterns of gang activity and violence (see Figure 8-3).[33]

A great deal of fluidity exists with gangs: they come in all shapes and sizes, they come together for a variety of purposes, and they often change their composition based on a number of factors. One of those factors is race and ethnicity. Most gangs are intraracial, with members from similar racial or ethnic backgrounds. Part of the reason stems from the geographic origin of gangs. In some areas of Texas, for example, Hispanic/Latino gangs are much more prominent, largely because of the density of the Hispanic/Latino population in the state. Hispanics/Latinos make up about half of the gang members in the United States. Blacks represent about 35 percent of the total, while whites represent about 9 percent. Popular at the turn of the twentieth century, at the height of immigration from Europe, white ethnic gangs, such as the Italians, the Irish, and the Jewish, have, for the most part, assimilated into mainstream American culture. Today, there are fewer white ethnic gangs in the United States,[34] and they are more likely to be present in rural areas than in large cities.[35]

BLACK GANGS

There are many black gangs in cities across the United States; however, cities like Los Angeles offer insight into the largest and best-known gangs: the Crips and the Bloods, with over 30,000 members, earning them the label *supergang*.[36]

The Crips

This Los Angeles–based gang has its roots in the radical group called the Black Panthers, who were popular among black Americans in the 1960s. This militant group became famous for its clashes with police and political leaders over the treatment of black Americans. While striving for the equal rights of black Americans, the Black Panthers created social programs, such as free breakfasts for children, that made them very popular with city residents.

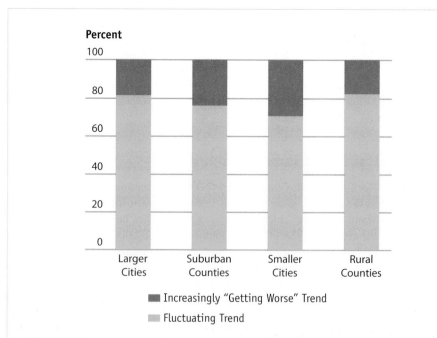

FIGURE 8-3 Assessment of the Gang Problem by Type of Community, 2002–2004
Why is there such a fluctuation in gang problems regardless of the area?

Source: U.S. Department of Justice, Office of Justice Programs, Office of Juvenile Justice and Delinquency Prevention. 2009. *National Youth Gang Survey Report.* Tallahassee, FL: Institute for Intergovernmental Research.

Spinoff groups such as the Avenues and Baby Avenues were created, the latter of which eventually became the Crips. The name "Crips" has been a source of curiosity. According to one story, when one of its leaders, Stanley "Tookie" Williams, wrote the word "Cribs," it was misinterpreted as "Crips." A different story explains that another founder of the group, Raymond Lee Washington, made a spelling mistake and wrote "Crips" instead of "Cribs." Regardless of its name origin, this group has been involved in a host of criminal activities including drug trafficking, armed robbery, and homicide. The Crips accept only black Americans as members and have branched out to other cities across the country.

Some gangs, such as the Crips, accept only African American members. These groups have particular "signs" to communicate with each other.

The Bloods

The Bloods, a much smaller gang than the Crips, are known for their violence against other gangs and for their involvement in the drug trade. The gang has its origins in Compton, California. While primarily made up of black Americans, the Bloods have accepted members from other racial groups, including Hispanics/Latinos, whites, and Asians. Like the Crips, the Bloods have expanded their operations across the country, and are particularly powerful as prison gangs, taking over much of the underground economy within the institutions and intimidating other inmates to join their organization. Because they are hated rivals, members of the Crips and the Bloods are sent to different prisons in California to avoid outbreaks of violence.

HISPANIC/LATINO GANGS

Given the growth in the number of Hispanics/Latinos in the United States, the number of delinquent gangs has also increased; however, there are significant differences between Hispanic/Latino gangs.

People Nation vs. Folk Nation

Two large gangs in the Midwest comprise what are generally known as the People and the Folks. The People Nation, a more racially heterogeneous group, is made up of many other subgangs that have their own names, structures, and allegiances. Moreover, these subgangs can switch affiliation to other supergangs. The largest People subgang is the Latin Kings. Folk Nation, another supergang formed by a somewhat odd coalition between a white gang, the Simon City Royals, and the Black Gangster Disciples. The Folks are aligned with the Crips while the People have connections to the Bloods.[37]

The Latin Kings

The Almighty Latin King and Queen Nation (ALKQN) was started in Chicago, Illinois, during the 1940s by a group of individuals of Hispanic/Latino descent in an attempt to overcome the prejudices they faced. This group wanted to rise above the racism and create an organization of so-called Kings equipped to fight off injustice and better themselves and their communities.

The ALKQN became one of Chicago's largest and most violent street gangs, targeting other gangs and even their own members. The Latin Kings use the colors black and gold to represent their gang, and commonly a crown symbol, which may have three or five points. They also make exclusive use of a trademark symbol known as the "master," often with a tear drop.[38] The Latin Kings are highly organized with a structure similar to the military: foot soldiers and ranking officers.[39]

Members of the Latin Kings follow particular rituals in terms of colors, symbols, and hand signs.

This sign represents the MS-13 gang. Many gangs flash "signs" as a form of identification and communication.

The MS-13

The MS-13 gang, also known as Mara Salvatrucha 13, has cliques, or factions, located throughout the United States and retains ties to its Central American counterparts. Its membership is estimated to total over 36,000 in Honduras alone. Like the Crips and the Bloods, MS-13 is involved in the drug trade, but it is also active in gun running, people smuggling, assassinations for hire, theft, arson, and extortion. Many MS-13 members have military training, making them an even greater threat to communities. In March 2004, the Maldon Institute, a Washington, DC–based think tank, released a report detailing the violent methods MS-13 used, including its increasingly typical "calling card." MS-13 often leaves behind dismembered corpses, complete with the decapitated head, at the scene of their murders, often with a note attached to the body.[40]

ASIAN GANGS

As with other ethnicities, there are differences among Asian gangs in terms of characteristics within the groups and influences on their communities.

Chinese Gangs

triads
Powerful community organizations that are closely associated with or control Chinese gangs.

Gang expert Ko-Lin Chin describes Chinese gangs as closely associated with or controlled by powerful community organizations called **triads.** An integral part of community life, these gangs are influenced, to a great extent, by Chinese secret societies and the triad norms and values. The primary activity of Chinese gangs is the pursuit of financial wealth. Members invest a considerable amount of money from their illegal enterprises in legitimate businesses in communities in which adult criminals serve as role models and mentors for gang members.

Although involved in drug trafficking, gang members themselves are generally not drug users. The establishment of Chinese gangs is intertwined with the economic and social structure of their communities. Additionally, Chinese gangs do not experience the deterioration and poverty that other types of gangs do. Rather, they grow and become economically prosperous by maintaining ties with the economic and political structure of their communities.[41]

Japanese Yakuza

"Yakuza" refers to an organized collection of all-male gangs that represent a contrast to traditional Japanese society. In Japan, there are 110,000 active Yakuza members, and in the United States, there are more than 200,000 members, divided into 2,500 families. The official Yakuza history portrays the group's ancestors as underdog folk heroes who stood up for the poor and the defenseless, just as Robin Hood supposedly helped the peasants of medieval England.

The Yakuza are proud to be outcasts, and the word *yakuza* reflects the group's self-image: in regional dialect, *ya* means 8, *ku* means 9, and *sa* means 3, numbers that add up to 20, which is a losing hand in the card game *hana-fuda* (flower cards). Yakuza members also favor tattoos, but unlike other gang tattoos, theirs are elaborate body murals that often cover the entire torso, front and back, as well as the arms and legs. Dragons, flowers, mountainous landscapes, turbulent seascapes, gang insignias, and abstract designs are typical body art images. The application of these extensive tattoos is painful and can take hundreds of hours, but the process is considered a test of a man's courage. Often involved in prostitution, gun smuggling, and human trafficking, in the United States, Yakuza members commit offenses against the Japanese-American community, largely because these immigrants do not trust local law enforcement for protection.

Offenses within the gang itself are treated harshly. When a Yakuza member violates the rules of the organization, he is required to perform a ceremony called *yubizume,* which involves the offender severing his little finger and presenting it to the insulted person as a form of apology. A repeat offense results in the offender being kicked out of the gang forever.[42] Jack Adelstein's *Tokyo Vice* explores the world of the Yakuza from an insider's point of view. A reporter with years of experience covering crime in Japan, Adelstein depicts the Yakuza as being similar in structure to a local business, with business cards giving the addresses and phone numbers of its members. The social acceptability of organized crime in Japan makes the Yakuza a relatively stable feature of the social and physical landscape.[43]

Vietnamese Gangs

Vietnamese youth gangs, especially in Southern California, are quite different from other Asian gangs. This group of immigrants, having experienced racism and discrimination both in the job market and in the classroom, has had a number of significant problems assimilating into mainstream American culture. Three themes best characterize Vietnamese gangs: mistrust, secrecy, and self-control.

Yakuza tattoos are different from other gang tattoos, with an emphasis on flowers and dragons, and typically covering almost the entire body.

A pervasive sense of mistrust runs through Vietnamese communities, which gang members exploit. For instance, distrust of American banks has led to valuables and money being kept at home. Because of this behavior, robbery of these families is a primary activity for these gangs. Drug dealing is perceived as too risky; therefore, it is not practiced. Drug use among members, however, is heavy.

Vietnamese gangs keep a low profile by avoiding conspicuous gang symbols such as tattoos and hand signals. Any indicator of gang affiliation is designed to be easily concealed. Moreover, in manners of dress, Vietnamese gangs tend to opt for clothing similar to other youths in Southern California. In this way, they are able to blend into the social landscape and to more easily avoid the attention of the police.[44]

WHITE GANGS

There are two major groups of white gangs in the United States: one is typically involved in drug use, and the other in racial purity.

Stoner Gangs

Members of stoner gangs are typically white, middle-class youths using drugs. Their involvement in criminal activities such as shoplifting, burglary, and drug dealing is simply to get money to buy more drugs. These gangs are not violent, do not declare "turf," and are only categorized as gangs based on their involvement in criminal activities to support their drug use. Essentially, this group embodies what was once referred to as *middle-class delinquency* in that these are youths who come from families with resources and engage in delinquency for reasons other than economic profit or the need to develop a street reputation.[45]

Skinheads

Skinheads are troubled youths easily identifiable with their typically shaved heads, steel-toed boots, straight-legged jeans, and racist agenda that promotes white superiority and purity. There are several versions of skinheads. Some see themselves as neo-Nazis and look upon Adolf Hitler as a visionary who understood the importance of racial purity. Other skinhead gangs protect what they see as threats to white culture: immigration, affirmative action, and interracial marriages. They are also violently opposed to homosexuality and same-sex marriage, largely because they believe it is unnatural and threatens the structure of society.[46]

TAGGERS

While there are a number of gangs that engage in serious criminal activity, many gangs have few organizational or economic goals. While they do not pose a serious threat to a community, some of these gangs remain problematic. For instance, while not engaged in serious delinquency, taggers do mark other people's property with graffiti. Crews compete to see who can put up the most graffiti in a given time period and/or area. Once a tool by street gangs to stake out their turf, tagging is now considered sport by a growing number of youths from all neighborhoods.[47]

According to police officials in San Jose, California, the situation has deteriorated so much that the public has been solicited in an attempt to reduce the number of tagging incidents. In 2006, the city experienced only 129 incidents of graffiti; however, in 2007 that number jumped to 2,594.[48] While this may give the impression that San Jose has a gang problem on its hands, especially when graffiti is used to "mark" a territory, only about 4 percent of the graffiti in the United States is gang-related.[49] Still, tagging contributes to a climate of fear due to the disorder it represents. In Los Angeles County, estimates suggest approximately 600 active crews and 30,000 taggers.[50] The Theory and Practice box on page 209 describes how some communities are attempting to address the issues associated with taggers.

FEMALE GANGS

The early literature on female gangs discussed membership in relation to male gang members as tomboys or sex objects. In 1950s New York City, virtually all female gangs were affiliated with male ones.[51] Their functions varied from sexual relations to weapons possession and spying. Twenty years later, criminologist Walter Miller identified three possible relations of female gangs to male ones: independent units, "coed" gangs, and auxiliaries of male groups.[52]

Whereas in the past female gang identity and social survival depended on affiliation with a male gang, that dependency has changed to some extent. Current research on female gangs shows that members regulate their own affairs, make their own decisions, and often use a system of norms similar to those of male gangs, such as sanctioning a member for failing to support another "homegirl" in a fight or failing to identify oneself as a gang member. While some research continues to identify female gangs as an appendage to their male counterparts, the evidence is far from conclusive. Female gang members tend to look and act similarly to their male counterparts, even in the use of violence.[53] In some ways, the reasons girls and women join gangs are similar to those of males: the need for a family-like atmosphere, companionship, camaraderie, and protection.

The process of joining a gang differs for females since some members become involved because of their boyfriends' gang affiliation or because of a family member's connection to one. As with male gangs, a status hierarchy determines a member's social position within the gang that goes beyond official leadership positions. Women who are "sexed in" to the gang are considered the lowest-ranking members since the method they used to become initiated involved having sex with several members of a male gang. This approach is considered demeaning, and as a result, these individuals are a source of contempt for other female gang members. Those who are initiated through traditional means, sometimes referred to as "jumped in," in which loyalty and courage are tested through a severe beating by several gang members at once, are accorded greater status because they proved their value and worth.[54] Walter's initiation ceremony is typical of that of many gangs, male or female:

For more on initiation, watch *Gang Initiation: Walter* at www.mhhe.com/mcnamarajd1e

THEORY AND PRACTICE WORKING TOGETHER

Community Responses to Graffiti Artists

Since taggers and their crews come from a wide range of backgrounds, how can parents determine if their child is involved in this activity? The Anti-Graffiti Program of San Jose's Parks, Recreation & Neighborhood Services offers the following indicators:

- The child, between twelve and eighteen years of age, stays out until early morning or all night, and sleeps during the day.
- The child is frequently deceitful about his or her activities.
- The child has paint or permanent marker stains on the tips of his or her fingers.
- The child possesses a large quantity of "My Name Is" stickers or other large stickers used for "sticker tagging."

- The child possesses graffiti paraphernalia such as markers, etching tools (e.g., sharp rocks, metal scribes, awls, screwdrivers), spray paint, bug spray (only shows up in the rain), and starch cans.
- The child has quantities of paint in cans but doesn't have the income to afford it.[55]

 THINK ABOUT IT **What can parents do if they discover their son or daughter is part of a tagger crew?**

So, I went over to his house and there was like 10 people there. There was a whole bunch of people, and, uh, he was just like, come here, man. Step in the garage. He opened the garage. I went in the garage. He was like, there were shelves and everything, no car in there, just shelves, and toolboxes and wire and all kinds of stuff. And uh, like, soon as I stepped in there, somebody hit me. I fell down on the ground. They started kicking me and stomping me. They started, uh—they beat me up for about, like, six minutes. And uh, they were—they, they helped me up. I got up. My eye was swollen, bruised, stuff like that, had a black eye, and, uh. . . . It was initiation into Imperial Gangster. So, he was like, you're in now.

Gang Structure

Early researchers noted that gangs traditionally had definitive characteristics or traits, such as clearly defined organization, leadership, turf, purpose, and social solidarity. More recent research indicates that while some gangs have these features, others are more fluid and lack structure.[56]

ORGANIZATION

There is a wide range of gang composition: some gangs are highly structured, resembling corporations, while others more closely resemble crowds than defined organizations. Gangs typically have ten to twelve core members. If the gang grows in size and activity, divisions, sometimes referred to as *cliques* or *subsets,* may be created. These cliques hold allegiance to the mother gang; however, they have their own structure and characteristics.[57] As Walter points out, some gangs have a structure that influences the types of activities members are required to engage in. There are also other reasons for being connected to the gang, such as status and protection:

Despite their changing nature, many gangs still focus on the use of violence and intimidation of community residents.

I did anything that my—well, the people that told me, they were higher than me in rank. If they told me to do something, I had to do it. I, I got—I was—I mean, I was pretty high. I could do what I had—I, I could tell, like, other lower gang members to do stuff. . . . If they wanted—like, um, if they wanted a couple stars, which is like couple steps towards your next rank, you know, I'd tell them, go beat that kid up, or go shoot at them, or rob somebody.

Types of Gangs

What are some of the commonalities among the different types of gangs described? What do these gangs hope to achieve, or what are their goals?

ANDRE'S CASE

Organization of the Black Cobras

Recall the purpose and structure of the Black Cobras:

- originally designed to protect its members from other gangs in the neighborhood
- not involved in serious criminal activities
- membership consists of longtime friends
- not affiliated with or tied to any of the known larger gangs in the area

While the members of the Black Cobras have formed tight bonds with each other, they do not have an organizational structure other than a leader. The group has only a few members, is not a subset of any complex organization, and does not have an agenda besides wanting some attention.

Some might question whether the Black Cobras are a "legitimate" gang, given their dynamics and membership. Compare the Black Cobras to some of the other gangs discussed in terms of their characteristics. Which ones do they resemble the most?

LEADERSHIP

Because the structure of gangs varies, the nature of leadership within them also varies. For some groups, there is one leader who has a chain of command similar to that found in the military or a large corporation. Particularly in smaller gangs, leaders are often charismatic and admired for their maturity, street savvy demeanor, physical prowess, and penchant for violence. In some cases, this combination of charisma and fear results in their holding onto their position despite a high turnover in membership.[58]

TURF

The importance of turf among gangs is reflected in issues of identity, control, and security. Many gangs lay social and physical claim to particular neighborhoods, parks, schools, and housing projects to establish geographic and social identities. These areas serve as places where gang members feel safe and in control. Today, however, the physical demarcations are becoming less significant as gang members are increasingly mobile. Given the greater tendency for gang members' families to relocate, the notion of turf has become less important.[59]

SOCIAL SOLIDARITY

Traditionally, youths joined gangs for camaraderie and enhanced status, and stayed in the gang out of loyalty, but some experts question whether this remains true today.[60] Gang members' lives are chaotic and lack focus and meaning. Many members are also insecure about their social standing. Given the more fluid organization found in today's gangs, some scholars argue that the sense of "brotherhood" among gang members is fading. The only sense of cohesion members feel toward one another may revolve around their delinquent activities.[61]

PURPOSE

According to conventional wisdom and based on early research, gangs exist for the purpose of criminal activities. While it is true that some gangs often specialize in a certain type of criminal activity, gang members do not spend a great deal of their daily activities engaged in crime—most spend the majority of their time simply hanging out like any other teenager. Fighting is also a common activity in the formation of a more structured gang, but as gangs become more established and as members get older, less emphasis is placed on fighting, and more on hanging out and partying.[62]

THE CHANGING NATURE OF GANGS

More recently, many of the reasons for joining a gang, such as the pseudo-family structure and loyalty to one's in-group, as well as social cohesion among its members, are changing. Some evidence exists of what are called **hybrid gangs,** which consist of members of different gangs who come together for a particular activity, such as drug dealing. Experts are witnessing instances in which rival gang members, even archrivals such as Bloods and Crips, interact and work together in various ways.[63]

Hybrid gangs became a part of the gang landscape in the 1980s and 1990s as gang migration patterns emerged. **Gang migration** is the movement of gang members from one region of the country to another. With physical relocation, the traditional understanding and parameters of gang structure began to change. While some experts contend that hybrid gangs have existed since the 1920s, they became much more pronounced over the past twenty years and impact not only the nature of gangs but also community and law enforcement responses.[64] Part of the challenge for law enforcement is that much of the training on gangs has become obsolete, as identifiers, patterns, and trends that once applied to gang activities do not apply to hybrid gangs.

A Bureau of Justice Statistics report identified Kansas City, Missouri, as one of the first cities to experience gang migration. In the early 1980s, Kansas City began to see a flood of gang members from Los Angeles–affiliated gangs, such as the Crips and the Bloods, who became immersed in the drug trade there. This was followed by a wave of Chicago-based gang members a short time later. Other cities in the Midwest began to experience a new gang presence as well. These hybrid gang members were not simply transferring the stereotypical structure of the gangs found at their home base: they were beginning to blur the traditional boundaries between rival gangs.[65]

Hybrid gangs may or may not have an allegiance to a traditional gang color. Much of the hybrid gang graffiti in the United States is a composite of multiple gangs with conflicting symbols. For example, Crips gang graffiti painted in red (the color used by the rival Bloods gang) would be unheard of in California but has occurred elsewhere in the hybrid gang culture.[66]

Gang members may also change their affiliation from one gang to another. It is not uncommon for a gang member to claim multiple affiliations, sometimes with rival gangs. For example, the police may encounter an admitted Bloods gang member who is also in another city known to be a member of the Gangster Disciples gang. Existing gangs may even change their names or merge with other gangs. Although many gangs continue to base membership on race and ethnicity, other gangs are increasingly diverse in terms of race, ethnicity, and gender. Hybrid gangs can also be homegrown and consider themselves to be distinct entities with no alliance to existing groups.[67]

Another change in the nature of gangs involves their presence in the military. In a 2009 report titled *Gang Activity in the U.S. Armed Forces Increasing,* the FBI documented the presence of members of nearly every major street gang, including the Bloods, Crips, Gangster Disciples, Hells Angels, Latin Kings, Mara Salvatrucha (MS-13), Mexican Mafia, Vice Lords, and various white supremacist groups, in military installations nationwide. Although most prevalent in the Army, the Army Reserves, and the National Guard, gang members can be found in all branches of the military and across most ranks. However, the report suggests that gang membership appears to cluster among the junior enlisted ranks.[68]

hybrid gangs
Groups that consist of members of different gangs, including rival ones, who come together for a particular purpose, such as drug dealing.

gang migration
The movement of gang members from one region of the country to another, which changes the traditional understanding and parameters of gang structure.

The extent of gang presence in the military is often difficult to determine since many gang members conceal their affiliation, and military authorities may not recognize certain gang characteristics. The military is also not required to report criminal activity occurring on its installations to the FBI, nor is it likely to do so, given that such activity reflects poorly on that particular branch of the service.

Some gang members may enlist in the military to receive weapons and combat training. Once they are discharged, gang members can then employ their skills against law enforcement officials and rival gang members. Another factor influencing gang presence in the military is the tendency for criminal courts to allow gang members to enlist in lieu of a prison sentence, a practice that violates military recruiting regulations. Judges see military service as a reasonable alternative in response to overcrowding in many U.S. prisons. The problem, however, is that once these individuals receive combat training, not to mention access to weapons and explosives, the threat they pose to the community upon their return is considerable. Further, if gang members maintain an allegiance to their gang while serving in the military, the safety of other soldiers and commanding officers is jeopardized. More globally, gang rivalries within the military can also compromise its ability to achieve its objectives in places like Iraq and Afghanistan.[69]

Increasing gang migration has led to a debate about why it is occurring. Some experts believe that the migration reflects the corporate expansion of gangs and their criminal activities. Just as businesses expand once they begin to prosper, gangs are tapping into areas traditionally insulated from gang-related criminal activities.[70] Another school of thought suggests that the increase in the number of communities reporting gang problems reflects either the changing definitions of gangs or the movement of youths from one part of the country to another for reasons other than gang expansion. For example, a gang member's family may relocate to a new location.[71]

THINK ABOUT IT

Gang Structure

How has the traditional gang structure changed? When you think about the changes in the role of women over the past thirty or forty years, do these changes contribute to the rise of female gangs? If so, how?

Gang Behavior

Many youths who are involved in gangs typically engage in some form of criminal behavior, and some gangs are exceptionally violent. The connection between gangs and drugs and between gangs and violence is a strong one. But what do we really know about these relationships?

DRUGS

Most researchers agree that drug use and drug dealing, especially by youths, are strongly related.[72] However, it is difficult to automatically associate these activities with gangs since gangs are quite diverse in their characteristics and behavior. While it is true that gang members are involved in drug use and dealing, and while it is true that these types of activities occur more often among gang members than other youths, gang membership does not necessarily lead to involvement in any of those crimes.

In some gangs, drug use is an important means of gaining social status, whereas in others, drug use is forbidden, especially if the gang is involved in selling them. Examples include the aforementioned Chinese gangs, which have strict rules regarding drug use. In other gangs, members are discouraged, but not prohibited, from using their product. In still other cases, gangs will forbid the use of the drug they sell but tolerate the use of other drugs. Then there are gangs that will use drugs but not deal in them at all. For example, Vietnamese gangs will use drugs, especially cocaine, but avoid dealing since it is considered too risky and will attract the attention of law enforcement.[73]

As the economic climate and opportunity structure have declined in many cities, the underground economy has begun to play an even more important role in lower-class communities. It would seem likely that youths in these neighborhoods would become involved in drug dealing. It would also seem likely that gangs, which in many cases have formed in response to these conditions, would organize themselves around money-making opportunities. However, the research is mixed.[74] In some cases, gangs have become highly organized around drug selling. Criminologist Jerome Skolnick makes a distinction between *instrumental, entrepreneurial,* and *cultural* gangs. This distinction is based upon the degree to which gang organization revolves around the drug business. Based on interviews with 100 young drug dealers and 100 law enforcement officers in California, Skolnick concluded that gangs, especially entrepreneurial gangs, dominate the drug trade in Northern California.[75] Other examples include the aforementioned black American gangs such as the Bloods and the Crips.

Other research suggests that while individual members may sell drugs, it is not necessarily a function of the group. While gang members may engage in drug dealing, it is essentially an individual activity, not in connection with the gang.[76] Researcher Cheryl Maxson, for instance, found that gang members accounted for only 27 percent of the 1,563 arrests for cocaine sales in two Los Angeles suburbs. She concluded that gang members' involvement in crack cocaine sales is not overwhelming, as some have thought, and the even lower rate of gang involvement with other drugs raises the question of the need for special concern for gangs and drugs. Maxson also asserted that the findings from her study have been replicated in other cities.[77]

While not all gangs are involved in drug selling, many use this as a primary source of revenue.

Whether it is drug use or drug selling, the research on the relationship between gangs and drugs has not been clearly defined or understood. A number of gangs are involved in using and selling drugs, while others are involved in one aspect and not the other. Fragmented gangs may have individual members dealing independently of the gang.

VIOLENCE

Of all the topics associated with gangs, perhaps none is more significant to the general public than violence, which evokes the greatest fear. As with the relationship of gangs to drugs, we have not yet developed a clear understanding of the relationship of violence to gangs.[78] Perhaps the act that best symbolizes the growing problem of gang-related violence is drive-by shootings. With its notoriety in the media, drive-by shooting has become synonymous with gang violence. In his book *Gangbangs and Drive-bys,* William Sanders describes the essential features of drive-by shootings and offers an explanation for its development. He contends that drive-bys are basically retaliatory measures against the offending gang based on the nature of the interaction between the groups. The value of participating in drive-bys is grounded in the need to maintain and enhance members' status. There is also an economic side to Sanders's explanation. He contends that as involvement in the drug trade expanded for a number of gangs, particularly in the 1990s, turf wars escalated as well. While the battle for turf has always been a common feature of intergang behavior, drug markets exacerbated the problem.[79]

Research on the causes of gang violence has tended to focus on two factors. One body of research argues that gangs become involved in violence as a result of gang leaders who are psychologically impaired. This perspective attributes the problem to the pathology of drugs, especially those that induce violent and psychotic behavior.[80] The second body of research most often cites *status deprivation* as the primary cause of violence. These studies conclude that most gang members feel they have been deprived by society of the status they are due; their use of violence is a means by which their standing is reintroduced. The logic behind this school of thought is the idea that violence emerges in low-income communities where it is seen as a natural by-product of social life. Violence, then, becomes the means by which physical and social goals are achieved.[81]

There is also a tendency to view gang-related violence as intertwined with the gang's effort to achieve its goals. While this may be true in some cases, such as when an organized gang involved in drug dealing seeks to punish a noncompliant customer, much of what we refer to as *gang violence* is committed by individuals who are members of gangs, but do not undertake this activity to further the gang's objectives.[82]

As in the case of the relationship between drugs and gangs, the best possible explanation of the relationship between gangs and violence is that it depends primarily on the organizational characteristics of the gang. Many studies of gangs have found that some gangs are organized to fight while others are formed to make money, and that the level of violence associated with each gang is dependent on its setup.[83]

 . . . it really started us fighting. And then it got to others. As we got older, we got to—we stopped fighting and got to shooting. But now there's no more of them. We ran them off, really.

SHUN

00:20 — 01:02

For more on gangs, watch *Gang Exposure: Jose* and *Getting Out of Gang Life: Walter* at www.mhhe.com/mcnamarajd1e

Another important variable in understanding the extent of gang violence is the direction of the gang's organizational structure. Gangs with a vertical/hierarchical organizational structure are likely to indulge in more organizational than individual violence, but they also tend to avoid violence and focus on their financial objectives. These gangs are able to exert greater control over their members, in large part because violence usually leads to law enforcement attention, which ultimately reduces the gang's profit margin.[84] In contrast, gangs with a horizontal/egalitarian structure tend to have less control over their members. While some of these gangs may be organized into cliques, which can be highly structured and are able to control their members, overall they form a loose collection of factions with limited organizational coordination.[85] While the organizational characteristics help to explain the incidence and prevalence of gang violence, not all gangs necessarily fit this description.

Gang members do not shun violence—it is a common theme of gang life. Conflicts can arise from intragang power struggles, intergang quarrels over turf (sometimes related to drug markets), and perceived threats to a gang's reputation.[86] What is especially disturbing is the increased firepower in the form of heavy automatic weapons, which makes outbursts of violence more deadly.

THINK ABOUT IT

Gang Behavior

Despite the wide variability in both drug involvement and the use of violence by gangs, the public seems to think that these two activities comprise most of what gangs do. Why is there this misperception? Is it because gangs are more prone to drug dealing and violent activities even though they do not make up the majority of drug-related and violent crimes?

Community Responses to Gangs and Public Policy

The review of the literature on gangs essentially leads to two important conclusions: gang activities are tied to the particular characteristics of the gang's community, and the sources of dangerous and illegal gang activities are found in the deteriorating economic conditions of inner cities.[87] With respect to the first point, interdiction efforts that have traditionally been employed have only a limited effect on the problem. As such, communities must take a more active role in developing less coercive intervention techniques that will complement the more traditional law enforcement approaches. We should also distinguish

ANDRE'S CASE

Conclusions about the Black Cobras

Recall the situation the Black Cobras find themselves in:

- They tried to insulate themselves from the threat of having to join a criminal gang.
- They now face the prospect of being treated like a legitimate gang.

Initially formed as a way of identifying themselves collectively, as well as generating feelings of importance in the neighborhood, the Black Cobras face an uncertain future. They may disband, perhaps resurfacing as another peer group with less of an emphasis on acting and looking like a "real" gang. Still, the risks associated with the pressure the Crips are putting on Black Cobra members will likely remain.

Are the Black Cobras a wanna-be gang, or do they exhibit enough characteristics to be considered a legitimate gang? Do gangs such as the Black Cobras suffer from the same pressures, resulting in the transiency of most gangs?

THINK ABOUT IT

hard-core gang leaders, who are involved in the most serious forms of criminal behavior, from peripheral members of a gang. One should be the focus of the criminal justice system, the other of community or diversion efforts.

A recurring theme in our discussion of delinquency is the importance of placing the problem in its proper context. Only then can we understand why the problem is occurring and develop solutions to address it. This contextual understanding applies to gangs as well. The structural explanations of delinquency and the solutions to the problems associated with gangs are inextricably woven into the changes in the economic structure of American society. Gang expert Ron Huff argued:

> Youth gangs are symptomatic of many of the same social and economic problems as adult crime, mental illness, drug abuse, alcoholism, the surge in homelessness, and multigeneration "welfare families" living in hopelessness and despair. While we are justly concerned with replacement of our physical infrastructure (roads, bridges, sewers), our *human* infrastructure may be crumbling as well. Our social, educational, and economic infrastructures are not meeting the needs of many children and adults. Increases in the numbers of women and children living in poverty (the "feminization" and "juvenilization" of poverty) are dramatic examples of this recent transformation. To compete with the seductive lure of drug profits and the grinding despair of poverty, we must reassess our priorities and reaffirm the importance of our neighborhoods by putting in place a number of programs that offer hope, education, job skills, and meaningful lives. It is worth the cost of rebuilding our human infrastructures since it is, after all, our children whose lives are being wasted and our cities in which the quality of life is being threatened.[88]

Deindustrialization, competition in the global economy, and relocation of many factories and even entire industries have led to the steep decline in jobs for unskilled or semi-skilled workers. This is especially true for teenagers in inner cities, whose unemployment rates are much higher than the national average.[89]

Researchers have examined the overall effectiveness of intervention programs to address the gang problem, and two basic strategies seem to be the most promising.[90] The first involves organizing neighborhoods in such a way that leads to a reduction in gang activity in a particular community. An example of this might be a form of Neighborhood Watch program, where residents patrol the streets and report any gang activity or presence of gang members.[91] The second strategy involves job creation and training, and other opportunities to lure individuals away from the gang life.[92] The Theory and Activity box on page 216 discusses how Homeboy Industries, a series of companies that employ and train former gang members, is having an impact on the gang problem in East Los Angeles, California.

THEORY AND PRACTICE WORKING TOGETHER

Homeboy Industries

How can communities work to solve gang problems in their neighborhoods? One innovative program was hatched in East Los Angeles in 1988 by a Jesuit priest, Father Greg Boyle, who wanted to offer gang members a way out of the gang life. He first created Jobs for a Future (JFF), a program at Dolores Mission parish, in an effort to address the escalating problems and unmet needs of gang-involved youths. Father Boyle and the community created an elementary school and a day care program, and attempted to find jobs for gang members who wanted to leave the gang.

In 1992, in response to a low success rate in finding jobs for former gang members, Father Boyle created Homeboy Bakery, a small business that would allow him to hire the most difficult-to-place young people while providing a safe environment. The hope was that they could learn important job skills and become more marketable for other jobs in the future. The success of Homeboy Bakery laid the groundwork for additional businesses and led to the creation of the nonprofit organization Homeboy Industries in 2001. Today Homeboy Industries includes a variety of businesses, such as Homeboy Silkscreen, which employs over 500 former gang members, often former rivals, who work side by side printing logos on apparel; Homeboy Maintenance, which provides landscaping and maintenance services; Homeboy/Homegirl Merchandise, which sells T-shirts, mugs, tote bags, and mouse pads with the Homeboy logo; and Homegirl Café, a small restaurant and catering service,

which provides a training ground for former female gang members in all aspects of the restaurant industry.

In addition, Homeboy Industries provides case management, legal services, mental health counseling, GED classes, tattoo removal, employment services, transitional programs, and twelve-step recovery programs. It even allows youths who are sentenced to community service to complete it onsite or under Homeboy Industries supervision. The organization attempts to holistically remove the barriers that prevent gang members from becoming contributing members of society.

In only a few years, Homeboy Industries has made an impact on the Los Angeles gang problem, employing young people from over half of the region's 1,100 known gangs. While a formal evaluation of the program has not been conducted, the fact that so many youths come to Homeboy Industries in search of a chance to get out of gang life and to get a job suggests that the cooperation between community and church can play a significant role in the lives of many youths. A popular saying among youths at Homeboy is "nothing stops a bullet like a job."

THINK ABOUT IT

What options do gang members have if they decide to quite the gang? Can they really make a successful transition without significant help from the community? Can programs such as Homeboy Industries serve as models for social reintegration?

Comprehensive Gang Initiative
An approach by the U.S. Department of Justice that involves several agencies or groups handling a number of facets of local gang problems and that focuses on not only suppression but also intervention and prevention.

A third strategy to combat the gang problem, an interdiction approach with arrest and incarceration as its primary features, is most commonly used.[93] This law enforcement strategy has a limited effect, although it is a necessary part of addressing the problem. Currently, there are more than 400 police gang units, most of which have been created in the last ten years.[94] This interdiction strategy, sometimes referred to as *suppression,* involves a number of activities, such as neighborhood sweeps and arrests with officers converging on an area where gang members are known to live. Another tactic involves saturation patrols, where officers identify known gang hangouts, aggressively stop and frisk gang members, and enforce curfew ordinances, truancy laws, and other statutes.[95]

The police often make use of injunctions or abatements, civil processes in which gang members are prohibited from engaging in public nuisance crimes, such as loitering or obstructing the use of public property. If gang members violate the injunction, they are issued a temporary restraining order. If they violate that, they can be held in contempt of court and charged in civil or criminal court.[96]

In addition to these basic strategies, various agencies may cooperate through an amalgamated approach by developing community-based solutions to the gang problem in that particular community, as well as having media campaigns to target potential gang members.[97] One example of this approach is found in the **Comprehensive Gang Initiative** (CGI) by the U.S. Department of Justice, which recognizes the variability in the study of gangs and offers assistance to communities facing gang-related problems. Its core approach involves several agencies or groups handling a number of facets of local gang problems and focusing not only on suppression but also on intervention and prevention. While the traditional community response is to increase the number of police officers, the CGI recognizes that the variation in the characteristics and activities of gangs calls for a more customized approach, which uses different strategies to target the different problems presented in those particular communities.[98]

Thus, the CGI encourages communities to focus on what can be described as *retail changes* instead of wholesale ones. When a community attempts to solve the "gang problem," there is a tendency to become overwhelmed with the large-scale implications of the problem. The CGI asserts that the focus of community programs should be on "small wins." This approach is designed to take large problems and break them into smaller ones so that manageable steps can be taken to deal with a particular aspect of the problem. If enough "small wins" occur, the global problem in that community is addressed.[99]

The "small wins" approach means that communities should reduce the problem of eliminating gangs into a series of specific problem statements and develop solutions for them. The success of each individual strategy will, in turn, increase the likelihood that the larger problem will be solved.[100]

The police are increasingly using innovative methods to interdict gangs and gang-related activities.

THE BIG PICTURE

Conclusions on Gangs and Delinquency

- Given the complexity of defining what gangs are and how they are structured, are taggers really gang members, or are they artists in an unconventional group? Explain.
- Why are hybrid gangs becoming so popular? If the main reason for joining a gang involves a certain sense of affiliation, why would gang members blur those lines?
- Why does the public believe that gangs are responsible for so much of the violence and drug dealing in this country when the data indicate otherwise?
- Do current community responses and public actions help to curb the growth of gangs and the violence associated with them?

Key Terms

co-offending	MS-13	skinheads
Crips	Chinese gangs	taggers
Bloods	triads	gang migration
People Nation	Yakuza	hybrid gangs
Folk Nation	Vietnamese gangs	
Latin Kings	stoner gangs	

Make the Call ▶ Gangs and Delinquency

Review the situation provided and decide on what you would do.

YOUR ROLE: Police officer on patrol

DETAILS OF THE SITUATION

- A new law allows police officers to detain gang members on mere suspicion instead of probable cause.
- Your department has outlined a list of characteristics for the various gangs in your city.
- Recently, an officer had failed to stop and search a suspect, a gang member, who ended up committing an armed robbery in which the store owner was shot and killed.
- You encounter a youth who appears to have flashed a known gang sign to another youth.
- The youth's appearance does not have any traditional gang symbols, colors, or affiliations.

WHAT DO YOU DO?

Even though on the surface, the youth does not display the traditional gang symbols outlined by your department, you have a strong suspicion that he is involved in a gang, and you believe you saw him flash a gang sign. Do you detain him and try to find a gang connection, or do you let him go because he does not meet any of the department's outlined characteristics of gang members?

Consider:

- Could this youth be a member of a hybrid gang?
- Could he simply be a neighborhood youth who has never been involved in status offenses or delinquency?
- Would arresting and interrogating him produce any meaningful information, or would it simply get one more kid off the street for a short period of time?

Apply Theory to Reality ▶ Understanding Gangs

While many delinquency theories focus on gang activity, the phenomenon of hybrid gangs presents new challenges in understanding them theoretically. Select one of the theories discussed in this text, and apply it to hybrid gangs. As with other theory exercises, first outline the theory and then apply it to explain the development of hybrid gangs.

Your Community ▶ Gangs and Delinquency

In addition to the information you glean from your readings, class lectures, and discussions, it is important to roll up your sleeves and immerse yourself in a topic as a researcher who gains an understanding of a problem or issue by observing or experiencing it firsthand. Through such methods, you gain a much greater appreciation of the magnitude of the problem than if you were only engaged in "armchair theorizing."

- Contact the local prison in your community, and ask permission to speak with correctional officers about

what they know about gangs and gang life. (They may only be able to comment on the impact of gangs in the institution and in prison in general.)

- Learn as much as you can about the life of a gang member in your community.

- After collecting your data, and drawing from relevant literature, prepare a report or a presentation of your findings and preliminary conclusions of gangs and gang life based on this initial research.

Notes

[1] U.S. Department of Justice, Federal Bureau of Investigation, 2006. *Crime in the United States, 2005.* Table 9: Expanded Homicide Data. Washington, DC: U.S. Government Printing Office.

[2] Catalano, S. M. 2006. *Criminal Victimization, 2005.* Washington, DC: Bureau of Justice Statistics.

[3] U.S. Department of Justice, Federal Bureau of Investigation. 2009. *Crime in the United States.* Washington, DC: U.S. Government Printing Office. Accessed at http://www.fbi.gov/ucr/ucr. htmhttp://www.fbi.gov/ucr/cius2008/offenses/expanded_information/data/shrtable_12.html.

[4] Steadman, J., and Weisel, D. 1998. *Addressing Community Gang Problems: A Practical Guide.* Washington, DC: U.S. Department of Justice, Office of Justice Programs, Bureau of Justice Assistance.

[5] Fagan, J. 1993. "The Political Economy of Drug Dealing among Urban Gangs." In Davis, R. C., Lurigio, A., and Rosenbaum, D. (eds.), *Drugs and Community.* Chicago: University of Chicago Press.

[6] See, for instance, Sanders, W. 1994. *Gangbangs and Drive-bys: Grounded Culture and Juvenile Gang Violence.* New York: Aldine de Gruyter.

[7] See http://www.miami-police.org/dept/overview.asp?dept=Juvenile.

[8] See http://www.lapdonline.org/search_results/content_basic_view/1396.

[9] See Klein, M. W., and Maxson, C. L. 2001. *Gang Structures, Crime Patterns, and Police Responses: A Summary Report.* Washington, DC: Office of Juvenile Justice and Delinquency Prevention. Available at http://www.ncjrs.gov/pdffiles1/nij/grants/188510.pdf.

[10] See, for instance, Hoge, R. 2001. *The Juvenile Offender: Theory, Research, and Application.* New York: Springer.

[11] Curry, G. D., and Decker, S. H. 1998. *Confronting Gangs: Crime and Community.* Los Angeles: Roxbury.

[12] Jankowski, M. 1991. *Islands in the Street: Gangs and American Urban Society.* Berkeley: University of California Press.

[13] Maxson, C., and M. Klein. 2001. "Street Gang Violence: Twice as Great or Half as Great." In Huff, C. R. (ed.), *Gangs in America.* Newbury Park, CA: Sage, pp. 71–102.

[14] Katz, C. 2003. "Issues in the Production and Dissemination of Gang Statistics: An Ethnographic Study of a Large Midwestern Police Gang Unit." *Crime and Delinquency,* 49: 406.

[15] Thornberry, T. P., and Krohn, M. D. (eds.). 2003. *Taking Stock of Delinquency: An Overview of Findings from Contemporary Longitudinal Studies.* New York: Kluwer.

[16] Ibid.

[17] Fagan, 1993.

[18] See LAPD Gang Unit website at http://www.lapdonline.org/search_results/content_basic_view/1396.

[19] Delaney, T. 2006. *American Street Gangs.* Upper Saddle River, NJ: Prentice-Hall.

[20] Ibid.

[21] See, for instance, Binder, A., Geis, G., and Bruce, D. 1997. *Juvenile Delinquency: Historical, Cultural, and Legal Perspectives,* 2nd ed. Cincinnati: Anderson.

[22] Ibid.

[23] Jankowski, 1991; Egley, A., Maxson, C., and Miller, J. 2006. *The Modern Gang Reader.* Los Angeles: Roxbury.

[24] Jankowski, 1991.

[25] Thraser, F. M. 1927. *The Gang: A Study of 1,313 Gangs in Chicago.* Chicago: University of Chicago Press; Shaw, C., and McKay, H. D. 1942. *Juvenile Delinquency and Urban Areas.* Chicago: University of Chicago Press.

[26] Thraser, 1927.

[27] Delaney, 2006.

[28] Miller, W. 1958. "Lower Class Culture as a Generating Milieu of Gang Delinquency."

Journal of Social Issues, 14: 5–19; Cloward, R., and L. Ohlin. 1960. *Delinquency and Opportunity.* Glencoe, IL: Free Press; Cohen, A. K. 1955. *Delinquent Boys: The Culture of the Gang.* New York: Free Press.

[29] Ibid.

[30] See Howell, 2003.

[31] Department of Justice, Office of Justice Programs, Office of Juvenile Justice and Delinquency Prevention. 2009. *Highlights of the 2007 National Youth Gang Survey.* http://www.iir.com/NYGS-/publications/2007-survey-highlights.pdf.

[32] Ibid. See also National Gang Center at http://www.nationalgangcenter.gov/Survey-Analysis/Gang-Related-Offenses.

[33] U.S. Department of Justice, Office of Justice Programs, Office of Juvenile Justice and Delinquency Prevention. 2009. *National Youth Gang Survey Report.* Tallahassee: Institute for Intergovernmental Research.

[34] Ibid.

[35] Office of Juvenile Justice and Delinquency Prevention. 2009. *National Youth Gang Survey Report.*

[36] Delaney, 2006.

[37] Ibid.

[38] See, for instance, Knox, G. 2000. *Gang Profile: The Latin Kings.* Peoria, IL: National Gang Research Center.

[39] Delaney, 2006.

[40] See, for instance, http://www.knowgangs.com/aboutus.php.

[41] Chin, K. 2000. *Chinatown Gangs: Extortion, Enterprise and Ethnicity.* New York: Oxford University Press.

[42] Delaney, 2006.

[43] Adelstein, J. 2009. *Tokyo Vice: An American Reporter on the Police Beat in Japan.* New York: Random House.

[44] Vigil, J. D. 2000. "Cholos and Gangs: Culture Change and Street Youth in Los Angeles." In

Huff, C. R. (ed.), *Gangs in America*. Newbury Park, CA: Sage, pp. 106–128.

[45] Wooten, W., and Blazak, R. 2000. *Renegade Kids, Suburban Outlaws: From Youth Culture to Delinquency*. Belmont, CA: Wadsworth.

[46] Hamm, M. 1994. *American Skinheads*. Westport, CT: Praeger.

[47] Wooten and Blazak, 2000.

[48] Kimbrel, J. 2008. "City Tags Graffiti Problem." *Spartan Daily,* February 26. Available at http://media.www.thespartandaily.com/media/storage/paper852/news/2008/02/26/News/City-Tags.Graffiti.Problem-3234554.shtml. Accessed July 22, 2008.

[49] Recycling and Waste Commission of Santa Clara County, CA. 2008. *Graffiti Q and A.* http://www.sccgov.org/portal/site/iwm/agencyarticle?path=%2Fv7%2FIntegrated%20Waste%20Management%20(DIV)%2FLitter%20and%20Graffiti&contentId=d28bdc18dfb34010VgnVCMP230004adc4a92. Accessed July 22, 2008.

[50] Wooten and Blazak, 2000.

[51] See Campbell, A. 1990 "Female Gangs." In Huff, C. R. (ed.), *Gangs in America.* Newbury Park, CA: Sage, pp.163–182. See also Finn-Aage, E., Deschemes, D. P., and Winfree, L. T. 2003. "Differences between Gang Girls and Gang Boys." In Peterson, R. (ed.), *Understanding Contemporary Gangs in America.* Upper Saddle River, NJ: Prentice-Hall.

[52] Moore, J., and Hagedorn, J. 2001. *Female Gangs: A Focus on Research.* Washington, DC: U.S. Department of Justice, Office of Juvenile Justice Delinquency Prevention. http://www.ncjrs.gov-/pdffiles1/ojjdp/186159.pdf. Accessed July 24, 2008.

[53] Finn-Aage, Deschemes, and Winfree, 2003.

[54] Moore and Hagedorn, 2001.

[55] "Profile of a Tagger," taken in part from "The Walls of San Jose" newsletter, published by the City of San Jose, California, Parks, Recreation & Neighborhood Services, Anti-Graffiti Program, Issue No. 9, Winter 1997.

[56] See Center for Study and Prevention of Violence. 2008. *Gangs and Youth Violence.* Available at http://www.colorado.edu/cspv/publications/factsheets/cspv/FS-001.pdf.

[57] See, for instance, Delaney, 2006.

[58] See, for instance, Shelden, R., Tracy, S., and Brown, W. 2004. *Youth Gangs in American Society,* 3rd ed. Belmont, CA: Wadsworth.

[59] Jankowski, 1991; Klein and Maxson, 2006.

[60] See, for instance, Klein and Maxson, 2006; Decker, S. 1996. "Collective and Normative Features of Gang Violence." *Justice Quarterly,* 13: 342–364. See also Amato, J., and Cornell, D. 2003. "How Do Youth Claiming Gang Membership Differ from Youth Who Claim Membership in Another Group?" *Journal of Gang Research,* 10: 13–23.

[61] Klein and Maxson, 2006.

[62] Center for Study and Prevention of Violence, 2008. See also Klein and Maxson, 2006; Schneider, J. "Niche Crime: The Columbus Gangs Study." *American Journal of Criminal Justice,* 26: 93–126; Delaney, 2006.

[63] Starbuck, D., Howell, J. C., and Lindquist, D. J. 2001. *Hybrid and Other Modern Gangs.* Washington DC: Office of Juvenile Justice and Delinquency Prevention. See also Miller, M., Ventura, H., and Tatum, J. 2004. "An Assessment of Gang Presence and Related Activities at the County Level: Another Deniability Refutation." *Journal of Gang Research,* 11(2): 1–22.

[64] Ibid.

[65] Miller, Ventura, and Tatum, 2004.

[66] Starbuck, Howell, and Lindquist, 2001.

[67] Ibid.

[68] National Gang Intelligence Center. 2009. *Gang Activity in the U.S. Armed Forces Increasing.* http://militarytimes.com/static/projects/pages/ngic_gangs.pdf.

[69] http://usmilitary.about.com/od/justicelawlegislation/a/gangs.htm.

[70] Shelden, Tracy, and Brown, 2004.

[71] Ibid.

[72] See, for instance, State of New York, Office of Alcoholism and Substance Abuse Services. 2009. *Youth Survey Reports Risk Factors for Alcohol and Drug Abuse.* Available at http://www.oasas.state.ny.us/pio-/press/pr-091609youthsurvey.cfm. See also Natarajan, M., and Hough, M. (eds.), *Illegal Drug Markets: From Research to Prevention Policy.* New York: Criminal Justice Press; Centers, N. L., and Weist, M. D. 1998. "Inner City Youth and Drug Dealing: A Review of the Problem." *Journal of Youth and Alcoholism,* 27(3): 395–411.

[73] See Gordon, R. A., White, N. A., Lahey, B. B., and Loeber, R. 2004. "Do Youth Gangs Produce Racial Differences in Adolescent Drug Selling?" Paper presented at the annual meeting of the American Sociological Association. See also Valdez, A., and Sifaneck, S. 2004. "Getting High and Getting By: Dimensions of Drug Selling Behavior among American Mexican Gang Members in South Texas." *Journal of Crime and Delinquency,* 41(1): 82–105.

[74] Delaney, 2006.

[75] Skolnick, J. H. 1995. "Gangs and Crime Old as Time: But Drugs Change Gang Culture." In Klein, M., Maxson , C., and Miller, J. (eds.), *The Modern Gang Reader.* Los Angeles: Roxbury, pp. 222–227.

[76] Valdez and Sifaneck, 2004. See also Howell, J. C. 1998. *Youth Gangs: An Overview.* Washington, DC: Office of Juvenile Justice and Delinquency Prevention. http://ojjdp.ncjrs.org/jjbulletin/9808/contents.html.

[77] Maxson, C. 1995. "Research in Brief: Street Gangs and Drug Sales in Two Suburban Cities." In Klein, M., Maxson, C., and Miller, J. (eds.),

The Modern Gang Reader. Los Angeles: Roxbury, pp. 228–235.

[78] Klein and Maxson, 2006.

[79] Sanders, 1994.

[80] Miller, 1958; Cloward and Ohlin, 1960.

[81] See Howell, 2003; Hoge, 2001.

[82] Ibid.

[83] Ibid.

[84] Delaney, 2006.

[85] Ibid.

[86] Shelden, Tracy, and Brown, 2004.

[87] Ibid.

[88] Huff, 1990, p. 536.

[89] See, for instance, Austin, A. 2008. *What a Recession Means for Black America.* Washington, DC: Economic Policy Institute. Available at http://www.epi.org/publications/entry/ib241/. See also Cochran, S. 2008. "Unemployment Report Reveals Unemployment Rates Highest for Teens, Lowest for Asians." Associated Content. Available at http://www.associatedcontent.com/article/1272999-/unemployment_report_reveals_unemployment.html?cat=3.

[90] See, for instance, U.S. Department of Justice, Office of Juvenile Justice and Delinquency Prevention. 2004. *Best Practices to Address Community Gang Problems.* Available at http://www.ncjrs.gov-/pdffiles1/ojjdp/222799.pdf.

[91] See National Crime Prevention Council. 2008. *Identifying and Addressing a Gang Problem.* Available at http://www.ncpc.org/training/powerpoint-trainings.

[92] See, for instance, U.S. Department of Justice, Office of Juvenile Justice and Delinquency Prevention. 2004. *Best Practices to Address Community Gang Problems.* Available at http://www.ncjrs.gov/pdffiles1-/ojjdp/222799.pdf. See also Gottfredson, G. D., and Gottfredson, D. C. 2001. *Gang Problems and Gang Programs in a National Sample of Schools.* Ellicott City, MD: Gottfredson. Also available on-line at http://www.gottfredson.com/gang.htm. See also Howell, J. C. 2002. *Youth Gang Programs and Strategies: Summary.* Washington, DC: U.S. Department of Justice. Also available on-line at http://www.ncjrs.gov/html/ojjdp/summary_2000_8/home.html.

[93] See, for instance, Loeber, R., and Farrington, D. P. 1998. "Never Too Early, Never Too Late: Risk Factors and Successful Interventions for Serious and Violent Juvenile Offenders." *Studies in Crime and Crime Prevention,* 17(1): 7–30. See also National Coalition for Effective Drug Policies. 2001. *Eight Steps to Effectively Controlling Drug Abuse and Drug Markets.* Available at http://www.csdp.or/news/news-/8steps.html; World Youth Report. 2003. *Juvenile Delinquency.* Available at http://www.un.org/esa-/socdev/unyin/documents/ch7.pdf; Clear, T. 2009. "The Collateral Consequences of Mass Incarceration." Paper presented to the School of Criminology and Criminal Justice, Arizona State

University, April. Available at http://ccj.asu.edu/downloads/asu-paper-3-todd-clear.

[94] Ibid.

[95] See Katz, C. 2001. "The Establishment of a Police Gang Unit: An Examination of Organizational and Environmental Factors." *Criminology*, 39: 37–74.

[96] See, for instance, Decker, S., and Curry, G. D. 2003. "Suppression without Prevention, Prevention without Suppression: Gang Intervention in St. Louis." In Decker, S. (ed.), *Policing Gangs and Youth Violence*. Belmont, CA: Wadsworth, pp. 191–213.

[97] See, for instance, Maxson, C., Henningan, K., and Sloane, D. 2005. "It's Getting Crazy Out There: Can a Civil Gang Injunction Change a Community?" *Criminology and Public Policy*, 4: 577–606.

[98] U.S. Department of Justice, Office of Justice Programs, Office of Juvenile Justice and Delinquency Prevention. 2007. *Comprehensive Gang Initiative*. Washington, DC: U.S. Government Printing Office. Online at http://www.ojjdp.ncjrs.gov/programs/antigang/.

[99] Ibid.

[100] Ibid.

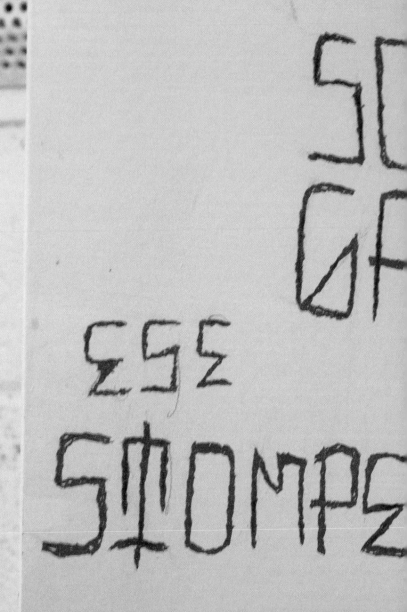

After reading this chapter, you should be able to:

- Identify the issues surrounding juvenile sex offenders.

- Demonstrate how certain factors would lead some juveniles to become

- fascinated with fires or to engage in arson.

- Debate the significance of chronic offending by juveniles.

- Select a special population and propose public policy to address delinquency in that population.

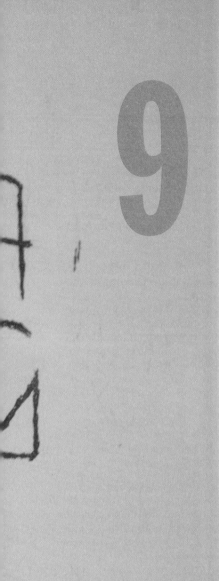

9

Special Populations and Delinquency

A common misperception of delinquency is that most delinquents are chronic offenders who begin their careers early and make the decision to commit criminal acts for some type of economic gain. While some delinquents do have economic motives, other incentives may be involved in the decision to engage in delinquency. Consider the following case.

Doug's profile:
- is a fifteen-year-old runaway
- has spent the last eighteen months on the street
- was supposed to go to a residential treatment facility for fire-starting

His father:
- physically abuses his mother
- also abuses Doug and his younger brother
- killed the family cat after it scratched the living room couch with its claws

Doug's recent behavior:
- never a strong student, was performing even worse academically
- withdrew socially from the other kids in the neighborhood
- became very aggressive toward others
- was avoided by most of his neighbors and peers
- after running away, began living on the streets of San Diego, California
- shoplifted food and other items that he either used or sold on the street
- began hanging around street youths, who introduced him to prostitution
- has been arrested several times for shoplifting and prostitution

Current status:
During his last visit to juvenile court, a judge ruled that Doug should be sent to a residential treatment facility. Doug escaped custody and has been living on the streets ever since. Last week, a man offered to pay

How does graffiti translate into criminal behavior for youths?

Doug $250 to burn down his abandoned warehouse. Doug agreed, but was caught and charged with arson.

The following are potential explanations for Doug's tendency to commit crimes and start fires:

- Doug has serious emotional problems that require professional intervention.
- Doug has made a rational decision to engage in a life of crime and must accept the consequences of his actions.
- Doug has consistently defied authority figures and is destined for a life of crime as an adult.
- Given the nature of his actions and the trauma he has experienced, there is very little that can be done to help Doug become a healthy, law-abiding adult.

 THINK ABOUT IT Do you agree with any of the four explanations given for Doug's situation? What is your reaction to what Doug is going through, and how would you explain his behavior?

While chronic and violent offenders have captured the attention of the public, most teenagers do not engage in violence and even fewer act violently on a regular basis. However, certain youths do merit special attention. This chapter examines a number of special juvenile populations, including sex offenders, male and female prostitutes, domestic abusers, fire-starters and arsonists, and chronic offenders. These populations are grouped in three main sections: sexual activity, mental illness, and chronic offending.

Sexual Activity

Almost all parents find it challenging to address the issue of sex with their adolescent children. This challenge is particularly problematic in American culture, which places a heavy emphasis on sexuality as a central aspect of identity, as well as playing an important role in the development of youths' social values and morality. Gender issues also relate to sexuality: boys who engage in frequent sexual activity and with multiple partners gain social status among their peers, while girls who engage in the same behavior are often scorned, ridiculed, or viewed as immoral. Sexual activity covers a wide range of behaviors, particularly for teenagers, including intercourse and activities involving coercion, manipulation, and force. Despite the fact that most information on adolescent sexual behaviors comes from the youths themselves, and despite the lack of uniform data collection protocols, research consistently suggests that many adolescents and preadolescents are engaged in some type of sexual activity (see Figure 9-1).

Teenage sexual activity is normal behavior, particularly for young adults. While this behavior is controversial for a number of reasons, for our purposes, the issue of adolescent sexual activity becomes problematic when youths are victims or perpetrators of sexual assault or dating and family violence. Also of concern are those who willingly sell their bodies or who are forced to engage in sex work. There has been a great deal of media attention, both in the United States and internationally, on the international trafficking of children. Such crimes have a deep and lasting impact on youths, and present significant challenges to society in general and to the juvenile justice system in particular. Three main areas of focus are juvenile sex offenders; juvenile prostitutes, particularly males; and the sex trafficking of children.

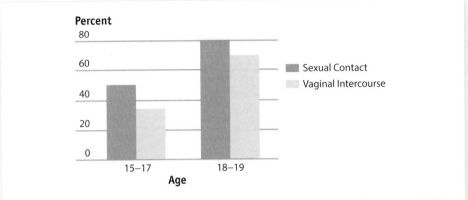

FIGURE 9-1 Adolescents Who Reported Engaging in Sexual Contact and Intercourse, 2002
Sexual contact includes kissing, hugging, fondling, oral sex, and vaginal intercourse.

Source: U.S. Department of Health and Human Services, National Center for Health Statistics. 2007. *Adolescent Health in the United States 2007*. http://www.cdc.gov/nchs/data/misc-/adolescent2007.pdf; http://www.cdc.gov/nchs/hus/child.htm.

JUVENILE SEX OFFENDERS

Few events evoke a more emotional reaction from both parents and the general public than the sexual victimization of children. Adult sexual offenders have received a great deal of media attention,[1] particularly in light of the numerous cases that have come to light of Catholic priests victimizing young boys in the United States,[2] but juvenile sex offenders also need to be considered.

The National Center on Sexual Behavior of Youth reports that adolescents accounted for approximately one-third of all reported sex offenses against children in 2005.[3] According to the Bureau of Justice Statistics, most offenders commit sex crimes around the age of 14.[4] Most juvenile sex offenders do not engage in aggressive or violent behavior. According to one estimate, 59 percent of the offenses involved touching or fondling, and 14 percent involved what are termed *noncontact offenses,* such as indecent exposure. Thus, nearly three-quarters of juvenile sex offender cases involve no force or threat of force. Where violence is used, such as in rape cases, generally, if the offender is under age eighteen, the victim is the same age as the offender or older.[5]

While conventional wisdom suggests that juvenile sex offending is a precursor to similar crimes when the perpetrator becomes an adult, the evidence suggests that this is often not the case, even with chronic young offenders.[6] Adult offenders generally begin their sex crimes later in life.[7] This finding runs counter to the notion that all adult sex offenders begin their crimes early and never stop victimizing children. In reality, most adult offenders did not engage in this activity as youths, and most juvenile sex offenders, even repeat ones, do not go on to commit these types of crimes as adults.[8]

In a study of 204 juvenile male sex offenders and 41 juvenile female sex offenders in Philadelphia, researchers found that only 10 percent of the boys committed another sex offense within eight years of their eighteenth birthday. Interestingly, none of the female offenders committed another sex offense in the same period.[9] Having committed a sex offense as a juvenile was not a strong predictor of committing one as an adult.[10] In another study, only 8 percent of adult sex offenders had been juvenile sex offenders,[11] while other research reports about half that number.[12] These findings are important because they raise questions about the value, let alone the need, of requiring juveniles to register as sex offenders.

Several researchers have attempted to create typologies of juvenile sex offenders in order to understand the motivations of the population. Perhaps the best known and most often cited system was developed by O'Brien and Bera (1986), who proposed seven categories of offenders, as summarized in Table 9-1.

TABLE 9-1 Seven Categories of Juvenile Sex Offenders

Naïve Experimenters	Young offenders, lacking in both social skills and knowledge about sex, who commit sex crimes based on the situational opportunity
Undersocialized Child Exploiters	Socially isolated and emotionally insecure youths with a poor self-image but no history of delinquent behavior
Sexual Aggressives	Juveniles with a history of delinquency and substance abuse, high levels of impulsivity, and lack of self-control, who are most likely to use force and violence during the offense
Sexual Compulsives	Offenders from very strict and socially disciplined households who tend to be quiet, anxious, and compulsive in their behavior, and who have deviant sexual fantasies that they eventually act on
Disturbed Impulsives	Offenders with severe psychological disorders stemming from a lack of self-control and impulsivity who act upon those feelings
Peer-Group-Influenced Offenders	Juveniles who commit offenses to impress their peers and are motivated by status and prestige more than by a sexually repressed need
Pseudo-Socialized Offenders	Intelligent individuals who lack the ability to be intimate with others, have only superficial relationships with people, and tend to be narcissistic in their decision making[13]

While it is helpful to use typologies to gain a greater understanding of the wide range of juvenile sexual offenses and the motivations behind them, typologies are not always mutually exclusive, as sex offenders do not usually specialize in a particular type of behavior. For instance, Sexual Aggressives may be motivated by the need to control their victims, but also by a desire to impress their friends or due to some other unmet need. Still, typologies are helpful in identifying the heterogeneity of this population of offenders.[14]

Some experts point to a biological explanation for sex offending: higher testosterone levels and stronger sex drives can result in criminal offenses.[15] Others point to environmental factors, whereby children who witness or experience sexual abuse are more likely to abuse others. Officials at the Safer Society Foundation, a nonprofit organization that works to protect children from predators, argue that some children who engage in sexual offending have simply learned how to commit and justify sex acts. Because this behavior is learned, it is possible to set offenders on another course of action through behavior modification therapy. According to other learning theories, sex offending occurs because these offenders never learned how to carry on appropriate, constructive relationships with others.[16]

Most experts agree that there are significant differences between adult and juvenile sex offenders. The deep-seated psychological problems seen in adult sexual offenders are not applicable to juveniles. Some studies, backed by the Association for the Treatment of Sexual Abusers, identify "nonsexual problems" as the most important factor behind serious sex crimes by child offenders:[17]

> Poor social competency skills and deficits in self-esteem can best explain sexual deviance in children, rather than paraphilic interests and psychopathic characteristics that are more common in adult offenders. There is little evidence that . . . these youths engage in acts of sexual penetration for the same reasons as their adult counterparts.[18]

Rather, juvenile sex offenders' motivations stem from other problems, such as learning disabilities, conduct disorders, sexual victimization, and abuse, all of which are amenable to treatment.[19] As Phillip describes his initial experiences with sex offending, he goes through some memory lapses and explains that everyone involved was too young to understand what was going on. Phillip contends that he believes he might have been sexually abused as a child, although he cannot recall with certainty that the event took place:

> I think when I started I was around 10, nine or 10. And I remember one time my brother Joe and I were in the same room together. . . . And so I offended against my brother, so . . . but and,

and I remember I exposed myself to him and he did it too. And he wasn't sure what was going on here. And I remember one time I was at the bottom of the stairs after one night when I set a fire on the chicken wire. . . . And I think, it's kind of a mixed up memory because I also remember my brother listening at the bottom of the stairs when my brother Xander was in my mom's room. And, and he was saying, "mom, mom, Phillip hurts Drew with his penis."

Because juvenile sex offenders are very different in their motivations from adults and generally do not continue this pattern of behavior as an adult, they are also more likely than adults to be successfully treated for their offenses. However, the general public and the media tend to view all sex offenders as a homogeneous category.

While the media tend to focus more on male offenders, a few cases involving female offenders have garnered attention. According to a recent report on female sex offenders by the Center for Sex Offender Management, information on this population can be unreliable because there is no single database from which to collect and analyze data.[20] Consequently, researchers draw from a variety of sources such as the Uniform Crime Reports (UCR), the National Crime Victimization Survey (NCVS), and self-report data, all of which are limited in their scope and comprehensiveness.[21]

Of all adults and juveniles who come to the attention of the police for sex crimes, females account for less than 10 percent of the cases. Of all adolescent sex offenses, females are responsible for 3 percent of forcible rape cases, 5 percent of other violent sex offenses, and 19 percent of nonviolent sex offenses.[22] Both male and female sex offenders have a history of family difficulties, poor coping skills, low self-esteem, substance abuse, and difficulty in sustaining relationships with intimate others. However, the history of sexual abuse among both juvenile and adult female offenders is greater and longer in duration compared to male offenders.[23] The main difference between males and females is the choice of victims. Juvenile female sex offenders usually target young children, typically within the female's family, and tend to act alone.[24]

The issues surrounding juvenile sex offenders are complicated, and available data are not sufficient to offer general conclusions about policy. Much of the offenders' behavior is learned, often as a result of experiencing similar trauma,[25] which suggests that if treatment is provided early enough, most juvenile offenders can change. The Theory and Practice box on page 228 offers insight into one promising strategy.

Another strategy that is used to address the threat posed by sex offenders involves **registry laws,** which require convicted sex offenders to make their whereabouts known by registering with the local police. Registry laws were first enacted in 1996, when President Clinton signed **Megan's Law,** named for Megan Kanka, who was killed at the age of seven by a neighbor and twice-convicted sex offender. Megan's Law is controversial because it requires released sex offenders to register with local police and for neighborhoods to be informed of the identity, criminal record, and address of offenders with a high-risk of reoffending. Depending on the perceived risk, different agencies are alerted. Only law enforcement is notified if the offender is considered a low risk; schools and day care centers are notified if the offender presents a moderate risk; and all neighbors are notified if the offender poses a high risk to the community. Registry is now required in all fifty states.[26]

Another law, the **Adam Walsh Child Protection and Safety Act,** signed by President Bush in 2006, integrates information from state sex offender registry systems so that offenders cannot evade detection by moving from state to state. The law strengthens federal penalties for crimes against children and provides grants to states to help them institutionalize sex offenders who have not changed their behaviors and are about to be released from prison. The act also created regional Internet Crimes against Children Task Forces to provide funding and training to help law enforcement combat crimes involving the Internet.[27]

For more on sex offenses, watch *Early Sex Experience & Offenses: Phillip* at www.mhhe.com/mcnamarajd1e

registry laws
Requirements for convicted sex offenders to make their whereabouts known by registering with local police.

Megan's Law
Named for seven-year-old Megan Kanka, who was killed by a neighbor and twice-convicted sex offender; the 1996 act introduced registry laws requiring released sex offenders to register with local police and neighborhoods to be informed of the identity, address, and criminal record of offenders with a high risk of reoffending.

Adam Walsh Child Protection and Safety Law
A law that integrates information from state sex offender registry systems so that offenders cannot evade detection by moving from state to state; also strengthened federal penalties for crimes against children.

THEORY AND PRACTICE WORKING TOGETHER

Treatment for Juvenile Sex Offenders

Juvenile sex offenders have received a great deal of attention in the media. This notoriety has influenced the public's perception of whether these individuals are curable. While most people generally agree that it is possible to change offenders' behavior, the public remains skeptical about some crimes, such as sex offenses. Public attitudes are often influenced by high-profile media coverage of extreme cases; however, a number of promising programs have demonstrated track records showing that releasing juvenile sex offenders into the community does not pose any risk to children.

One such program is called Counterpoint, a residential treatment facility in Portland, Oregon, managed by the Morrison Center for Children and Family Services. Counterpoint typically serves twenty boys between the ages of twelve and eighteen. Residents complete daily therapy sessions and attend the program year-round for approximately eighteen months. The program is selective—it only admits nonviolent youths who demonstrate a willingness to change. Another common feature of the program is that participants have been victims of abuse. Internal data show that 62 percent of the boys were sexually abused, 42 percent were physically abused, 79 percent experienced some form of abuse or neglect, and 40 percent were victims of multiple forms of abuse.

Counterpoint is based on a cognitive behavioral and relapse prevention therapy model. The key is for offenders to take responsibility for their behavior and to avoid the rationalizations they used to justify their abuse of another child. One therapeutic technique involves identifying triggers for disruptive behavior and making the link between emotion and behavior clearer to offenders. By being able to identify "triggers" or events that influence their emotions and actions, the youths can begin using deescalating techniques to curb those thoughts and feelings. National statistics show that although 35–50 percent of adult sex offenders reoffend after treatment, the recidivism rate for juvenile sex offenders is only about 6 percent.[28] The difference comes from the fact that adolescents have not yet completely formed their identities.

Research at Counterpoint shows a recidivism rate of only 4 percent after one year, better than the national average. Not all participants graduate from the program, however. One of the challenges that remains is accessibility—about 1,000 treatment programs such as Counterpoint exist around the country, and they can serve only a small number of youths. Inadequate funding for research and treatment programs means that many juvenile offenders wind up in correctional facilities without specialized therapeutic programs.

THINK ABOUT IT If juvenile sex offenders can be effectively treated, what are the reasons for the failure to provide therapy for them?

Jessica's Law
Named for nine-year-old Jessica Lunsford, who was abducted, assaulted, and buried alive by a convicted sex offender; the 2005 law requires more thorough monitoring of offenders, through such means as DNA samples, ankle bracelets, and GPS tracking.

Jessica's Law, passed in 2005, requires more thorough monitoring of offenders, through means such as DNA samples, ankle bracelets, and GPS tracking. The law was named for nine-year-old Jessica Lunsford, who was abducted from her Florida home by a convicted sex offender, sexually assaulted, and buried alive. Thirty-three states had passed some version of Jessica's Law by 2007.[29]

While registry laws may ease the concerns of parents and community residents about the threat of sex offenders, a number of issues are raised by requiring juvenile sex offenders to observe registry laws. Juveniles have lower recidivism rates than adults, but are usually included with adults under new laws. Should a teenager guilty of statutory rape be punished under the same law as an older man guilty of molesting young children? Do they need to register with their communities, and if so, for how long? Being on a registry list impacts offenders in many ways, such as their ability to obtain jobs.

JUVENILE PROSTITUTION

The phenomenon of juvenile prostitution, particularly male prostitutes, has, until recently, received only moderate attention. While the terms "child prostitution" and "juvenile prostitution" are used interchangeably, the vast majority of young sex workers are teenagers. This is because youths who run away from or are thrown out of home (see Chapter 3 for more on runaways and homeless youths) often find it difficult to earn money legitimately, particularly if they are too young to obtain a regular job. As a result, many turn to prostitution as a means of survival. Others become involved in the sex trade due to sexual and physical abuse at home. As with juvenile sex offending, juvenile prostitution can serve as a way of coping with the experience of sexual and physical trauma.[30]

While sexual and physical abuse contributes significantly to juvenile prostitution, substance abuse is also a factor; in fact, many young prostitutes have been abused in multiple ways. The decision to become involved in the sex trade is usually involuntary. Teenagers do not sit down, lay out all their options, and choose prostitution over some other career path. Often their decision is the least offensive or dangerous one from an assortment of unsavory options. Once they are on the street, teenage prostitutes face a host of other risks from clients, other sex workers, and, in some cases, pimps.[31]

While estimates of the juvenile prostitution population range from less than 1,500 to as many as 2.4 million, much of the data is questionable. Researchers at the Crimes Against Children Research Center (CACRC) at the University of New Hampshire estimate the size of this population to be at best a "guesstimate." Additionally, the CACRC discusses the tendency for the media to engage in the "Woozle Effect," whereby one media source reports a "hunch" about the size of the population, only to have another outlet cite the same source. This repeated use of the same source or figure results in the number becoming "factual" when in reality it is not.[32]

The CACRC does note that crime statistics, such as those from the Uniform Crime Reports, provide a plausible estimate of the population, largely because they are based on actual arrests, but even the UCR data are limited. Not all youths participating in prostitution are arrested, and not all are arrested for prostitution. According to the UCR, in 2008, there were 59,390 arrests for prostitution and commercialized vice. Of those, only a small percentage, about 2 percent, were individuals under the age of eighteen. There were 1,158 arrests for prostitution for individuals under eighteen years of age, 129 arrests for those under fifteen years of age, and a remarkable 8 arrests for those under ten years of age.[33]

A 2004 report by the Office of Juvenile Justice and Delinquency Prevention (OJJDP) on the patterns of juvenile prostitutes indicates that the nature of prostitution is changing.[34] While much attention is given to female prostitutes, especially juvenile females, who are often treated more as victims by police than as offenders, juvenile males are increasingly becoming a part of the statistical landscape. There is a wide range of prostitutes and activities, with some sex workers choosing to act as independent operators and others in groups, while still others are exploited by pimps. The OJJDP report documents that juvenile prostitution generally involves a single operator and is more likely to occur in homes or other private locations. This is in contrast to the more public nature of adult prostitution, which can occur in cars, streets, alleys and other more visible areas. Because of its "hidden" nature, juvenile prostitution is much more difficult to uncover and address.[35]

Male prostitutes tend to be different in many ways from female prostitutes: they tend to be older, are more likely to be arrested, and are most likely to be perceived by the police as an offender instead of a victim. Unlike females, male prostitutes tend not to use pimps. Nearly two-thirds of juvenile prostitutes are males, but this figure may be due to greater attention from and an increased likelihood of arrest by law enforcement officers. Official crime statistics notwithstanding, experts generally agree that about two-thirds of the juvenile prostitutes in this country are females.[36]

During the 1990s, research into juvenile prostitution was conducted largely due to the interest in risky sexual behavior and HIV/AIDS. Most of the studies focused on knowledge of the disease and the types of preventive steps young prostitutes used to avoid HIV infection. In one of the few in-depth ethnographic studies of male prostitutes, in New York City, sociologist Robert McNamara examined the lives of 35 male prostitutes ranging in age from fifteen to thirty, in an effort to understand the nature of male prostitution and the issues for many involved in the sex trade. He found that not

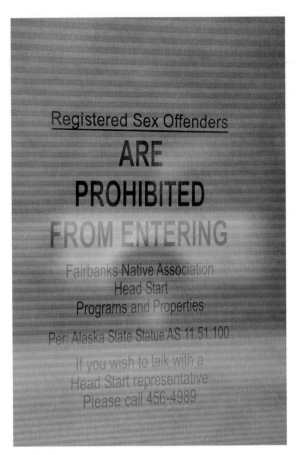

Given the consequences of being placed on a sex registry, should society consider which types of sex crimes are included?

What are some of the potential risks for juvenile prostitutes who work on the streets?

Why are male prostitutes more likely to be seen by the police as offenders rather than as victims?

hustlers
Individuals who engage in a host of legal and illegal activities, such as prostitution.

only did a community of **hustlers**—those who engage in a host of legal and illegal activities, such as prostitution—exist in the Times Square section of New York City, but also a number of cultural constraints placed many of the boys at risk for arrest, injury, or infection with HIV.

While most hustlers knew about HIV/AIDS and effective means of preventing infection, many used flawed protective strategies. For instance, some hustlers would use street reputation or frequent testing to avoid infection, but not condoms and more effective forms of protection. Individual hustlers felt a strong need for acceptance into the hustling subculture and would use what they knew to be ineffective prevention methods largely because that was the working norm or standard practice within the group.

Most of the hustlers in Times Square considered themselves to be heterosexual. These hustlers coexisted with homosexual hustlers who frequented Times Square and Greenwich Village in order to find clients. They distinguished themselves from gay hustlers by limiting the range and scope of activities they would engage in with clients. For instance, gay hustlers would perform virtually any sex act with a client if the price was right, but heterosexual hustlers were able to maintain their "manhood" by refusing to engage in such tactics. Whereas gay hustlers enjoyed homosexual activity (and got paid, too), heterosexual hustlers viewed their participation in prostitution as "working" or "hustling," in which they tried to elicit money from clients for as little sex as possible. In this way, the hustlers of Times Square could maintain their heterosexual identities. Similar assessments of the nature of both groups have been documented in other studies of the male prostitution population in other cities.[37]

DOUG'S CASE

Prostitution Problem

Recall Doug's family issues and recent behavior:

- His father physically abuses his mother, him, and his younger brother.
- His father killed the family cat after it scratched the living room couch with its claws.
- After being sentenced to a residential treatment facility, Doug ran away and has been living on San Diego streets for at least eighteen months.
- Doug has shoplifted food and other items, and has engaged in prostitution.
- Doug has been arrested and charged with arson for attempting to burn down an abandoned warehouse.

While it may initially appear that Doug is quickly turning into a "hard-core" delinquent, there are significant reasons for his getting into the sex trade as a source of income. Most youths who engage in prostitution are doing it as a means of survival and as a consequence of having few legitimate alternatives. Doug, like many other youths on the street, is more likely to get arrested than a young female working the streets. The prostitution arrest will likely cause him further problems since he has been arrested for other crimes and infractions, making him appear to be a more chronic offender.

THINK ABOUT IT

Are continual arrests the best answer to Doug's situation? How do we balance the need for treatment and assistance for troubled youths with accountability for breaking the law?

INTERNATIONAL TRAFFICKING OF CHILDREN

Recently, the media have paid greater attention to issues surrounding prostitution and public policy based on stories relating to the international **trafficking of children.** There is a difference between smuggling and trafficking, as outlined in Table 9-2. According to the U.S. Department of Health and Human Services, trafficking of human beings is a modern-day form of slavery, something former President George W. Bush called "a brutal crime that steals innocence and destroys lives."[38] Many victims of human trafficking are forced to work in the sex industry, but trafficking also occurs in forms of labor exploitation, such as domestic servitude, restaurant work, janitorial work, sweatshop factory work, and migrant agricultural work.

Traffickers use various techniques to instill fear in victims and to keep them enslaved. Some traffickers literally keep their victims under lock and key. But the more frequent practice is to use less obvious techniques, such as the following:

- Debt bondage, a modern-day version of indentured servitude, whereby the victims must pay off an exorbitant debt before they are free to leave.
- Isolation from friends, family, and the general public by limiting contact with outsiders and making sure that any contact is monitored or superficial in nature.
- Confiscation of passports, visas, and/or identification documents, making victims unable to flee.
- Threats or use of violence against family members to gain compliance.
- Threats of shaming victims by exposing their activities to family members.
- Threats of imprisonment or deportation for immigration violations if they contact authorities.
- Control of victims' income by claiming they are holding it for them, a common technique used by pimps on female prostitutes.[39]

While most trafficking cases involve the importation of children from developing nations, an increasing number of cases involve American children being trafficked to other countries. Within the United States, the problem usually involves immigrant children from Mexico, Thailand, and Guatemala, who are brought here to work as prostitutes. So much attention has

trafficking of children
A form of modern-day slavery whereby the victims are forced to work in the sex industry or to perform labor, such as domestic service, janitorial work, sweatshop factory work, or migrant agricultural work.

TABLE 9-2 Differences between Smuggling and Trafficking

Element	Smuggling	Trafficking
Type of crime	Crime against state—no victim by the crime of smuggling as such (violation of immigration laws/public order; the crime of smuggling by definition does not require violations of the rights of the smuggled migrants)	Crime against person/victim; violation of the rights of the victim of trafficking by definition (violation of a person's human rights; victim of coercion and exploitation that give rise to duties by the state to treat the individual as a victim of a crime and human rights violation)
Why do we fight it?	To protect sovereignty of the state	To protect a person against human rights violations; obligation of the state to provide adequate protection to its citizens
Nature of crime and duration of customer relationship	Commercial; relationship between smuggler and migrant ends after the illegal border crossing is achieved and the fee paid	Exploitative; relationship between trafficker and victim continues in order to maximize economic and/or other gains from exploitation
Rationale	Organized movement of persons for profit	Organized recruitment/movement and (continuous) exploitation of the victim for profit
Border crossing	Illegal border crossing a defining element	Purpose of exploitation is the defining element; border crossing is not an element of the crime
Consent	Migrant's consent to illegal border crossing	Either no consent, or initial consent made irrelevant because of use of force or coercion at any stage of the process

Why are both smuggling and trafficking important issues for us to address, especially with regard to their links to juvenile delinquency?

Source: http://www.antitrafficking.net/differencebetween-smugglingand.html.

been given to the issue of human trafficking that Congress passed the Trafficking Victims Protection Act (TVPA) of 2000, which defines human trafficking as a commercial sex act induced by force, fraud, or coercion, or in which the person influenced to perform such acts is a juvenile.[40]

While it is difficult to know the exact numbers, largely because much of this activity is covert in nature and goes unreported, according to the U.S. Department of State, about 1 million children per year are exploited by the global commercial sex trade.[41] Approximately 600,000–800,000 men, women, and children annually are trafficked across international borders, and an estimated 14,500–17,500 of those victims are trafficked into the United States. According to the International Labor Organization (ILO), a United Nations agency, millions more are trafficked within their own countries.[42]

According to another U.S. Department of State report, about 70 percent of trafficked female victims are forced into the commercial sex trade, and about a third are victims of forced labor.[43] The primary reason for such widespread trafficking is money: the yearly profits from the human trafficking industry have been estimated to be approximately $32 billion.[44] This phenomenon is so widespread that the U.S. Department of Health and Human Services estimates that not only is trafficking of humans the fastest-growing criminal industry in the world, but it remains tied with arms dealing as the second-largest enterprise, after drug dealing. Clearly, this industry represents a considerable threat to women and children across the globe, and is quickly becoming a topic for researchers who study prostitution, particularly juvenile prostitution.

While the issues stemming from juvenile prostitution are serious, generally, there are few resources available to deal with the problem. While some communities have programs to help runaway and homeless youths, such as shelters and counseling, programs to help youths avoid sex work are rare.

Because the problem of juvenile prostitution is related to poverty, running away, family discord, and other issues, many states have attempted to address the issue by enforcing strict curfew laws, creating more runaway shelters, and attempting to reconcile family problems. Rather than simply trying to minimize the effect of the particular problem, which will likely have limited results, noting *why* such behavior is occurring helps society reach the point where the origins of the problems emerge. In the case of juvenile prostitution, as well as juvenile sex offending, the real problem relates to family issues, such as abuse, neglect, and running away.

In 2008, an interesting twist emerged in the study of juvenile prostitution, potentially impacting decisions relating to public policy. Male prostitutes, who have historically been less visible and virtually ignored in the empirical literature, gained a national spotlight when the state of Nevada allowed male prostitutes to operate legally. What prevented male prostitution in the past was a technicality in the state law that mandated cervical exams for sex workers who legally operated in the state. When this requirement was lifted, male prostitutes were allowed to operate legally as well. The most noted criticism of the change came from brothel owners, who, somewhat ironically, thought that having homosexual prostitutes operating in brothels would tarnish the reputation of the industry in general and brothels in particular.[45]

THINK ABOUT IT

Sexual Activity and Delinquency

What can be done to help children living on the streets? What services are needed to prevent them from getting involved in prostitution?

Mental Illness

Like prostitution and sex offending, serious forms of delinquency are symptomatic of some larger problem, such as an emotional disorder. There are many dimensions to the relationship between mental illness and delinquency, such as concerns about violent offenders and mental illness as an explanation for criminal behavior.[46]

Our understanding of mental illness as it relates to delinquent behaviors has grown because of our awareness of the problem, as well as our ability to adequately diagnose and treat disorders. However, there is no discounting the extent of the problem: nationally, the prevalence of mental disorders is higher in the juvenile justice population than the general population.[47] Moreover, 70 percent of youths in the juvenile justice system have a diagnosable mental disorder. About one in five (20 percent) of these youths has a serious mental disorder.[48]

At the same time, emotional problems are difficult to manage, and many youths and families lack access to treatment. In 2003, 12,700 families relinquished custody of their children for the sole purpose of accessing mental health services for their child, 9,000 to the juvenile justice system.[49] Correctional facilities have become warehouses for mentally ill offenders. As an illustration, the rate of suicide among juveniles while incarcerated is four times that of youths overall.[50] Children and teenagers with mental health disorders are also at increased risk of victimization by others in juvenile detention centers.[51] Additionally, reports estimate that juvenile detention facilities spend $100 million each year to house youths who are waiting for mental health services.[52]

Without adequate community services, many youths end up in the criminal justice system. These environments are not designed to provide treatment on such a wide and in-depth scale, which exacerbates the problems for individual offenders. Because of staff shortages and a punitive philosophy, many of the institutional strategies, such as prolonged isolation, can increase the severity of the mental issue and escalate problem behaviors such as acting out, violating institutional rules, inflicting self-harm, and assaulting other offenders.

When it comes to assessing the relationship between mental illness and delinquency, we should distinguish between what are called *early-onset* and *later-onset* delinquents. Early-onset delinquents are usually males who have a history of aggression beginning as early as elementary school age. For this group, there may be some type of genetic link between mental illness and delinquency. Recall from Chapter 6 the discussion of a wide range of psychological disorders that youths experience and the possible biological connection between psychological disorders and delinquency.

Attention-Deficit/Hyperactivity Disorders, characterized by several symptoms including impulsiveness, and Conduct and Oppositional Defiant Disorders are linked to aggression and rule breaking. A significant number of early-onset delinquents have an exaggerated tendency to believe that others have hostile intentions toward them. This belief, along with the impulsiveness often associated with these types of disorders, can make it extremely difficult for these children and adolescents to appropriately evaluate perceived threats. This combination frequently leads to conflicts with family members and peers, as well as problems adjusting to different school situations.

Late-onset delinquents are often those who become involved in delinquent behavior during their teenage years but who rarely continue this behavior into adulthood. In these cases, it is likely that peer pressure or some other environmental factor such as inadequate supervision or lack of social boundaries by parents is the precipitating factor in their decision to engage in delinquency.[53]

While a host of delinquent behaviors have a relationship to mental illness, we will focus on two increasingly problematic ones: fire-starting and juvenile domestic violence. While some youths set fires simply for the thrill or excitement of it, often the behavior is connected to another set of problems. Juvenile fire-starting and arson are very similar in nature, while juvenile domestic violence is a growing problem for many states and has an assortment of links to adult violence as well.

FIRE-STARTERS

Setting fires might not seem like a serious act of delinquency, particularly in light of the media's focus on gangs and youth violence; however, statistics show that nearly 300 people die each year, 85 percent of whom are children, as a result of fires set by youths. Fires also cause over $600 million each year in destroyed property.[54] According to the UCR,

Why do so many youths have a fascination with fire?

arson is defined as "any willful or malicious burning or attempting to burn, with or without intent to defraud, a dwelling, house, public building, motor vehicle or aircraft, personal property of another, etc."[55] According to the UCR, in 2008, juveniles accounted for 47 percent of all people arrested for arson.[56] Despite the frequency with which youths engage in this activity, little empirical research has been conducted on it. This topic is one of the more fascinating and disturbing ones in the delinquency literature because of its obscurity and its offenders' psychological issues.

In comprehending fire-starting behavior, we should begin with a distinction between *fire play* and *fire-setting*. While both can result in damage to property and injury to victims, they differ in their intent. *Fire play* is a result of a fascination with fire. Youths start fires not to injure or damage property, but often out of curiosity. *Fire-setting*, on the other hand, is based on the intent to use fire as a means to achieve some objective. Moreover, fire-setting is more likely to be repeated behavior than fire play, making the latter less likely to become a chronic behavior for youths.[57]

A distinction can also be made between *fire interest* and *fire involvement*. As the term suggests, youths may be interested in fire but not necessarily start them. Fire involvement, on the other hand, suggests some type of participation. According to the United States Fire Administration, curiosity motivates a significant portion of fire involvement, as evidenced by studies reporting that 40 percent of all children have engaged in fire play.[58] These children are risk takers and learn by experience. A willingness to engage in risky behavior, combined with ready access to matches and lighters, a poor understanding of fire, and lapses in adult supervision, create a deadly formula that accounts for thousands of fires every year.[59]

According to the UCR, arson, a form of fire-setting, resulted in 10,784 arrests in 2008, with 47 percent (5,021) of the arrests consisting of offenders under the age of eighteen. The age group with the largest number of arson arrests was thirteen- and fourteen-year-olds, with 1,646 arrests (see Table 9-3). Unlike the situation with sex offenders, society tends to view juvenile arsonists differently from their adult counterparts. While teenagers might know the potential consequences of starting a fire, society does not assign them the same level of responsibility as adults who commit the same act because teenagers have not completely developed cognitively. Youths' lack of developed abstract reasoning causes authorities to look at treatment rather than punishment for juvenile fire-setters.[60]

TABLE 9-3 Arrests of Juvenile Arsonists, 2008

Age Group	Number of Arrests (total arrests: 10,784)
Under 18	5,021
17 years old	603
15 to 16 years old	1,516
13 to 14 years old	1,646
10 to 12 years old	885
Under 10 years old	291

The clearance rate, which consists of either an arrest or identification of a suspect, for juveniles was about 40 percent, the highest percentage of all offense clearances involving juveniles.[61] Do you believe that youths lack cognitive development and go unpunished for their actions?

Source: *Crime in the United States 2008*. Table 38. http://www.fbi.gov/ucr/cius2008/data/table_38.html.

The motivation to commit fire-setting/arson functions as a type of response to trauma rather than a calculated behavior.[62] Experts point to the concept of expressive and instrumental behavior: *expressive fire-setting* behavior reflects unresolved trauma, while *instrumental fire-setting* suggests that the fire was set to achieve an established goal. The distinction between expressive and instrumental fire-setting behaviors affects treatment and intervention strategies.[63]

Traumas can result from family dynamics that particularly affect adolescents. In a ten-year study on the impact of marital violence on children's mental health, researchers found a link between marital violence, parental abuse of animals, abuse of alcohol by parents, and childhood fire-setting behavior.[64] Walter's fire-setting behavior is an example of instrumental fire-setting. This instance is in response to a particular set of circumstances, where he is seeking revenge for a dispute with his brother:

Why do so many cases of arson involve juveniles?

> We were playing basketball and I shot it, and when I went up, my elbow hit him in the back of the head when he turned. He got mad and punched me in the jaw. So I was like, all right, I'm goin' to get him. So when he fell asleep, I took antifreeze and I put it on the corner of the bed and lit it on fire. And he, he—it didn't burn him none. It's just like the corner of the bed set on fire. He woke up. He was like, "what the—?" started cussing at me and got up and he beat me up. I don't know. I didn't care. It was, if you do something to me, I'm goin' to do something worse to you, just how I dealt with things.

In contrast, consider Phillip's experiences with fire-setting. While he has a history of engaging in this activity, this description might be considered an accident or curiosity fire-setting:

> One time I set a fire in the house on—well, I didn't mean to. I, I was, I had this laboratory in my room that I was showing my brothers. And I had done this a couple of times, where I'd done it myself. I took a Hot Wheels toy car. Thing. You know, one where you press the button and the cars go around the track. Well, I took the wire thing from it. The two prongs and put them in between the little plug-ins of another lamp. And put it in the outlet. And turned the lamp on. And I would push it down once, and a spark would fly out. And, but the reason why I did it was because it smelled good for some reason.

Because of difficult home environments with one or no biological parents present, adolescent fire-setters have higher levels of antisocial behaviors and aggression. They are, on average, about eleven years old, white, male, and often from middle-class backgrounds. The strongest predictor of recidivism is the juvenile being in a home with a significant number of family problems. Juvenile fire-setting is also related to poor school performance—depending upon the age of the offender, fire-setters may also have a history of truancy, disruptive behavior, hyperactivity, or lower academic achievement.[65]

00:20   01:02

For more on fire starting, watch *Fire Starting: Walter* at www.mhhe.com/ mcnamarajd1e

It is not surprising to find that juvenile fire-setters have poor relationships with peers and an inability to form close friendships. Besides conduct and aggression problems, many juvenile fire-setters suffer from depression and attention deficit disorders.[66] While some studies show a history of sexual abuse, these are limited, since few studies ever question the relationship between juvenile fire-setting and sexual abuse.[67]

DOUG'S CASE

Signs of Fire-Setting Behavior

Recall Doug's situation:

- His father physically abuses his mother, him, and his younger brother.
- His father killed the family cat after it scratched the living room couch with its claws.
- Doug has been living on the streets for over a year, has shoplifted, and has participated in prostitution.
- He showcases aggressive behavior and emotions, causing people to distance themselves from him.
- Recently, he accepted payment to burn down an abandoned warehouse, resulting in arrest and arson charges.

Doug has many characteristics of a juvenile fire-starter: he comes from a violent family, he witnessed his father killing the family pet, he shows classic signs of isolation, he is aggressive, and he does poorly in school.

 THINK ABOUT IT What significance does the family pet's death at his father's hands have in terms of Doug's fire-starting behavior?

The causes of fire-starting behavior translate into a range of options for treating the disorder. If fire-setting is a product of social learning or a response to blocked opportunities, then the goals of intervention and treatment can center on teaching the youths about the dangers of fire-setting and the reasons to avoid it. If fire-setting is more of a manifestation of a personality or behavioral disorder, then psychological counseling and treatment programs can focus on how and in what ways the fire is an expression of inner turmoil. However, juvenile fire-setting usually has multiple causes, and fire-setters have different personalities. What works with some individuals may not work with others because their behaviors may stem from different sources. Given the limited information available about this population, typologies or treatment models are more difficult to develop. But the fire-setting research literature clearly recognizes that successful intervention, control, and treatment involve multiple strategies.[68]

Media campaigns targeting fire prevention also have a long-standing history. The Smokey the Bear campaign, for example, has been used for decades. More recently, local agencies have implemented their own campaigns, including those presented at primary, middle, and secondary schools.

Some new education programs target only those juveniles who have been identified as *fire involved* in one way or another. However, these programs have confusion regarding the target audience, as well as inadequate evaluations of their effectiveness.[69] For instance, some experts question whether existing programs are designed with the particular motivations of offenders in mind. Youths who engage in fire play and fire-setting have different motivations, with some focused on fire interest and others on fire involvement, and programs need to reflect those variations.[70] Furthermore, rigorous evaluations of the effectiveness of many programs have not been completed.[71] Comparatively little research exists that addresses the success of intervention efforts according to the age of the fire-setter, the type of fire-setter, or the event characteristics—all of which are important for determining best practices for interventions.[72]

What role, if any, should the community play in addressing fire-setting among youths? Is this a behavior that requires more therapeutic treatment, or can social programs offer

Operation Extinguish

Operation Extinguish is a model program developed by the Montgomery County, Maryland, Department of Fire and Rescue Services in 1984 to provide intervention and educational services for juvenile fire-setters and their families. There are three main components of the program:

- an evaluation of the youths to assess their suitability for the program
- psycho-educational classes held at the public safety training academy
- recommendations for treatment after completion of the program

Juvenile fire-setters age seven to eighteen are charged and required to report to the Montgomery County Police Youth Division with their parents for screening. After interviewing the children and their parents, the screening officer decides whether to refer the child to the Operation Extinguish program, which consists of psychological evaluations of the children and their families and six hours of fire safety education. Over 1,000 youths have participated in the program since 1984, and only 1 percent had to go through it a second time as a result of repeated offending. Operation Extinguish has received an award from the National Association of Counties for being an outstanding juvenile justice program.

 THINK ABOUT IT Why is this program successful, especially given that motivations of fire-starting can vary from child to child?

help in curbing the behavior? The Theory and Practice box above discusses one promising strategy to help youths with this type of problem.

Our current level of understanding with regard to juvenile fire-setting may be similar to what we knew about child abuse more than twenty-five years ago. As we gained more understanding about the short- and long-term effects of child abuse, research on the topic began to reveal the causes and risk factors, and to produce effective treatment modalities to minimize its effects. Similarly, fire-setting research is developing in terms of its effects and correlations to other forms of delinquency.[73]

DOMESTIC VIOLENCE

One of the more interesting recent trends in the study of juvenile justice was the prediction of a "super predator" class of delinquents, who were expected to have a dramatic impact on crime in the United States.[74] But this supposed trend actually reflected changes in law enforcement policy and the recording of crimes. Another good example of this involves domestic violence.

In the 1980s, research confirmed that the best way to address problems stemming from domestic violence was a formal response from the justice system. Studies conducted by criminologist Larry Sherman showed that when police officers arrested a suspect for domestic violence, the likelihood of another incident decreased. These studies led police departments around the country to adopt mandatory arrest policies if probable cause indicated that domestic violence had occurred. Previously, the only way an officer could make an arrest was if the victim was willing to press charges. With the change in arrest policy, the officer became the complainant rather than the victim.[75]

What impact did this have on juvenile violent crime? While domestic violence is not usually considered a juvenile issue, this change in policy brought a large number of juveniles into the justice system. Fights with parents or siblings that had previously been ignored by law enforcement or handled as a status offense (e.g., incorrigibility or ungovernability) now resulted in an arrest for simple or aggravated assault. Consider Austin's relationship with his mother, one that led to criminal charges for parental violence. He thinks the incident stems from his belief that his mother never really loved him:

> Yeah, I, yeah, I, I pushed her once and then I got the cops called on me. And then, uh, charges got pressed. . . . I think, uh, we was arguing about me going to bed or something and, and I said no. And then she tried to grab me and pull—push me into my room. And I pushed her

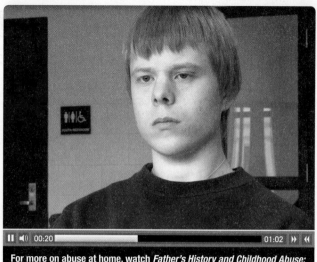

For more on abuse at home, watch *Father's History and Childhood Abuse: Austin* at www.mhhe.com/mcnamarajd1e

family violence
Hostile behaviors committed among siblings.

dating violence
Hostile altercations between unmarried partners.

back. And then she fell. . . . We'd argue a lot, but I never done that again. . . . That's not right to, you know, to punch my mom or push my mom. . . . She, she never—yeah, she'd never talk to me and do anything with me. She just—uh, she would do her own thing. . . .We'd never actually talk or anything, and have that, uh, bond with my mom. So, I grew up thinking that she didn't love me and didn't care.

These youths with serious family problems presented the juvenile justice system with a "new" type of juvenile offender.[76] As a result, researchers began to learn more about juvenile domestic violence.

While it is true that domestic violence committed by adults is different from what is known as **family violence** (violence committed among siblings) and **dating violence** (violence between unmarried, young partners), the implications of these crimes are significant for youths in the United States. Specific to dating violence, the Centers for Disease Control (CDC) has identified three main types of assault:

- Physical: includes when a partner is pinched, hit, shoved, or kicked.

- Emotional: occurs when a partner is threatened, teased, bullied, or isolated from family and friends. Emotional dating violence also includes any behavior that harms a partner's self-worth.

- Sexual: involves forcing a partner to engage in a sex act when she or he cannot or will not consent to participating in such activity.[77]

Dating violence is a significant issue in part because of the prevalence of the problem and the reluctance of many victims to report such incidents. For example, the CDC estimates that nearly 80 percent of eighth and ninth graders date, and 25 percent of adolescents report verbal, physical, emotional, or sexual abuse from a dating partner.[78] In a 2006 report for the National Institute of Justice (NIJ) titled *Juvenile Domestic and Family Violence: The Effects of Court-Based Intervention Programs on Recidivism,* researchers noted that the literature on dating and domestic violence had four consistent themes:

1. While a high percentage of adolescent women have been physically or sexually abused by a dating partner, dating violence has not been a priority of the justice system.

2. Dating violence is associated with long-term physical and emotional harm.

3. Dating and domestic violence is more prevalent for certain at-risk teens.

4. State laws have tended to overlook dating and domestic violence committed by minors.

In 2001, a study published in the *Journal of the American Medical Association* documented the significance of dating violence among adolescents. The study of adolescent girls in the ninth through twelfth grades reported that one in five female students reported being physically and/or sexually abused by a dating partner and that physical and sexual dating violence against adolescent girls is associated with increased risk of substance use, eating disorders, dangerous sexual behaviors, pregnancy, and suicide.[79] The authors concluded that "dating violence is extremely prevalent among this population, and adolescent girls who report a history of dating violence are more likely to exhibit other serious health risk behaviors."[80] While teen dating violence is becoming a topic of interest for some researchers, methodological problems, such as how to consistently define and measure the violence, preclude any broad conclusions about how often it occurs and why.[81]

What is known about dating/domestic violence among adolescents is that it can be linked to exposure to violence. Male high school students were more likely to inflict violence against a dating partner and to believe that male-female dating violence was justifiable when they had witnessed violence between parents.[82] Forms of mental illness, stemming from a history of maltreatment, alcohol and drug use, and attachment disorders, can help explain domestic violence.[83] Dating violence appears to begin early in the teenage years,[84] and juvenile domestic violence also appears to have a link to teen pregnancy. About 41 percent of young mothers become victims of intimate partner violence within twenty-four months after giving birth to their children.[85] More than 30 percent of the domestic violence offenders and victims had children together, and many of the victims reported that they had experienced violence while pregnant.[86] While some research is available that calls attention to the issues and challenges presented by youths who are involved in domestic violence, there is far too little information to make any confident statements about how to address the problem.

Why do so many young men think that abusing their girlfriends is acceptable behavior?

Domestic violence among youths is not unique to a particular race, ethnicity, or socioeconomic status.[87] Part of the problem in identifying and addressing dating violence or domestic violence among teenagers is that many states do not recognize this issue under its domestic violence laws, even if these minors are cohabiting. This lack of recognition carries over into intervention strategies since many states do not allow protection orders for victims who are minors. For instance, according to an NIJ report, only seventeen states provide a mechanism for underage victims of dating violence to apply for protective orders, and some of those states require the involvement of an adult. As a result, juvenile domestic violence has remained unidentified as an area of concern for policymakers.

Family violence, such as violence between siblings or a child and a parent, is another area of interest for researchers. As with dating violence among teens, currently, there are no reliable data or studies that clearly document the extent and impact of family violence. Some studies have shown that sibling violence is fairly common.[88] Out of the 15 percent of all violent incidents involving family members, the members involved are usually siblings or cousins. When asked to relate their experiences growing up, 65 percent of college students reported experiencing severe physical abuse by a sibling, with 17 percent reporting injuries as a result of the family violence.[89]

> When you sit there and see your parents do it all the time, it makes you do it when you're young. . . . I thought it was normal, really.
>
> **ZACHARY**

Similarly, the research on children who abuse their parents is mixed. Clearly, the problems of dating violence and family violence are significant and have many far-reaching implications. Given the lack of research on the subject, largely because these types of crimes go relatively unnoticed by juvenile justice officials, there is much to be learned not only about these specific crimes but also about chronic offending by juveniles.

Mental Illness and Delinquency

Why do you think there are so few studies of and programs available to address fire-starting behaviors and juvenile domestic violence among youths? Why are policymakers not giving more attention to these issues?

Chronic Offenders

One of the most important and consistent findings in the study of delinquency is that a small percentage of offenders are responsible for a large proportion of crime in the United States. The chronic offender, often cited in the discussion of the **career criminal,** is someone who has a long history of criminal activity lasting into adulthood. Unlike most youths who engage in delinquency and eventually stop, these individuals progress from delinquent activities to adult offenses and make crime a career.

The identification of chronic offenders stems from a famous study conducted in Philadelphia by criminologists Marvin Wolfgang, Robert Figlio, and Thorsten Sellin, who

career criminal
An individual who has a long history of criminal activity lasting into adulthood.

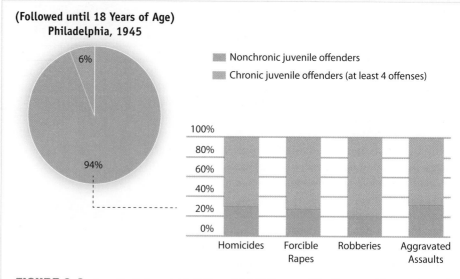

FIGURE 9-2 Juvenile Delinquent Activities of 9,945 Boys, and the Types and Percentages of Crimes Committed by Them

The acts of the "chronic 6 percent" were quite serious. A second study, which was larger and included more females, had about 7.5 percent of the sample responsible for most of the crimes of that overall group.

Source: Wolfgang, M. E., Figlio, R. M., and Sellin, T. 1972. *Delinquency in a Birth Cohort.* Chicago: University of Chicago Press; Wolfgang, M. E., Thornberry, T. P., and Figlio, R. M. 1987. *From Boys to Men, From Delinquency to Crime.* Chicago: University of Chicago Press.

examined the criminal activities of a group of boys born in Philadelphia in 1945 and followed them until they reached eighteen years of age. The researchers gathered personal background and school-related information, and police records on 9,945 boys. The results (see Figure 9-2) showed that about 6 percent of the sample or cohort (a group of individuals followed over time) were chronic offenders, meaning they had committed at least four criminal offenses.

Other studies have shown that these chronic 6 percent are most likely to become adult offenders.[90] The police recognize the existence of chronic offenders, as reflected in their use of directed patrol strategies to target this group. For example, Repeat Offender Programs (ROPs) direct patrol efforts to maximize the opportunity to arrest chronic offenders.[91] Similarly, police/community programs such as Weed and Seed, discussed in Chapter 4, are an effort to restore and revitalize disadvantaged neighborhoods touched by crime by "weeding" out the criminal element. These programs identify chronic offenders and focus attention on their activities. Once the criminals are removed, residents and businesses can then "seed" the area with opportunities for growth and restoration.[92]

VIOLENT OFFENDERS

Perhaps the smallest group of delinquents in the United States, but one that evokes the most fear, is violent juvenile offenders, who are primarily male and black American. These individuals accounted for 51 percent of all juveniles arrested for homicide in 2008. However, the level of violence may be decreasing. In 2008, the arrests for violent crime overall decreased about 9 percent from a decade earlier. Also in 2008, arrests of juveniles for rape decreased significantly, as did arrests for aggravated assaults. Thus, the data indicate that violent juvenile offenders have become less of an actual threat than is perceived by the public (see Table 9-4).

Violent juvenile offenders tend to have a history of truancy and dropping out of school, substance abuse problems, as well as mental health issues. Some evidence suggests that this population is getting younger, with some children as young as ten years old becoming involved. This was also the group that became the basis for the 1990s'

TABLE 9-4 Ten-Year Trend of Arrests for Violent Crimes by Suspects under Age 18 (1998–2008)

	1998	2008	% Change
Violent Crime Arrests	58,886	53,819	−8.6%
Murder	735	670	−8.8
Forcible Rape	2,539	1,848	−27.2
Robbery	15,673	19,651	+25.4
Aggravated Assault	39,939	31,650	−20.8
How would you account for the decrease in juvenile arrests?			

Source: *Crime in the United States 2008*. Available at http://www.fbi.gov/ucr/cius2008/data/table_32.html.

prediction of a "super predator" category of delinquents, with increases in crime and arrests, and the aforementioned social distortion of delinquency by the media. The leading proponents of this prediction were professors John DiLulio of Princeton University and James Fox of Northeastern University. Juvenile super predators were described as sociopaths with no moral conscience who saw crime as a rite of passage. They were youths who were not deterred by the sanctions that could be leveled against them by the juvenile justice system.

Some experts even argued that, as a result of maternal substance abuse during pregnancy, this new breed of offenders had different DNA than their predecessors.[93] The supporters of this argument also concluded that because this cohort of disturbed youths was so violent and irrational, the only reasonable solution would be to increase punitive sanctions and to treat them as the violent adults they would eventually become.[94]

In response to this growing "threat," nearly every state in the early 1990s changed how their justice systems responded to violent juveniles. Many states adopted legislation that required juveniles charged with certain violent crimes to be tried as adults or expanded the list of crimes that were excluded from juvenile court jurisdiction. Some states also gave prosecutors more discretion to file certain juvenile cases in either juvenile or adult court and lowered the age at which a juvenile court judge could transfer a youth to the criminal court.[95] As an illustration of the so-called super predator, consider Shun's experiences in school from an early age, where he initiated fights on a regular basis. Some might argue that this is reflective of the type of individual who will likely become an adult offender. Indeed, Shun's comments and behavior indicate that he may become an adult criminal, particularly given his gang affiliation:

> I just always stayed in trouble. If it wasn't for fightin', it was for something else. But, most of the time, it was for fightin'. I just started—I was starting—most—99 percent of the time, it'd be me startin' it over nothin'. I mostly started all of them. . . . I just pick on people, really. I, I—I'm—I did—I done a little more, but basically just make fun of people, uh, hit them, all kind of stuff like that—for no reason. . . . If I don't change my ways, and it's—that's almost a fact [that he will end up in prison].

While the super predator prediction failed to materialize, concerns about violent juvenile offenders remain high, and many of the associated policies and laws enacted have remained in effect.

The public's image of juvenile crime in general stems from sensational media accounts of gang members engaging in extreme forms of violence. Since public policy is often shaped by what is perceived to be the cause of the problem, in the case of these types of offenders, the "get tough" philosophy witnessed in the juvenile justice system comes largely from the perception that these individuals make up the bulk of the juvenile offender population. The impact of this trend can be seen in the increases in the number and size of prisons and in the decline in federal funding for delinquency prevention and rehabilitation programs.[96]

The fact that the public perceives violent offenders as pervasive does not mean that dramatic episodes do not occur, nor does it suggest that violent offenders are stoic, pathological criminals. In some instances, violence becomes a reaction to other violence. Consider

Anthony's experiences with attempted murder. While some might look at his situation as reflective of a stone-cold killer, notice the reasons for engaging in the crime and the emotions he experienced:

> Uh, it's just my life or his life. And I was with my little brother, and I couldn't see myself lettin' my little brother and me get shot. So, you point it [a gun], you shoot it, hopefully you hit what you aimin' for, because if you don't, you more than likely gonna get hit. . . . Like, I was, I was, I was mad. I had got jumped, somebody hit me in my head with a gun, so I really didn't care too much who I was—I just know it was these three people right here in this crowd. And I'm tryin' to hit everybody in that crowd, I wasn't—I was just shootin'. The only thing, it was like a little trance moment, the only thing that made me really start thinkin' when I heard the police sirens. When I heard the sirens, I just came back to and I ran. I couldn't focus. I just couldn't hear nothin', I was just panicking so hard. I didn't know what to do, I'm tryin' to hide the gun. I'm, I didn't know what to do.

DOUG'S CASE

Conclusions

Recall the situation that Doug is currently experiencing:

- an abusive home situation with a physically violent father
- a reluctance to attend a residential treatment facility
- homeless and living on the streets
- shoplifting, prostitution, and arson charges on his record

An initial view of Doug's behavior would indicate a youth who is destined for a career as an adult criminal. It would be easy to conclude that Doug is one of those youths who are not worth saving, largely because of the choices he has made with his life. It is worth noting, however, the context of those choices: what led him to engage in shoplifting, running away, setting fires, and engaging in prostitution? Consider the factors that played a role in his current situation.

 THINK ABOUT IT What makes using the "get tough" approach so easy with offenders like Doug? Why might he be so resistant to going to a residential treatment facility?

COMPUTER HACKERS

While computer hacking is not a typical topic for researchers who study delinquency, the available evidence suggests that it should be, given the disproportionate number of youths involved. There are several different frameworks to understanding hacking. *Cracking,* a term used to describe the tendency for hackers to break into secure databases, can also be understood on a continuum of motives: some do it for the challenge while others do it for "ethical" reasons, such as to point out the vulnerabilities of a database or agency.[97]

Experts on computer crime believe that hacking began with the creation of the interstate phone system and direct long-distance dialing in the late 1950s. The switching devices used to make the connections between phones were easily duplicated, and **phone phreaking,** in which calls are made without paying the appropriate toll or fee, began.[98] Phone phreaking is the oldest form of hacking. Hackers were also able to create phone numbers that would never be billed for service. With the advent of cellular phones, phreaking took on a new dimension—hackers began to use a combination of cellular and land-line phones to prevent the police from tracking them when they engaged in illegal activities.[99]

While the methods used to hack into computers are limitless, there are common ways hackers can gain access to a computer to steal information. *Spoofing* is the process by

phone phreaking
An offense in which calls are made without paying the appropriate toll or fee.

which a hacker gains access to a computer by pretending to be a legitimate user. Computer security systems perform limited checks to ascertain the identity of a user at the login phase. After access is granted, additional checks are rarely performed. Therefore, by feeding a minimal amount of information to the computer, a hacker can pose as a valid user. Even where security is more stringent, hackers can still get in.

Another method by which a hacker can spoof is called *social engineering*. In this case, a hacker pretends to be a user having trouble accessing the system. Finally, hackers can get knowledge of legitimate users' access information by *dumpster diving*. By searching through a company's trash, hackers can acquire login names, passwords, telephone numbers, and other confidential information.[100]

As with delinquents, there is no single type of hacker, and little empirical information is available on this population. In one study of 100 convicted juvenile hackers, criminologist Robert Taylor developed a typical profile: a white male, between the ages of fourteen and twenty, from a middle- to upper-class background, with an intact family and parents who love and care for him. Hackers tend to be loners, although they do have a wide assortment of friends via the Internet, especially other hackers. This virtual relationship is important as it provides insight, advice, and emotional support. Taylor found that hackers typically are highly intelligent and creative, although socially they feel most comfortable with other hackers, and even then, only in certain situations, such as the online environment. Despite high levels of intelligence, hackers tend to be underachievers at school, likely because of boredom, discomfort in the structured school environment, or difficulty interacting with others.[101]

Other experts focus on the psychology of hacking: they argue that hackers are emotionally insecure and that hacking allows them to feel in control of their world. The competition with other hackers, including attempts to "one up" each other, gives them a way to feel good about themselves.[102] Still other experts look at hacking as a form of childhood ritual, whereby adolescents explore areas simply because they are off limits and forbidden. Computer hacking is merely the latest version of a common act of delinquency or mischief, with a technological twist.[103]

The following typology presents a better grasp of the intent of hackers:

- **Visionaries:** these individuals are not necessarily hardcore criminals as much as they are fascinated with the ways in which technology can affect society.

- **Kickers/adventurers:** these hackers do not intend to inflict harm on any individual or society; rather, they are in it for the thrill and challenge.

- **Gamers:** these types of hackers focus primarily on defeating the software protection on computer games—defeating the software engineers at their own game becomes a source of status and prestige.

- **Destroyers:** these individuals focus on malicious and intentional destruction of other people's property—there is no apparent constructive gain involved.[104]

computer viruses
Programs designed to invade a computer's system to modify its operation, destroy or steal information, or call attention to problems within the system.

While some hackers are motivated by financial gain, most tend to be in it for the thrill and as a passive/aggressive reaction to the status quo. Hackers often commit their crimes by releasing **computer viruses,** programs designed to invade a computer's system to modify its operation, to destroy information, or to steal it. Other hackers release viruses as a way of calling attention to problems within the system.[105]

One of the most famous computer hackers in the United States was Kevin David Mitnick. Beginning his hacking career in suburban Los Angeles in the mid-1970s, Mitnick stole service from Pacific Bell's telephone system. In 1981, Kevin and two friends broke into the Pacific Bell phone center in downtown Los Angeles and stole company files. Eventually, Kevin was arrested, but he was a minor and so was treated as a delinquent instead of an adult criminal.

Of all the reasons youths engage in computer hacking, which one seems to be the most common?

In 1983, Kevin was again arrested by the campus police of the University of Southern California for using a university computer to hack into the ARPANET, the military version of the Internet at the time. He used the ARPANET to gain access to a computer located in the Pentagon. As a result of this offense, Kevin served six months in a juvenile prison in Stockton, California.

In 1987 and 1988, Kevin and a friend hacked into the computers of Digital Equipment Corporation in an effort to secure the source code for the company's operating system. After he was caught, Mitnick's defense was a psychological addiction to hacking. The case gained nationwide attention, and Kevin's attorney arranged a plea bargain that would send him to prison for one year and then to counseling for six months.

Despite these arrests and sentences, Mitnick continued hacking, and a federal judge issued a warrant for his arrest for violating the terms of his probation. Mitnick eluded the FBI until 1995, when he was finally caught and imprisoned.[106] Since his release, Mitnick has created a security firm that provides computer consulting to stop hackers, and he has written two books: *The Art of Intrusion,* a book on computer hacking, and *The Art of Deception,* a book focusing on personal security. [107]

The threats posed by computer hacking are serious and present numerous problems for society. While some hackers are only engaging in minor crimes, others have more ambitious goals. McAfee security software president Dave Dewalt said, "Last year we saw a 500 percent increase in malware . . . malicious software like worms or viruses. That was more than we saw in the last five years combined."[108] So dangerous is the threat of cybercrime that it became a priority during President Obama's administration. In 2009, the president created a new position of "Cyber Czar" to protect the nation's computer networks. Citing the risks to citizens' information and finance, as well as the potential cyberattacks by Al Qaeda and other terrorist groups, President Obama made cybercrime and hackers a priority.[109]

As it relates to juvenile justice, while there may be a tendency to treat hacking as an episode of youthful mischief, most hackers begin as juveniles and progress into adult offenders. This makes the challenge for juvenile justice officials a significant one since the behavior is not likely to end once the youth reaches a certain age. It also means that more punitive measures must be used to deter juveniles from engaging in hacking activities. This runs counter to the treatment orientation of the juvenile justice system, particularly since these offenders are nonviolent; however, the risks they pose to society are formidable.

THINK ABOUT IT

Chronic Offenders

Considering the extent of chronic offending and difficulty in treating chronic offenders, should society simply give up and treat them like the adult offenders they are likely to become?

Public Policy for Special Populations

While the study of juvenile delinquency typically focuses on issues relating to gangs, youth violence, and school and drive-by shootings, there are a wide variety of other populations, such as juvenile sex offenders, fire-starters, and hackers, that require attention. These youths are generally overlooked because the issues surrounding them are complex, and there have been few extended studies to adequately describe and explain these offenders and their motives for engaging in these types of offenses. Because of the lack of attention for and understanding of these special populations, few effective treatments or solutions are available to deal with the problems, which are widespread and growing.

While there are juvenile rapists, most juvenile sex offenders tend to be nonviolent and are typically amenable to treatment. But opportunities for treatment are limited due to a lack of resources and by a general perception that these offenders will never become healthy, productive adults. Most juvenile sex offenders are male, while female offenders typically victimize children in their care. Juveniles, whether they are males or females, engage in prostitution as a result of the need to survive or a substance abuse problem. They come from homes with long histories of physical, emotional, and/or sexual abuse, usually at the hands of parents or relatives.

Psychology plays a huge role in the motives and behaviors of children. While the delinquency literature covers a wide range of mental illnesses, two growing areas of interest are fire-starting and juvenile domestic violence. Although little information is available on them, fire-starting and juvenile arson represent a significant problem for juvenile justice officials and for society. There may be deep-seated psychological reasons behind the fascination with fire, but the damage arson inflicts on society is considerable. Nearly half of all arson arrests involve juvenile offenders.

Similarly, while Americans are concerned about domestic violence, the focus is usually on adults. A change in social policy with regard to addressing adult domestic violence has resulted in a number of juveniles being charged with violent crimes. Some acts, such as fights with siblings, which traditionally were handled informally, now end in arrests for many youths. Dating violence is also an increasingly challenging problem.

Chronic offenders evoke the greatest levels of fear. While they make up only a small segment of the offender population, this group is responsible for the vast majority of violence in society. The term often associated with repeat offenders is the "chronic 6 percent." Often these types of offenders go on to commit crimes as adults. Computer hackers are a part of the chronic offender group. Since much of this population consists of teenagers, and given that many of their acts constitute crimes, hacking and cybercrime has begun to interest researchers and experts on delinquency.

THE BIG PICTURE

Conclusions on Special Populations

- Why is it difficult to pinpoint the issues or factors that cause juveniles to engage in delinquent sexual activities such as prostitution?

- How does international trafficking of children factor into juvenile delinquency?

- Are registry laws an effective way of reducing juvenile sex offending? Why or why not?

- Is there a difference between fire-starters and arsonists? If so, what is the difference?

- Is dating violence as prevalent as the data suggest? Why has the juvenile justice system not done more to address juvenile domestic violence?

- Given limited public attention and policy to address these special populations and delinquency, what strategy comes to mind as a first step in terms of assisting these youths?

Key Terms

juvenile sex offender	hustlers	career criminals
registry laws	trafficking of children	chronic 6 percent
Megan's Law	fire-setting	phone phreaking
Adam Walsh Child Protection and Safety Act	family violence	computer viruses
Jessica's Law	dating violence	
	chronic offenders	

Make the Call ▶ Special Populations and Delinquency

Review the scenario and decide how you would approach this situation.

YOUR ROLE: Parent

DETAILS OF THE SITUATION

- Your son, age fourteen, has been arrested for setting fire to a neighbor's storage shed.

- You have always thought that your son had a fascination with fire, as evidenced by his behavior when you burn leaves in your backyard every autumn.

- You never thought the reaction was anything more than a "typical boy" behavior.

WHAT DO YOU DO?

The authorities may decide to charge your son with arson or vandalism. This means that the case may or may not be handled informally, which will affect your son's future. When you talk to your son, he says he did not really have a reason for setting the fire. Since he and your neighbor's son are best friends, he did not think it would be of consequence. How do you respond?

Consider:

- Does this appear to be a case of arson or fire-setting? If it is the latter, is it an example of instrumental or expressive fire-setting?

- Is there a psychological explanation for the boy's behavior?

- What are the appropriate steps to take to prevent the child from continuing to set fires or be involved in arson?

Apply Theory to Reality ▶ Katz's Theory

According to a 2009 ABC News report,[110] a recent trend among middle-school-aged boys is to start fires using the popular aerosol deodorant Axe. Fire department officials and emergency room and burn center physicians note that the boys typically turn the highly flammable products into explosives and miniature flamethrowers; they record their activities and post it on YouTube. What accounts for such obviously dangerous behavior? Jack Katz, a well-known criminologist, offers insight into the nature of this activity in his book *Seductions of Crime.* Use Katz's theory to offer an explanation of this type of fire-starting activity.

Your Community ▸ Juvenile Domestic Violence

In addition to the information you glean from your readings, class lectures, and discussions, it is important to roll up your sleeves and immerse yourself in a topic as a researcher who gains an understanding of a problem or issue by observing or experiencing it firsthand. Through such methods, you gain a much greater appreciation of the magnitude and scope of the problem than if you only engaged in "armchair theorizing."

■ Contact your local Department of Juvenile Justice, and see if you can schedule an interview with a caseworker to learn more about juvenile domestic violence.

■ Read local media reports on the problem, and ask about strategies in place in your community to address the problem.

■ After collecting your data, and drawing from the relevant literature, prepare a report or presentation of your findings and conclusions about your community's response to the issue of juvenile domestic violence.

Notes

[1] *Pedophilia* usually refers to an adult psychological disorder characterized by a preference for prepubescent children as sex partners, which may or may not be acted upon. *Child sexual abuse* describes actual sexual contact between an adult and someone who has not reached the legal age of consent. Not all incidents of child sexual abuse are perpetrated by pedophiles: in some cases, the offender may have other motives for his or her actions. See, for instance, http://psychology.ucdavis.edu/rainbow/HTML-/facts_molestation.html.

[2] See, for instance, Frawley-O'Dea, M. G. 2007. *Perversion of Power: Sexual Assault in the Catholic Church.* Nashville, TN: Vanderbilt University Press.

[3] National Center on Sexual Behavior of Youth. 2003. *What Research Shows about Adolescent Offenders.* http://www.ncsby.org/pages/publications/What%20Research%20Shows%20About%20Adolescent%20Sex%20Offenders%20060404.pdf. Accessed August 9, 2008; Baum, K. 2005. *Juvenile Victimization and Offending, 1993–2003.* Washington, DC: Bureau of Justice Statistics. http://www.ojp.usdoj.gov/-/bjs/pub/pdf/jvo03.pdf. Accessed August 9, 2008.

[4] Snyder, H. 2000. *Sexual Assault of Young Children as Reported to Law Enforcement: Victim, Incident, and Offender Characteristics.* Washington, DC: U.S. Department of Justice, Bureau of Justice Statistics. http://www.ojp.usdoj.gov/bjs/pub/pdf/saycrle.pdf. Accessed August 10, 2008.

[5] Davis, G. E., and Leitenberg, H. 1987. "Adolescent Sex Offenders, 101." *Psychology Bulletin,* pp. 417–419.

[6] Ibid.

[7] Vandiver, D. 2006. "A Prospective Analysis of Juvenile Male Sex Offenders: Characteristics and Recidivism Rates as Adults." *Journal of Interpersonal Violence,* 21(5): 673–688.

[8] Ibid.

[9] Zimring, F. 2007. "The Predictive Power of Juvenile Sex Offending: Evidence from the Second Philadelphia Birth Cohort Study." Cited in Human Rights Watch. 2008. *Sexual Violence in the U.S.,* pp. 13–14.

[10] Ibid.

[11] Zimring, 2007.

[12] Zimring, F., and Piquero, A. 2007. "Juvenile and Adult Sex Offending in Racine, Wisconsin," January 23, 2007. Cited in Human Rights Watch. 2008. *Sexual Violence in the U.S.*

[13] O'Brien, M., and Bera, W. W. 1986. "Adolescent Sexual Offenders: A Descriptive Typology." *Preventing Sexual Abuse: A Newsletter of the National Family Life Education Network,* 1(3): 1–4. See also Robertiello, G., and Terry, K. J. 2007. "Can We Profile Sex Offenders? A Review of Sex Offender Typologies." *Aggression and Violent Behavior,* 12(5): 508–518.

[14] Robertiello and Terry, 2007.

[15] Ibid.

[16] Ibid.

[17] See, for instance, Chaffin, M., and Bonner, B. 1998. "'Don't Shoot, We're Your Children': Have We Gone Too Far in Our Response to Adolescent Sexual Abusers and Children with Sexual Behavior Problems?" *Child Maltreatment,* 3(4): 314–316.

[18] Association for the Treatment of Sexual Abusers. 2000. *Position Statement: The Effective Legal Management of Juvenile Sexual Offenders.* www.atsa.com/ppjuvenile.html. Accessed August 10, 2008.

[19] Gordon, B., and Schroeder, C. S. 1995. *Sexuality: A Developmental Approach to Problems.* New York: Plenum Press.

[20] Ibid.

[21] See Fuller, J. R. 2010. *Criminology: Mainstreams and Crosscurrents.* New York: McGraw-Hill.

[22] Snyder, H., and Sickmund, M. 2006. *Juvenile Offenders and Victims: 2006 National Report.* Washington, DC: U.S. Department of Justice, Office of Justice Programs, Office of Juvenile Justice and Delinquency Prevention.

[23] Denov, M., and Cortoni, F. 2006. "Women Who Sexually Abuse Children." In Hilarski, C., and Wodarski, J. S. (eds.), *Comprehensive Mental Health Practice with Sex Offenders and Their Families,* pp. 71–99. Binghamton, NY: Haworth Press; Nathan, P., and Ward, T. 2002. "Female Sex Offenders: Clinical and Demographic Features." *The Journal of Sexual Aggression,* 8: 5–21.

[24] Bumby, N. H., and Bumby, K. M. 2004. "Bridging the Gender Gap: Addressing Juvenile Females Who Commit Sexual Offences." In O'Reilly, G., Marshall, W. L., Carr, A., and Beckett, R. C. (eds.), *The Handbook of Clinical Intervention with Young People Who Sexually Abuse,* pp. 369–381. New York: Brunner-Routledge; Frey, L. L. 2006. "Girls Don't Do That, Do They? Adolescent Females Who Sexually Abuse." In Longo, R. E., and Prescott, D. S. (eds.),

Current Perspectives: Working with Sexually Aggressive Youth and Youth with Sexual Behavior Problems, pp. 255–272. Holyoke, MA: NEARI Press; Glaze, L., and Bonczar, T. 2006. *Probation and Parole in the United States, 2005.* Washington, DC: U.S. Department of Justice, Office of Justice Programs, Bureau of Justice Statistics; Harrison, P. M., and Beck, A. J. 2005. *Prison and Jail Inmates at Midyear 2004.* Washington, DC: U.S. Department of Justice, Office of Justice Programs, Bureau of Justice Statistics; Robinson, S. 2001. "Adolescent Females with Sexual Behavioral Problems: What Constitutes Best Practice?" In Longo, R. E., and Prescott, D. S. (eds.), *Current Perspectives: Working with Sexually Aggressive Youth and Youth with Sexual Behavior Problems,* pp. 273–324. Holyoke, MA: NEARI Press; Vandiver, D. 2006. "Female Sex Offenders: A Comparison of Solo Offenders and Co-offenders." *Violence and Victims,* 21: 339–354.

[25] Robertiello and Terry, 2007.

[26] See http://www.klaaskids.org/pg-legmeg.htm.

[27] See http://juvienation.wordpress.com/2008/01/25/states-consider-costs-benefits-on-adam-walsh-act/.

[28] See, for instance, Baker, L. 2005. "For Juvenile Sex Offenders, Intensive Program Offers Chance to Change." http://www.connectforkids.org/node/3318. See also http://www.morrisonkids.org/resources/.

[29] See http://www.jmlfoundation.org/StatesJML-Law.htm.

[30] Finkelhor, D., and Ormrod, R. 2004. *Prostitution of Juveniles: Patterns from NBIRS.* Washington, DC: U.S. Government Printing Office. http://www.ncjrs.org/html/ojjdp/203946/page1.html. Accessed August 11, 2008.

[31] Ibid.

[32] Crimes against Children Research Center. 2008. *How Many Juveniles Are Involved in Prostitution in the U.S.?* Available at http://www.unh.edu/ccrc.

[33] *Crime in the United States* 2008. Available at http://www.fbi.gov/ucr/cius2008/data/table_38.html.

[34] While the Uniform Crime Reports system collects information on a limited number of Index crimes and gathers few details on each crime event (except in the case of homicide), the NIBRS collects a wide range of information on victims, offenders, and circumstances for a greater variety of offenses. Offenses include homicide, assault, rape, robbery, theft, arson, vandalism, fraud, and embezzlement, as well as a category called crimes against society, which include drug offenses, gambling, and prostitution. The NIBRS also collects information on multiple victims, multiple offenders, and multiple crimes that may be part of the same episode.

[35] Finkelhor and Ormrod, 2004.

[36] See Department of Justice, Federal Bureau of Investigation. 2007. *Crime in the United States.* Table 42. http://www.fbi.gov/ucr/cius2007/data/table_42.html.

[37] See McNamara, R. P. 1994. *The Times Square Hustler: Male Prostitution in New York City.* Westport, CT: Praeger. See also Reiss, A. J. 1961. "The Social Integration of Queers and Peers." *Social Problems,* 9(2): 102–120.

[38] U.S. Department of Health and Human Services. 2006. *HHS Fights to Stem Human Trafficking.* Available at http://www.hhs.gov/news/factsheet/humantrafficking.html.

[39] Ibid.

[40] Finkelhor and Ormrod, 2004.

[41] U.S. Department of State, *The Facts about Child Sex Tourism:* 2005.

[42] U.S. Department of Health and Human Services, 2006.

[43] U.S. Department of State, *Trafficking in Persons Report:* 2007.

[44] U.S. Department of Justice, *Assessment of U.S. Government Activities to Combat Trafficking in Persons:* 2004.

[45] Family Research Council. 2008. "Nevada Welcomes Male Prostitutes, Brothel Owners Not Happy." Opposing Viewpoints. Available at http://www.opposingviews.com/articles/opinion-Nevada-welcomes-male-prostitutes-brothel-owners-not-happy.

[46] For a discussion of the public's perception of mental illness, see the classic study by Szasz, T. S., and Alexander, G. J. 1968. "Mental Illness as an Excuse for Civil Wrongs." *Journal of Nervous and Mental Disease,* 147: 113–123.

[47] Joint Committee on Behavioral Health Care. 2001. "Studying Treatment Options for Offenders Who Have Mental Illness or Substance Abuse Disorders."

[48] Bazelon Center for Mental Health Law. 2004. "Thousands of Children with Mental Illness Warehoused in Juvenile Detention Centers Awaiting Mental Health Services."

[49] National Center for Mental Health and Juvenile Justice. "Key Issues."

[50] Bazelon Center for Mental Health Law, 2004.

[51] Koppelman, J. 2005. "Mental Health and Juvenile Justice: Moving toward More Effective Systems of Care." National Health Policy Forum, Issue Brief, 805. George Washington University.

[52] Ibid.

[53] Skowyra and Cocozza. 2007. "Blueprint for Change: A Comprehensive Model for the Identification and Treatment of Youth with Mental Health Needs in Contact with the Juvenile Justice System." Report by the National Center for Mental Health and Juvenile Justice in conjunction with the Office of Juvenile Justice and Delinquency Prevention.

[54] Putnam, C. T., and Kirkpatrick, J. T. 2005. *Juvenile Fire Setting: A Research Overview.* Washington, DC: Office of Juvenile Justice and Delinquency Prevention.

[55] U.S. Department of Justice, Federal Bureau of Investigation. 2007. *Crime in the United States.* http://www.fbi.gov/ucr/.

[56] National Association of State Fire Marshals. 2005.

[57] Putnam and Kirkpatrick, 2005.

[58] U.S. Fire Administration /Federal Emergency Management Agency. 1997. *Arson and Juveniles: Responding to the Violence.* A Review of Teen Fire Setting and Interventions, Special Report.

[59] Ibid.

[60] Putnam and Kirkpatrick, 2005.

[61] U.S. Department of Justice, Federal Bureau of Investigation. 2006. *Crime in the United States.* Table 38. Washington, DC: U.S. Government Printing Office. http://www.fbi.gov/ucr/cius2006/data/table_38.html. Accessed August 9, 2008. Do you believe that youths lack cognitive development and go unpunished for their actions?

[62] Stickle, T. R., and Blechman, E. A. 2002. "Aggression and Fire: Antisocial Behavior in Fire Setting and Non-fire Setting Juvenile Offenders." *Journal of Psychopathology and Behavioral Assessment,* 24(3): 177–193.

[63] Ibid.

[64] Becker, K., Stuewig, J., Herrera, V., and McCloskey, L. 2004. "A Study of Fire Setting and Animal Cruelty in Children: Family Influences and Adolescent Outcomes." *Journal of the American Academy of Child & Adolescent Psychiatry,* 43(7): 905–912.

[65] Ibid.

[66] Office of Juvenile Justice and Delinquency Prevention. 1997. *Juvenile Fire Setting and Arson. Fact Sheet 51;* U.S. Fire Administration / Federal Emergency Management Agency. 1993. *The National Juvenile Fire Setter /Arson Control and Prevention Program Fire Service Guide to a Juvenile Fire Setter Early Intervention Program;* U.S. Fire Administration/Federal Emergency Management Agency, 1997.

[67] Ibid. See also Campas, L., and Roe-Sepowitz, D. 2008. "Juvenile Male Arsonists: An Exploratory Study." Paper presented at the annual meeting of the American Society of Criminology, Atlanta.

[68] Becker et al., 2004.

[69] Kolko, D. (ed.) 2002. *Handbook on Fire Setting in Children and Youth.* Boston: Academic Press.

[70] Campas and Roe-Sepowitz, 2008.

[71] Ibid.

[72] Ibid.

[73] Putnam and Kirkpatrick, 2005.

[74] See, for instance, Becker, E. 2001. "As Ex-Theorist on Young Superpredators, Bush Aide Has Regrets." *New York Times,* February 9. Available at http://www.nytimes.com/2001/02/09/us/as-ex-theorist-on-young-superpredators-bush-aide-has-regrets.html.

[75] See, for instance, Sherman, L. W., and Cohn, E. C. 1989. "The Impact of Research on Legal Policy: Minneapolis Domestic Violence Experiment." *Law and Society Review,* 23: 117–127.

[76] See, for instance, http://www.law.jrank.org/pages/1548/Juvenile-Violent-Offenders-Causes-growth-decline-juvenile-violence.html.

[77] Centers for Disease Control. 2009. *Understanding Teen Dating Violence Fact Sheet.* http://www.cdc.gov/violenceprevention/pdf/TeenDatingViolence2009-a.pdfI.

[78] Ibid.

[79] Silverman, J. G., Raj, A., Mucci, L., and Hathaway, J. E. 2001. "Dating Violence against Adolescent Girls and Associated Substance Use, Unhealthy Weight Control, Sexual Risk Behavior, Pregnancy, and Suicidality." *Journal of the American Medical Association (JAMA),* 286: 572–579.

[80] Ibid.

[81] Foshee, L., Bauman, K. E., Linder, G. F., Benefield, T., and Suchindran, C. 2004. "Assessing the Long Term Effects of the Safe Dates Program and a Booster in Preventing and Reducing Adolescent Dating Violence Victimization and Perpetration." *American Journal of Public Health,* 94: 619–624.

[82] See, for instance, Arriaga, X. B., and Foshee, V. A. 2004. "Adolescent Dating Violence: Do Adolescents Follow Their Friends' or Their Parents' Footsteps?" *Journal of Interpersonal Violence,* 19: 162–184.

[83] Breslin, F. C., Riggs, D. S., O'Leary, K. D., and Arias. I. 1990. "Family Precursors: Expected and Actual Consequences of Dating Aggression." *Journal of Interpersonal Violence,* 5: 247–258.

[84] See, for instance, Arriaga and Foshee, 2004. See also Bank, L., and Burraston, B. 2001. "Abusive Home Environments as Predictors of Poor Adjustment during Adolescence and Early Childhood." *Journal of Community Psychology,* 29: 195–217; Breslin et al., 1990; Chapple, C. 2003. "Examining Intergenerational Violence: Violent Role Modeling or Weak Parental Controls?" *Violence and Victims,* 18: 143–162; Foo, L., and G. Margolin. 1994. "A Multivariate Investigation of Dating Violence." *Journal of Interpersonal Violence,* 10: 351–37; Marshall, L., and Rose, P. 1990. "Premarital Violence: The Impact of Family of Origin Violence, Stress, and

Reciprocity." *Violence and Victims,* 5: 51–64; Wolfe, D. A., and Feiring, C. 2000. "Dating Violence through the Lens of Adolescent Romantic Relationships." *Child Maltreatment,* 5(4): 360–363

[85] Harrykissoon, S. D., Rickert, V. I., and Wiemann, C. M. 2002. "Prevalence and Patterns of Intimate Partner Violence among Adolescent Mothers during the Postpartum Period." *Archives of Pediatrics and Adolescent Medicine,* 156(4): 325–330.

[86] Sagatun-Edwards, I., Hyman, E., Lafontaine, T., and Nelson-Serrano, E. 2003. "The Santa Clara County Juvenile Domestic and Family Violence Court." *Journal of the Center for Families, Children and the Courts,* 4: 91–113.

[87] Silverman et al., 2001.

[88] Uikert, B., Sagatun-Edwards, I., Crowe, A., Peters, T., Cheesman, F., and Kameda, D. 2006. *Juvenile Domestic and Family Violence: The Effects of Court-Based Intervention Programs on Recidivism.* Washington, DC: U.S. Department of Justice, Office of Justice Programs.

[89] Ibid.

[90] See Howell, J. C. 1995. *Guide for Implementing the Comprehensive Strategy for Serious, Violent, and Chronic Juvenile Offenders.* Washington, DC: National Institute of Justice, Office of Juvenile Justice and Delinquency Prevention. See also Wolfgang, M. E., Figlio, R. M., and Sellin, T. 1972. *Delinquency in a Birth Cohort.* Chicago: University of Chicago Press; Wolfgand, M. E., Thornberry, T. P., and Figlio, R. M. 1987. *From Boys to Men, From Delinquency to Crime.* Chicago: University of Chicago Press.

[91] See, for instance, Kappeler, V. 2005. *Policing in America,* 5th ed. Belmont, CA: Wadsworth.

[92] See U.S. Department of Justice, Office of Justice Programs, Community Capacity Development Office, Executive Office of Weed and Seed. http://www.ojp.usdoj.gov/ccdo/ws/welcome.html. Accessed August 11, 2008.

[93] Juvenile Violent Offenders—The Concept of the Juvenile Super Predator. http://law.jrank.org/pages/1546/Juvenile-Violent-Offenders-concept-juvenile-super-predator.html#ixzz0auiTs8YR.

[94] Ibid.

[95] Ibid.

[96] Ibid.

[97] Yar, M. 2005. "Computer Hacking: Just Another Case of Juvenile Delinquency?" *The Howard Journal of Criminal Justice,* 44(4): 387–399.

[98] Ibid.

[99] See Taylor, R. W. 2000. "Hacker, Phone Phreakers and Virus Makers." In Swanson, C. R., Chamelin, N. C,. and Territo, L. (eds.), *Criminal Investigation,* 7th ed. New York: McGraw-Hill.

[100] See, for instance, Kremen, S. 2008. Computer Forensics Online. Available at http://www.shk-dplc.com/cfo/articles/hack.htm.

[101] Ibid.

[102] Schmalleger, F. 2007. *Criminology Today,* 4th ed. Upper Saddle River, NJ: Prentice-Hall.

[103] Barlow, J. P. 1990. "Crime and Puzzlement: In Advance of the Law on the Electronic Frontier." *Whole Earth Review,* Fall, p. 44.

[104] Adapted from Maxfield, J. 1985. *Computer Bulletin Boards and the Hacker Problem. EDPACS, the Electronic Data Processing Audit, Control and Security Newsletter.* Arlington, VA: Automation Training Center.

[105] Selwyn, N. 2003. "Doing It for the Kids: Re-Examining Children, Computers and the Information Society." *Media, Culture and Society,* 15(3): 351–378.

[106] Kremen, 2008.

[107] See http://www.kevinmitnick.com/press.php.

[108] Selwyn, 2003.

[109] Sandell, C. 2009. "President Obama Says the Nation's Digital Security Is a Top Priority for His Administration." ABC News,, May 29. http://abclocal.go.com/kfsn/story?section=news-/politics&id=6839437.

[110] http://abcnews.go.com/US/story?id=7283537&page=2.

After reading this chapter, you should be able to:

- Understand the purpose of education as a socialization tool.

- Describe the burden placed on educational institutions to solve societal problems.

- Examine strategies used by educational institutions to reduce problems on school grounds.

- Measure the effectiveness of education and institutional policies in preventing delinquency.

10

Schools and Delinquency

In recent years, multiple school shootings have raised serious questions about issues associated with school violence, such as responding to bullying and carrying out threats of physical harm. In the wake of these tragedies, much has been learned about school violence and how it can be prevented. But questions remain as to the effectiveness of current policies and protective measures designed to keep students and teachers safe. Consider the case of Frankie, who goes to a school that has installed metal detectors, hired off-duty police officers to patrol school grounds, and enacted a zero-tolerance policy.

Frankie's profile:
- is a sixteen-year-old junior at an inner-city high school in Connecticut
- has a long history of disciplinary problems, including getting into fights, larceny, and drug dealing

His situation at school:
- is currently enrolled in the vocational program designed to prepare him for a job as an auto mechanic after graduation
- works at a local auto repair shop as part of his course requirements
- regularly skips class
- has been suspended many times for various types of inappropriate behavior

His current status:
A week ago, Frankie was caught with a handgun in his backpack. The gun was discovered after an altercation in the school restroom between Frankie and three known gang members, who were armed with knives and attempted to assault him. As part of a zero-tolerance policy, Frankie was arrested and expelled from school.

A concerned parent or school official might offer the following explanations for why students like Frankie would bring a gun to school:

- Frankie wanted to intimidate other students.
- Frankie was merely showing off.
- Frankie was afraid of being victimized.
- Frankie intended to use the gun on teachers, staff, and other students.

How effective are educational institutions in preventing juvenile delinquency, and why is there such a burden on them to solve societal problems?

THINK ABOUT IT Consider the role of educational institutions in the process of socialization. Based on the information provided, what reasons do you think Frankie might give for his behavior, and why?

social institutions
Organizations, such as schools, designed to meet societal needs.

To better understand situations like Frankie's, we will look at the larger context of delinquency in schools. Schools are **social institutions,** organizations designed to meet societal needs. In particular, schools play a primary role in the process of socialization. In order for socialization to be effective, its messages need to be consistently reinforced by other social institutions—the family, religious institutions, the media, the political and economic systems in place, and legal institutions.

Although the family is often the first agent of socialization, children's first experiences with society outside the family take place in educational institutions.[1] Schools are therefore charged with the task of preparing children and young adults to become productive members of society. Schools are also centers of character development, teaching lessons about integrity, honesty, and good citizenship, as well as critical thinking and problem solving.[2] Most of the time, these lessons are conveyed successfully—which is why most youths do not engage in delinquent, criminal, or deviant acts. For others, however, those messages are not received, are inconsistent, or are not effectively internalized.[3] Some sociologists believe that the problems all schools are facing may be attributable to the inconsistency with which children are socialized.[4]

As will be discussed in this chapter, delinquency and other school-related problems must be understood within the larger context of socialization. Schools, therefore, bear the bulk of responsibility for responding to delinquent behaviors, such as low academic performance, on-campus crime, and dropping out. In order to ensure that campuses are safe and conducive to learning, school officials must adopt strategies for handling these problems. This chapter will also examine these strategies, including how they function within schools and their surrounding communities, and their overall effectiveness in keeping students and teachers safe.

Structure of Public Education

Mass public education became compulsory around the beginning of the twentieth century in the United States. Previously, education had been a privilege of the wealthy. It was not so long ago that poor children were forced to leave school in order to work and help support their families. But in the early 1900s, as the government began to recognize the need for a skilled labor force, education for children became mandatory. Schools were then faced with an influx of students from different backgrounds and with varying levels of aptitude. Because compulsory education meant that all children should receive the same education, new requirements put pressure on teachers and administrators to standardize learning.

Administrators decided that the best way to standardize learning was to organize public schools bureaucratically.[5] While this new organization resulted in greater quality control, it also meant that schools were less flexible, and therefore less able to meet the individual needs of students. Thus, rigid policies and procedures were put into place to govern school operations and curriculum decision making.[6] Within this new system, many students found it even more difficult to achieve academically and socially.

social class bias
The advantages (social, economic, political) given to those who are from affluent families; often used in education to describe the differences between children from wealthy families, who receive a higher-quality education, and those whose families are poorer.

SOCIAL CLASS

Many low-income students lag far behind their more advanced and wealthier peers, a consequence that some would attribute to the bureaucratization of schools. Sociologists have argued that compulsory education serves to underscore an inevitable **social class bias** in education. Some students have better experiences in public schools than others, and much about the quality of that experience has been shown to depend on students' backgrounds and social statuses.

In his book *Class, Bureaucracy and Schools,* Michael Katz argues that public education in the United States has always been class-biased. Though it was introduced with the intention of opening up opportunities for all, public education is ultimately both a reflection of and a perpetuation of class inequalities. Katz argues that public schooling has historically functioned to secure advantages for children from affluent, white families. He also points out that generations of black Americans have been subjected to substandard educations in racially segregated schools—an injustice that society has only begun to address in the past three decades.[7]

Under the circumstances of compulsory education, some students are going to perform better than others. While students who perform well tend to go on to college, earn degrees, and find well-paying jobs, those who perform poorly often feel frustrated, angry, and rejected, and so turn to delinquent behavior.[8] In fact, school failure is a stronger predictor of delinquency than race or social class. Some research indicates that youths who do not like school, do not perform well in the classroom, and do not complete their homework are more likely to engage in delinquency than those children who do well in school, apart from any other problems they face at home, such as abuse or neglect.[9] Some experts argue that children who fail at school feel frustrated, angry, rejected, and alienated. Consequently, these students stop trying to succeed and turn to delinquency instead.[10]

Schools are not always prepared to address the issue of poor performance. Moreover, many schools are now mandated to administer high-stakes testing, further alienating students who struggle academically. Rather than have their average test scores adversely affected, some schools might even prefer that these students drop out. And for those underperforming students who remain in school despite their academic difficulties, the inflexibility of tracking, discussed below, discourages them from improving their social standing.[11]

In examining the physical differences between public schools, is it reasonable to think that the educational experiences of students is the same?

TRACKING

Historically, low-income children stopped attending school when they were old enough to work, in order to help support their families. This meant that the higher grades were made up of students from more affluent backgrounds.[12] When compulsory education became a matter of public policy, the composition of the student body was altered to include poor and working-class students, who stayed in school longer.

As the number of children in the labor pool decreased, new employment opportunities opened up for adults. With more parents working, the pressure on children to contribute to the family income lessened. Attitudes, too, began to change, influencing a belief that education was a way to improve one's social class position. In short, education—once a hardship for struggling families—was perceived as a potential path out of poverty.[13]

In an effort to accommodate growing numbers of students, educators came up with an innovative idea to organize high school curricula around a system of tracks. Each track was set up to prepare students for what they would most likely be doing upon graduation. This concept of **tracking** was based on the assumption that children from economically disadvantaged backgrounds were destined for similar futures. Thus, a vocational track was created for this group, while the affluent were steered into an academic track based on the assumption that they were likely to go to college or enter occupations in which academic skills would be useful.

School officials initially said that they were not using social class to determine the tracks of students. They claimed instead that placement was based on school performance. Since achievement levels tend to reflect the environmental advantages associated with social class backgrounds, the end result was the same: track placements reflected class differences.[14]

tracking
Organization of high school curricula to prepare students for what they would most likely be doing upon graduation; based on the assumption that children from economically disadvantaged backgrounds were destined for similar futures.

The tracking system allowed educators to argue that all children were receiving an equal opportunity to be educated. Their argument was based on the fact that schools had been reorganized to more efficiently assess and accommodate the varying abilities of students. But despite the use of a tracking system, the dropout and failure rates in public schools remained high.

Some have argued that high dropout and failure rates are symptoms of tracking. One study found that a number of demographic variables, such as race and social class, contribute to students' placement into academic or nonacademic tracks. In fact, students were being placed on vocational tracks even as the value of these tracks was being questioned.[15] Colin Greer, a noted expert on educational issues, argues that the failures of American education are attributable to an ulterior motive: the creation of a large pool of workers for low-paying and low-status jobs.[16] Whether or not one agrees with Greer's conclusions, it has become clear over time that tracking systems have their problems.

Tracking sets certain expectations for students. The stigma associated with certain tracks can have a significant impact on students' self-esteem and overall academic performance. In one study, researchers found that students felt stigmatized when they were not assigned to college prep tracks in high school. Students placed in a "general track" reported that it negatively affected their self-esteem and eroded beliefs in their own abilities. As a result, teachers and administrators expected far less of general-track students, and students responded by performing according to these expectations.[17]

Tracking also creates a set of expectations by teachers of their students' abilities. For example, one study found that while changes are being made with regard to perceptions of the value of vocational tracks, there remain a number of demographic variables, such as race and social class, that affect the placement of a student into academic or nonacademic tracks.[18]

The result of this differential treatment seems clear. Students from more affluent backgrounds, having been given preferential treatment in high school, will typically enter college. They will most likely get well-paying jobs and occupy a class position much like that of their parents. Low-income students, whether they are white or minority, are led to believe, through their track placement, treatment by teachers, and the evaluation of their performance, that they are not destined for success.

FRANKIE'S CASE

Identity and Status

Recall Frankie's situation:

- is a vocational-track student
- works off campus at an auto repair shop, in place of taking college prep classes
- skips classes and defies teachers' authority
- has been involved in several criminal incidents on campus

Consider Frankie's status among students, teachers, and school officials. His vocational track gives teachers the impression that he is not serious about school, and school officials have concluded that he is not college material. Additionally, his absence from class reinforces his reputation, among fellow students, of being "cool." Presumptions about Frankie's educational track have helped to shape his professional ambitions, even insofar as they conflict with his education. These presumptions have also established Frankie's reputation among classmates, which he in turn feels pressure to uphold.

 THINK ABOUT IT Recall Chapter 5's discussion of labeling theory. How would you compare the concept of labeling to that of tracking? What effects might labeling have had on Frankie's sense of identity? Do you think he would have behaved differently if he had been placed among college-track students?

NO CHILD LEFT BEHIND

In 2001, Congress passed the **No Child Left Behind Act** (NCLB), a controversial law designed to improve the academic performance and education of children at all levels in public schools. The approach is essentially twofold: increase accountability of schools, and give consumers—in this case, parents—more choices about which schools their children can attend.

The primary method of accountability is the standardized testing of all students. Proponents of the law contend that setting high expectations and establishing measurable goals can improve individual outcomes in education. They insist that all students in every grade should be learning the same age-appropriate information. The law therefore requires states to develop assessments in basic skills to be given to all students in certain grades. States that do not comply risk losing federal funding for their schools.[19]

The effectiveness of the law is a matter of great controversy. The goals of the law are to ensure that all students in all schools are receiving the same high-quality education and that skills are being taught effectively. The incentive is monetary. Principals and administrators of underperforming schools can be terminated, and teachers can be removed or reassigned to other schools. Successful schools, on the other hand, might receive financial incentives for teachers and administrators, as well as additional funding for their programs.[20]

The debate over NCLB centers on whether high-stakes testing is an effective means of measuring performance and ensuring that all students get a quality education. For example, critics point out that the program has failed because high-stakes testing pressures teachers to simply "teach the test" to students. In some circumstances, teachers under pressure to produce high scores have resorted to outright cheating or "coaching" students while they take the test. Similarly, administrators have been reported to manipulate test scores so as to give the impression of higher-level performance. Moreover, critics point out that throwing money at the problem does little to guarantee a better learning experience for students.[21]

A 2007 report by the U.S. Chamber of Commerce, in cooperation with the Center for American Progress and the American Enterprise Institute, titled *Leaders and Laggards: A State-by-State Report Card on Educational Effectiveness,* showed that some states are much further along than others in realizing improvements in their public education systems.[22] A more recent report from the Commission on NCLB has made several important recommendations for improving the legislation. In particular, these recommendations center on the accountability structures in place, including uniform definitions of high school graduation rates, realistic measures of teacher effectiveness (versus a reliance on qualifications), and issues relating to leadership and administration within schools.[23] Because so much is at stake, the problems involved in implementing NCLB create incentives for schools to misrepresent themselves. On the other hand, the proposed changes, if implemented, may be a step toward correcting those errors.[24]

No Child Left Behind Act
A law designed to improve the academic performance and education of children at all levels in public schools by increasing accountability of schools and giving parents more choices about which schools their children can attend.

Socialization in Public Education

How flexible are the tracks in most schools? Do you think a student could take courses outside his or her track? Why or why not?

THINK ABOUT IT

Problems in Schools

As we have seen in this chapter, the bureaucratic structure of education represents numerous challenges to educators and children alike. High dropout rates, poor academic performance, and acts of school crime, including bullying and intimidation, all have been linked to the inflexible standards set by public schools.

DROPOUTS

Dropping out and the associated sociological repercussions are of particular interest to experts in education, including sociologists and criminal justice scholars. Depending on one's definition, the dropout rate in the United States is around 11 percent for people between the ages of sixteen and twenty-four, a total of approximately 3.8 million young men and women every year.[25]

The short- and long-term effects experienced by young people who drop out of school can be difficult to overcome. For instance, there is a studied correlation between dropping out of high school and income earned in the years to follow. In 2005, the average income earned by persons between the ages of eighteen and sixty-five, who had not completed high school, was roughly $20,100. By contrast, the average income of persons in the same age group, who had completed their education with a high school credential, including a General Educational Development (GED) certificate, was nearly $29,700.[26]

A discussion of the relationship between dropout rates and degrees of poverty must also take into account rates of unemployment. High school dropouts are less likely to be in the labor force than those with a high school credential or higher.[27] A 2007 study conducted by the Center for Benefits-Cost Studies at the Teachers College at Columbia University confirms this trend. The researchers reported that two-thirds of Medicaid recipients and a substantial proportion of welfare recipients, including those receiving food stamps, housing assistance, and Temporary Assistance for Needy Families (TANF), were high school dropouts.[28] Another report from the National Center on Educational Statistics showed that youths from low-income families were approximately six times more likely to drop out of high school than their peers from high-income families.[29]

Other studies have explored the relationship between high school completion and measures of personal health. High school dropouts older than twenty-four years of age report being in worse health than adults who graduated from high school, regardless of income.[30] They also account for disproportionately higher percentages of the nation's prison and death row inmates. According to the Alliance for Excellent Education, in 2006, 75 percent of the inmates in state prisons, 59 percent of federal prisoners, and 69 percent of jail inmates were high school dropouts.[31]

Why, then, do students drop out? Many students drop out because social circumstances make it difficult for them to progress in their education. For example, when children are held back a grade, they are separated from their peers and grouped with students at least one year younger. Many children who are held back feel alienated from their friends. If students are held back a second or third time, the problem magnifies, and they tend to drop out when they are legally eligible. Although some students who drop out will return to school eventually or will earn a GED, many never go back.[32] Furthermore, the decision to drop out of school, and the experiences leading up to that decision, often serve to alienate children from education in general, a value they will likely pass down to their own children. Here is what Jose had to say about his experiences in the school system and what led him to drop out:

> I was doing okay, kindergarten, first, second, and third. But when I went to fourth, uh, when I started, I started flunkin' grades, flunked the fourth ones. I flunked the fifth ones. After that, they put me on a program, trying to skip me up a grade. That didn't, that didn't help. It was sixth grade, they put me in seventh. That didn't help either. . . . I tried to catch up. I, I know that I learned some stuff like, uh, the basic stuff, multiply and divide and subtract and all that stuff. And when, uh, I started getting it, I started learning stuff. But, it was like, only when I wanted to learn.

In contrast, Austin was actually a talented student, but his experiences with teachers, along with suspensions and expulsions, led him to drop out. Given the number of credits he needs to graduate with a diploma, completing his education at a high school seems unlikely:

> When I put forth effort, I was the Valedictorian for a couple years. So when I put forth effort, you know, I do good. But, I, I never really did put forth effort. I was always clownin' and acting up. Like I've gotten to the point where my teacher was afraid to send me out of class. . . . I only have four credits. I know if I can go back to school, I'm, uh, uh, I'm going to be there until I'm, like, nineteen, twenty. So I'm workin' on getting my GED.

Other more subtle factors contribute to students' dropping out. An example is learning difficulties. When learning disabilities go undiagnosed, or when the school does not have the resources to address these issues, children quickly fall behind their peers and are more likely to drop out. Social or cultural responsibilities likewise can lead to dropping out. Children whose parents own a business are sometimes pressured to leave school and work. As mentioned previously, some parents simply do not place a strong value on education and so are not supportive of their child's education; these parents may instead encourage their children to get a job and earn a living.[33] In some cases, race even plays a role, as when one member of a racial minority group accuses another of being a race traitor, or of "acting white," for working toward obtaining an education.[34] In these cases, pressures related to social and cultural identity strongly affect children's attitudes toward school.

Finally, many children find the routine of the school day boring and lacking in relevance to their lives. This is particularly true of schools organized bureaucratically, where rules seem unnecessarily restrictive and where too much emphasis is placed on discipline and too little on learning. Many children respond by skipping school to spend time with friends off campus. As we saw in Chapter 3, truancy is a gateway activity for chronic delinquency. The more often children miss school, the more likely they are to drop out.

It seems evident that a connection exists between dropout rates and problems associated with delinquency and crime. However, another relevant consideration pertains to how dropout data are interpreted. According to a 2007 report by the Alliance for Excellent Education titled *Understanding High School Graduation Rates*, there were eight different types of graduation rate calculations used by states across the country, many of which were used by schools to manipulate data, effectively obscuring low graduation or high dropout rates (see Figure 10-1).[35]

> " . . . but then I was like, screw school. I'm goin' to just be, uh, street smart. Uh, ever since then, I've been in the streets. "
>
> **LARRY**

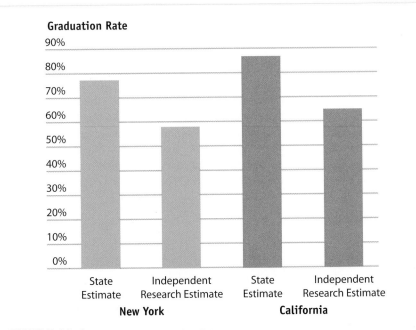

FIGURE 10-1 Calculating Graduation Rates

The Alliance for Excellent Education report highlights independent researchers' estimates of high school graduation rates and compares them to state estimates. The authors of the study point out that the different formulas used to calculate figures make it impossible to compare schools and state graduation rates, thereby obscuring the extent of the low graduation and dropout problem.

TABLE 10-1 Alternative Programs to Reduce the Dropout Rate

PROGRAM	FEATURES	RESULTS
The Perry Preschool Program	Student-teacher ratio of 5:1 Home visits Group meetings with parents Individualized education to prevent risky behaviors	Additional 19 graduates per 100 students
First Things First	Small classrooms Comprehensive school reform program More personalized approach Focus on student-teacher relationships Professional development for teachers Community participation	Additional 16 graduates per 100 students
The Chicago Child-Parent Center Program	Center-based preschool program Parental involvement and encouragement Outreach, and health and nutrition services	Additional 11 graduates per 100 students

Reducing class sizes in grades K-3 from 25 to 15 students per teacher results in an estimated additional 11 graduates per 100 students. A 10 percent increase in teacher salaries can result in an additional 5 graduates per 100 students.[36]

Whichever method schools choose to use to calculate dropout rates, most remain hard pressed to find a solution to the problem. A 2007 review of strategies being used to minimize dropout rates included the costs and benefits of implementing them. Table 10-1 describes some of the alternative programs used to address problems contributing to high dropout rates.

As the results in Table 10-1 clearly demonstrate, programs like the Perry Preschool Program and First Things First have the potential to substantially increase the number of youths who graduate from high school. While the costs of these programs are unavoidable, the benefits are significant and far-reaching. These programs can save the government and taxpayers considerable time, energy, and money—including lower government expenditures associated with crime, welfare, and health, and greater tax revenues as a result of increased employment rates.

When the costs associated with educational interventions are measured against the benefits that they would accrue, the answer seems simple. The net economic benefit would be more than twice the cost of the intervention.[37] Each new high school graduate results in $209,000 of government revenues and reduced government costs, while only $82,000 per graduate would be needed to provide the additional educational support and services. The success of the First Things First program in Kansas City schools is a case in point.

ACADEMIC ACHIEVEMENT

In 1983, the National Commission on Excellence in Education issued a report titled *A Nation at Risk,* which noted that only 40 percent of seventeen-year-olds could draw inferences from written material, a mere 20 percent could write a persuasive essay, and only 33 percent could solve mathematical problems requiring several steps.[38] Even today, many people lack basic literacy skills.

A 2004 report by the Center on Education Policy found that the majority of elementary school students were falling below standards in reading. While it was apparent that schools were making efforts to create safer campuses, it was also the case that less learning was taking place. According to the U.S. Department of Education, in 2008, one in eight children, upon leaving secondary school, demonstrated **functional illiteracy,** meaning they did not have the ability to read and write at a level necessary for everyday living. Moreover, the total number of functionally illiterate adults increases by approximately

functional illiteracy
The inability to read and write at a level necessary for everyday living.

THEORY AND PRACTICE WORKING TOGETHER

Kansas City Schools and First Things First

In 1997, Kansas City schools were experiencing high dropout rates and poor academic performance. In these schools, 77 percent of children qualified for free or reduced-price lunches. The student population as a whole consisted largely of minorities, and many showed little hope of finishing school. In response, the Kansas City School Board adopted the First Things First initiative.

Developed by the Institute for Research and Reform in Education (IRRE), First Things First is a comprehensive school reform model that seeks to address the poor academic performance and high dropout rates in secondary schools serving disadvantaged children. Its approach calls for a dramatic shift in the structure and operation of schools, including methods of instruction and evaluating accountability in disadvantaged middle and high schools.

The theoretical basis for this model was developed from research that identifies the essential features of school reform. The aim is to achieve significant academic improvement within disadvantaged student populations by using some of the features listed in Table 10-1, including smaller classrooms, a personalized approach to teaching, professional development activities for teachers, and the involvement of community groups whose resources contribute to a common goal.

By enlisting the aid of the entire community—businesses, government agencies, and nonprofit organizations—First Things First helped students feel valued. The fire department, area churches, and a local bank provided after-school care and tutoring on Wednesdays, giving teachers time for staff development and activity planning. Local businesses paid for school uniforms, provided computer equipment, and donated supplies. Even the Kansas City Chiefs football team pitched in by helping with a character education program for all middle school students.

Ten years later, evaluations deemed the program a success. First Things First dramatically reduced the dropout rate, improved students' overall academic performance, and brought the community together to work toward the common goal of educating its children. In 2004, the Kansas City public school system was given a Magna award by the *American School Board Journal* for its outstanding work.

THINK ABOUT IT — **Does this kind of effort generate a sense of social cohesion within the community?**

2.25 million persons every year.[39] People with functional illiteracy present some staggering statistics[40] (see Figure 10-2).

In his book *The Dumbest Generation*, Mark Bauerlein offers more evidence of underperforming.[41] Citing studies from governmental agencies, nonprofit organizations, foundations, and activist groups, Bauerlein reports consistent declines in reading and writing skills at all levels of education. His findings suggest that children who are not interested in reading, and who fail to read regularly, demonstrate poor reading skills, a general lack of knowledge, and poor performance in school. Additionally, Bauerlein points out that the proliferation of remedial reading and writing courses in colleges and in the labor market suggests a deficiency in the education process. He cites evidence that employers rank poor reading and writing skills as the second-highest deficiency among employees.[42]

It is not surprising to learn that students who do not perform well in school tend to engage in other activities, such as acting out, which can lead to suspension or expulsion. Underperforming students are also more likely to drop out if they do not feel as though they can learn. Thus, indicators of the decline in learning are perhaps the most significant measure of the problems of education in the United States. These conclusions have led many education experts to emphasize that the success of our education system, and the futures of our children, will depend on school administrations shifting their focus back to learning.

The ability to read and an interest in reading have a variety of influences on a youth's future.

SCHOOL CRIME

In the past ten years, a great deal of attention has been paid to the problem of **school crime,** offenses that take place on a school campus and disrupt the learning environment. In particular, media coverage of school shootings that have occurred across the country has reminded Americans that acts of extreme violence can take place almost anywhere, even in the classroom and the schoolyard.

school crime
Offenses that take place on a school campus and disrupt the learning environment.

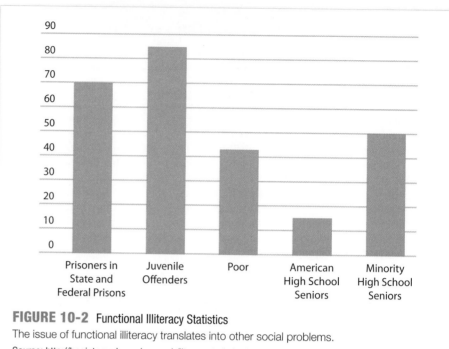

FIGURE 10-2 Functional Illiteracy Statistics

The issue of functional illiteracy translates into other social problems.

Source: http://begintoread.com/research/literacystatistics.htm

While school violence remains an issue, statistics show that the safety of public schools has improved, perhaps even as a result of increased awareness of the problem. Between 1995 and 2005, the percentage of students who reported avoiding one or more places in school declined from 9 to 4 percent.[43] According to the Bureau of Justice Statistics, in a report titled *Indicators of School Crime 2008,* school crime appears to be leveling off, with rates comparable to those in the previous four years. On the other hand, the same report noted that while children were less likely to be victims of crime at school, they were much more likely to be victimized off campus—for example, they were fifty times more likely to be murdered away from school than on campus (see Figure 10-3).

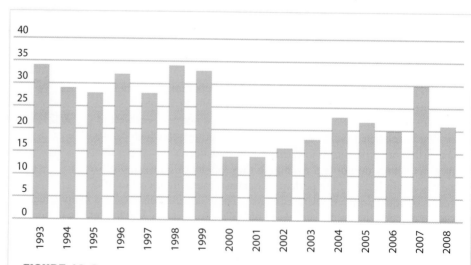

FIGURE 10-3 Number of Homicides on School Grounds

Each case in this chart represents an incident with one or more fatalities perpetrated by students on school grounds. Cases not involving school perpetrators or occurring off school grounds (i.e., near a school) are not included.

Source: Adapted from National School Safety Center. http://www.schoolsafety.us/. http://nces.ed.gov/programs/crimeindicators/crimeindicators2009/tables/table_01_1.asp?referrer=report).

Another indicator that experts on school violence use to assess fear of victimization is the percentage of students who carry a weapon to school. The lower percentage of weapons now found on school campuses can be attributed, at least in part, to safety measures taken by school officials. Between 1993 and 2005, the percentage of students in grades nine through twelve who reported carrying a weapon to school in the preceding thirty days declined from 12 percent to 6 percent.[44] In short, when students do not fear for their safety, they no longer feel the need to protect themselves with weapons. Nevertheless, given their experiences with school violence, bringing a gun to school is perceived by some to actually be a normal part of daily life on campus. When asked if he took guns to school, Shun said yes:

> Yeah. That's where—that's basically where it started up, 'cause I told you we was, we was, like, in elementary school when it started. But we was all cool. And then, it was summertime. And then, they—we came back to school and half of them had went to another school. So we started beefing with them. And it, it went from six-year-olds just competing at basketball, calling each other names to eighteen-, nineteen-year-olds shooting each other, the same kids, so . . .

For more on school environments, watch *School Environments: Jose* and *Public School Environment & Dress Code: Larry* at www.mhhe.com/mcnamarajd1e

BULLYING AND INTIMIDATION

In the past, **bullying and intimidation** were dismissed as a sort of rite of passage into adolescence. Today, however, bullying is considered a school crime. By definition, bullying and intimidation are forms of delinquency and school violence that include the physical, verbal, or emotional abuse of one student by one or several others over time. The traumatic effects of bullying on its victims include low self-esteem, anxiety, and other psychological disorders. As Table 10-2 shows, bullying tends to fall into four main categories: physical, relational, verbal and electronic.[45]

In 2005, a group of researchers examined more than 120,000 students from twenty-eight countries. They found that students who were bullied on a weekly basis were almost twice as likely as their nonbullied peers to experience headaches, stomachaches, backaches, or dizziness.[46] Furthermore, compared to nonbullied students, victims of bullying were two to eight times more likely to experience psychological symptoms such as loneliness, nervousness, and irritability, as well as symptoms related to depression, such as difficulty sleeping, tiredness, and feelings of helplessness.[47]

bullying and intimidation
Forms of delinquency and school violence that include the physical, verbal, or emotional abuse of one individual by one or several others over time.

TABLE 10-2 Categories of Bullying

PHYSICAL BULLYING	RELATIONAL BULLYING
Punching	Socially excluding
Kicking	Spreading rumors and gossip
Pushing	Writing and sending nasty notes
Tripping	
Confining	
VERBAL BULLYING	**ELECTRONIC OR CYBER BULLYING**
Name calling	Sending false emails, posts, tweets
Verbally intimidating	Using victim's name
Mocking	
Insulting	

The different types of bullying available indicate that victims have difficulty escaping their influence.

What are some of the psychological effects of bullying?

There is also growing evidence that bullied students avoid school. Between 6 and 8 percent of students reported staying away from school because of bullying, and victims of bullying were more likely to drop out of school altogether.[48] Bullied students also reported difficulties concentrating on their schoolwork and had lower levels of academic achievement than their nonbullied peers.[49]

According to the National Center for Education Statistics in a 2009 report on bullying and intimidation, both bullying and being bullied at school are associated with key violence-related behaviors, including carrying weapons, fighting, and sustaining injuries from fighting.[50] Bullying does not usually result in serious physical injury, although the psychological effects can be lasting. Of those students who reported bullying incidents that involved being pushed, shoved, tripped, or spit on, about a quarter of them also reported that they had sustained an injury as a result.[51] According to the same report, 79 percent of bullied students said the incidents had taken place inside a school building.

Another significant characteristic of bullying is the frequency with which victims are bullied. For some students, being bullied is a fairly regular occurrence. Of the students who reported being bullied during the previous six months, 53 percent said that they had been bullied once or twice during that period, while 8 percent said that they had been bullied almost daily (see Figure 10-4).[52]

Research shows that the percentage of students bullied at least once a week seems to have increased since 1999, although it is not clear if the increase reflects more incidents of bullying at school or perhaps greater awareness of bullying as a problem. In either case, this trend should not be taken as evidence that bullying is no longer an issue.[53]

Correlations between bullying and race and gender have also been studied. A 2007 report from the National Center for Education Statistics noted that white and black students were more likely than Latinos to report being bullied, and white students in particular were most likely to be bullied. Bullying also appears to bear a relationship to age and gender. In general, as grade level increased, students' likelihood of being bullied decreased. In 2007, about 43 percent of sixth graders, 31 percent of ninth graders, and 24 percent of twelfth graders reported that they had been bullied at school. Also, female students were more likely than male students to report being bullied (33.7 percent vs. 30.6 percent).[54]

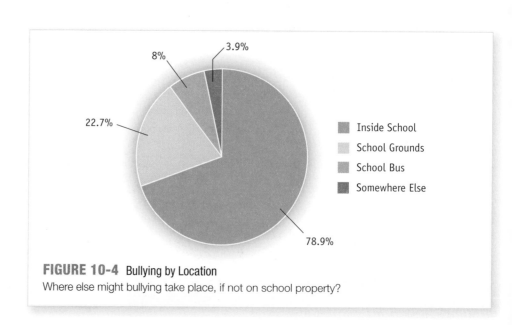

FIGURE 10-4 Bullying by Location
Where else might bullying take place, if not on school property?

Another place where bullying and intimidation occurs is on the Internet. **Cyber bullying** consists of sending or posting harmful material through the Internet or by mobile device. It differs from traditional forms of bullying because it can occur at any time, can reach a wider audience than a single victim, and allows offenders to remain anonymous. According to a 2008 report from the National Conference of State Legislatures, approximately 30 percent of sixth through eighth graders reported that they recently had either been cyber bullied or had done so to another student at least once.

Research shows that girls are about twice as likely as boys to be victims and perpetrators of cyber bullying, and that the most common method of cyber bullying is through instant messaging, followed by chat rooms, emails, and messages posted on websites.[55] As of 2007, thirty states had enacted harassment, intimidation, and bullying legislation, making it clear that the harmful effects of bullying—no matter where it occurs—must be addressed in meaningful ways.[56] Richard's experience with bullying is typical of many victims—sometimes students are targeted for the way they look or how they behave, and in some cases for no reason at all:

For more on bullying in schools, watch *Bullying in School: Richard* at www.mhhe.com/mcnamarajd1e

cyber bullying
The act of sending or posting harmful material through the Internet or by mobile device.

> Uh, elementary school was probably the best. Um, it was more fun. I got better grades. Um, people didn't pick on me. Everyone was more accepting. Um, when I got to middle school, thing—the work got harder, so my grades dropped. . . . And then, people started picking on me, and I got in trouble. Um, when I got in high school, it's—my grades started increasing a little bit. And um, I started acting better, but people still picked on me. And um, by the time I got to tenth grade, I—my grades went back up to what they were in elementary school, which was As and Bs. And uh, everyone still picked on me, because that—they thought I was the same. . . . [I]t could be the way I looked, um, the way I used to behave, because I was really immature before I became a Christian, um, just anything that they thought was different about me.

FRANKIE'S CASE

Motives for Carrying a Weapon to School

Recall Frankie's situation:

- held a reputation among his peers of being "bad"
- was being consistently harassed by gang members
- brought a gun to school for self-protection
- after gang members cornered him in the restroom, pulled out his gun to ward off the threat
- was arrested and expelled after the incident was reported

Much of the research on school crime suggests that while an increasing number of students bring guns to school, they usually do so out of fear of being victimized, and not with the intent to commit mass murder. Like many students who are concerned for their own safety, Frankie took drastic measures to protect himself on campus.

Do you agree that most students who carry guns on school property do so out of fear? If so, what strategies would you propose in order to reduce that fear?

THINK ABOUT IT

How has the fear of school shootings translated into school policies?

SCHOOL SHOOTINGS

Traumatic events, such as school shootings, often inspire fear in teachers and students that the incident will occur again. The media attention generated from high-profile cases, such as the mass murders at Columbine High School in Colorado and at Virginia Tech, has generated a level of fear that has prompted the implementation of zero-tolerance policies in schools around the country.

While school safety should always be a priority, empirical evidence, and not fear, should take precedence when determining the likelihood that school shootings will take place. Data that reflect the likelihood of such an event are a more reliable and accurate source of information than the media's sensational coverage of these events. According to the National School Safety Center, in 2005, there were twenty-one homicides at schools across the country; during the previous year, there were nineteen. While these are tragic incidents, one must take other factors into account—such as the total number of schools and students across the country—to see that the risks involved are quite low.[57]

THINK ABOUT IT

School Safety

In the absence of an obvious solution to maintaining order in classrooms and on campuses, what can administrators, teachers, and parents do to provide a safe and healthy learning environment for students?

Strategies to Reduce School Crime

Today, in response to many of the behavioral problems witnessed on campuses, school officials have implemented strategies designed to ensure greater control over the school environment. These can be narrowed down to three common strategies:

- dress codes and school uniforms
- zero-tolerance policies for misbehavior
- frequent use of out-of-school suspension and expulsion, or transfers to alternative schools

SCHOOL UNIFORMS

Over the past twenty years, more and more schools have begun requiring uniforms as a way of ensuring campuswide order and safety. In the 1980s, less than 1 percent of schools had a uniform policy. By 2002, the number had increased to 11 percent. In general, about 25 percent of U.S. public schools now require students to wear uniforms.[58] In many cases, uniform requirements have been enforced by school officials in response to the frequency with which students were fighting over designer clothing. In other cases, uniforms were a response to the fear of gang infiltration by nonstudents.

Advocates also argue that uniforms place students from different social classes on equal footing, as well as minimizing fighting over and theft of clothing. Moreover, many teachers report that students' grades improve.[59] Opponents of uniforms, on the other hand, assert that there is no evidence that uniforms make a difference in schools. In his 2004 book *The School Reform Movement and What It Tells Us about American Education: A Symbolic Crusade,* David Brunsma cites research that contradicts the claim that a uniform policy reduces violence and other problems. Brunsma argues that while some schools have achieved success, research shows that these schools' results are unique and that the majority of schools see little or no change in student behavior. He further contends that there is ample research to contradict the popular notion that uniforms result in improved academic performance.[60]

Do school uniforms make students safer?

With recent studies showing that uniforms do not have an effect on school performance, people are left to wonder why older studies promoted them in the first place. Brunsma claims that there is a simple explanation for this trend. When most of the studies were carried out, Brunsma points out, they were primarily focused on the comparison between Catholic schools, which required uniforms, and public schools, which did not. Most researchers assumed that if Catholic schools were outperforming public schools, the only major difference between the two schools was uniform policies. But, as Brunsma notes, there are other important differences between Catholic and public schools that perhaps more accurately explain discrepancies in academic performance. While research on the effectiveness of school uniforms and dress codes is still up for debate, uniforms remain a popular strategy for attempting to control the behavior of students.

ZERO TOLERANCE

The 1994 Gun-Free Schools Act requires that school officials expel any student found to be in possession of a firearm at school for one year. Such a policy is termed **zero tolerance,** which refers to the practice of automatically expelling students for violations of school safety rules. In recent years, these types of policies have been a first line of defense to student threats of violence.

zero tolerance
The practice of automatically expelling students for violations of school safety rules.

Although the Gun-Free Schools Act permits local school districts to modify the expulsion on a case-by-case basis, this provision is in keeping with the "get tough" approach of law enforcement and the criminal justice system generally. After the act was passed, schools took zero tolerance to extreme levels and began mandating automatic expulsions for all types of infractions, even minor ones that would not normally warrant severe punishment. Initially, zero-tolerance policies were intended to apply only to serious criminal behavior involving firearms or illegal drugs, but they have been extended to cover many more behaviors and circumstances.[61]

Zero-tolerance policies also tend to single out minority students. In 2007, more than 3.2 million students were suspended from school. Although African American children represented 17 percent of the public school enrollment that year, they accounted for 32 percent of the out-of-school suspensions.[62] Indeed, researchers have consistently found that minorities are disproportionately represented among students on the receiving end of exclusionary and punitive discipline practices. For example, African American students are overrepresented in the use of corporal punishment and expulsion, and they are underrepresented in the use of milder disciplinary alternatives. The overrepresentation of minorities in the application of harsh discipline appears to be related to the frequent use of suspensions: schools that rely most heavily on suspension and expulsion are also the ones with the highest rates of minority students.[63]

Opponents of zero tolerance contend that the central problem with these types of policies is that all threats of violence are treated as equally dangerous and therefore deserving of the same consequences. In other words, these kinds of policies provide no latitude for school authorities to consider the seriousness of the threat or degree of risk posed by the student's behavior. The result, of course, is that relatively minor infractions get punished out of proportion to their seriousness.

For example, according to the National Center for Education Statistics, data on suspensions consistently show that referrals for drugs, weapons, and gang-related behaviors account for only a small minority of suspensions. However, fighting among students is the single most frequent reason for suspension. This suggests that the majority of school

Have zero-tolerance policies resulted in safer schools?

suspensions occur in response to relatively minor incidents that do not threaten school safety.[64] One study of school expulsions in the United States found that the majority of offenses in the sample they investigated were committed by students who would not generally be considered dangerous to the school environment.[65]

Recall that the Gun-Free Schools Act permits local school districts to modify the expulsion on a case-by-case basis. Nevertheless, many school districts mandate automatic expulsion for all infractions, including toy weapons and objects that only appear to be weapons. For instance, in 1997 in Seattle, a ten-year-old boy was expelled from elementary school because he brought a one-inch plastic toy pistol—an accessory to his G.I. Joe action figure—to school. The boy discovered he had the tiny toy in his pocket when he checked to see if he had his lunch money.[66] Consider these other examples:

- A five-year-old in California was expelled after he found a razor blade at his bus stop, brought it to school, and gave it to his teacher.
- A nine-year-old in Ohio was suspended for having a one-inch knife in a manicure kit.
- A seventeen-year-old in Chicago was arrested and subsequently expelled for shooting a paper clip with a rubber band.
- In Ohio, a thirteen-year-old honor student was suspended for ten days after accepting two Midol pills from a classmate.
- In Virginia, a kindergartner was suspended for bringing a beeper from home and showing it to a classmate during a field trip.[67]
- In Arizona, a school suspended a thirteen-year-old boy for drawing a picture. The boy said it was a harmless doodle; the school said the drawing was of a gun. Since they have zero tolerance for guns, the boy was suspended.
- A second grader was suspended for bringing his grandfather's watch with a one-inch pocketknife attached for show-and-tell.
- A twelve-year-old honor student was banned from extracurricular activities because she shared her inhaler with another asthmatic student.
- A nine-year-old was punished because he included the phrase "you will die an honorable death" in a fortune cookie made as part of a class project.[68]

How well has zero tolerance worked? Although outcome measures are not easily defined, the most comprehensive and controlled study of zero-tolerance policies is the National Center for Education Statistics (NCES) study of school violence. The NCES survey asked principals to identify which of a number of possible components of a zero-tolerance strategy (e.g., expulsions, locker searches, the use of metal detectors, school uniforms) were employed at their school. Of the responding principals, 79 percent reported having a zero-tolerance policy for violence. Schools with no reported crime were less likely to have a zero-tolerance policy than schools that reported incidents of serious crime.[69]

From one perspective, this relationship is not surprising, since unsafe schools might well be expected to try more extreme measures. Yet the NCES found that schools that use zero-tolerance policies are still less safe than those without such policies.[70] Virtually no data suggest that zero-tolerance policies reduce school violence, and some data suggest that certain strategies, such as strip searches or the presence of undercover agents in school, may actually do emotional harm or encourage students to drop out.[71]

Expulsions and greater use of suspension as a part of zero-tolerance policies have a variety of long-term effects. In fact, the research on school suspension indicates that it is a strong predictor of whether students will drop out altogether. According to some studies, more than 30 percent of sophomores who dropped out of school had been suspended, a rate three times that of peers who stayed in school.[72] Dropping out of school is also a strong predictor of involvement in the criminal justice system. One study found that 52 percent of African American, male, high school dropouts had been incarcerated by their early thirties, while only 10 percent of white high school dropouts had been incarcerated.[73]

Indeed, the relationship between suspension and dropping out may not be accidental. In ethnographic studies, school disciplinarians report that suspension is sometimes used as a tool to *push out* particular students—to encourage "troublemakers," or those perceived as unlikely to succeed in school, to leave.[74]

In 2008, testimony given before the New York City Council Committees on Education and Civil Rights regarding the impact of suspensions on students' education rights pointed to evidence that some schools are removing problem students through suspension at an alarming rate.[75] There is also an issue of race to consider with regard to school suspensions. Nationwide, black students are 2.6 times more likely to be suspended than white students. Black students, who make up 17 percent of the nation's student population, account for 36 percent of school suspensions and 31 percent of expulsions.[76]

Recent advances in developmental psychopathology suggest other explanations for the relationship between suspension and dropping out. As early as their elementary school years, students at risk for developing conduct disorders exhibit disruptive behavior, below-average achievement, and poor social skills, causing them to become increasingly alienated from teachers and peers. As they reach the middle school years, these children become less interested in school and seek the company of other antisocial peers, and sometimes gangs. At the same time, their families often fail to monitor their whereabouts, allowing them more unsupervised time on the streets. In circumstances like these, it seems unlikely that suspension will positively influence the behavior of students. In fact, such punishment may even worsen the situation.[77] The Theory and Practice box on page 268 discusses one strategy offered by some schools in lieu of arrests, expulsions, or suspensions.

ALTERNATIVE SCHOOLS

Alternative schools offer a nontraditional education to students who do not show signs of succeeding in more traditional, and often less flexible, learning environments. Within the context of American public education, the concept of alternative schooling is not a new one. In the 1950s and 1960s, many school districts across the country had alternative schools for students who had already dropped out. However, educational leaders soon found that these schools had little effect on the dropout rate and so essentially discontinued them. In the 1970s, as school budgets began to shrink, nontraditional schools took another hit.[78]

Today there are more alternative schools in operation than ever before, and these schools are increasingly diverse. Many middle school or high school students attending alternative schools are underachievers lacking enough credits to graduate with students in their age groups. Typically, students participating in these programs either want to stay in school and earn diplomas or have been placed there by the court system. Some alternative schools offer unique parenting programs with special opportunities for teenage mothers who want to graduate but are unable to attend a traditional high school. While there are many different programs offered to students seeking an alternative education, one educational expert classifies alternative schools in the following way:

- **Schools of choice** offer specialized learning opportunities to a diverse student body, usually in what is known as a magnet school.

- **Last-chance schools** are designed to provide continued education program options for disruptive students.

- **Remedial schools** focus on students' need for academic remediation or social rehabilitation.[79]

There is considerable debate regarding the effectiveness of alternative school programs. Because these schools have relatively few universal standards, it is difficult to reach any overarching conclusions as to their effectiveness. A review of the research

alternative schools
Schools that offer nontraditional education to students who do not show signs of succeeding in more traditional, and often less flexible, learning environments.

THEORY AND PRACTICE WORKING TOGETHER

Operation CleanSWEEP

How can schools hold student offenders accountable while at the same time remaining consistent with the rehabilitative philosophy of the juvenile justice system? Operation CleanSWEEP, the San Bernardino, California, program for student offenders, presents an impressive model for accountability and rehabilitation.

Operation CleanSWEEP's success is owed in large part to its goal of keeping offenders in school and following a balanced punishment-incentive model. The list below describes the procedure followed by a CleanSWEEP school when responding to offenses committed by students on campus:

- Offending students are given a "ticket" or "summons," written by a vice principal or dean.
- The ticket places offending students in informal juvenile traffic court with their parents.
- There, students can tell the hearing officer their side of the story.
- The judge imposes a disposition, such as a dismissal, conviction, or conviction with a suspended sentence.
- Usually, the judge fines offenders anywhere from $30 to $400: students may waive these fines if they agree to certain sanctions, such as improving attendance or grades, providing community service, or attending diversionary programs, such as anger management or smoking cessation classes, depending on the nature of the offense.

The second part of the program involves a security assessment component, which has deputies conducting detailed analyses of the facilities for safety-related problems. The deputies distribute questionnaires to staff and students to gather input on safety-related issues. This way, they gain a snapshot of the school's general attitude on the subject of school security. The deputies then package all of this information together and present it to the principal.

The third element of Operation CleanSWEEP consists of speeches, classes, presentations, and promotional events designed to impart the best information possible about safety and security on campus. These events even include mock hostage scenarios, for instance, which prepare teachers and administrators in advance, should such an extreme situation occur.

Operation CleanSWEEP has proven extraordinarily successful, and in a relatively short period. Over time, calls for service to local police departments declined up to 57 percent, indicating that fewer crimes occurred on those campuses employing the program. At every CleanSWEEP school, the number of suspensions and expulsions also decreased, suggesting that fewer students were getting into trouble. Not only have measurably fewer fights and disruptive acts occurred on participating school campuses, but educators and students alike feel safer in their schools.

THINK ABOUT IT How might Operation CleanSWEEP appeal to those in opposition to zero-tolerance policies? What are the benefits associated with punishing and treating students on campus instead of through the juvenile justice system?

suggests that disciplinary-based alternative schools yield no positive long-term gains and may even increase negative outcomes. Some of the negative effects include teachers not wanting to teach in alternative schools, a lack of positive peer role models, and an atmosphere in which students feel labeled or ostracized from their peers attending traditional schools.[80]

In the 1980s and 1990s, there was little in the way of empirical evidence regarding the effectiveness of alternative schools. The studies that existed suffered from methodological problems, rendering their findings questionable.[81] But in 2001, the National Center for Education Statistics conducted perhaps the most comprehensive study of alternative schools. This study was also the first national one of public alternative schools and programs for students at risk of educational failure.[82]

When the study was conducted, there were 10,900 public alternative schools and programs for at-risk students in the nation. During the 2000–2001 school year, 39 percent of public school districts administered at least one alternative school or program. Not surprisingly, large urban school districts, especially those with more minority students, were more likely to have an alternative program for at-risk students (see Figure 10-5).[83]

About two-thirds of the districts had one alternative school or program, and large districts were more likely than smaller districts to have multiple programs or schools. Of those districts that offered alternative education, the majority focused on high school students, with over 90 percent of districts targeting that segment of the student population. About two-thirds of districts with alternative programs had alternative education available for middle school students, and about 20 percent had programs targeting at-risk

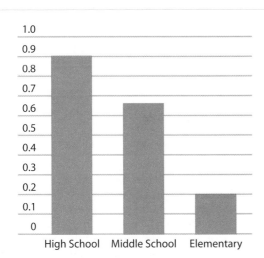

FIGURE 10-5 Alternative School Programs by Percentage

About two-thirds of the districts have one alternative school or program, and large districts are more likely than smaller districts to have multiple programs or schools. Of those districts that offer alternative education, the majority focus on high school students.

elementary school students. In all, the NCES study concluded that alternative schools provided a substitute for school officials, but the impact of such programs on students' achievement remained unanswered.[84]

A number of anecdotal studies have been done to measure the effectiveness of alternative schools in student retention. A 2004 study showed that alternative schools had been successful in reducing truancy, improving attitudes toward school, accumulating high school credits, and reducing behavioral problems.[85] In 2006, another study evaluated the effectiveness of a solution-focused alternative school (SFAS) in preventing students from dropping out of high school. The study showed that students in the experimental group earned significantly more credits over time than a comparison group, and more than half of the experimental group had entered a postgraduate education program after graduating from the SFAS.[86]

The SFAS appears to show promise as an intervention for reducing dropout rates for at-risk adolescents and enabling them to earn high school credits and eventually graduate. However, the research on the effectiveness of alternative schools remains mixed.[87] Part of the reason for this is the variability with which we define alternative schooling.

Critics of alternative schools contend that these schools discriminate against minority students by providing an inferior education to students who are more likely to drop out or be expelled. Furthermore, they argue that graduates of alternative schools are relegated to low-paying jobs and have fewer educational opportunities after high school. These problems often manifest in gang affiliations, acting out, poor anger management skills, and other behavioral problems. But perhaps the biggest challenge to the alternative school is to address these issues while also overcoming the educational deficiencies they create.[88]

SCHOOL SEARCHES

Schools are required to provide a safe learning environment for students. The problems discussed previously, such as school shootings, drugs, and gang activity, require that officials have the authority to search for evidence and apprehend offenders who threaten the safety of students and faculty. But the zero-tolerance approach raises questions about the ability of school officials to protect students' safety while also respecting their right to privacy.

According to the Center for Public Education, there are guidelines that teachers and school officials must follow when conducting searches of students' lockers or their

FRANKIE'S CASE

Drawing Conclusions

Recall the issues Frankie is facing:

- brought a gun to school
- pulled the gun on gang members in a school bathroom
- was reported to school officials
- was expelled from school

Consider what you have learned about the structure of schools and the various responses of school officials to student offenses. More and more, schools are responding to potential problems by trying to assert control over students, as they do with harsh measures like zero-tolerance policies.

Now reconsider Frankie's case. Frankie did not bring the gun to school to show off or to intimidate or bully others. Instead, his decision was informed by fear of victimization, along with the belief that school officials could not or would not protect him.

THINK ABOUT IT

Was Frankie wrong to bring a gun to school, or were his actions reasonable given the potential threat? Could Frankie have relied on school officials, teachers, or peers for protection?

Are police searches an invasion of students' right to privacy?

persons.[89] There are two legal mandates that provide the framework for these searches. One is the Fourth Amendment to the U.S. Constitution, which gives people the right to be free from unreasonable searches and seizures by the government. The second is the Fifth Amendment's due process clause, which requires school officials to have specific information and evidence about possible crimes committed by students. It also requires school officials to give accused students an opportunity to explain themselves and respond to the charges against them. The latter is known in legal circles as "notice and an opportunity to be heard."[90] Without following these due process steps, any punishment that is given—no matter how legitimate—can be overturned.[91]

The Fourth and Fifth Amendment provisions apply only to public schools. Because tuition and employment contracts dictate students' and employees' relationships with the school, private institutions have more leeway when it comes to conducting investigations. In public schools, however, the rules are different. Police K-9 units conduct searches on campus, including backpack, locker, and car searches, and athletes undergo routine drug tests. Generally, in the context of public schools, school safety often trumps the students' rights to privacy. However, there are limits to the extent that school officials can search.[92]

The standard for the Fourth Amendment is considerably lower on campus than off of it. Off campus, the law requires that police demonstrate that they have probable cause that a crime has been committed. Frequently, this means presenting evidence to a judge, securing a warrant, and then conducting the search. On campus, however—or when students are within the care of school officials, such as on a field trip—the standard is "reasonable suspicion," a much lower burden of proof. While privacy is still a factor, reasonable suspicion allows school officials to conduct searches that would normally not be allowed if conducted by the police.

Meanwhile, the U.S. Supreme Court has stated that a different standard is needed because school officials are responsible for the students in their care and must be allowed to ensure their safety. The following is a brief overview of when and how student searches are warranted by school officials. Note that the Plain View Doctrine, which allows police officers or other officials to seize contraband without probable cause or a warrant, as long as it is in plain view, applies whether on or off campus.[93]

- **Locker searches:** courts have generally upheld locker searches. Even though there is some expectation of privacy, the locker belongs to the school, and not students, and thus differs from a search of a student's home.

- **Searches of purses and book bags:** in 1985, the U.S. Supreme Court ruled that school officials must have reasonable suspicion to search these types of items. In *New Jersey v. T.L.O.,* an assistant principal opened and searched a purse after a student was accused of violating the school's no-smoking policy. The search revealed marijuana and other drug paraphernalia in addition to cigarettes. The Court concluded that school officials acted appropriately because they had reasonable grounds for suspecting that a search would turn up a violation of school rules—in this case, the possession of the cigarettes.

- **Body searches:** these usually consist of pat-down searches, which are less intrusive than strip searches. Some states have banned strip searches by school officials.

- **Dog-sniffing searches:** the courts have ruled that these are noninvasive since dogs search common areas such as hallways, and so there is no expectation of privacy.

- **Student drug testing:** this is more controversial since there is an absence of reasonable suspicion of a specific violation. However, the U.S. Supreme Court has ruled that because students voluntarily participate in athletics, they place themselves under the rule. The Court also noted that the test's purpose is not punishment, but remediation and health.[94]

DUE PROCESS

When students violate school policies, such as dress codes or possession of contraband, school officials have a variety of disciplinary measures at their disposal. Students may receive some form of in-school suspension, the contraband may be confiscated, or parents may be contacted and required to sign a disciplinary form before offenders are permitted to return to school. In other cases, they may be suspended from school or even expelled for serious violations. However, as the sanctions become more punitive, legal restrictions apply.

For instance, the Fifth and Fourteenth Amendments to the U.S. Constitution provide that people charged with a crime or infraction and who are thereby deprived of life, liberty, or property by the government are guaranteed **due process.** This means that some type of procedure must be used that outlines the rights to individuals in those circumstances. There are many cases in which the U.S. Supreme Court has considered due process as an issue in a criminal trial.

With regard to school suspension, the Supreme Court has ruled that students who face suspension have specific legal rights. In *Goss v. Lopez,* the Court ruled that schools must follow some type of due process procedure when suspending students from school for ten or fewer days. Students facing this type of suspension must receive oral or written notice of the charges against them and have an opportunity for a hearing to present their version of events that led to the charges.

The Court also ruled that the notice of charges and the hearing should be provided before the suspension is given, unless a student's presence in the school threatens the safety, property, or educational opportunities of others. In this particular case, which arose in Columbus, Ohio, several public high school students, including Lopez, were suspended from school for misconduct but were not given a hearing immediately before or after the suspension.

School authorities in Columbus claimed that a state law allowed them to suspend students for as long as ten days without a hearing. The students filed a petition with the court claiming that the statute was unconstitutional because it allowed school officials to deny students their right to a hearing. This violated the protections outlined in the due process clause of the Fourteenth Amendment.[95]

Since this ruling, each state has enacted a policy regarding long-term suspensions and expulsions. In these more serious cases, depending on the state's statutes, students' parents

due process
A term used to describe the way the legal system operates and provides a mechanism to ensure that the rights of the accused are protected.

or guardians have the right to appear at a meeting of the school board, or with an officer of the board, to discuss the charges. Parents or guardians must also be notified of this meeting by certified or registered mail or delivery of the notice in person. At the hearing, the students may be represented by attorneys who can present evidence and cross-examine witnesses on their behalf.[96]

CORPORAL PUNISHMENT

corporal punishment
The infliction of pain as a penalty for students who violate a school rule.

In previous eras, corporal punishment was used in schools by teachers and administrators, and was considered an effective means of disciplining students who misbehaved. **Corporal punishment** is defined as the infliction of pain as a penalty for students who violate a school rule. While corporal punishment was used as recently as the nineteenth century to control students in the classroom, today this practice is banned in every industrialized country except the United States, Canada, and Queensland, Australia. In the United States, only twenty-nine states have banned the use of corporal punishment in schools.[97]

In the 1977 case of *Ingraham v. Wright,* a junior high school student in Miami, Florida, named James Ingraham was punished for not leaving the stage of the school auditorium promptly. For this infraction, Ingraham was paddled twenty times by the school principal, Willie Wright. When Ingraham went home, his mother examined him and took him to a local hospital. The doctors prescribed pain pills and ice packs, and recommended that Ingraham stay home from school for one week. Ingraham filed legal action against the school and the principal, claiming his Eighth Amendment rights against cruel and unusual punishment had been violated, as had been the due process clause of the Fourteenth Amendment to the U.S. Constitution.

The U.S. Supreme Court ruled that the Eighth Amendment protection against cruel and unusual punishment does not apply to corporal punishment in schools, and that the due process clause of the Fourteenth Amendment does not require schools to give students notice before punishing them. The reasoning behind this ruling was that corporal punishment is a traditional method of maintaining discipline in public schools, so long as the punishment is reasonable. If the punishment is extreme, criminal charges may be brought against the offender.[98]

In 1987, this issue of excessive punishment was raised again in *Garcia v. Miera.* In this case, school officials in New Mexico used a broken wooden paddle and left welts, bruises, and permanent scars on a nine-year-old female student. In 1980, the Fourth Circuit Court of Appeals dealt with the issue of parents' objections to the use of corporal punishment in *Hall v. Tawney.* The court ruled that parents have no constitutional right to exempt their children from corporal punishment in public schools. Thus, even in those instances where parents do not believe in the use of corporal punishment—an issue we discussed in Chapter 7 on families and delinquency—if state law permits its use in public schools and parents allow their children to attend one, the children are subject to whatever disciplinary practices are commonly used in that school.

As was also discussed in Chapter 7, many questions remain about the effectiveness of corporal punishment, whether it is administered by parents or by school officials. What is known, however, is that some states, especially southern states, make greater use of it in public schools than other states do. Texas and Mississippi account for 40 percent of corporal punishment cases, and five states, including Georgia, Arkansas, and Alabama, account for nearly 75 percent of all school paddlings.[99]

FREE SPEECH

If schools across the country have responded to problems by exerting greater control over students, one of the most sensitive issues surrounding this tendency relates to the right of students to express their views. After all, educational institutions are supposed to be environments where the exchange of differing ideas and viewpoints is considered healthy and necessary in a civilized society. But how far can school officials go in regulating students' expressions without violating their First Amendment protections on free speech?

To begin with, no one in the United States has complete freedom of speech, a matter that has been articulated in early U.S. Supreme Court cases. For example, to yell "fire" in a crowded theater is not to practice protected speech, nor is using words to incite a riot or cause some other threat to public safety. Moreover, students, as minors, are not normally accorded the same measure of constitutional protections as adults. In the eyes of the law, minors cannot lawfully enter into a legal and binding contract, nor are they afforded all constitutional protections if they commit a criminal act. It makes sense, then, to think of free speech by minor students as somewhat different from that of their adult counterparts. Free speech in a school setting is more restricted than for adults off campus.

One of the more noteworthy cases involving free speech is *Tinker v. Des Moines Independent Community School District.* In this case, several students who wanted to protest U.S. involvement in the Vietnam War wore black armbands to school, which was in violation of the school's dress code. The U.S. Supreme Court ruled that wearing the armbands did not interrupt school activities, nor did it adversely affect school business or the lives of others.[100]

The issue gets more complicated when it involves actual speech by students. For instance, in *Hazelwood School District v. Kuhlmeier,* the issue was related to school publications— specifically, the school newspaper. This case involved a disagreement between students and school officials over the censorship of two pages in the school's student-run newspaper. The controversy stemmed from articles written about teenage pregnancy and divorce. The principal felt that the articles on these topics were written by students in such a way that it could lead to revealing the identity of the people involved, thus infringing upon their rights. The Supreme Court ruled in favor of the school district, stating that as long as the school funds the newspaper, and there is a compelling educational reason for doing so, censorship is permissible. The Court held that school officials can regulate the content of student publications, but only if doing so serves an educational purpose.[101]

In these and other cases, the Supreme Court has applied the educational value component in deciding whether students' First Amendment rights have been violated, as well as whether the activities occurred on school grounds, whether they interrupted school business in any way, or whether the school sponsored the activity. The third component to the free speech test is whether the words or displays infringe upon the rights of others on campus and, most importantly, other students.

Administrative Strategies

What are some of the administrative strategies schools use to curtail behavioral problems and improve academic performance? Thinking back to Frankie's case, for instance, how would you rate the effectiveness of these strategies?

THINK ABOUT IT

Public Policy Regarding Delinquency in Schools

Schools are faced with a host of challenges in their attempts to educate children while ensuring their safety. It is important to understand the context of the problems that occur on campuses, as well as how schools respond to them. For example, poverty can play a significant role in the quality and quantity of education children receive. As such, we need to recognize how this influences other, more symptomatic issues such as tracking, dropping out, and poor academic achievement, all of which have been shown to contribute to delinquency. Programs like Operation CleanSWEEP and First Things First have been successful in giving children an opportunity to get their education on track and to receive fair and effective treatment when they are delinquent. Policymakers also play an important role in how schools respond by proposing new legislation that will meet the needs of children who are at risk of delinquency. Among these are proposals for one-on-one mentoring opportunities and after-school programs for at-risk youths. Likewise, policymakers have proposed amendments to already-existing preventative legislation, such as the Juvenile Justice and Delinquency Prevention Act, to include new requirements for keeping status offenders out of adult correctional facilities.

THE BIG PICTURE

Conclusions on School and Delinquency

■ Have school officials misunderstood the factors that contribute to delinquency? Why do students turn to delinquent behavior, and what strategies can schools use to curb this behavior, improve school performance, and prevent dropouts?

■ What are the effects of labeling and tracking on students' expectations of themselves? Do teachers' expectations affect students' ability to learn? What role have race and class played in the labeling and tracking of students?

■ Are zero-tolerance policies effective in deterring delinquency, or are they a symptom of a larger problem? What alternative to zero-tolerance policies would you recommend?

Key Terms

social institutions
socialization
social class bias
tracking

No Child Left Behind (NCLB)
functional illiteracy
school crime
bullying and intimidation

cyber bullying
zero tolerance
alternative schools
corporal punishment

Make the Call ▶ Schools and Delinquency

Review the scenario below and decide how you might act.

YOUR ROLE: High school teacher in an urban community

DETAILS OF THE SCENARIO

■ You are teaching an elective course in sociology to a group of twenty-five high school students; most are from disadvantaged families.

■ You pride yourself on making a difference and helping students get a solid education, with the hope that some will go on to college.

■ Increasingly, you find that most of your time is spent maintaining order in the classroom rather than teaching the material.

■ On one particular assignment, a few students use a common text messaging reply "IDK," or "I don't know," as their entire response to the assignment.

■ Many of the students say that school is boring, teachers do not care, and they do not think they have a

bright future. Some even tell you that they think they will be either dead or in prison by the time they are twenty-five.

HOW DO YOU RESPOND?

Your students are already convinced that they cannot be educated, and some have even resigned themselves to delinquency. Responding to their poor performance with anger or harsh disciplinary action might only contribute to their belief that they are problems to be dealt with, rather than students who can learn. How do you respond productively to their expressions of apathy and frustration?

Consider:

■ What connections can you make between this scenario and this chapter's discussion about delinquency?

■ What might you do to reach these students?

■ What kinds of strategies can you employ to get them to develop their reading and writing skills?

■ Can you change their minds about education in general?

Apply Theory to Reality ▶ Social Structure Theory and Social Process Explanation

As discussed earlier in this chapter, there is a studied correlation between low academic achievement and race. For example, research shows that African American students are more likely to place little value on education in general, and are therefore more likely to drop out. Conduct a search of *social structural theory,* such as Merton's anomie, and *social process explanation,* such as social learning or labeling theory. Which theory would you use as a framework for understanding the relationship between race and academic performance, and why?

Your Community ▶ Inner-City Public Schools

In addition to the information you glean from your readings, class lectures, and discussions, it is important to roll up your sleeves and immerse yourself in a topic. That is, you gain an understanding of a problem or issue by observing or experiencing it firsthand. Through such methods, you gain a much greater appreciation of the magnitude and scope of the problem than if you were only engaged in "armchair theorizing."

- Using ten original photographs, produce a journalistic essay that clearly describes the differences in public

education for inner-city students as compared to wealthy suburban students.

- Present your photos in such an order that they "read" like an essay.

- In addition to your pictorial display, submit a report on the nature of your topic, including interviews with people who have experienced the phenomenon you are studying.

Notes

[1] Kornblum, W., and Smith, C. D. 2007. *Sociology in a Changing World.* 8th ed. Independence, KY: Wadsworth.

[2] Ibid.

[3] Ibid.

[4] For a general overview, see Levinson, D., Cookson, P. W., and Sadovink, A. R. 2002. *Education and Sociology: An Encyclopedia.* New York: Taylor and Francis.

[5] See, for instance, Tyack, D., and Cuban, L. 1995. *Tinkering toward Utopia: A Century of Public School Reform.* Cambridge, MA: Harvard University Press. See also Tyack, D. 1975. *The One Best System: A History of American Urban Education.* Cambridge, MA: Harvard University Press.

[6] This is also sometimes known as the "hidden curriculum." See Gatto, J. T. 2002. *Dumbing Us Down: The Hidden Curriculum of Compulsory School.* New York: New Society.

[7] Katz, M. 1975. *Class, Bureaucracy, and Schools: The Illusion of Educational Change in America.* Westport, CT: Praeger.

[8] Way, N., and Robinson, M. G. 2003. "A Longitudinal Study of the Effects of Family, Friends, and School Experiences on the Psychological Adjustment of Ethnic Minority, Low-SES Adolescents." *Journal of Adolescent Research,* 18(4): 324–346.

[9] Ibid.

[10] Ibid.

[11] See, for instance, Rozycki, E. G. 1999. "Tracking in Public Education: Preparation for the World of Work." *Educational Horizons,* 77(3): 113–116. See also the Educational Trust. 2009. *Education Watch: Tracking, Achievement, Attainment, and Opportunity in America's Public Schools.* http://www2.edtrust.org/EdTrust/Press+Room/EdWatch2009.htm.

[12] Tyack, 1975.

[13] Ibid.

[14] See, for instance, Hallinan, M. T. 2006. *Handbook of the Sociology of Education.* New York: Springer.

[15] See, for instance, Lewis, T., and Cheng, S.-Y. 2006. "Tracking, Expectations, and the Transformation of Vocational Education." *American Journal of Education,* 113: 1, 67–99. See also Van Houtte, M. 2004. "Tracking Effects on School Achievement: A Quantitative Explanation in Terms of the Academic Culture of School Staff." *American Journal of Education,* 110.

[16] See, for instance, National Center for Education Statistics. 2009. Fast Facts. http://nces.ed.gov/FastFacts/display.asp?id=16.

[17] Ibid.

[18] Rist, R. 1970. "Social Class and Teacher Expectations." *Harvard Educational Review,* 40(3): 411–451.

[19] Brown, C. G. 2007. "Beyond No Child Left Behind: Two New Reports Will Shake Up U.S. Education System." *Center for American Progress,* February 22. http://www.americanprogress.org/issues/2007/02/beyond_nclb.html/print.html. Accessed July 30, 2008.

[20] Thompson, T. G., and Barnes, R. E. 2007. *Beyond NCLB: Fulfilling the Promise to Our Nation's Children.* Washington, DC: The Aspen Institute. http://www.stand.org-/Document.Doc?id=821.

[21] Kozol, J. 2007. *The Shame of the Nation.* New York: Crown.

[22] Center for American Progress. 2007. *Leaders and Laggards: A State-by-State Report Card on Educational Effectiveness.* http://www.americanprogress.org/issues/2007/02/education_scorecard.html.

[23] See http://www.aspeninstitute.org/news/2009/08/19/commission-no-child-left-behind-expands-membership-launches-new-hearings-update-reco.

[24] Ibid.

[25] National Center for Education Statistics. 2009. *High School Dropout and Completion Rates in the United States 2007.* http://nces.ed.gov/pubsearch/pubsinfo.asp?pubid=2009064.

[26] U.S. Census Bureau. 2006. *Educational Attainment—People 18 Years Old and Over, by Total Money Earnings in 2005, Age, Race,*

Hispanic Origin, and Sex. Washington, DC: Author. Retrieved August 3, 2008, from http://pubdb3.census.gov/macro/032006/perinc/new04_001.htm.

[27] U.S. Department of Labor, Bureau of Labor Statistics. 2006. Retrieved August 3, 2008, from http://www.bls.gov/cps/cpsaat7.pdf.

[28] National Center for Education Statistics, 2009.

[29] Ibid.

[30] U.S. Department of Education, National Center for Education Statistics. 2004. *The Condition of Education 2004* (NCES 2004–077). Washington, DC: U.S. Government Printing Office.

[31] Curran, B. 2006. *Implementing Graduation Counts: State Progress to Date.* Washington, DC: National Governors Association. http://www.nga.org/Files/pdf/0608GRADPROGRESS.pdf.

[32] Ibid.

[33] Ibid.

[34] See, for instance, Cook, P. J., and Ludwig, J. 1998. "The Burden of Acting White: Do African Americans Disparage Academic Achievement?" In Jencks, C., and Phillips, M. (eds.), *The Black-White Test Score Gap.* New York: Brookings Institute, pp. 374–400.

[35] Whelan, D. L. 2007. "High-School Drop-Out Rates Are Higher Than Reported." *School Library Journal,* May 7. See also Alliance for Excellent Education. 2007. *Understanding High School Dropout Rates.* Washington, DC: Author.

[36] Belfield, L. H., Muenning, C. P., and Rouse, C. 2007. *The Costs and Benefits of an Excellent Education for All of America's Children.* New York: Columbia University Teachers College. http://www.cbcse.org/media/download_gallery/Leeds_Report_Final_Jan2007.pdf. Accessed July 31, 2008.

[37] Ibid.

[38] National Commission on Excellence in Education. 1983. *A Nation at Risk.* Available at http://www.ed.gov/pubs/NatAtRisk/index.html.

[39] U.S. Department of Education, Office of Adult and Vocational Education. http://www.ed.gov/about/offices/list/ovae/pi/AdultEd/readingabs2.html. Accessed August 4, 2008.

[40] http://slowdecline.wordpress.com/2007/10/06/the-united-states-of-america-and-the-functional-illiterates-who-contribute-to-its-decline/.

[41] Bauerlein, M. 2008. *The Dumbest Generation.* New York: Penguin.

[42] Ibid.

[43] Lin-Kelly, W., Dinkes, R., Cataldi, F., and Snyder, T. D. 2007. *Indicators of School Crime and Safety: 2007.* Washington, DC: Bureau of Justice Statistics. www.ojp.usdoj.gov/bjs/abstract/iscs07.htm.

[44] Ibid.

[45] Hawker, D. S. J., and Boulton, M. J. 2000. "Twenty Years' Research on Peer Victimization and Psychosocial Maladjustment: A Meta-analytic Review of Cross-sectional Studies." *The Journal of Child Psychology and Psychiatry and Allied Disciplines,* 41: 441–455.

[46] See Due, P., Holstein, B., Lynch, J., Diderichsen, F., Gabhain, S., Scheidt, P., Currie, C., and The Health Behaviour in School-Aged Children Bullying Working Group. 2005. "Bullying and Symptoms among School-Aged Children: International Comparative Cross Sectional Study in 28 Countries." *The European Journal of Public Health,* 1–5.

[47] Ibid.

[48] Kumpulainen, K. 1998. "Bullying and Psychiatric Symptoms among Elementary School-age Children." *Child Abuse and Neglect,* 22(7): 705–717; Fried, S., and Fried, P. 1996. *Bullies and Victims: Helping Your Child through the Schoolyard Battlefield.* New York: Evans.

[49] Beran, T. N., Hughes, G., and Lupart, J. 2008. "A Model of Achievement and Bullying: Analyses of the Canadian National Longitudinal Survey of Children and Youth Data." *Educational Research,* 50: 1, 25–39.

[50] Ibid.

[51] Ibid.

[52] Ibid.

[53] National Center for Education Statistics. 2009. *Indicators of School Crime and Safety 2009.* http://nces.ed.gov/programs/crimeindicators/crimeindicators2009/tables/table_11_2.asp. Accessed December 16, 2009.

[54] Ibid.

[55] National Conference of State Legislatures. 2008. *Educational Programs: School Bullying.* http://www.ncsl.org/programs/educ/bullyingoverview.htm. Accessed July 29, 2008.

[56] Ibid.

[57] See National School Safety Center Report http://www.schoolsafety.us/pubfiles/school_crime_and_violence_statistics.pdf.

[58] Stainbum, S. 2005. "Clothes-Minded." *Teacher Magazine,* 16(6): 14–15. See also Hill, S. 2007. "Should Public Schools Require Students to Wear Uniforms?" http://www.associatedcontent.com/article/235338/should_public_schools_require_students.html.

[59] Ibid.

[60] See Brunsma, D. 2004. *The School Reform Movement and What It Tells Us about American Education: A Symbolic Crusade.* Lanham, MD: Scarecrow Press; Snyder, S. 2004. "Uniform Approach to Conduct." *Philadelphia Inquirer,* September 24, pp. A1 + .

[61] The Civil Rights Project. 2000. *Opportunities Suspended: Devastating Consequences of Zero Tolerance and School Discipline.* Cambridge, MA: Harvard University.

[62] National Center for Education Statistics. 2007. Number and Percentage of Students Suspended from Public Elementary and Secondary Schools, by Sex, Race/Ethnicity, and State: 2004. Table 153. http://nces.ed.gov/programs/digest/d07/tables_2.asp. Accessed August 3, 2008.

[63] Skiba, R. J., Peterson, R. L., and Williams, T. 1997. "Office Referrals and Suspension: Disciplinary Intervention in Middle Schools." *Education and Treatment of Children,* 20: 295–315.

[64] National Center for Education Statistics, 2007.

[65] Morrison, G. M., and D'Incau, B. 1997. "The Web of Zero Tolerance: Characteristics of Students Who Are Recommended for Expulsion from School." *Education and Treatment of Children,* 20: 316–335.

[66] "Boys Suspended for Tiny G.I. Joe Guns; District's Zero-Tolerance Policy Bars Inch-Long Plastic Toy." *Seattle Times,* January 8, 1999.

[67] Skiba, R., and Peterson, R. 1999. "The Dark Side of Zero Tolerance: Can Punishment Lead to Safe Schools?" *Phi Delta Kappan,* 80(5): 372–381.

[68] Knowlton, B. 2000. "Zero-Tolerance Injustices Multiplying, Critics Say: A Backlash in the U.S." *International Herald Tribune,* February 14. http://www.iht.com/articles/2000/02/14/rlash.2.t.php. Accessed August 4, 2008.

[69] Nolle, K. L., Guerino, P., and Dinkes, R. 2007. *Crime, Violence, Discipline, and Safety in U.S. Public Schools: Findings from the School Survey on Crime and Safety: 2005–06* (NCES 2007-361). Washington, DC: National Center for Education Statistics, Institute of Education Sciences, U.S. Department of Education.

[70] Ibid.

[71] Ibid.

[72] See Weissman, M., Wolf, E., Sowards, K., Abate, C, Weinberg, P., and Marthia, C. 2005. *School Yard or Prison Yard: Improving Outcomes for Marginalized Youth.* Washington, DC: Center for Community Alternatives; Skiba, and Peterson, 1999; Western, B., Pettit, B., and Guetzkow, J. 2002. *Economic Progress in the Era of Mass Imprisonment. Collateral Damage: The Social Cost of Mass Incarceration.* Washington, DC: Center for Community Alternatives; Ekstrom, R. B. 1986. "Who Drops Out of High School and Why? Findings from a National Study." *Teachers College Record,* Spring, pp. 356–373.

[73] Weissman et al., 2005.

[74] Bowditch, C. 1993. "Getting Rid of Trouble-makers: High School Disciplinary Procedures and the Production of Dropouts." *Social Problems,* 40: 493–507; Fine, M. 1986. "Why Urban Adolescents Drop into and out of Public High School." *Teachers College Record,* Spring, pp. 393–409.

[75] Testimony of Donna Lieberman on Behalf of the New York Civil Liberties Union before the New York City Council Committees on Education and Civil Rights Regarding the Impact of Suspensions on Students' Education Rights, January 2008. http://www.nyclu.org/node/1602. Accessed August 4, 2008.

[76] Ibid.

[77] Patterson, G. R. 1992. "Developmental Changes in Antisocial Behavior." In Peters, R. D., McMahon, R. J., and Quinsey, V. L. (eds.),

Aggression and Violence throughout the Life Span, pp. 52–82. Newbury Park, CA: Sage.

[78] See, for instance, Rutherford, R. B., and Quinn, M. M. 1999. "History and Issues of Alternative Schools." *Education Digest,* 64: 47–51.

[79] Raywid, M. 1994. "Alternative Schools: The State of the Art." *Educational Leadership,* 52(1): 26–31.

[80] King, L., Silvey, M., Holliday, R., and Johnston, B. 1998. "Reinventing the Alternative School: From Juvenile Detention to Academic Alternative." *High School Journal,* 8(4): 229–232.

[81] Rutherford and Quinn, 1999.

[82] National Center for Education Statistics. 2001. *District Survey of Alternative Schools and Programs.* Washington, DC: Author.

[83] Ibid.

[84] Ibid.

[85] Cash, T. 2004. "Alternative Schooling." In Smink, J., and Schargel, F. P. (eds), *Helping Students Graduate: A Strategic Approach to Dropout Prevention.* Larchmont, NY: Eye on Education.

[86] Franklin, C., Streeter, C. L., Kim, J. S., and Tripodi, S. J. 2007. "The Effectiveness of a Solution-Focused, Public Alternative School for Dropout Prevention and Retrieval." *Children and Schools,* 29(3): 133–144.

[87] Ibid.

[88] See, for instance, Harris, W. 2009. "A Growing Expulsion Pipeline." *The Notebook,* 17(3). Available at http://www.thenotebook.org/winter-2009/091943/growing-expulsion-pipeline.

[89] See, for instance, Darden, E. C. 2006. *Search and Seizure, School Searches, Due Process and Public Schools.* Washington, DC: Center for Public Education.

[90] Ibid.

[91] Ibid.

[92] Ibid.

[93] Ibid.

[94] Ibid.

[95] *Goss v. Lopez,* 419 U.S. 565 (1975).

[96] See, for instance, http://www.law.umkc.edu/faculty/projects/ftrials/conlaw/dueprocessstudents.htm.

[97] Center for Effective Discipline. 2008. U.S. Corporal Punishment and Paddling Statistics by State and Race. Available at http://www.stophitting.com.

[98] *Ingraham v. Wright,* 439 U.S. 651 (1977).

[99] Center for Effective Discipline, 2008.

[100] *Tinker v. Des Moines Independent Community School District,* 393 U.S. 603 (1969).

[101] *Hazelwood School District v. Kuhlmeier,* 484 U.S. 260 (1988).

OBJECTIVES

After reading this chapter, you should be able to:

- Define the differences between gender and sex.

- Discuss the rise in female crime and delinquency.

- Differentiate the various feminist paradigms and explain how they relate to female delinquency.

- Interpret the ways in which the justice system has historically treated female offenders versus males.

- Explore female delinquency and its implications for public policy.

11

Gender and Delinquency

Increasingly, the public, policymakers, and even some researchers have begun adhering to the belief that women are becoming involved in more violent crimes. Consider the following case about Fiona:

Fiona's profile:

- is a sixteen-year-old student
- grew up in a rough neighborhood
- was sent to military school by her parents for the education and safety it would provide her

Fiona's situation since attending military school:

- Male cadets often ridicule her and question her physical and academic abilities.
- Officers are excessively critical during inspections and other military exercises.
- She has difficulty keeping up with her academic responsibilities and struggles in her classes.
- She feels socially, physically, and academically inadequate.
- She withdraws from interaction with others.

Current status:
One night, after a particularly difficult day, an officer threatens to have Fiona expelled from school for insubordination. In response, Fiona attacks the officer, punching and kicking him, causing him considerable embarrassment in front of his peers, but no real injuries.

The next day, the commandant of the school, who is in charge of all nonacademic matters on campus, reviews Fiona's case. After reviewing the charges and reports from witnesses, the commandant mentions that he has recently read a government report of an alarming trend of female violence, both on college campuses across the country and among teens in general. He thinks Fiona's situation is an example of this larger trend. In keeping with the school's honor code, which regulates all student conduct, he presses criminal charges against Fiona and begins expulsion proceedings against her.

What role does gender play in the discussion of delinquency?

When trying to determine the cause of an outburst by a young woman like Fiona, a school official might offer the following explanations:

- Fiona is emotionally unbalanced, and her violent episode is a manifestation of extreme trauma.

- Fiona's behavior is reflective of the increased use of violence by young women, particularly those from inner-city neighborhoods.

- Fiona's behavior would be perceived differently if she were a male; however, because of her gender, she is being singled out for discriminatory treatment.

- The military school's strict honor code requires Fiona to be expelled, and its zero-tolerance policy on violence means the police must be involved. The result is an apparent increase in crime on and off campus, particularly with regard to violence committed by females.

 THINK ABOUT IT Is this situation a result of Fiona suffering from a psychological disorder or is it the result of an unreasonable honor code? Are there societal/structural factors at work here?

It is easy to observe behavior like Fiona's and conclude that her situation fits into a larger trend of increased involvement of women in the adult criminal and juvenile justice systems. But doing so fails to take into account a larger set of circumstances. As we will see, the changing roles and perceptions of women in American society significantly impact reported rates of crime and the administration of justice.

As more and more women begin taking on traditionally male roles, it is reasonable to assume that they will engage in some of the same behaviors as men or will be perceived as being more like their male counterparts. The contexts for these behaviors range from the professional to the criminal.

While it is reasonable to conclude that violence among women is a problem, we need first to consider the possibility that criminal behavior by women might be a symptom of other problems or trends. We should also consider the means by which we explain female delinquency. Traditionally, researchers and experts have assumed that theories used to explain male delinquency can be applied to female delinquency as well. Though this assessment might be true, it is based on the assumption that the motivations for male behavior are the same as, or similar to, those for the behavior of women. Moreover, there may be very different reasons for why women commit crimes. As long as we continue to treat male and female offenders the same, we may not come around to discovering these reasons.

In 2007, around 27 percent of the U.S. population consisted of youths under the age of eighteen. Of these roughly 83 million youths, approximately half were females.[1] These numbers reinforce the importance of studies like the ones discussed in this chapter, which seek to explain the apparent rise in female delinquency. This chapter will also discuss the treatment of women in the juvenile justice system and explain some of the ways in which this treatment is similar to or different from that given men. In doing so, we will compare rates of criminal activity for each gender and examine the question of gender as it relates to delinquent behaviors like truancy and violence. Just as the changing role of women in society helps us to understand the dynamics of delinquency, it also helps to develop our understanding of the reasons for apparent increases in crime and violence perpetrated by women.

Definition of Sex and Gender

Sex refers to the biological characteristics that distinguish males and females. **Gender,** on the other hand, is a social distinction that refers to the behavioral, physical, and psychological traits typically attributed to one sex. While the concept of gender exists across cultures, the characteristics associated with masculinity and femininity vary from one group to another. With the labels *male* and *female* come expectations for our behavior as well as our physical traits and features. While we inherit our sex, we are socialized into our gender by the expectations and standards of the culture in which we live.[2] In turn, these labels often guide our behavior.

sex
The biological characteristics that distinguish males and females.

gender
A social distinction that refers to the behavioral, physical, and psychological traits typically attributed to one sex.

DIFFERENCES BETWEEN BOYS AND GIRLS

Boys and girls are biologically and sociologically different. But in what ways does socialization influence youths' perceptions of the world and of themselves? Long before children begin making decisions about their lives and who they will become, cultural influences shape their worldviews and set behavioral standards for them based on their gender. For example, being "a man" in our culture means possessing masculinity, a trait that encompasses physical strength, courage, and mental and physical toughness. Being "a man" in this sense also means not displaying weaknesses.

One implication of this standard is that men are supposed to have jobs that embrace masculinity. Consider the stigma associated with being a male nurse, an occupation that has traditionally been associated with women and femininity. Men who deviate from the standards set by their culture are not considered "real men," and can be mocked for their choices.[3] Many people think that there is something inherent about the differences between men and women, and to some extent this is true. However, we must be careful not to attribute too much of this difference to biology.

What are some additional examples of popular cultural stereotypes of masculinity? Can you think of examples that break this mold?

Physical Differences

Whatever one believes with regard to the differences between men and women, it is true that men and women have different physical abilities. On average, males are 10 percent taller, 20 percent heavier, and 30 percent stronger, especially in their upper bodies, than women. Women tend to live longer than men, by roughly five years; on average, women live 79.8 years, compared to 74.4 years for men.[4] It is popular to contend that women are smarter than men, but research shows that there are no overall differences in intelligence between the sexes. Together, these findings suggest that while there are biological differences between men and women, there is no evidence to suggest that one sex is naturally superior to the other.[5]

Boys and girls also differ in their developmental progress. Girls learn to speak earlier and faster, and are more adept overall in their verbal skills than boys. Cognitively, boys tend to develop their mechanical and dexterity skills faster than girls. Furthermore, cognitive differences increase in scope as boys and girls are socialized, making these natural inclinations some of the most significant markers of the differences between the two sexes.[6]

Specialized Differences

Children are taught from an early age about the differences between men and women. They also learn which behaviors are appropriate in masculine or feminine terms. Gender, therefore, also shapes our thoughts, feelings, and behaviors.

Besides eating disorders, depression, and low self-esteem, what other problems might girls experience as a result of negative self-image?

For example, girls between the ages of eight and eleven years generally view themselves as strong and confident, and are not afraid to say what they think. But as they enter adolescence, girls feel pressure to adopt the more traditional roles associated with women: they become concerned with how they are supposed to behave and with their physical and sexual attractiveness. These social pressures often impose negative self-images onto young girls and manifest in problems like eating disorders, depression, and low self-esteem.[7]

Some would argue that societal-based gender roles are the source of these feelings. For example, our culture defines males as ambitious and competitive, and as such we expect them to play team sports and to aspire to be leaders. By contrast, our culture defines women as emotional and deferential, and so we expect them to be supportive helpers of men and to be quick to show their feelings. Research shows that even parents send gender messages to their sons and daughters.[8] For example, several studies have shown that female children are held more tenderly and with greater affection, while male children are often treated more playfully and aggressively.[9] In general, our culture, our parents, and our peers send the message that women should be passive and emotional while men should be independent and action-oriented.[10]

In her book *The Beauty Myth,* Naomi Wolf argues that American culture serves to damage women's self-esteem by teaching them to measure themselves in terms of physical appearance. American standards for beauty are largely unrealistic, and the inability to meet those standards results in lowered self esteem for many women.[11] The same myth that designates standards for women's physical appearance, argues Wolf, also defines their roles in relationships with men. In short, women are evaluated based on physical appearance, and they gain status by using their physical traits to attract men. In social terms, such standards effectively reduce women to the status of objects.[12]

Carol Gilligan, a psychologist at Harvard University, has helped to clarify some of these issues by examining gender in terms of behavior. In trying to answer the question of whether girls are more naturally nurturing than boys, she argues that much of the difference can be explained through the process of socialization. For example, Gilligan argues that boys and girls use different strategies for making moral decisions (see Table 11-1).

Like Wolf, Gilligan also found that self-esteem issues can be discussed in relation to gender. She found that young girls are often much more self-confident than girls reaching, or going through, adolescence. Gilligan attributes this difference to the ways in which young women are socialized in American culture, as well as to the culture's lack of strong female role models.[13]

In the late 1990s, the American Psychological Association created a task force to address the issues faced by adolescent girls. In particular, they were interested in answering key questions relating to gender, self-esteem, relationships, sexuality, and public policy. The result of their research, as well as a review of the literature, was a book titled *Beyond*

TABLE 11-1 Making Moral Decisions

	Males	Females
Perspective	Justice	Care and responsibility
Description	Reliance on formal rules to develop sense of morality	Reliance on compassion and sense of responsibility for others
Example	Objection to stealing because it breaks the law	Sympathy for the offender by asking why someone would steal in the first place

According to Gilligan's argument, boys and girls will react differently to situations because of different viewpoints.

Appearance: A New Look at Adolescent Girls.[14] One issue of particular significance to this study is body image. Given the unrealistic standards set forth by the media's image of the "perfect body," many young women feel inadequate and express dissatisfaction with their own bodies. Studies have shown that these feelings contribute to a host of pathologies, such as eating disorders and depression.[15]

Another important dimension of female identity involves maintaining relationships. Girls experience a great deal of pressure to be popular among their peers, and this pressure can manifest in negative behaviors, including delinquency.[16] Thus, while relationships are essential to the overall well-being of young girls, and are important to the development of their identities, they are also one of the more stressful experiences of growing up. Some experts refer to the manifestations of this stress as "relational aggression," characterized by negative behaviors like spreading rumors, threatening or withdrawing from friendships, and reacting to power issues within a group.[17] Sometimes girls inflict forms of hazing and social isolation on their female peers, which can result in emotional trauma. It can also lead to delinquent acts as girls attempt to fit in and be part of the group.[18]

Organizations whose focus is the health and safety of young girls are responding to the growing need to teach girls to withstand some of the cultural pressures of adolescence and develop positive self-images. One example of such a program is described in the Theory and Practice box on page 284.

HISTORICAL OVERVIEW

Until relatively recently, women in the United States were not regarded as men's equals. In fact, for a long time, women were actually considered to be the property of men. Their status often limited them to the traditional roles of wife and mother. While these roles were, and still are, valued by society, they did not afford women the equal rights enjoyed by men. For example, women were not protected by the Nineteenth Amendment to the U.S. Constitution, which provides equal protection under the law.[19] Further, it was not until 1920 that American women were given the right to vote.[20]

Women's struggle for equal rights has spanned much of our nation's history and has laid the groundwork for the advancement of women to their present-day social status. Today, the continuous efforts and campaigns promoting the belief that males and females should be politically, socially, and economically equal are often referred to as **feminist movements.**[21] Generally, **feminism** is a belief or doctrine that advocates equality in the social, economic, and political treatment of women in society. Feminist scholars discuss these movements as having occurred in three waves[22] (see Figure 11-1).

The first wave of feminism occurred in the nineteenth and early twentieth centuries, and focused on women's legal rights. This wave occurred in response to the rise of modern industrial society, which saw an increase in economic and political opportunities for women, and inspired many to begin questioning their traditional status in society. This wave culminated in women winning the right to vote—a logical first step toward equality.

During the period following World War II, the U.S. economy experienced a boom. Both world wars had brought women into the workforce in large numbers, and as a result, inequities between the sexes became more apparent. Within the workplace, these inequities were measured in terms of pay, job security, benefits, and the overall treatment of employees. In general, women began demanding that society allow them to take on more important roles.[23]

feminist movements
Efforts and campaigns promoting the belief that males and females should be politically, socially, and economically equal.

feminism
A belief or doctrine that advocates equality in the social, economic, and political treatment of women in society.

Wave 1: 1900–1950	Wave 2: 1960–1970	Wave 3: 1980 on
Right to vote	Emerging Identities for Women	Holistic Role of Women

FIGURE 11-1 Feminist Movements
Have the issues for feminists changed as more equality has been granted?

THEORY AND PRACTICE WORKING TOGETHER

Friendly PEERsuasion

Traditional stereotypes about gender can trigger or exacerbate problems already associated with growing up. As we have discussed, these problems include low self-esteem, depression, anxiety, and the desire to fit in. Problems of delinquency can also be traced back to the pressures imposed by gender stereotypes, manifesting in behaviors such as substance abuse, aggressiveness toward peers, and early or self-destructive sexual activity.

A nationwide program called Friendly PEERsuasion has shown progress in helping young women face the problems so often associated with adolescence and growing up. Friendly PEERsuasion, offered by Girls Inc., a nonprofit organization dedicated to helping girls across the country to become role models for others, approaches these problems as peer issues, using the positive influence of young people to model healthy behavior.

In the first phase of the program, girls ages eleven through fourteen learn decision-making, assertiveness, and communication skills, including practicing how to walk away from situations in which they feel pressured to use alcohol or drugs. Through games, group discussions, and role-playing, girls learn about the short- and long-term effects of substance abuse, begin to recognize how media and peer

pressure influence drug use and poor decision-making, and practice better ways to manage stress. In the second phase of the program, the newly trained "PEERsuaders" plan substance-abuse prevention activities for groups of children ages six through ten. Looked up to as leaders, the older girls' commitment to staying drug- and alcohol-free is reinforced.

An independent evaluation showed that Friendly PEERsuasion helped to delay eleven- and twelve-year-old girls' use of harmful substances by giving them the skills to leave situations in which their peers were using drugs. Furthermore, the Office of Juvenile Justice and Delinquency Prevention (OJJDP) concluded that this program has made significant progress in reducing female delinquency.

THINK ABOUT IT Consider the correlation between low self-esteem and delinquent behaviors among young women. What are some examples of delinquent behaviors linked to low self-esteem? What other measures might a program like Friendly PEERsuasion take to counteract these behaviors?

As more women entered the workforce following World War II, inequities between men and women became more apparent. How might you account for the differential treatment of men and women in the workplace, then and now?

The second wave of the feminist movement peaked in the 1960s and 1970s, and focused on the emergence of a formal identity for women. This wave coincided with other movements, such as the Civil Rights Movement and anti–Vietnam War protests in the United States. The 1964 Civil Rights Act had recognized and guaranteed equal protection under the law for minorities. Feminist groups observed these movements and found inspiration in the experiences of minorities. The struggle of minorities to achieve basic civil rights had a profound effect on women and influenced their perspectives regarding their own rights. Borrowing techniques from the Civil Rights Movement, such as demonstrations, political lobbying, and awareness raising, women sought to make progress of the kind achieved by other groups who had historically fought their own oppression.[24]

In the 1970s, women's groups, like the National Organization for Women (NOW), sought to overturn laws that enforced discrimination in matters such as contracts, property rights, employment, and wages. Perhaps the greatest effort of this period was the attempt to pass the Equal Rights Amendment (ERA), a constitutional amendment that would have granted women equal protection under the law, and which had been denied in Congress since its proposal in 1923. While the ERA is yet to be made into law, feminists continue to use it to pressure legislators to address women's issues.[25]

The third wave of feminism began in the 1980s and continues today. Though it bears much resemblance to earlier feminist movements, third-wave feminism differs fundamentally in its approach. Many third-wave feminists choose to address issues of equal rights from *within* the political and legal establishments, rather than criticizing them from the outside as feminists had previously been known to do. This mostly younger generation of feminists also stresses the need to broaden the scope of feminism, emphasizing global networking, human rights, and a more holistic understanding of the role of all women in society.[26]

Conflicts within the feminist paradigm are most readily apparent in this third wave. Some experts and feminist scholars point out that much of the momentum gained by the second wave of feminism in the 1970s has been lost to a greater focus on individualism, whereas previously the focus of feminism was on the larger collective effort. In a 2002 conference at Barnard College in New York City, sponsored by the group Veteran Feminists of America, feminist scholars from around the country discussed the growing conflict between two generations of feminists, questioning whether women in their twenties and thirties appreciate what their historical counterparts have done.[27] At the same time, the conference focused on the lack of collective effort and the reduced political voice of women in society, both of which were emphasized by previous generations of feminists. In fact, many older feminists argue that their younger counterparts have a strong sense of entitlement to rights and privileges that were only obtained by the sacrifices made by previous generations. These older activists lament that the momentum of change has stalled as more women seek to address issues on an individual level rather than as part of a much larger, cooperative format.

With so much support for the values upheld by the Equal Rights Amendment, why do you think it remains to be ratified?

Other feminists tend to focus on how feminism has become a stigma. Kalpana Krishnamurthy, co-director of the Third Wave Foundation, a New York–based feminist organization, said that the reason for the conflict between newer and older generations of feminists might have to do with the greater freedom of choice now afforded to younger women. According to Krishnamurthy, third-wave feminists can choose to focus on a wider range of topics rather than limiting themselves to the central issues of the past, which often related to employment and abortion.[28]

Gender and Sex

How does a person's gender and socialization influence the decision to commit a delinquent act?

THINK ABOUT IT

Females and Delinquency

According to the Uniform Crime Reports (UCR) for 2008, girls under the age of eighteen represented approximately 19 percent of all arrests for females. UCR data also show a trend in the types of crime for which this age group tends to be arrested (see Table 11-2). As the table shows, girls are more likely to be arrested for status offenses, such as violating curfew, or underage drinking, than for any other type of crime, and at a higher rate than boys.

According to the UCR data, in 2008, nearly a quarter, or 24.7 percent, of arrests of females under the age of eighteen were related to status offenses. Larceny made up the next-largest category of arrest charges for females, accounting for about 20 percent of all arrests. Much of what constitutes larceny for women consists of shoplifting.[29] On the other hand, it has been shown that the police often prefer to handle certain kinds of female delinquency informally. What this means is that for certain types of delinquency, girls are given greater leniency, such as when they run away, as officers often understand that these girls are fleeing chaotic or abusive home environments. One reason for this difference when it comes to females might be an overarching concern for the well-being

TABLE 11-2 Arrests of Females by Type of Crime

Offense Charged	Total All Ages	Ages under 15	Ages under 18
Total	2,714,361	128,883	460,927
Total percent distribution*	100.0	4.7	17.0
Murder and non-negligent manslaughter	1,020	8	69
Forcible rape	208	23	45
Robbery	11,919	547	2,523
Aggravated assault	72,905	3,056	9,747
Burglary	35,109	1,945	6,863
Larceny-theft	463,508	30,641	116,330
Motor vehicle theft	11,408	683	2,646
Arson	1,617	308	552
Violent crime	86,052	3,634	12,384
Violent crime percent distribution*	100.0	4.2	14.4
Property crime	511,642	33,577	126,391
Property crime percent distribution*	100.0	6.6	24.7
Other assaults	269,736	21,327	59,135
Forgery and counterfeiting	25,425	57	504
Fraud	69,393	293	1,762
Embezzlement	7,177	9	203
Stolen property; buying, receiving, possessing	17,300	711	2,811
Vandalism	38,504	3,814	9,782
Weapons; carrying, possessing, etc.	10,511	1,112	2,767
Prostitution and commercialized vice	39,437	82	844
Sex offenses (except forcible rape and prostitution)	5,337	528	1,109
Drug abuse violations	242,414	4,142	21,002
Gambling	904	1	38
Offenses against the family and children	22,332	354	1,295
Driving under the influence	251,695	70	2,668
Liquor laws	128,132	3,952	34,049
Drunkenness	78,141	504	2,814
Disorderly conduct	139,315	16,744	44,722
Vagrancy	5,655	164	601
All other offenses (except traffic)	696,621	17,595	67,793
Suspicion	424	10	39
Curfew and loitering law violations	27,504	7,442	27,504
Runaways	40,710	12,761	40,710

Why do you think females are more likely to be arrested for minor offenses than boys?

*Because of rounding, the percentages may not add to 100.0.

of young women, who are at greater risk of victimization than their male peers.[30] But as we will learn later in this chapter, there are several reasons for this discrepancy, not all of which stem from a concern for the well-being of young women. For instance, a five-year trend analysis of official arrest data by the FBI showed consistent female involvement in the justice process—and in some cases, more so than males (see Figure 11-2).

According to the 2009 UCR, while juvenile arrests generally decreased, the proportion was greater in some areas for boys than for girls. In fact, arrests for some crimes, such as larceny, actually increased for females while they decreased for males—a 4.2 percent decrease for males, but a 6.1 percent increase for females. Other crimes, such as embezzlement, showed a general increase for both males and females, but a larger increase in arrests for females than males—9.2 percent for males, but 35.7 percent for females. In other cases, both males and females showed a decline in the percentage of arrests, but the decrease was smaller for females. One example is simple assault, which saw a decrease of 6.3 percent for males, but only 1.5 percent for females.[31]

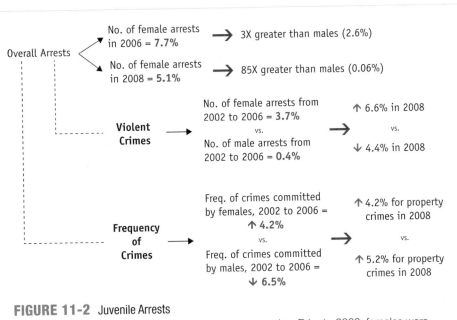

FIGURE 11-2 Juvenile Arrests
Data since 2006 show more arrests for females than males. Prior to 2006, females were arrested for more violent crimes than males, but recent data show a reversal trend. While more males are being arrested for property crimes than females, women continue to show a willingness to commit crime in large numbers.

While it may appear that the rates of female delinquency have increased, many questions remain as to whether this is an actual trend or is based on other factors. In 2007, the OJJDP created a study group made up of the country's leading experts on delinquency to examine the apparent rise in female delinquency. The report, *Violence by Teenage Girls: Trends and Context,* published in 2008, explored the issue in greater detail. The study group examined arrest statistics from the UCR and victimization data from the National Crime Victimization Survey (NCVS), as well as self-reported data from the Monitoring the Future study, a national survey of high school students conducted annually to report on drug use and other topics.

Data from the UCR showed an alarming trend. By 2006, females accounted for nearly 30 percent of all juvenile arrests, and female arrests for some offenses increased significantly. As Table 11-3 indicates, in some cases, arrests for females increased more than males over a ten-year period, but in other cases, decreases in arrests were lower than those for males. This can be interpreted as an actual increase for females—even though both groups witnessed decreases in the number of arrests, females decreased at a slower pace than males.[32]

The UCR statistics on juvenile arrests for assault point to certain conclusions about the seriousness of girls' use of violence. One of the reasons boys are more likely than girls to be charged with aggravated assault is that boys use weapons more frequently and physically inflict more injury on their victims. Although girls' rates of arrest for simple assault have increased over the past decade, their arrest rates for aggravated assault have not. Despite dramatic changes in the number and rate of arrests, the OJJDP study group concluded that it is unclear whether these trends signify a real change in girls' underlying violent behavior or reflect methodological changes in the way crimes are defined, prosecuted, or analyzed.

The OJJDP study group also examined data from the NCVS. Unlike UCR data, these data showed that ratios of simple assault and aggravated assault are stable. Additionally, the NCVS data showed

How might the appearance of a female delinquent affect the outcome of her case?

TABLE 11-3 Changes in Juvenile Arrests from 1999 to 2008[33]

Offense	Female	Male
Violent Crime Index	−10%	−8%
Robbery	38	24
Aggravated assault	−17	−22
Property Crime Index	1	−28
Burglary	−3	−16
Larceny	−4	−29
Motor vehicle theft	−52	−50
Vandalism	3	−9
Weapon possession	−1	−3
Drug abuse violations	−2	−8
Liquor law violations	−6	−29
DUI	−7	−34
Disorderly conduct	18	−5

It appears that the changes for females are more dramatic than for males. Is this due to recording practices, or is it a result of actual offending patterns?

that both boys' and girls' rates of assault have dropped significantly in recent years, in contrast to the UCR data that showed a decline for males only. This might indicate that the rates of arrests of females are a function of the attention paid to females by the police, and not of actual crimes taking place.[34]

Finally, the OJJDP study group examined self-reported data to assess whether a dramatic increase in female delinquency has occurred. Analyses of the Monitoring the Future data showed that assault rates among girls and boys were relatively unchanged between 1980 and 2003, with female assault levels consistently lower than male levels. In sum, the OJJDP study group concluded that the gender differences relating to crime are not as large as first indicated, nor do the data indicate a substantial increase in female assaults or other violent crimes.[35]

Other researchers examined data concerning the apparent increase in female delinquency and tried to use other measures, in addition to official crime statistics, to explain the increase. The findings showed similar patterns to those revealed in the OJJDP study.[36] Consistent with the OJJDP report, the Monitoring the Future study showed little change in female violence over the past twenty years. As demonstrated in Figure 11-3, between 1992 and 2003, the percentage of female juveniles who reported they had assaulted someone represented between 15 and 18 percent of all assaults by juveniles during this entire period.[37]

Similarly, the National Youth Risk Behavior Survey of high school youths showed a decrease in female fighting from 35 percent in 1991 to 25 percent in 2003.[38] This trend continued in 2007, when the percentage increased slightly to 26.5 percent.[39] Thus there

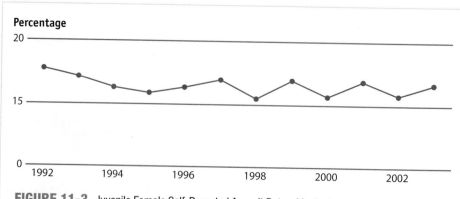

FIGURE 11-3 Juvenile Female Self-Reported Assault Rates, Monitoring the Future, 1992–2003

What factors might have contributed to the difference in assaults reported by law enforcement and self-reported assault rates?

Source: Analysis by J. Schwartz of *Monitoring the Future Survey* (1993–2004).

remain a number of questions about whether a crime wave among young women is in fact taking place.

INCREASE IN FEMALE CRIME

Women account for a smaller proportion of delinquent activities than men do, which might be interpreted to mean that they commit fewer crimes than men. However, another reason for the lower incidence of females in delinquency statistics is the differences in how they are treated within the juvenile justice system.

As we have seen already in this chapter, the way society perceives women in general, and female delinquents in particular, influences the outcome of criminal activity. One example of this kind of outcome occurs when police officers or judges are more inclined to handle minor crimes by females informally rather than process them through the juvenile justice system. Another instance in which the perception of female delinquents affects the outcome of their crimes can be seen in responses to statistics showing that females are becoming involved in criminal and delinquent activities more commonly associated with males.

In what ways might movies like *Lara Croft: Tomb Raider* and *Kill Bill* empower women viewers? Which of the feminist perspectives would most likely agree with this reading of these films? Which would tend to disagree?

Being Like Males

In July 2008, a fight broke out during a professional basketball game. For most basketball fans, this would not stand out as an unusual occurrence. NBA players are known to get into fights with other players, coaches, and, in rare instances, fans. In this instance, however, the fight occurred during a WNBA game, between female professional basketball players.

In trying to piece together an explanation for the events, commentators and other experts consistently referenced the fact that the WNBA is a competitive league and that fighting is symptomatic of the strong desire to win. Former NBA players who were interviewed by the media noted that players in the WNBA were similar in many ways to their male counterparts in the NBA. Some analysts even suggested that this might signal a trend in female athletes acting increasingly like male players.[40]

Consistent with strain theories, discussed in Chapter 4, some delinquency experts blame the increased arrest rates for girls on the breakdown of social institutions like the family, church, community, and school. They argue that girls are more likely to act out because the lines designating traditional gender roles for men and women have become blurred. Hollywood capitalized on this explanation, creating movies and television shows depicting women who revel in violence, such as *Charlie's Angels, Lara Croft: Tomb Raider,* and the *Kill Bill* movies.[41] One of the problems with this explanation is that it associates higher crime rates involving women with the values of the women's movement, which promotes independence, feelings of empowerment, and the equality of women and men.

Paternalism and Females

Not all experts attribute the increase in female delinquency to the rise of feminism, the increasingly blurred gender lines between men and women, or the perception that women are changing their response to blocked opportunities. Instead, some sociologists believe that the changes in crime statistics, and specifically those that indicate a rise in violent female offenses, are the result of different recording practices that no longer reflect the traditional paternalism of the juvenile justice system. Moreover, these changes may signify a change in approach on the part of the system: instead of handling female offenders differently by not formally charging or processing them, the system may be moving toward a more equal-handed approach.

Because some jurisdictions have reclassified simple assaults as violent crimes, the statistics of arrests for crimes like aggravated assault appear to be on the rise. Given what you know about the social pressures imposed on adolescent girls, how do you think this reclassification affects female delinquents in particular?

Still other research, such as that conducted by the OJJDP study group, contests the supposed increase in violence among girls. These experts blame policy changes, such as more aggressive policing of low-level crimes, as well as redefinitions of certain activities as crimes, for the apparent rise in female delinquency. In other words, they argue that these policy changes give only the appearance of an alarming trend, not the reality.

For instance, the OJJDP study group argues that police are more willing to arrest female offenders than they were in the past. Also, the criteria for arrest have changed in some jurisdictions. As a result, law enforcement agencies are using broader definitions of violence that include more minor incidents. Disorderly conduct, harassment, and resisting arrest are now often categorized as simple assaults.[42] Some jurisdictions are also classifying simple assaults as violent crimes or aggravated assaults in their crime statistics. This classification is problematic in that these behaviors do not fit the definition of aggravated assault, which typically involves the use of a weapon or some behavior that can cause serious bodily injury. In short, changes in recording and arrest practices have given the impression of a dramatic increase in violent female offenders.[43]

As we saw in Chapter 3 on status offenses, bootstrapping also occurs, whereby youths are held in detention and adjudicated as delinquents for acts that should not be considered criminal. The reasons for this practice, as we have seen, often involve attempts to prevent recidivism, as well as to get youths to comply with court orders. Faced with so many cases of noncompliance, juvenile court judges have increasingly elevated the status of youths in order to make them eligible for more severe sanctions. Consequently, when youths are reclassified and adjudicated as delinquents, crime rates will appear to be on the rise.[44]

Schools are also more likely to refer misconduct to the police for intervention. As was discussed in Chapter 10, many school districts are employing zero-tolerance policies, which require officials to report even minor violations to the police. In general, this practice incites significant fears of crime on campus and, in particular, a fear of school shootings.[45] In fact, many experts argue that this trend bears some resemblance to the myth of the "super predator" class of delinquents discussed in Chapter 1. Misinformation can easily create a climate of fear, and overly punitive reactions to that fear are often reflected in policy.[46] These experts would likely argue that it is critical to carefully examine the data reflecting yearly increases in female delinquency. Finally, these data should be analyzed over time, so as not to incite fear and lead to drastic policy change when results are misconstrued.

FIONA'S CASE

Gender and Delinquency

Recall Fiona's situation:

- is a sixteen-year-old student
- attends a predominantly male military school
- is treated differently than her male peers
- is withdrawn and unhappy
- lashes out at an officer after being threatened with expulsion

Consider Fiona's behavior within the context of our larger discussion of female delinquency. Traditionally, it has been thought that boys are more aggressive than girls, and so tend to solve conflict through physical action. However, some experts see individual acts of female violence as part of a growing trend. Others believe that the issue of female delinquency is more complicated, that it involves many more factors than can be accounted for by gender alone.

THINK ABOUT IT

How might you explain the reasons for Fiona's actions and her expulsion? In what ways might she be treated differently if she were a male cadet?

The Rise of Female Delinquency

Consider the ways in which women are treated differently within the juvenile justice system. In particular, how does the perception of young women affect the ways in which they are treated in this system? What effects do these biases have on the larger problem of female delinquency?

THINK ABOUT IT

Theories of Female Delinquency

Many of the theories discussed in previous chapters use male behavior as a model; likewise, many studies use males as samples for their findings. Here we will weigh the relevance of these theories to the study of female delinquency.

EARLY BIOLOGICAL AND PSYCHOLOGICAL EXPLANATIONS

In 1903, using a biological perspective, Cesare Lombroso offered one of the earliest explanations of crime and delinquency. His book *The Female Offender* provided new insight into the nature of female criminality. Lombroso argued that female offenders were a throwback to an evolutionary type of human, that they were even more primitive and less intelligent than men. He asserted that most women were born with innate intellectual limitations that predisposed them to live dull and conforming lives. Moreover, according to Lombroso, female offenders inherited some male characteristics, such as excessive body hair, larger heads, and a genetic predisposition toward violence.[47] Women were said to be particularly vicious, even more so than male criminals. Lombroso also concluded that women were incapable of feeling pain, and this meant that they lacked a sense of moral and social responsibility for hurting others. One might argue that in his attempt to explain female criminal behavior, Lombroso effectively characterized women as the first true sociopaths.[48]

In 1923, in *The Unadjusted Girl,* W. I. Thomas wrote about female delinquency in terms of prostitution, borrowing heavily from a physiological explanation of female offending. Thomas argued that female delinquency was a normal response to a set of conditions women might face. Women who engaged in delinquency, he said, were driven by three main ambitions: an attraction to new experiences and adventure, the need for stability and security in their lives, and the desire for recognition. As it specifically relates to his study, Thomas believed that women engaged in prostitution and other forms of delinquency based on their need for love and for the recognition it provided them.[49]

In 1950, Otto Pollak published *The Criminality of Women,* in which he argued that women were often involved in what he described as "hidden" crimes, meaning that they frequently went unnoticed by the public. These crimes, he thought, were largely related to the types of jobs women held, since their deviant activity could be concealed in the performance of their everyday activities as maids, nurses, and teachers. Pollak also argued that women were inherently deceitful and devious, and so were also able to capitalize on men's stereotypical perceptions of them.[50]

It is fair to say that the early history of research on the psychology of female delinquency was seriously flawed. For the most part, this research was conducted under the assumption that women were weak, deceitful, narcissistic, and dependent.

SOCIOLOGICAL EXPLANATIONS

Sociological theories of female delinquency have suffered from several limitations. As previously mentioned, the data informing these theories have focused almost exclusively on males. This has led to the assumption that men and women share the same motivations for engaging in certain behaviors. Many criminologists argue that the structural conditions that affect men are just as compelling when used to explain female delinquency.[51] While these conditions may apply in some cases, however, understanding female delinquency calls for a more nuanced approach.[52]

Most scholars today argue that the traditional theories used to explain delinquency are insufficient to explain female delinquency.[53] Others have criticized the theoretical explanations of crime and delinquency for overlooking women entirely. At the same time, some scholars argue that these theories may actually have more applicability to female delinquency than ever before. In her classic book *Sisters in Crime* (1975), Freda Adler argued that a rise in female criminality, for both adults and juveniles, was linked to the opportunity structure that existed in American society. By her account, female crime occurred for many of the same reasons that strain theorists used to explain male criminality.[54]

Adler cited changes in crime statistics that reflected a shift from females engaging in minor crimes, such as running away, incorrigibility, and promiscuity, to more conventional and violent crimes. She argued that this shift was the result of women beginning to think and act more like men, meaning they had become more aggressive and competitive. Adler therefore agreed with the argument that the Women's Liberation Movement was in part responsible for the rise in female crime.[55]

However, critics of Adler's theory have pointed out that most female offenders are poor, unemployed minorities, who are largely uneducated. For them, the decision to commit crime has less to do with ideology—trying to be more like men and gain equal footing in society—and more to do with meeting their needs for survival. Other critics have pointed out that the Women's Liberation Movement had little actual impact on female criminality since the trend of female crime has been gradual and has not occurred as dramatically as Adler suggests.[56]

FIONA'S CASE

Acting like a Boy?

Recall Fiona's school situation:

- is struggling to fit in a mostly male military school
- is withdrawn, behavior that is misunderstood by fellow cadets and officers
- lashed out when threatened with expulsion

Consider the factors contributing to Fiona's situation. Some experts suggest that females are increasingly acting like males, which would explain the apparent rise in female delinquency. In fact, it would seem that this trend informed the commandant's decision to expel Fiona for her behavior. But individual motivations for committing crimes are often more complicated than such theories can account for. It is unlikely that Fiona's actions can be explained so simply.

 THINK ABOUT IT Consider the ways in which female offenders, historically, have been treated differently than male offenders. How might Fiona's sex influence the way she is treated by her peers and superiors? Do you think her violent behavior reflects a larger trend in female delinquency?

FEMINIST PERSPECTIVES

Gender is one of the strongest variables in measuring delinquency. To apply feminist doctrine to the topic of female delinquency represents an attempt to understand how gender influences criminal behavior, as well as why the criminal justice system responds the way it does. When biological, psychological, and sociological explanations fail to account for female delinquency, some scholars have turned to feminist perspectives for a means of understanding.

As we have noted, women tend to receive differential treatment within the criminal justice system. Feminist explanations can help account for the ways in which this treatment affects delinquency rates. For instance, feminist scholars recognize that race and poverty, in addition to gender, are interrelated. All three must therefore be considered when attempting to understand crime. Not all feminist scholars agree on the ways in which traditional stereotypes of gender, race, and poverty affect female delinquency and the system's response to it.[57] However, most feminist perspectives support five general principles:

1. **Equality.** Feminist ideology is critical of the status quo and tries to change the perception and treatment of women.

2. **Human choice.** Feminists maintain that cultural notions of gender limit individuals' choices. For instance, it is traditionally presumed that certain traits belong to the female domain—such as nurturing and cooperation—while traits like rationality and competition belong to the male domain. These preconceptions, reinforced by culture, influence the personal and professional decisions of men and women alike. Feminists, on the other hand, believe that people, regardless of their gender, should feel free to make choices based on the things that matter most to them.

3. **Elimination of gender-based stratification.** Feminists are opposed to laws that limit economic, political, and social opportunities for women. While the Equal Rights Amendment was defeated in the 1970s in Congress, this legislation has given momentum to other women's rights efforts.

4. **Elimination of sexual violence.** Many feminists argue that in our male-dominated society women are generally seen as sexual objects. They would further argue that violence against women, such as domestic violence, rape, sexual harassment, and pornography, are symptoms of this perception of women.

5. **Sexual freedom.** Feminists support the idea of women having control over their own bodies, particularly as this control relates to reproduction. The decision whether to bear children or to terminate a pregnancy, for instance, is referred to by many feminists as "a woman's right to choose." One aspect of sexual freedom on which some feminists disagree, however, is prostitution. While feminists defend a woman's right to choose what to do with her body, many argue that prostitution is not a choice. Instead, these feminists believe that women turn to prostitution in response to economic hardship and as a means of survival in a society that otherwise limits opportunities for women.[58] The topic of sexual freedom as it relates to prostitution and pornography is a contentious one in feminist circles, and one that has gathered more nuanced opinions in feminism's third wave.

Generally, there are five perspectives or versions of feminist theory: liberal feminism, phenomenological feminism, socialist feminism, Marxist feminism, and radical feminism. As demonstrated by the general principles of feminism outlined above, all of these perspectives share certain core beliefs, while differing in terms of degree and focus.

Liberal Feminism

This perspective focuses on equal opportunities for women and the freedoms that allow women to make decisions about their lives. Liberal feminists do not believe that the political system is inherently biased or that discrimination against women is institutionalized or systematic. They instead believe in the idea of equality and in the promise that men and women can work together cooperatively. By their standards, policies such as affirmative action and fair labor laws, as they apply to women, demonstrate that it is possible for men and women to find common ground when it comes to equal treatment and protection under the law. The ideas that Adler articulated in *Sisters in Crime,* when she argued that adolescent females are imitating males in order to achieve similar economic and social goals, could be described as adhering to a liberal feminist agenda.[59]

Phenomenological Feminism

When it comes to female delinquency, phenomenological feminism focuses on how women and girls are treated by the system. Phenomenological feminists examine the issues of discriminatory treatment of female delinquents by the juvenile justice system and how some laws penalize female offenders. For instance, as we saw in Chapter 3 on status offenders, females are much more likely to run away than males, but they are also much more likely to be arrested and adjudicated for that offense. The reasons for this may stem from a chivalrous approach to treating female offenders. That is, officials may be attempting to protect females either by dealing with criminal offenses informally, thus keeping them out of the system, or by punishing them more severely, so that they recognize the error of their ways and begin to engage in more appropriate conduct.[60]

Socialist Feminism

Given how class and gender are interrelated, socialist feminists argue that it makes no sense to think of only one of these variables at a time. Looking at the larger picture, socialist feminists suggest that crime results from the lack of access to political power for women. Female delinquency occurs because women are more likely to be poor, and so lack the same professional and educational opportunities as men. Lacking social opportunities often means lacking political influence as well. As a result, socialist feminists believe that women's needs and concerns are often ignored by policymakers and government officials.[61]

Marxist Feminism

Drawing heavily from the theories of Karl Marx, this version of feminist theory contends that the control of private property in the early days of capitalism set in motion a series of events whereby men controlled the social institutions of society. Because most of the economic, political, and social power belonged to men, women were left without sufficient opportunities to achieve societal success. As with the *lumpenproletariat* in Marx's theory—the segment of society that consisted of vagrants, criminals, and other people without resources—crime for women became one of the only means by which economic survival was possible, largely because men controlled the means of production and excluded women from benefiting from a capitalistic system. Thus, Marxist feminists explain female involvement in economic crimes, such as shoplifting and prostitution, as the symptom of a society that systematically discriminates against women.[62]

Radical Feminism

Radical feminists view the control of society by males to be the source of all social inequality. According to this perspective, a **patriarchal society,** or one in which males dominate every aspect of economic, social, and political life, has resulted in women's oppression throughout history. Masculine control of society has also resulted in the objectification of women, with women's sexuality valued above all. As a result, the oppression of women is more widespread and has become internalized in the attitudes, values, and beliefs of American culture. Radical feminists are often hypervigilant and sensitive to women's oppression and men's domination of women. They also contend that eradicating this type of discrimination is exceptionally difficult and requires women to maintain a heightened sensitivity to abuse.[63]

Meda Chesney-Lind applies a radical feminist perspective to gain insight into female delinquency. She argues the following:

- Girls are frequently the victims of violence and sexual abuse, often by male relatives. However, the way parents, the criminal justice system, and even the victims themselves interpret the events surrounding their victimization is colored by the second-class status of women in our society.

- Perpetrators of physical and sexual abuse of young females often use the law and the criminal justice process to keep their daughters at home and vulnerable.

- Girls often run away from abusive homes, largely due to sexual abuse and neglect.

- While on the streets, young females are forced to engage in petty crimes such as shoplifting, panhandling, or even prostitution, in part because they cannot declare their emancipated status (until a certain age) and because they fear being caught and returned home.

- Research suggests that prostitutes and incarcerated female offenders have a history of sexual and physical abuse. The reasons for this stem from the fact that parents, and in particular fathers, are in control of their minor daughters, even when they are victimizing them.[64]

patriarchal society
A situation in which males dominate every aspect of economic, social, and political life.

Feminist Principles and Perspectives

Recall the five general principles of feminism, and consider how these principles unify the feminist cause. Now consider some of the major issues on which feminists disagree. Why do you think some feminists are uneasy about the decision of women to engage in prostitution? Which feminist perspectives would be most likely to embrace a woman's decision to engage in prostitution? Which would most likely oppose this decision, and why?

Gender and the Juvenile Justice System

Studies have consistently demonstrated a pattern of differential treatment of females, whether adult or juvenile, within the criminal justice system.[65] Early studies found that police officers, juvenile justice officials, and judges all practiced a sexual double standard. For some offenses, female offenders were more likely than their male counterparts, who committed the same offenses, to be petitioned to court and to be detained prior to and after adjudication hearings. At the same time, however, police were less likely to arrest females suspected of other crimes. Furthermore, if they were arrested, they were less likely than males to be formally charged with a criminal offense, and if they were charged, they were less likely than males to be incarcerated for their crimes.[66]

One explanation for this treatment has already been discussed in this chapter: girls are perceived by officials as weaker, more helpless, and less threatening than boys. Instead of seeing females as "real" offenders, officials often attempt to minimize the impact of the justice process by giving them lighter sentences. This tendency is sometimes referred to as the **chivalry hypothesis.** The other tendency, the obverse of chivalry, is the **evil-woman hypothesis,** which applies to women who are more likely to look, think, and act like male offenders. These individuals are likely to be treated more harshly by the justice system and not be granted the same consideration by police officers, judges, and other officials.[67]

chivalry hypothesis
The perception that girls are weaker, more helpless, and less threatening than boys, and so are not seen as "real" offenders and are given lighter sentences.

evil-woman hypothesis
The tendency of police officers and criminal justice officials to give harsher treatment to women viewed as more likely to look, think, and act like male offenders.

FIONA'S CASE

Conclusions

Recall Fiona's background:

- grew up in rough neighborhood
- was sent to military school, where she was treated unfairly
- responded to isolation and mistreatment with violence

Consider the precipitating factors leading up to Fiona's violent outburst. Fiona's behavior may have been out of line, but it would be unfair to judge her case without considering her background and the environment in which the violence took place. Moreover, the decision to expel Fiona was based, in part, on a misconception of rates of violence among women.

As we saw in Chapter 10 on schools and delinquency, fear of a supposed epidemic often leads to extreme reactions, often having little impact on the problem but having serious consequences for offenders. How do you think the school's zero-tolerance policy impacted the decision to expel Fiona? How does the outcome of Fiona's case help to shape preconceptions of female delinquency more generally?

Even when police officers decide not to handle encounters with females informally, if offenders go to court, they are more likely to be released to their parents than boys (assuming a safe home environment). Girls who appear to be sexually promiscuous are more likely to be detained than boys. Even if the case goes to the adjudication stage, there is a wealth of evidence to suggest that girls are treated more leniently by judges than boys—girls are more likely to get probation for a given offense, while boys are more likely to be detained for the same crime.[68]

While gender is a significant factor in the processing of cases, the overriding consideration is whether the offender appears and acts in a stereotypical manner. As it relates to race, white females are more likely to receive leniency in their punishment than minority females.[69] A review of the existing literature has found that almost two-thirds of the studies examined demonstrate that the racial and ethnic status of youths affected decision-making in the juvenile justice system.[70]

Female Delinquency and Public Policy

As girls and young women have encountered the juvenile justice system—as some believe, in increasing numbers—the system and its policies have had to undergo some adjustments. As we have seen in this chapter, not all of these changes have been made with regard to the well-being of female juvenile delinquents. At the same time, individuals and organizations have made great strides in creating policies that see to the social, psychological, and physical needs of girls and young women. As discussed earlier in this chapter, Girls Inc. is one example of an organization whose programs have had a positive effect on public policy. Another notable example is the Girl Scouts of America, which, since 1912, has made concerted efforts to positively affect the development and socialization of young women—from character-building, to teaching skills, to empowerment.

Girl Scouts Beyond Bars is a program that attempts to keep families intact to ensure interaction between parents and daughters, even under the extraordinary circumstance of incarceration. Created in 1992 through a partnership with the National Institute of Justice, this program now serves approximately 800 girls age five to seventeen in seventeen states. One of the Girl Scouts' many programs that make girls' social development a top priority, Girl Scouts Beyond Bars provides girls with an opportunity to visit their incarcerated mothers weekly or monthly, and participate in the following activities:

- Participants attend mother-daughter Girl Scout troop meetings.
- Incarcerated mothers lead troop meetings and develop skills in leadership, conflict resolution, and parenting, all of which are critical to success in returning to family life and employment after their release.
- Girls and their mothers have facilitated discussions about family life, violence, and drug abuse prevention.
- In addition to these weekly or monthly meetings, daughters of incarcerated women meet weekly with their troops, to encourage a sense of continuity between visits.

Another program, Girl Scouting in Detention Centers, targets female delinquents who have been adjudicated, are wards of the court, or are court-referred. This program is often court-mandated for teens. It provides them with opportunities to be resocialized and to learn what it means to be a productive citizen. The program also offers life-skills programs that foster independence and healthy lifestyles. This program serves over 10,000 girls age twelve to seventeen living in detention facilities in twenty states. Girl Scouts Beyond Bars and Girl Scouting in Detention Centers have been successful in carrying out the missions of the Girl Scouts organization. Moreover, the OJJDP has identified both as model programs with demonstrated track records of success.

THE BIG PICTURE

Conclusions on Female Delinquency

- Explain the double standard that exists in the treatment of female delinquents. Why do you think this double standard exists?
- How would you explain the differences in behavior between males and females? Do you subscribe to biological explanations or socialization theories?
- Have rates of female delinquency increased, or might the data reflect a redefinition of certain crimes and aggressive enforcement practices?
- Which of the five feminist perspectives are most appealing to you, and why?

Key Terms

gender

sex

feminist movements

feminist

National Organization for Women

masculine

feminine

liberal feminism

phenomenological feminism

socialist feminism

Marxist feminism

radical feminism

patriarchal society

chivalry hypothesis

evil-woman hypothesis

Make the Call ▶ Female Delinquency

Review the scenario below and decide how you would approach this case.

YOUR ROLE: consultant to the mayor of a town

DETAILS OF THE CASE

- The mayor of a small town with low crime has recently noticed an increase in the number of females arrested, primarily for assault.
- The police chief also noticed an increase in female crime, for delinquents in particular. Moreover, juvenile court personnel report an increase in the number of females being processed and detained for criminal activity.
- The mayor, who must decide how to allocate resources to address social problems, has hired you as a consultant to examine the delinquency problem in this town. You are required to present to her an overall assessment of female delinquency, as well as to make recommendations based on your analysis.

WHAT IS YOUR ASSESSMENT?

Recall what you have learned in this chapter and the situation as presented above. Provide an assessment to the mayor and offer recommendations.

Consider:

- Is the mayor convinced there is a problem and so is looking for a solution? Or is she still in the fact-finding stage of assessing the problem?
- What data are being consulted by criminal justice officials regarding a possible female delinquency crime wave in this town?
- Will you try to convince the mayor to look at the problem comprehensively, or will you simply give her the recommendations she is looking for?

Apply Theory to Reality ▶ Unequal Punishment

The *Wall Street Journal* recently noted a correlation between the increasing numbers of women in the professional labor force and the increased tendency for women to engage in crimes like embezzlement. Moreover, women engaging in fraudulent behaviors are not sentenced to prison with the frequency or duration of men convicted of the same crimes. Use one of the theories discussed in an earlier chapter to explain this unequal punishment. Likewise, use this theory to explain the trend of increased frequency of embezzlement by females.

Your Community ▶ Female Delinquency

In addition to the information you glean from your readings, class lectures, and discussions, it is important to roll up your sleeves and immerse yourself in a topic as a researcher who gains an understanding of the problem by observing or experiencing it firsthand. Through such methods, you gain a much greater appreciation of the magnitude and scope of the problem than if you only engaged in "armchair theorizing."

■ Schedule a visit to an elementary, junior high, or high school.

■ Observe the way girls learn and interact with others compared to boys. What examples can you point to that indicate a difference? Who are the leaders in the classroom? On what subjects do girls seem to excel? Which ones do they struggle with?

■ After making your observations, schedule an interview with teachers, and ask them about the value of single-sex education, as well as how they teach students based on gender. If possible, you should also consider interviewing principals, superintendents, and educational experts on the differences between learning styles of males and females.

■ After collecting your data and drawing from the relevant literature, prepare a report highlighting your observations. Consider how the issues of gender differences in the classroom relate to female delinquency.

Notes

[1] See *The World Factbook*. 2008. https://www.cia.gov/library/publications/the-world-factbook/.

[2] Ibid.

[3] See Savran, D. 1998. *Taking It like a Man: White Masculinity, Masochism, and Contemporary American Culture*. Princeton, NJ: Princeton University Press. See also Kimmel, M. 1997. *Manhood in America: A Cultural History*. New York: Free Press.

[4] See U.S. Department of Health and Human Services, Health Resources and Services Administration. 2008. "Life Expectancy." *Women's Health 2008*. Available at http://mchb.hrsa.gov/whusa08-/hstat/hi/pages/207le.html.

[5] See, for instance, Tavaris, C., and Wade, C. 2001. *Psychology in Perspective*, 3rd ed. Upper Saddle River, NJ: Prentice-Hall. See also Ehrenreich, B. 1999. "The Real Truth about the Female Body." *Time*, 153(9), pp. 56–65.

[6] See, for instance, Halpern, D., and LaMay, M. 2000. "The Smarter Sex: A Critical Review of Sex Differences in Intelligence." *Educational Psychology Review*, 12: 229–246.

[7] See, for instance, Jackson, T., and Hong, C. 2007. "Sociocultural Predictors of Physical Appearance Concerns among Adolescent Girls and Young Women from China." *Sex Roles*, 58(5–6): 402–411. See also Wolfe, W. L., and Maisto, S. A. 2000. "The Relationship between Eating Disorders and Substance Abuse." *Clinical Psychological Review*, 20(5): 617–631; Reel, J., Soohoo, S., Franklin Summerhays, J., and Gill, D. 2008. "Age before Beauty: An Exploration of Body Image in African American and Caucasian Adult Women." *Journal of Gender Studies*, 17(4): 321–330.

[8] See Lippa, R. A. 2005. *Gender, Nature and Nurture*. New York: Routledge. See also Freeman, N. H. 2007. "Preschoolers Perceptions of Gender Appropriate Toys and Their Parents' Beliefs about Genderized Behaviors, Miscommunication: Mixed Messages or Hidden Truths?" *Early Childhood Education Journal*, 34(5): 357–366.

[9] See, for instance, Coon, D., and Mitterer, J. O. 2008. *Psychology: Modules for Active Learning*, 11th ed. Belmont, CA: Cengage. See also Henslin, 2003.

[10] Henslin, 2003.

[11] See, for instance, Dunham, M. G. 2002. *The Lolita Effect: Why the Media Socialize Young Girls*. New York: Overlook Press. See also Greenfield, L., and Brumberg, J. J. 2002. *Girl Culture*. San Francisco: Chronicle Books; Maine, M., and Kelly, J. 2005. *The Body Myth*. New York: John Wiley.

[12] Wolf, N. 1990. *The Beauty Myth: How Images of Beauty Are Used Against Women*. New York: Morrow.

[13] Gilligan, C. 1990. *Making Connectiions: The Relational Worlds of Adolescent Girls at Emma Willard School*. Cambridge, MA: Harvard University Press.

[14] Johnson, N. G., Roberts, M. C., and Worell, J. (eds.). 1999. *Beyond Appearance: A New Look at Adolescent Girls*. Washington, DC: American Psychological Association.

[15] Ibid.

[16] See, for instance, Greenfield and Brumberg, 2002; Maine and Kelly, 2005.

[17] Ibid.

[18] Dunham, 2002.

[19] See Kraditor, A. S. 1981. *The Ideas of the Women's Suffrage Movement, 1890–1920*. New York: Norton.

[20] Muraskin, Roslyn. 2007. "Ain't I a Woman?" In Muraskin, R. (ed.), *It's a Crime: Women and Justice*, pp. 2–12. Upper Saddle River, NJ: Prentice-Hall.

[21] See, for instance, Flexner, E. 1976. *Century of Struggle: The Women's Rights Movement in the U.S.* Cambridge, MA: Harvard University Press.

[22] See, for instance, Wandersee, W. D. 1988. *On the Move: American Women in the 1970s*. New York: Twayne.

[23] Kraditor, 1981; Flexner, 1976. For a good discussion of the history of the feminist movement, see http://www.womensenews.org/article.cfm/dyn/aid/920/context/cover. Accessed August 5, 2008.

[24] Ibid.

[25] Wandersee, 1988.

[26] Ibid.

[27] Friedlin, J. 2002. "Second and Third Wave Feminists Clash over Future." *We News*, May 26.

[28] Ibid.

[29] Ibid.

[30] See Puzzanchera, C. 2008. *Juvenile Arrests 2007*. Washington, DC: Office of Juvenile Justice and Delinquency Prevention. Available at http://www.ncjrs.gov/pdffiles1/ojjdp/225344.pdft/.

[31] Ibid. See also U.S. Department of Justice, Federal Bureau of Investigation. 2009. *Crime in the United States 2008*. Table 35. Available at http://www.fbi.gov/cius2008/data/table_35.html.

[32] Adams, B., and Puzzanchera, C. 2007. *Juvenile Justice System: A National Snapshot*. Pittsburgh: National Center for Juvenile Justice.

[33] https://www.ncjrs.gov/pdffiles1/ojjdp/228479.pdf.

[34] Zahn, M. A., Brumbaugh, S., Steffensmeier, D., Feld, B. C., Morash, M., Chesney-Lind, M., Miller, J., Payne, A. A., Gottfredson, D. C., and Kruttschnitt, C. 2008. *Violence by Teenage Girls: Trends and Context.* Washington, DC: Office of Juvenile Justice and Delinquency Prevention, p. 10.

[35] Ibid, p. 10.

[36] See, for instance, Centers for Disease Control, National Center for Chronic Disease Prevention and Health Promotion. 2007. *Youth Risk Behavior Surveillance System, Sex Subgroups Fact Sheet.* Atlanta. http://www.cdc.gov/HealthyYouth/yrbs/index.htm. Accessed August 6, 2008.

[37] Ibid.

[38] Ibid.

[39] Ibid.

[40] "WNBA Fight Leads to Four Ejections." http://msn.foxsports.com/wnba/story/8368564/WNBA-fight-leads-to-four-ejections#. Accessed September 6, 2008.

[41] See, for instance, Chesney-Lind, M., and Pasko, L. 2004. *The Female Offender: Girls, Women and Crime.* Thousand Oaks, CA: Sage.

[42] See Schwartz, J., Steffensmeier, D. J., and Feldmeyer, B. 2009. "Assessing Trends in Women's Violence via Data Triangulation: Arrests, Convictions, Incarceration and Victim Reports." *Social Problems,* 56(3): 494–525. See also Steffensmeier, D. J., Schwartz, J., Zhong, H., and Ackerman, J. 2005. "An Assessment of Recent Trends in Girls Violence Using Diverse Longitudinal Sources: Is the Gender Gap Closing?" *Criminology,* 43(2): 355–405.

[43] Ibid.

[44] See McNamara, R. H. 2008. *The Lost Population.* Durham, NC: Carolina Academic Press.

[45] See, for instance, Morrison, G. M., and D'Incau, B. 1997. "The Web of Zero Tolerance: Characteristics of Students Who Are Recommended for Expulsion from School." *Education and Treatment of Children,* 20: 316–335; Skiba, R., and Peterson, R. 1999. "The Dark Side of Zero Tolerance: Can Punishment Lead to Safe Schools?" *Phi Delta Kappan,* 80(5): 372–381; Knowlton, B. 2000. "Zero-Tolerance Injustices Multiplying, Critics Say: A Backlash in the U.S." *International Herald Tribune.* February 14. http://www.iht.com/articles/2000/02/14/rlash.2.t.php. Accessed August 4, 2008; Weissman, M., Wolf, E., Sowards, K., Abate, C., Weinberg, P., and Marthia, C. 2005. *School Yard or Prison Yard: Improving Outcomes for Marginalized Youth.* Washington, DC: Center for Community Alternatives.

[46] Ness, C. N. 2004. "Why Girls Fight: Female Youth Violence in the Inner City." *The Annals of the American Academy of Political and Social Science,* 595: 32–48.

[47] Lombroso, C. 1903. *The Female Offender.* New York: Appleton.

[48] Ibid.

[49] Thomas, W. I. 1967. *The Unadjusted Girl.* New York: Harper and Row.

[50] Pollack, O. 1950. *The Criminality of Women.* Philadelphia: University of Pennsylvania Press.

[51] See Miller, J., and Mullins, C. W. 2006. "The States of Feminist Theories of Criminology." In Cullen, F. T., Wright, J. P., and Blevins, K. R. (eds.), *Taking Stock: The Status of Criminology Today,* pp. 217–249. New Brunswick, NJ: Transaction.

[52] Chesney-Lind, M., and Shelden, R. G. 2004. *Girls, Delinquency, and Juvenile Justice,* 3rd ed. Belmont, CA: Wadsworth.

[53] See Cullen, F. T., Wright, J. P., and Blevins, K. R. (eds.). *Taking Stock: The Status of Criminology Today.* New Brunswick, NJ: Transaction.

[54] Adler, F. 1975. *Sisters in Crime.* New York: McGraw-Hill.

[55] Ibid.

[56] See, for instance, Brown, B. 1983. "Female Crime: The Dark Figure of Criminality." *Economy and Society,* 15:355–402; Carlen, P. 1983. *Women's Imprisonment: A Study of Social Control.* London: Routledge; Smart, C. 1979. "The New Female Criminal: Reality or Myth?" *British Journal of Criminology.* 19: 50–59.

[57] See Jaggar, A. M., and Rothenberg, P. (eds.). 1984. *Feminist Frameworks.* New York: McGraw-Hill. See also Adler, 1975.

[58] See, for instance, Macionis, J. 2005. *Sociology,* 10th ed. New York: McGraw-Hill.

[59] Jaggar and Rothenberg, 1984.

[60] See McNamara, 2008.

[61] Jaggar and Rothenberg, 1984.

[62] Ibid.

[63] Ibid.

[64] Chesney-Lind, M. 1987. "Girls Crime and Woman's Place: Toward a Feminist Model of Female Delinquency." Paper presented at the annual meeting of the American Society of Criminology, Montreal.

[65] See, for instance, McNamara, R., and Burns, R. 2008. *Multiculturalism in the Criminal Justice System.* New York: McGraw-Hill.

[66] See, for instance, Bishop, D. M., and Frazier, C. E. 1992. "Gender Bias in the Juvenile Justice System: Implications of the JJDP Act." *Journal of Criminal Law and Criminology,* 82: 1167.

[67] See, for example, Knox, G. W. 2008. *Female Gang Members and the Rights of Children.* Chicago: National Gang Crime Research Center.

[68] See Yiff, R. M. 2008. "Discrimination of Female Juvenile Delinquents: A Consideration of the Police and Court Processing Practices in the State of Florida." Paper presented at the annual meeting of the Southern Political Science Association, New Orleans. http://www.allacademic.com/meta-/p213022_index.html. Accessed August 5, 2008.

[69] See, for instance, Yiff, 2008; Young, V. D. 1986. "Gender Expectations and Their Impact on Black Female Offenders and Victims." *Justice Quarterly,* 3: 305–328. See also McNamara and Burns, 2008.

[70] Yiff, 2008.

After reading this chapter, you should be able to:

- Outline the history of delinquency prevention and its importance.

- Understand the different ways to categorize delinquency prevention.

- List the different types of risk factors, and justify the solutions employed to address these risks.

- Assess the various programs that target delinquents at different stages of development.

- Envision the future of delinquency prevention in the United States.

12

Delinquency Prevention

Discussions of delinquency prevention tend to focus on programs like Neighborhood Watch, D.A.R.E., and Scared Straight. However, the actual impact these programs have had on delinquency is largely misunderstood. Consider the following scenario:

A community has a high rate of crime, especially juvenile delinquency, which prompts the mayor to hire a new police chief. The police chief's plan for community improvement consists of three main points:

- taking measures (expansion of Block Watch programs and increase in police patrols) to prevent delinquency
- instituting educational programs (D.A.R.E.) for youths that focus on decision-making skills
- preventing recidivism in delinquent youths (Scared Straight programs)

The community responds positively to this plan, since it appears to be a comprehensive one that will address many community needs. These are some possible outcomes from the new chief's plan:

- Because it is comprehensive and considers many factors for why youths commit delinquent acts, the plan will likely work.
- The plan sounds good, but it is too early to tell if the police department will follow through with it.
- The plan is a political ploy to get the public to think the department is doing something about crime and delinquency, but in reality, little will be accomplished.
- Some parts of the plan sound logical, but it is unclear if they will actually have an impact on crime and delinquency.
- Very few of the strategies offered by the department will be effective in reducing delinquency.

Mentoring and other youth programs, such as the Boy Scouts, which teach the importance of pro-social behavior and concern for others, are critical to successful prevention of delinquency. What other programs address delinquency prevention?

THINK ABOUT IT   What outcome do you anticipate based on the information given and what you know about prevention tactics?

A thorough examination of delinquency will help us to better judge the effectiveness of preventive strategies like the ones proposed above. For example, a deeper understanding of the problems of poverty, inadequate education, and issues relating to family makeup, housing, and employment can help us determine why delinquency happens, as well as how to prevent it. We must also understand how the public perceives delinquency prevention programs, since public policy and funding decisions are influenced by the beliefs of policymakers, politicians, and the public at large.

Discussions of delinquency prevention are fueled largely by the public's fear of victimization. This fear is driven in part by a general misunderstanding of the nature of delinquency, as well as an overall tendency to sensationalize its occurrences. While it is true that highlighted incidents of delinquency occur, it is also the case that misinformation and slanted exposure in the media help to incite fear in the minds of many citizens about the extent, nature, and scope of delinquency. Often, these misunderstandings undermine the programs that aim to solve delinquency. The discussion of the panacea phenomenon that follows illustrates how fear influences public policy surrounding delinquency issues.

Current Delinquency Prevention in the United States

Preventing delinquency has become a formidable challenge for communities. Some experts have argued that the most logical way to overcome delinquency in individual communities is to employ programs that prevent it from occurring in the first place. This strategy, it is argued, curtails the social, economic, and political costs associated with delinquency. While this seems a simple enough policy, other factors must be taken into consideration.

As with most social problems, when it comes to crime, the American public tends to want a quick and simple solution. Delinquency expert James Finckenauer describes the public's attempt to find a single answer to the problems relating to delinquency as the **panacea phenomenon.** By definition, a panacea is a cure-all, a single solution to a wide variety of problems. Figure 12-1 illustrates Finckenauer's idea that the pursuit of a

panacea phenomenon
The public's attempt to find a single, cure-all answer to the problems relating to delinquency.

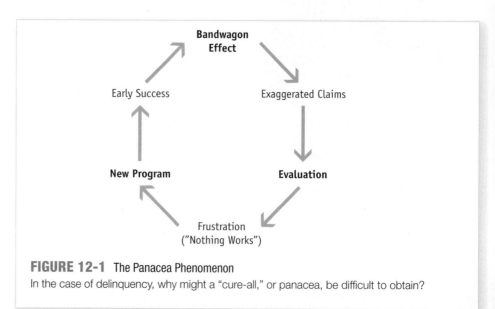

FIGURE 12-1 The Panacea Phenomenon
In the case of delinquency, why might a "cure-all," or panacea, be difficult to obtain?

single answer creates a cycle wherein, in the case of delinquency, Americans experiment with many programs only to be disappointed with the results.[1]

According to Finckenauer, the initial stages of any delinquency prevention program, simply because it is new, will show signs of promise. Rarely do programs fail immediately. As the success of a particular program is noted, excitement builds, and other people become involved in supporting it. Politicians, the public, and social activists, inspired to "jump on the bandwagon," promote the program as the long-sought-after solution.

As time passes, this new solution is expanded to incorporate all types of offenders. As the hype reaches its highest point, with models of the program implemented in many jurisdictions, claims of success become exaggerated, and usually without any empirical proof to support them. When an empirical evaluation is finally conducted, the program reveals itself to be not nearly as effective as its advocates claimed. The frustration felt by the general public feeds the attitude that "nothing works." This feeling lingers until the next panacea is proposed and the entire process begins anew.

The panacea phenomenon is critical to understanding the nature of delinquency and the social programs that have been designed to respond to it. Alongside the attitude that "nothing works," the panacea phenomenon has a negative effect on the public's understanding of the problem of delinquency. For example, the hype and eventual disappointment that accompany this phenomenon distract the public from more far-sighted solutions. Moreover, these attitudes distort the public's perspective, leading some individuals to dismiss programs that are effective with some groups but not with others.

There are hundreds of delinquency prevention programs that target youths. One categorization of these programs is according to age, meaning that certain programs target offenders at different age levels. Another way of categorizing these programs is by the type and frequency of delinquent behaviors they target, as when, for example, a particular program addresses chronic delinquents versus first-time offenders.

Historically, criticism of prevention programs has focused on their perceived effectiveness or lack thereof. A review of the literature on delinquency prevention programs in the 1970s, for example, suggested that many prevention programs were largely ineffective.[2] As we will see, many still face this criticism today. Another criticism is that prevention programs contribute to what some experts refer to as **net widening,** the use of diversion programs to keep delinquent youths under the control of the juvenile justice system when the courts would normally dismiss their cases.[3] **Diversion** is a term used to describe a wide range of programs to keep juveniles who commit crimes out of the formal juvenile justice process. Diversion programs, therefore, are designed to keep youths out of trouble with the law.

Some opponents of delinquency prevention programs contend that many existing programs target particular dimensions of delinquency while failing to examine the larger issues that lead to it. Others argue that these programs ignore the constitutional rights of juveniles. They point out that much of what constitutes diversion and prevention occurs without the benefit of due process normally afforded youths in juvenile court proceedings.[4] The conclusion by many experts is that the failure of prevention programs, past and present, is primarily the result of a focus on reacting to crime rather than trying to prevent it.[5]

In the 1990s, the Office of Juvenile Justice and Delinquency Prevention (OJJDP) attempted to address these criticisms by formulating a comprehensive strategy for delinquency prevention and targeting violent and chronic offenders. A multifaceted approach was established using pilot programs that address key risk factors in youths' lives and emphasize the factors that contribute to their healthy physical and emotional development. These programs involve intensive contact with at-risk youths and build on individuals' strengths instead of focusing on their weaknesses. These programs also attempt to balance accountability with intensive rehabilitative services, an approach designed to prevent youths from becoming involved in the formal juvenile justice system.[6]

In 2002, the revision of the 1975 Juvenile Justice Delinquency Prevention Act refocused policymakers' attention on prevention and identifies five crucial areas related to the prevention of delinquency:[7]

net widening
The use of diversion programs to keep delinquent youths under the control of the juvenile justice system when the courts would normally dismiss their cases.

diversion
A wide range of programs to keep juveniles who commit crimes out of trouble with the law and the formal juvenile justice process.

1. **Community-based alternatives:** programs for youths needing temporary placement with services like crisis intervention, **shelter care,** or **aftercare.** These are also for youths who need some type of long-term residential placement, such as foster care or group homes.

2. **Community-based programs:** programs that work with parents and other family members to strengthen families. These programs include parent self-help groups that aim to keep juveniles in their homes and safe. Other community-based programs work with juveniles during their incarceration to ensure a safe return to their homes upon release. Still others work to strengthen families with limited English-speaking abilities, to help them better communicate their needs to agencies dedicated to helping them.

3. **Comprehensive prevention programs:** programs designed to work collaboratively with a variety of local institutions and agencies, such as schools, courts, law enforcement agencies, child protection agencies, mental health agencies, welfare services, health care agencies, and private nonprofits. Comprehensive prevention programs take a holistic approach to meeting the needs of youths.

4. **Victim services:** programs that focus on providing treatment to juvenile offenders who are the victims of child abuse or neglect, and to their families, in order to reduce the likelihood that offenders will commit future crimes.

5. **Educational programs:** as part of a comprehensive approach, programs providing youth activities that reduce offenders' motivations to commit crimes.[8] These include athletic programs like the Police Athletic League and the Boys and Girls Clubs of America.

Crime prevention can be divided into three approaches: primary, secondary, and tertiary. Each type addresses crime and delinquency at a different stage of development. **Primary crime prevention** programs focus on making crime more difficult to commit or increasing the likelihood of the offender getting caught. This approach to crime prevention is based on the belief that most crimes are committed by offenders who take advantage of low-risk opportunities that require little effort. **Routine activities theory,** a popular explanation for delinquency, suggests that youths commit delinquent acts after identifying a target based on its vulnerability. Because of people's routine activities, meaning their work schedules and other daily behavior, the target is an easy one because it is insufficiently protected—either by a surveillance network or by some measure that makes that target more formidable.[9]

Consequently, primary crime prevention efforts are designed to *harden* a target, or make it more difficult for offenders to take advantage of it. This includes strategies such as improving lighting in trouble spots, installing deadbolt locks on doors, and implementing crime prevention through environmental design (CPTED), discussed in detail later in this chapter. **CPTED** refers to the design of buildings and locations in such a way as to limit the opportunities for crime. Other programs, such as Neighborhood Watch, attempt to deter criminals through increased surveillance in a neighborhood or community.[10]

If primary crime prevention focuses on reducing youths' opportunities to commit crimes, **secondary crime prevention** focuses on removing or reducing their desire to engage in criminal acts. Examples of secondary crime prevention include sports-related programs such as the Police Athletic League, discussed in Chapter 13, and the Boys and Girls Clubs of America. The idea is to alter youths' motivation levels by giving them something else besides criminal behavior to occupy their time and on which to focus their energies.

Tertiary crime prevention deals with individuals who have already committed crimes. This is the third line of defense in crime prevention in that these types of programs focus not only on preventing initial acts but on ensuring that youths who have already committed crimes will not engage in similar activities in the future. In some cases, this may include treatment and rehabilitation, while in others, a combined incarceration and treatment approach is used. Tertiary crime prevention programs are usually found in departments of corrections, probation, and parole. Examples include boot camps and wilderness programs.[11]

shelter care
Residential program for youths needing temporary placement.

aftercare
Programs for youths needing temporary placement with services like crisis intervention or shelter care, and for youths who need some kind of long-term residential placement, such as foster care or group home.

primary crime prevention
Efforts to make crime more difficult to commit or to increase the likelihood of the offender getting caught.

routine activities theory
The theory that crime occurs because offenders take advantage of the typical, everyday behavior of their victims.

CPTED
The design of buildings and locations in such a way as to limit the opportunities for crime.

secondary crime prevention
Methods, such as sports-related programs, to aid in removing or reducing youths' desire to engage in criminal acts.

tertiary crime prevention
Programs that focus not only on preventing initial criminal acts but on ensuring that youths who have already committed crimes will not engage in similar activities in the future.

Regardless of its focus, care must be taken with any type of delinquency prevention program to assess not only the motivation of the offender but the type of crime as well. It is also important to distinguish between property offenses, where security devices and street designs can protect a target, and personal crimes, where security devices do not work. The latter often occur in the home or in other places where citizens and the police cannot patrol.[12]

History of Delinquency Prevention

Consider what you know about the history of delinquency prevention. How might you compare the public's approach to delinquency prevention and its attitude toward the juvenile justice system in general? Do you think this attitude informs public policy?

THINK ABOUT IT

Primary Delinquency Prevention Programs

When trying to understand why youths commit crimes, it is important to consider the social, physical, and economic factors at play. Much of what happens to individuals as children impacts their social and intellectual abilities, even as they mature. For instance, children's exposure to nicotine, alcohol, marijuana, and other drugs has been linked to problems with their verbal functioning, including reading, writing, speech, memory, and problem-solving skills.[13] Drug use and poor nutrition can also contribute to health problems in children, such as inadequate sleep and a lack of adequate immunizations. Health problems, moreover, contribute to poor academic performance. For all of these reasons, proponents of delinquency prevention emphasize that early intervention methods are essential.

Good parenting skills are imperative to ensuring that children grow up with healthy behaviors. Infanthood is the most critical period in children's psychological development, and mothers are the primary emotional providers at this stage. The love, care, and physical contact that mothers give have lifelong effects on the behaviors and choices of their children, even into adulthood.[14] Preventive programs that address these issues fall under the general category of primary delinquency prevention.

PRENATAL CARE FOR EXPECTANT MOTHERS

Research has shown that the most effective programs for delinquency prevention are aimed at children in the earliest stages of life.[15] Consequently, a number of prenatal programs have emerged, as well as those that focus on early childhood development.

One prenatal program is the Elmira Prenatal/Early Infancy Project. This program, which began in the 1970s, is based on the idea that many of the problems seen in older youths stem from poor or nonexistent prenatal care, which can result in low birth weight and a lack of adequate social support for the child and the family.[16] To alleviate these problems, nurses visit expectant mothers in an effort to improve their health and nutrition during pregnancy. These visits typically take place during the end of the first trimester of pregnancy and continue for two years. The target population consists of low-income, first-time mothers. The goals of these visits are to encourage mothers to avoid or dramatically reduce the use of nicotine, alcohol, and illegal drugs, as well as provide examinations to identify pregnancy-related complications.

Nurses in the program also offer insight into the nature of normal child development and help mothers to become responsible and nurturing parents. An evaluation of this program has shown that mothers who receive visits have fewer low-birth-weight and prematurely born babies than a comparison group. Moreover, participants have improved diets, provide better nutrition for their children, smoke less, and have fewer subsequent pregnancies.[17]

Another program that shows significant promise is the Yale Child Welfare program, located in New Haven, Connecticut. This program provides services to a number of pregnant black women expecting their first child. The program caters to low-income clients and provides services until children are thirty months old. Clinicians make home visits and counsel expectant mothers about good nutrition and housing, as well as how to make important decisions about future goals, like those regarding the education of children and career paths for mothers. In addition, information about normal child development is provided for mothers, and children receive pediatric services.

The long-term impact of the Yale Child Welfare program is seen in a ten-year follow-up study that showed that participating children were less likely to be truant, needed fewer remedial educational programs, were less likely to act out either in school or off campus, and were considered by teachers to be better adjusted socially than a comparison group of children. The impact on participant mothers was also significant: measured against a comparison group of mothers, most of the families were self-supporting by the time their first child was twelve years old. Moreover, mothers who participated had fewer children and waited longer to have subsequent children. Thus, the program demonstrated significant positive long-term effects on both the children and the family.[18]

While this particular program is no longer in operation, Yale University's Edward Zigler Center in Child Development and Social Policy has continued to conduct research on these and other issues relating to child development. Most recently, it has begun to focus on a comprehensive strategy that combines prenatal and early childhood development with educational programs that provide parents with the tools they need.[19]

EARLY CHILDHOOD AND PRESCHOOL PROGRAMS

Research consistently shows that children's emotional, cognitive, and social development is essential to their achieving adequate knowledge and skill development. Preschool programs are a vital component of that process. This is particularly true for children from disadvantaged backgrounds, since the failure to fully develop at an early age often results in delinquency later in life.[20]

The Head Start program is well known for addressing just these needs. Head Start was created in 1965, by Edward Zigler, the same person who created the Child Welfare program at Yale University and the founder of the School of the 21st Century (21C), discussed below. As part of President Lyndon Johnson's War on Poverty, Head Start was designed to address the educational difficulties experienced by many low-income and poor students, and to adequately prepare them to enter kindergarten.

Officially, Head Start consists of two core programs, Head Start (HS) and Early Head Start (EHS). HS is a comprehensive early childhood development program primarily serving low-income, preschool-age children and their families. Established during the 1994 reauthorization of HS, EHS was created as a comprehensive early childhood program serving primarily low-income children, prenatal to age three; pregnant women; and their families.

Funding for these programs is provided directly from the federal government to local grantees. The federal government provides 80 percent of the yearly costs to operate HS and EHS programs, while the remaining 20 percent must come from what are called in-kind contributions, which may be in the form of monetary contributions, donations of goods or services, or volunteer hours.

In 2008, there were over one million children and pregnant women enrolled in HS and EHS programs: approximately 976,000 in HS and 95,000 in EHS, at an average cost per child of about $7,100 for HS and $10,200 for EHS. Contrary to correlations between minorities and poverty, less than one-third of participants were black or African American (see Table 12-1).[21]

The HS program provides a variety of comprehensive services to children age three to five, including meals and nutritional services, and medical and dental checkups; for parents, the program offers assistance in accessing social service agencies in their communities. Additionally, as a key component of these programs, parents become involved in their child's preschool education by classroom visits or spending a day assisting the teacher in the class.

TABLE 12-1 Race and Ethnic Distribution of Participants: Head Start and Early Head Start, 2009

Race or Ethinicity	Participants
White	39%
Black or African American	29
Biracial or multiracial	7
American Indian or Alaska Native, Hawaiian or Pacific Islander, Asian, or other	7
Hispanic or Latino origin	36
Non-Hispanic or non-Latino origin	64

In previous chapters, we have noted that minorities represent a disproportionately high number of youths involved in the juvenile justice system. What does this table tell us about the racial and ethnic makeup of the Head Start and Early Head Start programs? How might you explain this disparity?

The Head Start programs generally achieve small to moderate gains, particularly in the areas of reading, writing, and vocabulary.[22] However, the long-term effects of these programs, as seen over the span of participants' educational careers, are worth noting. In particular, HS children are more likely to complete high school and attend college than children who did not participate in the program. HS children are also less likely to repeat a grade or be arrested for committing a crime, either as youths or as adults.[23]

Another well-known primary prevention program is the HighScope Perry Preschool program, which began in 1962 as an educational program based on the theories of developmental psychologist Jean Piaget. Piaget emphasized that children are active learners who learn most effectively when they are engaged in activities they plan, carry out, and review. In the HighScope Perry Preschool program, classroom activities are combined with home visits by staff. During these visits, parents are taught to support and encourage their children's classroom activities.[24]

As part of a long-term study conducted alongside this program, data were collected from police and court records to show that rates of juvenile delinquency were significantly lower for participants in the program. By contrast, by age twenty-seven, nonparticipants were found to be five times more likely to be arrested, and by age forty, they were twice as likely to be arrested for violent crimes. Data also showed that participants performed better academically, were more likely to graduate from high school, and earned higher salaries upon entering the workforce.

A cost-benefit analysis of the study also shows that the program produces a savings to taxpayers of more than seven times the initial investment per child. That means that for every $1 spent on the program, there is a return savings of over $7. These savings are seen in fewer costs related to welfare assistance and criminal justice, as well as in the savings afforded to victims of crime. Finally, these savings are measured in increased tax revenues from individuals who work instead of receiving funds from the government.[25]

PARENTING SKILLS

As we saw in Chapter 7 on the relationship between families and delinquency, most people raise their children using methods similar to those their parents used, whether or not those methods were effective or nurturing. Parents who were neglected or abused as children, or even those who merely grew up poor, often have inadequate training in good parenting skills. In some families, this leads to a cycle of abuse, neglect, and problem behaviors.

Programs that improve parenting skills, and that focus on the use of discipline in particular, can have a significant impact on mothers' behaviors. Home visitation programs to educate parents on normal child development have a similar impact. For instance, one study found that participation in such programs reduced not only charges of abuse and neglect against mothers but also subsequent criminal and delinquent activity on the part of their children.[26]

One program that has shown considerable success in helping parents is the Nurturing Parents Program (NPP). This program typically targets families considered to be at higher risk for abuse and neglect and families in recovery for alcohol and other drug abuse. The program is based on research that suggests four common traits among abusive and neglectful parents. The traits discussed below stem from the parents' lack of understanding about the needs and capabilities of children, as well as from their own experiences of how they were raised:

- **Inappropriate expectations of the child:** parents sometimes mistakenly expect their children to behave in ways that are developmentally inappropriate for their ages. For example, young children, who are not old enough to do so, are expected to help with household chores or to be able to care for themselves without adult supervision.
- **Lack of empathy regarding children's needs:** when parents are unable to understand the emotional needs of a child, or respond to those needs in an inappropriate way, they display a harmful lack of empathy towards the needs of their children. For example, abusive parents often ignore their children because they do not want to spoil them.
- **Parental role reversal:** in instances of parental role reversal, parents sometimes look to their children to fill an emotional void, which often originates from their own childhoods. In these cases, parents have the unrealistic expectation that children can take on a nurturing role and provide the care and comfort they need. When the child fails to meet these needs, parents experience even greater disappointment and begin to see their children as inadequate. Their frustration might be taken out on children in the form of physical abuse, belittling, and outright neglect.[27]
- **Physical punishment:** among abusive parents, there tends to be a strong belief in the value of corporal punishment. Using corporal punishment fulfills the need of an abusive parent to feel in control of the child and to reinforce obedience. This use of corporal punishment is often a reflection of how parents were treated as children, thus perpetuating a cycle of violence as a problem-solving tool.

For children, the burden of their parents' unrealistic expectations can be significant. Unable to meet their parents' expectations, children perceive themselves as failures, a perception that can continue into adulthood and manifest as a sense of worthlessness. These feelings begin as a result of poor socialization, but they result in chemical changes in children's brains, affecting levels of anxiety and empathy and problem-solving skills. Therefore, abused children are more likely to repeat similar abuses with their own children. These changes in brain chemistry represent one more example of how the cycle of abuse, described above, continues over generations.[28]

NPP believes that parenting is a learned behavior. In response to these and other trends among abusive parents, NPP attempts to divert negative thoughts, feelings, and behaviors in children, using a variety of formats that are applied based on children's ages. The program is guided by six elements that attempt to address the four critical traits mentioned above. These elements consist of the following:

- **The family is a system.** In order for a family to function effectively, all members must participate in its growth and improvement.
- **Empathy is critical to effective parenting.** Empathy is the ability to be aware of the needs of others and to value those needs. There is an inverse relationship between empathy and abuse: the more empathy that exists within a family, the lower their incidents of abuse.
- **Parenting exists on a continuum.** While no family is perfect, and all families experience some level of unhealthy behaviors and interactions, the goals of NPP are to minimize their impact and to capitalize on healthy relationships.
- **Learning is cognitive and affective.** This means that interventions to help families have to be informative and emphasize the emotional component of interactions.
- **Children with high self-esteem are nurturing parents.** Because children who feel good about themselves are more capable than those who do not, and because such children are also more likely to become nurturing parents, NPP makes enhancing self-esteem and feelings of self-worth a major goal.

■ **No one benefits from abuse.** Family members would, if given the choice, rather have happy and healthy relationships. The health and happiness of families has a societal impact as well, since the problems of unhealthy families can impact entire communities.[29]

NPP offers thirteen different programs to accommodate all types of families and children of different ages. The program achieves its objectives by using group and individual counseling sessions for both parents and children, teaching age-specific parenting skills through role-playing, instructional videos, and individual assessment exercises. Group-based sessions typically last about three hours once a week, while home-based sessions run about an hour and a half in the same intervals. In their groups, parents are taught to develop skills in the following areas:

- philosophies of discipline, and appropriate uses of it
- nurturing and empathy for their children and others, including ways to nurture others through praise and communicating through touch
- improved communication by understanding feelings and by redirecting or ignoring some behaviors exhibited by the child
- the relationship between anger, alcohol, and abuse
- proper child development, such as when to toilet train
- ways to baby-proof a home
- establishment of morals, values, and rules[30]

An evaluation of NPP by the National Institute of Mental Health showed that 93 percent of participants modified their abusive parenting techniques, and parents reported being more empathetic to their children's needs. Parents also demonstrated greater self-confidence and enthusiasm, and lower levels of anxiety about raising their children.[31]

Levels of self-confidence and enthusiasm have been shown to significantly impact an individual's ability to learn. How do programs like NPP use self-esteem-building techniques for teaching both children and their parents?

Programs like HighScope Perry and NPP are essential to changing children's and parents' behavior. Moreover, by decreasing parents' dependency on government assistance and services, these programs also cut costs.[32] A study published in the *Journal of the American Medical Association* (JAMA) found that in a fifteen-year follow-up, low-income families who participated in a comprehensive education, family, and health services program in Chicago had higher rates of high school completion and lower rates of juvenile arrests and violent crime, particularly in the case of boys. As this and other studies suggest, early intervention in the form of structural and procedural changes in family interaction can have a significant impact on later delinquency.[33]

The Center for the Study and Prevention of Violence at the University of Colorado at Boulder has identified ten programs that demonstrate consistent effectiveness in preventing or reducing violence among youths. These programs, called the Blueprints Model Programs, were selected from a review of over 450 violence prevention programs.

As it relates to early intervention, home visit programs, such as those that occur between a woman's pregnancy and the two years that follow, show substantial reductions in maternal criminal activity, as well as fewer juvenile arrests up to fifteen years later. In addition, the costs of the home visitation program are recouped within four years of a family's involvement in the program. At a cost of $3,200 per family, such programs are a bargain compared to the significant costs of incarcerating a youth, which can be as high as $40,000 per year.[34]

Perhaps the most ambitious attempt to address the issues surrounding families and youth development is 21C, the school affiliated with the Edward Zigler Center in Child Development and Social Policy at Yale University. 21C is a comprehensive program that targets the many needs of working and poor families. These needs include nutrition for parents and children, early education programs, parenting skills training, and a wide range of information and service agency referrals for families. The goal of 21C is guided by five principles to promote the optimal development of all children:

- high-quality, noncompulsory programming
- universal access to programs
- strong parental support and involvement
- professional advancement opportunities for child care providers
- focus on the social, emotional, and intellectual development of children[35]

community crime prevention programs
Community efforts to combat crime, mostly sponsored by police departments, which conduct home security surveys and hold community meetings to organize and plan neighborhood group activities.

target-hardening measures
Prevention methods that include installing deadbolt locks on doors, adding window locks, improving the lighting around homes and streets, and implementing Block Watch programs, where citizens patrol their neighborhoods and report suspicious activity to the police.

What distinguishes 21C from other programs is that it offers comprehensive services to parents and their children from birth through school age, and across a diverse range of issues. Access to these services is universal, meaning they are available to all children. Finally, the 21C program has the flexibility to adapt to local community conditions. This means it can be tailored to address particular problems in different regions of the country. There are nearly 1,400 21C schools in states across the country, including Connecticut, Arkansas, Missouri, and Kentucky.[36] Evaluations of the 21C program show that it improves the academic achievement levels of participating children, enhances their social and emotional development, improves parent-teacher relationships, and reduces stress levels for both parents and teachers.[37]

In addition to individual early childhood prevention efforts, which have clear links to reduced delinquency, there are community efforts broadly categorized as **community crime prevention programs.** These programs consist of citizen groups that come together to combat crime in their neighborhoods. Most community crime prevention groups are sponsored by police departments, which conduct home security surveys and hold community meetings to organize and plan neighborhood group activities. Much of what constitutes community crime prevention consists of **target-hardening measures,** which include installing deadbolt locks on doors, adding window locks, improving the lighting around homes and streets, and implementing Block Watch programs, where citizens patrol their neighborhoods and report suspicious activity to the police.[38]

NEIGHBORHOOD/BLOCK WATCH

Currently, there are approximately 24,000 Neighborhood Watch (NW) groups involved with over 2,500 law enforcement agencies in the United States.[39] NW groups share information about local crime problems, exchange crime prevention tips, and make plans for engaging in surveillance of neighborhoods and reporting suspicious activities.

Most NW groups do not engage exclusively in informal surveillance. Other activities include engraving property, conducting household security surveys, and improving street lighting. NW programs operate as a supplement to the police and do not attempt to replace them. In essence, they become the "eyes and ears" of the police.

NW groups have had only modest success in reducing crime and have reported difficulty in keeping their members involved over time. One reason for these setbacks might be attributable to the fact that residents rarely encounter a crime in progress while on patrol. Another reason might be that many of the activities of NW groups are one-time efforts: installing deadbolts, improving lighting, engraving property, and so on do not need to be regularly repeated, which sets the expectation that the group's purpose has been quickly fulfilled. Perhaps as a result of all these factors, many residents believe that their efforts to patrol the neighborhood do not yield any tangible positive results.[40] Although their presence has the potential to create a deterrent effect, this effect is not always apparent to residents, and it is difficult to measure empirically.

Neighborhood Watch groups are thought to be the "eyes and ears" of local law enforcement. What other effects, besides curbing crime, might target-hardening measures have on a community?

TARGET-HARDENING MEASURES

Target-hardening measures are intended to make it more difficult for offenders to victimize residents and businesses, thereby reducing the opportunity to commit crimes. One way to do this is to have the police department conduct home security surveys to assess residents' risks.[41] Normally, this would include recommendations to reduce the chances of victimization, like those described above.

Another type of target-hardening measure is called Operation ID. This is a program that allows residents to permanently mark their property in the event that it is stolen. Police departments loan community groups engravers with which residents mark their property. This accomplishes two goals: the owner of the property can identify it if it is stolen, and the markings serve as evidence against the offenders at trial to demonstrate that the property does not belong to them.[42]

CRIME PREVENTION THROUGH ENVIRONMENTAL DESIGN (CPTED)

This form of primary crime prevention involves the physical design of neighborhoods to decrease the chances of victimization. The idea is to design buildings so that residents create a surveillance network, allowing them to easily recognize strangers. Examples include building neighborhoods in cul de sacs and redesigning public spaces such as intersections by using one-way streets and speed bumps.

The basis of CPTED is outlined in the classic 1972 book on community design and city planning, *Defensible Space,* by Oscar Newman. Based on the results of a study of crime in public spaces, Newman's book argued that constructing low-rise buildings with courtyards and other small public spaces creates a sense of cohesion among residents. At the time of this study, residents of low-rise projects experienced lower crime rates than residents of high-rise buildings. Newman attributed this disparity to the personal responsibility that residents feel when they have a sense of ownership of their physical space and community. Residents of well-designed communities, therefore, are more likely to take on the role of ensuring its well-being and to look out for one another as a result.[43] Moreover, this approach sends a symbolic message to the criminal population that the area is defended by residents and should not be targeted.[44] Of all the programs available under the general category of community crime prevention, only CPTED has been shown to have a consistent and positive impact on reducing victimization.[45]

What do you think of Newman's theory about the relationship between the design of community spaces and crime? Consider the space in which you currently live. Does its design lend itself to a sense of community and safety?

Delinquency Prevention Measures

Recall each of the delinquency prevention programs described so far in this chapter. In general, how are these programs categorized? How does this method of categorization help to ensure that at-risk groups are targeted for services?

Secondary Delinquency Prevention Programs

Recall that secondary crime prevention programs are designed to reduce the motivation of youths to commit crimes. One of the first ways that experts attempted to achieve this goal was by examining the risk factors that place certain youths in jeopardy of committing crimes alongside the protective factors that shield them from such behavior. This method is an example of a risk model.

risk models
Methods of examining the risk factors that place certain youths in jeopardy of committing crimes alongside the protective factors that shield them from such behavior.

Risk models borrow heavily from the area of public health that places an emphasis on preventing disease before it occurs. In the same way that one does not wait until one has a heart attack before taking preventive steps, the risk model suggests that communities should not wait until delinquency occurs before responding to it. This proactive approach has resulted in research that identifies the strongest risk factors for youths to become involved in delinquency. Table 12-2 assesses the risk factors for various ages.[46]

A risk factor is broadly "anything that increases the probability that a person will suffer harm."[47] Although researchers use risk factors to predict whether youths will commit crimes, many youths with multiple risk factors never commit delinquent or violent acts—in other words, risk factors increase the chance of something happening, but they do not guarantee it.[48]

In contrast to risk factors are protective factors, influences or variables that *reduce* youths' chances of offending. In other words, protective factors insulate or *protect* youths from the risks engaging in criminal behavior. Protective factors operate by either reducing risky behavior, improving self-esteem and confidence, or creating constructive opportunities that keep youths out of trouble.[49]

TABLE 12-2 Risk Factors Associated with Delinquent Behavior by Age Group

	Risk Factor		
Domain	**Early Onset (age 6–11)**	**Late Onset (age 12–14)**	**Protective Factor***

Individual	General offenses
	Substance use
	Being male
	Aggression**
	  Hyperactivity
	  Problem (antisocial) behavior
	Exposure to television violence
	Medical, physical problems
	Low IQ
	Antisocial attitudes, beliefs
	Dishonesty**
		General offenses
		Restlessness
		Difficulty concentrating**
		Risk taking
		Aggression**
		Being male
		Physical violence
		Antisocial attitudes, beliefs
		Crimes against persons
		Problem (antisocial) behavior
		Low IQ
		Substance use
			Intolerant attitude
			  toward deviance
			High IQ
			Being female
			Positive social
			  orientation
			Perceived sanctions for
			  transgressions

Family	Low socioeconomic status/
	  poverty
	Antisocial parents
	Poor parent-child relationship
	Harsh, lax, or inconsistent
	  discipline
	Broken home
	Separation from parents
	Other conditions
	Abusive parents
	Neglect
		Poor parent-child relationship
		Harsh or lax discipline
		Poor monitoring, supervision
		Low parental involvement
		Antisocial parents
		Broken home
		Low socioeconomic status/poverty
		Abusive parents
		Family conflict**
			Warm, supportive relationships
			  with parents or other adults
			Parents' positive evaluation of
			  peers
			Parental monitoring

School	Poor attitude,
	  performance
		Poor attitude,
		  performance
		Academic failure
			Commitment to school
			Recognition for involvement in
			  conventional activities

Peer group	Weak social ties Antisocial peers	Weak social ties Antisocial, delinquent peers Gang membership	Friends who engage in conventional behavior
Community		Neighborhood crime, drugs Neighborhood disorganization	

What is the difference between a risk factor and a protective factor based on your observations of this table?

* Age of onset not known.
** Males only.

Source: Adapted from Office of the Surgeon General, 2001.

THEORY AND PRACTICE WORKING TOGETHER

Future Problem Solving Program of Connecticut (FPSPofCT)

Community-based prevention programs encourage participants to develop a sense of ownership of their community, emphasizing that each participant is personally invested in its present and future well-being. While not a traditional delinquency prevention program, FPSPofCT represents a community-based approach to engaging children and youths in large-scale thinking about their roles in society.

FPSPofCT is a nonprofit education organization governed by a board of directors consisting of teachers, parents, and past participants. FPSPofCT prepares students for the future by teaching essential problem-solving skills, with an emphasis on creativity, analytical thinking, and leadership, and by improving oral and written communication skills. Participants hone these skills while learning about complex social and scientific issues. Currently, FPSPofCT offers several options for students, with the program broken down into three divisions based on age:

- junior division (grades four–six)
- middle division (grades seven–nine)
- senior division (grades ten–twelve)

FPSPofCT offers two types of programs: competitive and noncompetitive. Students participating in the competitive program break into teams of four (or fewer) and evaluate a future scene using a six-step problem-solving process. Students prepare reports and submit them to the state office for evaluation. Top teams in each division compete for an invitation to an international conference. In the noncompetitive program, students are divided in the same way as the competitive program and submit reports for review, but do not participate in the international conference.

Another component of the program is called Community Problem Solving (CmPS). In CmPS, teams work together to identify a problem locally, in their school or community, or globally. They then use the problem-solving process to determine the underlying causes of the problem and to generate and evaluate possible solutions. Once this is accomplished, the team implements a creative program to minimize or eliminate the problem they have identified.

As part of FPSPofCT, students engage in problem-solving activities that impact their communities in positive ways. Can you think of some problem-solving activities students could participate in that have the potential to effect real change, locally or globally?

Secondary Prevention Strategies

Recall the table of risk factors associated with delinquency. How do the examples of secondary prevention programs described in this chapter address particular risk factors? Do these same programs make efforts to replace risk factors with protective factors?

Tertiary Delinquency Prevention Programs

Recall that tertiary prevention programs target individuals who have already committed a delinquent act. The goal here is to prevent youths from engaging in further delinquency.[91] This is accomplished by diverting them from formal prosecution.

Diversion programs are designed to correct or prevent youths from experiencing more serious problems in the future by keeping them out of the formal juvenile justice process. Based on the assumption that most youths will commit some sort of delinquent act, diversion programs try to avoid the stigma associated with becoming involved in the juvenile justice process. They do this by finding ways of handling these matters less formally. This practice also relieves the juvenile justice system of the burden of minor delinquency and allows it to dedicate time and energy to serious offenders.[92]

While a wide range of programs can be classified as diversionary, most states have restrictions on what types of offenders can participate in such programs. Usually, the criteria are that youths be of a certain age, usually under fourteen years old; have committed a minor offense; and be a first-time offender. Additionally, youths must agree to participate in some sort of treatment-based program in exchange for avoiding the formal

THEORY AND PRACTICE WORKING TOGETHER

South Carolina's Community Juvenile Arbitration Program (JAP)

JAP, which began in 1983, is designed to allow first-time juvenile offenders who commit minor crimes to have their records purged if they agree to participate in an individualized program administered by a volunteer arbitrator. The use of community members as volunteer arbitrators allows paid Department of Juvenile Justice (DJJ) staff to concentrate more time and energy on serious and chronic offenders.

When juveniles are charged with crimes, the cases are sent to the DJJ. For cases that are appropriate for arbitration, the DJJ reviews prior records and forwards the files to JAP. The director of the program then sets a hearing date, usually within three weeks of arrest, and informs the juvenile, his or her parents, the victim, and the arresting officer. If the offender or parents do not agree to participate in the program, the case is then forwarded to the prosecutor's office for formal disposition in the juvenile justice system. Those who accept arbitration meet with the arbitrator and the parties involved in the case. At the hearing, the arbitrator determines the facts of the case and determines an appropriate sanction. The arbitrator also attempts to determine if the juvenile's family is in need of assistance from available resources (counseling, crisis intervention, assessments, family services, etc.).

Examples of sanctions can include requiring the youth to visit a correctional institution, attend substance abuse counseling or similar program, make restitution to the victim, participate in community service, or write a letter of apology to the victim and his or her family. The arbitrator assigned to the case also monitors the progress of the juvenile in completing the requirements. When all requirements are satisfied, the arbitrator notifies the program director, who then informs the prosecutor's office that no record needs to be created. According to its website, JAP has been 91 percent successful in reducing recidivism statewide, meaning only 9 percent of youths who participated in the program were subsequently re-arrested.

THINK ABOUT IT

Consider the value of a program that requires offenders and victims to meet face to face. Do you think a requirement like this could be effective in reducing recidivism? Why or why not?

---

justice process. If youths fail to complete the designated program, prosecution can then be instituted against them.[93]

One example of a diversion program is the Community Juvenile Arbitration Program (JAP), which targets first-time offenders and requires them to submit to the sanctions of the volunteer arbitrator. This program is highlighted in the Theory and Practice box above.

Diversion programs often employ a wide variety of strategies. For example, teen and drug courts have become popular ways to hold youths accountable for their actions. Teen courts, also referred to as youth courts, are a relatively recent development, and several versions are in operation across the country. In only a short time, they have become popular alternatives for first-time offenders.

One version of teen court involves an adult judge who rules on court procedures while youths serve in other capacities, such as attorneys, clerks, and bailiffs. Another variation uses teens in every position, including as the judge. A third option uses a tribunal in which youth attorneys present their client's case to a panel of three youth judges, who, upon hearing the evidence, rule on the case in the absence of a jury. Finally, peer juries involve adult or youth attorneys, though jury members can question the defendant directly.[94]

According to the OJJDP, most teen courts use adult judges to handle first-time minor offenders charged with crimes such as possession of alcohol, disorderly conduct, or theft. Very few teen courts accept offenders with a prior criminal record, and the sentences handed out typically involve community service and letters or essays of apology to victims.[95]

In terms of their overall effectiveness, advocates point to the educational value of the teen court experience, both for defendants and for youths who partake in the court process. Teen courts have been praised for increasing youths' understanding of the judicial process, as well as their sense of morality and accountability.[96] As further evidence of their effectiveness, advocates also point to lower recidivism rates for participants in teen courts.[97] On the other hand, because there are no standard testing criteria for these programs, the empirical evidence of their effectiveness is mixed. For example, some studies found recidivism rates of less than 10 percent for participants, while other studies have shown it can be as high as 20 percent.[98]

Critics of teen court programs argue that because only a certain segment of the offender population is selected to participate, a self-selection, or "creaming," of participation occurs, which ensures high rates of success.[99] By selecting offenders less likely to commit another crime in the first place, teen courts and programs like it virtually ensure success in instances when doing nothing might yield similar results. Skeptics also worry that the availability of such a popular alternative actually encourages local officials to arrest and process very young and low-risk offenders, thus leading to the practice of net widening.[100]

Juvenile drug courts are another popular practice. These courts give offenders an opportunity to change their behavior and stop using illegal drugs before becoming chronic offenders, who are eligible for much more severe sanctions.[101] Drug courts are popular in part because federal funding for such programs gives local governments an incentive to create them.

State and local jurisdictions began establishing juvenile drug courts in the mid-1990s. In November 2003, there were 294 such courts in forty-six states and the District of Columbia; in 2006, there were 430 programs.[102] However, the effectiveness of drug courts for juveniles, like that of teen courts, remains unclear. Some of the research regarding drug courts also indicates that the recidivism rate of participants is higher than for those in conventional programs.[103]

Some experts, such as Jeffrey Butts, director of the Urban Institute, argue that instead of spending time labeling youths by participation in a drug court, a more effective approach would be to divert the youth from the risk factors that led him or her to engage in this behavior in the first place.[104] At the same time, efforts should be made to focus more heavily on protective factors such as constructive recreational opportunities, job preparation, and family counseling programs that encourage and support youths' positive decision making.[105]

Since the 1990s, drug courts have become an increasingly popular method of dealing with juvenile drug offenders. Are you a proponent of juvenile drug courts, or do you think drug offenses are better handled by the criminal justice system?

Programs Targeting Delinquents

THINK ABOUT IT

Most juvenile delinquents do not become chronic offenders or progress to adult crime. Based on your reading of this chapter, do you think this suggests that diversion programs are effective? Do you believe they are more effective at certain stages in an offender's development, and less so at other stages?

THE NEW POLICE CHIEF'S CASE

Conclusions on His Plan

Recall some of the programs and ideas involved in the police chief's plan:

- D.A.R.E.
- Scared Straight
- Block Watch expansion

The chief's plan, while comprehensive in its scope, fails to focus on effectiveness. It instead focuses on those programs that have earned more notoriety. Many of the programs that focus on primary prevention have limited impacts. The same can be said for tertiary programs that target offenders who have already committed an offense. Some primary programs that show promise can perhaps be best understood as structural programs designed to alleviate larger problems like poverty and family dysfunction, and to model proper behavior in youths. Secondary programs that focus on providing positive role models, job training, and school-based programs that target youths who are on the verge of becoming chronic offenders tend to be more promising.

Given what you have read about the impact of prevention programs, particularly programs like D.A.R.E. and Scared Straight, what do you think of the potential for the new chief's plan to succeed?

THINK ABOUT IT

Delinquency Prevention and Public Policy

While there exist many programs that have been shown to effectively reduce delinquency, the search for panaceas often leads people to ignore or minimize the effectiveness of these programs. While it may seem cost-effective to expand programs to include more clients, thus yielding greater results while reducing the costs of the program, in the case of these programs, doing more with fewer youths seems to have a greater impact. This is similar to the argument discussed in Chapter 10, whereby many educators believe that smaller classes result in greater learning opportunities for students. The reasons for this are the same as they apply to juvenile justice programs: a smaller client base ensures more one-on-one care for individuals and greater long-term impacts.[106]

Scare tactics have become a popular, though largely ineffective way to prevent delinquency. Their popularity derives from the general perception that juvenile crime in the United States is rising because youths do not fear the consequences of the justice system. As a result, a "law and order" campaign aimed at juveniles and juvenile crime has emerged. Examples include the tendency for juvenile courts to waive jurisdiction to adult criminal court for youths who commit violent crimes. Such "get tough" approaches are based on the logic that the fear of imprisonment will reduce juvenile crime rates. However, this relationship is a weak one: youths who have been placed in the adult system actually have higher recidivism rates than those placed in juvenile detention facilities.[107]

As a preventive strategy, the philosophy supporting scare tactics is based on the idea that the threat of punishment will prevent youths from getting involved in crime in the first place. Scare tactics also make people feel as though something constructive is being done about juvenile crime. But programs based on fear have not proved effective in preventing delinquency.

Three notable examples of programs based on scare tactics are juvenile boot camps, D.A.R.E., and Scared Straight. In **juvenile boot camp programs,** "at-risk" youths are placed in intense, structured environments that are modeled after military boot camps. Boot camps were originally intended to enhance participants' ability to define goals, improve their self-esteem, and learn the importance of structure, discipline, and self-confidence.[108] The ultimate goal was to reshape a youth's identity in such a way that when he or she returned home and was exposed to delinquency-producing influences and other criminals, the participant would be able to resist peer pressure. Unfortunately, for many youths, the programs fail to achieve these goals.[109]

Boot camps have three primary goals: reduce recidivism, reduce the size of the prison population, and decrease costs. Evaluation studies by the National Institute of Justice (NIJ) consistently show that boot camps have little to no effect on recidivism. Part of the reason might be the fact that the program's duration is too short, typically between 90 and 120 days—far too brief a period to have a lasting impact on youths' future behavior. NIJ studies also show that boot camps have no effect on reducing the size of the prison population. One reason for this is the restrictive nature of the programs, which take only a certain type of offender. Because the type of offender eligible for a boot camp intervention represents a small number of the entire population, the program's ability to reduce the prison population is severely limited. Finally, because boot camps cannot take many offenders, and because the length of stay is short, little in the way of cost savings actually occurs.[110]

D.A.R.E., which stands for Drug Abuse Reduction through Education, is a cooperative effort among law enforcement agencies, educators, students, parents, and local communities. The curriculum consists of seventeen weeks of drug prevention lectures targeted at fifth- and sixth-grade students, and delivered by specially trained law enforcement officers. The curriculum focuses on the negative impact drugs have on users and offers students a basis on which to make informed decisions regarding their own nondrug use.

The D.A.R.E. program was created in 1983 as a collaborative venture of the Los Angeles Police Department and Los Angeles Unified School District. Building on this partnership, D.A.R.E. has become the largest and most popular drug prevention curriculum

juvenile boot camp programs
Intense, structured environments that are modeled after military boot camps to enhance at-risk youths' ability to define goals, improve their self-esteem, and learn the importance of structure, discipline, and self-confidence.

D.A.R.E.
Drug Abuse Reduction through Education, a cooperative effort among law enforcement agencies, educators, students, parents, and local communities, consisting of drug prevention lectures targeted at fifth- and sixth-grade students, and delivered by trained law enforcement officials.

in the world. D.A.R.E. reaches more than 80 percent of all school districts nationwide, and an estimated 18,000 law enforcement officers have received training in the D.A.R.E. curriculum.[111]

In the 1990s, D.A.R.E. came under scrutiny for being less effective than what advocates claimed. Evaluations of the program found that it had no impact on the rate of drug use by children who went through D.A.R.E. training.[112] Defenders of D.A.R.E. cited methodological problems with these studies and claimed students benefited from the D.A.R.E. experience. D.A.R.E. officials pointed to other studies that showed a short-term positive impact on drug-related knowledge, attitudes, and behaviors. However, experts argue that most of these studies were poorly designed, contained nonrepresentative samples, and employed inadequate data collection and data analysis procedures.[113]

More recent studies of D.A.R.E., using more sophisticated research techniques (e.g., large samples, random assignment, and longitudinal follow-up), have shown that D.A.R.E. has little or no impact on drug use, particularly beyond the initial post-test assessment. As some experts have noted, when stronger research designs are used to evaluate the program, the results show that D.A.R.E. has an even lesser impact on drug-using behavior. In fact, in 2001, the Surgeon General of the United States placed the D.A.R.E. program in the category of "Does Not Work."[114]

Another program, **Scared Straight,** brings parole and probation youths into maximum-security prisons to interact with adult prisoners. The original Scared Straight program began in the 1970s. Inmates serving life sentences at Rahway State Prison in New Jersey launched a program in which they would "scare" at-risk or delinquent children using an aggressive depiction of the violence that characterizes social life in prison. This original program generated a great deal of media attention and a television documentary touting a 94 percent success rate. Subsequent programs modeled after Scared Straight reported success rates ranging between 8 and 90 percent.[115]

While popular with politicians and policymakers, and even declared successful by many practitioners, one evaluation of Scared Straight programs showed that participants were actually more likely to be arrested than nonparticipants.[116] To underscore this initial finding, a rigorous review of Scared Straight programs was conducted in 2002. From the 500 studies conducted on these types of programs, nine met a complicated set of criteria to ensure that the programs and their evaluations were conducted properly. The results again showed that the youths who went through the Scared Straight programs had higher recidivism rates than those who did not.[117]

There may be a number of reasons why boot camps, D.A.R.E., and Scared Straight programs do not work. Perhaps exposure to scare tactics desensitizes youths to the negative impact of such outcomes. That is, by seeing what prison life really looks like, youths may come to feel as though they will be able to cope with its negative effects. This experience can easily negate whatever deterrent value the program might have had on them.

The lack of impact of these programs in terms of reoffending can also be explained by the fact that some youths may find that the prison experience or the drug-using culture provides a haven into which they feel they fit—meaning they readily identify with drug users or prison inmates and their behavior. Still another explanation may be that the drama and intensity of the experience, along with the dangers described, might be seen as a challenge to youths—to prove they can handle the adversity of the boot camp, prison, or drug subculture.[118]

Many of the programs offered by the juvenile justice system are tertiary in nature; that is, they are designed to prevent delinquents from committing future crimes. Some experts argue that this provides juvenile justice officials with an opportunity to focus on changing the attitudes, values, and beliefs of youths while they are being detained. Advocates of such an approach contend that behavioral changes are more likely to occur when youths are confined and are not influenced by outside factors. This is part of the logic of boot camps—by changing the environmental conditions, counselors and therapists can have a

Do you think that boot camp programs can positively affect the character and self-esteem of at-risk youths?

Scared Straight
A program that brings parole and probation youths into maximum-security prisons to interact with adult prisoners, thereby discouraging them from future risky behavior that would land them in such an environment.

much better chance of changing youths' behavior. Programs involving what is sometimes referred to as *milieu treatment,* whereby residents of a detention facility are rewarded for engaging in appropriate behavior, can be successful in the short term. Once youths are released from institutions and returned to their neighborhoods and friends, however, any positive effects of the program all but disappear.[119]

Even one-on-one counseling—even when it occurs as part of a youth's aftercare following detention—has been shown to be ineffective. To be fair, some of these results may be attributable to the characteristics of particular youths. It is much more difficult to effect attitude and behavioral changes with hard-core, chronic, and violent offenders than with first-time delinquents. Finally, even when individual counseling is coupled with close supervision of delinquent youths, along with an array of social services to address many of the issues and problems discussed in this chapter, it often fails to have a positive impact on recidivism.[120]

Complicating matters still further is the manner in which many of the programs are managed. Politics, underfunding, and mismanagement all contribute to the inability of government-run programs to effectively meet the needs of a wide range of offenders, making it unlikely that many programs will achieve their particular goals. Moreover, in this era of reduced funding, any program, no matter how well managed or how well it identifies the needs of its clients, will face significant challenges.

THE BIG PICTURE

Conclusions on Delinquency Prevention

- Why do you think the public and policymakers focus so much on finding a single solution to a problem as complex as delinquency?
- Which programs do you think are most effective: primary, secondary, or tertiary? Explain.
- Are teen courts useful in reducing delinquency? Or do they engage in "creaming," as some critics claim, thus guaranteeing success even though their impact might be limited?
- What value do you place on the presence of mentors or positive role models in the lives of delinquents? Do you think that mentor relationships can actually prevent delinquency in at-risk youths?

Key Terms

panacea phenomenon
net widening
community crime prevention programs
target-hardening measures
primary crime prevention
secondary crime prevention

tertiary crime prevention
risk factors
protective factors
mentoring programs
Job Corps program
diversion

teen courts
drug courts
juvenile boot camp programs
D.A.R.E.
Scared Straight programs

Make the Call ▶ Delinquency Prevention

Review the scenario below, and decide how you would approach this case.

YOUR ROLE: Volunteer for a juvenile arbitration program

DETAILS OF THE CASE

- A young man, age thirteen, tried to steal a pair of sneakers from a local department store.
- He was arrested for shoplifting.
- He is a first-time offender who has never been in trouble at school, and his parents assure you that this is not typical behavior.
- The store has a zero-tolerance policy and so wants to press charges.
- The boy seems remorseful, and his parents promise to provide better supervision.

WHAT TYPE OF SANCTION DO YOU EMPLOY?

You have a wide range of options, including restitution, a letter of apology to the managers of the store, and community service.

Consider:

- Has the child committed a crime before?
- Has he displayed delinquent behavior at school or elsewhere?
- What reasons might he have had for behaving the way he did?
- Is it appropriate to press charges against the child, and is this sanction necessary to teach him not to steal again in the future?
- What other sanctions might achieve this end without harming the child's record?

Apply Theory to Reality ▶ Social Cohesion Theory

All delinquency programs share a relationship to the idea of social cohesion, by which we create ties and connections between individuals and society, and vice versa. Explore the work of Emile Durkheim. How might you apply his ideas to explain why delinquency prevention programs emphasize social cohesion among their participants and their communities?

Your Community ▶ Delinquency Prevention

In addition to the information you glean from your readings, class lectures, and discussions, it is important to roll up your sleeves and immerse yourself in a topic as a researcher who gains an understanding of a problem or issue by observing or experiencing it firsthand. Through such methods, you gain a much greater appreciation of the magnitude and scope of the problem than if you were only engaged in "armchair theorizing."

- Contact a local chapter of Big Brothers/Big Sisters, the Boys Club of America, or another mentoring program in your community, and ask to interview representatives of that chapter.

- Interview volunteers to get a sense of their experiences spending time with youths. What do they say about the impact of their efforts on youths? Have they seen any significant behavior changes or evidence that youths are using different strategies to solve problems since they were assigned as mentors?

- If it is appropriate to do so, interview youths and try to learn more about what having a mentor means to them.

- After collecting your data, and drawing from the relevant literature, prepare a report that highlights your experiences with one or more of these programs. Connect your experience to the discussion of delinquency prevention in this chapter.

Notes

[1] Finckenauer, J. 1982. *Scared Straight and the Panacea Phenomenon.* Englewood Cliffs, NJ: Prentice-Hall.

[2] See, for instance, a review of nearly forty delinquency prevention programs, Lundman, R. J., and Scarpetti, F. R. 1978. "Delinquency Prevention: Recommendations for Future Projects." *Crime and Delinquency,* 24: 207.

[3] See, for instance, Taylor, R. W., Fritsch, E. J., and Caeti, T. J. 2007. *Juvenile Justice,* 2nd ed. New York: McGraw-Hill.

[4] Macallair, D. 2002. *Widening the Net in Juvenile Justice and the Dangers of Prevention and Early Intervention.* San Francisco: Center on Juvenile and Criminal Justice.

[5] See Lundman, R. J. 2001 *Prevention and Control of Juvenile Delinqu*ents, 3rd ed. New York: Oxford University Press.

[6] See, for instance, Dryfoos, J. G. 1990. *Adolescents at Risk: Prevalence and Prevention.* New York: Oxford University Press.

[7] Juvenile Justice and Delinquency Prevention Act, 2002 revision. Available at http://ojjdp.ncjrs.gov/about/ojjdpact2002.html.

[8] Juvenile Justice and Delinquency Prevention Act as amended, Pub. L. No. 93-415 (1974).

[9] Schmallenger, F. 2007. *Criminolog,* 8th ed. Upper Saddle River, NJ: Prentice-Hall.

[10] Lab, S. 2007. *Crime Prevention,* 7th ed. Cincinnati, OH: Anderson

[11] Ibid.

[12] Gaines, L. K., Kappeler, V. E., and Vaughn, J. B. 1994. *Policing in America.* Cincinnati, OH: Anderson.

[13] See, for instance, Lanphear, B., Wright, R., and Dietrich, K. 2005. "Environmental Toxins." *Pediatrics Review,* 26: 191–196.

[14] See, for instance, Carnegie Task Force on Meeting the Needs of Young Children. 1994. *Starting Points: Meeting the Needs of Our Youngest Children.* New York: Carnegie Corporation of New York.

[15] Ibid.

[16] Olds, D., Hill, P., Mihalic, S., and O'Brien, R. 1998. *Nurse-Family Partnership: Blueprints for Violence Prevention, Book Seven.* Boulder, CO: Center for the Study and Prevention of Violence.

[17] Olds, D., Hill, P., Mihalic, S., and O'Brien, R. 1993. "Effect of Prenatal and Infancy Nurse Home Visitation on Government Spending." *Medical Care,* 31: 155–174.

[18] Seitz, V., Rosenbaum, L., and Apfel, N. 1985. "Effects of Family Support Intervention: A Ten-Year Follow-Up." *Child Development,* 56: 375–391.

[19] See Henrich, C., Ginicola, M. M., and Finn-Stevenson, M. 2006. *The School of the 21st Century Is Making a Difference: Research in Brief.* New Haven, CT: Yale University. Available at http://www.yale.edu/21C/documents/2006_issueBrief_webversion.pdf.

[20] See, for instance, the U.S. Department of Education, Institute of Education Services, What Works Clearinghouse, at http://ies.ed.gov/ncee/wwc. See also Promising Practices Network on Children, Families, and Communities at http://www.promisingpractices.net/default.asp; National Center for Children in Poverty at http://www.nccp.org/index.html.

[21] Basic Head Start Facts. Available at http://www.nhsa.org/files/static_page_files/399A3EB7-1D09-3519-ADB004D2DAFA33DD/BasicHeadStartFacts.pdf.

[22] See http://www.nhsa.org/research/full_research_studies.

[23] Ibid.

[24] Parks, G. 2000. *The High/Scope Perry Preschool Project.* Washington, DC: Office of Juvenile Justice and Delinquency Prevention.

[25] Ibid.

[26] Olds, D. L. 1998. "Long-Term Effects on Nurse Home Visitation on Children's Criminal and Antisocial Behavior: 15 Year Follow Up of a Randomized Controlled Trial." *Journal of the American Medical Association,* 280: 1238–1244. See also www.colorado.edu/cspv/blueprints/model/programs/nfp.html.

[27] Bavolek, S. 2001. *The Nurturing Parenting Programs.* Washington, DC: Office of Juvenile Justice and Delinquency Prevention.

[28] See Perry, B. 1997. "Incubated in Terror: Neuro-developmental Factors in the Cycle of Violence." In Osofsky, J. D. *Children, Youth and Violence: Searching for Solutions.* New York: Guilford Press.

[29] Bavolek, 2001.

[30] Ibid.

[31] Ibid.

[32] Greenwood, P.W., Model, K. E., Rydell, C. P., and Chiesa, J. 1996. *Diverting Children from a Life of Crime: Measuring Costs and Benefits.* Santa Monica, CA: Rand Corporation.

[33] Reynolds, A. J., Temple, J. A., Robertson, D. L., and Mann, E. A. 2001. "Long-term Effects of an Early Childhood Intervention on Educational Achievement and Juvenile Arrest." *Journal of the American Medical Association,* 285: 2339–2346.

[34] See the Center for the Study and Prevention of Violence at the University of Colorado at Boulder at http://www.colorado.edu/cspv/blueprints/model/programs/nfp.html.

[35] See the parameters, philosophy, and scope of the 21C program at http://www.yale.edu/21c/news.html.

[36] Ibid.

[37] Ibid. See also Henrich, Ginicola, and Finn-Stevenson, 2006.

[38] Lab, 2007.

[39] While there is no way to determine an exact number of members, largely because participants in programs like Neighborhood Watch fluctuate a great deal, these figures are estimates by the Neighborhood Watch Program, which is sponsored by the National Sheriffs' Association. See "Celebrating the Success of 35 years of Neighborhood Watch" at http://www.usaonwatch.org/resource-/publication.aspx?PublicationId=49.

[40] Bennett, T., Holloway, K., and Farrington, D. P. 2006. "Does Neighborhood Watch Reduce Crime? A Systematic Review and Meta-Analysis." *Journal of Experimental Criminology,* 2: 437–458.

[41] See Lab, 2007.

[42] While every state has its own version of this program, the basics of Operation ID can be found at http://www.opid.org/.

[43] Newman, O. 1972. *Defensible Space: Crime Prevention through Urban Design.* New York: Macmillan.

[44] See, for instance, Crowe, T. D. 2000. *Crime Prevention through Environmental Design and Space Management Concepts.* New York: Butterworth-Heinemann.

[45] See, for instance, Sherman, L. 2002. *Evidence-Based Crime Prevention.* New York: Routledge.

[46] Farrington, D. P. 2000. "Explaining and Preventing Crime: The Globalization of Knowledge, The American Society of Criminology 1999 Presidential Address." *Criminology,* 38(1): 1–24.

[47] Office of the Surgeon General. 2001. *Youth Violence: A Report of the Surgeon General.* Washington, DC: U.S. Department of Health and Human Services.

[48] Shader, M. 2003. *Risk Factors for Delinquency: An Overview.* Washington, DC: Office of Juvenile Justice and Delinquency Prevention. Available at http://www.ncjrs.gov/html/ojjdp-/jjjournal_2003_2/index.html.

[49] Rutter, M. 1987. "Psychosocial Resilience and Protective Mechanisms." *American Journal of Orthopsychiatry,* 57(3): 316–331.

[50] See Shader, 2003; Herrenkohl, T. L., Maguin, E., Hill, K. G., Hawkins, J. D., Abbott, R. D., and Catalano, R. F. 2000. "Developmental Risk Factors for Youth Violence." *Journal of Adolescent Health,* 26(7): 176–186.

[51] Herrenkohl et al., 2000.

[52] McCord, J., Widom, C. S., and Crowell, N. A. (eds.). 2001. *Juvenile Crime, Juvenile Justice. Panel on Juvenile Crime: Prevention, Treatment and Control.* Washington, DC: National Academy Press.

[53] See, for instance, Garzon, D. L., Huang, H., and Todd, R. D. 2008. "Do Attention Deficit Hyperactivity Disorder and Oppositional Defiant Disorder Influence Preschool Unintentional Injury Risk?" *Archives of Psychiatric Nursing,* 22(5): 288–296. See also Vitulano, M., Fitz, P. J., and Rathert, J. L. 2009. "Delinquent Peer Influences on Child Delinquency: The Moderating Effect of Impulsivity." *Journal of Psychopathology and Behavioral Assessment.* Available at http://www.springerlink.com/content-/b7062623825160r5/fulltext.pdf?page=1; Vaughn, M. G., Beaver, K. M., and DeLisi, M. 2009. "A General Biosocial Paradigm of Antisocial Behavior." *Youth Violence and Juvenile Justice,* 7(4): 279–298. Available at http://yvj.sagepub.com/cgi/content/abstract/7/4/279.

[54] Ibid.

[55] Wasserman, G. A., and Seracini, A. G. 2001. "Family Risk Factors and Interventions." In Loeber, R., and Farrington, D. P. (eds.), *Child Delinquents: Development, Intervention and Service Needs,* pp. 165–189. Thousand Oaks, CA: Sage. See also Bavolek, 2001.

[56] Ibid.

[57] Ibid.

[58] See Loeber, K., Burke, J., and Pardini, D. A. 2009. "Development and Etiology of Disruptive and Delinquent Behavior." *Annual Review of Clinical Psychology,* 5: 291–310. See also Laird, R. D., Pettit, G. S., Dodge, K. A., and Bates, J. E. 2005. "Peer Relationship Antecedents of Delinquent Behavior in Late Adolescence: Is There Evidence of Demographic Group Differences in Developmental Processes?" *Developmental Psychopathology,* 17(1): 127–141. See also Hawkins, J. D., Smith, B. H., and Catalano, R. F. 2002. "Delinquent Behavior." *American Academy of Pediatrics,* 23(11): 387–391.

[59] Lipsey, M. W., and Derzon, J. H. 1998. "Predictors of Violent or Serious Delinquency in Adolescence and Early Adulthood: A Synthesis of Longitudinal Research." In Loeber, R., and Farrrington, D. P. (eds.), *Serious and Violent Juvenile Offenders: Risk Factors and Successful Interventions,* pp. 86–105. Thousand Oaks, CA: Sage.

[60] See Shader, 2003; Herrenkohl et al., 2000.

[61] The National Research Council and the Institute of Medicine. 2000. *From Neurons to Neighborhoods: The Success of Early Childhood Development.* Washington, DC: National Academy Press. See also Sweeten, G. 2006. "Who Will Graduate? Disruption of High School Education by Arrest and Court Involvement." *Justice Quarterly,* 23(4): 462–479.

[62] Ibid.

[63] McCord, Widom, and Crowell, 2001, p. 89.

[64] See Shader, 2003; Herrenkohl et al., 2000.

[65] See, for instance, Larson, R. 1975. "What Happened to Patrol Operations in the Kansas City? A Review of the Kansas City Preventive Patrol Experiment." *Journal of Criminal Justice,* 3(4): 267–297. See also Coupe, T., and Blake, L. 2005. "The Effects of Patrol Workloads and Response Strength on Arrests at Burglary Emergencies." *Journal of Criminal Justice,* 33(3): 239–255.

[66] See Flanagan, C. A., Webster, N. S., and Perkins, D. F. 2006. *Encouraging Adult Voluntarism among Young People.* New York: Springer. See also Ingersoll, S. 1997. The National Juvenile Justice Action Plan. Washington, DC: Office of Juvenile Justice and Delinquency Prevention. Available at http://ojjdp.ncjrs.gov/jjjournal/jjjournal997/plan.html.

[67] See Big Brothers/Big Sisters program at http://www.bbbsa.org. Accessed July 1, 2008.

[68] See http://www.colorado.edu/cspv/blueprints/query/default.htm. Accessed July 1, 2008.

[69] http://www.rightofpassage.com. Accessed July 1, 2008.

[70] Ibid.

[71] Ibid.

[72] See U.S. Department of Labor. 1999. National Job Corps Study: Report on the Process Analysis. Washington, DC. Available at http://wdr.doleta.gov/opr/fulltext/document.cfm?docn=6065.

[73] Ibid. See also Job Corps website at http://www.jobcorps.gov/cdss.aspx.

[74] Ibid.

[75] See Schochet. P. Z., Burghardt, J. A., and McConnell, S. 2008. "Does Job Corps Work? Impact Finding in the National Job Corps Study." *American Economic Review,* 98(5): 1864–1886.

[76] Ibid.

[77] Ibid.

[78] See, for instance, Due, P., Holstein, B., Lynch, J., Diderichsen, F., Gabhain, S., Scheidt, P., and Currie, C. 2005. "Bullying and Symptoms among School-aged Children: An International Comparative Cross-sectional Study in 28 Countries." *The European Journal of Public Health,* 1–5; Kumpulainen, K. 1998. "Bullying and Psychiatric Symptoms among Elementary School-aged Children." *Child Abuse & Neglect,* 22(7): 705–717; Fried, S., and Fried, P. 1996. *Bullies and Victims: Helping Your Child through the Schoolyard Battlefield.* New York: Evans, M., Beran, T. N., Hughes, G., and Lupart, J. 2008. "A Model of Achievement and Bullying: Analyses of the Canadian National Longitudinal Survey of Children and Youth Data." *Educational Research,* 50: 1, 25–39.

[79] See, for instance, Wilson, J. Q., and Loury, G. C. (eds.). 1987. *Families, Schools, and Delinquency Prevention.* Secaucus, NJ: Springer-Verlag.

[80] See, Gottfredson, D. E., Gottfredson, G. D., and Weisman, S. A. 2001. "The Timing of Delinquent Behavior and Its Implications for After-School Programs." *Criminology and Public Policy,* 1: 61–86.

[81] See Sherman and Eck, 2002; Wilson and Loury, 1987; Kumpulainen, 1998; Beran, Hughes, and Lupart, 2008. See also http://www.stopbullyingnow.com.

[82] Olweus, D., Limber, S., and Mihalic, S. 1999. *Blueprints for Violence Prevention, Book Nine: Bullying Prevention Programs.* Boulder, CO: Center for the Study and Prevention of Violence.

[83] Ibid.

[84] Ibid.

[85] See, for instance, Sherman and Eck, 2002; Wilson and Loury, 1987; Kumpulainen, 1998; Beran, Hughes, and Lupart, 2008. See also http://www.stopbullyingnow.com.

[86] See overview of program at http://www .ridgeviewacademy.com/rva/site/default.asp.

[87] Ibid.

[88] http://www.rightofpassage.com. Accessed July 1, 2008.

[89] Mendel, R. 2000. *Less Hype, More Help: Reducing Juvenile Crime: What Works and What Doesn't.* Washington, DC: American Youth Policy Forum. Available at http://www.aypf.org/publications/mendel-/index.html.

[90] Ibid.

[91] Lab, 2007.

[92] Mendel, 2000.

[93] Herman, M. 2003 *Juvenile Justice Trends in 2002 Teen Courts—A Juvenile Justice Diversion Program.* National Center for Safe Courts. Available at http://www.ncsconline.org/WC/Publications/KIS_JuvJus_Trends02_TeenPub.pdf.

[94] Ibid.

[95] American Bar Association. 2002 "The Sudden Popularity of Teen Courts." *The Judges' Journal,* 41(1); Butts, J., Hoffman, D., and Buck, J. 1999. "Teen Courts in the United States: A Profile of Current Programs." *OJJDP Fact Sheet.* Washington, DC: Office of Juvenile Justice and Delinquency Prevention.

[96] Herman, 2003.

[97] Butts, J. A., and Roman, J. (eds.). 2004. *Juvenile Drug Courts and Teen Substance Abuse.* Washington, DC: Urban Institute.

[98] Herman, 2003. See also Butts, J. A., Buck, J., and Coggershall, M. B. 2002. *The Impact of Teen Court on Young Offenders.* Washington, DC: Urban Institute.

[99] Butts and Roman, 2004.

[100] American Bar Association, 2002.

[101] Herman, 2003; Butts, Buck, and Coggershall, 2002.

[102] http://www.ncjrs.gov/spotlight/drug_courts/facts.html.

[103] See, for instance, Butts, Buck, and Coggershall, 2002; Butts and Roman, 2004.

[104] Ibid.

[105] Butts and Roman, 2004.

[106] See, for instance, Garry, E. M. 1999. *A Compendium of Programs That Work for Youth,* OJJDP Fact Sheet #121. Washington, DC: Office of Juvenile Justice and Delinquency Prevention. See also American Probation and Parole Association. 2008. *How Do We Reduce Recidivism? A Look at Research Based Best Practices.* Available at http://www .supremecourt.az.gov/jjsd/SPEP/docs/2008-/How_do_weReduce_Juvenile_Recidivism.pdf.

[107] Ibid.

[108] Parent, D. 2003. *Correctional Boot Camp: Lessons from a Decade of Research.* Washington, DC: U.S. Department of Justice, Office of Community Oriented Policing Services.

[109] See Mendal, 2002; Krisberg, 2005.

[110] Parent, 2003.

[111] For an overview of the D.A.R.E. program, see http://www.dare.com/home/documents-/2008AnnualReport.pdf.

[112] *Past and Future Directions of the D.A.R.E. Program: An Evaluation Review,* Draft Final Report by Research Triangle Institute September 1994. See also Harmon, M. A. 1993. *Reducing the Risk of Drug Involvement among Early Adolescents: An Evaluation of Drug Abuse Resistance Education (DARE).* College Park, MD: Institute of Criminal Justice and Criminology, University of Maryland.

[113] Rosenbaum, D. P., and Hanson, G.S. 1998. "Assessing the Effects of School-Based Drug Education: A Six-Year Multi-Level Analysis of Project D.A.R.E." *Journal of Research in Crime and Delinquency,* 35(4): 381–412.

[114] Office of the Surgeon General, 2001.

[115] Finckenauer, J. O. 1982. *Scared Straight and the Panacea Phenomenon.* Englewood Cliffs, NJ: Prentice-Hall; Petrosino, A., Turpin-Petrosino, C., and Buehler, J. 2003. "'Scared Straight' and Other Juvenile Awareness Programs for Preventing Juvenile Delinquency." In *The Campbell Collaborative Reviews of Intervention and Policy Evaluations (C2-RIPE).* Philadelphia: Campbell Collaboration.

[116] Ibid.

[117] Petrosino, A., Turpin-Petrosino, C., and Buehler, J. 2003. "Scared Straight and Other Juvenile Awareness Programs for Preventing Juvenile Delinquency: A Systematic Review of the Randomized Experimental Evidence." *The ANNALS of the American Academy of Political and Social Science,* 589: 41–62

[118] Finckenauer, 1982.

[119] See Surgeon General's report on delinquency prevention at http://mentalhealth.samhsa.gov-/youthviolence/surgeongeneral/SG_site/chapter 5/sec 4.aspineffectiveprimaryprevention.

[120] Ibid.

After reading this chapter, you should be able to:

- Identify the early forms of policing and how they relate to the treatment of delinquents.

- Understand the complex dynamic between social work and crime control for police officers.

- Apply constitutional rights afforded to juveniles at various stages of an encounter with law enforcement.

- Differentiate the types of police-sponsored delinquency prevention programs and their impact.

13

Law Enforcement and Delinquency

It is a common assumption that most encounters that occur between juveniles and law enforcement are the result of some type of misbehavior. However, there is a growing expectation that officers interact socially with the youths in their communities in order to better understand, and ultimately to prevent, juvenile crime. Consider the following case about Jai:

- is a sixteen-year-old boy living with his parents in a middle-class suburban neighborhood
- father is a corporate executive for Dell computers
- mother works for a nonprofit organization
- older twin sisters recently moved out to attend college
- has broken into neighbors' homes while they were away on vacation, eaten their food, stolen from them, swam in their pools, and vandalized their properties
- has also tagged a number of buildings in the community with graffiti and displayed bullying behaviors at school

All of Jai's offenses and crimes have gone unprosecuted because the police have not caught him in the act. His peers will not report him to the police, and none of the community members have first-hand knowledge of his activities. Given that many of these crimes could be classified as felonies, Jai presents a real problem to his community.

When trying to understand why an entire community, including its law enforcement, has failed to address Jai's behavior, the following explanations might come to mind:

- The police department's "style" of policing focuses on serious offenses only. While Jai's behavior is troublesome, it is unlikely to become a law enforcement priority.
- Patrol officers do not know many of the youths in the neighborhood, so they are unaware of Jai's activities.
- Jai is such a violent offender that community members are afraid to report his crimes to the police.

There are a variety of factors that determine how the police respond to an encounter with a juvenile. What are some factors the police and the community need to consider when dealing with a minor?

- The police lack options for dealing with Jai, since there are no programs to prevent or curtail his behavior.
- The police are limited in what they can do. Because there is no complainant, the police do not have probable cause to arrest Jai.

THINK ABOUT IT

How can the police department collaborate with community members to prevent delinquency?

In examining the relationship between youths and law enforcement, we should not limit our discussion to procedures following arrest. Of all the agencies that affect the lives of juveniles, it can be argued that law enforcement plays the most pivotal role. Interactions with law enforcement officers are usually the entry point by which youths become involved in the juvenile justice system.

This chapter will explore the nature of interactions that take place between law enforcement officers and juveniles. These interactions can be divided into three broad categories:

police discretion
The subjective use of judgment by officers in deciding whether to invoke the justice process.

- social interactions with juveniles, which involve the use of **police discretion,** or the subjective use of judgment by officers in deciding whether to invoke the justice process
- procedural requirements that officers must follow, should formal intervention become necessary
- prevention strategies designed to address issues involving juveniles before they become problems

Historical Overview

In its earliest forms, policing relied on citizens to address crime. Until the beginning of the Industrial Revolution, law enforcement in England, for instance, was a local matter. Citizens had a social obligation to maintain order in their communities. During this era, England was primarily rural and agrarian, and did not have a formal police force. While the king was the ultimate authority, who designated certain key officials to maintain order and deal with criminals, much of what constituted policing was done informally. The primary law enforcement mechanism from 1066 until well into the 1300s was called the frank-pledge system. The **frankpledge system**—also referred to as the mutual pledge system— was a type of informal social control, mandating that each community member over the age of twelve had a responsibility to protect the community, and each other, in times of need (see Figure 13-1).

frankpledge system
The primary law enforcement system—also referred to as the mutual pledge system—from 1066 until well into the 1300s, mandating that each community member over the age of twelve protect the community, and each other, in time of need.

Under this system, communities were divided into ten-family groups called *tithings.* Cities as we know them did not exist, so each tithing was responsible for maintaining peace within its own boundaries. It was each citizen's duty to let others know when a crime was committed and to gather his neighbors and pursue the offender. Every ten tithings formed a *hundred,* headed by a constable, who was appointed by a local noble-man to be in charge of weapons and equipment. The hundreds, in turn, were grouped together to form a *shire,* whose size was comparable to what we know as a county. For each shire, the king appointed a supervisor, called a *shire reeve,* from which the modern term *sheriff* is derived.[1] This system of mutual responsibility and shared penalties— in the form of fines levied by the king when the offender was not apprehended—was designed to ensure that all members of the community made a conscientious effort to control crime.[2]

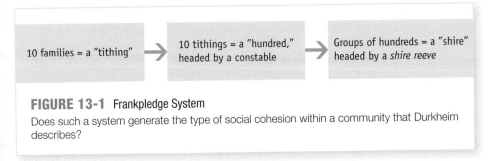

10 families = a "tithing"	→	10 tithings = a "hundred," headed by a constable	→	Groups of hundreds = a "shire" headed by a *shire reeve*

FIGURE 13-1 Frankpledge System
Does such a system generate the type of social cohesion within a community that Durkheim describes?

In 1285, another advance was made toward an organized system of policing. A new law established the **watch and ward system** to help constables in their law enforcement efforts. The watch and ward system required men from each town to take turns standing watch at night. If any criminals were caught, they were turned over to the constable for trial the following day.[3] Like the frankpledge system, which monitored crime during daylight hours, the watch and ward system emphasized community responsibility for crime control.

This dual system of law enforcement, based on the frankpledge system and supplemented by the watch and ward, was in effect for several hundred years. Gradually, however, it lost community support. Watchmen were generally incompetent; they often drank while on duty, fell asleep, or simply failed to report crimes that occurred. For the most part, community-based crime control efforts were ineffective, and crime continued to plague England's cities.

In 1822, Sir Robert Peel assumed the office of Home Secretary in a nation that had suffered many years of violence and disorder, not to mention a public that had a general distrust of politicians and the justice process. In 1829, Peel introduced a bill in Parliament, referred to as the Metropolitan Police Act, which sought to improve policing in cities. The act provided for a single authority that would be responsible for a seven-mile radius from the heart of the city.

On September 29, 1829, 6,000 officers were brought together to form the first organized police force in England. They were called the Metropolitan Police of London, the New Police, or the Preventive Police. Peel's vision was to have this new force serve as a vehicle for restoring order and social harmony in the community. The operation of the new police force was very different from that of the watch and ward system. It emphasized strict supervision to ensure that officers would actually perform their duties and not sleep, drink, or otherwise act irresponsibly while on duty. Instead, the city was to be patrolled by officers who were assigned specific territories, or beats. Peel also wanted to employ military principles to organize what had traditionally been a civilian force. Thus, the Metropolitan Police were distinguished by their patrol of specific areas, and by their paramilitary organization, which was designed to maintain discipline.[4]

To avoid comparisons to military personnel, while still restoring order and harmony to London's residents, Peel chose not to arm his officers with guns. Instead, they carried nightsticks. Because the public was generally opposed to the use of standing armies as a means of enforcing civil laws, Peel's officers, although dressed in uniforms and organized according to a paramilitary model, did not act like soldiers. These officers performed a number of non–law enforcement tasks designed to improve the quality of life in the London area. These included lighting street lamps, calling out the time during the night, and providing care to the needy. Thus, under Peel, what began as an informal community response to social problems like crime evolved into a more formal mechanism of enforcing community norms and laws.[5]

THE JUVENILE JUSTICE SYSTEM AND POLICING IN THE UNITED STATES

Early policing in the United States imitated England's model. However, during this period, American citizens had strong feelings of distrust toward law enforcement. In particular, they felt that officers represented a form of military presence that infringed

watch and ward system
A system that required men from each town to take turns standing watch at night; if any criminals were caught, they were turned over to the constable for trial the following day.

upon their privacy and freedoms.[6] Moreover, U.S. law enforcement held a reputation for incompetence, corruption, political patronage, and an inability to solve crime.[7]

At about the same time that formal policing was established in the United States, the official treatment of juveniles in the criminal justice system also evolved.[8] As we discussed in Chapter 1, when it came to crime, early law enforcement generally treated juveniles as adults. In the 1800s, the Child Savers Movement advocated for a separate system of justice for juveniles. Advocates argued that treating young offenders like their adult counterparts would lead to their becoming adult offenders. To address this potential outcome, a separate system was created that focused not on punishment but on treatment, with the goal of helping juveniles become productive citizens. By the mid-1920s, every state had a separate justice system for juveniles.

The creation of the juvenile justice system resulted in a host of new challenges for law enforcement. For example, police departments struggled to cope with the two systems and their differing offender populations. In response, many departments created juvenile or youth divisions to handle juvenile matters.[9]

POLICE MATRONS AND DELINQUENTS

police matrons
Women assigned to deal with juveniles, as well as to take on administrative duties and parking enforcement.

The philosophy of the juvenile court differed from that of the criminal court in that it focused on the treatment and rehabilitation of offenders. Because women were thought to be more maternal and nurturing, they were also expected to be better equipped to deal with juvenile offenders than were male officers. The result was the designation of **police matrons,** who were assigned to deal with juveniles, as well as to take on administrative duties and parking enforcement. Police matrons were assigned based on the belief that they could best meet the needs of all types of juvenile offenders (e.g., they were more nurturing, compassionate, and sensitive to the needs of children). In fact, some experts point out that the rise in delinquency was one of the main reasons for the inclusion of women in law enforcement.[10]

PROFESSIONALIZATION OF POLICING AND DELINQUENCY

In 1900, the only criteria used to select police officers were physical fitness and a political connection to the police department.[11] By the 1930s, only about 15 percent of police officers in the United States had participated in any type of training program. However, in the 1960s and 1970s, police departments began making a concerted effort to improve standards and training, and to professionalize policing as a career. In what has since been described as "the progressive era of policing," several presidential commissions were created to focus on the improved operation of the criminal justice system as the best way to reduce crime.[12]

During this period, dedicated efforts were made to transform policing into a desirable career. For example, the first crime labs were established, and elaborate investigative techniques were developed. Also, selection and training methods were created and enhanced to improve the quality of officers. While police departments around the country attempted to enhance their public image, the treatment of juveniles remained essentially unchanged. It was only after the passage of the Juvenile Justice and Delinquency Prevention Act in 1975 that changes in the treatment of juvenile offenders began to take effect.

One of the unfortunate effects of the efforts to professionalize policing in the 1960s and 1970s was that police officers lost touch with citizens in their communities. In an effort to be objective, competent, and professional, officers were instructed to interact with the public in very specific ways and only in particular types of situations. The image of law enforcement officers as "professionals" was not received well by communities, whose members felt that this new professionalism meant that officers

In the early days of the juvenile justice system, women were thought to be better equipped to deal with the juvenile offender population. Think back to Chapter 10's discussion of the stereotypical traits women are supposed to display. How might these stereotypes have contributed to the creation of the role of police matron?

were less concerned with their well-being. In fact, many residents began to believe that the police focused only on serious street crimes, and not on the community as a whole. In the 1970s, demonstrations and riots occurred in many cities across the country, sending a clear message to law enforcement that officers needed closer contact with the people they served. It became increasingly apparent that the public wanted more from its officers than a traditional focus on crime fighting. This need was backed by research that focused on the effectiveness of the police and the importance of citizen-police encounters.[13]

As we discussed in Chapter 12, a new emphasis on community policing has helped remedy some of the conflicts and tensions between the police and the community. Community policing is based on a service-oriented style of law enforcement, which differs significantly from the traditional focus on serious street crimes. This type of policing also focuses more broadly on disorder in the community, crime prevention, fear reduction, and community support for organized prevention and enforcement efforts. This new focus on prevention has had significant implications for the way officers handle juveniles and interact with them.[14] It has also led to the development of particular "styles" of law enforcement. These were developed largely from the work of James Q. Wilson, whose book *Varieties of Police Behavior* (1968) proposed three different models, or styles, of policing:

1. **Watchman:** the watchman style emphasizes the order maintenance function of police officers. Officers using this style are concerned with public order and serious crime, but are not overly attentive to minor infractions. For example, there is a certain expectation that juveniles are going to "act up," so unless they commit felonies, most officers are not likely to arrest them without mitigating factors. Watchman-style officers typically take a familial view toward juveniles and use court referrals only as a last resort. Similarly, domestic squabbles are viewed as a private matter that need not involve the police, unless a crime has occurred. This style is characteristic of lower-class neighborhoods where the police intervene only when it is necessary to control behavior.

2. **Legalistic:** this style of policing focuses more strictly on law violations, rather than on maintaining order. Departments adopting this style usually require officers to enforce one set of uniform standards on the public. In this particular style, the exercise of discretion by officers is discouraged. Instead, all citizens, regardless of circumstances, are to be treated the same. The reason for this narrow interpretation of the police function is that discretion is viewed as a possible first step to police corruption. Under the legalistic style, the police respond to calls for service, act only if there is probable cause of serious violations, and generally avoid intervention in problems that are not crimes. However, because they are often not allowed to exercise discretion, if a crime occurs, officers tend to implement the criminal justice process, and offenders rarely escape sanction. Officers in these types of departments write a lot of tickets and arrest and detain people even for minor violations.

3. **Service:** this style approaches law enforcement from a broad problem-solving perspective. Police departments practicing this style of policing are usually found in homogeneous, middle- and upper-class communities. These departments and officers emphasize providing services to community residents. They consider all calls to be serious, regardless of their nature, but invoke the justice process only when necessary. Officers try to correct problems that are symptomatic of crime, such as loitering, public intoxication, and domestic arguments. These social problems are addressed both through direct intervention and through referrals to other social agencies. Service-style departments often resemble private security companies, with an emphasis on public and community relations.[15]

Wilson's styles are useful in classifying and understanding police departments today. There are numerous examples of each of the styles. For instance, a campus police department might adopt a watchman style; a tourist community might use a service style; and an industrial city might be more legalistic in its approach to law enforcement. We should also keep in mind that some departments use a combination of all three styles. Think of a beachfront community, in which officers may adopt a service style of policing during spring break or tourist season, and revert to a watchman style after the summer is over.[16]

incident-based policing
An approach in which officers wait for crimes to occur and respond with arrests.

Today, an even greater emphasis has been placed on community policing, with officers encouraged to examine underlying issues in a community and to address them proactively. In contrast to **incident-based policing,** in which officers wait for crimes to occur and respond with arrests, this more holistic approach focuses on the contexts in which problems exist, such as poverty, substandard housing, and unemployment.[17] Advocates of community policing believe that crime is a symptom of these larger problems, and so cannot be prevented through arrests alone.

JAI'S CASE

Styles of Policing and Jai's Behavior

Recall Jai's situation:

- is sixteen years old and lives in a middle-class suburban neighborhood
- has committed numerous acts of delinquency, including break-ins and vandalism, and exhibits bullying behaviors
- has never been caught by law enforcement or had charges pressed against him

It is possible that the police in Jai's community have adopted an incident-based policing strategy, meaning that until Jai commits a serious crime and is caught in the act, they are likely not to take action. Instead of being proactive and trying to understand the root causes of Jai's behavior, the department seems satisfied to take a more reactive approach.

THINK ABOUT IT

According to Wilson's three styles of policing, incident-based policing is more common in industrial cities or lower-class neighborhoods than in upper-middle-class communities like Jai's. What other factors, besides class, might inform the policing style used in Jai's community?

Are there any abandoned lots or buildings in your neighborhood? How do you think these areas came to look the way they do? Have any efforts been made to repair or repurpose these areas?

Community policing is based on the broken windows philosophy, which argues that small problems can quickly become bigger ones if left unaddressed. For example, suppose there is an abandoned warehouse in your community. One day, a kid throws a rock through a window of the warehouse. If the window is not repaired, the building will appear uncared for. Given how much fun it can be to throw rocks through windows, soon many kids are doing the same thing. Next, a graffiti artist sees the broken windows and concludes that the abandoned warehouse is a clean canvas on which to display his art. The building and the area around it now look very different. The building's new image gives people in the community the impression that they can abandon things, like old furniture, on this lot. Residents come to view the area as unsafe and avoid it. As a result, drug dealers and addicts begin to use parts of the warehouse for illegal activities.

According to the broken windows theory, when police officers focus only on answering calls for service in a particular area, the problems in that area worsen. Only when law enforcement takes a proactive approach—addressing small problems before they become big ones—can it have an impact on crime in that community. The same logic can be applied to juvenile delinquency. By addressing minor problems, the police can have an impact on the larger issues. Think of minor offenders as broken windows: they can be repaired and restored, or they can be left alone until the problems fester and grow, making it more difficult for the police to resolve them.

History of Policing

Recall this chapter's discussion of early police practices. How might you compare today's emphasis on community policing to Robert Peel's early vision of an organized police force?

THINK ABOUT IT

Law Enforcement–Juvenile Interactions

The problems arising from delinquency are complex. Police officers are now required to have a more holistic understanding of crime and community concerns. One of the concerns that is deserving of a holistic understanding is the tension that exists between juveniles and law enforcement officers. This tension leads to difficult encounters that are, ultimately, counterproductive to both juveniles' best interests and law enforcements' goals of reducing crime. In order to better understand these interactions, and to train law enforcement accordingly, researchers have looked into why this tension exists.

JUVENILES' PERCEPTION OF LAW ENFORCEMENT

Assessing youths' perceptions of law enforcement has not been an easy task. Unlike research that has been conducted on adults' perceptions of the police, studies of juveniles' attitudes have produced mixed results. For instance, a number of studies have concluded that juveniles generally hold unfavorable attitudes toward the police. Generally, in places where poverty and crime are prevalent, fear levels relating to victimization are high. The same is true for communities in which neighborhood conditions are on the decline. As a result of these circumstances, adolescents in poor communities tend to mistrust the police and feel they cannot rely on them for help when needed.[18] They express a mistrust of officers, as well as a lack of understanding of the role of the police in society.[19] Other youths have expressed a high level of unhappiness with the way they are treated by the police. They feel unfairly harassed by them and believe that officers are slow to assist them when they need help.

Then there are studies reporting that some youths feel the police contribute to the social and physical decline of their neighborhoods.[20] As an illustration of this perception of the police by some youths, consider Larry's comments. He was selling drugs, which made his relationship with the police a contentious one:

> The cops is heavy in my neighborhood, out west, and they be ducked off, because they know every move—every, every movement every time, what time of the day, what, what day it is, whether it's morning or night. And it was just a lot of chaos going on over there, lot of drug dealers, crack heads, NARCS [informants], it's a lot of stuff. . . . At one point in time, I thought that the police was on my back, 'cause I used to sell drugs, too. And I thought they was on me. But they was on my next-door neighbor. . . . They're not going to help nobody like random, like me, or somebody that's educated, 'cause, for one, they're going to be like, we don't communicate with y'all. So, it'll mostly be the, the fiends that, uh, really get helped, more than regular people.

Still other studies conclude that a surprising number of juveniles express indifference toward the police.[21] And a few studies have even found that juveniles have generally positive attitudes toward the police and other forms of authority.[22]

While we might assume that race and gender are important components in juveniles' perceptions of the police, the data on these variables are inconclusive. What seems to be the most consistent factor in terms of understanding the relationship between juveniles and the police is the quality of the contacts youths have with officers. This includes personal contact, such as individual interactions, as well as what is referred to

For more on perception of law enforcement, watch *Perception & Role of Police: Larry* and *Police Presence: Jose* at www.mhhe.com/mcnamarajd1e

vicarious contact
Communications from other youths about unpleasant experiences with the police.

as **vicarious contact,** as when youths hear about unpleasant contact with the police from other youths. Interestingly, the research indicates that negative contact with police officers has a greater significance in the minds of youth than positive contact.[23]

Consider the relationship between juveniles and law enforcement in general. What more could law enforcement do to earn the trust of the youths in their communities?

Why do you think police officers are more likely to take on a crime-fighting role in their interactions with juveniles?

LAW ENFORCEMENT'S PERCEPTION OF JUVENILES

The police mandate requires officers to prevent and reduce crime, as well as to maintain order and help citizens. Given that so many crimes are committed by juveniles, particularly crimes involving drugs and gangs, officers have frequent contact with them. While most officers would prefer to steer wayward youths toward more productive lifestyles, they often choose not to deal with youths unless they have committed serious crimes.[24]

Many officers report that their encounters with juveniles are rarely positive and that they have few opportunities to develop social relationships with them. Instead, their encounters with youths tend to result in arrests.[25] An illustration of the focus on serious offenders is highlighted by Anthony B., with whom many officers have had interactions:

> Uh, they think I'm going to be in prison for the rest of my life. I don't know. They don't think I'm going to ever change. . . . Because they all—they deal with me for about four years now. They know, I don't—I run from them every time they try to stop me. I'm always stealing, stealing people's cars and stuff, drugs, you know?

Officers also tend to believe that the juvenile justice system does not sufficiently punish delinquent youths. Therefore, responding to minor crimes feels like a waste of their time. Problems like running away, curfew violations, and truancy qualify as minor crimes that create an inordinate amount of paperwork and produce very little in the way of positive behavioral results.[26]

Thus, officers generally tend to avoid dealing with juveniles or they refer cases to officers assigned to a specialized unit within the department that targets youthful offenders, if the department has one. In fact, many police officers spend less time with juveniles and delinquency prevention activities than they do on making arrests and answering calls for service. In other words, these officers practice incident-based policing.[27] By avoiding these interactions or failing to address the problems of youths, even when they commit minor offenses, officers increase the chances that these juveniles will progress to more serious crimes as they get older.

According to the Office of Juvenile Justice and Delinquency Prevention (OJJDP), about 50 percent of police calls involving juveniles are related to public disturbances, family violence, complaints from the elderly, traffic enforcement, and vandalism. This figure refers to only those calls for which formal contact results.[28] According to an estimate that includes informal contact, 70–90 percent of police-juvenile encounters involve maintaining order or providing some sort of social service.[29] While in some cases arrest and traditional policing are appropriate and necessary responses, the data indicate that officers might have a greater impact on reducing or preventing crime if they adopted a social worker role with youths.[30]

LAW ENFORCEMENT OFFICERS AND SOCIAL WORKERS

It is often the case that in a given community, police officers and social workers interact with many of the same families. In either role, the goal is to try to improve the conditions of people's lives within that community. However, because they tend to address social

JAI'S CASE

Law Enforcement–Juvenile Interactions

Recall Jai's situation:

- displays delinquent behavior on a regular basis, but has never been caught
- poses a threat to the community that will likely worsen with time

Consider our discussion of law enforcement–juvenile interactions, then reflect on Jai's situation. Many police officers avoid interactions with youths because they expect those interactions to be unpleasant and unproductive. Some experts would argue that if the officers in Jai's neighborhood established a better relationship with local youths, they would be perceived as trustworthy and could do their jobs more effectively as a result. For example, when youths trust law enforcement, they are more likely to report crimes like Jai's.

Consider the concept of community policing from the perspective of law enforcement. How might an officer go about improving his or her relationship with the youths in a community? What potential roadblocks might he or she face? What are some of the possible positive outcomes of these relationships?

THINK ABOUT IT

issues from different perspectives, the relationship between law enforcement and social workers can be tense.

Many police officers do not believe that social workers take a sufficiently rigid stance in dealing with their clients. They argue that accountability is important and that, although social workers typically mean well, they do not really understand the culture of the people they serve. From their perspective, social workers are manipulated by their clients and end up enabling them instead of providing them with structure in the form of consequences.[31]

Social workers, too, tend to view the role of law enforcement with some skepticism. While officers accuse social workers of being too flexible and open-minded with their clients, social workers think that officers view social problems too narrowly.[32] Social workers argue that there are many more ways of solving the problems of juveniles than simply arresting and processing them. From a social worker's perspective, police officers lack an understanding of the larger issues families face, and the wide range of solutions that can be applied to them. In other words, accountability and consequences are important, but they are not the only answer.

One of the earliest studies of the relationship between law enforcement and social work found that the police think social workers have little understanding of how to alter people's behavior[33] (see Table 13-1). Instead, social workers approach their cases from an overly academic perspective, or from what police respondents in one study called "ivory towers." Another study assessing the differences between the types of people who become police officers and those who become social workers found that police officers scored higher than social workers on scales measuring perseverance, orderliness, moral absolutes, and role conformity. Officers also preferred external control, directive leadership, and routine operating procedures. In contrast, social workers scored higher than police officers on scales that measured planning ahead, independence, participative leadership, social interaction, intellectual achievement, and delegative leadership.[34]

One other study asked police officers to identify a single term to describe social workers. In answer to this question, officers offered the term "wishy-washy." They also felt that social workers were too lenient in carrying out their duties. In describing themselves, on the other hand, many officers used the terms "realistic" and "courageous." They felt that when the situation called for it, officers would do whatever was necessary to solve a problem.[35]

While their perceptions of each other are somewhat negative, in reality, there is a great deal of overlap between the work of law enforcement officers and that of social workers. Researchers have estimated that 70–90 percent of officers' time is devoted to activities that are also performed by social workers. Examples include settling domestic disputes,

TABLE 13-1 Philosophical Differences between Police Officers and Social Workers

Police Officers	Perseverance
	Orderliness
	Moral absolutes
	Role conformity
	External control
	Directive leadership
	Routine operating procedures
Social Workers	Planning ahead
	Independence
	Participative leadership
	Social interaction
	Intellectual achievement
	Delegative leadership

How do the philosophical differences between social workers and police officers translate into how they interact with community members?

protecting children, and providing information to community residents.[36] Some experts even argue that the functions of the two professions are so closely related that the police should be referred to as "all-around social workers."[37] At the same time, social workers often find themselves in a law enforcement role. For instance, the child protection movement, and changes in state and federal laws regarding the safety of children, has required social workers to become more mindful of their role as law enforcers.[38]

Still, each organization has objectives and missions that cause it to focus on different aspects of the same problems. The police, for example, have a mission to protect society as a whole. This is not to say that officers are unconcerned about individuals or their problems, but that their focus must remain on the problems that threaten the entire community.[39] Police officers also tend to view child abuse and neglect cases as criminal matters. In these types of cases, officers typically spend time collecting evidence for criminal prosecution. Unless they have been trained in the philosophy of child protection, officers will generally see little value in family preservation. In fact, most officers would probably argue that parents who abuse or neglect their children should lose those rights and privileges, and be sanctioned through incarceration. This point is illustrated by a study that found that in cases of suspected child abuse, where the police were the first to respond to the scene, children were much more likely to be separated from their families than if social workers preceded them.[40]

In contrast, the social work mission focuses on helping the individual. Social workers, also known in some states as child protective services (CPS) workers, maintain a focus on the protection of the child from further abuse and neglect, as well as maintaining the integrity of the family. When dealing with child endangerment cases, the primary objective of CPS workers is protecting the family and lessening the risk of endangerment. Consequently, the intervention strategies used by CPS workers are usually rehabilitative in nature. Their mission is consistent with state and federal laws that support the preservation or the reunification of the family.

Despite evidence pointing to a contentious relationship, there is, in fact, a high degree of cooperation and collaboration between the police and social workers. Most of the examples are problem-specific, such as partnering with each other to deal with the mentally ill, to address juvenile delinquency issues, or to respond to the sexual abuse of children.[41] In fact, as early as 1976, researchers were pointing to collaborative efforts by both agencies to preserve families.[42] Generally, these efforts were of two types. One focused on providing training for police officers so that they would be better able to

While police work focuses on whole communities, social work tends to deal with individuals within that community. Can you think of any scenarios in which these roles might be seen as collaborative or complementary?

THEORY AND PRACTICE WORKING TOGETHER

Law Enforcement–Social Work Collaboration: Partners for Family Solutions

Family preservation has been the guiding principle of state and federal law for children and families since 1980, with the passage of the Adoption Assistance and Child Welfare Act. Since then, family preservation training has focused primarily on social workers, attorneys, and judges. However, in general, police have not been considered a vital component of family preservation.

The Partners for Family Solutions (PFS) program began as an attempt to improve police training in family services. Because the police and the Department of Children and Families (DCF) have frequent contact with the same families in a given community, cooperation between the two can be vital. For example, police officers can provide information, insight, and even protection to social workers when they visit the homes of families at risk. Conversely, when police officers are not aware of the theory and practice of family preservation, the efforts of DCF workers can be unnecessarily inhibited.

PFS was designed to develop a training model for police departments to improve their understanding of family preservation, as well as to develop protocols to articulate how police departments should handle family preservation cases. This model also emphasizes the development

and enhancement of a collaborative working relationship with child welfare agencies. To accomplish these goals, police officers and social workers are provided with opportunities to develop better working relationships through cross-training workshops and informal gatherings to share information and ideas.

CPS workers are also encouraged to participate in a ride-along program, in which they accompany officers as they answer calls and conduct preventive patrol. To a similar end, officers can ride along with CPS workers when they make home visits. The ride-along program helps both groups to understand the problems and issues faced by each agency. An overall assessment of the program showed an improved relationship between agency personnel, as well as a decrease in the number and types of calls for service reported by both organizations.

 THINK ABOUT IT Some people compare the role of the police officer to that of an "all-around" social worker. In what ways might a social worker be expected to take on a law enforcement role? How does a program like PFS encourage an overlap in these roles?

help people they encountered on patrol. This type of crisis intervention training involved a number of issues, such as juvenile offenses, domestic violence, and suicide. Because mental health professionals were not always available when crises developed, this type of police training took on special importance.

The second type of collaborative effort involved the development of social work teams within police departments. These teams were staffed with veteran social workers who had knowledge of police procedures and served as liaisons between the police department and other social services agencies. These teams also assessed clients referred to them by police officers and were responsible for providing in-service training to officers in crisis intervention.[43]

While police officers always have the authority to invoke formal means for solving problems, most of what they do with regard to juveniles can be characterized as social work. Moreover, social workers, particularly those working for CPS divisions, often have law enforcement powers when they discover parents or guardians who are abusing or neglecting children. While the two groups have differing philosophies, with social workers acting in the best interests of the child and the police focusing on protecting society and maintaining order, they converge when it comes to dealing with families and children. One example of productive collaboration between law enforcement and social workers is described in the Theory and Practice box above.

LAW ENFORCEMENT DISCRETION

When it comes to deciding whether to take juveniles into custody or to handle matters informally, officers have a wide range of options. This decision is left largely to police officers' discretion.

Over the years, a number of studies have attempted to determine how officers respond to situations involving youths. The research shows that the number of juveniles formally charged and referred to juvenile court is very small when compared to the total number of law enforcement–juvenile encounters that take place. This is the case even when the seriousness of the crime is taken into account.[44] While there are a multitude of factors that go into an officer's decision on how to proceed, the following variables play particularly important roles in the outcome of an interaction:

- the seriousness of the offense
- the youth's gender
- the youth's race
- the youth's social class
- whether injuries occurred as a result of the action
- the number of prior contacts with the police and the juvenile justice system
- whether the youth is affiliated with a gang
- whether parents or guardians are willing to take responsibility for the youth
- whether the officer knows the youth and/or the youth's family
- the availability of diversion and detention programs
- the policing style of the officer and the officer's department
- policies and procedures regulating certain encounters with the youth
- the individual officer's intuitive sense of the situation[45]

However, the most consistent factor in determining an officer's actions is youths' appearance and demeanor. Youths who are neatly dressed are less likely to be stopped, questioned, or arrested than those who are poorly dressed or who appear to be members of a gang. In such instances, baggy clothes, lots of jewelry, various-colored rags, hats, or sneakers signify delinquency to officers and can determine the type of encounter that will take place.[46] Retired NYPD Lieutenant Patrick Igneri explains how the police uses discretion:

[W]here the discretion comes in is with violations or low level misdemeanors or when there's no victim like public drinking or disorderly youths or disorderly groups. Then the police officer has the discretion. He can warn and admonish. He can make a referral to the, to the various specialized units. He can write up a juvenile report. . . that's almost like an intelligence report that the officer fills out and they keep on file in the precinct . . . and use that if there's any further incidence.

For more on police interaction and perception of youths, watch *Practitioner Patrick Igneri* at www.mhhe.com/mcnamarajd1e

How youths respond to being stopped by officers makes a big difference in the outcome of that interaction. Youths who are polite and respectful and who do not take an aggressive posture toward police are much less likely to be arrested or referred to juvenile court. The research also shows that minority youths who act in a suspicious manner or who live in or loiter around high-crime neighborhoods are more likely to attract police attention than those who do not display these characteristics and behaviors. Thus, attitude and appearance are key variables in the outcome of law enforcement–juvenile encounters.[47]

When it comes to improving the nature of these interactions and their outcomes, police training has proved vital. The program described in the Theory and Practice box on page 341 has demonstrated some promise in retraining officers to understand the value of developing relationships with juveniles.

RACIAL AND GENDER BIASES

Because some experts argue that profiling is discretionary, a great deal of controversy and debate surrounds its practice. For example, some believe that the decision to make an arrest is based largely on law enforcement's judgment of suspects' characteristics, and in particular

THEORY AND PRACTICE WORKING TOGETHER

The Juvenile Justice Center

New Approaches to Police Youth Interactions, created by the Juvenile Justice Center (JJC) at Suffolk University Law School in Boston, Massachusetts, is one of the more promising programs addressing the problems of law enforcement–juvenile relations. The JJC seeks to establish a sense of trust between youths and officers, as well as with residents in the community. Its training program provides officers with information regarding the cultural and psychological basis of youths' behavior, including the way they process information and the factors that influence their worldviews. Officers learn "ice-breaking" techniques for interacting with difficult youths and skills for reducing the stress that often accompanies these interactions. This training also gives officers critical insight into how youths respond to youths during the course of social encounters.

This in turn helps them to assert their authority while also reducing conflicts with youths.

An evaluation of the JJC police officer training revealed a reduced number of juvenile arrests by participating officers. Interactions between law enforcement and the community at large were likewise improved as youths and residents began to understand the constraints placed on the police, and officers learned more about issues of concern to residents.

THINK ABOUT IT

Think back to the discussion in Chapter 4 on Durkheim's theory of social cohesion. Why is trust one of the most important elements of social solidarity?

---

their race and gender. Others argue that race and gender do not play a role, but that suspects' behaviors determine the outcomes of law enforcement–juvenile interactions. Despite debate and disagreement, there is evidence to suggest that even the perception of differential treatment can negatively affect the outcome of law enforcement–juvenile interactions.

One study explored the racial factors that appeared to play a role in youths' getting hassled by police. This perception comes from youths who personally experienced a negative interaction with an officer, witnessed such an event, or knew someone who had been involved in a similar experience. According to the study, African Americans are more likely to perceive they are being hassled by the police. Nearly one-half of African Americans in the study had experienced a negative police interaction, and two-thirds knew someone who had a similar experience. Only 10 percent of white people reported having experienced this type of treatment. While such a discrepancy could be a result of a difference in patrol practices, and in particular those that focus on minority neighborhoods, it could also be that officers perceive African Americans and other minorities as more likely to commit crimes and warrant police attention.[48]

Hassling can also involve verbal abuse. Many complaints are filed each year against officers who verbally abuse citizens. The Christopher Commission, created to investigate allegations of abuse in Los Angeles following the beating of Rodney King by white officers, found that officers frequently use abusive language during their interactions with citizens, as well as among themselves. For example, the commission's investigation discovered computer messages sent to officers that contained racially offensive comments. With regard to abusive language toward citizens, research on police behavior suggests that derogatory comments are used as a way for officers to control suspects. While unprofessional and inappropriate, profanity by police officers serves several functions: to gain the attention of suspects, to keep suspects at a social distance during an interaction, and to achieve psychological dominance.[49]

The issue surrounding discriminatory treatment of African Americans in particular extends beyond serious offenses and includes minor forms of abuse, like harassment and profiling. In fact, one might argue that minor forms of abuse create a climate of fear and hostility between the police and minorities. These indignities are significant because of what they represent, regardless of how one judges their immediate impact on suspects. For example, some attribute the tense relationship between law enforcement and minorities to the frequency with which these types of interactions occur.[50] Moreover, unlike more serious forms of abuse, discretionary practices, such as racial profiling, leave no tangible evidence that the incident occurred. These interactions usually take place on the street and often involve no witnesses, which makes sustaining allegations very difficult.

While the study conducted by the Bureau of Justice Statistics noted large gaps in the types of encounters with law enforcement experienced by whites and racial minorities, it did not state the reasons for these discrepancies. What types of questions might you ask participants in the study in order to come to a better understanding of the reasons for their treatment? To the same end, what might you ask members of law enforcement?

In April 2005, a report on racial profiling was released by the Department of Justice's Bureau of Justice Statistics. Based on interviews with 80,000 people conducted in 2002, the study found that nationwide that year white, black, and Hispanic drivers were stopped by the police at about the same rate of roughly 9 percent. However, the Justice Department report also found that once they were stopped, Hispanic drivers were searched or had their vehicles searched by the police 11.4 percent of the time, and blacks 10.2 percent of the time, as opposed to only 3.5 percent for white drivers. The study also found that officers were more likely to threaten or use force against blacks and Hispanics than against whites, and that they were much more likely to issue tickets to Hispanics rather than give them a warning.

The authors of the study said that they were not able to draw any conclusions about the reason for the differing rates, but that the gaps were notable. The report concluded with evidence that black drivers were more likely to be arrested, to be searched, or to have force used against them during traffic stops than were white drivers. The inflammatory nature of these findings allegedly led to the Justice Department trying to suppress some of the information or to change the findings. While strenuously arguing that the results should not be altered for political purposes, the director of the Bureau of Justice Statistics was demoted.[51]

While this study revealed little about law enforcement's motivations for abuse, its conclusions remind us that the relationship between the police and minorities is complex. For instance, while it may be the case that African Americans are arrested disproportionately, in part, because of their more frequent involvement in criminal activities, such discrepancies may also have to do with the way African Americans respond to police contact. For example, structural issues such as poverty and overcrowding in urban areas may contribute to greater police contact, as well as to higher levels of tension between residents and law enforcement. It is also the case that some officers believe minorities are more likely to become involved in criminal activities, and so feel they merit greater police attention.

Gender also plays a role in law enforcement–juvenile interactions. Many experts argue that the police treat male and female offenders differently. As discussed in Chapter 11, while some experts argue that the police are likely to act paternalistically toward young girls and not arrest them, others believe that officers are more likely to arrest females who act counter to gender stereotypes.[52] There appears to be some truth to this gender bias. In particular, females are less likely to be arrested by the police for traditional delinquent acts, while they are more likely to be arrested for status offenses.[53]

THINK ABOUT IT

Interactions between Law Enforcement and Juveniles

Based on your reading, what can officers do to develop positive relationships with juveniles? Is it possible for officers to improve their relationships with youths while also being tasked with holding them responsible for their actions?

Procedural Rules Governing Juveniles

Procedural rules for handling juveniles apply to arrests, searches, and interrogations. For example, in the case of arrests, juveniles must be afforded many of the same constitutional protections that apply to adults.

ARREST

The juvenile justice process can be understood as a series of "if-then" statements. What this means is that what happens at each stage of the process depends on a wide range of factors. Whenever possible, most officials in the system will attempt to handle matters informally, without involving juveniles in the formal justice process.[54] However, when officers encounter situations with juveniles that cannot be resolved informally, they might resort to making arrests.

When we employ the phrase "taken into custody" with regard to juveniles, we do not necessarily mean an **arrest** was made. Historically, this phrase was used to describe what happened to juveniles in lieu of arrest, in order to shield them from the stigma of the criminal justice process. An officer might take a youth into custody in order to detain him or her until his or her parents could be contacted. However, given the recent trends in how juveniles are treated, "taken into custody" and "arrest" have come to be used interchangeably.[55]

The basis of a legal arrest is referred to as **probable cause,** which can be defined as facts and circumstances that would lead a reasonable person to believe that a crime has been committed and that the suspect is responsible for that crime. Another way to think of probable cause is as something beyond mere suspicion but short of absolute certainty. In order for officers to make a legal arrest, they must have probable cause to do so. This is true whether the suspect is an adult or a juvenile; however, police officers have more latitude in controlling juveniles' behavior. The standard for taking youths into custody is a **preponderance of evidence.** The difference between this burden of proof and probable cause is that a preponderance of evidence refers to the facts and circumstances that point to the suspect, no matter how inconsequential those facts may seem.[56]

While less compelling than probable cause, a preponderance of evidence is used when the goal is to protect youths' best interests. The legal term that is sometimes used to describe the wide latitude is called *in loco parentis,* which is Latin for "in place of the parents."[57] According to *in loco parentis,* the state recognizes that there are instances in which the police must act as the parent in a given situation and should therefore be given the authority to provide necessary services. This includes taking youths into custody when it is for their own good.[58]

Once individuals are taken into custody or arrested, the constitutional safeguards provided by the Fourth and Fifth Amendments apply to juveniles and adults alike. Given that juveniles are increasingly being treated like adult offenders, these protections have become even more important in the processing of juveniles. For instance, traditionally, confidentiality laws prohibited the fingerprinting and photographing of juvenile suspects, in order to spare them the stigma associated with being arrested and treated like a criminal.[59] But some states are now allowing this, treating juveniles more like adults.[60] Without protections provided by the Fourth and Fifth Amendments, juveniles processed in this way would risk losing their right to privacy.

SEARCH AND SEIZURE

The Fourth Amendment to the U.S. Constitution is one of the most important in the Bill of Rights, particularly as it relates to law enforcement. The Fourth Amendment states:

> The right of the people to be secure in their persons, houses, papers, and effects, against unreasonable searches and seizures, shall not be violated, and no warrants shall issue, but upon probable cause, supported by oaths or affirmations, and particularly describing the place to be searched, and the persons or things to be seized.[61]

The same **search and seizure** guidelines used to search adults also apply to juveniles. In most cases, searches should not take place unless a warrant is obtained from a judge that outlines the area to be searched and the items officers are looking to find.

There are, however, exceptions to this rule. For example, the U.S. Supreme Court has ruled that the evidence seized in **warrantless searches** is legal, even when such searches are conducted on juveniles. Specifically, warrantless searches are legal under the following circumstances:

- The search consists of the officer patting down the outer clothing of a suspect after a stop, in an effort to determine whether the suspect poses a risk to the officer.[62]

- Contraband is observed in plain view by the officer, such as drugs or weapons lying on the back seat of a suspect's vehicle.[63]

arrest
Now used interchangeably with "taken into custody" with regard to juveniles; historically, the phrase used to describe what happened to juveniles in lieu of arrest, in order to shield them from the stigma of the criminal justice process.

probable cause
The basis of a legal arrest; the facts and circumstances that would lead a reasonable person to believe that a crime has been committed and that the suspect is responsible for that crime.

preponderance of evidence
The facts and circumstances that point to the suspect, no matter how inconsequential those facts may seem.

in loco parentis
Instances in which the police must act as the parent in a given situation and should therefore be given the authority to provide necessary services, such as taking youths into custody when it is for their own good.

search and seizure
Guidelines that searches should not take place unless a warrant is obtained from a judge that outlines the area to be searched and the items officers are looking to find.

warrantless search
The finding and seizing of evidence without warrants or court orders.

- The suspect knowingly and voluntarily consents to a search.[64]
- An arrest has been made, in which case the officer may conduct a full search of the suspect and the area within his or her immediate control, sometimes referred to as a **search incident to a lawful arrest.**[65]
- Probable cause exists; the officer can conduct a search of an automobile, driver, passenger, and even closed containers in the trunk, as long as the search is reasonable.
- Electronic searches can be conducted if the suspect has no expectation of privacy.[66]

search incident to a lawful arrest
A full search following arrest of the areas within the suspect's immediate control.

Should the police conduct an illegal search and find evidence leading to the suspect's arrest, the suspect's attorney can file a pretrial motion to identify the search as illegal and to exclude any evidence that was obtained in the process. In legal terms, the evidence obtained from an illegal search is sometimes referred to as "fruit from the poisonous tree"—meaning that if the search is illegal, then, like a poisonous tree, anything that is produced by it is similarly tainted.[67]

CUSTODIAL INTERROGATION

Given the somewhat unique nature of the juvenile justice system, the balance between treatment and punishment is a slippery one. As we increasingly apply constitutional protections to juveniles, questions are inevitably raised as to the appropriateness, and the implications, of their application. In Chapter 14, we will discuss some of the most significant cases decided by the U.S. Supreme Court on this issue. One of these cases is referred to as *In re Gault,* in which the Fifth Amendment was applied to juveniles, giving them constitutional protections against self-incrimination.

The Miranda warning is given when suspects are taken into custody, as a means of informing them of their constitutional rights under those circumstances. Most of us are familiar with the terms of the Miranda warning, if only from hearing it recited on television and in movies. That is, the suspect has the right to remain silent; if a suspect gives up that right, anything he or she says can be used against him or her in court. The suspect also has a right to an attorney, and if he or she cannot afford one, the state will provide one at no charge.

But what does it mean to read these rights to a juvenile who is being taken into custody? Some experts have raised questions about juveniles' ability to determine whether to waive their rights, as well as whether to have an attorney present once that decision is made. Most courts have ruled that parents or attorneys do not need to be present for juveniles to waive their rights, and the general rule is that while they can do so, the validity of this waiver is determined by what is known as the **totality of circumstances.** This means that the question of whether youths have the capacity to waive their rights will be determined by a number of factors including the method of interrogation, the suspect's educational level, whether the suspect understands the nature of the charges, and whether the suspect has been allowed to consult with family or friends.[68]

totality of circumstances
The validity of youths' waiver of rights without the presence of parents and attorneys based on the method of interrogation, the suspect's educational level, whether the suspect understands the nature of the charges, and whether the suspect has been allowed to consult with family or friends.

Two controversial cases relating to the waiver of Miranda rights by juveniles have addressed these issues. In *Fare v. Michael C,* the U.S. Supreme Court ruled that if a child asks to speak to a probation officer, it is not the same as speaking to an attorney, which provides protection under the attorney-client privilege. The Court ruled that statements made to the probation officer and to the police were admissible in court.[69] As an example, consider Phillip's situation, in which his parents brought him to the police department for sexually abusing his brother. Throughout the entire interrogation, Phillip was not accompanied by an attorney:

> I'm like, Dad, what's wrong? And he said, Phillip, I'm not taking you to the play. I'm taking you to the police station. And that's when I got taken there. And I was asked if I needed a lawyer. And I, I didn't want one because I thought I was all big and tough and all that. And I thought I could handle it, and I was smarter than everybody else. And so I sat down with this guy named, I was interrogated for about almost like two to four hours or something like that.

In another case, *California v. Prysock,* the U.S. Supreme Court ruled that the protections provided by the Miranda warning have been met even when it is given in a different language, as long as the meaning of the Miranda warning is easily understood, even by a youth.[70]

Many legal experts dispute these rulings, arguing that youths have less cognitive ability than adults and are often vulnerable to deception and trickery by the police.[71] Some experts also point to new scientific evidence suggesting that a teenager's brain is underdeveloped until late adolescence, which explains why so many youths engage in impulsive and risky behaviors.[72]

In addition, some psychological research shows that juveniles are less able to foresee and comprehend the consequences of their actions. This is in part because of youths' distorted understanding of time.[73] Psychologists generally believe that adolescent thinking is present-oriented and so tends either to ignore or to discount future events and implications. To the extent that adolescents do consider the implications of their choices, they often consider only short-term consequences, perceiving and weighing longer-term consequences to a lesser degree if at all.[74]

The inability to perceive and weigh long-term consequences can make juveniles much more susceptible to deceptive interrogation techniques than adults. This explains why police frequently, and falsely, tell juveniles they can go home if they confess—and why juveniles so often fall prey to this tactic.[75] To many juveniles, the opportunity to end a grueling interrogation by confessing represents immediate gratification, while the risks of prosecution, conviction, and sentencing are further in the future, and their impact may not be felt for some time.[76]

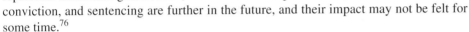

For more on interrogation, watch *Arrest & Interrogation: Phillip* at www .mhhe.com/mcnamarajd1e

Finally, some evidence shows that juveniles have a greater tendency than adults to make decisions based on emotions, such as anger or fear, rather than logic and reason. Additionally, stressful situations exacerbate the emotional nature of decision-making for juveniles.[77] Interestingly, those who believe that youths should not be allowed to waive their rights without counsel argue that courts already use this line of thinking in other juvenile matters. For instance, in cases of emancipation, in which youths attempt to gain financial, social, and legal independence from their parents, courts often take into consideration the fact that youths do not always have the capacity to grasp or understand the significance of their decisions.[78] This lack of cognitive ability is easily applied to custodial interrogation, leading some to question why juveniles should be allowed to waive their rights during interrogation, a decision that has a potentially profound effect on their futures.[79]

Juveniles and Constitutional Rights

During what stages of law enforcement–juvenile interaction should the constitutional rights of youths be considered? Are there any stages of this process at which you believe these rights should not be applied? Do you believe youths have different reasoning capabilities than adults? Are there any circumstances under which you think it is appropriate for the police to interrogate a juvenile without an attorney or parent present?

THINK ABOUT IT

Delinquency Prevention Strategies

A third area of law enforcement–juvenile relations focuses on delinquency prevention programs. Some officers dislike dealing with juvenile offenders, either because they do not think they should be spending time on juvenile matters or because of the tension that exists between law enforcement and the juvenile justice system. Other law enforcement officers believe strongly in the concept of prevention. As exemplified by community policing efforts and better understanding of the broken windows philosophy, some officers recognize that the only way to minimize the effects of delinquency is to prevent it from occurring in the first place. When that is not possible, then aggressive patrol tactics should be considered to minimize the impact delinquents can have on the community.[80] Retired NYPD Lieutenant Igneri says that the role of the police in preventing delinquency is two-fold:

> The NYC police department has done a good job with that [prevention] . . . they have all these specialized units. The sector guys on patrol, they can't do that. The patrol guys are the first line of defense. They may wanna get involved with the kid on the street corner that they think may need a good talking to or may need a referral, but the odds are, especially in, especially in precincts that have a high level of radio runs, they just don't have the time. They can't do it. And it's not gonna happen so, so the police department has created the precinct youth officers.

G.R.E.A.T.

Gang Resistance Education and Training; a program modeled after its precursor, D.A.R.E., in which police officers visit schools and work with elementary and middle school children to develop the skills and attitudes that will help them resist involvement in drugs and gangs.

Two of the most prominent delinquency prevention programs are D.A.R.E. and **G.R.E.A.T.,** both of which bring officers into schools to interact with juveniles and teach lessons and skills related to drug and delinquency prevention. Many police agencies also operate boot camps, or military-style detention facilities for youths. While the success of these strategies has been questioned, many departments continue to sponsor them, and the federal government continues to fund them. The reasons for this may have much to do with politics and economics, but they may also have something to do with the lack of adequate alternatives. As we discussed in Chapter 12, there are many effective programs that prevent certain types of delinquency, but the continuous search for a single cure to all delinquency may actually prevent policymakers from addressing these problems successfully.

The participation of law enforcement in prevention activities can be traced back to the 1960s, when officers first came into the public schools with the aim of preventing delinquency. At the same time, they also became involved in truancy programs, drug abuse rehabilitation, and recreation programs. Because these efforts coincided with a renewed understanding of delinquency, it made sense that the police, who were being given the responsibility of supervising delinquents, would be at the forefront of these prevention efforts.

Recall our discussion of delinquency prevention programs in Chapter 12. In what ways was the D.A.R.E. program less effective than advocates had claimed?

However, during the 1970s and even into the 1980s, police departments began to eliminate juvenile divisions because of inflation and budgetary constraints. It was during this time that most of the country was focusing on the rehabilitation of juveniles, while police departments, because of a lack of resources, were focused almost exclusively on neglected and abused children. During the late 1980s and into the 1990s, a growing concern about rising juvenile crime rates increased police participation in school-based programs. Some have described this era as being personified by former First Lady Nancy Reagan, who instituted a "Just Say No" substance abuse prevention campaign. In response, most police prevention programs focused on preventing drug use or diverting substance abusers from the juvenile justice system. The D.A.R.E. program, which was discussed at length in the previous chapter, was a popular program developed during this campaign.

In the 1990s, with escalating concern about school violence, federal laws, such as the Gun-Free School Zones Act, were designed to reduce the number of students who brought guns to campus and to address the problem of gang-related violence at school.[81] As Chapter 10 describes, this legislation was instrumental in shaping school policies regarding crime, including implementation of zero-tolerance policies and the increased use of expulsion of students.

G.R.E.A.T.

G.R.E.A.T. (Gang Resistance Education and Training) is modeled after its precursor, D.A.R.E., with both having the primary objective of preventing delinquency and gang involvement. About once a week, officers participating in the G.R.E.A.T. program visit schools and work with middle school and elementary school children on developing the skills and attitudes that will help them resist involvement in drugs and gangs. The program consists of four components, each with its own age-appropriate curriculum:[82]

- Middle school component: a thirteen-week skills-based curriculum with a focus on behavioral and attitudinal risk factors

- Elementary school component: the precursor to the middle school component; a six-week curriculum that prepares students for the more intensive and cooperative training they will receive in middle school

- Summer component: a program that gives students a positive outlet for social interaction and an alternative to gang involvement over the summer months

- Family component: a program that engages parents and their children, age ten to fourteen, in activities promoting strong family relationships

G.R.E.A.T. initially began as an eight-week program for middle school students. Evaluations of that version of the program showed mixed results in its ability to reduce gang involvement and delinquency. Some studies found that students who completed the program had lower rates of gang membership and delinquency than those who were not exposed to G.R.E.A.T., while other studies showed that, four years later, no significant differences in terms of gang membership or delinquency existed.[83] This means that whatever initial effect G.R.E.A.T. might have had, it did not last. A newer version of G.R.E.A.T., which began in 2000, has shown some promise, but the overall effectiveness of the program continues to be questioned by researchers.[84]

THE POLICE ATHLETIC LEAGUE

The Police Athletic League (PAL) is a police-based crime prevention program that attempts to provide opportunities for police officers and local youths to interact and form relationships. With officers participating in and facilitating sports programs for community youths, the youths are given the much-needed opportunity to have shared experiences with officers who also act as mentors. Youths who participate in the program report feeling more comfortable seeking officers out for advice and counsel on and off the field.[85] They also begin to view officers not simply as enforcers of the law who punish them, but as people who care about them and want to see them succeed.[86] Advocates of PAL believe that if children can develop friendly relationships with police officers, they will be more likely to become responsible and productive members of society.

The concept for PAL originated in 1910, through the efforts of Lieutenant Ed Flynn of the New York City Police Department. After witnessing increasing vandalism by youth gangs, Flynn realized that there was a lack of productive outlets for youths. Flynn interviewed gang members, who complained that the police continued to harass them but did not offer any constructive alternatives to misbehavior. In response to these complaints, Flynn found an available playground and began organizing baseball teams for local youths, all under the supervision of the police.[87]

Building upon Flynn's success, Captain John Sweeney, a precinct commander, created the Police Athletic League in 1914. Today, over 65,000 youths participate in PAL programs in New York City alone, playing basketball, baseball, flag football, and soccer. PAL has become the largest juvenile delinquency prevention program in the United States, with over 3 million members in over 500 cities and towns.[88]

Several studies have found that recreational and sports-related programs can have a significant positive impact on youths' behavior.[89] This is one reason why the Boys and Girls Clubs of America have had such great success in steering youths away from drugs, gangs, and delinquency. Using sports to channel children's energy in positive directions, programs like these have reported success in encouraging children to lead healthy and productive lives.[90]

More recently, PAL has built on its success with athletic programs like midnight basketball leagues and academic programs such as after-school tutoring, computer skills classes, and other education-based activities. In doing so, PAL has sought to provide

JAI'S CASE

Conclusions

Recall Jai's situation:

- is sixteen years old
- displays frequent delinquent behavior, to which police and community residents do not respond
- poses a threat to the community and to himself

It is possible that the community tolerates Jai's behavior either out of fear or out of concern for creating a scandal. Law enforcement in Jai's community may overlook juvenile behaviors that do not constitute serious crimes, believing that they are a waste of their time and resources. If neither the community nor its law enforcement responds to Jai's behavior, it is likely that it will continue. It might even become more serious as he matures. If Jai is caught soon, he will be processed by the juvenile justice system. But if law enforcement puts off addressing Jai's problems, he may experience more serious consequences in the future.

 THINK ABOUT IT Parental responsibility laws exist in most states, whereby they can fine or even imprison parents for their children's behavior. Do you think Jai would change his behavior if the police were to arrest his parents and hold them accountable for his actions? Or do you think that Jai should be held accountable for his own criminal behavior?

Given that most police departments struggle with limited resources, in what ways might communities pitch in to facilitate programs like PAL?

a more holistic approach to addressing youths' problems. Although very few studies have actually assessed the effectiveness of PAL programs, they continue to be very popular with the police and their communities.[91]

POLICE CADET PROGRAMS

Police cadet programs are another type of program designed to break down some of the barriers between the police and juveniles. Often affiliated with the Boy Scouts of America, these programs seek to teach youths about the role of law enforcement and the importance of volunteering in the community.[92] Cadet programs usually target older adolescents and even college students, and involve them in serving as volunteers in a law enforcement capacity. Cadets work with the police department and learn many of the skills needed to become a police officer, including arrest techniques and the laws and procedures on search and seizure. Cadets also participate in ride-alongs with officers each month. This type of program not only exposes youths to the problems in the community from the law enforcement perspective, particularly as these problems relate to delinquency, but also serves as a recruiting tool for departments, since cadets receive valuable training while participating in the program.[93]

AGGRESSIVE PATROL

A popular approach to assessing and dealing with crime is **hot spots analysis.** Hot spots are locations in a community that have a concentrated level of criminal activity in a given period. Once hot spots have been identified, aggressive patrol tactics are used there, such as **saturation patrols** (the increase of police presence in a given area to deter criminal activities), crackdowns, and other strategies that focus attention on particular neighborhoods. Another tactic is to aggressively enforce truancy and curfew

hot spots analysis
An approach to assessing and dealing with crime in which locations in a community that have a concentrated level of criminal activity in a given period are targeted aggressively.

saturation patrols
The strategy used by police departments of placing numerous officers in a given area to maintain a high visibility, to deter criminal activities, and to increase the likelihood of catching offenders.

laws in an effort to identify and arrest gang members. These strategies are also known as **directed patrol.**

Zero-tolerance policing is another common strategy. As the term suggests, zero-tolerance policing provides no exceptions to violations of the law. Although it has been popular in recent years, research on this strategy fails to show any significant level of effectiveness. While zero-tolerance policing may increase arrests for some crimes over the short term, a long-term impact of general crime prevention has not been achieved.[94]

directed patrol
A tactic that aggressively enforces truancy and curfew laws in an effort to identify and arrest gang members.

zero-tolerance policing
Enforcement that provides no exceptions to violations of the law.

COMMUNITY POLICING AND PROBLEM-ORIENTED POLICING

In its purest form, community policing represents a change in philosophy about how the police should fulfill their responsibilities to the public. In fact, part of the official definition of community policing, given by the Office of Community Policing Services, stipulates that it is not simply a tactic or strategy to be used, but is a new orientation for addressing community concerns. The relationship between citizens and the police is critical to the issue of preventing and addressing crime; the police cannot solve the crime problem without cooperation and assistance from community residents.

A related topic within the larger community policing framework is problem-oriented policing (POP). Sometimes referred to as *problem-solving policing,* POP attempts to identify and resolve underlying causes of problems rather than simply treat their symptoms. Incident-based policing, which is characteristic of the traditional model of law enforcement, does little, if anything, to address the reasons why crimes occur; officers simply wait until an incident takes place and then respond where appropriate. POP takes a different approach by asking officers to conduct social science research to learn about the factors that contribute to the problems they are approaching. In doing so, officers may be able to minimize or even eliminate problems completely.

Where incident-based policing is reactive, POP is a proactive form of law enforcement. The basic model used by officers in "doing" POP is called SARA, which stands for scanning, analysis, response, and assessment.

1. **Scanning:** this first step involves identifying residents' issues of concern, even those that are not crime-related, and narrowing them down to specific, concrete issues. Instead of solving the drug problem in a community, officers are trained to focus on one type of drug activity, in a specific location, at a specific time, by specific individuals. By making the problem smaller and more easily identifiable, the chances of success in addressing it are improved.

2. **Analysis:** at this stage, officers learn more about why certain behaviors are occurring in a given location. Recall our discussion of hot spots analysis: crime occurs for a reason, and if officers can address those underlying causes, the problem behavior is more likely to decrease or stop.

3. **Response:** this is the stage where officers attempt to come up with innovative ideas to solve or minimize the problem they have identified. Because of limited resources and funding, it is important that officers think "outside the box" for creative solutions.

4. **Assessment:** in this final stage, officers attempt an evaluation of the impact of the response. Often programs and solutions are implemented without our ever really knowing if they are effective. Assessments can consist of changes in calls for service, decreases in crime statistics, resident satisfaction surveys, or another tool to evaluate the strategy employed.

Community policing and POP have been used in a number of programs around the country, particularly to address violence among youths. For example, Project Safe Neighborhoods is designed to bring federal, state, and local law enforcement agencies together with community leaders to address gun-related crime by serious juvenile offenders. POP can be used to solve simple quality-of-life issues for residents as well. Its real value is in diagnosing community concerns and targeting the cause of the problem, rather than simply using standard law enforcement practices that have not been successful.[95]

Police-Sponsored Delinquency Prevention

In your opinion, which of the police-sponsored delinquency prevention programs discussed in this chapter shows the most promise for directing youths' energies away from criminal activity? What other types of activities might you suggest for achieving the same goal?

Law Enforcement and Juvenile Public Policy

The police are the agency primarily responsible for implementing public policy regarding the treatment of youths who commit crimes. Given that it is impossible to enforce every law all the time, it is left to the discretion of the police to selectively enforce those laws and policies that provide the greatest level of public safety. As we have seen, however, many of the day-to-day police interactions with juveniles are limited, either because the police prefer not to approach youths or because they do not have the time and resources to make these interactions possible. A variety of factors influence an officer's decision to arrest a juvenile, with subjective factors such as the race, gender, and appearance of the youth and his or her attitude toward the officer playing important roles. As the police increasingly view the juvenile justice system as ineffective and inefficient, coupled with an overall "get tough" public policy regarding delinquents, it should not be surprising to learn that many officers avoid interacting with youths (because they do not feel the system will hold them accountable for their actions), and make arrests only for serious crimes (where the youths involved are more likely to be tried as adults). Thus, a policy shift, such as the one that occurred in the 1990s regarding juvenile delinquency, results in a set of police practices that avoid the holistic approach in treating youths in favor of more punitive practices. Current police practices, along with the overall "get tough" approach to delinquency, may make the problem worse by not investing sufficient time or energy in solving smaller problems before they become bigger ones.

THE BIG PICTURE

Conclusions on Law Enforcement–Juvenile Interactions

- Do you think that the police should adopt a zero-tolerance policy regarding youthful offenders, or should they be allowed to practice discretion on a case-by-case basis? What are the implications and potential problems related to either strategy?

- Should law enforcement be responsible for delinquency prevention, or is its job simply to enforce the law as society defines it?

- What are some of the most important factors in determining whether a delinquent gets taken into custody?

- Why do you think so few of the prevention programs discussed in this text show sufficient levels of effectiveness in reducing delinquency?

Key Terms

frankpledge system
watch and ward system
police matrons
broken windows philosophy

appearance and demeanor
probable cause
preponderance of evidence
in loco parentis

warrantless searches
G.R.E.A.T.
Police Athletic League (PAL)
zero-tolerance policing

Make the Call ▶ Law Enforcement and Delinquency

Review the scenario below, and decide how you would approach this case.

YOUR ROLE: Police officer

DETAILS OF THE CASE

- After 11 pm, you receive a call about a disturbance from an elderly woman complaining that there is a group of teens making a lot of noise near her home.

- When you arrive the teens scatter, except for one African American youth, about fifteen years old.

- You ask him what he and his friends were doing out, since there is a curfew in place that prohibits unaccompanied youths in the community after 10 pm on weekdays.

- The boy is dressed neatly, is very polite, and answers all of your questions. He explains that he and his friends were celebrating their high school football team's victory over a rival team, and they had lost track of time.

- When you ask where he lives, he tells you he lives with his grandmother nearby.

WHAT ACTION DO YOU TAKE?

Since the young man is in violation of the curfew law and has contributed to disturbing the peace, you have grounds for taking him into custody. You could also let him go with a warning that he should obey the curfew in the future. On the other hand, you are reasonably sure that the neighbor is going to file a formal complaint.

Consider:

- What factors would contribute to your decision to arrest this youth?

- Does this young man qualify for a break, or should he be taken into custody?

- Does he appear to pose a threat to himself or the community?

- Is your objective to punish the youth for his misbehavior or to provide him with an important lesson?

- Should he alone be held accountable for the behavior of everyone in the group?

- Does the fact that he did not run when you arrived and answered all of your questions matter to you in making your decision? Why or why not?

Apply Theory to Reality ▶ Law Enforcement and Delinquency

Juveniles' and officers' reluctance to interact with one another creates a self-fulfilling prophecy by which delinquency is more difficult to prevent. Select one of the social process theories discussed in this text, such as labeling theory or social learning theory, and discuss this theory in terms of how it relates to the nature of law enforcement–juvenile interactions.

Your Community ▶ Officers' Perspectives of Juveniles

In addition to the information you glean from your readings, class lectures, and discussions, it is important to roll up your sleeves and immerse yourself in a topic as a researcher who gains an understanding of a problem or issue by observing or experiencing it firsthand. Through such methods, you gain a much greater appreciation of the magnitude and scope of the problem than if you were only engaged in "armchair theorizing."

- Contact a local police department and ask the chief for permission to interview patrol officers about their perspectives on juveniles.

- In your interviews, ask questions aimed at determining officers' attitudes toward juveniles. Do they routinely try to interact with juveniles, or do they focus only on those who commit crimes? Do you get the sense that officers refrain from getting involved because of a lack of resources, or do they give another reason?

- Because police officers can be a bit cautious when being interviewed, be prepared to do some probing and rephrasing of questions in order to learn as much as you can about the issues your community faces.

- After collecting your data, and drawing from the relevant literature, prepare a report that discusses the relationship between youths and law enforcement in your community.

Notes

[1] See Gaines, L. K., Kappeler, V. E., and Vaughan, J. P. 2007. *Policing in America.* Cincinnati, OH: Anderson.

[2] Ibid.

[3] Ibid.

[4] See Peak, K. 2005. *Policing in America,* 5th ed. Belmont, CA: Wadsworth.

[5] Ibid.

[6] Gaines, Kappeler, and Vaughn, 2007.

[7] Ibid.

[8] See Taylor, R. W., Fritsch, E. J., and Caeti, T. J. 2007. *Juvenile Justice: Policies, Programs and Practices,* 2nd ed. New York: McGraw-Hill.

[9] Ibid.

[10] Ibid.

[11] Gaines, Kappeler, and Vaughn, 2007.

[12] Peak, 2005.

[13] Ibid.

[14] Ibid.

[15] Wilson, J. Q. 1968. *Varieties of Police Behavior.* New York: Free Press.

[16] Ibid.

[17] Peak, 2005.

[18] Ibid.

[19] See, for instance, Nihart, T., Lersch, K. M., Sellers, C. S., and Mieczkowski, T. 2005. "Kids, Cops, Parents and Teachers: Exploring Juvenile Attitudes toward Authority Figures." *Western Criminology Review,* 6(1): 79–88.

[20] Ibid. See also Hurst, Y. G. 2007. "Juvenile Attitudes toward the Police." *Criminal Justice Review,* 32(2): 121–141.

[21] See, for instance, Hurst, Y. G., and Frank, J. 2001. "How Kids View Cops: The Nature of Juvenile Attitudes toward the Police." *Journal of Criminal Justice,* 28(3): 189–202. See also Taylor, T. J., Turner, K. B., Finn-Aage, E., and Winfree, L. T. 2001. "Coppin' an Attitude: Attitudinal Differences among Juveniles toward the Police." *Journal of Criminal Justice,* 29(4): 295–305.

[22] Nihart, Lersch, Sellers, and Mieczkowski, 2005.

[23] Ibid.

[24] Myers, S. 2002. *Police Encounters with Juvenile Suspects: Explaining the Use of Authority and Provisions of Support.* Washington, DC: National Institute of Justice.

[25] See Schulenberg, J. L. 2009. "Patterns in Police Decision Making with Youth: An Application of Black's Theory of Law." *Criminal Law and Social Change.* Available at http://www.springerlink.com/content-/v23853uu342320n8/fulltext.pdf?page=1.

[26] Myers, 2002.

[27] Bullock, K., and Tilley, N. 2003. *Crime Reduction and Problem-Oriented Policing.* London: Willan.

[28] U.S. Department of Justice, Office of Justice Programs, Office of Juvenile Justice and Delinquency Prevention. 1999. "OJJDP Research: Making a Difference for Juveniles." Available at http://www.ojjdp.ncjrs.gov/pubs/makingadiffer/intro.htmlbout.

[29] Myers, 2002.

[30] Peak, 2005.

[31] While there is little recent research on the perceptions of police officers of social workers, much of this debate is discussed by Strang, D. 2003. "To See Ourselves as Others See Us." Keynote speech, Association of Directors of Social Work, annual conference, May 22, Dunblane, Scotland.

[32] Finney, R. K. 1972. "A Police View of Social Workers." *Police,* 16: 59–63.

[33] Penner, G. L. 1959. "An Experiment in Police and Social Agency Cooperation." *The Annals of American Academy of Political and Social Science,* 322: 79–88.

[34] Trojanowicz, R. C. 1971. "The Policeman's Occupational Personality." *Journal of Criminal Law, Criminology and Police Science,* 62: 555.

[35] Finney, 1972.

36 See, for instance, Bell, D. J. 1982. "Police-women: Myths and Realities." *Journal of Police Science and Administration,* 10: 112–120; Waddington, P. A. 1993. *Calling the Police: Police Interpretation of and Response to Calls for Assistance from the Public.* Aldershot, UK: Avebury.

37 Fielding, N. G. 1991. *The Police and Social Conflict: Rhetoric and Reality.* London: Athlone.

38 Vernon, S. 1990. *Social Work and the Law.* London: Butterworth.

39 Morgan, R. 1989. "Policing by Consent: Legitimating the Doctrine." In Morgan, R., and Smith, D. J. (eds.), *Coming to Terms with Policing.* London: Routledge.

40 Sireman, J., Miller, B., and Brown, H. F. 1981. "Child Welfare Workers, Police, and Child Placement." *Child Welfare,* 60(6): 413–422.

41 See, for example, Colbach, E. M., and Fosterling, C. D. 1976. *Police Social Work.* Springfield, IL: Charles Thomas; Stephens, M. 1988. "Problems of Police–Social Work Interaction: Some American Lessons." *The Howard Journal,* 22(2): 81–91; Conte, J. R., Berliner, L., and Nolan, D. 1980. "Police and Social Worker Cooperation: A Key in Child Sexual Assault Cases." *FBI Law Enforcement Bulletin,* 49(3): 7–10.

42 See, for instance, Bard, M., and Berkowitz, B. 1969. "Community Psychology Consultation Program in Police Family Crisis Intervention: Preliminary Impression." *International Journal of Social Psychology,* 15: 209–215; Bennett, A. 1980. "Team Aids Police Officers, Works with Rape Victims." *Practice Digest,* 32(2): 5–7; Roberts, A. R. 1978. "Training Police Social Workers: A Neglected Area of Social Work." *Journal of Education for Social Work,* 14(2): 98–103.

43 Ibid.

44 Myers, S. 2002. *Police Encounters with Juvenile Suspects: Explaining the Use of Authority and Provisions of Support.* Washington, DC: National Institute of Justice.

45 See, for instance, Worden, R. E., and Myers, S. M. 2001. *Police Encounters with Juvenile Suspects.* Albany: Center for School of Criminal Justice, State University of New York at Albany. See also Black, D. J., and Reiss, A. J., Jr. 1979. "Police Control of Juveniles." *American Sociological Review,* 35: 63–77.

46 Ibid.

47 Ibid.

48 Browning, S. L., Cullen, E. T., Cao, L., Kopache, R., and Stevenson, T. J. 1994. "Race and Getting Hassled by the Police: A Research Note." *Police Studies,* 17(1): 1–11.

49 White, M. F., Cox, T. C., and J. Basehart, J. 1991. "Theoretical Considerations of Officer Profanity and Obscenity in Formal Contacts with Citizens." In Barker, T., and Carter, D. L. (eds.), *Police Deviance,* 2nd ed., pp. 275–297. Cincinnati, OH: Anderson.

50 Delone Walker, S., Spohn, C., and Delone, M. 2007. *The Color of Justice: Race, Ethnicity, and Crime in America.* Belmont, CA: Wadsworth.

51 Lichtblau, E. 2005. "Profiling Report Leads to Demotion." *New York Times,* August 24, p. B1. Available at http://www.nytimes.com/2005/08/24/politics/24profiling.html.

52 See, for instance, Bishop, D. M., and Frazier, C. E. 1992. "Gender Bias in the Juvenile Justice Processing: Implications of the JJDP Act." *Journal of Criminal Law and Criminology,* 82: 1167. See also Knox, G. W. 2008. *Female Gang Members and the Rights of Children.* Chicago: National Gang Crime Research Center; Yiff, R. M. 2008. "Discrimination of Female Juvenile Delinquents: A Consideration of the Police and Court Processing Practices in the State of Florida." Paper presented at the annual meeting of the Southern Political Science Association, New Orleans. http://www.allacademic.com/meta-/p213022_index.html. Accessed August 5, 2008.

53 Ibid.

54 See Kupchick, A. 2006. *Judging Juveniles.* New York: New York University Press.

55 Taylor, Fritsch, and Caeti, 2007.

56 http://legal-dictionary.thefreedictionary.com/preponderance+of+the+evidence.

57 http://www.legal-dictionary.org/legal-dictionary-i/In-loco-parentis.asp.

58 Ibid.

59 See, for instance, Mason, J. 2004. *Confidentiality in Juvenile Delinquency Proceedings.* Chapel Hill: University of North Carolina School of Government.

60 Synder, H., and Hickman M. 2007. *Juvenile Offenders and Victims 2006 Report.* Washington, DC: National Center for Juvenile Justice.

61 http://caselaw.lp.findlaw.com/data/constitution/amendment04/.

62 Ross, D. L., and Myers, J. J. 2009. "Officer Safety Trumps Passenger Privacy." *Criminal Justice Review,* 34(3): 468–481.

63 *Arizona v. Hicks,* 480 U.S. 321 (1987).

64 *Stafford Unified School District v. Redding,* 557 U.S. (2009). http://www.oyez.org/cases/2000-2009/2008/2008_08_479.

65 *Arizona v. Gant,* 556 U.S. (2009). Available at http://www.oyez.org/cases/2000-2009/2008/2008_07_542.

66 "Unknown Facts Justify Warrantless Search." 2004. *Juvenile Justice Digest,* March 1.

67 http://dictionary.law.com/definition2.asp?selected=795.

68 See Grisso, T. 1980. "Juveniles' Capacity to Waive Miranda Rights: An Empirical Analysis." *California Law Review,* 68:1134.

69 *Fave v. Michael,* 422 U.S. 707, 99 S. Ct 2560 (1979).

70 *California v. Prysock,* 451 U.S. 1301 (1981).

71 Scott-Hayward, C. S. 2007. "Explaining Juvenile False Confessions: Adolescent Development and Police Interrogation." *Law and Psychology Review,* 53: 1–21.

72 McMullen, P. M. 2005 "Questioning the Questions: The Impermissibility of Police Deception in the Interrogations of Juveniles." *Northwestern University Law Review,* Winter: 971–1005.

73 Scott-Hayward, 2007.

74 Ibid.

75 See Alpert, G. P., and Noble, J. J. 2008. "Lies, True Lies, and Conscious Deception." *Police Quarterly.* Available at http://www.deadlyforce.com/Lies%20and%20Deception%20(PQ)-1.pdf.

76 Ibid.

77 McMullen, 2005.

78 See Zerby, S. 2008. "Legal Issues, Rights, and Ethics for Mental Health in Juvenile Justice." *Child and Adolescent Psychiatric Clinics of North America,* 15 (2): 373–390.

79 Ibid.

80 Whitaker, G. P., Phillips, C. D., Haas, P. J., and Worden, R. E. 2008. "Aggressive Policing and the Deterrence of Crime." *Law and Policy,* 7(3): 395–416.

81 See revised Gun-Free School Zones Act, enacted September 30, 1996, at http://www.cs.cmu.edu/afs/cs/usr/wbardwel/public/nfalist/gun_free_school_zones.txt.

82 See http://www.great-online.org/. Accessed September 7, 2008.

83 Esbensen, F. 2004. *Evaluating G.R.E.A.T.: A School-Based Gang Prevention Program.* Washington, DC: National Institute of Justice.

84 See, for instance, Ramsey, A. L., Rust, J. O., and Sobe, S. M. 2003. "An Evaluation of the G.R.E.A.T. Program: A School-Based Prevention Program." *Education,* 124(2): 297–310.

85 See http://www.palnyc.org.

86 Ibid.

87 Ibid.

88 Ibid.

89 See, for instance, Mulvey, E. P., Arthur, M. W., and Reppucci, N. D. 1997. "The Prevention of Juvenile Delinquency: A Review of the Research." *The Prevention Researcher,* 4(2): 1–4. Available at http://www.tpronline.org/article.cfm/The_Prevention_of_Juvenile_Delinquency__A_Review_of_the_Research. See also Grossman, J., and Bulle, M. 2009. "Review of What Youth Programs Do to Increase the Connectedness with Adults." *Journal of Adolescent Health,* 39(6): 788–799; Witt, P. A., and Crompton, J. L. 1996. "The At-Risk Youth Recreation Project." *Journal of Park and Recreation Administration,* 14(3): 1–9.

90 Ibid.

91 Ibid.

92 http://www.learningforlife.org/exploring/lawenforcement/.

93 See, for instance, the San Jose, CA, Police Department police cadet program at http://www.sjpdpal.com/Cadets/Default.asp. Retrieved September 7, 2008.

94 See, for instance, Fritsch, E., Caeti, T., and Taylor, R. 1999. "Gang Suppression through Saturation Patrol, Aggressive Curfew and Truancy Enforcement: A Quasi-Experimental Test of the Dallas Anti-Gang Initiative." *Crime and Delinquency,* 45: 122–139.

95 http://www.psn.gov/about/index.html.

After reading this chapter, you should be able to:

- Identify the issues surrounding the differences between the juvenile justice system and the adult justice system.

- Describe the changes to the way juveniles today are prosecuted for crimes.

- Recognize the key participants and construct the process for juvenile justice.

- Explore the issue of "waiver" to adult courts for serious offenses.

- Organize the steps involved in the juvenile justice system with a discussion of constitutional protections at each stage.

14

The Juvenile Court System

Because juveniles can be sent to prison for committing criminal offenses, the general public believes that they should have the same constitutional protections as adults once they enter the juvenile justice system. However, consider Andrew's situation.

His profile:

- is sixteen years old
- was arrested for possession of drugs with the intent to distribute them on school grounds
- assaulted another youth who attends the same school

His situation:

Andrew was given his Miranda warning, but neither his parents nor an attorney were present when he was questioned. After a lengthy interrogation by detectives, Andrew signed a confession and was charged with both drug possession and assault. When he appeared in court, he was not given the opportunity to cross-examine the prosecution's witnesses, nor was he allowed to present evidence in his defense. The judge heard testimony only from the prosecutor. Andrew was adjudicated a delinquent and was sent to a juvenile detention center for a period of three years.

What are some differences between juvenile and adult court systems? What are the rights for young people at each stage of the justice system?

Upon learning the details of Andrew's case, we might ask ourselves the following questions:

- Does an attorney or parent need to be present when youths are being interrogated?
- Was Andrew's due process denied by the juvenile court judge?
- Was the judge justified in his actions based on the best interests of the child?
- If the judge erred, what rights should have been afforded to Andrew?
- Does Andrew have a constitutional right to an appeal?

In 2005, an estimated 1.7 million delinquency cases were handled in juvenile courts nationwide.[1] While most delinquency matters are handled informally within the juvenile courts, there are times when youths are brought to court for formal processing. This chapter will examine the participants in the juvenile court system, the constitutional rights of delinquents, and the sequence of events by which youths are formally processed. This chapter will also discuss changes in legislation that allow youths to be waived into the adult criminal courts according to circumstances and criteria that differ from state to state.

Historical Overview

Prior to the creation of the first juvenile court in 1899 in the state of Illinois, the legal treatment of juveniles in the United States was based on England's system. During this period, children who committed crimes were categorized and treated according to the following three age categories:

- Children younger than age seven were presumed to be incapable of criminal intent and could not be prosecuted or punished for their crimes.
- Children between the ages of seven and fourteen could mitigate their intent for committing the crime by using the "infancy defense," which involved showing a limited ability to construct intent.
- Children over the age of fourteen were treated as if they were adult criminals.[2]

In the United States, this treatment of children by the court system attracted critical attention. In particular, members of the Society for the Prevention of Cruelty to Animals argued that animals were treated better, and given more protection by society, than children. This movement helped to bring about the creation of the first juvenile court.

By 1925, all but two states had established juvenile courts based on *parens patriae.* This philosophy promotes the idea that not every child in every situation should receive exactly the same treatment. According to *parens patriae,* the court should be responsible for balancing the needs of children, their families, and the community—with a focus on the offender and not the offense. This approach led to a judicial process with the following features:

- Juvenile judges and other officials attempt to handle most cases informally.
- Judicial hearings are less formal than adult trials—they resemble business meetings more than formal court proceedings.
- Hearings are closed to visitors and observers, and juvenile court records are sealed from public access. This provides the court with the ability to maintain the confidentiality of youths involved.
- Attorneys are generally not present, except in trials or in the most serious cases.
- Dispositions or sentences are assessed on a case-by-case basis, with treatment as the guiding philosophy rather than automatic or mandatory sentences.[3]

Together, these features represent what some have called *individualized justice,* a distinguishing characteristic of the juvenile justice system. Although the juvenile court considers the facts of the offense when determining the proper course of action, the specific needs and circumstances of the individual youth are emphasized above all else. From the beginning, it was believed that such consideration would give youths the greatest chance of becoming productive citizens.[4]

While the doctrine of *parens patriae* continues to be the guiding principle behind the actions of the juvenile court, problems remain concerning the treatment of children. It might be helpful to think of the way juveniles were handled in the past as doing the wrong thing for the right reason. In other words, while treatment traditionally was the goal in dealing with delinquents, the emphasis on subjectivity and individuality, as well as the potential punishment involved, led to many instances in which juveniles were not afforded constitutional protections during judicial proceedings. This raised questions about due process for juveniles who might face imprisonment. Thus, concern over the arbitrary nature of the juvenile justice process led to a series of U.S. Supreme Court cases addressing juveniles' rights.

The first case was *Kent v. United States* (1966). On September 2, 1961, Morris Kent entered the apartment of a woman in the District of Columbia, took her wallet, and raped her. The police found fingerprints in the apartment that matched Kent's. Three days later, Kent was taken into custody by the police. Kent was then sixteen years old and eligible to be tried as an adult. Upon being apprehended, Kent was taken to police headquarters where he was interrogated by police officers. He admitted his involvement in the crime and volunteered information about similar offenses involving home invasion, robbery, and rape. His interrogation lasted about seven hours, after which he was taken to a detention center for juveniles. The next morning he was released to the police for further interrogation at police headquarters, which lasted all day. Kent was detained at the center for several days. There was no arraignment during this time, nor was there a determination by a judicial officer of probable cause for the arrest.

Finally, on September 6, Kent's mother showed up with an attorney, who had Kent examined by two psychiatrists and a psychologist. Kent's attorney then filed a motion with the juvenile court for a hearing about the waiver, as well as Kent's suitability to stand trial. The juvenile court judge did not rule on the motions made by Kent's attorney, held no hearings, and did not interview Kent, his mother, or anyone else. The judge ruled that there was sufficient reason to transfer jurisdiction to adult criminal court, although no explanation was given for it.

This was the first time the U.S. Supreme Court had dealt with a juvenile court case. The Court established that youths transferred to adult criminal court must have due process and that youths must be represented by an attorney who has access to youths' juvenile records. More specifically, the Court ruled that Kent should have been afforded an evidentiary hearing during the transfer hearing; that Kent should have been present when the court decided to waive jurisdiction; that Kent's attorney should have been permitted to examine the social worker's investigation of the case, which the judge used to waive jurisdiction; and that the judge should have recorded a statement explaining the reasons for the transfer.[5]

The second case was *In re Gault* (1967). On June 8, 1964, police arrested fifteen-year-old Gerald Gault and his friend Ronald Lewis after a verbal complaint was made by a neighbor that the two youths had made lewd or indecent remarks to her over the phone. At the time of the arrest, neither of Gault's parents were at home, and they were not notified of their son's arrest. Gault's parents searched for their missing child and later found out through a friend that he had been arrested. The arresting officer filed a petition with the court the next day, on June 9, 1968, but it was not seen by anyone until the habeas corpus hearing on August 17, 1964.

At the trial, Gault's father was not present, nor was the complainant. Other omissions of procedural guidelines included the fact that no one was sworn in at the trial and no records of the proceedings were kept. The judge sentenced Gault to the state industrial school for six years, until he turned twenty-one. An adult charged with the same crime would have received a maximum $50 fine and two months in jail. Gault's lawyers filed a writ of habeas corpus but were denied by both the Superior Court of Arizona and the Arizona Supreme Court.

The U.S. Supreme Court overruled the Arizona Supreme Court for its dismissal of a writ of habeas corpus. This case, perhaps more so than any other, brought constitutional protections to juveniles. The ruling established that juveniles have the constitutional right to notice of the proceedings, the right to counsel, the right to confront and cross-examine accusers, the right against self-incrimination, and the right to appeal a decision of the juvenile court. Collectively, these constitutional protections are referred to as *due process rights.*[6]

Next was *In re Winship* (1970). When he was twelve years old, Samuel Winship was arrested and charged as a juvenile for breaking into a woman's locker and stealing $112 from her pocketbook. Had Winship's act been committed by an adult, it would have constituted the crime of larceny. A family court found Winship guilty, despite acknowledging that the evidence did not establish his guilt beyond a reasonable doubt. Winship's appeal stated that the court's use of preponderance of evidence as a burden of proof was unconstitutional. This argument was rejected in both the Appellate Division of the New York Supreme Court and in the New York Court of Appeals, before the U.S. Supreme Court heard the case.

In this case, the U.S. Supreme Court decided that juveniles are entitled to a burden of proof that is beyond a reasonable doubt. In ruling that preponderance of evidence is an insufficient basis for a judicial decision when youths are charged with criminal offenses, the Court recognized that some flexibility in the judicial process for juveniles is needed at times. However, on other issues, such as when youths face the possibility of the loss of freedom, the burden of proof standards used for adults should apply.[7]

The fourth case was *McKeiver v. Pennsylvania* (1971). In 1968, Joseph McKeiver, then sixteen years old, was arrested and charged with robbery, larceny, and receiving stolen goods. McKeiver's offense was his participation—with twenty or thirty other youths—in pursuing three young teenagers and taking twenty-five cents from them. McKeiver had never been arrested and had a record of gainful employment. In addition, the court found the testimony of two of the victims somewhat inconsistent and "weak" in credibility. At the time of the adjudication hearing, McKeiver was represented by counsel. However, his request for a jury trial was denied, and his case was heard by a family court judge. McKeiver was adjudicated a delinquent and placed on probation.

In this case, the Supreme Court moved in the opposite direction of the trend to protect youths when it determined that there is no constitutional right to trial by jury in juvenile proceedings.[8] The rationale for this decision was based on the idea that a jury trial makes the proceedings a more adversarial process, negating the need for a separate juvenile justice system with an emphasis on treatment and individualized justice.[9]

Finally, there was *Breed v. Jones* (1975). On February 9, 1971, a petition was filed in the Superior Court of California, alleging that Breed, then seventeen years old, had committed armed robbery. The following day, a detention hearing was held, at the conclusion of which Breed was ordered to remain in detention pending a hearing on the petition. After taking testimony from Breed and two prosecution witnesses, the juvenile court judge adjudicated Breed a delinquent. The dispositional hearing was scheduled for a later date, and Breed remained in custody. At the dispositional hearing, the court ruled that Breed could not be adequately treated in a juvenile justice facility and should be tried in adult court. Breed's attorney objected, arguing that no mention of such a ruling had been made in the adjudication hearing and that he had no time to prepare a response to these new charges. The court rescheduled the dispositional hearing for one week later. Having considered only the report of the probation officer assigned to the case and her testimony, the judge declared Breed "unfit for treatment as a juvenile" and ordered that he be prosecuted as an adult.

double jeopardy
A situation centered on the question of whether a juvenile can be prosecuted as an adult for the same crime after being adjudicated a delinquent.

The central issue in this case was Breed's transfer to adult court. Unlike the *Kent* case, however, the constitutional issue in *Breed* was **double jeopardy,** meaning that it centered on the question of whether a juvenile can be prosecuted as an adult after being adjudicated a delinquent. The increased use of transfers to adult court made this issue an important one. The U.S. Supreme Court ruled that Breed's case did, in fact, constitute double jeopardy—a juvenile court cannot adjudicate a case and then turn it over to adult court for processing on the same offense.[10] What makes the Breed case significant is that it forces prosecutors to decide which court in which to prosecute youths—they only get one chance.

ANDREW'S CASE

Constitutional Protections of Juveniles

Recall Andrew's case:

- is sixteen years old
- was arrested for possession of drugs with the intent to distribute them on school grounds and assaulting another youth
- was interrogated and signed a confession without a parent or attorney present
- was sentenced to three years in a juvenile detention facility

When juveniles commit crimes, they do not automatically have the same constitutional protections as adults. For example, Andrew does not have a constitutional right to an appeal. Moreover, it is not considered unconstitutional for the police to interrogate Andrew if he has been given his Miranda warning and decides to cooperate. This is true even in instances where the police are intent on using deception to elicit a confession.

Should Andrew have been given the opportunity to call an attorney before his interrogation began? Do you think that Andrew, at sixteen years old, should be able to waive his rights in response to the Miranda warning?

THINK ABOUT IT

Historical Overview of the Juvenile Justice System

THINK ABOUT IT

Describe the historical basis for the differences between juvenile and adult criminal justice systems. Do you think juveniles should have all the constitutional protections that adults have? Why or why not?

Recent Changes

The 1960s and 1970s constitute a significant period in the history of the juvenile justice system. As more cases were heard by the U.S. Supreme Court, juveniles were afforded more due process and constitutional protections. Also during this time, the concern for youths' well-being led to the deinstitutionalization of status offenses, as discussed in Chapter 3.

In the 1980s, another set of court decisions brought about additional changes in the ways in which juveniles were treated by the system. In light of concerns about a rising juvenile crime rate, legislatures began making three types of changes to the way the juvenile court handled cases. These changes represented a significant departure from the treatment-orientation of the juvenile justice system, and a movement toward a more punitive approach to juvenile crime.

CRIMINAL COURT TRANSFERS

Historically, only certain types of offenses, under specific and unusual circumstances, were transferable to adult criminal court. However, in the 1980s and 1990s, fears of rising juvenile violence and the anticipation of the "super predator" class of delinquents prompted a number of states to pass laws requiring automatic waivers to criminal court for specified offenses. Some states also lowered the age at which youths could be transferred to criminal court. In the past, laws generally did not permit the transfer of youths to criminal court if they were under the age of fourteen.

What might be some of the benefits and drawbacks to trying juveniles as adults?

As concerns about juvenile violence grew, policymakers responded with changes in other laws as well. A number of states even revoked the juvenile court's authority to determine whether it had jurisdiction over certain cases. Thus, not only were judges required to waive specified offenses, but in some states, the law gave prosecutors the discretion to file an offense in either juvenile or adult criminal court. Some of these laws made the automatic waiver age specific: if a youth committed a particular offense by a certain age, the case was automatically transferred to adult criminal court.[11] Michael Corriero, former judge of New York County Supreme Court and now Executive Director of New York Center for Juvenile Justice, offers insight into the criminal transfer process in New York State:

> New York is kind of a unique state in the nation in terms of its methodology and its legal framework in terms of adjudicating cases of young people under 18 years of age. New York's age of criminal responsibility is, for example, 16 . . . New York further permits the prosecution of children as young as 13 who are accused of murder and children as young as 14 who are accused of robbery and other serious crimes automatically in the first instance in the adult court pursuant to New York's juvenile offender law.

To better understand how New York (and North Carolina) set 16 as the age, Corriero provides a historical context:

> Prior to 1978, New York prosecuted the cases of all children under 16 years of age regardless of the severity of the crime in the juvenile court and family court where they could be placed for no more than 5 years or until they reached the age of 21. And this proved to be a mistake because in 1978 along came a young man by the name of Willie Bosket who murdered two people on a subway before he reached the age of 16. And when the public became aware, now wait a minute Willie Bosket is gonna go to the family court, the juvenile court where he can only be placed for 5 years or until he reaches the age of 21? This is scandalous. How are we dealing with children who are capable of such violence?

Such changes were experienced by many of the youths interviewed for this text. For instance, Anthony was sent to a juvenile detention facility rather than being waived to adult court as part of a plea bargain agreement:

> . . . my first, my first court hearing was . . . they, um, told me, uh, I was going up for waiver. And uh, my attorney, she was representing me, she told me, you can get, "you can do 2 to 8 years for every—all of these charges." And I had two C felonies, a misdemeanor, and she's like was like that's 16 to 40 years. I'm like, "I can't do that, that's too much time." She was like, "well, we gonna see what they tell me about a plea bargain." I'm like, would it, would I be able to do something less? She's like "no, because they tell me my crime was violent and it'd be non-suspendable," so I had to do whatever they gave me. And I, I went back to the court, I ended up, I was so frustrated, like, "I don't care no more, I'm going to prison anyways." I fought a detention staff and that didn't make it no better. I picked up a D felony, I got three felonies and a misdemeanor. And the judge is like "I'm gonna help you." And I thought I was really going to get away with it. I started doing good, started hearing me talking to the man [God], he came through. I went to my um, I went to my disposition and stuff . . . they let me sign a plea to come here for two years.

For more on the criminal transfer process in New York State, watch
Practitioner Michael Corriero at www.mhhe.com/mcnamarajd1e

CONFIDENTIALITY LAWS

In addition to the shift in laws regarding the jurisdiction of juvenile court, many other traditional features of juvenile court proceedings have changed as well. For instance, confidentiality was always considered an important dimension of the juvenile justice process. The stigma that communities associate with juvenile criminal activity is incongruent with the treatment and rehabilitative philosophy of the court. In fact, prior to the 1990s, delinquency court hearings, and information related to those hearings, were generally off-limits to the press and the public.[12]

Since the 1990s, this perspective has changed. Many state legislatures have removed the confidentiality restrictions and have determined that the community's right to know is more important than protecting youths from being stigmatized. Today, in many jurisdictions, unless it is shown that opening proceedings would significantly harm youths, the juvenile justice process is open to the public.[13]

The U.S. Supreme Court has ruled on three separate cases that have significantly changed the way juveniles are protected with regard to confidentiality. Specifically, affording juveniles certain protections has become less important than addressing the fears and concerns of the general public.

In *Davis v. Alaska,* the issue involved an effort to obtain testimony from a juvenile on probation, who was a witness in a criminal trial. Initially, the prosecution made a motion in a lower court to prevent the defense counsel from making any reference to the juvenile's record. However, the U.S. Supreme Court ruled that the right to completely cross-examine an adverse witness is more important than any potential or real injury that might occur to the juvenile by revealing information contained in his juvenile record.[14]

Oklahoma Publishing Co. v. District Court involved an eleven-year-old boy suspected of homicide. The boy appeared at a detention hearing where photographs were taken by news reporters and published in local newspapers. When the district court judge learned of this, he prohibited the newspapers from publishing the photos. In response, the publishing company argued that this was an infringement on First Amendment protections regarding freedom of the press. The U.S. Supreme Court ruled that a state court does not have the authority to restrict the dissemination of information obtained at an open juvenile proceeding.[15]

Finally, in *Smith v. Daily Mail Publishing Co.* the U.S. Supreme Court ruled on those instances in which a media source publishes the identity of a juvenile even if there are state statutes prohibiting the practice. Now, if newspapers obtain information about the identities of juveniles through legal means, they have the right to publish them. This ruling suggests that the Court has concluded that the need for the public to be aware of certain crimes committed by youths is more important than the safeguards offered to protect them.[16]

The rulings by the U.S. Supreme Court on the issue of confidentiality not only involve those cases where the identities of juvenile offenders becomes known, but also extend to access to juvenile records. In the past, juvenile records were kept confidential. However, the information contained in the reports could be opened by court order in some states. Increasingly, states are allowing noncriminal justice personnel access to defendants' juvenile records. The reasons for this relate to the public's right to know, as well as the need to have all of the facts in making a decision about a particular case. Many first-time adult offenders committed crimes as juveniles. This information would normally not be available to adult court judges when passing sentence unless states allowed them such access.[17] As with the practice of revealing the identities of juveniles, many experts and legislatures contend that the public's right to know more about defendants' past records is more important than protecting juveniles from the embarrassment of others viewing their records.[18]

blended sentencing
A sentence that is both treatment-oriented and punishment-oriented, involving both juvenile and adult facilities.

TOUGHER JUVENILE SANCTIONS

While the U.S. Supreme Court has provided many constitutional protections for juveniles charged with crimes, particularly in the area of due process, many states have increased the level of accountability for convicted offenders. For example, some have lowered the age at which youths can be held in secure detention, as well as that at which they can be sent to secure correctional institutions.

States have also expanded the options related to **blended sentencing.** In blended sentencing, which we will discuss in greater detail in Chapter 15, a judge can impose a sentence that is both treatment-oriented (juvenile) and punitive-oriented (adult). One type of blended sentence stipulates that if offenders successfully complete the juvenile portion of the sentence, the adult criminal sentence may be set aside and not enforced. Another type of blended sentence occurs when juveniles are ordered to serve time in a juvenile facility until reaching the age of majority; they are then transferred to an adult facility to complete the sentence.[19]

What are the three major goals of BARJ? Can you think of any treatments or punishments designed to achieve these goals?

Balanced and Restorative Justice Model (BARJ)

A model that gives equal consideration to protecting the community, holding offenders accountable for their actions, and helping offenders to develop the skills and attitudes they need to succeed in becoming law-abiding and productive members of society.

While some legislatures have changed their laws to reflect a "get tough" approach to juvenile crime, other states have explored the use of the **Balanced and Restorative Justice Model (BARJ).**[20] This model gives equal consideration to the following:

- protecting the community
- holding offenders accountable for their actions
- helping offenders to develop the skills and attitudes they need to succeed in becoming law-abiding and productive members of society[21]

The basic assumption underlying this model is that crime cannot be dealt with effectively if only justice system officials are involved. The input and participation of the entire community is needed to effectively address crime. The model begins with the larger notion that all human beings have dignity and worth. If that dignity and worth are threatened or harmed in some way, restoration—repairing the harm and rebuilding relationships in the community—should be the primary goal of the juvenile justice system.

Restorative justice argues that all parties should take part in responding to crimes, including the victim if he or she wishes, the community, and juvenile offenders. The victim's perspective is central to deciding how to repair the harm caused by the crime. Also, juveniles must learn accountability by accepting responsibility and acting to repair the harm they have done. Results are measured by how much repair was done rather than by how much punishment was inflicted. The Office of Juvenile Justice and Delinquency Prevention (OJJDP), in its *Guide for Implementing the Balanced and Restorative Justice Model* (see Figure 14-1), offers insight into the philosophy of restorative justice, as well as how communities around the country can implement this model into their juvenile justice system.[22] As former Judge Corriero states, while many states approach the problem by increasing the use of transfers to the adult system, he had a different solution:

> We would focus the limited resources that we had available to us to try and identify those children that we thought we could safely channel out of the system by placing them in alternatives to incarceration programs which were essentially privately funded, not institutionalized

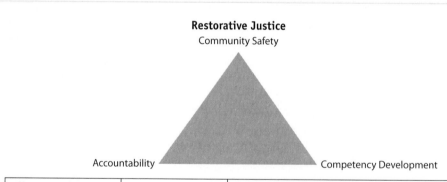

Clients/Customers	Goals	Values
Victims	Accountability	When an individual commits an offense, the offender incurs an obligation to individual victims and the community.
Youth	Competency development	Offenders who enter the juvenile justice system should be more capable when they leave than when they entered.
Community	Community safety	Juvenile justice has a responsibility to protect the public from juveniles in the system.

FIGURE 14-1 Balanced Approach Model

A balanced approach of combining treatment and punishment traditionally has been the foundation of the juvenile justice system.

Adapted from Maloney. D., Romig, D., and Armstrong, T. 1998. *Juvenile Probation: The Balanced Approach.* Reno, NV: National Council of Juvenile and Family Court Judges.

but . . . who were kind of coming at the court to lobby judges for kids they thought fit their profile of someone that they could work with . . . And this was important this idea of earning youthful offender, giving them the opportunity to develop a historical record of improving their behavior so that when I decided to grant youthful offender treatment I would have a reasonable basis to do that in the record because every decision to grant youthful offender treatment was appealable by the prosecutor.

Many of the changes described in this section give the impression that the United States is returning to an era in which the public, the police, legislators, and policymakers view juvenile delinquents like miniature adults. With changes in the justice process, a decreased emphasis on treatment and rehabilitation, and an increased willingness to transfer juveniles to adult court, it appears that we have adopted a punishment philosophy to solve our delinquency problems. In response to these and other issues involved in the processing of juvenile offenders, a recent report issued by the National Council of Juvenile and Family Court Judges, titled *Juvenile Delinquency Guidelines: Improving Court Practices in Juvenile Delinquency Cases,* makes a series of recommendations aimed at improving the way juveniles are processed and explaining the rationale behind decisions at each stage of the judicial process. The types of offenders entering the system, as well as the wide range of family and educational issues they present, make it difficult for juvenile courts to balance the needs of the individual with the concerns of the community. The council's report also acknowledges that little has been done in recent decades to evaluate and assess the impact of some of the changes that have taken place and whether they constitute the best interests of the children they aim to serve.[23]

00:20   01:02

For more on youthful offender treatment, watch *Practitioner Michael Corriero* at www.mhhe.com/mcnamarajd1e

ANDREW'S CASE

Considering His Sentence

Recall Andrew's case:

- is sixteen years old
- was arrested for possession of drugs and assault
- was denied due process
- was sentenced to three years in a juvenile detention facility

The judge's decision to open Andrew's trial to the public is one example of the types of changes taking place in the juvenile justice system, with regard to confidentiality. Traditionally, courts have tried to protect youths from the stigma of being adjudicated a delinquent. Changes such as these, which treat juvenile offenders more like their adult counterparts, have also been accompanied by tougher sentencing practices.

Assume that the judge was within his authority to open the hearing to the public, as a result of a change in state law. Do you think the judge made the right decision? Is opening the case to the public in Andrew's best interests, or do you think Andrew's rights have been violated?

THINK ABOUT IT

Changes in the System

Consider the changes that have taken place in the way juveniles are prosecuted for crimes. Should states be allowed to determine if the *parens patriae* philosophy is no longer applicable? In such cases, should states pass laws that treat juveniles like adults?

THINK ABOUT IT

Juvenile Justice Participants

Juvenile court proceedings involve a number of key players, ranging from state-appointed attorneys to volunteer court advocates such as guardians ad litem. In theory, each of these roles exists to ensure the best interests of juveniles.

JUDGES

In the juvenile court, the judge is the ultimate decision maker. Given that judges are responsible for keeping the framework of *parens patriae* as a guideline for how cases are decided, they do not simply rule on the facts of the case. Instead, they need to have a wide range of options available in order to render a decision. Juvenile judges also rule on pretrial motions, such as arrest, search, and seizure; the admissibility of evidence; transfer issues; and whether the youth in question should remain in detention until the case is resolved. Although judges may use court administrators to handle some of their responsibilities, their most important job is the disposition stage of cases.

Juvenile court judges also manage the court in terms of hiring and firing staff, budgeting, and performing other administrative duties. Additionally, they set the tone for the type of cases that have priority in their jurisdiction. For instance, as we discussed in Chapter 3, there is some debate about whether status offenders should be under the control of the juvenile court. Some judges feel this is inappropriate and decide that such cases be diverted from their court. Depending on the state, and on whether transfer is done by statute, judges may also influence which types of offenders are sent to adult court for processing.

Some judges are elected officials, making them sensitive to community concerns. Other judges are appointed by the governor or state legislature. There is a long-standing debate regarding the election of judges. Some experts believe that judges should be appointed so that they can be insulated from public opinion and decide cases based on their merits, rather than on what their constituents want. Others argue that elections are beneficial because they force judges to consider the community's needs when rendering decisions.[24]

Some judges are appointed by what is known as the Missouri Plan. That is, they are appointed by governors for a fixed term and then run for reelection in uncontested elections. If a judge is reelected, then he or she serves another term, usually four to six years. If a judge is not elected by voters, then the governor of the state appoints another judge and the process begins again.[25]

REFEREES

Many juvenile courts make use of a referee, who assists judges in the processing of individuals through the juvenile court system (see Table 14-1). Many states use the term *Master* or *Commissioner,* and assign them varying levels of responsibility regarding

TABLE 14-1 General Difference between Juvenile Court Judge and Juvenile Court Referee[26]

	Judge	Referee
Obtain Position	Elected or appointed by governor	Appointment by presiding judge as a subordinate
Types of Cases	All types of cases	Vast majority minor juvenile cases
Public Persona	Wears robe Is addressed as "Your Honor"	Wears robe Is addressed as "Your Honor"
Authority	Hears cases, rules on orders, and makes final decisions	Certain orders must be reviewed by a judge; a party in a case can ask for rehearing by a judge.

Functionally, there is generally no difference between the referee and a judge performing the same work.

Would it be better if more cases were heard and handled by referees first?

cases. These individuals may or may not have legal training or be members of the national or state Bar Associations, which are the governing bodies for attorneys. Typically, referees hear cases at the fact-finding stage and sometimes at detention hearings; this allows judges to dedicate their time to dispositional hearings, which is a critical stage of the process.[27]

PROSECUTORS

The role of the prosecutor is changing, particularly as it relates to the juvenile justice process. Typically, the prosecutor represents the state in juvenile proceedings. He or she decides what charges are to be brought against an individual, depending on whether the case moves forward or is handled informally. The prosecutor also brings about a disposition, either through an adjudication hearing or through plea bargaining. Prosecutors are usually responsible for initiating the transfer proceedings that waive juveniles to adult court for trial. Increasingly, as the juvenile justice process becomes more punitive in its philosophy, this role is evolving to become more like the prosecutor's role in adult court.[28]

DEFENSE ATTORNEYS

In juvenile cases, the role of the defense attorney is similar to that in adult court. The defense attorney's job is to present the best case possible to either the judge or a jury, to negotiate a plea agreement, and to protect the constitutional rights of juveniles during the process. As in the adult system, if the offender is indigent and cannot afford an attorney, the court appoints one for him or her. These provisions were brought about as a result of the *In re Gault* case, described previously. However, research has shown that less than half of juveniles accused of delinquency make use of an attorney.[29] Because most juvenile cases are handled informally, attorneys are not always needed.[30]

PROBATION OFFICERS

Probation officers perform three essential roles in juvenile court: intake, preparation of predisposition reports, and supervision of probationers. During intake, wherein juveniles first come into contact with the juvenile justice system, probation officers determine if a case is to be handled informally or if the youth goes to the next phase of the justice process. Probation officers also prepare presentence or predisposition reports, which are used by judges in rendering disposition or sentence for adjudicated youths. Finally, probation officers provide supervision to youths who are sentenced to probation to make sure they are meeting the conditions of their probation agreement with the court.[31]

COURT ADVOCATES

In some cases, there are special circumstances that court personnel normally cannot address. In those cases, a volunteer who receives special training may be appointed as a **Court Appointed Special Advocate (CASA).** These individuals provide assistance and advice to the court about the appropriate placement of youth. One example of a type of CASA volunteer is a guardian ad litem. These volunteers are commonly used in abuse and neglect cases in which Child Protective Services (CPS) officials bring a case to family court against a parent or guardian. Unlike CPS workers, who have heavy caseloads, guardians take only one or two cases at a time. This allows them to investigate the case more thoroughly, to interview and visit the child more often, and to provide insight into the case that normal procedures do not allow.[32]

 The CASA program began in 1977, when a Seattle judge decided to use trained community volunteers to advocate for the best interests of abused and neglected children in court. In 1990, the U.S. Congress encouraged the expansion of CASA programs with passage of the Victims of Child Abuse Act.[33] Currently, CASA consists of 59,000 volunteers who serve 243,000 abused and neglected children through over 900 local programs

Court Appointed Special Advocate (CASA)
Volunteers who receive special training to provide assistance and advice to the court about the appropriate placement of youths.

Why do you think guardians ad litem and CASA volunteers are so effective?

across the country.[34] In a 2007 report on the effectiveness of CASA programs, the U.S. Department of Justice Office of the Inspector General (OIG) reported the following:

- Children with a CASA volunteer were substantially less likely to spend time in long-term foster care, defined as more than three years in care (13.3 percent for CASA cases vs. 27 percent of all children in foster care).[35]

- When a CASA volunteer was involved, both children and their parents were more likely to receive services ordered by the court. The report concluded that this was an indication that "CASA is effective in identifying the needs of children and parents."[36]

- Cases involving a CASA volunteer were nearly twice as likely to be "permanently closed," meaning the children were less likely to reenter the child welfare system. The report showed that about 9 percent of CASA children reentered the system compared to 16 percent of those without a CASA volunteer.[37]

These findings, as well as other studies evaluating the effectiveness of CASA programs, indicate that they play an essential role in ensuring that children receive the proper attention and care from the juvenile court system.[38]

Participants in the Juvenile Justice System

Recall the role of CASA volunteers in the juvenile courts. Why do you think CASA volunteers have such a significant impact on cases? How does a court advocate's role differ from that of a probation officer?

Juvenile Court Process

The juvenile court process, like its adult counterpart, is a series of decisions that determine how far an offender moves through the system. At any stage of the process, officials in the system may decide to simply drop the charges or to handle matters informally. This is consistent with the rehabilitative philosophy of the court, as well as with the goal of serving the best interests of children. According to the OJJDP report *Juvenile Court Statistics 2005,* there were approximately 1,697,900 juvenile cases in 2005, most of which were being handled formally (see Figure 14-2), an increase of 46 percent since 1985.

In terms of the outcome of the experience in juvenile court, probation continues to be the most common sanction. In 2005, about 60 percent of all adjudicated delinquency cases were ordered to formal probation, 20 percent of all adjudicated delinquents were ordered to residential placement, and 18 percent of cases resulted in offenders making restitution, performing community service, or seeking treatment or counseling.[39]

INTAKE

intake
The first step in the juvenile justice process, usually preceded by referrals to court by police or probation officers.

The general steps in the juvenile justice process are intake, petition, adjudication, and disposition. **Intake** usually proceeds with a referral to juvenile court. These referrals are made by police officers, who handle the vast majority of cases; by school officials, who witness a crime on campus; by parents, who might not be able to control their children; by victims of crimes; and even by probation officers, when youths violate the terms of their probation agreements.[40]

After a case has been referred to juvenile court, it is sent to intake, which is usually conducted by a probation officer. Similar to the decision in the adult system, the intake officer must determine whether to immediately detain offenders and whether to bring

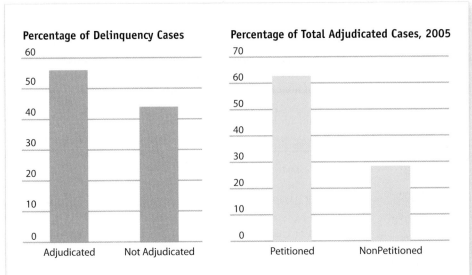

Percentage of Delinquency Cases

Percentage of Total Adjudicated Cases, 2005

FIGURE 14-2 Data for Delinquency Cases, 2005

Data suggest that when a case gets to juvenile court, it is most likely to result in formal processing. Of those cases where a petition was filed, two-thirds resulted in offenders being adjudicated delinquents. Only about 1 percent of cases involving youths under the age of fifteen resulted in waiver to adult court. A majority of juvenile offenders (57 percent) are under the age of sixteen, a larger majority are male (63 percent), and nearly two-thirds (64 percent) are white.

formal charges against them. In the juvenile system, this is referred to as a **petition.**[41] A petition states the allegations against juveniles and requests that the court intervene and adjudicate them delinquents.

Detention

Youths can be held in a **detention** facility under the following circumstances:

- if they are a threat to the community
- if they are flight risks, who may not appear at hearings
- if their parents cannot be located

According to the OJJDP report *Juvenile Court Statistics 2005,* only about 11 percent of juveniles were held in detention facilities at some point between referral to court and case disposition. In fact, in most cases, even violent offenders will not be detained prior to adjudication.[42] As seen in Table 14-2, the likelihood of detention varies by general offense category. In 2005, person offense cases were the most likely to involve detention (25 percent), followed by public order offense cases (24 percent). In comparison, juveniles were less likely to be detained in drug offense cases and property offense cases.[43]

Public order offenses include activities such as loitering, curfew violations, or underage drinking.[44] When youths are detained prior to an adjudication hearing, a detention hearing must be held within twenty-four to seventy-two hours. At this hearing, a judge decides whether to release offenders. About half of all detained juveniles are released after a detention hearing.[45]

petition
The determination of whether to detain offenders and whether to bring formal charges against them and request that the court intervene and adjudicate them delinquents.

detention
Facilities that hold youths if they are a threat to the community, if they are flight risks before their hearing, or if their parents cannot be located.

TABLE 14-2 Offense Profile of Detained Delinquency Cases, 1985 and 2005

Most Serious Offense	1985	2005
Person	19%	25%
Property	52	16
Drugs	7	18
Public order	22	24

These findings suggest that violent crime has become an important issue compared to property crimes, and the likely response is detention.

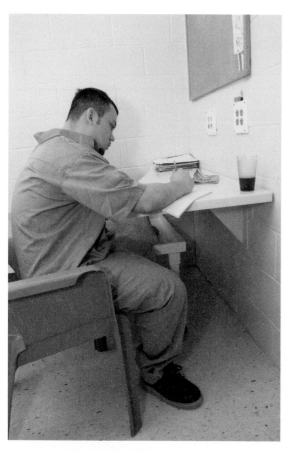

Under what circumstances might youths be held in detention centers prior to adjudication? Can you think of an example in which detention prior to adjudication is in juveniles' best interests?

Once intake receives a referral, intake officers have three options: dismiss cases and release the offender to his or her parents or guardians; handle matters informally by placing the juvenile on probation; or petition the case to the juvenile court for a formal disposition of the matter. The decision to petition is usually made by a probation officer, although increasingly prosecutors are playing a role in this phase of the process—perhaps due to the increasing similarities between the juvenile and adult criminal justice processes.[46]

Typically, first-time offenders and youths who commit minor crimes are dismissed, as are those against whom there is a lack of evidence. Usually, dismissals come with a warning to youths about the ramifications of returning to the system a second time. According to the OJJDP, in 2005, 18 percent of all delinquency cases were dismissed at intake, generally for lack of evidence. An additional 26 percent of cases were handled informally, with juveniles agreeing to some sort of voluntary sanction, like restitution.[47]

If intake officers opt to handle matters informally, they have a wide range of options available to them, such as placing youths on informal probation, requiring them to perform community service, or otherwise imposing a sanction that offenders agree to perform in lieu of formal processing of their cases. As we discussed in Chapter 12, many delinquency prevention programs require youths to make restitution, perform community service, or write letters of apology, all of which are popular alternatives to formal disposition by the courts. If juveniles do not complete the criteria set out in the agreement, the case can be sent to juvenile court for a more formal outcome. If an intake officer decides to move forward in the justice process, the prosecutor receives the case and can either decide to dismiss the charges, handle the matter informally, or petition the case to the juvenile court. Another option might be to waive the juvenile to adult court for processing.

When intake officers decide to offer restitution to offenders, there are programs in place to help juveniles carry out their sanctions. A program in New Hampshire that targets first-time offenders offers insight into the informal handling of juvenile cases. New Hampshire's Juvenile Conference Committee and Earn-It are described in the Theory and Practice box.

Bail

bail
The amount of money, normally set at the initial court appearance and related to the seriousness of the crime and potential of the defendant to flee, that must be paid to the court to ensure that the accused will return for subsequent hearings or trial.

Bail is the amount of money that must be paid to the court to ensure that the accused will return for subsequent hearings or trial. The price of bail is normally set at the initial appearance and is related to a number of factors, including the seriousness of the offense and whether the court believes the accused is likely to flee the jurisdiction of the court. In other words, the sole purpose of bail is to guarantee that suspects will return when commanded by the court. A secondary objective of bail is that, while free, individuals can contribute to their own defense by collecting evidence to show their innocence. However, if the accused cannot afford bail, they are remanded to custody until the trial.[48]

While the Eighth Amendment guarantees adults the right to reasonable bail in noncapital cases, most states refuse to grant juveniles that same right. The reason for this relates to the philosophy of the juvenile justice system, whose proceedings are civil, and not criminal, in nature. Another reason that this right is not granted in juvenile cases is that detention is part of a rehabilitative strategy, not a punitive one. In many states, laws already exist that allow juveniles to be released into the custody of their parents.

State laws vary quite a bit on this topic. However, there are generally three types of laws relating to bail: those that grant bail to juveniles, those that give the court the authority and discretion to grant bail to juveniles, and those that deny it completely. This wide range of laws means that there is a general lack of continuity, from state to state, regarding bail.

One reason for this disparity is the fact that the U.S. Supreme Court has never ruled on the issue of juvenile bail. However, the Court has ruled that the state has the right to practice

THEORY AND PRACTICE WORKING TOGETHER

New Hampshire's Juvenile Conference Committee and Earn-It

The Juvenile Conference Committee (JCC) is an intervention program for first-time juvenile offenders. JCC's goal is to minimize youths' involvement with the justice system and to encourage a sense of responsibility and accountability among offenders.

JCC considers each case to ensure individualized justice, and has established a process by which this type of justice is achieved.

- Dispositions are arranged that fit the needs of juveniles, victims, and their communities.
- Contracts are created and established that youths must complete as part of their disposition.
- Activities and conditions include in-person apologies by offenders to victims, community service work, research papers, restitution, contracts relating to school performance and to home behavior, and curfews.

As a condition of participating in JCC, youths must be willing to admit their involvement in the delinquent act to the Juvenile Coordinator and JCC, and be held accountable and responsible for their behavior. While participation in the program is voluntary, the Juvenile Coordinator is responsible for deciding whether the case is appropriate for diversion;

moreover, it is the decision of minors and their parents, guardians, or custodians whether they wish to participate in the program. Internal evaluations of the JCC program indicate that 92 percent of offenders complete the program and 94 percent have not returned to juvenile court within a year of participating in the program.

A related program, called Earn-It, helps youths who have been ordered to pay restitution find jobs. Earn-It is a positive sentencing alternative first implemented in 1979, when a frustrated judge determined that traditional sentencing options for young first-time offenders—dismissal of charges or detention in jail—were failing the victims, the juvenile offenders, and their communities. Since 1988, Earn-It has served eighteen communities, and youths in the program have earned thousands of dollars to pay off their debts. Evaluations of the Earn-It program show a 91 percent completion rate, with 88 percent of offenders not returning to juvenile court within a year of participation.

THINK ABOUT IT What are the long- and short-term advantages of Earn-It? What do programs like JCC and Earn-It teach youths about accountability?

---

preventive detention, whereby dangerous youths remain confined until their adjudication hearings. In 1984, in *Schall v. Martin,* the Court ruled that the overriding concern for public safety allows states to take extreme steps in some cases, and to hold youths indefinitely before trial.[49]

In December 1977, Gregory Martin was arrested in New York City on charges of robbery, assault, and criminal possession of a weapon. Martin also lied about his address, and because the arrest occurred near midnight, Martin was kept in detention overnight and brought to juvenile court the next day for an initial appearance. The family court judge ruled that because of the seriousness of the charges, particularly the possession of a loaded weapon, and the obvious lack of adult supervision, Martin would be held in detention until trial. This decision was consistent with New York state law, which authorized pretrial detention if it could be shown that the youth in question would not be likely to show up for trial, or would potentially commit another crime while free on bail. Later, at trial, Martin was adjudicated a delinquent and sentenced to two years' probation.[50]

While Martin was detained prior to his adjudication hearing, attorneys filed a class action suit against the state, claiming that this type of detention violated the due process protections of the Fifth and Fourteenth Amendments to the U.S. Constitution. The New York appellate courts upheld Martin's claim, stating that since most delinquents were released or placed on probation after their adjudication hearing, it was unfair to detain them before trial. The prosecution brought the case before the U.S. Supreme Court. After hearing arguments, the Court upheld the state's right to place juveniles in preventive detention, noting that such a practice need not be considered punishment. Moreover, since procedural safeguards were already in place, such as a notice and a hearing before a youth was placed in detention, preventive detention did not violate any constitutional protections. In other words, not only is preventive detention a reasonable strategy for dangerous offenders, there are procedural safeguards in place to prevent abuse of the practice.[51] Preventive detention remains a controversial topic, with critics of the practice arguing that it unfairly deprives some youths of their freedom, a determination that is based on what they might do in the future, something no one can adequately predict.[52]

Plea Bargaining

A **plea bargain** is a strategy whereby the offender pleads guilty to an offense in exchange for a lower sentence. This is usually a negotiation that occurs between the prosecutor and the defense attorney at some point in the criminal justice process, though usually toward the beginning. Theoretically, everyone wins in such a situation: the offender is granted some leniency in punishment, the prosecutor obtains a guilty plea without having to go to trial and incur the time and expense to the state, and the defense attorney gets his or her client a "good deal." In the adult system, plea bargaining is a significant part of the process: more than 90 percent of all adult defendants plead guilty, and the U.S. Supreme Court has ruled that plea bargaining is an acceptable practice.[53]

In the juvenile justice system, the language used to describe this type of plea is a bit different. Unlike in the adult system, juveniles generally do not enter guilty or not-guilty pleas. In most states, youths either agree to a finding of the facts or deny the petition. If they agree with the finding of the facts of the case, the court rules on the appropriate outcome. If they do not agree, then the case moves to the trial stage. What makes the notion of plea bargaining challenging in the juvenile system is that while a high percentage of youths enter guilty pleas, meaning they admit to the facts of the petition, we cannot know what percentage of these pleas are a result of plea bargaining. This is because there are fewer constitutional protections for juveniles, such as the right to an attorney, and because no data are collected on the circumstances surrounding them.

In theory, plea bargaining in juvenile cases should not be necessary, since there are no juries, trials, or long sentences. Also, the court's mandate to act in the best interests of children seems to render the incentive to engage in plea bargaining unnecessary. However, the advantages of plea bargaining have become more evident over time. Specifically, plea bargaining results in lower court costs and greater efficiency within the justice process. Cost and efficiency are important matters considering the increasing number of cases that have come to the attention of the juvenile court in recent decades.

With the development of more punitive measures for juveniles, where serious offenses have been committed, plea bargaining has become more popular. This is in part because it allows the juvenile court to retain jurisdiction over cases that might be transferred to the adult system. While the research on the extent of plea bargaining in the juvenile system is scant, and while it is difficult at the present time to know how often plea bargaining is used, it seems reasonable that this practice will increasingly be used by prosecutors as the system is faced with more serious offenders.[54]

What does it mean for a juvenile to agree to "a finding of the facts"?

Transfer Procedure

There are five types of waivers that allow youths to be prosecuted in adult court, some of which overlap in their criteria:

- **Judicial waiver:** in forty-five states, juvenile court judges have the discretion to have juvenile cases tried in the adult criminal court.[55]

- **Prosecutorial waiver or direct file:** when prosecutors become involved and want suspects tried as adults, this is referred to as a prosecutorial waiver or direct file. Currently, fifteen states allow prosecutors the discretion to have youths' cases tried in the adult criminal court.[56]

- **Mandatory waiver:** juvenile court judges are required to automatically transfer youth cases to adult criminal court for certain offenses or because of the details of their prior records. Currently, fifteen states have mandatory waiver.

- **Statutory waiver:** youths' cases are automatically moved to criminal court based on the age of the youth, the type of crime, or both. Currently, twenty-nine states employ statutory exclusion.[57]

- **Age of majority status:** some states automatically prosecute offenders as adults once they reach a certain age. Three states—Connecticut, New York, and North Carolina—automatically prosecute sixteen- and seventeen-year-olds as adults. However, in 2008, Connecticut, which had exceptionally high incarceration rates for youths under the age of eighteen, changed its strategy on age of majority status.[58] Ten states—Georgia, Illinois, Louisiana, Massachusetts, Michigan, Missouri, New Hampshire, South Carolina, Texas, and Wisconsin—automatically prosecute seventeen-year-olds as adults.[59]

Waivers to Adult Court

The purpose of waiving juveniles to adult court is to impose longer sentences than are allowed within the juvenile justice system or to remove chronic and violent offenders from the system. Whether waivers work depends on their intended outcome, or on what states expect to accomplish by waiving juveniles to adult court. According to the OJJDP, in 2005, juvenile court judges waived jurisdiction over an estimated 6,900 delinquency cases. This represents less than 0.5 percent of all delinquency cases handled. As Table 14-3 shows, in 2005, half of waived cases involved person offenses.[60]

Research on the outcomes of juvenile cases that have been moved to adult criminal court has been mixed. Some studies have found that juveniles waived to adult court are more likely to be sentenced to prison than any other type of sanction. Other studies have found that juveniles who are waived are about equally as likely to receive prison sentences or probation, or to have their cases dismissed.[61] While the reasons for waiving juveniles are often related to the violent nature of their offenses and the need for more severe punishments than the juvenile system can provide, the results of these studies show that there is no guarantee that waivers ensure harsher punishments. This is likely because waived juveniles are often viewed as first-time offenders whose age mitigates sentencing decisions. On the other hand, studies have found that if a juvenile is waived to adult court and is then sentenced to prison, the sentence is usually longer than what a juvenile court would give.[62]

ADJUDICATION

The next step in the juvenile justice process involves an arraignment and an **adjudication hearing.** At the arraignment, juveniles are notified of the charges and informed of their constitutional rights. These include:

- the right to counsel and court-appointed representation, if needed
- the right to an adjudication hearing
- the right to confront and cross-examine witnesses
- the right to have witnesses testify on their behalf[63]

adjudication hearing
Much like a trial in the adult system; only a small percentage of delinquency cases actually involve this stage.

TABLE 14-3 Waived Cases to Criminal Court, 1985 and 2005

Type of Offense	1985	2005
Person	33% (7,200)	51% (6,900)
Property	53% (2,400)	27% (3,500)
Drugs	5% (400)	12% (800)
Public order	9% (600)	10% (700)

One explanation for the use of waivers could be related to legislation passed by many states that excludes serious offenses from juvenile court jurisdiction. On the other hand, some states have passed legislation that permits prosecutors to file certain cases directly in criminal court, thus negating the need for a waiver.[64]

Juveniles are also asked to enter a plea at this stage. Most cases involve a guilty plea, after which a sentence is imposed. Only a small percentage—approximately 5 percent of all delinquency cases—actually involve an adjudication hearing.[65] Should the case go to the adjudication stage, a hearing takes place, which is much like a trial in the adult system. At that time, a judge hears evidence and testimony from the prosecuting and defense attorneys, and determines if proof beyond a reasonable doubt exists about whether the youth committed the offense in question. The process imitates the adult system, with the prosecuting attorney going first, presenting evidence, followed by cross-examination by the defense attorney, who, after the prosecution rests its case, begins its own presentation.[66]

During the defense attorney's presentation of the case, youths can testify on their own behalf and present witnesses in order to give their side of the story. Summaries from both attorneys are offered at the end, with the judge or court referee rendering a decision. However, despite its increasingly legalistic format, and in addition to constitutional protections about legal representation, less than half of juveniles make use of an attorney.[67] As Zach points out, at times the disposition stage can be the point of entry for detention for some youths, who do not think they will be sent to a detention facility:

For more on court interactions, watch *Experience with the Court & Judge: Larry, Experience with the Court & the Prosecutor: Anthony B.,* and *Experience with the Court & the Prosecutor: Anthony J.* at www.mhhe .com/mcnamarajd1e

I was in a courtroom, and they told me I was going to DOC [Department of Corrections]. I mean, I was upset because I heard all the stories about this place and didn't wanna come. And then once I got up here and stuff, it's—it's cool. You just do your programs, stick to yourself, and you're gonna get out of here. You ain't gonna have any problems. Well, you're gonna have minimum problems.

Early in the development of the juvenile justice system, it was believed that guilty verdicts would stigmatize youths, whereas adjudicating them as delinquents demonstrated a much more paternalistic approach to accountability.[68] Today, if a judge ruling on a case believes that proof beyond a reasonable doubt exists with regard to whether the suspect committed the offense in question, he or she is not found guilty, but is "adjudicated" a delinquent.

DISPOSITION

The **disposition hearing** takes place at the completion of the adjudication hearing. This is similar to a sentencing hearing in the adult system. In the disposition stage, a judge may ask for a presentence or predisposition report. This report, typically prepared by the probation department, provides a more holistic picture of youths' background and particulars of a case that may not have been discussed at the adjudication hearing.

In preparing the predisposition report, a probation officer usually interviews youths' parents, teachers, employers, and other agency staff who may have some type of relationship with them. The report also includes information about the juveniles' physical and emotional health, family and home situation, friends, previous involvement with the juvenile justice system, and any history of alcohol or drug use.[69] Information such as mitigating or aggravating factors in the commission of the crime is also considered, as are recommendations about the best course of action for individual youths—consistent with the notion of individualized justice for juveniles.

disposition hearing
The next step, similar to a sentencing hearing in the adult system, following the completion of the adjudication hearing.

The judge has a wide range of options in deciding how to dispose of the case. In some cases, the judge decides not to make a ruling at all. This is sometimes called *suspending judgment,* whereby the judge postpones the decision on the case if the youth agrees to follow certain conditions. This practice is similar to the informal probation that is used at the intake stage.[70]

Judges may also allow juveniles to be released on probation, usually for some specified period of time. This is perhaps the most widely used sanction by the juvenile court.[71] In addition to probation, judges often include a requirement of attendance at certain types of treatment facilities, such as anger management programs or drug or alcohol treatment. If youths comply, cases are completed and no further actions are taken. If youths do not comply with the parameters of probation, or if they fail to complete the additional requirements, cases are returned to the court, and a judge may impose more punitive measures.[72]

Currently, juveniles do not have a constitutional right to an appeal, although practically every stage grants an **appellate review** or **process** to juveniles. The reason for this relates back to the *In re Gault* decision by the U.S. Supreme Court, which ruled that juveniles should be treated with many of the same protections as adults, particularly the equal protection clause of the Constitution. Consequently, most state legislatures passed laws granting appeals to juveniles.[73]

What are some of the major differences between juvenile and adult court proceedings? Are waivers to adult court ever in juveniles' best interests?

Sentences

Sentences can be categorized as **determinate** or **indeterminate,** which means they either have a fixed time period of punishment or do not. Traditionally, when youths are adjudicated delinquents, the maximum punishment available to judges is confinement in a detention center until juveniles reach the age of majority, usually meaning twenty-one years of age. The only way to impose a longer sentence is to waive youths to adult court and apply adult sanctions. However, problems with these practices have led many states to experiment with what are known as *blended sentences,* which combine punishment from both the juvenile and the adult court systems.

In other words, certain offenders processed in juvenile court may receive adult punishments, and others who have been waived to adult court may receive sentences used in the juvenile system. This is a significant development in the juvenile justice system, because it serves as a reasonable alternative to simply treating juveniles as adults, and it blurs the traditionally strict lines between the adult and juvenile systems of justice.

There are essentially five types of blended sentences, three of which involve an offender being processed by the juvenile court and receiving adult-like sentences. The varying sentences are based on where the case originated and what sentencing options are available in that particular court system.

1. **Juvenile-exclusive blend:** in this type of sentence, youths are eligible to receive a sentence in either the juvenile or the adult correctional system. That is, judges must decide between either a juvenile- or an adult-level sanction.

2. **Juvenile-inclusive blend:** here, a judge can impose both a juvenile- and an adult-level punishment. The adult sanction is usually suspended, unless youths commit more crimes, at which point they must complete the adult portion of the original offense, as well as any sentences for new offenses. This is a type of "carrot and stick" approach in that the juvenile sanction is usually less severe than the adult sentence and its application is contingent upon youths' behavior. That is, if they comply and stay out of trouble, the adult sentence is not carried out. If they engage in further criminal activity, however, the full weight of the adult punishment will be felt.

3. **Juvenile-contiguous blend:** in this case, a judge may impose a sentence that goes beyond what the juvenile court normally imposes (which is age-limited). The way it works is that once juveniles reach the age limitation for detention set by state statute, they are transferred to the adult system to fulfill the remainder of the sentence.

4. **Criminal-exclusive blend:** when a judge must decide whether to impose a juvenile or adult sanction after a youth has been waived and convicted in adult court, he or she may decide on a criminal-exclusive blended sentence. It is similar in many ways to the juvenile-exclusive blend, except that the offender has been tried and convicted in adult courts.

appellate review or process
The right for juveniles to appeal a case, particularly serious ones; generally, juveniles do not have a constitutional right to appeal a case, but most states provide for it.

determinate sentence
A sentence with a fixed period of punishment, in contrast to indeterminate sentences; part of a more punitive philosophy suggesting that everyone should be punished equally if they commit the same crime.

indeterminate sentence
A sentence that has no fixed period of confinement; based on the rehabilitation/treatment philosophy of punishment.

5. **Criminal-inclusive blend:** this type of sentence is similar to the juvenile-inclusive blended sentence in that the judge imposes both a juvenile- and an adult-level punishment after a youth has been convicted in adult court. Usually, the adult sanction is suspended, unless the offender commits other offenses, in which case the more severe sanction is imposed.[74]

Death Penalty

A full discussion of the treatment of juvenile offenders as adults raises the question of whether the ultimate sentence of death can be imposed on juveniles. Historically, there have been 366 documented executions of juveniles, which make up 2 percent of all executions in American history. Since 1973, 226 juveniles under the age of eighteen have been executed. This is in contrast to the 1,234 adults who have been executed during that same time.[75] The age of juveniles at the time they committed their crimes is important, since some states recognize sixteen- or seventeen-year-olds as adults. The age at the time the crime is committed is also important for the U.S. Supreme Court in determining if capital punishment for young offenders violates the Eighth Amendment of the U.S. Constitution, which prohibits cruel and unusual punishment.

In *Thompson v. Oklahoma* (1988), the U.S. Supreme Court ruled that executing juveniles who were under the age of sixteen at the time of their offense violates the protections against cruel and unusual punishment. This meant that juveniles could not be executed for an offense that they committed when they were fifteen years old or younger.[76] This ruling led many to raise the question of what would happen to youthful offenders who were sixteen or seventeen years old, particularly those who committed crimes in states that considered them adults under certain circumstances.

One year later, in *Stanford v. Kentucky* (1989), the Supreme Court ruled that the execution of an offender who was sixteen or older at the time of the offense did not violate the Eighth Amendment protection against cruel and unusual punishment.[77] The Court felt that states lacked clear standards regarding the execution of young offenders. In other words,

ANDREW'S CASE

Conclusions

Recall Andrew's case:

- was arrested for possession of drugs and assault
- was tried in juvenile court
- was denied due process
- was sentenced to three years in a juvenile detention facility

Juveniles do not have all of the same rights as adults during the criminal justice process. While juveniles are treated like their adult counterparts with regard to custodial interrogation, for instance, whether they will have the right to appeal is another matter.

Andrew does have certain constitutional rights, within his age group and his state. For example, during the adjudication stage of the criminal justice process, the judge denied Andrew the right to confront his accusers and to cross-examine witnesses, rights that were outlined in the *Gault* case. Also, the judge made a disposition without hearing recommendations from the prosecutor, the defense attorney, or the probation officer assigned to the case. On the other hand, within the state where Andrew committed his crimes, he has no constitutional right to appeal.

 THINK ABOUT IT Recall our discussions of *parens patriae*, individualized justice, and the overall increase in the punitive sanctions for juveniles who commit crimes. How might the judge defend his decisions based on the ideas outlined in this chapter? What impact do you think a "get tough" approach will ultimately have on juvenile crime?

since many states thought it was acceptable to sanction the death penalty for sixteen- or seventeen-year-olds, there was no compelling reason to ban the practice.

As a result of this ruling, the United States became one of only eight countries in the world that allowed the execution of youthful offenders. The other countries are Iran, Pakistan, Saudi Arabia, Yemen, Nigeria, the Congo, and China, none of which have a positive track record with regard to human rights. Moreover, all of these countries have essentially abolished the practice.[78]

In 2005, the U.S. Supreme Court reversed its decision in the *Stanford* case and struck down the constitutionality of the death penalty as it applies to juvenile offenders. In *Roper v. Simmons,* the Court ruled that society's sense of morality has evolved to such a degree that most people would agree that executing youths is inappropriate. More formally, the Court ruled that the execution of juveniles who were under the age of eighteen when their crimes were committed violates the Eighth and Fourteenth Amendments to the U.S. Constitution. This ruling had a significant impact on the seventy-two juveniles who had been on death row prior to the *Roper* decision in 2005.[79]

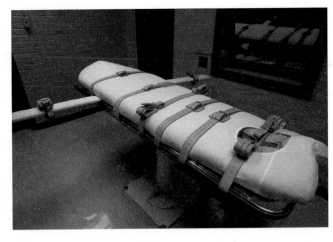

Do you think capital punishment, as it applies to youthful offenders, should be considered cruel and unusual punishment? Why or why not?

The Court Process

Recall the five types of waiver by which juveniles can be transferred to adult criminal court. Why do you think certain waivers apply in some states and not in others? How might you account for their differences and overlaps in criteria?

Juvenile Courts and Public Policy

In the early years, the juvenile justice system focused on treatment and rehabilitation, in keeping with the belief that children are too young to grasp and recognize the consequences of their actions. Consequently, punishing children and teens for behaviors they do not really understand seems harsh and unreasonable. Some psychologists point to evidence that even violent youthful offenders have lower levels of maturity and competency compared to adults—which means they are incapable of realizing the impact of their behavior on others, and punishment is unlikely to have a significant influence on their behavior.[80]

On the other hand, some experts argue that an increasing number of teenagers, some as young as fourteen or fifteen, are engaging in violent adult behaviors and should be held accountable. According to this position, youths do in fact understand the significance of their actions, and mild treatment by the juvenile justice system is not sufficient to deter their behavior.[81]

Experts who argue from this point of view also point out that the system does not seem to have any meaningful way of dealing with these types of youths. As such, the only safe and reasonable way to address this problem is to take them off the streets and punish them more severely.[82] If the juvenile justice system is responsible for controlling and correcting the behavior of youths who violate the law, the recidivism rate suggests that it is not fulfilling its mission. This debate also runs parallel to political lines: conservatives generally want a "get tough" approach to juvenile crime, believing that punishing delinquents like adults is acceptable, while liberals tend to believe that not all juveniles are alike and so should be handled on an individualized basis. For instance, from a liberal standpoint, status offenders should be handled differently than juveniles who commit more severe violent acts.[83]

My first time I'm like, what is this place? I never been here. And it kind of touched me, but it didn't. And I was like, well, since it's my first time coming, I'm going to get used to it, 'cause I kept coming back and forth.

LARRY

The most extreme position is to abolish the juvenile court entirely. This argument has gained some support recently, as juvenile courts increasingly take on the characteristics of adult systems. Some proponents of this position argue that if there are no real differences in the constitutional safeguards afforded defendants, if the punishments are the same, and if the public demands accountability for serious offenders, then it is redundant to have two identical systems. Barry C. Feld, a noted law professor and specialist in juvenile law, has argued that there is no reason why the adult system cannot take into account some of the unique aspects of juvenile crime and protect youths who commit serious crimes from further harm while at the same time holding them strictly accountable for their actions.[84]

> I do advocate for two separate systems but I'm not ignoring the tremendous challenges that our juvenile courts currently have. We have to improve them; we have to re-invest in them . . . [W]e need to revisit the way in which we view children. We need to reinvigorate the family court.
>
> **MICHAEL CORRIERO**

This argument is further enhanced when one looks at the fragmentation of the juvenile justice system. While this system mirrors the adult version—the police, courts, and correctional methods, for example—there is a wide range of state laws governing the treatment of juveniles, as well as jurisdictional issues regarding youthful offenders, not to mention the extensive range of diversion programs. While this variability could be seen as individualized justice, in that each state decides for itself what its youthful offenders need and how they should be processed, critics argue that it results in an absence of consistency across states in terms of how juveniles are held accountable.[85] This debate about whether a separate juvenile court is effective or necessary is ongoing while the public's concern about the increase in violent crime continues to grow. For now, the guiding principle places an emphasis on treatment, although increasingly the system as a whole seems to be moving toward treating juvenile offenders like their adult counterparts.

THE BIG PICTURE

Conclusions about the Juvenile Court System

- Should juveniles be given the same constitutional protections as adults when they are brought into the juvenile justice system?

- Do you think the CASA and guardian ad litem programs are really that effective in terms of making decisions that are in the best interests of children? Why or why not?

- What are the elements of restorative justice? Do you think they should be the guiding principles of the juvenile court?

- Do you think there should continue to be a separate court for juvenile offenders? Why or why not?

- Currently, the U.S. Supreme Court says that the death penalty constitutes cruel and unusual punishment, if applied to juveniles. However, ten years ago, the Court ruled that it was acceptable. How do you feel about capital punishment with regard to youthful offenders?

Key Terms

parens patriae
Kent v. United States
In re Gault
In re Winship
McKeiver v. Pennnsylvania
Breed v. Jones
double jeopardy

blended sentencing
Balanced and Restorative Justice
  Model (BARJ)
Roper v. Simmons
Court Appointed Special Advocate
  (CASA)
intake

petition
adjudication
disposition

Make the Call ▶ Juvenile Justice System

Review the scenario below, and decide how you would approach this case.

YOUR ROLE: Faculty member at a local university, and an expert on juvenile delinquency

DETAILS OF THE SITUATION

- You are asked to give a speech to a group of community members and local politicians on the effectiveness of waiving juvenile offenders to adult court.

- The governor of your state has introduced legislation to impose an automatic waiver for offenders who commit crimes under the age of seventeen.

- The public is in support of these measures as they have read news accounts of the growing problem of violent youthful offenders.

WHAT WILL YOU SAY?

You are speaking to an auditorium filled with community residents, police officers, politicians, activists, and others who are concerned about the growing problem of delinquency in your community. Imagine that your university president is also in favor of waivers and has publicly stated that he supports the governor's legislation. What do you say about the nature of juvenile crime, about waivers in general, and about what the evidence seems to suggest?
  Consider:

- Is your audience familiar with your research in juvenile delinquency? Would they have read any of your articles or attended other talks you have given on the topic?

- What evidence might you present to demonstrate the effectiveness or ineffectiveness of such waivers?

- Have incidents of youthful crime risen in this community? Have any incidents in particular heightened public awareness of the issue of waivers?

- Who do you wish to influence most with your speech—community members, local politicians, activists, or your university president?

Apply Theory to Reality ▶ Punishment and Deterrence

Deterrence theory focuses on how certain punishment that is swift and severe can change behavior. While this is one theory or framework used to justify punishing offenders, there are several others, including rehabilitation and incapacitation. Select one of these philosophies of punishment, and use it to explain how it impacts the disposition stage for juvenile court judges who must pass a traditional sentence on an offender.

Your Community ▶ Interviews with Juvenile Court Judges

In addition to the information you glean from your readings, class lectures, and discussions, it is important to roll up your sleeves and immerse yourself in a topic as a researcher who gains an understanding of a problem or issue by observing or experiencing it firsthand. Through such methods, you gain a much greater appreciation of the magnitude and scope of the problem than if you were only engaged in "armchair theorizing."

- Schedule an opportunity to observe juvenile court in session, with the aim of learning more about what actually happens during a case.

- Next, interview juvenile court judges to gain more insight into how they see their role in the process. What do they see as the main issues in handling cases? Do they believe that, in general, the punitive approach has its desired effect? Also ask judges about the challenges they experience and their approaches to the legal and ethical dilemmas they face.

- After collecting your data and drawing from the relevant literature, prepare a report about the processes and outcomes in the juvenile court you observed.

Notes

[1] Sickmund, M. 2009. *Delinquency Cases in Juvenile Court 2005.* Washington, DC: Office of Juvenile Justice and Delinquency Prevention. http://www.ncjrs.gov/pdffiles1/ojjdp/224538.pdf.

[2] National Council of Juvenile and Family Court Judges. 2005. *Juvenile Delinquency Guidelines: Improving Court Practices in Juvenile Delinquency Cases.* Reno, NV. http://www.ncjfcj.org/images-/stories/dept/ppcd/pdf/JDG/juveniledelinquencyguidelinescompressed.pdf. Accessed August 17, 2008.

[3] Ibid.

[4] Ibid.

[5] *Kent v. United States,* 383 U.S. 541, 86 S. Ct. 1045, 16L Ed. 2d 84 (1966).

[6] *In re Gault,* 387 U.S. 1, 18 L. Ed. 2d 527, 87 S. Ct.1428 (1967).

[7] *In re Winship,* 397 U.S. 358, 90 S. Ct. 1968, 25 L. Ed. 2d 368 (1970).

[8] *McKeiver v. Pennsylvania,* 403 U.S. 528, 535 (1971).

[9] Ibid.

[10] *Breed v. Jones,* 421 U.S. 519, 95 S. Ct. 1779 (1975).

[11] Campaign for Justice. 2008. *Fact Sheet: Trying Juveniles as Adults.* http://www.campaignforyouthjustice.org/Downloads/KeyResearch/FactSheetTryingYouthAsAdults.doc. Accessed August 14, 2008.

[12] See, for instance, Greacen, J. M. 2008. "Confidentiality, Due Process, and Judicial

Disqualification in the Unified Family Court." *Family Court Review,* 46(2): 340–346.

[13] See U.S. Supreme Court ruling in *Davis v. Alaska,* 425 U.S. 308 (1974); 94 S. Ct. 1105.

[14] *Davis v. Alaska,* 425 U.S. 308 (1974); 94 S. Ct. 1105.

[15] *Oklahoma Publishing Co. v. District Court,* 430 U.S. 97 (1977); 97 S. Ct. 1045.

[16] *Smith v. Daily Mail Publishing Co.* 443 U.S. 97, 99 S. Ct. 2667, 61 L.Ed. 2d 399 (1979).

[17] See Myers, D. L. 2008. "Accountability in Juvenile Justice: Policy and Research." *Criminal Justice Policy Review,* 19(3): 255–263.

[18] Rosenheim, M. K., Zimring, F. E., Tanenhaus, D. S., and Dohrn, B. 2001. *A Century of Juvenile Justice.* Chicago: University of Chicago Press.

[19] See, for instance, National Juvenile Justice Network. 2008. *Advances in Juvenile Justice Reform.* Available at http://www.jjustice.org/pdf/Advances%20in%20Juvenile%20Justice%20Reform%202007-2008.pdf.

[20] National Council of Juvenile and Family Court Judges, 2005.

[21] Pranis, K. 1998. *Guide for Implementing the Balanced and Restorative Justice Model.* Washington, DC: Office of Juvenile Justice and Delinquency Prevention. http://ojjdp.ncjrs.org/pubs/implementing/intro.html. Accessed August 17, 2008.

[22] Ibid.

[23] Ibid.

[24] See Annie E. Casey Foundation. 2009. *A Road Map for Juvenile Justice Reform.* Available at http://www.aecf.org/~/media/PublicationFiles/AEC180essay_booklet_MECH.pdf. See also Sims, B., and Preston, P. (eds.). 2006. *Handbook of Juvenile Justice.* Boca Raton, FL: Taylor and Francis.

[25] U.S. Department of Justice, Office of Justice Programs, Office of Juvenile Justice and Delinquency Prevention. 1999. *Focus on Accountability: Best Practices for Juvenile Court and Probation.* Available at http://ojjdp.ncjrs.org/pubs/jaibgbulletin/over.html.

[26] This example is drawn from the Los Angeles California Juvenile Justice System. Available at http://www.smartvoter.org/2010/06/08/ca/la/vote/hammock_r/paper2.html.

[27] See, for instance, Chawla, M. J. 2006. "The Role of Referees in District Court." *The Hennepin Lawyer.* Available at http://hennepin.timberlakepublishing.com/article.asp?article=1079&paper=1&cat=148.

[28] See, for instance, Backstrom, J. C. 2006. *The Expanding Role of the Prosecutor in Juvenile Justice.* Dakota County, MN: Dakota County District Attorney's Office. Available at http://www.co.dakota.mn.us-/NR/rdonlyres/00000987/qmxaroespdbzrghotrwyasnzjhzkfbou/ExpandingRoleProsecutorJuvenileJustice.pdf.

[29] Sims and Preston, 2006.

[30] Sterling, R. W. 2009. *The Role of Juvenile Defense Counsel in Delinquency Court.*

Washington, DC: National Juvenile Defender Center. Available at http://www.njdc.info/pdf-/role_of_juvenile_defense_counsel.pdf.

[31] Most probation offices are organized and operate in a similar manner. For a good description of one and its programs, see the Lancaster, Pennsylvania's Office of Juvenile Probation's website at http://www.co.lancaster.pa.us/courts/cwp/view.asp?a=472&Q=389322.

[32] See a description of Florida's Guardian ad Litem program at http://www.guardianadlitem.org. Accessed August 15, 2008.

[33] The Victims of Child Abuse (VOCA) Act, Public Law 101-647, November 29, 1990, as amended by Public Law 102-586, November 4, 1992.

[34] For more information on CASA Guardian ad Litem programs, see Court Appointed Special Advocates at http://www.casaforchildren.org/site/c.mtJSJ7MPIsE/b.5301295/k.BE9A/Home.htm.

[35] U.S. Department of Justice, Office of Inspector General. 2007. *National Court-Appointed Special Advocate Program, Audit Report 07-04.* Available at http://www.justice.gov/oig-/reports/OJP/a0704/index.htm.

[36] Ibid.

[37] Ibid.

[38] See CASA's website at http://www.casaforchildren.org/site/c.mtJSJ7MPIsE-/b.5301295/k.BE9A/Home.htm. Accessed August 17, 2008.

[39] Puzzanchera, C., and Sickmund, M. 2009. *Juvenile Court Statistics 2005.* Washington, DC: Office of Juvenile Justice and Delinquency Prevention. http://www.ncjrs.gov/pdffiles1/ojjdp/224538.pdf.

[40] Sickmund, 2009.

[41] Ibid.

[42] Puzzanchera and Sickmund, 2009.

[43] Ibid.

[44] Ibid.

[45] Ibid.

[46] Sims and Preston, 2006.

[47] Ibid.

[48] Sims and Preston, 2006.

[49] *Schall v. Martin.* 104 S. Ct 2403 (1984).

[50] Ibid.

[51] Ibid.

[52] Puzzanchera and Sickmund, 2009.

[53] See Willrich, M. 2003. *Dickering for Justice: Power, Interests, and the Plea Bargaining Juggernaut.* Baltimore: Johns Hopkins University Press.

[54] See, for instance, Shepard, R. E. 2003. "Pleading Guilty in Delinquency Cases." *ABA Journal,* available at http://www.abanet.org/crimjust/juvjus/cjmpleaguilty.html. See also Rosenheim, Zimring, Tenenhaus, and Dohrn, 2001; Sanborn, J. 1993. "Philosophical, Legal, and Systematic Aspects of Juvenile Court Plea Bargaining." *Crime and Delinquency,* 39: 509–527.

[55] Fagin, J., and Guggenheim, M. 1996. "Preventative Detention and the Judicial Prediction of Dangerousness for Juveniles: A Natural Experiment." *Journal of Criminal Law and Criminology,* 86(2): 415–448.

[56] Ibid.

[57] Ibid.

[58] Hammond, S. 2008. "Adults or Kids? States Debate What Is the Best Response to Teens Who Commit Crimes." http://realcostofprisons.org/blog/archives/2008/05/adults_or_kids.html. Accessed August 14, 2008.

[59] Campaign for Justice, 2008.

[60] Sickmund, 2009.

[61] National Council of Juvenile and Family Court Judges, 2005.

[62] Ibid.

[63] Rosenheim, Zimring, Tanenhaus, and Dohrn, 2001.

[64] Sickmund, 2009.

[65] Puzzanchera and Sickmund, 2009.

[66] Sims and Preston, 2006.

[67] Ibid.

[68] Puzzanchera and Sickmund, 2009.

[69] Sickmund, 2009.

[70] Sims and Preston, 2006.

[71] Snyder and Sickmund, 2006.

[72] Puzzanchera and Sickmund, 2009.

[73] Rosenheim, Zimring, Tanenhaus, and Dohrn, 2001.

[74] Sickmund, 2009.

[75] See The Death Penalty Information Center, Fact Sheet. Available at http://www.deathpenaltyinfo.org-/documents/FactSheet.pdf.

[76] *Thompson v. Oklahoma,* 487 U.S. 815 (1988).

[77] *Stanford v. Kentucky,* 492 U.S. 361 (1989).

[78] See International Justice Project at http://www.internationaljusticeproject.org.

[79] *Roper v. Simmons,* 543 U.S. (2005).

[80] See Bishop, D. M. 2009. *Reforming Juvenile Justice.* New York: Springer.

[81] Ibid. See also Rhule, D. M. 2005. "Take Care to Do No Harm: Harmful Interventions for Youth Problem Behavior." *Professional Psychology: Research and Practice,* 36(6): 618–625.

[82] See Underwood, L. 2006. "Treatment and Post-release Rehabilitative Programs for Juvenile Offenders." *Child and Adolescent Psychiatric Clinics of North America,* 15(2): 539–556. See also Lipsey, M. W., Wilson, D. B., and Cothern, L. 2000. *Effective Interventions for Serious Juvenile Offenders.* Washington, DC: Office of Juvenile Justice and Delinquency Prevention. Available at http://www.ncjrs.gov-/pdffiles1/ojjdp/181201.pdf; Winoker, K. P., Smith, A., Bontrager, S. R., and Blankenship, J. L. 2008. "Juvenile Recidivism and Length of Stay." *Journal of Criminal Justice,* 36(2): 126–137.

[83] See, for instance, King, A., and Maruna, S. 2009. "Is a Conservative Just a Liberal Who Has Been Mugged? Exploring the Origins of Punitive Views." *Punishment and Society,* 112: 147–169. See also Carmichael, J. T. 2006. *The Political Sociology of Juvenile Punishment: Treating Juvenile Offenders as Adults.* Doctoral dissertation, Ohio State University; McGarmel, E. F. 2004. "The Ideological Bases and Functions of Contemporary Juvenile Law Reform: The New York State Experience." *Crime, Law, and Social Change,* 113(2): 163–187.

[84] See Feld, B. 1997. "Abolish the Juvenile Court: Youthfulness, Criminal Responsibility and Sentencing Policy." *Journal of Criminal Law and Criminology,* 88(1): 60–78.

[85] Bishop, 2009.

After reading this chapter, you should be able to:

- Recall the history of juvenile corrections.

- Describe community alternatives to incarceration, such as wilderness and vocational programs.

- Differentiate the institutional facilities available for juveniles, and determine the effectiveness of each.

- Discuss the rights of detained juveniles, and debate whether

juveniles should have similar rights as adults.

- Assess the future of corrections for juvenile delinquents in terms of public policy.

15

Corrections and Delinquency

CASE STUDY ON PHIL

Approximately one-third of juveniles sent to long-term detention facilities are there for committing violent crimes.[1] However, the prevailing assumption is that the majority of juveniles in long-term detention have been committed for acts of violence. Consider the following scenario about Phil:

Phil's situation:

- is fifteen years old and lives in a remote area of North Dakota
- has been involved in several minor fights at school
- has been arrested for vandalism, a charge dismissed because of a lack of evidence
- has also been arrested for shoplifting a video game; the case was handled informally when Phil agreed to make restitution

Last year, Phil was arrested for burglarizing a neighbor's home. He was adjudicated a delinquent for this crime and received two years of probation. Last week, Phil missed his appointment with the probation officer and skipped school as well. Officers found him in a pool hall and brought him before a juvenile court judge.

The predisposition report indicates that Phil lives with his mother, a single mom who works at a diner during the day and as a cocktail waitress at night. Phil is the only child in the home, and he is generally left to take care of himself. After reviewing his record and the current offense, the judge sentences Phil to a year of detention at a medium-security facility.

What kinds of detention facilities and what rights are available to detained juveniles?

THINK ABOUT IT

Upon hearing Phil's case and reviewing the predisposition report, we might ask ourselves the following questions:

- Is Phil a serious threat to the community?
- Do his actions warrant this type of confinement?
- What part of Phil's record is of most concern to the judge?
- Were there other options available to the judge that might have been as effective as incarceration? If so, what are they?
- What will Phil be like when he returns from detention?

In Chapter 9, we saw that chronic offending is a consistent problem for a small group of youths, and the negative impact they can have on a community is considerable. This group inspires high levels of fear about juvenile violence, for which many laws, such as mandatory waivers, have been passed. These types of offenders are referenced most often by critics of the juvenile justice system, who point to the failures of the system for their repeat delinquency.

This chapter will examine traditional approaches to juvenile corrections, such as detention in secure facilities. It will also discuss the methods applied to community-based sanctions. Given what appears to be an alarming recidivism rate for juvenile offenders, critics question the effectiveness of a community-based approach.[2] However, far more common than sentences of long-term incarceration are strategies that are applied effectively outside of detention facilities.

As the name suggests, community-based corrections consist of treatment within the community, in contrast to institutional-based corrections, which generally calls for the incarceration of delinquents in more formal detention facilities. Examples of community-based corrections include probation, day treatment (sometimes called outpatient treatment), and residential facilities that offer more structured care. The other alternative is institutional placement, which includes training schools (which can be minimum-, medium-, or maximum-security facilities), ranches and forestry camps, boot camps, jails, and even, in extreme cases, adult prisons.

As noted previously, the juvenile justice system makes greater use of community-based corrections as a guiding principle for dealing with delinquency.[3] According to the Office of Juvenile Justice and Delinquency Prevention (OJJDP), the use of residential placement constituted about 25 percent of all adjudicated delinquency cases in 2006, while the use of probation doubled between 1985 and 2002. This means that the juvenile courts handle the majority of cases with probation or other nonincarceration sanctions. Typically, formal probation is the sanction of choice for most judges. Sanctions such as restitution—when offenders repay money or provide services to their victims—and community service have also increased dramatically in recent years.

Historical Overview

Community-based corrections originated from the concept of juvenile parole, or juvenile aftercare. In the 1820s, Houses of Refuge had the authority to release youthful offenders as they saw fit. While some juveniles were returned to their families, others were placed in the community to serve as apprentices in various trades, such as carpentry, plumbing, or masonry. Upon completion of their term, youths were given their release, with marketable skills.

In the United States, the idea of probation began in the 1800s with John Augustus, a volunteer who posted bail for youthful offenders and convinced judges to release delinquents into his custody. By the mid-1800s, Augustus had supervised thousands of offenders and reported to the juvenile court on a regular basis. Augustus, credited with being the "father" of probation, developed many strategies that are characteristic of modern probation. When the first juvenile court was established in 1899, Augustus's work ensured that a system was in place to work with delinquent youths.[4]

In the early twentieth century, juvenile aftercare programs shared many of the characteristics of adult parole. However, unlike adult parole, juvenile aftercare did not involve a parole board. Instead, in many states, aftercare officers decided when youths could return to the community, a practice that is consistent with the idea of individualized justice.[5] What had begun as a practice of unfettered discretion carried out by the superintendents of Houses of Refuge was transformed into one of authority without accountability. Around the same time, community volunteers often took on the roles of community-based corrections, including that of probation officers.

In the 1950s, greater attention was given to the constructive treatment of juveniles, and many states began hiring formal full-time probation officers. The popularity of residential programs began to increase as well. In the 1960s and 1970s, the certification and training of probation officers became important to the provision of juvenile justice.[6] In the late 1980s and 1990s, many residential and day treatment facilities faced severe budget cuts because of decreases in federal funding. What followed was a shift in policy regarding the treatment of youthful offenders. Probation, aftercare, and training facilities remained the three main methods of community-based corrections, but many training schools were forced to close. A hard-line approach was mandated to probation and aftercare officers, who were now trained to enforce punishment as opposed to treatment.[7]

In what ways might training facilities and farming be a useful tool for teaching discipline and the value of hard work?

Historically, it was believed that a well-adjusted family could provide a model for children that would lead them to becoming productive members of society. In 1825, the New York House of Refuge, the first juvenile correctional institution, reflected this model. The goal was to have the institution give the appearance of a well-organized family, complete with discipline, accountability, love, and respect. While the New York House of Refuge is acknowledged as the first of its kind, many other states followed suit in the decades following. The majority focused on providing housing for males, with an average capacity of about 200 boys per house.

Also in keeping with the family-oriented philosophy, the cottage system consisted of a series of small groups of youths—between twenty and forty—who were housed in separate buildings. These facilities were often located in rural areas where farming skills could be taught to youths alongside the values of discipline and hard work.[8] Today cottages are called "training schools" or "industrial schools."

The twentieth century also saw a greater effort to make juvenile corrections more holistic and treatment-oriented. Individual and group therapy, classification systems, furloughs and work release programs, and educational and vocational programs were implemented. Also, the first ranches and forestry camps were created, as were traditional prisons for juveniles.

Despite noble intentions, juvenile training schools began to take on the characteristics of miniprisons, and juvenile experts who studied these schools found evidence of violence and the exploitation of youths. In the late 1980s and 1990s (see Table 15-1), more youths were sent to detention facilities. Perhaps as a result of overcrowding, training schools became violent places. Increasingly, minorities were overrepresented, and in particular, drug offenders. Private institutions, which would normally provide space for nonserious offenders, began admitting violent offenders as well. As a result, more juveniles are now being waived to adult criminal court and serving longer prison sentences.[9]

Increasing Use of Punishment

Have we given up on the rehabilitation or treatment of juveniles, as evidenced by the greater use of punishment for adjudicated delinquents?

THINK ABOUT IT

TABLE 15-1 History of Community-Based Corrections

1820s	New York House of Refuge Development of juvenile aftercare
1900s	Individual and group therapy Vocational programs Work release Furloughs Therapeutic ranches and forestry programs
1950s	First full-time probation officers Increased use of residential programs
1960s–1970s	Enhanced training and certification of probation officers
1980s–1990s	Residential and day treatment programs eliminated Greater use of incarceration and detention

The focus has changed from helping wayward youths to punishing them as a guiding policy.

Community-Based Corrections

As we discussed in Chapter 14, restorative justice places an emphasis on restitution versus punishment. This philosophy informs many strategies and sanctions for juvenile offenders that focus on repairing what was damaged rather than on simply punishing offenders for their behavior. While restorative justice can be used as a guiding principle in traditional detention facilities, its primary focus is on community-based correctional strategies.

PROBATION

probation
The courts' release of juveniles to parents or legal guardians, provided youths meet certain conditions.

The vast majority of cases that are adjudicated by the juvenile court involve judges rendering decisions or dispositions that include **probation.** As a sanction, probation consists of the courts releasing juveniles to parents or legal guardians, provided youths meet certain conditions. While there is a wide range of criteria by which youths are granted this freedom, the underlying framework promotes a balance between rehabilitation and treatment, while preserving the safety of the community.

Probation is used with virtually all first-time offenders. As Table 15-2 shows, in 2005, probation was used as a sanction in about a third of all cases in the system. Another third of those cases were dismissed, about 27 percent were handled through other means, and about 8 percent of youths entering into the system overall were detained. Among petitioned cases that are adjudicated, probation is used about 60 percent of the time, with detention occurring in about 22 percent of the cases. Probation remains a cost-effective strategy that aims to hold youths accountable at a much lower cost than residential placement. This is true even for extreme forms of probation, such as shock probation or electronic monitoring.[10]

Most youths who have been adjudicated have committed status offenses or property crimes, making them eligible for probation with minimal supervision. When youths commit additional acts or refuse to abide by the conditions of their probation agreements—which can include attending school regularly, paying restitution to victims, obeying parents, or undergoing special counseling—they can be brought back into court for further processing. While probation is often used for first-time offenders, some repeat offenders may also be given probation as part of their disposition, either owing to extenuating circumstances in their cases or because of overcrowding in detention facilities.

Despite the frequency with which probation is used in the juvenile courts, it is not without its problems. Some experts argue that probation does not provide any significant means of accountability for youths, unless they violate the conditions of their probation agreements. In their view, probation as a disposition is too mild to prevent delinquency or address the problem of recidivism.[11]

TABLE 15-2 Cases Processed in Juvenile Court, 2005

Case	Resolution
Total number of cases: 1,697,800	
Nonpetitioned cases: 748,500	Dismissed: 301,200 Other: 283,400 Probation: 164,000

Petitioned cases: 949,300	Waived: 6,900
	Nonadjudicated: 318,500
	    Dismissed: 238,500
	    Other: 60,900
	    Probation: 19,100
	Adjudicated: 623,900
	    Probation: 373,400
	    Placed (detention): 140,100
	    Other: 110,400

The data show that most cases are handled informally, using dismissal or probation as an outcome. How does this relate to the popular "get tough" approach to delinquency?

On the other hand, probation is a broad-based tactic that can include a host of stipulations to make treatment more individualized. It is also less expensive than formal detention, and evidently, it is effective—most juvenile offenders do not commit additional crimes.[12] One of the advantages of probation is its versatility. Judges can use a number of combined sanctions with probation, holding the youth accountable while providing some form of treatment.

INTENSIVE PROBATION

As the name suggests, this type of probation focuses on the supervision of juvenile offenders. Intensive probation is usually considered an alternative to formal detention in secure facilities. It is used when offenders have committed serious crimes or when they are more likely to commit additional crimes if released under normal probation guidelines. Intensive probation may also be used with chronic offenders—those who have committed multiple offenses, both status and delinquent. These individuals typically have not successfully completed previous probation requirements.[13]

One challenge of intensive probation is selecting juveniles who will benefit the most from it. Recall our discussion of bootstrapping in Chapter 3. Bootstrapping classified status offenders as delinquents when they violated court orders or ignored escape petitions. Consequently, these youths were treated more like traditional delinquents. For example, a repeat status offender would be eligible for intensive probation, despite the fact that this is not the type of offender this strategy seeks to identify. In research terms, we would refer to this result as a **false positive,** meaning these youths look like target offenders but have been misclassified. By contrast, the term we would use for youths who should be identified for intensive probation but who fall through the cracks of the system is **false negative.**[14]

There is a wide variety of intensive probation programs. Some focus more on treatment and services while others emphasize supervision and control. The real question about intensive probation is whether it is effective in reducing recidivism. However, as we have seen with other studies of delinquency, the research on intensive probation does not clearly demonstrate its overall impact. Some research has found that youths who participated in intensive probation programs have lower rates of recidivism compared to those who did not receive it. Other studies have contradicted these findings.[15]

Generally, the research tends to show that intensive probation is really no more effective than the levels of probation assigned for repeat offenses. This is true despite the fact that many intensive programs claim to have a greater impact on reducing recidivism among youths than normal probation programs.[16]

false positive
A situation in which offenders are misclassified and are given intensive probation but do not need it.

false negative
A situation in which youths who should be identified for intensive probation fall through the cracks in the system.

In sum, it is unclear whether intensive supervision works, and the studies on its overall impact have a number of problems, which mask its true effect on recidivism.[17] For example, in some studies, it remains unclear whether intensive probation was implemented properly. Likewise, in other studies, it is difficult to determine if the goals and objectives of the program were achieved. Finally, these assessments also call into question whether or not youths actually received higher levels of supervision than other probation groups.

SHOCK PROBATION

Shock probation combines more punitive measures with the treatment goals of traditional probation. Often, with this type of probation, judges sentence youths to a detention facility for a short period of time and then follow that detention with a lengthier period of traditional probation. The objective is to influence youths with the "shock" of detention, which is followed by their subsequent release. The shock youths experience upon detention and release can help them to connect the negative, tangible consequences of their actions with their behavior.[18]

Some states that employ shock probation do not inform youths of their impending release; other states make youths aware of the format of the treatment to help them understand the relationship between detention, release, and their delinquent behavior. Shock probation can be used at many different stages of the juvenile justice process, such as right after adjudication, or during treatment, if youths are not fulfilling their responsibilities in terms of their probation agreements. In some cases, judges may place youths in a detention facility for a weekend or longer to send a message about what will happen if they fail to comply with their treatment plans, as spelled out in the disposition hearing.[19]

SCHOOL-BASED PROBATION

In school-based probation, traditional forms of supervision are used within a school environment. This strategy allows probation officers to provide more direct and consistent supervision of youths, since both parties are on campus during the day. Being on campus also allows probation officers the opportunity to develop stronger ties to the juveniles under their care.

School-based probation essentially takes two forms. The first is a more holistic approach, in which probation officers are responsible for all aspects of cases, from intake through disposition. A variation on this approach is when administrative staff process the paperwork related to the case, allowing the probation officer more time to supervise clients. Research on the use of school-based probation has shown that it results in lower caseloads for probation officers, it is less expensive than traditional probation programs, and it can reduce recidivism.[20]

HOUSE ARREST

When juveniles commit crimes and are suspected to be flight risks, judges can order them to stay at home under house arrest. This can take the form of a preadjudication order, while youths are awaiting an adjudication hearing, or it can be part of a larger probation disposition. While under house arrest, youths are not allowed to leave their homes, except to attend school, work, or religious services, or undergo treatment. Probation officers monitor them by placing them on schedules and making random visits and phone calls. House arrest is often used as an early condition of probation, or when juveniles fail to comply with a court order.[21]

electronic monitoring
A variation on house arrest in which a juvenile is fitted with a device around the ankle that triggers an alarm and notifies probation officers should the juvenile stray outside the range of the device.

A variation on house arrest is **electronic monitoring,** in which juveniles are fitted with a device around their ankles. This device works in conjunction with a monitoring system that is located in the home and is connected to a phone line. The basic operating principle is that if youths stray outside the range of the device, an alarm will sound and probation officers will be notified.

As is the case with house arrest, the juveniles' parents or guardians must agree to electronic monitoring. Also, juveniles and their families often are required to pay for the costs of the bracelet and the monitoring fees, unless they cannot afford to do so. Compared to the costs associated with incarceration, the use of electronic monitoring is a cost-effective strategy for monitoring juveniles.[22]

RESTITUTION

One of the most popular dispositions used in conjunction with probation is restitution. Typically, victims will provide the court with a list of the costs they incurred as a result of the crime committed. These lists are then used to sentence juveniles in such a way that costs are covered or damages repaired. For example, for juveniles who tag the outside walls of businesses, their sentences might be to repaint the walls and to pay for the materials needed.[23]

Sometimes judges use restitution as a means of shaming or embarrassing offenders into refraining from committing crimes in the future. While there are potential problems with this strategy, there is some evidence that recidivism decreases when restitution is used. For example, some studies have found that youths who were required to make restitution had lower levels of reoffending than those who committed similar crimes but were not required to pay the victim back.[24]

COMMUNITY SERVICE

Another community-based sanction often given to youthful offenders is community service. Like the other strategies outlined here, this type of disposition can take on a variety of forms. It can include requiring juveniles to pick up trash on state highways, sweep out subway stations in large cities, volunteer to help the elderly, serve food in a homeless shelter, or plant trees in a local community space. Judges will typically attempt to customize the service to the crime committed, and in some cases to the neighborhood where the offense occurred.

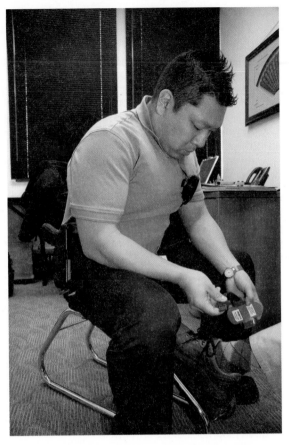

In your opinion, is electronic monitoring a fair and safe strategy for monitoring juveniles? Can you think of cost-effective alternatives to detention?

MEDIATION PROGRAMS

Another community-based alternative is to divert youths toward one of the many mediation programs in existence across the United States, a few of which were described in Chapter 12. For example, a variety of teen courts and drug courts focus on particular types of offenses and offenders. Also, juvenile arbitration programs offer a cost-effective way of handling first-time offenders for status offenses and other minor crimes, without forcing youths through the juvenile justice process.

In South Carolina, the Community Juvenile Arbitration Program uses volunteers to handle first-time offenders, in lieu of sending cases to juvenile court for processing. Volunteer arbitrators have had offenders write letters of apology to victims, make restitution for damages, and fulfill community service obligations, thereby holding youths accountable for their actions while also allowing them to learn from their mistakes.[25]

DAY TREATMENT FACILITIES

Day treatment facilities are usually reserved for probationers who are having difficulty meeting the criteria of probation or who have particular needs such as drug treatment. Many programs require youths to participate during the day and return home in the evening.

In addition to making amends to victims, what are some of the other benefits of restitution and mediation programs?

THEORY AND PRACTICE WORKING TOGETHER

Outward Bound

The goal of wilderness programs is to provide treatment and therapeutic interventions for youths before they become chronic or hard-core delinquents. They do this by challenging youths physically and mentally in an unfamiliar environment.

Outward Bound is a nonprofit educational organization with five core programs:

- Outward Bound Wilderness
- Expeditionary Learning Schools Outward Bound
- Outward Bound Professional
- Outward Bound Urban Centers
- Outward Bound Discovery

Outward Bound courses take participants who typically have no wilderness experience to a remote wilderness area and engage them in group activities focusing on team-building, self-reliance, and communication.

The components of the course include:

- **Skills education:** survival skills and teamwork skills are integral to the Outward Bound program, in which members set goals and make decisions as a group to build trust in and reliance on others. The program also teaches leadership skills to help participants develop initiative, good judgment, and self-reliance.
- **Challenge activities:** participants learn about mental fortitude through activities like climbing and rappelling, and they gain problem-solving skills by mastering an obstacle course of beams and cables suspended in the air. By the end of the course, instructors begin to take on a secondary role. Teams of participants take over the leadership of the expedition, making virtually all decisions about where to go and how to get there.
- **Solo:** this unique phase of the course requires participants to spend time alone in the wilderness, for periods ranging from a few hours to up to three days, depending on the length of the trip. Participants are encouraged to use their time alone to engage in self-reflection. Food, shelter, and supervision by instructors are provided.
- **Service:** this component of the program focuses on serving others. Participants clean campsites, teach skills they have mastered, or provide emotional support to others in the program. In the process of serving, they learn about building connections with others and with society as a whole.
- **Homeward Bound:** at the end of a course, a celebration ceremony gives participants a chance to say goodbye to each other, as well as to celebrate their achievements and the skills developed over the course of the program.[26]

Programs like Outward Bound have proven successful in treating some youths. On the other hand, because it is a short-term, one-time intervention, with little in the way of follow-up, its effects do not always last.

THINK ABOUT IT Why do you think community-based programs have had some success in treating delinquency? Do you believe that delinquent youths have not been adequately educated regarding their roles in society? How do wilderness programs like Outward Bound work to educate youths about their societal roles?

What types of skills can be taught most effectively in a wilderness environment?

Day treatment programs are economical because they do not provide living and sleeping quarters, they require fewer staff, and they are less coercive and punishment-oriented than other residential placements. Nonresidential day programs usually serve male offenders, although increasingly, programs that target female offenders are being developed.

Project New Pride is one example of a day treatment program that targets serious offenders. Located in Denver, Colorado, Project New Pride meets clients' needs by offering a three-month intensive treatment program and a nine-month period during which aftercare officers follow up with youths. The program has four main components:

- education, which consists of diagnostic assessment, assignment to a local alternative school or a center for learning disabilities, and school reintegration and maintenance assistance
- cultural enhancement, designed to expose clients to a variety of cultural experiences in the surrounding Denver area
- counseling and intensive supervision
- job training and help finding employment

The goals of the program are to reduce recidivism, find employment for clients, address academic deficiencies, and return clients to school so they can complete the requirements for graduation from high school. Project New Pride has been replicated and used in many states, and some evidence suggests that it has achieved its goal of reducing recidivism.[27]

Residential programs are a variation on the type of community treatment exemplified by Project New Pride and other programs like it. Residential programs typically involve group homes or foster care. Some programs are also operated like halfway houses and serve the function of aftercare when youths are released from formal detention and have no place to go. **Group homes** aim to provide a nurturing home environment for adjudicated youths. An alternative to incarceration, group homes allow probation and aftercare officers to deal with youths' community problems and act as an intermediary for youths who are returning to the community following incarceration. Most group homes limit how many youths can participate. Many have long waiting lists, since residents typically stay longer than they would in training schools. While some argue that programs like these provide adjudicated youths with the supervision and services they need, others question whether group homes are merely a less punitive alternative to juvenile institutions.[28]

Wilderness programs are short-term residential programs that use rigorous outdoor activities, such as survival training, to teach adjudicated youths the importance of setting and achieving goals. In the process of teaching self-reliance and building self-confidence, these programs also provide adjudicated youths with alternative paradigms or frameworks to understand the world and their place in it. Outward Bound, described in the Theory and Practice box, is one of the more popular wilderness programs in the United States.[29]

group homes
A nurturing home environment for adjudicated youths that is an alternative to incarceration and that allows them to mainstream back into the community and learn to cope with problems while developing independent living skills.

wilderness programs
Short-term residential programs that use rigorous outdoor activities, such as survival training, to teach adjudicated youths the importance of setting and achieving goals and to provide these youths with alternative paradigms or frameworks to understand the world and their place in it.

PHIL'S CASE

Detention

Recall Phil's situation:

- is fifteen years old, an only child from single-parent home
- was arrested last year for burglarizing a neighbor's home
- was adjudicated a delinquent and received two years of probation
- was sentenced to a year of detention at a medium-security facility after missing an appointment with his probation officer

While Phil was serving time in the detention facility, he began to experience panic attacks while sitting in his cell. He also showed signs of depression. Increasingly, Phil became socially withdrawn: he did not socialize with other youths, he said very little to correctional officers, and he generally seemed despondent and morose. About two weeks into his sentence, Phil attempted to commit suicide. Fortunately, a staff member found Phil in his cell before he could do so. As a result, Phil was sent to a secure treatment facility, where staff members incorrectly diagnosed him as a paranoid schizophrenic who requires high doses of medication.

Based on your reading, do you think the judge's ruling was more focused on treating Phil or on punishing him? What other strategies, besides probation, might the judge have used to treat Phil's delinquency?

THINK ABOUT IT

Community-Based Corrections

Does the use of alternative measures such as probation, community service, and house arrest contribute to the perception that the juvenile justice system is "soft" on crime and does not hold offenders sufficiently accountable?

THINK ABOUT IT

Institutional Corrections

As we have seen so far in this chapter, despite their frequent successes, community-based programs do not always work. Some offenses are too serious to warrant a restorative justice approach. In these instances, more formal detention might be required.

Institutional facilities are generally designed to serve youths awaiting a detention or adjudication hearing, or those who were committed by a juvenile court or some other administrative body such as a social service agency. Youths referred to detention facilities under these circumstances are sometimes called *voluntary placements,* because either their parents turned them over to a social service agency or the agency placed them there because they committed juvenile acts but were not formally adjudicated.

Voluntary placements are rare, consisting of less than 1 percent of all detained youth.[30] Far more common are situations in which judges order youths to residential facilities. There is a wide range of options for institutional detention, including reception centers, ranches and forestry camps, boot camps, traditional training schools, and even adult prisons.

According to the OJJDP, in 2006, there were 94,558 juveniles in residential placements in the United States (see Figure 15-1). About 35 percent of these youths were detained for violent crimes, 26 percent for property crimes, and only 8 percent for drug offenses.[31] In most cases, delinquents are held in publicly operated facilities; most status offenders are held in private ones. While about 80 percent of public juvenile detention facilities are considered secure, only about 20 percent of private institutions are high-security facilities.[32]

States vary in their use of secure detention for juveniles. According to the National Center for Juvenile Justice, the District of Columbia has the highest juvenile custody rate in the country, with 625 per 100,000 juveniles; followed by Wyoming, with 606 per 100,000 juveniles; and South Dakota, with 564 per 100,000 juveniles. In contrast, Vermont has the lowest rates of detention, with 72 per 100,000 juveniles, followed by Hawaii, with 97 per 100,000 juveniles.[33]

The number of juveniles serving time in detention centers has decreased since 2003, when the total number was nearly 97,000 youths. However, this number may not accurately reflect all youths who are detained. For example, the data do not include many minors who were incarcerated after they were waived to adult courts, nor do they include those who were tried as adults. Moreover, some youths may be placed in private mental

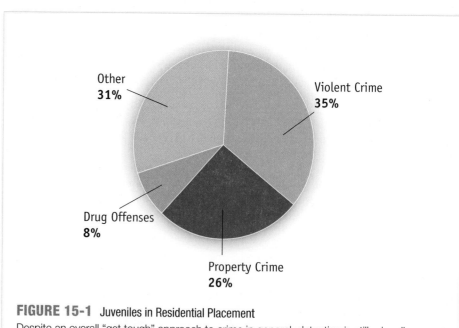

FIGURE 15-1 Juveniles in Residential Placement

Despite an overall "get tough" approach to crime in general, detention is still primarily reserved for violent offenders.

TABLE 15-3 Juveniles in Residential Facilities by Offense, 2006

Type of Crime	Race/Ethnicity					
	White	Black	Hispanic/Latino	American Indian	Asian	Other
Violent crime (22,958)	33.9%	42.7%	19.3%	1.7%	1.1%	1.0%
Property crime (17,004)	38.7	36.1	20.8	1.9	1.2	1.0
Drug offenses (5,673)	32.6	42.9	21.0	1.4	1.0	0.9
Status offenses (3,635)	50.9	32.9	7.7	4.7	0.8	2.8
Public order crime (6,878)	37.2	37.1	21.1	1.9	1.6	0.9
Technical violations (8,410)	36.3	36.6	22.1	2.0	1.0	1.5

Why do you think more white youths are arrested for status offenses than any other group?

hospitals and substance abuse clinics, but these are not typically included in official statistics on juveniles in detention.[34]

Race also plays a role in detention statistics: black Americans represent 16 percent of the population but constitute 29 percent of all juvenile arrests.[35] Table 15-3 demonstrates that for all offenses, black Americans are more likely than any other race to be detained.[36] According to a recent report by the OJJDP, the racial disparity in the juvenile justice system can be seen in the proportion of cases in the court system that involve minorities, as well as in the outcomes of these cases. Black Americans are more than three times more likely than white Americans to be charged with violent crimes, more than twice as likely as whites to be charged with property or public order crimes, and about one and a half times more likely to be charged with drug offenses.[37]

In addition to being more likely to be sent to detention facilities, black Americans are disproportionately represented in the juvenile justice system, particularly with regard to arrests. In fact, one of the amendments to the Juvenile Justice Delinquency Prevention Act of 1974 included a provision mandating that states investigate whether there is a racial bias in their juvenile justice system, collect data to document such a trend, and develop effective solutions for reducing a bias.[38]

The research suggests the early stages of case processing contribute to this disparity. Black youths are less likely to be diverted from the court system and more likely to receive sentences involving detention. About 60 percent of all juveniles in custody are minorities, as are almost three-fourths of youths held in custody for violent crimes.[39] Using data from 2008, Table 15-4 helps to illustrate the extent to which black Americans are disproportionately involved in the juvenile justice system.

TABLE 15-4 Proportion of Juvenile Arrests for Black Americans, 2008[40]

Crime	% of Black Juveniles Arrested for the Crime
Murder	58%
Forcible rape	37
Robbery	67
Aggravated assault	42
Simple assault	39
Burglary	35
Larceny-theft	31
Motor vehicle theft	45
Weapons violation	38
Drug abuse violation	27
Vandalism	19
Liquor law violations	6

Clearly, black juveniles are more likely to be arrested than white juveniles. Is this due to a greater likelihood of offending for this group of youths, or are there other factors at work?

How might you explain the disproportionate numbers of black and minority youths who are diverted to detention facilities? What factors might contribute to the discrepancy between treatment of black and white youths, for example?

Juveniles who are serious offenders can be sent to training schools or state institutions for longer periods of detention. They can also be sent to adult prisons, depending on a number of factors, such as the seriousness of the crime, the age of the offender, the offender's prior record, and state statute that mandates waiver to adult court. The main difference between an adult prison and a training school is that juvenile facilities place a greater emphasis on rehabilitation and counseling than do adult prisons. What both types of facilities have in common is an emphasis on maintaining order and control of individual behavior.[41]

Correctional treatment in juvenile facilities is designed to alter individuals' behavior so that they do not commit additional crimes in the future. Because participants in these programs have committed serious offenses or are repeat offenders, success is a relatively difficult concept to evaluate. The fact that many serious offenders may go on to adult careers in crime is not necessarily an indication that these facilities are ineffective. It is possible that the population they serve is the most difficult to change.[42]

The vast majority of juveniles who come into contact with the juvenile justice system do not commit additional crimes. This should suggest that while the system is imperfect, its philosophy and strategic approach make a difference. It also suggests that the public's fear of delinquents in general might be distorted. For example, few hard-core offenders progress to adult careers in crime. Moreover, they represent a very small segment of the entire delinquent population: only about 20 percent of youths sentenced to secure detention have committed violent crimes.[43]

Training schools are an expensive way to handle delinquent youths. This is the case whether they resemble prisons, college campuses, or home environments. Training schools face other challenges similar to those in adult institutions. For example, like adult prisons, training schools suffer from overcrowding and increased gang activity.[44] Despite the challenges of cost and crowding, training schools are becoming an increasingly popular solution for housing juveniles.

SHORT-TERM FACILITIES

There are two types of short-term facilities. The first are those that house youths awaiting adjudication or dispositional hearings; these are similar in many ways to jails. There are also short-term facilities that house adjudicated offenders, such as boot camps, forestry camps, or ranches.

Forestry camps and ranches are minimum-security or nonsecure facilities designated for first-time offenders or those who have been committed through private placements. In 2006, there were twenty-nine camps and ranches operating in the United States.[45] Because these programs effectively combine the general maintenance of state parks and other government facilities with treatment of youths, forestry camps have grown in popularity.

The average length of stay at a ranch is about six months. While there, youths participate in horseback riding, take care of livestock, and learn other farming skills. Youths tend to prefer forestry camps or ranches to training schools, largely because of the amount of freedom they are given on the grounds of a farm or ranch.[46] These camps also provide youths an opportunity to mainstream back into society by gradually immersing them in the local community.

Another short-term strategy involves boot camps. First used in the 1980s and emphasizing military discipline and physical training, boot camps peaked in popularity in the mid-1990s, with hundreds of them in operation across the country. Boot camps employ a strict regime of marching and military protocol, which is enforced by military drill-sergeant instructors. These programs typically range between 30 and 120 days, and are designed to shock individuals out of their delinquency, while also attempting to restore self-confidence and self-esteem. The goal is to return youths to their neighborhoods with the tools to withstand peer pressure and stay out of trouble.[47]

Boot camps are generally a midrange type of sanction, targeting those who have failed under probation agreements but are not sufficiently hardened to warrant more serious detention arrangements. Like their minimum-security counterparts, boot camps for juveniles contain some type of work detail, but most allocate more than half of the day to education and counseling. Additionally, most participants can expect to undergo some version of intensive probation following graduation.

Much of the research on boot camps demonstrates that they have not significantly reduced recidivism or otherwise had many long-term, positive effects on juveniles. This lack of effectiveness has led many states to abandon or significantly scale back their boot camp programs.[48] One of the

How have the media portrayed boot camp scenarios involving youth? Given what you have just read about boot camps as a means of treatment, how do these portrayals differ from the reality of these programs?

problems with these programs is that they offer too little in the way of therapy. As a result, they do not correct the behavior that caused the youth to be arrested in the first place. Moreover, like wilderness training programs, boot camps have no system for following up with youths; instead, youths are sent back to the environments and neighborhoods from which they came without sufficient tools for coping with the problems that contributed to their behavior.[49]

INSTITUTIONAL LIFE

Despite the coercive nature of institutional life, detention facilities are intended to be places where youths can make progress and learn to behave constructively. Because many youths come to detention facilities from dysfunctional families, where living arrangements are chaotic and lack meaningful structure, some might consider incarceration a form of **upward social mobility.** What this means is that these youths' social standing improves by their being incarcerated, if only because the institution provides them with the bare essentials of shelter, food, and clothing.[50] This issue of upward social mobility is highlighted in Zach's comments about how life is better inside prison for some youths than when they are at home:

upward social mobility
Improvement in social standing through means such as incarceration in which detention facilities offer structure and bare essentials that dysfunctional families do not.

. . . there's a kid, recently, who, who, uh, he's been here, uh, in DOC for about three years. And he's told me he don't want to go home. You know, he don't want to go home. He's always getting in trouble. He does all kinds of stuff, and stupid stuff. And I think that's being institutionalized, where you don't care about going home, even though your family wants you home. You don't care. You're willing to stay here. . . . It's free food. It's a free place to sleep, free clothes. Like some kids, it's better in here for 'em than on the outs [outside prison] because they have problems on the outs with people, not a good lifestyle, don't have food, clothes. So most of the kids in here, they'll get in trouble on purpose to stay here.

Adjusting to institutional life can be difficult for many youths, even those whose lives were difficult prior to incarceration. The structure of institutional life is inflexible, meaning that inmates' regimen is strictly regulated by others. For some youths, detention is their first encounter with this type of inflexibility and lack of freedom. Moreover, detention introduces youths to new experiences, such as finding ways to spend idle time and confronting difficult issues in therapy sessions.[51]

For more on life on the inside, watch *Detention and Treatment: Austin* and *Prison Life: Zachary* at www.mhhe.com/mcnamarajd1e

"Privacy, you ain't got none. You shower, there's a little stall. You can see—they see from your chest up. That's one of the best places you get."
ANTHONY

For more on institutional life, watch *Institutional Life: Zachary*, *Institutional Life: Anthony B.*, and *Institutional Life: Anthony J.* at www.mhhe.com/mcnamarajd1e

Institutionalized youths are likely to suffer from under-developed social skills, as well as various forms of mental illness. Institutions are therefore structured to force youths to interact with one another in constructive ways and to provide encouragement and support as they learn these skills.[52] While every institution varies in the structure and routine it provides, here is one youth's description of the day-to-day existence inside the institution:

Well, it's definitely changing the environment, because on the outs [outside prison] you can do whatever you want, whenever you want. There may be some consequences, but you could still do whatever. But, in here, you wake up, they tell you when you can go to the bathroom, when you have to eat, when you can rec [recreation], when you go to sleep, when you wake up. And it sucks, because they make you wake up, like, 4:30 in the morning. Some of the staff do, but we're really supposed to get up at 5:30. But, today, we got woke up at like 4:30. And I have a job, though, so—'cause I took the GED test. So I stay on the unit a lot more than everybody else does, when they go to school in the unit, and I read and stuff. But, this really ain't a place to be. You know, it's, it's different. And especially if your family don't live close and they can't come see you, and you can only visit certain days of the week.

Mental Illness and Detention

Statistics show that many youths, upon entering the prison system, suffer from a host of emotional and psychological disorders. One meta-analysis of the literature on psychological and mental disorders in juvenile detention facilities found that adolescents, and particularly boys, were ten times more likely to suffer from psychosis than the general population. Girls in detention were most often diagnosed with major depression, but males were more likely to be diagnosed with ADHD, conduct disorders, bipolar disorder, and other illnesses.[53] According to some studies:

- Between 50 and 90 percent of youths in confinement suffer from conduct disorders, about half from attention deficit disorders.
- Approximately 40 percent suffer from anxiety disorders.
- Approximately 50 percent are substance abuse dependent.
- Approximately 80 percent suffer from affective disorders.
- Between 1 and 5 percent suffer from a psychotic disorder.[54]

All of these figures are higher than for youths in the general population.[55]

Each of these disorders can lead to disciplinary problems in detention facilities. They can also limit youths' participation in programs designed to address their mental health issues. Because youths are increasingly being detained for the purposes of accountability and punishment, and less so for treatment, most public institutions are facing challenges to the provision of such services. Unfortunately, given the number of juvenile inmates who suffer from these disorders, cutting mental health services will likely result in higher rates of recidivism.

Gangs

The influence of gangs in juvenile detention facilities presents another set of problems. For example, because gangs are often divided along racial and ethnic lines, overcrowded facilities experience heightened tensions, which often results in incidents of violence.[56] For many youths, dealing with gangs on the street is difficult enough; avoiding gang members in an institutional setting presents an even greater challenge.

Female Inmates

Historically, female offenders were handled informally by the juvenile justice system. For this reason, issues related to their presence in detention facilities have been largely ignored. As we saw in Chapter 11, girls are much less likely to be arrested than boys.

offenders who come to the attention of the juvenile justice system. As such, they bring with them unique problems, behaviors, and perspectives that may make them at higher risk for extreme behavior such as suicide. These findings underscore the need for staff working in confined environments to receive additional training to handle these types of offenders.[79]

Privatization of Juvenile Corrections

Another increasing trend is the **privatization of corrections,** whereby private companies, instead of state agencies, provide detention services for juveniles. Of the 2,861 juvenile facilities in existence in 2006, about 59 percent were privately owned and operated. These institutions house approximately 28 percent of all juvenile offenders in the United States. Thus, while there are slightly more private facilities than public ones, the latter are responsible for the majority of juvenile offenders.[80]

Private for-profit corporations, such as Wackenhut or Corrections Corporation of America, currently operate secure juvenile facilities in at least twenty-three states and the District of Columbia. With its recent acquisition of Youth Services International, CSC has emerged as the dominant player in the juvenile corrections segment of the market.[81] Proponents of privatization cite the benefits of free enterprise, pointing out that competition may lead to superior products, lower costs for states, and lower levels of recidivism. In theory, private corporations, with their attention to profit margins and greater levels of accountability, can provide a higher-quality set of services to incarcerated youths at a savings to states.

Opponents of privatization claim there are a number of issues with this theory. The first issue involves the practice known as *creaming.* Creaming occurs when private companies select only those youths who pose the fewest problems while incarcerated, thus making it easier and cheaper to provide space for them. Creaming also results in private companies being able to show fewer disciplinary problems with inmates, thus creating an image that the private sector is better suited for rehabilitating youths. Obviously, creaming leaves the more difficult youths in public facilities, where the costs of housing and treating them are much higher, as are the number of incidents of rule violations.[82]

Opponents also claim that the supposed primary advantage of privatization—cost savings—is not always conducive to creating innovative programs or strategies for rehabilitation. Rather, facilities save money by hiring fewer, and less qualified, staff and reducing the services offered. When staff levels are too low, or when facility workers are poorly trained or inexperienced, more incidents involving violence, injury, and excessive use of restraint and isolation occur. When disciplinary problems emerge in these facilities, rehabilitative programs are often sacrificed to accommodate tight security and controls.[83]

A third problem with regard to privatization relates to the oversight of agencies. Given that public facilities for juveniles are often inadequate and poorly monitored, critics wonder who will be responsible for ensuring that private agencies will be held to minimum levels of care. A lack of oversight, they claim, will inevitably lead to cost-cutting measures, which in turn often leads to the abuse or neglect of youths.[84] For example, privately owned facilities have a strong incentive to keep their census at maximum capacity, often bringing in prisoners from other states to achieve this objective. In doing so, these facilities make it difficult to ensure that youths who are transferred to them will be in close proximity to their families and will be reintegrated to their home communities following detention.

Finally, critics question the type of sanctions states can use if privately owned facilities do not support prevention programs that attempt to reduce recidivism. After all, privately owned facilities actually benefit from recidivism by providing a steady stream of clients.[85]

From a policy standpoint, there has been little research documenting the effectiveness of privately owned facilities. While some research has shown the economic benefits and savings to states that use them, few studies have compared recidivism rates between privately owned facilities and public ones. Moreover, of the studies that have been done, methodological problems with their overall evaluations make it difficult to accurately

privatization of corrections
A trend toward using private companies, instead of state agencies, as providers of detention services for juveniles.

interpret the data. For example, some studies have shown that inmates from privately funded facilities have somewhat lower recidivism rates than those coming from public ones. This is an encouraging finding for advocates of privatization, but it is far from conclusive.[86]

INSTITUTIONAL PROGRAMS FOR DETAINED YOUTHS

Nearly all institutions that target delinquents have some form of treatment program, such as educational and vocational training, counseling, recreational programs, or religious components. All of these programs are designed to help rehabilitate youths and send them back into the community as productive citizens. However, most programs fail to achieve their desired goals. This is in part because few programs are implemented effectively. Institutional programs face a host of challenges, including a lack of well-trained staff members, budgetary constraints, and a focus on punishment instead of rehabilitation.[87]

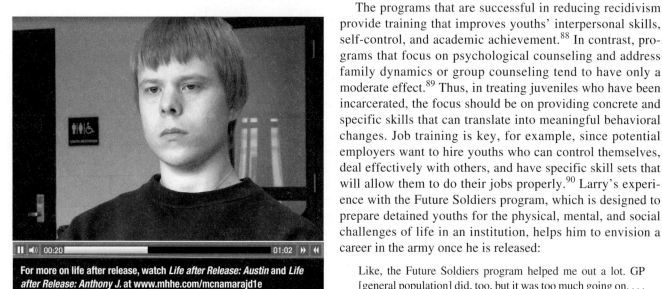

For more on life after release, watch *Life after Release: Austin* and *Life after Release: Anthony J.* at www.mhhe.com/mcnamarajd1e

The programs that are successful in reducing recidivism provide training that improves youths' interpersonal skills, self-control, and academic achievement.[88] In contrast, programs that focus on psychological counseling and address family dynamics or group counseling tend to have only a moderate effect.[89] Thus, in treating juveniles who have been incarcerated, the focus should be on providing concrete and specific skills that can translate into meaningful behavioral changes. Job training is key, for example, since potential employers want to hire youths who can control themselves, deal effectively with others, and have specific skill sets that will allow them to do their jobs properly.[90] Larry's experience with the Future Soldiers program, which is designed to prepare detained youths for the physical, mental, and social challenges of life in an institution, helps him to envision a career in the army once he is released:

> Like, the Future Soldiers program helped me out a lot. GP [general population] did, too, but it was too much going on. . . . Stronger minded then as in talking stronger out your mouth.

Education and Vocational Training

Institutional life presents a great opportunity for detained youths to improve their educational achievement while also receiving therapeutic intervention. Unlike public schools, where teachers may not always have the incentive or the resources to focus on individual youths' education, in detention facilities, teachers are able to work more closely with students and to coordinate their activities with other staff in the institution.

Unfortunately, the majority of delinquents do not return to school after their release from an institution.[91] One way to provide youths with marketable skills that do not require a high school diploma is to offer vocational training. This type of training ensures that individuals will be able to offer marketable skills to their community and to find employment upon release.

Recreational Programs

As we saw in Chapter 12 on delinquency prevention, recreational programs can have a significant impact on youth behavior. These programs are an important part of the overall treatment plan for incarcerated youths, in that they provide youths with a means of coping with the stress of incarceration. They also help to relieve boredom and give juveniles something to look forward to at the end of the day. Many secure facilities, including those that have multiple cottages or dormitories, have basketball teams, allowing youths to compete against one another. Other recreational activities include weight lifting, baseball, and football.

Counseling and Therapy

Because treatment is a principal goal of detention, incarcerated youths are given many opportunities to receive counseling, in the form of both individual and group therapy. Individual counseling is perhaps the most common treatment and is used, in some form, by virtually all juvenile correctional institutions.

The goals of individual and group therapy differ in ways that are often misunderstood. When a therapist begins a treatment dialogue with individual youths, the goal is to help them identify and cope with some of the issues that lead to inappropriate behavior. By learning to identify emotional triggers that signal anxiety, fear, or anger, youths can better cope with the problems they face and can choose more constructive alternatives.

Some approaches to therapy encourage youths to understand the origins of their problems by looking closely at their childhood years and family dynamics. Behavior modification is another commonly used strategy, wherein youths are provided with a set of appropriate behavioral expectations along with rewards and consequences when they meet or fail to live up to them. By rewarding youths for prosocial behavior, for example, therapists hope that these behaviors will be internalized and adopted. Likewise, therapists withhold rewards when youths display antisocial behaviors, and they encourage youths to be accountable for poor decisions. The goal of this type of treatment is to teach youths how to live up to society's expectations.[92]

Group therapy is also frequently used in juvenile correctional institutions. There are many types of group therapy. Milieu therapy attempts to blur the lines between inmates and staff, and focuses more intensively on making the environment a part of the treatment. By emphasizing youths' relationships with their peers and therapists, this type of therapy aims to create a conscience within youths, as well as a sense of dependence on their communities. In each type of group therapy, youths are encouraged to hold each other accountable while at the same time providing each other with emotional support and insight. In these sessions, the therapist steers the conversation along therapeutic lines and helps youths to realize that there are others who share their problems and who are willing to help.[93]

While educational, vocational, recreational, and counseling programs can be effective in helping youths to avoid future involvement in the juvenile justice system, the research has consistently shown that incarcerating youths is expensive (approximately $200–300 per inmate per day) and usually does not lead to behavioral changes. When officials resort to incarceration, it can often be assumed that it is because they are dealing with a particular type of offender. However, questions remain about how to identify the right type of offender for incarceration, as well as whether there are more effective ways to address the problems offenders present.

In February 2007, a report published by the National Association of Counties on Juvenile Detention Reform highlighted the importance of reducing the reliance on detention for youths who commit crimes. The report concluded that detaining children does not promote public safety, is costly, and has adverse effects on youths. This report was supported by research conducted over the last decade that found that, for most juveniles, detention does little in the way of rehabilitation and does not contribute to keeping communities safe. Furthermore, the study found that detention can increase the likelihood that youths will reoffend. The research also showed that detention was increasingly being used as an alternative when treatment and services were unavailable. While this report indicated that detention facilities play an important role in juvenile justice, it also emphasized that detention should be reserved for youths who pose the greatest risk to public safety and who cannot be otherwise safely diverted.

As part of a pilot program by the Annie E. Casey Foundation, New Jersey is employing an innovative strategy for addressing the problem of treating youthful offenders. The program, discussed in the Theory and Practice box on page 400, is called the Juvenile Detention Alternatives Initiative.

THEORY AND PRACTICE WORKING TOGETHER

The Annie E. Casey Foundation's Juvenile Detention Alternatives Initiative

In 2003, New Jersey's Juvenile Justice Commission responded to alarming trends involving the increasing number of youths inappropriately detained in the state's seventeen county detention centers and the overcrowding that existed in those facilities. The result was the formation of Juvenile Detention Alternatives Initiative (JDAI), whose guiding principle is to appropriately channel youths into less restrictive settings that will help them become productive citizens.

Nationwide, budget cuts have led many states to close detention facilities or to combine inmate populations. As New Jersey's efforts to divert youths from detention have yielded economic savings, the state has used that money to invest in other nondetention-related strategies, such as electronic monitoring, gang prevention programs, nonresidential treatment–based programs, and after-school programs that continue to hold youths accountable in a setting that is educational and therapeutic rather than punitive.

Other state counties have adopted this initiative, such as Santa Cruz and Bernalillo Counties in New Mexico, and Cook County in Illinois. The findings of a related research report have shown that substantial reductions in the number of juveniles detained were achieved by this initiative—in some cases by as much as 66 percent. Moreover, juvenile crime rates in all of the JDAI sites have seen a dramatic decrease, as have levels of racial disparity in inmate populations.

 THINK ABOUT IT

What do you think the success of a program like JDAI can tell us about the types of offenders the juvenile justice system should detain? According to the research cited above, under what circumstances might you suggest detention as a strategy for effectively treating delinquent youths?

 THINK ABOUT IT

Institutional Corrections

What are the various institutional facilities available for juveniles who are facing detention? How do they differ from one another? Do they have any features or goals in common? What feature might you require all facilities to offer detained juveniles?

Constitutional Rights of Detained Juveniles

Even if programs like the Annie E. Casey Foundation's JDAI can screen out youths who do not belong in detention facilities, many serious offenders do require treatment. As a consequence of the recent trend of treating juveniles more like adult offenders, the nature of treatment for juveniles in detention has changed.

Once youths are confined, they retain certain rights. The problems of overcrowding, gang activity, and assaults that occur in juvenile detention facilities have led to a number of lawsuits that resulted in constitutional protections for youths who are incarcerated. In the past four decades, the courts affirmed two major rights of delinquents: the **right to treatment** and the right to be free from cruel and unusual punishment, as the U.S. Supreme Court ruled in *Roper v. Simmons,* for example, with regard to capital punishment.[94] Other legal decisions have mandated that a juvenile cannot simply be warehoused in a correctional center, but must receive proper care and treatment in their rehabilitation.

For instance, the case of *Inmates of the Boys' Training School v. Affleck* brought to light many of the inhumane conditions of juvenile detention facilities. In this particular case, a lower court ruled that practices such as solitary confinement, strip searches, and a lack of educational opportunities for youths confined to state training schools constituted a violation of the Eighth Amendment protection against cruel and unusual punishment. In

right to treatment
A legal right to receive proper care and treatment that youths retain once confined.

1974, two years after *Affleck,* in *Nelson v. Hayne,* an appellate court in Indiana ruled that excessive and unnecessary corporal punishment, the use of tranquilizing drugs to control behavior, and the failure to provide rehabilitative treatment violated youths' Eighth and Fourteenth Amendment rights. This case was the first appellate court decision that guaranteed juveniles a right to treatment.[95]

The methods used to maintain order in juvenile facilities have also come under scrutiny.[96] In *Morales v. Turman,* a court found that the use of CS gas, a stronger version of tear gas, extended periods of forced silence by inmates, segregation, and the excessive use of corporal punishment were inappropriate sanctions. It also found that the state of Texas had an obligation to rehabilitate youths.[97] In 1995, in *Alexander v. Boyd and South Carolina Department of Juvenile Justice,* plaintiffs argued that four institutions in the state routinely used practices that violated youths' constitutional rights. These practices included:

- using CS gas and lockup tactics as disciplinary measures
- placing youths in padlocked cells, which violates state fire safety codes
- serving food containing cockroaches and other foreign substances
- failing to provide adequate medical care or living space for inmates
- failing to provide adequate programming or educational opportunities for inmates

In this case, a federal district court stated that the purpose of the institution was to provide rehabilitation and treatment, and that the existing practices did not accomplish any of those objectives. In addition, such practices violated juveniles' constitutional protections. The judge ordered the state to create an acceptable plan for addressing the existing deficiencies and promoting the rehabilitation of youths.[98]

While the lower courts have ruled on the right to treatment, they have done so on a case-by-case basis, rather than as a matter of policy. Furthermore, the U.S. Supreme Court has not ruled on a case involving juveniles' right to treatment. For these reasons, problems like those outlined above are likely to be found in other states and in other

PHIL'S CASE

Conclusions about His Sentence

Recall Phil's situation:

- is fifteen years old
- has previous arrests for vandalism, shoplifting, and burglary
- was sentenced to a year in medium-security detention after missing probation appointments for a previous arrest
- in detention, experienced panic attacks and depression, and attempted to commit suicide
- has been sent to a secure treatment facility, where he is misdiagnosed and heavily medicated

Research on the adverse effects of incarceration raises questions as to its rehabilitative effects. In Phil's case, the judge had many options at his disposal, detention in a medium-security facility being only one of them. Some would argue that the adverse effects of incarceration have actually made Phil more of a burden to society than a potential asset. Had the judge sent Phil to some other type of facility, such as a therapeutic group home, foster care, or a wilderness camp, Phil might have gotten the message and changed his ways.

Do you think there should be limits to the use of discretion by juvenile court judges? Keeping in mind the juvenile justice system's goal of "individualized justice," under what circumstances might you restrict judges' authority?

THINK ABOUT IT

institutions. Nevertheless, these cases have set the tone for many state laws concerning the minimum levels of care for juveniles in detention centers. These include minimum standards for assessing educational skills and programs to advance inmates' education, the delivery of medical and psychiatric care to confined juveniles, and the provision of a humane environment.[99] Thus, in many ways, the prisoners' rights movement found in adult prisons many years ago, which assured inmates certain rights and constitutional protections against mistreatment by correctional officials, has gradually filtered into juvenile institutions.[100]

Lawsuits are one way to ensure proper treatment of juveniles in detention facilities. Another involves the invocation of federal law for violations of inmates' civil rights. In 1980, the Civil Rights of Institutionalized Persons Act (CRIPA) gave the U.S. Department of Justice the authority to investigate civil rights violations against inmates in state or local facilities. According to some experts, this act has also been used to start investigations of alleged abuse of youths in juvenile detention facilities.[101] However, the act applies only to publicly operated facilities, meaning that although private agencies are still bound by federal law, the CRIPA is not applicable to them. As many states begin to explore the privatization of correctional facilities, this distinction will have a significant impact on the treatment of detained juveniles.

THINK ABOUT IT

Constitutional Rights

How would you describe the prisoners' rights movement? Do you think this movement has set precedents on which detained juveniles' rights might eventually be based?

Reentry and Aftercare

According to one estimate, approximately 100,000 youths are released from the juvenile justice system each year. These youths are sent from detention facilities back to families that have a wide assortment of problems, to neighborhoods with high rates of poverty and crime, and to school districts that often fail to meet federal performance guidelines. These youths often do not have adequate life-skills training, employment assistance, or help in reintegrating back into school or the community in any meaningful way. Under these circumstances, not surprisingly, many youths end up back in the juvenile justice system or living on the streets. According to a recent estimate, almost half of homeless youths between the ages of ten and seventeen had recently been in a correctional facility.[102]

Each of the many problems we have discussed in previous chapters—including poverty, family dysfunction, learning disabilities and educational deficiencies, mental health issues (including cognitive disorders), and unemployment—contributes to our understanding of juvenile delinquency. When youths are sentenced to secure facilities, they encounter new problems that impact their worldviews and behaviors. These include the stress and anxiety of incarceration, feelings of isolation, depression, and exposure to gang violence. By the time they are released, most youths are ill-equipped to handle the transition back into society.

When youths are sent to state training schools, the state normally retains authority over them until they are released. Parole, also known as aftercare, incorporates programs that address some of these reintegration problems and that aim to help youths adjust to life in their communities. Reentry services are sometimes available to youths who have been completely released from the system.

The decision to parole youths is usually made by institutional staff, although a number of states give other agencies the authority to parole juveniles.[103] Early release from training schools is often the result of overcrowding in those facilities and is rarely a decision based on youths' rehabilitation and preparedness for reintegrating into society.[104]

However, not all cases are decided this way. A number of factors contribute to the decision to release detained youths, including:

- the seriousness of offenses
- offenders' prior records
- the length of time they have been detained
- their adjustment to institutional life
- their general attitudes toward the institution, its staff, and treatment programs

The type of offense is also an important consideration. For example, it is much easier to justify the early release of offenders who committed property crimes than those who are chronic and violent offenders, or who present a significant threat to their communities.[105]

Moreover, youths are not sent into the community without supervision. The supervision provided by aftercare workers or parole officers is designed to help youths make the transition back into society as seamless as possible. This can be difficult for many youths, particularly those who have been detained for an extended period of time.

The emphasis on treatment, even for offenders who have been incarcerated, remains at the forefront of the efforts of aftercare. These efforts include emotional and psychological support during the readjustment period following release. Because communities can view released youths with suspicion and mistrust, another important role of the aftercare worker is to act as an intermediary between youths in their care and the community. Aftercare workers facilitate interactions between youths and community residents, work with agencies and employers to help them find jobs, and in general help youths transition from the role of inmate to that of citizen. In addition, the aftercare worker creates treatment plans for youths, outlining what they should accomplish in a particular time frame, including enrolling in school and attending classes, acquiring job skills or training, finding employment, or attending anger management and other types of counseling.

In response to many of the challenges presented by juveniles who are released from detention facilities, the Youth Reentry Task Force of the Juvenile Justice and Delinquency Prevention Coalition, a collection of agencies committed to helping youths to become productive citizens, issued a report outlining what was needed to help youths in such situations. Their recommendations included the following:

- **Strengthen the Juvenile Justice and Delinquency Prevention Act to incorporate the reentry stage of youth development in the juvenile justice system.** This would require states to develop some type of plan and program for the release of youths, regulated by federal law.

- **Eliminate barriers to medical and mental health services for reentering youths.** The emotional problems that youths experience while incarcerated do not usually disappear upon release. These youths often require further therapy, medication, or other types of treatment.

- **Provide funding to local organizations to offer a broad range of services for reentry youths.** The logic behind this recommendation is that the entire community has an incentive to see released youths succeed, especially those who have been incarcerated. This effort can only come from within the community, since limited governmental resources have yielded inadequate results.

- **Provide incentives to states to reduce long-term incarceration and increase the use of reentry services.** As we have seen with the JDAI, states are hard pressed to absorb the costs of detaining youths. Public policy has focused more on accountability and punishment, which requires that states make use of detention. In the end, there is a general agreement that no one wants to see youths commit additional acts. This recommendation attempts to balance the need for states to hold youths accountable while recognizing the serious limitations associated with detention. The goal is to offer meaningful programs to all youths to be mainstreamed back into their communities.[106]

Another important contribution to aftercare for juveniles is called the Intensive Aftercare Program (IAP) model.[107] The IAP was initially designed to help correctional agencies implement effective aftercare programs for chronic and serious juvenile offenders. This model stresses intensive surveillance and services, as well as a combination of positive incentives and negative consequences to help youths adjust to life outside the juvenile justice system. Five basic principles underlie this model:

1. Help youths to achieve increased levels of responsibility and freedom in the community.

2. Develop ways for youths to become more involved and interact with members of the community.

3. Assist youths in developing the necessary skills, attitudes, and values needed to make a successful transition back into the community.

4. Develop and enhance new and existing resources depending on the youth and the situation.

5. Implement case planning, including monitoring youths' skill development and their connections with community groups.[108]

Over the past fifteen years, a number of cities have adopted the IAP model, including Denver, Colorado; Norfolk, Virginia; and Las Vegas, Nevada. In Denver, for example, community providers meet weekly with youths while they are incarcerated and offer counseling and life skills services. They continue to provide these services during aftercare. Two months prior to release, youths are permitted to take graduated supervised trips into the community, with overnight or weekend home passes given within thirty days of release. When youths are paroled, the program mandates several months of day treatment services and a highly structured schedule. As time progresses and youths show improvement, supervision is relaxed.

In Las Vegas, once the treatment plan is completed, IAP participants begin a thirty-day prerelease phase, in which they are given structured programs on life skills and substance abuse. The first thirty days of release involve intensive supervision and service. Youths are also subject to frequent drug testing and surveillance by aftercare workers. If youths successfully complete this initial phase of the program, the next two months involve three contacts per week with a case manager. This is reduced to two contacts per week for the following two months and then once a week during the last month of parole.

In Norfolk, the central feature of the IAP is the use of group home placements. Upon being granted parole, youths enter group homes for either thirty or sixty days. During that time, life skills and counseling services are provided, as is intensive supervision. Like in Denver and Las Vegas, as time progresses and the youth responds favorably to the treatment plan, the level of supervision is gradually relaxed.

While the evaluation of the IAP model in these cities has shown mixed results, the program implementers are currently integrating more in the way of parental involvement, employment and educational skills, and improved relationships between the program and community resources.[109]

During the aftercare process, youths are placed under the supervision of an aftercare or parole officer, who monitors them and provides them with a list of rules they must follow. These might include obeying parents and not fleeing their custody, being home at a certain time each night, attending school in accordance with state law, refraining from operating an automobile without permission, avoiding contact with other delinquents, avoiding the use of alcohol and other illegal substances, and reporting to the aftercare officer as required.

In many ways, the parameters set up for juveniles in aftercare are similar to those for adult parolees. Should youths fail to follow the rules of their aftercare programs, many jurisdictions will follow through with formal procedures for revoking aftercare, which are similar to adult parole revocation hearings.[110] If a field agent or aftercare worker begins revocation proceedings against a youth, given the Fourteenth Amendment rights relating to due process, the youth is entitled to a hearing before an impartial judge who is an attorney. Youths facing revocation are also entitled to have legal counsel, at state expense if necessary, and they have the right to confront and cross-examine witnesses, and to introduce their own evidence and witnesses who can testify on their behalf.[111]

Juvenile Corrections and Public Policy

The public's fears and concerns about serious juvenile offenders have often led to practices that focus more on punishment than on treatment. Programs for detained youths have also been limited by the public's perception of who these youths are and what they need.

The research suggests that detention does little to effectively rehabilitate youths and that perhaps the need for accountability supersedes any therapeutic benefit. The long-term effects of a get-tough approach to delinquents also deserve attention. Inmates eventually must be released into society, and in the absence of effective methods for reintegrating them, many will return to criminal behavior and to the juvenile and criminal justice systems. Unfortunately, for serious and violent juvenile offenders, there are not always effective alternatives to detention. For these youths, incarceration, at times in adult facilities, is the only viable option.

THE BIG PICTURE

Conclusions about Juvenile Corrections

- Do you think that the juvenile justice system is too "soft" in its treatment of offenders? Should the system mimic its adult counterpart by emphasizing punishment instead of treatment? Why or why not?
- Why do you think probation is used so frequently with juveniles? Are there ways to make probation strict by having youths comply with the stipulations of their probation agreement? What could we do differently?
- Should juvenile detention facilities screen inmates for gang affiliation so that rival gang members are segregated from the general population?
- What kind of long-term effect do you think programs like boot camps and Outward Bound have on youths' behavior? Are these programs best applied to specific offenders, or can any offender benefit from such programs?

Key Terms

juvenile aftercare	shock probation	upward social mobility
probation	house arrest	group homes
intensive probation	electronic monitoring	day treatment programs
false positive	restitution	wilderness programs
false negative	shaming	privatization of corrections

Make the Call ▶ Corrections and Delinquency

Review the scenario below, and decide how you would approach this case.

YOUR ROLE: Counselor at a secure detention facility for juvenile offenders

DETAILS OF THE CASE

- You are new to this facility and have worked there for only a few months.
- You are approached by a youth who tells you that he is a member of MS-13, the dominant gang in the institution.
- He asks you to look the other way during visiting time so that colleagues can pass drugs off to inmates.
- In exchange for your cooperation, the gang member offers you $500 per week.
- When you refuse, he tells you that gang members on the outside know where you live, and he even provides you with detailed information about your family.

WHAT DO YOU DO?

Given how many drugs enter the institution, you might consider taking the money. It would double your salary and would not require you to engage in drug dealing directly. Accepting his offer might also keep your family safe. On the other hand, you would lose your job and your license to practice if your cooperation were ever discovered. Consider:

- Do you immediately report the incident to your supervisor?
- Do you agree to take the money but then report it to your supervisor, who can then begin an investigation?
- Do you ask your supervisor for a transfer to another facility?
- What do you risk, professionally and personally, by cooperating? What do you risk if you do not cooperate?
- What type of training might help you navigate threatening situations like these?

Apply Theory to Reality ▶ Detention and Recidivism

As we have seen in this chapter, detention and other punitive measures are likely to increase recidivism rather than prevent it from occurring. We also know that detention has a negative effect on youths in terms of an increased level of violence. Which of the theories discussed in this text offers the best explanation for what happens to youths who are sent to detention? Some questions to consider might include the following:

- Is the increase in recidivism and violence a function of labeling by society?

- Is it a result of socialization with other violent offenders?

- Is it other structural factors, such as poverty, racism, and inadequate education, that leave youths with no choice but to commit further crime?

- Is it a combination of factors and theories?

Select one of the theories discussed in this text, and discuss how it relates to the nature of detention, punishment, and juvenile offenders.

Your Community ▶ Probation, Aftercare, and Delinquency

In addition to the information you glean from your readings, class lectures, and discussions, it is important to roll up your sleeves and immerse yourself in a topic as a researcher who gains an understanding of a problem or issue by observing or experiencing it firsthand. Through such methods, you gain a much greater appreciation of the magnitude and scope of the problem than if you were only engaged in "armchair theorizing."

- Contact a local department of juvenile justice, and ask permission to interview probation and parole officers to gain their perspectives on juveniles and what can be done to minimize delinquency.

- In your interviews, ask questions aimed at determining officers' attitudes toward juveniles and their role in the juvenile justice process. Do the officers attempt to get to know the youths and their backgrounds, which gives them a chance to target the larger issues in youths'

lives? Or do the officers simply provide supervision in an effort to catch the youths if they commit another crime? Do you get the sense that probation and/or parole officers refrain from getting involved because of a lack of adequate resources, or do they identify another reason?

- Be aware that the answers to these questions may not be directly presented to you, especially since these officers may be concerned about what they say and how their responses will be used. Therefore, be prepared to do some probing and rephrasing of questions in order to learn as much as you can about the issues your community faces.

- After collecting your data, and drawing from the relevant literature, prepare a report that discusses the relationship between probation and parole and delinquency in your community.

Notes

[1] Office of Juvenile Justice and Delinquency Prevention. 2006. *Census of Juveniles in Residential Placement 2006 Databook.* Washington, DC: OJJDP. http://www.ojjdp.ncjrs.org/ojstatbb/cjrp-/asp/Offense_Committed.asp. Accessed September 9, 2008.

[2] Ibid.

[3] Snyder, H., and Sickmund, M. 2006. *Juvenile Offenders and Victims: 2006 National Report.* Washington, DC: Office of Juvenile Justice and Delinquency Prevention. http://www.ojjdp.ncjrs.gov/ojstatbb/nr2006/-downloads/chapter6.pdf.

[4] Roberts, A. R. (ed.). 2004. *Juvenile Justice Sourcebook: Past, Present and Future.* New York: Oxford University Press.

[5] Ibid.

[6] Ibid.

[7] Ibid.

[8] Rothman, D. L. 1971. *The Discovery of the Asylum.* Boston: Little, Brown.

[9] Ibid.

[10] Puzzanchera, C., and Kang, W. 2008. "Juvenile Court Statistics Databook." Available at http://ojjdp.ncjrs.gov/ojstatbb/jcsdb/.

[11] See, for instance, Feld, B. C. 1995. *Violent Youth and Public Policy: A Case Study of Juvenile Justice Law Reform.* 79 MINN. L. REV. 965, 1009.

[12] Ibid.

[13] See, for instance, Champion, D. J. 2005. *Corrections in the United States: A Contemporary Perspective,* 4th ed. Upper Saddle River, NJ: Prentice-Hall.

[14] Turner, S., Petersilia, J., and Deschenes, E. P. 1992. "Evaluating Intensive Supervision Probation/Parole (ISP) for Drug Offenders." *Crime and Delinquency,* 38(4): 539–556.

[15] Lane, J., Turner, S., Fain, T., and Seligal, A. 2005. "Evaluating an Experimental Intensive Juvenile Probation Program: Supervision and Official Outcomes." *Crime & Delinquency,* 51(1): 26–52.

[16] See, for instance, Lane, J., Fain, T., and Sehgah, A. 2007. "The Effects of an Experimental Intensive Juvenile Probation Program on Self-reported Delinquency and Drug Use." *Journal of Experimental Criminology,* 3(3): 201–219.

[17] Ibid.

[18] See, for instance, Champion, 2005.

[19] Ibid.

[20] Lipsey, M. W., and Cullen, F. T. 2007. "The Effectiveness of Correctional Rehabilitation: A Review of Systematic Reviews." *Annual Review of Law and Social Science,* vol. 3. Available at http://www.vanderbilt.edu/VIPPS/ER&M/LipseyCullen_Offender_Rehabilitation.pdf. Accessed September 9, 2008.

[21] Ashton, J. 2005. "Family Law: Child Support Dockets Benefit from Using Problem-Solving Court Principles." *NASJE Quarterly,* 21(1): 1–3. http://nasje.org/news/newsletter0601/resources_03.htm. Accessed September 9, 2008.

[22] Ibid.

[23] See Schneider, P. R., and Griffith, W. R. 1982. "Juvenile Restitution as a Sole Sanction or Condition of Probation: An Empirical Analysis." *Journal of Research on Crime and Delinquency,* 19(1): 47–65.

[24] Greenwood, P. 2006. *Changing Lives: Delinquency Prevention as Crime Control.* Westport, CT: Greenwood.

[25] See http://www.juvenilearbitration.org/about .html. Accessed September 9, 2008.

[26] See http://outwardboundwilderness.org/ whatis.html. Accessed August 26, 2008.

[27] Blew, C. H., McGillis, D., and Bryant, G. 1977. *Project New Pride: Denver Colorado.* Washington, DC: U.S. Department of Law Enforcement Assistance Administration.

[28] Ryan, J. P., Marshall, J. M., Herz, D., and Hernandez, P. M. 2008. "Juvenile Delinquency in Child Welfare: Investigating Group Home Effects." *Children and Youth Services Review.* Available at http://www.cwla.org/programs/juvenilejustice/grouphomeeffects.pdf.

[29] Bedard, R. M., Rosen, L. A., and Vacha-Hasse, T. 2003. "Wilderness Therapy Programs for Juvenile Delinquents: A Meta-Analysis." *Journal of Therapeutic Wilderness Camping,* 3(1): 7–13.

[30] Snyder and Sickmund, 2006. http://www .ojjdp.ncjrs.gov/ojstatbb/nr2006/downloads/chapter6.pdf.

[31] Ibid.

[32] Office of Juvenile Justice and Delinquency Prevention, 2006.

[33] Ibid.

[34] See McNamara, R. H. 2008. *The Lost Population: Status Offenders in America.* Durham, NC: Carolina Academic Press.

[35] Snyder and Sickmund, 2006.

[36] Office of Juvenile Justice and Delinquency Prevention, 2006.

[37] Snyder and Sickmund, 2006.

[38] For a description of the racial disproportionality clause of the JJDPA, see http://www.njjn. org/-federal_activity_156.html.

[39] Office of Juvenile Justice and Delinquency Prevention, 2006.

[40] Puzzanchera, 2009. *Juvenile Arrests 2008.* Washington, DC: Office of Juvenile Justice and Delinquency Prevention.

[41] See Taroola, S. M., Wagner, E. F., Rabinowitz, J., and Tubman, J. L. 2002. "Understanding and Treating Juvenile Offenders: A Review of Current Knowledge and Future Directions." *Aggression and Violent Behavior,* 7(2): 125–143.

[42] See Haapanen, R., Britton, L., and Croisdale, T. 2007. "Persistent Criminality and Career Length." *Crime and Delinquency,* 53(1): 133–155.

[43] Snyder and Sickmund, 2006.

[44] Ibid.

[45] Ibid.

[46] Ibid.

[47] As was mentioned in Chapter 12, boot camps began in the 1980s and emphasized military discipline and physical training. These programs typically range between 30 and 120 days and are designed not only to shock the individual out of his or her delinquent ways but also to restore self-confidence and self-esteem in youths, so that they can withstand peer pressure once they return to their own neighborhoods.

[48] See Mendel, R. A. 2002. *Less Hype, More Help: Reducing Juvenile Crime: What Works and What Doesn't.* Washington, DC: America Youth Policy Forum. See also Krisberg, B. 2005. *Juvenile Justice: Redeeming Our Children.* Los Angeles: Sage; Mackenzie, D. L. 2006. *What Works in Corrections.* Boston: Cambridge University Press, pp. 271–303.

[49] See Mackenzie, D. L. 2006. *What Works in Corrections: Reducing the Criminal Activities of Offenders and Delinquents.* Cambridge, MA: Cambridge University Press.

[50] For some inmates, life improves substantially when they are incarcerated in that their immediate needs are met. For an interesting discussion of the economics of incarceration, see Vera Institute of Justice. 1996. *The Unintended Consequences of Incarceration.* Available at http://www.cejamericas.org/-doc/documentos/eeuu-vera-incarceration.pdf#page=96.

[51] See, for instance, Petersen-Badali, M., and Koegl, C. J. 2002. "Juveniles' Experiences with Incarceration: The Role of Correctional Staff in Peer Violence." *Journal of Criminal Justice,* 30(1): 41–49.

[52] Ibid.

[53] Faze, S., Dole, H., and Angstrom, N. 2008. "Mental Disorders among Adolescents in Juvenile Detention and Correctional Facilities: A Systematic Review and Meta Regression Analysis of 25 Surveys." *Journal of American Academy of Child and Adolescent Psychiatry,* 48(9): 1010–1019.

[54] Otto, R., Greenstein, J., Johnson, M., and Friedman, R. 1992. "Prevalence of Mental Disorders among Youth in the Juvenile Justice System." In *Responding to the Mental Health Needs of Youth in the Juvenile Justice System.* Seattle, WA: National Coalition for the Mentally Ill in the Criminal Justice System, pp. 7–48. See also Edens, J., and Otto, R. 1997. "Prevalence of Mental Disorders among Youth in the Juvenile Justice System." *Focal Point* (Spring):1–8.

[55] See, for instance, Coosa, J., and Skiwear, K. 2000. "Youth with Mental Health Disorders: Issues and Emerging Responses." *Juvenile Justice,* 7(1):3–13.

[56] Snyder and Sickmund, 2006.

[57] Myers, S. 2002. *Police Encounters with Juvenile Suspects: Explaining the Use of Authority and Provisions of Support.* Washington, DC: National Institute of Justice.

[58] Ibid

[59] Arias, I. 2004. "Report from the CDC. The Legacy of Child Maltreatment: Long-Term Health Consequences for Women." *Journal of Women's Health,* 13(5): 468–473.

[60] Avoca, L., and Deadly, K. 1998. *No Place to Hide: Understanding and Meeting the Needs of Girls in the California Juvenile Justice System.* San Francisco: National Council on Crime and Delinquency.

[61] U.S. Department of Justice, Office of Justice Programs, Office of Juvenile Justice and Delinquency Prevention. 2005. *Guiding Principles for Promising Female Programming.* Washington, DC: Author. Available at http://www.ojjdp.ncjrs .gov/publications/index.html.

[62] Obeidallah, D. A., and Earls, F. J. 1999. *Adolescent Girls: The Role of Depression in the Development of Delinquency.* Washington, DC: U.S. Department of Justice, Office of Justice Programs, National Institute of Justice. Available at http://www.ncjrs.gov/pdffiles1/fs000244.pdf.

[63] Hayes, L. M. 2009. *Juvenile Suicide in Confinement: A National Study.* Washington, DC: Office of Juvenile Justice and Delinquency Prevention. Available at http://www.ncjrs.gov/pdffiles1-/ojjdp/213691.pdf.

[64] See, for instance, Belenko, S., Sprott, J. B., and Petersen, C. 2004. "Drug and Alcohol Issues among Minority and Female Juvenile Offenders: Treatment and Policy Issues." *Criminal Justice Policy Review,* 15(1): 3–36.

[65] See, for instance, Belenko, Sprott, and Petersen, 2004.

[66] American Bar Association and National Bar Association. 2001. *Justice by Gender: The Lack of Appropriate Prevention, Diversion and Treatment Alternatives for Girls in the Justice System.* See also Maniglia, R. 2003. *Meeting the Needs of Juvenile Female Offenders: Pre-program Assignment.* Longmont, CO: National Institute of Corrections.

[67] Ibid.

[68] Carmona, R.H. 2005. *Suicide Prevention among Native American Youth.* Prepared remarks of Richard H. Carmona, M.D., M.P.H., F.A.C.S., Surgeon General, U.S. Public Health Service, U.S. Department of Health and Human Services. Testimony before the Indian Affairs Committee, U.S. Senate, June 15, 2005; Department of Health and Human Services. 1999. *The Surgeon General's Call to Action to Prevent Suicide, 1999.* Washington, DC: U.S. Department of Health and Human Services.

[69] Substance Abuse and Mental Health Services Administration. 2001. *Summary of Findings from the 2000 National Household Survey on Drug Abuse.* NHSDA Series: H-13, DHHS Publication No. SMA 01-3549. Rockville, MD: U.S. Department of Health and Human Services, Substance Abuse and Mental Health Services Administration.

[70] Hayes, L. 1995. "Prison Suicide: An Overview and a Guide to Prevention." *The Prison Journal,* 75(4): 431– 455. Hayes, L. 1999. *Suicide Prevention in Juvenile Correction and Detention Facilities: A Resource Guide.* South Easton, MA: Council of Juvenile Correctional Administrators.

[71] Parent, D., Leiter, V., Kennedy, S., Livens, L., Wentworth, D., and Wilcox, S. 1994. *Conditions of Confinement: Juvenile Detention and Corrections Facilities.* Washington, DC: U.S. Department of Justice, Office of Justice Programs, Office of Juvenile Justice and Delinquency Prevention.

[72] Morris, R., Harrison, E., Knox, G., Tromanhauser, E., Marquis, D., and Watts, L. L. 1995. "Health Risk Behavioral Survey from 39 Juvenile Correctional Facilities in the United States." *Journal of Adolescent Health,* 17(6): 334–344.

[73] Robertson, A., and Husain, J. 2001. *Prevalence of Mental Illness and Substance Abuse Disorders among Incarcerated Juvenile Offenders.* Jackson: Mississippi Department of Public Safety and Mississippi Department of Mental Health.

[74] Ibid.

[75] Kempton, T., and Forehand, R. 1992. "Suicide Attempts among Juvenile Delinquents: The Contribution of Mental Health Factors." *Behaviour Research and Therapy,* 30(5): 537–541; Alessi, N., McManus, M., Brickman, A., and Grapentine, L. 1984. "Suicidal Behavior among Serious Juvenile Offenders." *American Journal of Psychiatry,* 141(2): 286–287; Morris et al., 1995.

[76] Ibid. See also Esposito, C., and Clum, G. 2002. "Social Support and Problem-Solving as Moderators of the Relationship between Childhood Abuse and Suicidality: Applications to a Delinquent Population." *Journal of Traumatic Stress,* 15(2):137–146.

[77] Anno, B. 1984. "The Availability of Health Services for Juvenile Offenders: Preliminary Results of a National Survey." *Journal of Prison and Jail Health,* 4(2): 77–90.

[78] Goldstrom, I.,J., Henderson, M., Male, A., and Manderscheid, R. 2001. "The Availability of Mental Health Services to Young People in Juvenile Justice Facilities: A National Survey." In *Mental Health, United States, 2000.* Washington, DC: U.S. Department of Health and Human Services, Substance Abuse and Mental Health Services Administration, pp. 248–268.

[79] Hayes, 2009.

[80] Ibid.

[81] Ibid.

[82] Armstrong. G. A. 2001. *Private vs. Public Operation of Juvenile Correctional Facilities.* Chicago: LFB Publishing.

[83] Bayer, P. J., and Pozen, D. E. 2005. "The Effectiveness of Juvenile Correctional Facilities: Public versus Private Management." *Journal of Law and Economics,* 48: 549–589.

[84] Benson, B. 1998. *To Serve and Protect: Privatization and Community in the Criminal Justice System.* New York: New York University Press.

[85] Ibid. See also Bayer and Pozen, 2005.

[86] For a review of the literature on private versus public recidivism, see Bales, W. D., Bedard, L. E., and Quinn, S. T. 2003. *Recidivism: An Analysis of Public and Private State Prison Releases in Florida.* Available at http://www.dc.state.fl.us/pub/recidivismfsu/RecidivismStudy2003.PDF. See also Austin, J., and Coventry, G. 2001. *Emerging Issues on Privatized Prisons.* Washington, DC: U.S. Department of Justice, Bureau of Justice Assistance; Amstrong, 2001; Bayer and Pozen, 2005; Curran, D. J. 1988. "Destructuring, Privatization, and the Promise of Juvenile Diversion: Compromising Community-Based Corrections." *Crime and Delinquency,* 34: 363; Robert, B., Levinson, R. B., and Taylor, W. J. 1991." Studies Privatization in Juvenile Corrections." *Corrections Today,* 53: 242–248.

[87] See, for instance, Holman, B., and Ziedenberg, J. 2006. *The Dangers of Detention: The Impact of Incarcerating Youth in Detention and Other Secure Facilities.* Washington, DC: Justice Policy Institute. http://www.justicepolicy.org/images/upload/06-11_REP_DangersOfDetention_JJ.pdf. Accessed September 9, 2008.

[88] See Burns, B. J., Howell, J. C., Wiig, J. K., Augimeri, L. K., Welsh, B. C., Loeber, R., and Petechuck, D. 2003. *Treatment, Services, and Intervention Programs for Child Delinquents.* Washington, DC: Office of Juvenile Justice and Delinquency Prevention. Available at http://schoolsafetyclearinghouse.org-/Resources/July07/July07/child%20delinquency-treatment.pdf.

[89] Ibid.

[90] See Sue, D. W., and Sue, D. 2003. *Counseling the Culturally Diverse: Theory and Practice,* 4th ed. New York: Wiley.

[91] Wiebush, R. G., Wagner, D., McNulty, B., Wang, Y., and Le, T. N. 2005. *Implementation and Outcome Evaluation of the Intensive Aftercare Program Final Report.* Washington, DC: Office of Juvenile Justice and Delinquency Prevention.

[92] See Goldenberg, I., and Goldenberg, H. 2003. *Family Therapy: An Overview.* New York: Thomson/Brooks Cole.

[93] Ibid.

[94] See Alexander, R. 1995. "Incarcerated Juvenile Offenders' Right to Rehabilitation." *Criminal Justice Policy Review,* 7(2): 202–213.

[95] *Nelson v. Hayne,* 491 F.2d 352 (1974).

[96] *Inmates of the Boys' Training School v. Affleck,* 346 F. Supp. 13154, 1366 (D.R. I. 1972).

[97] *Morales v. Turman,* 430 U.S. 322 (1977).

[98] *Alexander v. Boyd and South Carolina Department of Juvenile Justice,* 876 F. Supp. 773, 778 (D.S.C. 1995).

[99] Alexander, 1995.

[100] Civil Rights of Institutionalized Persons Act (CRIPA); 42 U.S.C. § 1997a et seq.; Elrod, P., and Ryder, S. 2005. *Juvenile Justice: A Social, Historical and Legal Perspective,* 2nd ed. Boston: Jones and Bartlett.

[101] Ibid.

[102] See Nellis, A., and Wayman, R. H. 2009. *Back on Track: Supporting Youth Reentry from Out-of-Home Placements to the Community.* Washington, DC: Youth Reentry Task Force of the Juvenile Justice and Delinquency Prevention Coalition.

[103] Ibid.

[104] Ibid

[105] Elrod and Ryder, 2005.

[106] See Nellis and Wayman, 2009.

[107] See U.S. Department of Justice, Office of Justice Programs, Office of Juvenile Justice and Delinquency Prevention. 2007. *Recent Juvenile Aftercare Initiatives: OJJDP's Intensive Aftercare Program.* Available at http://www.ojjdp.ncjrs.gov/jjbulletin/9907_3/ojjdp.html.

[108] Ibid.

[109] Wiebush, R. G., Wagner, D., McNulty, B., Wang, Y., and Le, T. N. 2005. *Implementation and Outcome Evaluation of the Intensive Aftercare Program.* Washington, DC: Office of Juvenile Justice and Delinquency Prevention.

[110] Elrod and Ryder, 2005.

[111] *Morrissey v. Brewer,* 408, U.S. 471, 92 S. Ct. 2593, 33 L. Ed. 2d 484 (1972).

Glossary

academic achievement (or academic performance) Success in school that opens the door to better job opportunities and a better quality of life, although educational opportunities are not equally distributed.

Adam Walsh Child Protection and Safety Act A law that integrated information from state sex offender registry systems so that offenders cannot evade detection by moving from state to state. It also strengthened federal penalties for crimes against children.

adjudication hearing Much like a trial in the adult system; only a small percentage of delinquency cases actually involve this initial stage.

aftercare Programs for youths needing temporary placement with services like crisis intervention or shelter care, and for youths who need some type of long-term residential placement, such as foster care or group homes.

age of onset The time period when juveniles begin committing offenses and crimes.

aging out process The process by which juvenile offenders engage in less delinquent and criminal activity as they begin to mature.

alternative schools Schools that offer nontraditional education to students who do not show signs of succeeding in more traditional, and often less flexible, learning environments.

anomie Normlessness; occurs when rules, laws, or norms no longer apply to people's lives or their behavior.

appellate process or appellate review The right for juveniles to appeal a case, particularly serious ones; generally, juveniles do not have a constitutional right to appeal a case, but most states provide for it.

arrest Now used interchangeably with "taken into custody" with regard to juveniles; historically, the phrase used to describe what happened to juveniles in lieu of arrest, in order to shield them from the stigma of the criminal justice process.

atavisms Assumed physical features, such as large ears, protruding jaws, large canine-looking teeth, tattoos, scars, and broad cheekbones, of those prone to crime.

Baby Boomers The generation born post–World War II, representing about 76 million Americans responsible for some of the most dramatic social changes in American history, such as the Vietnam War protests, the Civil Rights Movement, and the rise of feminism.

bail The amount of money, normally set at the initial court appearance and related to the seriousness of the crime and potential of the defendant to flee, that must be paid to the court to ensure that the accused will return for subsequent hearings or trial.

Balanced and Restorative Justice Model (BARJ) A model that gives equal consideration to protecting the community, holding offenders accountable for their actions, and helping offenders to develop the skills and attitudes they need to succeed in becoming law-abiding and productive members of society.

bifurcated hearing (or bifurcated process) A type of hearing where the offender is given a sentence that contains both juvenile sanctions and adult ones. Offenders may serve part of their sentence in a juvenile facility and then transfer to an adult prison once they reach majority age.

biosocial theorists Those who believe in the interaction between biology and the environment as an explanation for delinquency.

blended sentencing A sentence that is treatment-oriented and punitive-oriented involving both juvenile and adult facilities.

bootstrapping A process whereby a juvenile court classifies a status offender as a delinquent after repeated violations of the same offense.

bourgeois Capitalists or owners of the means of production whose goal is the pursuit of profit.

broken home A family situation in which family members are separated, either due to divorce, separation, or criminal charges against one or more parents. Children from broken homes often end up in foster care or living with relatives.

broken windows theory A theory that explores how small problems and signs of disorder or social control, such as graffiti, trash, and broken windows, can become bigger ones if left unaddressed.

bullying and intimidation Forms of delinquency and school violence that include the physical, verbal, or emotional abuse of one individual by one or several others over time.

career criminal An individual who has a long history of criminal activity lasting into adulthood.

child abuse Any act or failure to act on the part of a parent or caregiver that results in death, serious physical or emotional harm, sexual abuse, or exploitation of a minor.

Child Savers Movement Individuals consisting primarily of philanthropists and social reformers who felt that the exploitation of children ultimately resulted in juvenile crime and a host of other problems, and who sought to enact laws that would allow children to be placed in reformatories or other institutions.

Children In Need of Supervision (CHINS) Youths who should be under the authority of the juvenile justice system or social services agencies.

Children's Aid Society Established by Reverend Charles Loring Brace in 1853; assisted homeless children, orphans, runaways, and throwaway children. Today, it helps all children in need and their parents through counseling, housing, health care, and preparatory programs.

chivalry hypothesis The perception that girls are weaker, more helpless, and less threatening than boys, and so are not seen as "real" offenders and are given lighter sentences.

chronic 6 percent Chronic recidivists or serious repeat offenders responsible for more than half of all offenses.

chronic offenders Individuals who violate the law early and continue at a high rate well into adulthood, and who are resistant to change despite having gone through punishment.

class consciousness The awakening of the workers in recognition of their contributions to the economy led to demands for better working conditions and higher wages, but the bourgeois resisted because any increase in wages would be subtracted from their profits.

Classical School of Criminology The particular conception of crime and criminal justice that emerged in the eighteenth century with a focus on lawmaking and legal processing.

clearance rate The percentage of crimes solved by arrest.

cocaine An alkaloid extracted from coca leaves that is commonly used as an illicit drug.

cognitive theory The theory that delinquents use a template for problem solving that tells them how to interpret and process information, as well as which conclusions to draw and the appropriate behavioral response.

collective conscience The way a group or society responds to moral or ethical situations; when the group's sense of morality is clear, everyone agrees on what is and is not acceptable.

community crime prevention programs Community efforts to combat crime, mostly sponsored by police departments, which conduct home security surveys and hold community meetings to organize and plan neighborhood group activities.

community service A variety of tasks, such as picking up litter on public roads, sweeping subway terminals, planting trees, or painting graffiti-covered buildings, required as part of a sentence in lieu of imprisonment.

complaint A formal charge against a suspect.

Comprehensive Gang Initiative An approach by the U.S. Department of Justice that involves several agencies or groups handling a number of facets of local gang problems, and that focuses on not only suppression but also intervention and prevention.

computer viruses Programs designed to invade a computer's system to modify its operation, destroy or steal information, or call attention to problems within the system.

co-offending The act of committing offenses or crimes with others, but not necessarily as part of a gang.

corporal punishment The infliction of pain as a penalty for students who violate a school rule.

cottage system A shelter program that offers a small, safe environment where participants are also residents.

Court Appointed Special Advocates (CASA) Volunteers who receive special training to provide assistance and advice to the court about the appropriate placement of youths.

covering The attempt to minimize the effects of a disability and the stigma connected to a label.

CPTED The design of buildings and locations in such a way as to limit the opportunities for crime.

crack A cheaper, yet more potent and pure, form of cocaine that solidifies in the purification process to assume a rocklike form; is often smoked and is considered highly addictive.

Crime Index Seven main classifications of violent crime, including murder and non-negligent manslaughter, forcible rape, robbery, aggravated assault, property crimes such as burglary and larceny, and motor vehicle theft.

cultural deviance theory or cultural transmission theory A theory that the values of a group, in this case delinquents or criminals, transmit from one generation to the next.

curfew violations Status offenses involving ordinances that prohibit youths of certain ages from being in a public place during late evening or nighttime hours unless they are accompanied by an adult or are traveling to or from some acceptable activity.

cyber bullying The act of sending or posting harmful material through the Internet or by mobile device.

D.A.R.E. Drug Abuse Reduction through Education; a cooperative effort among law enforcement agencies, educators, students, parents, and local communities, consisting of drug prevention lectures targeted at fifth- and sixth-grade students, and delivered by specially trained law enforcement officers.

dark figure of crime Unknown crime that may not be present in UCR findings, resulting in an inability to have the entire crime picture.

dating violence Hostile altercations between unmarried partners.

definitions Justifications from youths to rationalize certain inappropriate behaviors, which allow them to square their self-images with the obvious harm of their actions.

deindustrialization The process through which companies either get out of a certain market entirely or outsource their operations to lower-wage countries resulting in fewer jobs, more competition for remaining ones, and the emergence of new industries, primarily in technology, which require specialized training.

delinquency prevention Various programs to either discourage youths from engaging in delinquency or keep delinquency from occurring in the future.

detention Facilities that hold youths if they are a threat to the community, if they are flight risks before their hearing, or if their parents cannot be located.

determinate sentence A sentence with a fixed period of punishment, in contrast to indeterminate sentences; part of a more punitive philosophy of punishment suggesting that everyone should be punished equally if they commit the same crime.

determinism The belief that delinquency is not a result of free will, but is determined by other factors beyond the control of the individual.

differential association A theory arguing that crime is a behavior learned from others, such as family members and delinquent peers, who feel that criminal behavior is acceptable.

differential opportunity The concept that because legitimate means of success are blocked and illegitimate ones may be as well, the path juveniles choose to follow is dependent on the nature of the community and the opportunities it offers.

differential reinforcement A concept that relates to social learning theory, which states that certain types of rewards and punishments have different effects on certain types of people.

directed patrol A tactic that aggressively enforces truancy and curfew laws in an effort to identify and arrest gang members.

disposition hearing The next step, similar to a sentencing hearing in the adult system, following the completion of the adjudication hearing.

diversion A wide range of programs to keep juveniles who commit crimes out of trouble with the law and the formal juvenile justice process.

double jeopardy A situation centered on the question of whether a juvenile can be prosecuted as an adult for the same crime after being adjudicated a delinquent.

dramatization of evil The process by which society's reaction to a negative label results in further criminal or delinquent behavior on the part of offenders.

drift theory The theory that offenders learn rationalizations in an effort to protect themselves against the condemnation of society by downplaying the negative impact of their crimes.

dropout A student enrolled in school who voluntarily chooses not to return and complete the requirements for graduation.

due process A term used to describe the way the legal system operates and provides a mechanism to ensure that the rights of the accused are protected.

ectomorphs Thin and frail-looking individuals who tend to be more introverted and shy.

electronic monitoring A variation on house arrest in which a juvenile is fitted with a device around the ankle that triggers an alarm and notifies probation officers should the juvenile stray outside the range of the device.

encoding The process of acquiring the information needed to make a decision and redefining the information until it is understood.

endomorphs Round and overweight individuals who tend to be outgoing but lazy.

evil-woman hypothesis The tendency of police officers and criminal justice officials to give harsher treatment to women viewed as more likely to look, think, and act like male offenders.

false consciousness A situation in which the proletariat accepts the exploitation by the bourgeois as a condition of employment.

false negative A situation in which youths who should be identified for intensive probation fall through the cracks of the system.

false positive A situation in which offenders are misclassified and are given intensive probation but do not need it.

family A group of individuals related by blood, marriage, or adoption who meet its members' needs for food, shelter, and intimacy, as well as providing socialization and the transmission of culture from one generation to the next.

family violence Hostile behaviors committed among siblings.

feminism A belief or doctrine that advocates equality in the social, economic, and political treatment of women in society.

feminist movements Efforts and campaigns promoting the belief that males and females should be politically, socially, and economically equal.

focal concerns Core values of autonomy, excitement, fate, smartness, trouble, and toughness that play an important role in youths' decisions to become involved in crime and delinquency.

foster care A system where the state provides care to neglected, abused, or abandoned children in place of their parents.

frankpledge system The primary law enforcement mechanism—also referred to as the mutual pledge system—from 1066 until well into the 1300s, mandating that each person over the age of twelve protect the community, and each other, in times of need.

free will Often associated with choice theory and rational decision-making, the ability of an individual to choose a particular course of action.

functional illiteracy The inability to read and write at a level necessary for everyday living.

gang A small group of adolescents who loiter on a street corner, but also applicable to graffiti artists, drug users, neo-Nazi Skinheads, or any group of highly organized youths whose purpose is to generate money from drug dealing or other criminal activity.

gang cycles Consistently changing patterns of gang activity and violence.

gang migration The movement of gang members from one region of the country to another, which changes the traditional understanding and parameters of gang structure.

gang-related An often misused term to describe the criminal activities of an individual member rather than the coordinated activities of the gang itself.

gender A social distinction that refers to the behavioral, physical, and psychological traits typically attributed to one sex.

general strain theory A theory of how crime and delinquency are adaptations to stress coming from different sources of strain, such as the disjunction between just or fair outcomes and actual ones, the removal of positively valued stimuli from the individual, and the presentation of negative stimuli.

gentrification An influx to inner-city neighborhoods of affluent people who want to enjoy the advantages of living near a downtown metropolitan area, where they are likely to work, creating an environment with the strong sense of responsibility and purpose that comes from home ownership, but also causing property values and real estate taxes to increase.

good parenting Behaviors, such as honesty, empathy, self-reliance, kindness, cooperation, and self-control, that parents can display that protect or insulate youths from engaging in delinquent acts.

G.R.E.A.T. Gang Resistance Education and Training; modeled after its precursor, D.A.R.E., in which police officers visit schools and work with middle and elementary school children on developing the skills and attitudes that will help them resist involvement in drugs and gangs.

group homes Nurturing home environment for adjudicated youths that is an alternative to incarceration and that allows them to mainstream into the community and learn to cope with problems while developing independent living skills.

heroin A highly addictive narcotic that is more potent than morphine and is used illegally for its euphoric effects.

heterogeneity Diversity of attitudes, values, and beliefs about how things should be accomplished, as well as what is acceptable and unacceptable behavior.

hidden delinquents Detained status offenders who rarely show up in official statistics because they are detained in treatment facilities, such as mental hospitals and substance abuse treatment centers, which does not violate the mandates of the JJDPA.

hierarchical line Rank-ordering of offenses for the UCR count.

homeless youths Young people up to the age of twenty-one who do not have a safe living space outside of or within a relative's home.

homogeneity Shared or similar views of the world, as well as what is acceptable and unacceptable behavior.

hot spots analysis An approach to assessing and dealing with crime in which locations in a community that have a concentrated level of criminal activity in a given period are targeted aggressively.

Houses of Refuge Started in 1825 in New York; facilities exclusively for children, whether poor, orphaned, incorrigible, or wayward.

hustlers Individuals who engage in a host of legal and illegal activities such as prostitution.

hybrid gangs Groups that consist of members of different gangs, including rival ones, who come together for a particular activity, such as drug dealing.

illusion of invulnerability The tendency of teenagers to believe that they are immune to the negative consequences of high-risk activities.

imitation The decision to engage in crime by modeling other criminals' behavior.

impression management Creating a favorable impression of oneself for others.

in loco parentis Instances in which the police must act as the parent in a given situation, and should therefore be given the authority to provide necessary services, such as taking youths into custody when it is for their own good.

incident-based policing An approach in which officers wait for crimes to occur and respond with arrests.

incorrigibility The habitual disobedience of juveniles toward their parents or guardians.

indeterminate sentence A sentence that has no fixed period of confinement; based on the rehabilitation/treatment philosophy of punishment.

individualized justice A guiding principle of the juvenile justice system that each case should be decided on its own merits and the punishment or treatment be tailor-made to a particular offender.

Industrial Revolution A transition, beginning in the late eighteenth century in Great Britain and afterward spreading throughout the world, from a simple, preindustrial society to a complex, modern, multicultural one.

informal social control The process by which community residents solve their own problems without the use of formal agents of control, such as the police.

inhalant Any toxic substance, such as glue or paint thinner, whose fumes are inhaled for their euphoric effect.

intake The first step in the juvenile justice process, usually preceded by referrals to court made by police officers or probation officers.

Jessica's Law Named for nine-year-old Jessica Lunsford, who was abducted, assaulted, and buried alive by a convicted sex offender; the 2005 law requires more thorough monitoring of offenders, through such means as DNA samples, ankle bracelets, and GPS tracking.

Job Corps program A residential education and training program that prepares disadvantaged youths by giving them the opportunity to earn their GED, and by teaching them vocational skills with which they can obtain rewarding jobs.

juvenile aftercare Also sometimes referred to as juvenile parole or juvenile reentry, these include a variety of services provided to youths upon their release from detention.

juvenile boot camp programs Intense, structured environments that are modeled after military boot camps to enhance at-risk youths' ability to define goals, improve their self-esteem, and learn the importance of structure, discipline, and self-confidence.

juvenile delinquency Behavior that violates the criminal code and is committed by youths who have not reached majority age.

Juvenile Delinquency Prevention and Control Act (1968) An act that prohibited states from incarcerating status offenders and required them to detain juvenile offenders in separate facilities from adult offenders

Juvenile Justice Delinquency Prevention Act (JJDPA) of 1974 A pioneering act that made a legal distinction between youths who committed criminal acts and status offenders so that status offenders did not suffer from the stigmatizing label "juvenile delinquent," and that turned care of status offenders over to community agencies.

labeling theory The societal reaction or interactionist perspective which asserts that society creates criminals, delinquents, and deviants based not on the harm caused by their acts but on the way in which society labels such behavior.

latchkey kids Children age six to twelve who spend five or more hours per week unsupervised or in the care of an older sibling, and who are at much greater risk for engaging in delinquent behavior than children who have an adult provider in the home.

life chances Extensive opportunities for individuals who grow up with solid social networks, usually those in the middle class or the wealthy.

mandatory sentence A sentence that requires a particular type of punishment; often used for serious offenders who are waived to adult court, mandatory sentences are determined by law and do not allow judges to alter or modify the sentence.

marijuana A drug, usually smoked, that is derived from the dried leaves and female flowers of the hemp plant.

maturational effect An aging out process whereby offenders engage in less delinquent and criminal acts as they get older.

means of production The resources, such as factories, equipment, land, and raw materials, needed to produce wealth.

mechanical solidarity A type of social connection to others where there is a similarity of attitudes, values, and beliefs. This type of social cohesion traditionally was derived from the fact that most people performed the same tasks such as farming, lived in sparsely populated areas, and tended to know their neighbors.

Megan's Law Named for seven-year-old Megan Kanka, who was killed by a neighbor and twice-convicted sex offender; the 1996 act introduced registry laws requiring released sex offenders to register with local police and neighborhoods to be informed of the identity, criminal record, and address of offenders with a high-risk of reoffending.

member-based definition Classification of an incident as gang-related simply because the individual involved is a gang member.

mentoring programs Secondary prevention programs designed to reduce the interests in and motivation of potential offenders to commit delinquent acts by providing positive adult role models who can steer youths away from criminal influences and help them change their attitudes and behaviors.

mesomorphs Muscular and athletic individuals who are active, confident, and assertive. The somatyping theory suggests these individuals are more likely to commit crimes.

minimal brain dsyfunctions (MBD) Neurological imbalances in or damage to youths' brains as an explanation for aggressive behavior.

Minors in Need of Supervision (MINS) Adolescents who should be under the control and supervision of the juvenile justice system.

motive-based definition Classification of an incident as gang-related if offending individuals act on behalf of the gang.

multiple-partner fertility The tendency of mothers to have children by different fathers.

National Crime Victimization Survey (NCVS) A telephone survey of victims that gives policymakers and researchers a better idea of the extent and scope of crime.

near poor Those who have incomes that are too high to qualify for government assistance but not high enough to cover basic expenses for food, clothing, and shelter.

negative reinforcement Refraining from certain behaviors because of an absence of reward or the application of punishment.

neglect A situation created when parents or guardians do not provide the kind of care needed, even though they have the ability to do so.

net widening The use of diversion programs to keep youths under the control of the juvenile justice system when the courts would normally dismiss their cases.

neutralization theory Also referred to as the drift theory; involves the rationalizations offenders learn in an effort to protect themselves against the condemnation of society.

No Child Left Behind Act A law designed to improve the academic performance and education of children at all levels in public schools by increasing accountability of schools and giving parents more choices about which schools their children can attend.

nuclear family A smaller unit composed of parents and their children, but not including grandparents, uncles, aunts, and others living in the household.

organic solidarity A type of cohesion based on interdependence and need of residents in a society. This type of solidarity comes as a result of the Industrial Revolution and the division of labor in society.

Orphan Trains The vehicles used to transport city youths to rural farms, where families assumed custody of and responsibility for them as apprentices.

panacea phenomenon The attempt to find a single, cure-all answer to the problems relating to delinquency.

parens patriae The foundation for the state to intervene and to provide protection for children whose parents did not provide adequate care or supervision.

Part I crimes Seven main classifications of violent crime, which are known as the Crime Index, that include murder and non-negligent manslaughter, forcible rape, robbery, aggravated assault, property crimes such as burglary and larceny, and motor vehicle theft.

Part II crimes Offenses that provide a broad picture of less serious and dangerous crimes, such as simple assault, fraud, forgery, counterfeiting and embezzlement, vandalism, gambling, disorderly conduct, liquor law violations, offenses against family members, weapons possession, vagrancy, curfew violations, and status offenses.

passing The process by which people will attempt to hide potentially stigmatizing attributes.

patriarchal society A situation in which males dominate every aspect of economic, social, and political life.

Persons In Need of Supervision (PINS) Individuals, who may have reached majority age, who should be under the control and supervision of the justice system.

petition The determination of whether to detain offenders and whether to bring formal charges against them and request that the court intervene and adjudicate them delinquents.

phone phreaking An offense in which calls are made without paying the appropriate toll or fee.

plea bargain A strategy whereby an offender pleads guilty to the offense in exchange for a lesser sentence, usually the result of negotiation between the prosecutor and the defense attorney early in the criminal justice process.

police discretion The subjective use of judgment by officers in deciding whether to invoke the justice process.

police matrons Women assigned to deal with juveniles, as well as to take on administrative duties and parking enforcement.

positivism A scientific approach to understanding and identifying the biological connections to criminal behavior.

preponderance of evidence A burden of proof that places value on the facts and circumstances of a case that is more than suspicion but less than proof beyond a reasonable doubt.

present orientation An inability to think about or plan for the future; a living-for-the-moment mentality.

primary crime prevention Efforts to make crime more difficult to commit or to increase the likelihood of the offender getting caught.

primary deviance The type of behavior that goes unnoticed or, if the individual is caught, the impact of which is minimized or explained.

privatization of corrections A trend toward using private companies, instead of state agencies, as providers of detention services for juveniles.

probable cause The basis of a legal arrest; the facts and circumstances that would lead a reasonable person to believe that a crime has been committed and that the suspect is responsible for that crime.

probation The courts' release of juveniles to parents or legal guardians, provided the youths meet certain conditions.

proletariat Those who have only their labor to sell; the working class.

proportionality of crime A concept whereby the punishment given is related to the seriousness of the offense.

protective factors Influences or variables that reduce youths' chances of offending and minimize the risks to which they are exposed.

recidivism The repeated criminal behavior by an offender, usually measured by the re-arrest rate of an offender.

reentry The transition back into mainstream society from being detained or incarcerated.

registry laws Requirements for convicted sex offenders to make their whereabouts known by registering with local police.

residential programs Out-of-home placements that provide an alternative to detention centers and state schools and are not subject to JJDPA deinstitutionalization guidelines.

resiliency The social adaptability of people and youths in the face of adversity.

right to treatment A legal right to proper care and treatment that youths retain once confined.

risk factors Behaviors and events that place youths at higher risk to engage in delinquency.

risk models Methods of examining the risk factors that place certain youths in jeopardy of committing crimes alongside the protective factors that shield them from such behavior.

routine activities theory The theory that crime occurs because offenders take advantage of the typical, everyday behavior of their victims.

runaways Youths who leave home without permission for more than twenty-four hours.

saturation patrols The strategy used by police departments of placing numerous officers in a given area to maintain a high visibility, to deter criminal activities, and to increase the likelihood of catching offenders.

Scared Straight A program that brings parole and probation youths into maximum-security prisons to interact with adult prisoners, thereby discouraging them from future risky behavior that would land them in such an environment.

school crime Criminal offenses that take place on a school campus and disrupt the learning environment.

search and seizure Guidelines that searches generally should not take place unless a warrant is obtained from a judge that outlines the area to be searched and the items officers are looking to find.

search incident to a lawful arrest A full search conducted following arrest of the areas within the suspect's immediate control.

secondary crime prevention Methods, such as sports-related programs, to aid in removing or reducing youths' desire to engage in criminal acts.

secondary deviance The kind of systematic deviance that comes as a result of labeling.

self-fulfilling prophecy A condition that is created in which a false prediction actually becomes true because of the actions of the people involved.

self-report studies Primarily surveys or interviews that ask individuals about their experiences with criminal activity.

sex The biological characteristics that distinguish males and females.

shaming The public embarrassment of offenders for engaging in inappropriate behavior; sometimes used to refrain youths from committing crimes in the future.

shelter care Residential program for youths needing temporary placement.

social capital The development of networks that provide opportunities for well-paying jobs and a chance to succeed.

social class bias The advantages (social, economic, political) given to those who are from affluent families; often used in education to describe the differences between children from wealthy parents, who receive a higher-quality education than those whose families are poor.

social control theory A theory that suggests most people internalize the norms of society and engage in conforming behavior most of the time. However, some individuals are not adequately socialized and do not develop a sense of responsibility to societal laws. Such individuals are more likely to commit crime or delinquent acts.

social disorganization A sociological theory that asserts a community's lack of structure and ability to control its residents' behaviors.

social ecology model A sociological theory derived from plant ecology to explain the growth and expansion of the urban landscape, as well as how problems like delinquency are a normal part of society.

social institutions Organizations, such as schools, designed to meet societal needs.

social solidarity The connectedness people feel for the larger group.

social structural theories Explanations of how delinquency and crime that attribute these behaviors to societal problems that influence people's decisions on how to act.

socialization The process by which people in a given culture learn the accepted attitudes, values, beliefs, and behaviors of that group.

status offenders Those who engage in activities that could be committed only by youths, such as truancy, running away, or underage drinking.

status offenses Acts, such as truancy, incorrigibility, and curfew violations, that are considered against the law, but are not viewed as criminal, based on the status or age of the offenders.

strain The sense of anxiety in people who want to achieve certain societal goals but who do not have access to the institutional means to do so.

street youths Individuals who live and interact on the streets and in other high-risk, nontraditional locations, such as under bridges, in abandoned buildings, or in vehicles.

subcultural theories Explanations for delinquency that consider a group's influence on a youth's decision to commit a crime.

subculture of violence The assumption that the use of violence is consistent with a group's beliefs that it can serve as a problem-solving tool.

symbolic interaction A paradigm in sociology that explains the nature of social relationships and communication by the use of symbols.

tagging The assignment of a label to delinquents

target-hardening measures Prevention methods that include installing deadbolt locks on doors, adding window locks, improving the lighting around homes and streets, and implementing Block Watch programs, where citizens patrol their neighborhoods and report suspicious activity to the police.

telecommuting The ability for a full-time employee to work from home.

tertiary crime prevention Programs that focus on ensuring that youths who have already committed crimes will not engage in similar activities in the future.

throwaway youths Young individuals who either are asked to leave home by parents or other adults in the household or who are away from home overnight and prevented from returning.

totality of circumstances The standard used by the juvenile court in assessing whether a youth's rights have been violated. It considers all the variables involved to determine if the agent of the juvenile justice system acted appropriately.

tracking Organization of high school curricula to prepare students for what they would most likely be doing upon graduation; based on the assumption that children from economically disadvantaged backgrounds were destined for similar futures.

traditional family values The family structure of the 1950s, when women stayed home to raise the children.

trafficking of children A form of modern-day slavery whereby the victims are forced to work in the sex industry or to perform labor, such as domestic servitude, restaurant work, janitorial work, sweatshop factory work, or migrant agricultural work.

training schools Larger facilities that place a greater emphasis on education and vocational training.

transfer The turning over of youths charged with violating criminal laws to criminal court to be tried as adults.

Transitional Zone A concentrated blighted urban area, usually near the central business district, with affordable housing and job opportunities, but undergoing rapid social change.

triads Powerful community organizations that are closely associated with or control Chinese gangs.

truancy The act of skipping school.

twin studies Research, using identical twins separated at birth, that would identify genetic links to delinquency.

unfounded crimes Incidents in which a crime has been reported but no evidence has been found to indicate one has occurred.

Uniform Crime Reports A system created by the International Association of Chiefs of Police (IACP) in 1927 to document a number of crimes. Its data are used to determine how best to allocate law enforcement resources and to identify effective strategies to reduce crime.

upward social mobility Improvement in one's social standing through various means. While most people achieve upward social mobility through obtaining an education, career advancement, or some other means, ironically, some juvenile and adult offenders achieve upward social mobility through incarceration. This is due to the fact that detention facilities offer structure and bare essentials that dysfunctional families do not.

valid court order amendment Legislation that allows juveniles being tried as adults for felonies or juveniles with felony convictions to be sent to an adult jail or lockup and to be held for six hours in urban areas and up to twenty-four hours in rural ones, if secure detention is required and no alternative arrangements can be made.

verbal assault Yelling at or disparaging children.

vicarious contact Communications from other youths about unpleasant experiences with the police.

victimization The situation in which individuals become the receivers of crime and are sometimes made to feel embarrassed, think they should have known better, or feel partially responsible for their trauma by the retelling of their story to several parties.

waive jurisdiction The move of a youth from juvenile to criminal court, where he or she would be tried as an adult.

warrantless searches The finding and seizing of evidence without warrants or court orders.

watch and ward system A system that required men from each town to take turns standing watch at night; if any criminals were caught, they were turned over to the constable for trial the following day.

wilderness programs Short-term residential programs that use rigorous outdoor activities, such as survival training, to teach adjudicated youths the importance of setting and achieving goals and to provide those youths with alternative paradigms or frameworks to understand the world and their place in it.

zero tolerance The practice of automatically expelling students for violations of school safety rules.

zero-tolerance policing Enforcement that provides no exceptions to violations of the law.

Photo Credits

Cover: Photo © Richard Ross/www.juvenile-in-justice.com

Chapter 1 Opener: Photo © Richard Ross/www.juvenile-in-justice.com; Page 11: © David R. Frazier Photolibrary, Inc.; p. 12: © Hill Street Studios/Matthew Palmer/Blend Images LLC RF; p. 13: © Ryan McVay/Getty Images RF.

Chapter 2 Opener: © Brand X Pictures RF.

Chapter 3 Opener: © Punchstock/Image Source RF; p. 59: © Ingram Publishing RF; p. 62: © JGI/Jamie Grill/Getty Images RF; p. 66: © Purestock/Getty Images RF; p. 69: © Doug Menuez/Photodisc Green/Getty Images RF; p. 70: © PunchStock/Image Source RF; p. 73: © Corepics VOF/Cutcaster RF; p. 74: © Steve Helber/AP/Corbis.

Chapter 4 Opener: Library of Congress Prints and Photographs Division (LC-DIG-nclc-01379); p. 83: © Jeff Greenberg/Alamy; p. 85: © ZUMA Press/Newscom; p. 86: Library of Congress Prints and Photographs Division (LC-DIG-nclc-01379); p. 90: © PhotoAlto RF; p. 96: © Comstock/PunchStock RF; p. 99: © Hjack Star/PhotoLink/Getty Images RF; p. 100: © Doug Menuez/Getty Images RF.

Chapter 5 Opener: Photo © Richard Ross/www.juvenile-in-justice.com; p. 112: © BananaStock/PunchStock RF; p. 121: © imagenavi/PunchStock RF; p. 122(top): © AP Photo/King Co. Sheriff's Department; p. 122(bottom): © BananaStock/PunchStock RF; p. 125: © AP Photo/Eau Claire Leader-Telegram, Dan Reiland; p. 126: © David R. Frazier Photolibrary, Inc.; p. 131: Centers for Disease Control.

Chapter 6 Opener: Photo © Richard Ross/www.juvenile-in-justice.com; p. 139: © Historical Picture Archive/Corbis; p. 142: © Mary Evans Picture Library/Alamy; p. 143: © BananaStock/PunchStock RF; p. 144: © Stockbyte/PunchStock RF; p. 149: © Keith

Brofsky/Getty Images RF; p. 154: © The McGraw-Hill Companies Inc./Ken Karp, photographer.

Chapter 7 Opener: Photo © Richard Ross/www.juvenile-in-justice.com; p. 167: © The McGraw-Hill Companies Inc./John Flournoy, photographer; p. 174: © Comstock Images/Jupiter Images/Alamy RF; p. 179: © Comstock/PunchStock RF; p. 180: © Sandro Di Carlo Darsa/PhotoAlto/Corbis; p. 181: © David H. Wells/Corbis; p. 184: © Ocean/Corbis.

Chapter 8 Opener: Photo © Richard Ross/www.juvenile-in-justice.com; p. 205(top): © Daniel Lainé/Corbis; p. 206(bottom): © Andrew Lichtenstein/Corbis; p. 206: © Trevor Snapp/Corbis; p. 207: © Gideon Mendel/Corbis; p. 209: © Mikael Karlsson; p. 213: © Brand X Pictures RF; p. 217: © Photodisc/Getty Images RF.

Chapter 9 Opener: Photo © Richard Ross/www.juvenile-in-justice.com; p. 229(top): © Ashley Cooper/Corbis; p. 229(bottom): © The McGraw-Hill Companies, Inc./Christopher Kerrigan, photographer; p. 230: © Creasource/Corbis; p. 234: © Randy Allbritton/Getty Images RF; p. 235: © Greg Henshall/FEMA; p. 239: © BananaStock/PunchStock RF; p. 243: © Nick Cardillicchio/Corbis.

Chapter 10 Opener: Photo © Richard Ross/www.juvenile-in-justice.com; p. 253: © Neville Elder/Corbis; p. 259: © Hill Street Studios/Blend Images LLC RF; p. 262: © Design Pics/Don Hammond RF; p. 264: © Ed Andrieski/AP/Corbis; p. 265: © Design Pics/Darren Greenwood RF; p. 266: © Jimi Lott KRT/Newscom; p. 270: © Mikael Karlsson.

Chapter 11 Opener: Photo © Richard Ross/www.juvenile-in-justice.com; p. 281: © Design Pics/Kristy-Anne Glubish RF; p. 282, p. 284: © Ingram Publishing RF; p. 285: © The McGraw-Hill Companies, Inc./Ken Cavanagh, photographer; p. 287: © BananaStock/

PunchStock RF; p. 289(top): © Aaron Roeth Photography; p. 289(bottom): © David R. Frazier Photolibrary, Inc.

Chapter 12 Opener: © David R. Frazier Photolibrary, Inc.; p. 309: © BananaStock/PictureQuest RF; p. 310: © S. Meltzer/PhotoLink/Getty Images RF; p. 311: © Creatas RF/PunchStock RF; p. 313: © Monkey Business Images Ltd/Photolibrary RF; p. 315: © Najlah Feanny/Corbis; p. 319: © Colleen Cahill/Design Pics/Corbis; p. 321: © Robert King/Newsmakers/Getty Images.

Chapter 13 Opener: © Mikael Karlsson; p. 332: Jesse Brown Cook Scrapbooks Documenting San Francisco History and Law Enforcement, Volume 9, UC Berkeley, Bancroft Library. © 2009 The Regents of The University of California; p. 334: Carol M. Highsmith's America, Library of Congress, Prints and Photographs Division; p. 336(top): © David R. Frazier Photolibrary, Inc.; p. 336(bottom): © The McGraw-Hill Companies Inc./Ken Karp, photographer; p. 338: © Ralph Barrera/American-Statesman/World Picture News; p. 342: © Brand X Pictures RF; p. 346: © Jeff Greenberg/PhotoEdit Inc.; p. 348: © Kathy Willens/AP/Corbis.

Chapter 14 Opener: Photo © Richard Ross/www.juvenile-in-justice.com; p. 359: © Brand X Pictures RF; p. 361: © BananaStock/PunchStock RF; p. 366: © David Joles/ZUMA Press/Corbis; p. 368: © Mikael Karlsson; p. 370: © Comstock/Jupiterimages RF; p. 373: © David R. Frazier Photolibrary, Inc.; p. 375: © Greg Smith/Corbis.

Chapter 15 Opener: Photo © Richard Ross/www.juvenile-in-justice.com; p. 383: © Hulton-Deutsch Collection/Corbis; p. 387(top): © David R. Frazier Photolibrary, Inc.; p. 387(bottom): © Will & Deni McIntyre/Corbis; p. 388: © Joshua Berman; p. 392: © Royalty-Free/Corbis RF; p. 393: © Robin Nelson/ZUMA Press/Corbis; p. 395: © Mikael Karlsson/Alamy.

Index

A

abandonment, 182
Abbott, Henry Jack, 115
A Better Chance (ABC) program, 18
abuse. *See* child abuse; sexual abuse
academic achievement, 17, 62, 160, 258–259, 265. *See also* schools
accommodation, 150
Accountability Courts, 62, 63
Adam Walsh Child Protection and Safety Act, 227
Adelstein, Jack, 207
ADHD (Attention-Deficit/Hyperactivity Disorder), 154–155, 233
adjudication hearing, 371–372
Adler, Freda, 292
adolescence-limited offenders, 152
adolescents
    cognitive skills of, 149–150
    community experience of, 22
    developmental assets of, 169–171
    engaging in sexual activity, 225
    female delinquency and early puberty, 145
    gender and self-image, 282
    generational differences in, 14–15
    illusion of invulnerability in, 17–18
    increasing population in U.S., 10
    law enforcement's perceptions of, 336
    perceptions of law enforcement, 335–336
    population distribution by age, 10
    protective factors for, 18
    risk factors for, 17–18
    social problems and, 16–17
    typical behaviors of, 13–14
Adoption Assistance and Child Welfare Act, 339
adult courts, 8, 9, 19–20. *See also* transfer (to adult courts); waive jurisdiction
adult gangs, 199
adventurers (hackers), 243
African Americans. *See* race or ethnicity
aftercare, 304, 383, 402–404
age
    arson arrests by, 234
    bullying and, 262
    correlates to delinquency, 40
    of first marriage (median), 172
    for juvenile court jurisdiction, by state, 4–5
    maturational effect, 40
    multiple-partner fertility and, 172
    of onset, 40, 233
    physical abuse rates by, 44, 184
    population distribution by, U.S., 10
    risk factors for delinquent behavior by, 312
    status offenses based on, 52, 53

Aggression Replacement Training (ART), 118, 119
aggressive patrol, 348–349
aging out process, 40, 201
Akers, Ron, 117–118
alcohol. *See* drugs and alcohol
Alexander v. Boyd and South Carolina Department of Juvenile Justice, 401
Alliance for Excellent Education, 256
Almighty Latin King and Queen Nation (ALKQN), 205
alternative schools, 258, 267–269
American Academy of Pediatrics, 13
American Civil Liberties Union, 67
American Dream, 94, 95, 100
American Indians, 37
Anderson, Elijah, 102
anger control training, 119
Annie E. Casey Foundation, 399, 400
anomie, 94. *See also* strain theories
antisocial behavior, genetics and, 143–144
appearance, police discretion and, 340
appellate review or process, 373
arrest, defined, 343
arrests of juveniles
    arsonists by age, 234
    for curfew violations, 66
    females, by type of crime, 286
    females, for status offenses, 285–286, 395
    females vs. males, 287–288
    gang members, 216
    homicide trends, 35
    percentage by offense, 33
    percent change in (1999–2008), 37
    procedural rules governing, 343
    property crime trends, 34
    racial bias in, 340–341, 391
    search incident to a lawful arrest, 344
    ten-year trend for violent crimes, 241
    violent crime trends, 34
arson, 233–237
ART (Aggression Replacement Training), 118, 119
The Art of Deception (Mitnick), 244
The Art of Intrusion (Mitnick), 244
Asian Americans. *See* race or ethnicity
assimilation, 150
atavisms, 141
attachment, in bonding theory, 121
Attention-Deficit/Hyperactivity Disorder (ADHD), 154–155, 233
Augustus, John, 382
autonomy, 92–93, 100, 169

B

Baby Boomers, 14
bail, 368–369
Balanced and Restorative Justice Model (BARJ), 362–363
Bandura, Albert, 148
bandwagon effect, 302, 303
Bauerlein, Mark, 259
The Beauty Myth (Wolf), 282
Becker, Howard, 123, 124
Behavioral Monitoring and Reinforcement Program (BMRP), 148
behavioral theory, 146, 147–148
behavior therapy for ADHD, 155
belief, in bonding theory, 121
The Bell Curve (Wilson & Herrnstein), 145
Bera, W. W., 225
Big Brothers/Big Sisters programs (BBBS), 149, 314
biochemical factors in delinquency, 142–143
biological factors in female delinquency, 291
biosocial theorists, 142
biosocial theory, 142–145
bipolar disorder, 156–157
birth order and delinquency, 176, 177
Black Cobras gang, 197, 202, 210, 215
Black Panthers, 204
Blackstone, William, 5–6
blended families, 166
blended sentencing, 361, 373–374
Bloods gang, 205
body image, gender and, 282–283
body searches, 271
bonding theory, 121–122
book bag searches, 271
boot camps, 392–393
bootstrapping, 54
bourgeois, defined, 130
Boyle, Greg, 216
Boy Scouts of America, 314
Brace, Charles Loring, 6
Braithwaite, John, 127, 128
Breed v. Jones, 358
Broad Scope Runaways, 57
broken homes, 7
broken windows theory, 88, 334
Brunsma, David, 264–265
bullying and intimidation, 201, 261–263, 316
Bumfights (video), 122
Bureau of Justice Statistics, 198, 211, 225
Burgess, Ernest, 91
Byofsky v. Borough of Middletown, 68

C

ISBN-13: 978-1-259-72137-3
ISBN-10: 1-259-72137-X